CONSUMER ECONOMIC ISSUES IN AMERICA

Fourth Edition

by

E. Thomas Garman

DAME
Publications, Inc.
Houston, TX

Artist & Proofreader:	**Pamela S. Porter**
Cover Design:	**Naika R. Malveaux**
Cover Photos:	**© Corel Professional Photos**. Images may have been combined and/or modified to produce final cover art.

ISBN 0-87393-590-X
Library of Congress Catalog No. 96-085536

Printed in the United States of America

Table of Contents at a Glance

Preface xix
Foreword by Virginia H. Knauer xxxii
About the Author xxxiv

Part One: **Some Perspectives**

Chapter 1   What Is the Consumer Interest?   1
Chapter 2   The Consumer Movement Continues to Evolve   29

Part Two: **Facing Consumer Problems Successfully**

Chapter 3   Consumer Rights, Responsibilities and Remedies   55
Chapter 4   Ripoffs and Frauds in the Marketplace   85
Chapter 5   Laws That Help Consumers   131

Part Three: **The Challenging Market Place**

Chapter 6   The Capitalistic American Marketplace   179
Chapter 7   Economic Concepts Critical to Consumer Success   209
Chapter 8   Consumers in the Global Marketplace   231
Chapter 9   Government Regulation of Economic Interests   261
Chapter 10   Government Regulation of Consumer Interests   289

Part Four: **Information Processing**

Chapter 11   How to Analyze Consumer Issues   319
Chapter 12   Decision Making in Today's Complex Society   349
Chapter 13   The Planned Buying Process   387

Part Five: **Consumer Economic Issues**

Chapter 14   Food Issues   423
Chapter 15   Health Care Issues   453
Chapter 16   Product Safety Issues   487
Chapter 17   Banking, Credit, and Housing Issues   515
Chapter 18   Insurance and Investment Issues   553

Appendix   Careers in Consumer Affairs   581
Index   589

Table of Contents

Preface xix

Foreword by Virginia H. Knauer xxxii

About the Author xxxiv

Part One: Some Perspectives

Chapter 1   What Is the Consumer Interest?   1

Economic Activities Performed by Consumers 2
    Earning 3
    Consuming 3
    Utilizing 4
    Borrowing 4
    Saving 4
    Investing 5
    Taxpaying 5
Sovereignty in the Marketplace 5
Consumer Problems in a World of Imperfectly Competitive Markets Where the
    Interests of Sellers and Consumers Conflict 6
    What Are "Consumer Problems"? 6
    Consumers Shop in Imperfectly Competitive Markets 7
    The Seller-Consumer Conflict Will Always Exist 7
The Consumer Interest Viewed in a Price-Quality Model: A Useful but
    Incomplete Perspective 8
    Everyone in the Market Wants a Good Deal 8
What Really Is the Consumer Interest?—Value for Money and Equity 9
    Consumer Interest #1: Seeking Value for Money (While Constantly
        Making Tradeoffs) 10
    Consumer Interest #2: Seeking Equity for All Consumers 11
    Seeking Equity Sometimes Requires a Paternalistic Attitude 12
    Who Determines the Consumer Interest? 13
Consumers Achieve Their Interests by Securing, Protecting and Asserting Their
    Eight Important Consumer Rights 13
The Consumer Interest As a Special-Interest Group 14
The Public Interest Differs from Both the Consumer Interest and the Business
    Interest 15
    The Public Interest 17
    One's Consumer and Public Roles Differ 17
    Business and the Consumer Interest 18
Government's Challenging Public Interest Responsibilities 18
    Government's Economic/Political Biases in the United States 19
    Government Making Public Policy Decisions 19
    Government Resolving Public Interest Disputes 19
    Government and the Consumer Interest 20

Conflicts between the Public and Consumer Interests Are Usually Caused
 by Potential Price Increases 21
Consumers Must Look Out for Their Consumer Interests 22
 Businesses and Governments Sometimes Help Consumers 23
 How Consumers Pursue Their Interests 23
 The Challenge of Being an Effective Consumer 24
Review and Summary of Key Terms and Concepts 26
Useful Resources for Consumers 27
"What Do You Think" Questions 28

Chapter 2 The Consumer Movement Continues to Evolve 29

The Early Periods of the Consumer Movement 30
 Awakening to Consumer Problems: Before 1890 30
 Early Consumer Movement: The 1890s through the 1920s 31
 Renewed Consumer Interest: 1929 through the 1950s 32
Consumerism: The 1960s and Early 1970s 33
Responses to Consumerism in the 1970s and 1980s 35
 Business Response 35
 Government Response 37
What Makes Consumer Movements Successful? 39
 Rising Expectations of Consumers 39
 Scandals and Dramatic Crises 39
 Charismatic People 40
 Active Government Organizations 41
 Active Private Organizations 42
 Poor Economic Conditions 44
Today's Consumer Movement is Strong 44
The Major Players Influencing the Consumer Movement 46
 Sellers 46
 Governments 47
 Consumer Organizations 48
 Consumers Themselves 49
The Future of the Consumer Movement is Bright 50
Review and Summary of Key Terms and Concepts 52
Useful Resources for Consumers 54
"What Do You Think" Questions 54

Part Two: Facing Consumer Problems Successfully

Chapter 3 Consumer Rights, Responsibilities and Remedies 55

Legal Rights of Consumers 56
 Implied Warranty Rights Are Powerful Legal Rights 56
 Express Warranty Rights are Enforceable 58
 Lots of Other Legal Rights Also Exist 59
Moral Rights of Consumers Are Legitimate Expectations 60
 General Moral Rights 60
 President Kennedy's Consumer Bill of Rights 61
 A List of Consumer Rights for All Americans 61
Responsibilities of Consumers 62
 Regarding *the right to choose*, consumers have the responsibility to 63
 Regarding *the right to safety*, consumers have the responsibility to 64
 Regarding *the right to information*, consumers have the responsibility
  to 64

Regarding *the right to voice* (or *to be heard*), consumers have the
    responsibility to 64
Regarding *the right to redress or remedy*, consumers have the
    responsibility to 65
Regarding *the right to environmental health*, consumers have the
    responsibility to 65
Regarding the *right to service*, consumers have the responsibility to 66
Regarding *the right to consumer education*, consumers have the
    responsibility to 66
Why People Don't Complain 67
Remedies to Resolve Consumer Problems 68
How to Complain Effectively 69
The Complaining Process Should Follow a Sequence 69
    1. The Local Business 70
    2. The Manufacturer 70
    3. Self-Regulatory Organizations 71
    4. Consumer Action Agencies 73
    5. Small Claims and Civil Courts 74
Use Small Claims Lawsuits to Sue When Necessary 75
How Consumers Can Break a Contract 76
Damages to Ask for When Suing 77
Use a Class Action Lawsuit When Many Are Wronged 77
Techniques of Last Resort: How to Fight Back—And Win!—Against Ripoffs
    and Frauds 78
Review and Summary of Key Terms and Concepts 80
Useful Resources for Consumers 81
"What Do You Think" Questions 82
Appendix 3A: Writing a Letter of Complaint 83

Chapter 4   Ripoffs and Frauds in the Marketplace   85

How Ripoffs and Frauds Work against Consumers 86
Why Ripoffs and Frauds Exist in the Marketplace 87
What Do Ripoffs and Frauds Have in Common? 88
General Guidelines to Avoid Ripoffs and Frauds 89
    Be Cautious in Marketplace Dealings 89
    Ask Lots of Questions 90
    Things Never to Do 90
    Be Informed Before Going Shopping 91
    Know Your Rights 91
    Be Alert to Signs of Being Ripped Off 91
    When in Doubt 91
Ripoffs—and There Are Many—Are *Not* Illegal 92
    Negative Option Buying Plans—Ripoffs? 93
    Rental Car Insurance—A Ripoff Industry? 94
    Credit- and Debit-Card Registration Services—Ripoffs? 95
    Health Products—Ripoffs? 96
    Weight-Loss Plans—Ripoffs? 96
    Telephone Company Ripoffs 97
    Insurance (Health, Cancer, and Life)—Ripoffs? 99
Fraud Also Exists in the Marketplace 103
Untrue, Deceptive, and Misleading Advertising Also Exists 104
    Bait and Switch Advertising Is Illegal 105
    Puffery Is *Not* Illegal 105
Economic Frauds of Large Corporations 105
Telemarketing and Mail Scams 106
    Mail Fraud 106
    Telemarketing to Get Your Money 107
    Sweepstakes 108

Prizes and Free Gifts 109
Contests 110
Postcards and Letters Saying, "You Definitely Have Won!" 111
Many Charities Are *Not* What They Claim to Be 112
Buying Ripoffs and Scams 113
Buying Clubs 114
Rent-to-Own 115
Coupon Books 116
Vacation Certificates 116
Scholarship Aid 117
Vehicle Sales and Repairs 118
Fictitious List Prices 118
High-Balling the Value of the Trade-in Allowance 119
Low-Balling the Price of a New Vehicle 119
Automobile Repair Scams 119
Investment Swindles 120
The Investment Swindler's Game 121
Tips on How to Avoid Financial Swindles 122
Ponzi Schemes Are Illegal 123
Pyramid Schemes Are Illegal 124
Multi-Level Network Marketing Investments Are Legitimate 126
Chain Letters Are Illegal Pyramid Schemes 126
Referral Rebate Sales Are Illegal Pyramid Schemes 127
Work-at-Home Scams 127
Review and Summary of Key Terms and Concepts 128
Useful Resources for Consumers 130
"What Do You Think" Questions 130

Chapter 5   Laws That Help Consumers   131

Laws on Sales Transactions 132
Telemarketing Solicitations Regulations of the FCC and FTC 132
"900-Number" FCC Regulations 134
Unordered Merchandise Regulations of the Postal Service 135
Negative Option Mail-Order Rule of the FTC 136
Mail-Order Merchandise Regulations of the FTC 136
COD (Cash on Delivery) Rule of the Postal Service 137
Door-to-Door Sales Regulations of the FTC 138
Door-to-Door Sales Cooling-Off-Period Laws in States 139
Cooling-Off Laws for Health Spas, Timeshares, Campground Contracts,
Mortgage Refinancing, Etc. 139
Consumer Leasing of Automobiles 139
Airline Delayed Arrivals 140
Airline Bumping Regulations 140
Airline Regulations on Lost Baggage 141
Pet Lemon Laws 141
Weight-Loss Center Laws 142
Rent-to-Own Laws 142
Deliveries and Installations Laws 142
Laws on Vehicles 143
Odometer Fraud Law 143
Motor Vehicle "Buyer's Orders" Laws 143
Lemon Laws for New Vehicles 143
Used Vehicle Lemon Laws 144
Used Vehicle Lemon Branding Laws 145
Vehicle Repair Laws 145
Secret Warranty Disclosure Laws for Vehicles 145
Federal Trade Commission Used Car Rule 146
Laws on Warranties 152

Magnuson-Moss Warranty Act 152
Standards for Companies that Offer Warranties 153
What Some Confusing Phrases in Warranties Really Mean 153
Disclaiming Implied Warranties Is Prohibited Except When Something Is
    Sold "As Is" 154
Full and Limited Warranties May Be Offered 154
Informal Dispute Procedures Are Encouraged 155
Laws on Housing 155
Renter's Security Deposits 156
Late Possession of the Rental Property 156
Habitability of Rental Unit 156
Interstate Land Sales 157
Community Reinvestment Act 157
Fair Housing Act 157
Home Mortgage Disclosure Act 157
State Housing Discrimination Laws 158
Laws on Credit 158
Limited Liability on Credit Cards 158
Electronic Funds Transfer Act 159
Automatic-Billing Disputes 160
Fair Credit Reporting Act 161
Fair Credit Billing Act 162
Equal Credit Opportunity Act 166
Fair Debt Collection Practices Act 166
Fair Credit and Charge Card Disclosure Act 167
State Laws on Credit Card Disclosures 167
Home Equity Loan Consumer Protection Act 168
Home Ownership and Equity Protection Act 169
Summary of Key Terms and Concepts 170
Useful Resources for Consumers 172
"What Do You Think" Questions 172
Appendix 5A: Sample Letters Challenging Credit Card Charges 173

Part Three: The Challenging Market Place

Chapter 6   The Capitalistic American Marketplace   179

How an Economic System Functions 180
Socialism As an Economic System 181
Capitalism As an Economic System 182
Mixed Economic Systems Predominate Today 184
Allocating Resources in the U.S. Economy 184
Types of Resources 185
Resource Availability 186
How Resources Are Allocated 187
The Price Mechanism at Work 189
The Circular Flow of Economic Activity 190
The Multiplier Effect 191
How the U.S. Government Tries to Manage the Economy 191
Fiscal Policies: Taxing and Spending 191
Monetary Policies: Managing Money and Credit 192
Broad Social and Economic Goals of American Society 195
The U.S. *Assumes* Scarcity, Democracy, and Capitalism 196
Primary Goal: Economic Freedom 197
Primary Goal: Economic Efficiency 197
Primary Goal: Full Employment 198

Primary Goal: Price Stability 199
Primary Goal: Economic Growth 199
Primary Goal: Economic Productivity 202
Primary Goal: Economic Security 203
Primary Goal: Economic Justice 204
Review and Summary of Key Terms and Concepts 205
Useful Resources for Consumers 207
"What Do You Think" Questions 207

Chapter 7   Economic Concepts Critical to Consumer Success   209

Demand in a Market Economy 210
How Demand Affects Prices 210
The Demand Curve Slopes Downward and to the Right 211
Demand is Characterized by Its Elasticity 213
Supply Affects Prices 215
The Supply Curve Slopes Upward to the Left 215
Several Non-Price Determinants of Supply Exist 216
Market Equilibrium Is the Ideal Where Price Meets Supply 216
When Supply and Demand Does Not Work 219
Farm Prices Often Are Not Set by Supply and Demand 219
Price Ceilings Are Occasionally Imposed by Government 219
Price Fixing Eliminates the Competitive Forces of Supply and Demand 220
Income and Substitution Effects 220
Opportunity Cost 220
Marginal Cost 221
Diminishing Marginal Utility 224
Review and Summary of Key Terms and Concepts 227
Useful Resources for Consumers 227
"What Do You Think" Questions 228
Appendix 7-A: The Life Cycle and Permanent Income Hypotheses 229

Chapter 8   Consumers in the Global Marketplace   231

World Economic Problems 232
Economic Problem: Damaging Pollution 233
Economic Problem: Excessive Population Growth 233
Economic Problem: Persistent Poverty 234
Economic Problem: Excessive Military Spending 234
Economic Problem: Crime, Corruption and Anarchy 235
Economic Problem: Growing External Debt 235
What Are the Key Economic Concepts Important to Understanding Global
Trade? 236
Pareto Efficiency: Economic Trade Is a "Win-Win" Situation 237
Economies of Scale 237
Absolute Advantage 237
Comparative Advantage 238
Challenges Facing the United States in World Trade 238
The Growing U.S. National Debt 240
Getting Americans to Invest More 241
Which Way Should a Nation Go: Free Trade or Industrial Policy? 242
Benefits of Free Trade 243
Barriers to Free Trade 243
Industrial Policy—A New Paradigm for the U.S. 246
Regional Trade Agreements and the World Trade Organization 248
North American Free Trade Agreement 249
European Union 250
The World Trade Organization 251

The International Consumer Movement 252
    Consumers International 252
    International Codes for Proper Corporate Behavior 255
    United Nations Guidelines on Consumer Protection 256
    The Future of the International Consumer Movement 257
Review and Summary of Key Terms and Concepts 258
Useful Resources for Consumers 260
"What Do You Think" Questions 260

Chapter 9   Government Regulation of Economic Interests   261

The Economic Role of Business in Society 262
    Why Businesses Operate As They Do 262
    Social Responsibilities of Business 263
Self-Regulation Is Essential to Good Business Practices 264
    Purposes of Self-Regulation 265
    Examples of Self-Regulation 265
Why Governments Regulate 267
    Governments Attempt to Create External Benefits 269
    Governments Encourage or Discourage Certain Behaviors 270
    When Is it Desirable for Government to Control the Market? 271
The Historical Culture of Government Regulation in the U.S. 274
    Separation of Powers 274
    A Nation of Laws 274
How Government Promotes Fair Competition 275
    Effects of Little or No Competition—Economic Fraud 275
    Government Sometimes Prohibits Competition 276
    Government Gets Businesses to Sign Consent Agreements 277
Government Laws That Promote Fair Competition 278
    Sherman Antitrust Act 278
    Clayton Act 281
    Federal Trade Commission Act 283
    Robinson-Patman Act 284
    Cellar-Kefauver Act 284
    Hart-Scott-Rodino FTC Improvements Act 285
Four Primary Antitrust Tools That Government Uses to Promote Competition 285
Review and Summary of Key Terms and Concepts 286
Useful Resources for Consumers 288
"What Do You Think" Questions 288

Chapter 10   Government Regulation of Consumer Interests   289

U.S. Government Goals and the Consumer Interest 290
    Goal: A Free and Competitive Economic Marketplace 290
    Goal: To Promote Public Well-being and Safety 290
    Goal: To Demand Adequate Information for Consumers 291
    Goal: To Set Uniform Standards 291
    Goal: To Protect Consumers from Economic Frauds 291
    Goal: To Provide Sources of Redress 292
    Consumers Often Gain When Government Regulates to Pursue the Public
        Interest 292
The Role of Special-Interest Groups 293
    Lobbyists Are Important to Effective Government 293
    Consumers Also Have Lobbying Organizations 295
    "Neg-Reg": A New Form of Regulation 295
How Government Regulates to Benefit Consumers 296
    Administrative Agencies: The "Fourth" Branch of Government 296
    Executive (Dependent) and Independent Agencies 298

Powers of Regulatory Agencies 298
Some Regulatory Agencies Have the Powers of All Three Branches of
Government 301
How States and Local Governments Protect Consumers 301
Deregulation and the Consumer Interest 305
The Backlash against Regulation 305
The Concept of Deregulation 307
Deregulation Has Critics, But It Will Continue 308
The Powers of the Federal Trade Commission 308
Quasi-Judicial Powers 309
Quasi-Legislative Powers 310
Benefits and Costs of Government Regulation 311
Benefit-Cost Analysis Is a Tool 311
The Many Costs of Government Regulation 312
How Government Uses Cost-Benefit Analysis 313
Regulating with Specification and Performance Standards 313
Sources of Regulatory Inadequacy 314
Review and Summary of Key Terms and Concepts 315
Useful Resources for Consumers 317
"What Do You Think" Questions 317

Part Four: Information Processing

Chapter 11   How to Analyze Consumer Issues   319

Policymaking in the United States 320
Power Clusters 320
Attentive Public and Latent Public 321
How Public Policy Is Shaped 322
Power Cluster Behaviors 323
The Effects of Economic Ideology and Political Beliefs 323
The Neoclassical Belief System 324
The Managerial Belief System 326
The Reformist Belief System 327
Political Belief Systems 328
Support for Consumer Protection Proposals 332
Analyzing and Resolving Consumer Issues 334
Constructive Thinking 334
Purposeful Analytical Thinking 334
Preparing Alternative Solutions 336
Government Action in Resolving Alternatives 337
How to Lobby the Government Decision Making Process 338
Resolution of Consumer Issues Through Cooperation 339
Issues That Would Strengthen the Balance of Power Between Consumers and
Sellers 341
1. Fully Fund Regulatory Agencies 341
2. Encourage Public Participation in Regulatory Proceedings 341
3. Create Financial Consumer Associations 342
4. Encourage Corrective Advertising 342
5. Broaden the Use of Mediation and Arbitration 342
6. Expand Consumer Education 343
Review and Summary of Key Terms and Concepts 344
Useful Resource for Consumers 346
"What Do You Think" Questions 346
Appendix 11-A: Proposed Consumer Protection Legislation and Regulations 347

Chapter 12 Decision Making in Today's Complex Society   349

Reasons Why Decision Making Is Getting More Difficult 350
  The Consumer Search for Value 350
  Consumer Dissatisfaction Occurs 351
  The Number and Complexity of Products Is Increasing 351
  To Cope With the Challenging Marketplace, Many Consumers Blindly
      Follow Rules of Thumb 352
  Consumer Make Many Irrational Marketplace Decisions 352
  Consumers (Irrationally) Often Ignore the Discount Rate 353
  Information Processing for Consumers Is Difficult, But It Has Very High
      Potential Payoffs 353
  Price Discrimination Exists and Is Taken Advantage of by Informed
      Consumers 355
  Time Is Limited for Decision Making 355
  Searching? Comparison Shopping? Maybe, Maybe Not 356
  Some Shop for "*Good* Buys" Instead of "*Best* Buys" 357
  Lifestyles and Values Affect Decision Making, Including Those That Are
      Politically Correct 357
The Geistfeld Model of Consumer Choice 358
  Indifference Curves 358
  Budget Constraint 361
  Optimal Purchases: Maximizing Satisfaction 361
  Inadequate Information and Purchase Decisions 363
  Consumers Need Two Types of Information 363
Understanding How to Be a Pro-environmental Consumer 366
  Many Consumers Use Environmental Factors in Decision Making 367
  Consumers Sometimes are "Free Riders" When It Comes to Pollution 368
  A Decision Making Matrix for Pro-Environmental Consumers 370
Advertising and Consumers 374
  How Advertising Is Regulated 375
  Types of Truth and Exaggeration in Advertising 376
  Types of Advertisements: Informational and Puffery 377
  Misleading Advertising Negativelly Affects Decision Making 378
  Deceptive Advertising Is Illegal, but Not Until a Government Agency Says
      So 379
  "Advertising Dollars"—A Form of Censorship That Attacks the Consumer
      Interest 380
  Television Advertising Directed at Children 381
  Needed: A More Knowledgeable Media Consumer 383
Review and Summary of Key Terms and Concepts 384
Useful Resources for Consumers 385
"What Do You Think" Questions 386

Chapter 13 The Planned Buying Process   387

General Buying Behaviors of Consumers 388
  Habit Buying 388
  Impulse Buying 388
  Conspicuous Consumption 389
Planned Buying for Important Purchases 391
Sources of Buying Information for Consumers 393
  Source: Consumer Testing Magazines 394
  Source: Consumer-Oriented Magazines 395
  Source: Seals and Certification Program Information 395
  Source: Mass Media 398
  Source: Government Agency Information 398
  Source: Facts from Better Business Bureaus 398
  Source: Point-of-Purchase Information 399

Defining the Problem 399
Identifying Personal Values and Goals 400
    Can Bonnie Afford to Buy an Automobile? 400
    How Much Can Bonnie Get for Her Money? 401
Identifying Possible Alternatives 402
Comparing Costs and Benefits 403
    Warranties 405
    Service Contracts/Extended Warranties Are Bad Deals 407
    Leasing Is a Good Choice for Some Consumers 409
    Financing Options 410
    Choosing Priorities 411
Negotiating 413
    The Goal of Negotiation 413
    The Process of Negotiation 414
    Determining the Price You Want to Pay 415
    Automobile Brokers and Buying Services 416
Selecting the Best Alternative 417
    Accepting and Evaluating the Decision 418
Review and Summary of Key Terms and Concepts 419
Useful Resources for Consumers 420
"What Do You Think" Questions 421

Part Five: Consumer Economic Issues

Chapter 14   Food Issues   423

American Eating Habits 424
    Calorie Intake 425
    The Poor Quality of American Diets 425
    The Importance of Low-Fat Eating to Good Health 428
    Some Americans Are Trying to Improve Their Diets 430
    Eating Healthy Isn't Difficult 430
    Nutritional Labeling and Education Act 431
    USDA's Food Guide Pyramid 433
Questionable Food Selling Practices 433
Anti-Competitive Practices in the Food Industry 435
    Calendar Marketing Agreements Squeeze Out Competitors 435
    Allocation Agreements for Shelf Space 436
    Agricultural Marketing Orders 436
    Economic Concentration in the Meatpacking Industry 437
Agencies and Specialized Laws Protecting Food Consumers 437
    U.S. Department of Agriculture 437
    The Food and Drug Administration 438
    The Food Additives Amendment 439
    The Miller Pesticide Chemicals Amendment 442
    The Delaney Clause 443
    The Color Additive Amendments 444
Assessing Consumer Risks: Does Everything Cause Cancer? 445
    Research and a Risk-Free Society 446
    Research Conducted on Animals 446
How Consumers Get Confused When Food Shopping 447
Review and Summary of Key Terms and Concepts 449
Useful Resources for Consumers 450
"What Do You Think" Questions 451

Chapter 15　Health Care Issues 　　　　　453

The Challenges of Purchasing Health Care Services 454
Guidelines on How to Purchase Services 455
What Is Wrong with the U.S. Health Care System 457
　　Health Care Costs in the U.S. Are the Highest in the World 457
　　One-Quarter of Americans Are Without Health Insurance 458
　　We Already Pay—Through Hidden and Real Taxes—the Health Care
　　　　Costs of the Uninsured 459
Calls to Reform the U.S. Health Care System 459
　　Why National Health Care Reform Failed 459
　　Calls to Reform Health Care Are Answered by Some States 460
　　Those Who *Have* Health Care Coverage Utilize Managed Care and
　　　　Managed Competition 462
Prescription Drugs 464
　　What Are Drugs? 464
　　Premarket Review of Prescription Drugs 465
　　Generic Drugs 466
　　Generic Substitution Laws 467
　　Some Pharmacists Prescribe Drugs 468
Over-the-Counter Drugs 468
　　Problems and Dangers 469
　　Aspirin and Similar Pain Relievers 470
　　Vitamins and Food Supplements 474
Smoking and Health 475
　　Smoking and Death 476
　　Related Negative Effects of Smoking 477
　　The Tobacco Companies Lied for Fifty Years 478
　　Secondhand Smoke Kills 40,000+ Every Year 478
　　What About Smoking Is Harmful? 480
　　Surprise (NOT!), Nicotine Is As Addictive As Heroin 480
　　The Future of Smoking 480
Alcohol and Health 482
Review and Summary of Key Terms and Concepts 485
Useful Resources for Consumers 486
"What Do You Think" Questions 486

Chapter 16　Product Safety Issues 　　　　　487

Product Safety and Effectiveness 488
　　Many Products Cause Injuries 488
　　Causal Factors in Injuries 489
Cost-Benefit Analysis and Safety 490
　　How Much Risk Is Acceptable? 491
　　Measuring Risk for Public-Policy Decisions 491
　　Criticisms of Cost-Benefit Analysis 492
　　Using Benefit-Cost Analysis 493
　　Factors to Consider in Making Product Safety Decisions 493
　　Products Needing Safety Regulations 494
Product Liability Lawsuits—A Powerful Weapon of Consumers 495
　　Punitive Damages Penalize the Worst Manufacturers 496
　　Today's Product Liability Laws 497
　　Critics of Product Liability Lawsuits 499
　　Supporters of the Consumer's Right to Sue 499
The Consumer Product Safety Commission 500
　　CPSC Legal Mandates and Responsibilities 500
　　CPSC Authorities and Powers 501
　　CPSC Injury Data-Collection System 503
　　CPSC Rulemaking Procedures 503

The National Highway Traffic Safety Administration 505
   NHTSA Legal Mandates and Authorities 505
   NHTSA Programs 506
   NHTSA Recalls 507
   NHTSA Vehicle Crashing and Testing 509
   NHTSA Safety Standards 509
Criticisms of Government Product Safety Efforts 511
   Few People Respond to Recalls 511
   Serious Time Delays Exist 511
   Too Much Reliance on Voluntary Efforts 511
   Too Much Politics 512
   Inclination Not to Prosecute 512
   Not Enough Resources to Do the Job Properly 512
Review and Summary of Key Terms and Concepts 513
Useful Resources for Consumers 514
"What Do You Think" Questions 514

Chapter 17   Banking, Credit, and Housing Issues   515

Banking Problems and Issues 516
   Truth in Savings, Almost 516
   Deregulation of Banking 517
   Rising Fees 519
   Discrimination Against Small Depositors and Nondepositors 520
   Basic Banking Is a Reality in Some States, But Not All 521
   Paying for the Savings and Loan/Banking Scandal 523
Credit Problems and Issues 525
   Unnecessary Credit-Card Solicitations 525
   Paying Interest Rates That Are Too High 526
   Making Credit Payments Increases Total Costs 527
   Paying Only the "Low Minimum Monthly Payment" 527
   Grace Periods Are Confusing Because the Methods of Assessing Interest
      Are Perplexing 530
   The "Two-Cycle Method of Assessing Interest" Legally Doubles the
      Effective Interest Rate 531
   The "Rule of 78s" Is a Prepayment Penalty 532
   Credit- and Debit-Card Registration Services 533
   Credit Insurance (Life/Disability/Unemployment) 533
   Mistakes in Credit Files 534
   Privacy 536
Housing Problems and Issues 538
   Discrimination in Housing and Credit 538
   Redlining 540
   The High Cost of Housing in America 541
   Appraisers Are Regulated, but Not for Most Consumers 544
   Mandatory Defect-Disclosure Laws 545
   Laws to Require Agents to Disclose to Buyers Whom They Represent 545
   Bargaining Is Necessary to Reduce Sales Commissions 546
   Kickback Fees to Help Arrange Other Services 546
   Locked-in Mortgage Loans 548
   Settlement Date May Lack Meaning 548
   Escrow Ripoffs Exist 549
   Canceling Private Mortgage Insurance 549
Review and Summary of Key Terms and Concepts 550
Useful Resources for Consumers 552
"What Do You Think" Questions 552

Chapter 18   Insurance and Investment Issues   553

Consumer Problems and Issues in Insurance 554
    The Insurance Consumer's Bill of Rights 554
    The Automobile Insurance Rebellion and Resulting Reforms 555
    Insurance Industry Accounting Logic 556
    Anti-Group Laws 557
    Insurance Industry is Exempt from Anti-trust Laws 557
    Price Fixing Among Insurers is State Approved 558
    Price Fixing Between the Automobile Repair and Insurance Industries 558
    No-Fault Automobile Insurance 560
    Which Remedy for the Auto Insurance Mess Do You Want? 562
    Good Buys in Term Life Insurance 564
    Beware of Life Insurance Being Sold as a Retirement Plan 565
    Title Insurance for Homes: A Ripoff 565
    What Happens When Insurance Companies Go Broke? 566
    The Coming Insurance Industry Scandal 567
Consumer Problems and Issues in Investments 568
    The Investing Consumer's Bill of Rights 568
    Banks Sell Investments That Are *Not* Federally Insured 569
    Consumers Buying Bank Investments Are Misinformed 571
    Most Financial Advisors Are Biased 571
    Method of Compensation Indicates Potential Bias 572
    Insider Trading 573
    Fairness in Arbitration 574
    State Guarantee Funds Often *Exclude* So-Called "Guaranteed Investment
        Contracts" 575
    Some Retirement Investment Pensions Are at Risk 575
    Workers' Pensions Can Get "Stolen" in Leveraged Buyouts 577
    Timesharing Vacation Real Estate Is *Not* An Investment 577
Review and Summary of Key Terms and Concepts 579
Useful Resources for Consumers 580
"What Do You Think" Questions 580

Appendix   Careers in Consumer Affairs   581

Career Opportunities in Consumer Affairs 581
    Job Responsibilities 581
    Career Development Opportunities 582
    Career Options 583
    Curriculum Requirements 584
    Competencies of Graduates 585
    Sample Letters for Employment 585

Index   589

Preface

Thanks to the support of many instructors and students around the United States, the fourth edition of *Consumer Economic Issues in America* is now a reality. You must share the belief that consumer issues are important and that all consumers must be empowered with sufficient knowledge about consumer economics. Such information helps consumers clarify their values, goals, interests, and priorities about how the world works, what needs to be done to improve it, and how they can do their part to help make it better.

These times are bringing change to the consumer's world. While the consumer movement has long been interested in strengthening the power of consumers in the seller-consumer relationship, this emphasis is gathering steam. The decade of the 1990s is experiencing increased citizen activism, especially by students. Energetic and informed participation by consumers in the issues of the day is increasingly accepted as a form of patriotism.

In the years ahead, the consumer movement will address such issues as increasing (or decreasing) government regulation, breaking up large corporate monopolies, demanding more fairness in advertising, increasing the availability of useful purchasing information, preventing frauds and misrepresentations, keeping unsafe foods and drugs out of the marketplace, banning dangerous consumer products, improving automobile safety, making more remedies available for consumers with problems, and providing consumers with a greater voice in government and corporate policy matters.

While the consumer movement continues to broaden and mature, individual consumers keep asking such questions as, "How can I get my money's worth?" "How can I live the good life?" "How can I personally help improve the world in which I live?"

Your students already possess considerable experience in answering these questions. Each student is now probably in the first part of what is expected to be a long life of making consumer decisions. Most decisions will be good, but some might not be so good. A sound understanding of the principles and concepts of consumer economics is absolutely vital if students are to avoid the pitfalls of poor consumer decision making and deal effectively with the marketplace. At the very least, students need to know what questions to ask.

Accordingly, I believe it is essential to provide much more than a simplistic "how to" approach to consumer economics. I want students to learn enough to become knowledgeable and assertive consumers who are able to efficiently and effectively satisfy personal needs and wants, as well as be prepared to help improve the functioning of the American economic marketplace for all consumers. What students learn should be practical and have a favorable impact on the resources, health, and safety of consumers. In the words of actor and comedian Bill Cosby when talking about education, "It doesn't mean anything if you can't take what you know and make America a better place."

Students today have the academic training, maturity, and freedom in America to find out who they are. In all likelihood, they will do well in life. The field of consumer economics demands that they become involved in societal issues, and in addition to doing well in life, they also do some good. Consumer economics is a subject that encourages students to calculate the benefits and costs of alternatives. Some will argue that it also has to do with honor, kindness, decency, fairness, and compassion.

Approach is Normative

Experts agree that consumer economics must include emphasis on buying skills, money management, and consumer-citizenship responsibilities. I strongly agree! One cannot become an effective citizen-consumer without being aware of the facts, understanding and applying principles and concepts, developing favorable attitudes and a personal code of ethics, and making a commitment to helping create positive changes in the American marketplace.

This book argues on a theoretical base of critical theory that rejects the assumption that consumer economics should be value-free knowledge. There are no correct answers; both knowledge and truth are qualitative. Society was created by humans and is subject to change by them.

Consumer economics demands that consumers become involved in the quality of lives of the people in society. The normative approach in consumer economics asks that students respond to the high expectations that the best of America holds for them.

Develops informed Citizen-Consumers

Knowledge and information is power. Consumers need to get that knowledge and information, and use it to their advantage. Accordingly, this book seeks to develop informed citizen-consumers who have a right and a duty to protect their own interests as well as those of other consumers. Informed citizen-consumers who make wise decisions in the marketplace ultimately help raise the level of living for all consumers while also contributing to improvement in the morality of the marketplace. Consumers also must learn that they have many important responsibilities, as well as rights. Such empowerment permits consumers to foment change as well as create forces for change.

Promotes the Consumer interest

In order to think systematically and properly function as a consumer, one first needs to understand the concept of consumer interest. Therefore, broadly defined, the **consumer interest** involves efforts to secure, protect, and assert consumer rights in the marketplace in order that all consumers receive an acceptable quality of goods and services at fair or low prices. Note that the consumer interest is first and foremost concerned with price and quality. It is also concerned with questions of equity. Accordingly, this book emphasizes fundamental, real-life consumer issues and problems.

Takes a Pro-Consumer Viewpoint

The viewpoint taken in *Consumer Economic Issues in America* is pro-consumer and normative in that it reveals the vested economic interests of businesses, governments, and consumers. This book also is appropriately critical of each interest, and this perspective becomes apparent as the book pursues, illuminates, and illustrates the consumer interest in over 100 consumer issues. A special effort is made to introduce key economic concepts as they apply to consumer decision making situations, as well as to the analysis of issues. This requires only a basic appreciation of economic concepts that anyone can comprehend.

Uses Economic Concepts to Develop Higher-Order Thinking

This book depends heavily on economics—presented in an uncomplicated manner—because applying economic concepts is a form of **higher-order thinking**. The term describes the process of learning how to learn. One's success in life depends less on what is learned in school and more on learning how to apply what is known in a world that is constantly changing. Thus, to help develop higher order thinking skills in consumer economics, it is important for students to find structure in what appears to be disorder. That mode of thinking assists the students to analyze consumer issues, deal effectively with complex public policy proposals, recognize different approaches to thinking and problem solving, and be able to develop multiple solutions when appropriate. Models to assist in analyzing problems and issues are provided.

Uses an Issues Approach

Consumer Economic Issues in America examines basic issues that have arisen between consumers and sellers. Although the short-run interests of consumers and sellers are different, and often very much at odds, they are interdependent. Consumers and sellers have to cooperate for long-run satisfaction and economic survival. In effect, the consumer movement desires to maintain a "creative friction" between consumers and sellers where both accept certain responsibilities to effectively resolve consumer issues for the betterment of all.

This book focuses on many important and fundamental consumer issues. It also tries to go beyond concern about today's "issue of the moment." An attempt is made to expose the underlying forces, interests, and problems among consumers, sellers, and governments. This book tries to clarify the scope and depth of consumer issues, and to suggest what direction the future likely holds for resolution of the concerns.

The approach is to provide a book that contains adequate treatment of virtually all consumer interest topics in order that students be properly informed. The book examines issues in economics, consumer economics, family economics, decision making, and money management. Problems are examined in these fields as well as in the areas of resource management, marketing, psychology, sociology, and political science. Students need to be familiar with a breadth of consumer concerns in order to develop a full understanding of how to effectively protect and promote the consumer interest. Also included is an in-depth discussion of the analysis and resolution of consumer issues so that students can appreciate and learn the process of constructive cooperation, rather than resort to a confrontational approach.

Includes Chapters Plus Appendices

As part of an important conceptual approach, some chapters have one or more appendices. This allows flexibility. The reader can simply read each chapter as presented and gain the essentials in consumer economics. The appendices then supply supplementary materials that offer more depth in subject matter, provide additional practical advice, or examine public-interest concerns.

Utilizes a Multi-Disciplinary Approach

For greater effectiveness, *Consumer Economic Issues in America* takes a multi-disciplinary approach. This strategy can be effective in such courses as consumer economics, consumer education, consumer problems, consumer issues, consumer finance, money management, and consumer protection. Some instructors will find that there is sufficient information in this fourth edition for two courses.

Goals of This Text

Two broad goals defined the efforts in writing *Consumer Economic Issues in America:* (1) to develop competence in understanding consumer economic issues, and (2) to develop confidence in dealing with consumer economic concerns.

To Become Competent

To become competent in understanding consumer economic issues, the reader must be provided wide scope. I have endeavored to make this the most comprehensive textbook available by including all traditional topics and some of particular importance (such as health and product safety issues). The book attempts to make clear the nature of the issues as well as solutions, both present and proposed.

A unique learning feature called "Consumer Update" appears throughout the text. These are brief inserts, typically two to three paragraphs in length, that provide **up-to-date information** on approximately one hundred consumer problems, issues, or laws. Sometimes these offer relevant asides or additional details that add depth to the topics examined.

Another feature is called **Did You Know?...** which is a series of boxed inserts that offers interesting data related to consumer topics.

Competence also requires an **in-depth examination** of a subject. Students need to understand how the economic marketplace is designed to serve consumers as well as how it sometimes fails to serve consumers; students must comprehend the nature of the economic system and its impact on them as consumers. Supportive of this understanding is an underpinning of **technically correct legal information** on dozens of federal, state, and local consumer protection laws and regulations. Further, this book helps **bridge the differences in viewpoints** between consumers and sellers. After completing this book, readers should **be prepared to dialogue intelligently** on the issues with government personnel, businesspersons, consumer activists, and "real" everyday consumers.

WHAT IS THE MOST IMPORTANT THING A CONSUMER SHOULD KNOW?

In the collective words of some consumer economics students: "I don't have to accept less than adequate products, services, or business/government inattention to the interests of consumers. That goes go me and everyone else out there. I can demand better quality and prices, and my fellow consumers can demand the same. Together, we can make the institutions of society better attend to the interests of consumers."

To help readers become competent in understanding consumer economic issues, this book **provides some perspectives** on the changing economic marketplace and some **useful tools** for success as consumers. Students need to know what personal economic goals they have and how to achieve them. Thus, students have to come face to face with their values, goals, and dreams and then give them priorities so that they can manage their choicemaking in those directions. This book encourages more rational decision making. *Consumer Economic Issues in America* helps students learn how to manage their resources to reach their goals. It also can serve as a useful reference or resource book.

To Become Confident

To become confident in dealing with consumer economic concerns, the reader needs to be led **through**, not simply **to**, the material. This book attempts to acquaint the reader with the subject matter **logically** and to offer no unanticipated surprises. Assuming that most students in consumer economics have little background in economics, family economics, and sociology, the book **provides appropriate background knowledge** when necessary. **Numerical examples** are always explained parenthetically, and I have endeavored to discuss the **benefits and costs** of different consumer decisions.

Key words and concepts—which are printed in bold type—are clearly and completely defined when they first occur in the text and again in later chapters, in case the chapters are read out of sequence. Many standard terms are defined too, in recognition of the fact that American English is not the native tongue of many college students. This book emphasizes the importance of understanding **new vocabulary and basic concepts**, since these are the tools used to confidently master the principles of consumer economics.

Throughout the text there are a number of **tables, charts, and illustrations** to aid understanding. These make the text more **enjoyable to read** and provide visual clarification of important concepts. Objectives open each chapter to bolster student confidence in the subject matter of consumer economics by focusing on what is important. The "Review and Summary of Key Terms and Concepts" questions at the end of each chapter emphasize **applying** the concepts and principles to **everyday real-life** consumer decision making situations. **Principles** that are well learned, particularly in applied situations, have long lives. As students **better understand themselves**, they develop more expertise in dealing with consumer economic concerns. Thus, the student becomes a more **informed citizen-consumer** who is better able to become involved in advocating the consumer interest.

Organization and Topical Coverage

I surveyed over 100 instructors across the country and conducted two focus groups to discover what they wanted in a quality textbook on this subject. The clearest message I heard was that instructors wanted a straightforward book to **emphasize the basics: the fundamental consumer economic issues affecting all consumers**.

Consumer Economic Issues in America has a bias toward consumer economic issues that help keep the American marketplace **competitive, free, and fair** for the benefit of sellers and consumers alike. I believe in supporting **the self-regulatory efforts** of business and at the same time looking carefully at what government is doing and can do for consumers. This book emphasizes **understanding our American economic system, the concepts of consumer sovereignty and the consumer interest, evaluative criteria** by which products and services are judged, tools for living, how to analyze issues, money management, and the factors that affect buying decisions. This book includes consideration of **environmental issues** because many consumer decisions in the marketplace have environmental aspects which are thought by some to be important. This book provides in-depth coverage of the **consumer protection efforts by federal, state, and local governments**. I think the topical coverage in *Consumer Economic Issues in America* is what consumer economics instructors will want for their students.

As can be seen in the table of contents, this book approaches topical coverage in a manner that provides a **full explanation of the fundamentals** of a topic before commencing further study. While each of the eighteen chapters has a place in the overall sequence, **each chapter also is complete in itself**. Thus, the chapters can be rearranged to be read in another developmental sequence with minimal loss of comprehension.

Part One provides an introduction to consumer economics by offering **Some Perspectives**. Chapter 1 focuses on the question "What is the consumer interest?" Surprisingly, no textbook addresses this question in a meaningful way. Chapter 2 provides an appreciation of why the consumer movement has changed and how the role of consumers will continue to evolve; the chapter reviews the problems, concerns, and issues faced by the consumer movement over the past 100 years and suggests future directions.

Part Two, **Facing Consumer Problems Successfully**, contains three chapters. Chapter 3 discusses the rights and responsibilities of consumers as well as the remedies available to consumers when seeking to correct any wrongs encountered. Chapter 4 provides a virtual encyclopedia of information on avoiding the most popular ripoffs and frauds in the American marketplace. Chapter 5 offers an "appendix format" of about 60 key laws and regulations that protect consumers and help them obtain redress.

Part Three, **The Challenging Marketplace**, contains five chapters. Chapter 6 examines capitalism and how resources are allocated in the American marketplace. Chapter 7 details a number of economic concepts critical to consumer success. Both chapters 6 and

7 are especially useful for readers who may not have completed a course in economics. Chapter 8 examines consumers in a global economic marketplace, and surveys the related topics of free trade, industrial policy, regional trading agreements, and the international consumer movement. Chapter 9 examines the enormous function of government in regulating economic interests while Chapter 10 overviews government regulation of the interests of consumers.

Part Four, **Information Processing**, has three chapters. Chapter 11 presents an introduction to the breadth of current concerns of consumer interest plus a model and a framework useful in analyzing and resolving consumer issues. Chapter 12 focuses on rational decision making and how this process is affected by factors such as concerns about the environment and advertising. Chapter 13 provides a detailed illustration of the planned buying process for major expenditures, using an automobile purchase as an example.

Part Five, consisting of five chapters, focuses on **Consumer Economic Issues**. Chapter 14 is aimed at helping students better understand the food issues affecting consumers and how they can deal with them. It emphasizes the laws, regulations, and agencies protecting the consumer interest in the area of food. The important and controversial subject of health care issues is examined in Chapter 15, including using alternative health care services and understanding the effects of using tobacco and alcohol.

No consumer economics book would be complete without a chapter focusing on product safety issues, the subject of Chapter 16. In this chapter, the effectiveness of two government agencies is scrutinized: the Consumer Product Safety Commission and the National Highway Traffic Safety Commission. Chapter 17 focuses on consumer problems and issues in banking, credit and housing, such as basic banking, the infamous savings and loan scandal, redlining and other forms of discrimination in access to credit, and the high costs of housing. Chapter 18 examines consumer problems and issues in insurance and investments. Examples include new ideas to confront overpricing of automobile insurance, what happens when insurance companies go bankrupt, and some dangers to consumers' personal pension plans.

Major Revisions for the Fourth Edition

Numerous changes were made to the fourth to make the book more up-to-date, to more tightly focus on consumer issues, to facilitate student readability, and to shorten its overall length. To update this book, over 1,400 pieces of print information (over 150 each on heath care reform and finding truth in the tobacco industry) were carefully reviewed and over 600 changes were made.

A new feature, **Useful Resources for Consumers**, was added, and it provides the interested student addresses to write, telephone numbers to call, and Internet addresses to search. Over thirty new **Consumer Updates** were added. Several new **Did You Know?** boxed inserts were added. **Updates were made to every chapter** to reflect changes over the past year, including many of the proposals and actions by President Bill Clinton. More updates are identified below.

Learning Aids

This book offers a number of learning aids for each student:

- **Objectives** beginning each chapter.

- **Narrative Introductions** that give a rationale for study and summarize the contents of each chapter.

- **End-of-Chapter Review of Key Terms and Concepts** that allows the student to **apply** the concepts presented and gain confidence in using the knowledge outside the classroom. Students responding to these questions will have reviewed **all** important concepts in each chapter. Since it is not just a simple listing, these are appropriate for instructors to use in class when orally reviewing the material.

- A **new** feature is **"Useful Resources for Consumers"** which provides addresses to write, telephone numbers to call, and Internet addresses to search.

- **"Consumer Update" Boxed Inserts**, more than 100 of them, spotlight important information and present it in a concise manner. They add emphasis and stimulate interest as they illustrate additional relevant concepts, problems, issues, and controversies that underscore the practical aspects of consumer economics. Examples include:

  "Who is Ralph Nader, the Nation's Consumer Spokesperson?"
  "Ameristroika: The Future of Capitalism? Managers and Workers Own Part of the Company"
  "Capital Flight Damages the Economies of Less Developed Countries"
  "On the Difference Between an Environmentalist and a Consumer Advocate"
  "Yes, the Poor are Disadvantaged in the Marketplace"
  "Do Consumers Value Style or Substance?"
  "High Skills or Low Wages: America's Choice."
  "Advertising Foods to Kids"
  "Privacy (?!) at the Checkout Counter"
  "Court Secrecy Masks Safety Issues"
  "How to Organize a Boycott"
  "Teenage Shoppers Are Discriminated Against"
  "Theater Popcorn, Healthy or Not?"
  "All Consumer Deposits Are Not Covered By FDIC Insurance"
  "Baumol's Disease Explains Why Government Takes On So Many Jobs"
  "The Real Bogeyman is Productivity Not Foreign Competition"
  "Access to Consumer Credit Should Be A Consumer Right"
  "How to Identify Discrimination: Examples"
  "Consumers Consistently Make Purchasing Decisions Ignoring the Discount Rate"
  "Searching for a Used Car on the Information Superhighway"

- New **"Consumer Update" Boxed Inserts**, more than 30 of them, are included in the fourth edition:

  "Classified Ads Are Full of Lies"
  "The Dishonor Roll of Unfair Competitors"

"Your Current Homeowner's/Renter's Insurance *Already* Covers the Liability for Lost Credit and Debit Cards"
"The U.S. Exports Its Values Around the World"
"Cartels Are Created to Overcharge All Customers"
"Questions to Ask Your HMO"
"Top Ten Reasons NOT to Take a Consumer Economics Course"
"Consumers Sometimes Are 'Free Riders' When It Comes to Pollution"
"Consumers in Developing Countries Are at Risk to the 'Dark Side' of Marketing"
"Ideal Weight Guidelines"
"Yes! You Can Get Out Of Many Contracts"
"Some Things That Government Does Right!"
"P.J. O'Rourke on Democrats and Republicans"
"Anger and Cynicism About the Ugliness of the Political Process"
"Which Deal is Better: The Auto Dealer's Cash Rebate or a Low Interest Rate?"
"The Medical Care Market Has Characteristics that Make it Difficult to Reform"
"How to Refinance Your Education Loans"
"Your Right to Privacy is Being Invaded"

■ **"Did You Know?..."** is a series of boxed inserts for the fourth edition that offer interesting data related to consumer topics. Examples include:

"The Chances of Unemployment in Industrialized Countries"
"Just Who is Getting Those Big Subsidies?"
"The United States Saves Less Than It Invests"
"What is Most Favored Nation Trade Status?"
"The Gifts and Prizes... What They Really Are"

■ **"An Economic Focus On..."** is a series of special boxed inserts that carefully describes and illustrates a **single economic concept** which is related to the content of each chapter. These explanations—written by experts around the country—are presented in a **non-technical manner** so that all students can understand the essence being presented. Examples include:

"The Effects of Protectionistic Trade Quotas"
"Standard and Level of Consumption and Living"
"The Propensity to Consume"
"How the Supply of and Demand for Labor Affects Wage Rates in Developing Countries"
"Indifference Curve and Budget Line Analysis"
"Externalities and Air Pollution"
"Large-Scale Production and Price Regulation"
"Information Search in the Buying Process"
"Usury Laws and the Supply and Demand for Consumer Credit"
"The Economics of Discrimination Are Against the Consumer Interest"
"The International Consumer Movement and the Consumer Interest"
"A Proposal to End Discrimination in Automobile Insurance: Use the Odometer as the Exposure Unit"
"The Uniqueness of the Medical Care Market Makes It Difficult to Reform"
"The Geistfeld Model of Consumer Decision-Making"

■ **Key Terms and Concepts** are reinforced in several ways. All key terms—over 1200—are highlighted in bold type the first time they are used, then they are clearly defined! In the index, the key words and the numbers of the pages on which they are defined and discussed are in **bold** in the index.

- **An Index** appears at the end of the book and it is the most thorough of all books on the market—over 3000 entries in all—numbering 16 pages.

- **Headings and Subheadings** in bold print, four levels in all, are used to improve readability and reinforce the organization of the topics.

Supplements to Text

Accompanying this text is an **Instructor's Manual with Test Bank**, updated by Sheila Stogdale. This manual contains several components:

- **Organizing the Course** Suggested course syllabi and outlines are offered to emphasize a consumer protection, a buying skills, a money management, or a consumer issues approach to the subject

- **Suggested readings** for further study from a variety of both popular and academic sources

- **Suggestions on teaching/learning methods and techniques**

- **Outside research class assignments**

- **Answers to end-of-chapter questions**

- **Computerized Test Bank** of the 2500 questions from the **Instructor's Manual** with Test Bank available to adopters.

- **Transparency masters** of all the pertinent graphics from the text

Acknowledgments

I realize that an instructional text of this breadth and depth could not be created without the assistance of many people. I should, of course, mention my reviewers, who offered helpful suggestions and criticisms of the text while it was being developed and revised. The text has unquestionably been strengthened by their contributions. I am deeply appreciative of the generous assistance for the previous editions given by:

Ralph H. Alexander, Jr., Executive Director, National Advertising Review Board
William Bailey, Assistant Professor, University of Arkansas
Stephen J. Brobeck, Executive Director, Consumer Federation of America
James Brown, Director, Center for Consumer Affairs, University of Wisconsin
John R. Burton, Professor, University of Utah
Patrick Butler, Director, Insurance Project, National Organization for Women
Elizabeth Dolan, Associate Professor, University of New Hampshire
Joye J. Dillman, Associate Professor, Washington State University
Sidney W. Eckert, Professor, Appalachian State University
Meredith M. Layer, Senior Vice President, American Express

Mary Ellen Fise, Product Safety Specialist, Consumer Federation of America
Vicki Schram Fitzsimmons, Associate Professor, University of Illinois
Paul S. Forbes, President, The Forbes Group
Raymond E. Forgue, Associate Professor and Department Head, University of Kentucky
Steve Hamm, Administrator, Department of Consumer Affairs, South Carolina
Barbara Heinzerling, Professor, University of Akron
Donna Iams, Associate Professor, University of Arizona
Jane Kolodinsky, Assistant Professor, University of Vermont
Virginia H. Knauer, Special Assistant to Presidents Nixon, Ford, and Reagan
Jeffrey H. Krasnow, Attorney at Law
Carole J. Makela, Professor, Colorado State University
Richard L.D. Morse, Professor Emeritus, Kansas State University
Jeffrey O'Connell, Professor, University of Virginia
Joseph G. Painter, Jr., Attorney at Law, Blacksburg, Virginia
Claudia Peck, Professor and Associate Dean, University of Kentucky
Esther Peterson, Special Assistant and Consumer Affairs Advisor to Presidents
    Kennedy, Johnson, and Carter
R. David Pittle, Technical Director, Consumers Union
Mary E. Pritchard, Professor, Northern Illinois University
Warren J. Prunella, Chief Economist, Consumer Product Safety Commission
S. Lee Richardson, Jr., Professor and G. Maxwell Armor Eminent Scholar, University of
    Baltimore
Mary Ellen Rider, Associate Professor, University of Nebraska
Margaret Sanik, Professor, The Ohio State University
David Schmeltzer, Associate Director of Compliance and Administrative Litigation, Con-
    sumer Product Safety Commission
Jane Schuchardt, Program Director, United States Department of Agriculture Coopera-
    tive Extension Service
William B. Schultz, Public Citizen Litigation Group
Mark Silbergeld, Director of the Washington Office, Consumers Union of the United
    States
Mary Frances Stephanz, Executive Director, Better Business Bureau of Western Virginia
James S. Turner, Attorney, Swankin and Turner
Clinton Warne, Professor, Cleveland State University
Dorothy West, Professor, Michigan State University
Richard Widdows, Professor, Purdue University

Over thirty reviewers made specific suggestions. Their advice was largely accepted. Some who helped include:

Anne W. Bailey, Miami University
Peggy S. Berger, Colorado State University
Mary Ann Block, Tarleton State University
Jan Bowman, Lousiana State University
Gregory E. Brown, Central Missouri State University
Marilyn L. Cantwell, Assistant Professor, Louisiana State University
Nina Collins, Bradley University
Ellen Daniel, Harding University
Judith Durrand, University of Houston
Judy A. Farris, South Dakota State University
Linda Kirk Fox, University of Idaho
Victoria Marie Gribschaw, Seton Hill College
Gong-Soog Hong, Purdue University

Virginia Junk, University of Idaho
Lauren Leach, State University of New York College at Oneonta
Carole J. Makela, Colorado State University
Drew E. Mattson, Anoka-Ramsey Community College
Martin Machowsky, Issue Dynamics Incorporated
Carol B. Meeks, University of Georgia
James L. Morrison, University of Delaware
Kathleen Morrow, Syracuse University
Aimee D. Prawitz, Northern Illinois University
Sue Unger, Pittsburg State University
Lynn B. White, The Texas A&M University System
Jing-jian Xiao, The University of Rhode Island

A number of friends around the country have taken the time to generously contribute to this text by writing boxed inserts titled "An Appendix Issue," "A Consumer Update On..." or "An Economic Focus On..." Each has strengthened the text. The contributors include:

Raymond E. Forgue, Associate Professor, University of Kentucky
Helen Foster, Assistant Professor, State University of New York at Oneonta
Mohamed Abdel Ghanny, Professor, University of Alabama
Sherman Hanna, Professor, Ohio State University
Gong-Soog Hong, Assistant Professor, Purdue University
Carole J. Makela, Professor, Colorado State University
Julia Marlowe, Associate Professor, and *Joan Koonce Lewis*, Associate Professor, The University of Georgia
Robert N. Mayer, Professor, The University of Utah
E. Scott Maynes, Professor Emeritus, Cornell University
Tamra Minor, Assistant to the Vice President, The Ohio State University
Mark Silbergeld, Director, Consumers Union, Washington Office
Jing-jian Xiao, Assistant Professor, The University of Rhode Island
Zhiming Zhang, Economist, People's Republic of China

Other friends contributed **new** "Consumer Update" boxed inserts or sections of text for this edition. The contributors included:

Raymond E. Forgue, Associate Professor, University of Kentucky
Lucy S. Garman, Nutritional Counselor, Newport, Virginia
Gong Soog Hong, Assistant Professor, Purdue University
Robert Kerton, Professor, University of Waterloo
Joan Kinney, Lecturer, University of Wisconsin-Madison
Greg O'Donoghue, Manager, Personal Financial Management Program, Seymour Johnson Air Force Base, North Carolina
Sheila Stogdale, Graduate Student, Virginia Tech
Carol Ann Walker, Personal Finance Manager/Air Force Aid Officer, Peterson Air Force Base, Colorado

A special note of appreciation is given to *Loren V. Geistfeld*, Professor, The Ohio State University, for contributing "The Geistfeld Model of Consumer Choice."

In addition, I wish to thank the thousands of students who had the opportunity to read, critique, and provide research inputs for *Consumer Economic Issues in America*. Some have written letters offering suggestions as well as criticism, and I deeply appreciate each communication. Special thanks go to *Paul Camp*, Purdue University and *W. Kurt Schumacher*,

Board of Governors of the Federal Reserve System for their especially helpful suggestions. *Michael D. Cox* (Virginia Tech), *Katherine Lee* (University of Delaware), and *Sheila Stogdale* (Virginia Tech) helped with the proofreading.

Also deserving of thanks are the more than 80 instructors of consumer economics who have been generous enough to share their views on what should and should not be included in a high-quality textbook. In addition, a number of suggestions have come from directors of Centers for Economic Education, directors of State Offices of Consumer Affairs, and Media Consumer Affairs Experts, especially *News 5 reporter Elizabeth Owen in Nashville, Tennessee*. I have attempted to meet the collective needs in every way possible.

A note of appreciation is due the mentors of my academic and professional life: *William Boast*, *Ronald West*, and *John Binnion*. By their examples and instruction, they have given me motivation, direction, and the tools to seek excellence. Thanks are due also to *William McDivitt* for allowing me to register for college with less than a dollar in my pocket on two separate occasions. *Ray Forgue* similarly deserves my thanks for both his friendship and his brilliant questions that get my mind thinking at a higher level.

Finally, *Lucy S. Garman* has helped me clarify my thoughts on many consumer issues (especially in nutrition and health) over our candlelit, evening meals together. She has regularly added to the quality of this book. As my partner in life, she has been wonderful in her total support of my passion for the labor of love it takes to write *Consumer Economic Issues in America*.

Consumer Economic Issues in America is a challenge. It is controversial. It is informative. It is factual. It is honest. It is a book to be selected by teachers who care deeply about their students and want them to read newspapers, watch public television specials, listen to National Public Radio news, and become involved in truly understanding issues of concern to consumers. I believe that the approach of this book will make the reader an informed consumer who in turn will help shape a continually improving world for others. I believe that this is an interesting text that students will enjoy reading. I hope I have succeeded because I have the strong bias that students need to learn consumer economic concepts and principles thoroughly so that they may apply them effectively and successfully in their personal lives. This will improve their personal levels of living and the lives of other consumers.

E.T.G.

P.S. Dear Students: If you are going to save any of your college textbooks, be certain to save this one. Especially valuable are the chapters on laws and regulations and how to remedy wrongs against consumers. Also, you may want to present the book as a gift to a spouse or a parent. My e-mail address is TGARMAN@VT.EDU for those who wish to communicate electronically.

Foreword by Virginia H. Knauer*

We are a nation of more than 265 million consumers. Whatever type of work we do, wherever our homes may stand, whoever we are, we are all consumers. Although our needs and desires are diverse, this common role causes us to share many interests. Underlying these is the sincere belief that our moral and ethical consumer rights are as important as our legal rights. We expect equal standing with sellers in marketplace transactions. And we hope for a marketplace that is guided by principles, rules, and standards of good conduct, whether fashioned by business or government. In short, we want to shop in a marketplace that knows right from wrong.

We are also realists. We recognize a natural tension between consumers, who want the best value for their money, and sellers, who want to make as much profit as they can and stay in business. Yet we know that without consumers to buy products and services, there is no market for the products and services that manufacturers and sellers promote. So we can see that if we become informed consumers, if we learn and exercise our marketplace rights, then we can help shape the competitive marketplace to meet our needs. This, then, is how we pursue our consumer interest.

Consumer Economic Issues in America represents a breakthrough in communicating to the public perspectives of what the consumer interest is truly about. It looks broadly at the important responsibilities of business, government, private voluntary groups, and individual consumers in helping to promote and protect the consumer interest. It provides insights into the essence of consumerism and presents both its history and a glimpse of its future. It explains the government decision making process so that consumers can become more involved in the formation of public policy. It provides useful everyday tools consumers can use to help analyze consumer issues and better understand their own rational (and sometimes irrational) decision making. And it details many key consumer responsibilities that accompany consumer rights in the marketplace.

The overwhelming majority of businesses in America are trying honestly and diligently to meet the needs of consumers today. Increasing competition from foreign marketers, better-informed consumers, and rapid developments in advanced technology—in short, the realities of the modern marketplace dictate this posture. Evidence of this long-term trend is found in the increased emphasis on customer service, proactive complaint-handling, better-quality products, and the development of partnerships between consumers, business, and government aimed at searching out and meeting consumers needs.

When fraud does occur, however, the consumer must be well prepared to spot it, avoid it, and help prevent it from victimizing others. The material in the chapters on frauds and misrepresentations is frightening upon first reading. The staggering number and variety of fraudulent schemes are limited only by the creativity of the scam artists behind them. However, the purpose is not to frighten, but to enlighten; to boost consumers' awareness of the signs of fraud so that they will do a little checking before they believe an offer that sounds too good to be true. This will reduce the number of people who fall victim to these scams and, in turn, the number of scams out there.

Another important element of this book is its detailed attention to the many current consumer issues. No book of this type would be complete without a detailed discussion of food and health issues. American consumers want to know about such topics as how to acquire good eating habits, how to use nutritional and diet-food labeling, where to learn about additives in food, which government agencies and programs are designed to help consumers, how to find information about the services of alternative health care providers, when to buy generic drugs, and how tobacco and alcohol products affect the body. *Consumer Economic Issues in America* addresses these and many other topics.

Indeed, dozens of important issues are examined in this book. It is not necessarily a neutral presentation, and perhaps not all would subscribe to the author's endorsements. But this book strives to offer all sides of the issues. For instance, the importance of self-regulation in product safety and effectiveness is made clear along with suggested appropriate roles for governments and consumers. This book also carefully examines the issues of benefit-cost analysis, product liability laws, disclosure laws, and warnings, and ingredient labeling; it discusses criticisms of product safety efforts. The same degree of depth is seen in every chapter of *Consumer Economic Issues in America*.

This book plays an important role in advancing the consumer interest. It can be a major contribution to our universal goal of a competitive marketplace that works, a nation of businesses and governments that are able to satisfy consumers, and a country of consumers who are able and willing to cooperate with businesses and governments in positive partnership efforts where consumer interests are paramount in the marketplace.

If you are a student, I recommend this book to you. And when you have finished reading it, I urge you to further your studies with a look at consumerism in other nations. Our marketplace is increasingly global in nature, and the decisions and issues affecting governments in far corners of the world-whether they concern trade policy, agricultural policy, safety regulations, or whatever-have everyday implications for the marketplace choices we enjoy in America. Once this becomes clear, you will begin to see that consumerism changes and matures as economies develop. And you will recognize that an adequate consumer education requires more than one course. It is a lifelong process. This excellent book is but a strong beginning for your own consumer education.

Virginia H. Knauer

Virginia H. Knauer is former White House Special Assistant for Consumer Affairs for President Ronald W. Reagan, President Gerald R. Ford, and President Richard M. Nixon. Mrs. Knauer is currently a member of Anderson, Benjamin, Read & Haney, a Washington, D.C. consulting firm that boasts a nationally recognized consumer relations program.

About the Author

E. Thomas Garman is a successful writer, lecturer, consultant, and teacher. He is a professor of Consumer Affairs at Virginia Polytechnic Institute and State University in Blacksburg, Virginia. He holds bachelors and masters degrees from the University of Denver and a doctorate from Texas Tech University. Garman's experience includes work for a United States Senator in Washington, retail sales management in Colorado, economic development project management in West Africa, and teaching for thirty years, including summer workshops for ten different universities and eight "Consumer Issues in Washington" classes on location in the nation's capital. Garman has taught in eight states and three countries. He is a professor who truly enjoys teaching.

In 1994, Garman received the Stewart Lee Consumer Education Award from the American Council on Consumer Interests in recognition of his lifetime achievements in consumer education. In 1995, that same organization elected him a "Distinguished Fellow."

Professor Garman has authored or co-authored fifteen books, including the currently available **Consumer Economic Issues in America** (Dame Publications), **Regulation and Consumer Protection** (Dame Publications), **Ripoffs and Frauds: How to Avoid and How to Get Away** (Dame Publications), **Personal Finance** (Houghton Mifflin Company; also the best selling text in the field), and **The Consumer's World** (McGraw Hill Company). His current writing project is **Consumerism: Issues and Perspectives**.

He has published over 110 refereed articles and proceedings publications. Articles have appeared in the *Journal of Consumer Affairs, Advancing the Consumer Interest, Mobius* (the journal of the Society for Consumer Affairs Professionals in Business), *Proceedings of the American Council on Consumer Interests, Journal of Retailing, Journal of Business Communications, Business Education World, Journal of Home Economics, Death Education, Delta Pi Epsilon Journal, The Balance Sheet, Journal of Business Education, College Student Journal, Financial Planning and Counseling, and Journal of Home Economics and Consumer Studies.*

He has made over seventy major speeches to professional groups in twenty-three states and three foreign countries. Garman is a past president of one state professional association, the Consumer Education and Information Association of Virginia, and two national organizations, the Association for Financial Counseling and Planning Education and the American Council on Consumer Interests.

Garman has been a consultant to over forty corporations, trade associations and government agencies. He recently completed appointed terms of service for the National Advertising Review Board, the Consumer Advisory Council of the Board of Governors of the Federal Reserve System, and the National Advisory Council on Financial Planning for the International Board of Standards and Practices for Certified Financial Planners. He currently is a consultant for the U.S. Navy and the Department of Defense.

Garman teaches both graduate and undergraduate courses in consumer affairs and family financial management, fields in which his textbooks are widely used. Garman has two grown children, and he lives with his wife in their home located on Gap Mountain near Newport, Virginia.

Chapter 1

What Is the Consumer Interest?

OBJECTIVES

After reading this chapter, you should be able to

1. Describe the basic economic activities performed by consumers.

2. Discuss why consumers are not sovereign in the economic marketplace.

3. Recognize that consumer problems exist in a world of imperfectly competitive markets where the interests of sellers and consumers conflict.

4. View the consumer interest in a price-quality model to provide a useful but incomplete perspective.

5. Understand what really is the consumer interest—value for money and equity for all consumers.

6. Recognize that the consumer interest is a special-interest group and consumers themselves must pursue their own consumer interest objectives.

7. Discuss the differences between the public interest and the consumer interest and recognize that both business and government sometimes support the consumer interest.

8. Appreciate government's challenging public interest responsibilities.

9. Understand that consumers themselves must look out for the consumer interest and identify how a variety of people go about pursuing their consumer interests.

In order to understand better the consumer interest and your role in it, you need to understand what the consumer interest is. Many people confuse the narrow interests of consumers with the broader concerns of the general public, which is also known as the public interest. It is crucial for those teaching or studying consumer economic issues, as well as for those working in the consumer interest, to have a clear understanding of the perspectives because the consumer interest and the public interest differ sharply. In addition, it is important for all of us to understand our multiple roles in the social-political-economic marketplace and to know something about the other players in the economy.

This chapter begins by reviewing how consumers satisfy their economic goals in the economy: earning, consuming, borrowing, saving, investing, taxpaying and utilizing. The question of consumer sovereignty versus producer sovereignty is then examined. Next, the problems of consumers are examined in the context of a world where the interests of sellers and consumers will always conflict. Then the consumer interest is differentiated from both business and public interests through an examination of a price-quality continuum, a useful but incomplete perspective. The consumer interest is then carefully defined, explained and more correctly viewed in a value-for-money/equity model. How consumers attempt to achieve their consumer interests is by securing, protecting, and asserting their several consumer rights. It then becomes apparent that the consumer interest is a special-interest group and consumers themselves must pursue their own consumer interest objectives because no one else can do it as well as they can. Further clarifications are also made on the interests of consumers, governments and businesses, especially in a capitalistic form of an economic system. The chapter concludes with some reflections about how consumers go about pursuing their special interests.

Upon completion of this chapter, you should realize that you can achieve your own agenda in life (and it is hoped that includes vigorously protecting the consumer interest) better because you will more clearly understand the agendas of business, government, and the public. Once the consumer interest is clear in your mind—value for money and equity for all consumers—you can then spend the rest of your life looking out for your own and your fellow consumers' interests.

Economic Activities Performed by Consumers

The American marketplace is where we satisfy our personal economic goals. It is a **market price system** where the economy is driven by supply and demand and that is what determines which goods and services are produced and the prices at which they are sold. Individuals in society play three roles in economic life: (1) worker, (2) consumer, and (3) citizen. As a worker, you are probably concerned about having a job and future growth of income. As a consumer, you are likely interested in spending, saving and the rising cost of goods. As a citizen, you are expected to be concerned about practices and laws that affect your income, spending, saving, investment, and employment opportunities.

As we go through life, each of us is constantly engaged in economic activities, such as earning an income, spending money on food and borrowing money to finance an automobile or a home. We can seek and reach our personal economic goals in the marketplace more easily when we understand and use a few useful concepts related to our economic activities.

A **consumer** is one who acquires goods and services for ultimate consumption or use by a person, family, or household. Consumers go shopping and purchase goods and services in their efforts to accomplish their own economic goals. The ultimate purpose of all economic activity is to satisfy consumer wants. **Satisfaction** is defined individually by each person when his or her desires and needs are fulfilled or gratified. Consumers must be involved in economic activities in order to accomplish their personal goals and achieve satisfactions.

People's personal economic goals are often in conflict, and sometimes consumers must make difficult decisions among alternatives. For example, as an earner, you may want to demand a higher salary. This conflicts with your desire to not spend too much because prices are pushed up by increasing labor costs. While you may want the government to put ceilings on interest rates for consumer loans to reduce your borrowing costs, this conflicts with your desire to earn a high interest rate on your savings account. The economic activities performed by consumers are described below.

Earning

Earning, a basic economic activity for most people, is the gain derived from the performance of service, labor, or work, such as the salary or wages of a person, the profits of a business enterprise, and returns from an investment. Earning is production in the marketplace, and it is usually essential for survival. Since consumer goods and services cost money, most people work to earn money income so that they can spend.[1] American earners are tremendous producers of goods and services.

Consuming

Consumption is the expenditure made by consumers and nonprofit institutions for goods and services. At the consumer level, consumption is the acquisition and utilization of goods, such as commodities and services, directly to satisfy wants. This is a natural and fundamental act by consumers.

Consumers are the driving force in the American economy, making up 65 percent of total spending; businesses and governments contribute 35 percent. Americans are the greatest consumers in the world as they use (and dispose) enormous quantities of goods and services. This high level of consumption occurs because the level of living for so many people is quite high.

Consumption by consumers for goods to be used in consumption helps provide guidance to the economy. Over 200 years ago, philosopher Adam Smith wrote that "Consumption is the sole end and purpose of production and the interest of the producer ought to be attended to, only so far as it may be necessary for promoting that of the consumer."

Consumers in the United States typically pay the one price marked, and if that price is too high, many go elsewhere to shop for a fairer price. Most consumers would prefer, if possible, to buy it on sale (i.e., at a low price). For expensive products, such as automobiles, most consumers haggle for a lower price than the vehicle's sticker price.

---

[1]Household production, while extremely valuable to the family and to society in general, does not produce money income or earnings in the traditional economic sense.

It is in their role as consumers that Americans typically consume for over seventy years of their lifetime, while their economic role of earning often lasts for less than forty years. (During the earliest years of life, when they are too young to work, the sole task of humans is to consume.) Consumers, therefore, by the observable essence of their marketplace behavior, are strongly interested in pursuing their consumer interest in seeking an acceptable quality of goods and services at fair or low prices. The quest for value for money is pursued by consumers every day in numerous transactions.

Moreover, this suggests that instead of the consumer role being not nearly as important to consumers as their role as producers, as has been wrongly suggested by others, one's consuming interest role is in fact quite important relative to other economic activities.

Utilizing

Utilizing can be defined as using for a certain purpose. In an economic sense, it is effectively making use of all one's economic and non-economic resources. Utilizing involves disposing of material resources, such as money and property, as well as using up the nonmaterial resource of time. Utilizing also involves the reaping of benefits of personal economic activities. In our affluent American society, time becomes scarcer with increasing material consumption. In economist Staffam Burenstam Linder's classic book *The Harried Leisure Class*, he observed that consumers have time pressures to earn more money to buy more goods, which then take increasing time for their use, care, and maintenance. Consumers are always faced with choices on how to effectively utilize.

Borrowing

Most consumers must borrow at one time or another. **Borrowing** is obtaining or receiving something on loan with the promise or understanding of returning it or its equivalent. About two-thirds of all Americans own their homes, and most of them had to borrow money to make such an expensive purchase. About 95 percent of adults own automobiles, and nearly three-quarters financed their automobile purchase. Just over half of all Americans use credit cards, another form of borrowing, to make a variety of consumer purchases.

Saving

Saving is the act of setting aside for future use, and in an economic sense, it is income not spent for consumption. Saving arises from not spending all current income. Consumers save by putting money into a savings or checking account at a financial institution, buying a government savings bond, putting cash into a money market fund, or buying a certificate of deposit (CD). People who save for their retirement years are trying to achieve an optimal pattern of consumption throughout their lifetimes. As a nation, the savings rate in recent years has been about 4 percent. People also save by putting money into tangible items, such as their homes, which may increase in value over a number of years.

Investing

Investing is committing money or property to a productive use (such as for equipment and machinery) to be used in producing goods or services in order to profit in the form of interest, dividends, rent, capital gains, or other income. Investment adds to the nation's stock of capital goods. Savings is not the same as investing, since the former arises from not spending and the latter results from putting money into productive use. The intent of investing is to increase future income and help maximize enjoyment of life. Investments do have an element of risk, since money is placed in assets that do not guarantee return of principal or earnings.

Taxpaying

Taxpaying is yet another economic activity performed by consumers. This is the effort to pay a variety of taxes to any number of governments, such as local, state and federal. **Taxes** are compulsory charges imposed by a government on people. In the United States, approximately 32 percent of personal income goes for taxes. Examples include federal income taxes, social security taxes, state (and sometimes local) income taxes, sales taxes, use taxes (gasoline, cigarettes, liquor, etc.), real estate taxes, personal property taxes, and gift and estate taxes. Most economists would argue that taxpaying is simply another spending economic activity.

Sovereignty in the Marketplace

As mentioned earlier, a consumer is one who acquires goods and services for ultimate consumption. Consumers are people like you and me. We go shopping and purchase goods and services for our personal and family use. **Consumer choice** is a market condition that exists when a consumer is presented with options from which he or she can choose to buy or not. If consumers have the freedom to decide what to buy and how to use it, then consumer choice exists.

Consumer sovereignty is a market situation where consumers have the power to ultimately decide which products and services society will produce and consume. Neither producers nor politicians dictate consumer tastes, rather, as economists like to say, "the consumer is king." When consumer sovereignty exists production in the economy is directed by millions of consumers making buying decisions with their dollar votes. Recognize that you can have consumer choice but not consumer sovereignty, such as occurs with the laws that require us to buy automobile insurance and to acquire drivers licenses.

An alternative view of consumer decision making called **producer sovereignty** also exists. This is where the producers have the power to decide which products and services society will produce and consume. Some people believe that consumers are mere puppets who are easily manipulated into spending their economic dollars on products and services for which manufacturers create demand. This view holds that the consumer is a pawn to be directed and exploited.

Which theory of consumer participation in the market is correct? Is the consumer sovereign in the marketplace where the consumer is king? Or is the consumer led, directed, and manipulated by artificial demand where the consumer is no more than a puppet?

Reality probably lies somewhere in between. In our imperfectly competitive market economy, neither complete consumer sovereignty nor complete producer sovereignty can exist. Producers decide what products and services will come into the market, given whatever information they have available to help them make such decisions, but the powerful consumer clearly decides what products and services will survive in the marketplace.

Consumer Problems in a World of Imperfectly Competitive Markets Where the Interests of Sellers and Consumers Conflict

Consumers must confront a variety of problems when shopping in a market-driven economic system. These difficulties exist because markets are imperfectly competitive and because the interests of sellers and consumers differ.

What Are "Consumer Problems"?

Consumer problems exist in the marketplace. Mayer defines **consumer problems** as "conditions that cause dissatisfaction in the process of selecting, using, or disposing of goods and services."[2] Four consumer problems exist in society:

1. "Most problems of consumers," says Thorelli,[3] "originate in the inability, or unwillingness, of producers to satisfy fully consumer needs and interests." This results in things consumers do not want, such as dangerous and defective products, price gouging, product performance failures, delivery failures, deceptive advertising, dishonored promises and warranties, and frauds and ripoffs.

2. A lack of consumer information also exists on such important matters as performance, durability, likelihood of defects, health and safety threats. It is difficult to get your money's worth in a marketplace that often offers insufficient information for effective choicemaking. For example, consumers experience problems in making healthy food choices, selecting good medical care, finding adequate and fairly-priced housing and transportation, avoiding high costs for banking and credit, and any number of services where quality is difficult to objectively measure. Information is crucial for consumers because it empowers them to effectively seek their interests.

3. The market system, observes Maynes,[4] generally does not resolve consumer grievances very easily or effectively.

---

[2]Mayer, R. N. (1991). Gone today, here today: Consumers issues in the agenda-setting process. *Journal of Social Issues.* 47, 21.

[3]Thorelli, H. (1988). *The Frontier of Research in The Consumer Interest*, 525.

[4]Maynes, E. S. (1976), *Decision-Making for Consumers* (MacMillan), 256-257.

4. The consumer interest is underrepresented in government to the point where too many public policy decisions (laws, regulatory actions, and regulations) favor producers.[5]

Consumers Shop in Imperfectly Competitive Markets

Consumer problems always have existed because the world always has had imperfectly competitive markets. The deviations, or **market failures**, "mostly involve costs to society external to the unit producing them, like pollution and erosion that fills up reservoirs, through monopoly and other restraints of trade..."[6] Market failures often involve the underproduction of public goods and an overproduction of public bads. They include (1) a lack of competition among sellers, (2) **negative externalities** (the harms caused by some marketplace transactions, such as pollution, that are difficult to avoid), (3) imperfect information, and (4) the overuse of public goods. Examples of market failures are underproviding positive aspects (i.e., information, safety, representation, competition, redress) and overproviding negative aspects (i.e., resource depletion, pollution, frauds, misrepresentations, corporate profiteering).

To address these market failures, consumers tend to seek a fairer marketplace. They seek laws and regulations to combat misrepresentations and deceptions, to mandate disclosures on information, to enforce antitrust standards, to obtain health and safety protection, and occasionally (as in the case of utilities) to seek economic regulation. Businesses (sellers) typically resist government intervention, unless they believe it will help them. These imperfections in the marketplace and "maldistributions of power" are precisely "what brought the consumer movement into being."[7]

The Seller-Consumer Conflict Will Always Exist

While sellers and consumers are mutually dependent on each other, the essence of the relationship is that they have different motivations. Sellers are interested in revenues and profits. Consumers are interested in satisfying their needs, with little, if any, regard for the interests of the sellers. Thus, a **seller-consumer conflict** will always be present in market transactions, suggests Feldman.[8]

To compound the resolution of these matters, sellers and consumers usually perceive consumer issues differently. Getting agreement on or even defining the nature and extent of a consumer problem is often difficult. Their differences remain apparent when consumers and sellers work together in attempting to find suitable remedies for problems.

For example, many businesspeople endorse a model of our marketplace that is not reality, but rather is an ideal. The premise is that competitive forces are sufficient to regulate the relationship between sellers and consumers in the marketplace. This model

---

[5]Ibid.

[6]James N. Morgan, "Twenty-two Serious Policy Proposals in the Consumer Interest," October 18, 1994, private correspondence to the author.

[7]John Kenneth Galbraith, "Esther Peterson and the Consumer Movement," address to the Consumer Federation of America and the American Council on Consumer Interests, Washington, DC, March 17, 1995.

[8]Part of the logic in developing this section was taken from L. P. Feldman (1980). *Consumer Protection: Problems and Prospects*, 2nd ed. (pp. 21-34). St. Paul, MN: West.

is based on the assumption that any seller who offers shoddy products or services or who treats customers poorly will lose out to competitors. In reality, this does not happen. One reason is that most businesses try to attract new customers and do not necessarily need to retain all their previous customers. Another reason is that few consumers or even consumer advocacy groups are influential enough in spending their economic dollars to force manufacturers to change their perspective. Moreover, consumers are not truly sovereign.

The viewpoints of sellers and consumers will never be reconciled. The task is to reduce the level of the conflict to the point where the groups talk to each other in a calm effort to find areas of agreement where both interests can benefit or be mutually maximized.

The Consumer Interest Viewed in a Price-Quality Model: A Useful but Incomplete Perspective

An **interest** in the sense examined here is a regard for one's benefit or advantage; a self-interest. An interest can be exhibited by a person, group, organization or government.

Everyone in the Market Wants a Good Deal

The process of consumption at its most fundamental level involves consumers buying products and services in the marketplace. Each player in the market, every single buyer and seller, is hoping to get a **good deal**. The sellers hope to get the most they can for what they have to sell. The buyers hope to pay as little as possible for what they buy. This dynamic interaction of economic advantage is at the heart of understanding the consumer interest.

Consumer advocate and attorney James S. Turner describes one major aspect of the consumer interest using a **price-quality conceptual model**, as illustrated in Table 1-1. He suggests that one can readily see that the *consumer interest* (assuming for a moment that there is only a single consumer interest) is to obtain goods and services of the highest quality at the lowest possible prices. The *business interest,* on the other hand, is to try to sell goods and services at the highest price possible for the lowest quality. The *public interest,* suggests Turner, involves selling goods and services of fair quality (including safe use) at fair prices. ("Fair" and "low" are normative terms and subject to change over time.) Turner argues further that the idea of fair price for fair quality "is the generic objective of an entire local, national and global economy with production and consumption working in tandem."[9] In short, this model suggests that the consumer interest lies in getting value for money expended; therefore, it focuses upon consumer efficiency in marketplace transactions.

The price-quality model demonstrates the fundamental differences in perspectives and agendas of business, consumers, and the public by drawing attention to the basic

---

[9]A broader discussion of these concerns can be found in J. S. Turner (1984), Whither consumerism? *At Home With Consumers* (The Direct Selling Education Foundation), *5*(4).

	Consumer	Public	Business
Price	Low	Fair	High
Quality	High	Fair	Low

TABLE 1-1   A Price-Quality Model Illustrating Fundamental Differences Among Interests

importance of price and quality in marketplace transactions. Observation of reality suggests that the interests of businesses and consumers are not quite as compartmentalized as presented in this model. For example, it should be recognized that businesses sell goods and services of low, medium, and high quality and they do so at a variety of prices. Therefore, the **business interest**, more accurately than suggested above, is to sell goods and services of whatever quality at the highest possible prices given the competitive forces at work in the marketplace.

While the price-quality model is useful in the abstract because it docs accurately draw attention to the essence of the consumer interest, albeit imprecisely, the price-quality model is further limited because it focuses solely on a concern for personal consumer efficiency. Even though price and quality concerns are important to consumers, the consumer interest embraces much more than value for money.

What Really Is the Consumer Interest?—Value for Money and Equity

The **consumer interest** is concerned with securing, protecting, and asserting consumer rights primarily in marketplace transactions in order that all consumers receive an acceptable quality of goods and services at fair or low prices. Thus, the consumer interest has to do with both value for money for oneself and equity for others. The emphasis of the definition on the consumer interest occurring "primarily in marketplace transactions" is because that is where consumers predominately do what they do when they perform the consuming function. Note also that each consumer has his or her own definition of **acceptable quality**. Thus, one consumer might only purchase goods which are considered friendly to the environment or made by someone who was paid a fair wage. Another consumer might demand that the worker be employed in safe working conditions by a socially responsible company that did not discriminate in hiring practices or neglect the needs of the economically disadvantaged. Yet another consumer might ignore such considerations when making a purchase. Each individual consumer has his or her own definition of a **fair** or **low price**, and these vary over time for each product or service purchased.

Consumer Interest #1: Seeking Value for Money (While Constantly Making Tradeoffs)

Americans spend a lot of time in their consuming role, such as going to shopping malls, buying groceries, eating meals in restaurants, buying automobiles, paying for gasoline, and living in homes. They are looking for good values for their money. In that search, consumers constantly make tradeoffs between price and quality in marketplace transactions where there is imperfect information available to consumers (virtually all the time). A **tradeoff** is the act of giving up one good or activity in order to obtain another good or activity. This involves an exchange of one thing in return for another, especially a giving up of something desirable, as a benefit or advantage, for another benefit or advantage regarded more desirable.

Unfortunately, consumers often make **inefficient tradeoffs**. Here consumers make poor quality or price decisions. This occurs because consumers operate in a complex and technological marketplace where, during marketplace transactions, they are often lacking in legal strength, product knowledge, capacity, resources, organization, and willingness. Thus, they frequently operate at a disadvantage to the sellers who are experts in sophisticated production and selling techniques. Misrepresentations and deceptions exist which confound consumers in the marketplace. In sum, consumers occupy a weak position relative to producers, distributors, advertisers and retailers. This reduces the consumer's success in obtaining value for money.

A great number of consumers do not always insist on buying at the lowest possible price. For example, not all consumers think it imperative that they always pay the lowest price. Fair and/or somewhat low prices are oftentimes acceptable and usually desirable, given a certain minimum amount of quality. Some consumers, however, seem to have an inclination towards preferring to pay high prices. Observation of consumer decision making in the marketplace reveals that very few consumers ever tell a seller to "Please sell me something at the highest price you want to charge," and even fewer tell sellers to "Please take this amount of money and sell me any level of quality."

Most people occasionally act irrationally in their consumer decision making. There are some areas where consumers have "persistently biased perceptions of risk, or notions about what cost to count. They may not believe the odds in a gamble even if they are told."[10] All of this suggests that consumers cannot make good decisions for themselves unless they are educated so they know how to act on appropriate information.

Moreover, the consumer interest in value for money has to do with obtaining an acceptable quality of goods at fair or low prices with a minimum of unintended negative consequences and to do so expecting the benefits of a competitive marketplace. This is illustrated in Table 1-2 which offers a model of the consumer interest using the constructs of value for money and equity.

---

[10]Morgan, J. N. (1985). What is in the consumer's interest? In K. P. Schnittgrund (Ed.) *The Proceedings of the American Council on Consumer Interests* (p. 3). Columbia, MO: University of Missouri.

VALUE-FOR-MONEY INTERESTS	EQUITY INTERESTS
Obtaining an acceptable quality of goods and services at fair or low prices	Seeking equity between sellers and buyers provided by a mutual recognition of several consumer rights
Expecting the benefits of a competitive marketplace	Pursuing equity for all consumers in their access to acceptable goods and services

TABLE 1-2   The Consumer Interest Using Value-for-Money/Equity Model

Consumer Interest #2: Seeking Equity for All Consumers

The emphasis on rights for consumers invites the concept of a consumer goal of equity to a discussion of the consumer interest. **Equity** is what is right and what is wrong; those are the ideals of justice, impartiality and fairness for consumers in circumstances not typically provided for by law. A consumer **inequity** occurs when benefits and burdens are not distributed fairly. For example, a fully loaded tractor-trailer weighs about the same as 25 automobiles, yet, while causing as much damage to highways as 10,000 cars, the truck pays only a small fraction of its fair share in road taxes. An emphasis on equity for all consumer encourages consideration of a *morality aspect* to the consumer interest. This suggests that consumers should have or develop a moral perspective and concern about the economic marketplace. Mayer says that the concept of consumerism is beneficial for people to understand because as consumers seek to improve their self interest (get value for money expended) they also improve their social consciousness.[11]

Kroll contends that an equity aspect of the consumer interest has to do with "opportunity rights," as well as "benefit rights" as solutions to consumer problems.[12] **Opportunity rights** are those which improve "the opportunity for effective exercise of individual responsibility in securing benefits" such as the right to information and choice and disclosures for product ingredients, product life, care instructions, comparative prices, comparative performance, and health and safety warnings. **Benefit rights** are those "which provide benefits to members of some group without the exercise of individual responsibility," such as mandated automobile safety standards and low-cost banking services. Thus, the equity aspect of the consumer interest also has to do with **non-economic issues** (i.e., health, safety, quality, ethics, equity) and **economic concerns** (i.e., buying efficiency, credit availability).

Thus, the equity aspect of the consumer interest focuses first on asserting consumer rights for individual consumers and their families. The equity interest then broadens to include encouraging access for all consumers to acceptable goods and services. Examples of this are check cashing at banks by economically poor non-depositors, availability of generic prescription drugs for the elderly, and subsidized housing loans for low-income

[11]Mayer, R. N. (1989), *The Consumer Movement: Guardians of the Marketplace* (Twayne Publishers), 9 and 31.

[12]Kroll, R. J. and R. W. Stampfl (1981), The new consumerism, *Proceedings of the American Council on Consumer Interests* (pp. 97-98); and Kroll, R. J. and R. W. Stampfl (1986), Orientations toward consumerism: A test of a two-dimensional theory, *The Journal of Consumer Affairs*, 20,2, 214-230.

families. In sum, the consumer interest in equity has to do with seeking equity between sellers and buyers through a mutual recognition of several consumer rights, as well as with pursuing equity for all consumers in their access to acceptable goods and services at fair or low prices. This is illustrated in Table 1-2.

Seeking Equity Sometimes Requires a Paternalistic Attitude

The equity outlook also suggests that consumers can be paternalisticly forced to accept some protection against negative consequences of their own behaviors because their choices may be restricted or prohibited. For example, the only rotary lawnmowers available in the marketplace today are those which adhere to government-mandated safety standards. As another example, low-income consumers have no choice other than to purchase the same three-pronged electrical safety extension cords as do more affluent consumers. Also, people of all income levels must buy new automobiles which meet government safety standards. Thus, the less affluent and several other types of **vulnerable consumers** (those who are most likely to suffer abuse in marketplace transactions, including children, elderly, mentally retarded, severely handicapped, and non-English speaking) are forced to accept certain benefits (such as safety or information) whether or not they want to pay for them.

CONSUMER UPDATE: The Values Emphasized in Consumer Economics Should Be Based on the Consumer Interest

Normative public policies that should be adopted by those studying consumer economics are those that promote the consumer interest. These concerns are primarily about questions of personally obtaining value for money and seeking equity for all consumers. A suggested list of values that might be examined when studying consumer economics classes are honesty, trust, loyalty, goodwill, civility, dignity, opportunity, rights, justice, fairness, decency, tradition, stability, individuality, conformity, change, practicality, economy, saving, education, investment, self gratification, social prestige, equality, choice, tolerance, personal responsibility, honor, financial success, and financial security. It can be argued that most of the above named values are some of the fundamental values of civilized society.

This equity aspect of the consumer interest is generally limited to situations where the majority of consumers will themselves experience only very low additional costs or very small decreases in quality in order to provide specific access benefits to other consumers through **cross-subsidization** or **cost-shifting**. This is the process of shifting the costs of supporting one segment of a business with the income from another. Typically, cross subsidization supports a service for the less affluent with the income (or taxes) from the affluent.

Who Determines the Consumer Interest?

The equity perspective implies that there is but one single normative consumer interest which presumably can be determined by a consumer czar. However, such a conclusion is false. The nation's 265 million consumers live in a changing society where yesterday's societal norms are certainly not today's rules and probably will not be tomorrow's standards. Equity for consumers is first defined by each individual consumer, and the *true* spokespersons for the consumer interest are the individual consumers themselves.

Different perceptions about the consumer interest are held by various individuals and groups. The consumer interest in equity issues (as well as value-for-money issues) is, therefore, determined by other concerned groups, including businesses, trade associations, church groups, unions, and state governments. For examples of the diversity of views on the consumer interest, consider whether the consumer perspective of the American Association of Retired Persons is the same as the Philadelphia Consumer Protection Association or the AFL/CIO Consumer Issues Committee. There can be no doubt that the consumer interest is seen in the eye of the beholder. The diversity of consumers results in many different interpretations of the consumer interest.

Consumers Achieve Their Interests by Securing, Protecting and Asserting Their Eight Important Consumer Rights

Consumers try to achieve their interests by securing, protecting, and asserting their consumer rights. The rights which are important aspects of the consumer interest include those suggested and sanctioned by American Presidents Kennedy, Johnson, Nixon, Ford, and Clinton as well as most consumer advocates:

1. **Choice** where consumers have the right to make an intelligent choice among products and services;

2. **Information** where consumers have the right to accurate information on which to make a free choice, thus they are provided access to the facts with which to make informed choices while also being protected against fraudulent, deceptive, and misleading information, advertising, labeling, and related practices;

3. **Safety** where consumers have the right to expect the health and safety of the buyer will be taken into account by those seeking patronage, thus consumers should be able to assume that products will perform as intended without being hazardous to health or life;

4. **Voice** (or the right to be heard) where the interests of consumers will be given full and fair consideration in government policy-making situations;

5. **Redress** (or the right to remedy) where consumers are provided with easily accessible, understandable and cost-efficient mechanisms through which consumer grievances and dissatisfactions can be addressed;

6. **Environmental health** where consumers may consume in an environmentally sound manner and be protected from the ill effects of pollution of the air, earth, and water which may occur in the performance of everyday marketplace transactions;

7. **Service** where consumers may expect convenience, courtesy, and responsiveness to consumer needs and problems and all the steps necessary to ensure that products and services meet the quality and performance levels claimed for them.

8. **Consumer education** where consumers are provided the right to consumer education, without which consumers cannot gain the full benefit of the other seven consumer rights. This helps all consumers to maximize their resources, become more effective in the marketplace and achieve the greatest personal satisfaction.[13]

Consumer rights are not simply given to people. Once articulated and secured for citizens by consumer leaders, presidents, educators, or whomever, consumer rights must be protected, as well as asserted.

AN ECONOMIC FOCUS: The Critical Role of Information and Understanding in Assessing the Consumer Interest*

To best understand and assess the consumer interest, one must underline the critical role of information and understanding. As an example, under existing partial information and understanding, many consumers have a preference for *Bayer's* rather than some other brand of aspirin. They may argue that *Bayer's* has been around for decades and has stood the test of the market and therefore must be "better" than other aspirins. Others, understanding that aspirin is simply acetylsalicylic acid that is manufactured according to formula, will know that "aspirin is aspirin." Hence, *Bayer's* is no better than other aspirin and you should not pay a higher price for it. As to price, some may be unaware of the true range of prices in the market and may view as "good" a price that is clearly "high" under full information. It must be argued that all qualities, all prices, and all policies should be assessed, *for normative purposes*, under the assumptions of *full information and full understanding*. Why? Only then can we expect preferences for qualities, prices, and policies to be stable. They will change only as a result of new developments in the market or as outcomes of new technologies.

*Contributed by E. Scott Maynes, Professor Emeritus, Cornell University

---

The Consumer Interest As a Special-Interest Group

A **special-interest group** is a group of persons who attempt to influence the statutory, regulatory, economic, and political decisions of government as they appeal for special consideration for their particular concerns. Often the concerns of special-interest groups center around economic self-interest. Groups with a special interest include computer chip manufacturers (who want protection from foreign competition), physicians (who want to keep their incomes high), prescription drug manufacturers (who want the legal right to market their inventions for a number of years), and hundreds of others. As former U.S. Senate Commerce Committee Chairman Warren Magnuson used to say after a long day of listening to lobbyists, "All anyone ever wants is a fair advantage!"

Understand that the consumer interest is also biased toward its self-interest. It can be advocated on the individual level in daily marketplace transactions, as well as in the public policy arena of social issues and government decisions. The consumer's special-interest perspective is that of a self-interested economic player who first wants value for

---

[13]As human rights are more fundamental to civilized society than consumer rights, these are excluded from this list. **Human rights** are those factors fundamental to civilized humanity, such as the rights of all people to food, clothing, shelter, health care, sanitation, education, employment, worker safety, fair wages, safe environment, and peace.

money. The consumer interest in equity for all consumers has its roots in the community values of truth, reciprocity, trust, fair dealing, equality, value for money and social justice.

These goals are pursued by **citizen-consumers**, people who seek to promote the interests of consumers by striving with a great deal of civic concern for the betterment of their community and society. The special-interest perspectives of the civil rights and environmental movements are similar in that regard. In this role, active citizen-consumers become political persons who try to influence laws, regulations, and the allocation of public goods. It is good for a society to have an active citizenry and good for consumers to live by values embedded in the consumer interest.

The consumer interest functions to see that the concepts of choice, safety, information, voice, redress, environmental health, service, and consumer education are present and effective in an economy where people seek value for money in their purchases and equity for all consumers. Consumers and consumer groups get particularly awakened when business or government disregards, ignores, forgets, or overrides the consumer interest rights of special groups of consumers, such as women, minorities, children, the elderly, the physically handicapped, and the poor. When the consumer interest is not properly attended to, and that is often, consumers and consumer groups are quick to challenge decisionmakers to consider the public interest to be certain that the consumer interest is protected.

The Public Interest Differs from Both the Consumer Interest and the Business Interest

As stated in the preamble to the Constitution, the purpose of the federal government in the United States is to, "provide for a more perfect union." Government does this by providing for the national defense, making social welfare programs accessible to many, caring for the needy, subsidizing space research, and providing for other public needs. What government does is all designed to help the public and, when necessary, provide the people with **public goods**. These are goods which exhibit a jointness of supply or consumption to the extent that the number of consumers does not affect the consumption of the good by others, i.e., clean air, ample supplies of water, state recreation parks, radio and television broadcasts, police protection, national defense. The **public** is all of us: consumers, taxpayers, business people, government employees, children, elderly, physicians, sugar beet growers, computer chip manufacturers, and many other categories of special-interest groups. Whenever possible, citizens generally desire a great amount of public goods (maximum output) while they want to limit their payment for public goods (minimize payment).

This latter concept, **free riding**, occurs when people have an incentive to enjoy the benefits of a good without paying for them. For example, those who enjoy public television without contributing money to the station are getting a free ride from the people who donate. Free riders have an incentive not to pay for public goods, and the common ownership of such goods sometimes results in overutilization. When a good is determined to be important to the community, government often claims ownership of the public good and intervenes to ensure that it remains available.

AN ECONOMIC FOCUS: The Economics of Discrimination Are Against the Consumer Interest*

In the absence of discrimination, all consumers in the market for a particular good x face the same market Demand, D_t, and Supply, S_t, curves. The resulting equilibrium Price is P_t as shown in Figure 1-1. (The vertical axis represents the increase in price while the horizontal axis represents the increase in quantity, as one moves away from 0.) With discrimination, some sellers will not sell to the group of consumers (group A) that they are discriminating against. In this case, those being discriminated against face a reduced Supply, S_a. The result of this reduced supply is that consumers being discriminated against must pay a higher Price, P_a, than they would without discrimination in order to purchase what they desire.

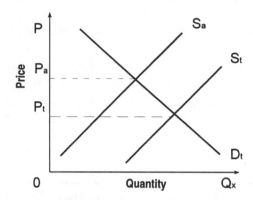

Figure 1-1: Discrimination Against Group A

There is evidence that blacks face higher prices with respect to low-income rental housing in the South as a result of discrimination.[1]

Discrimination also hurts sellers, because those sellers who refuse to sell to a particular group face a decreased Demand curve, D_b; see Figure 1-2. Consumers not being discriminated against (group B) pay a lower Price, P_b. Thus, the seller receives a lower price in order to satisfy his/her "taste for discrimination."

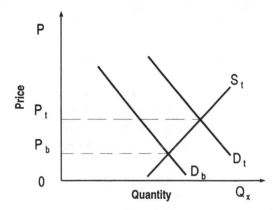

Figure 1-2: No Discrimination Against Group B

---

[1]See Lewis, J.K. and J. Marlowe. "Evidence of a Black Tax Dispelled in Some Markets, but Found with Low-Income Rental Housing," *The Western Journal of Black Studies*, (forthcoming).

*Julia Marlowe, Associate Professor, and Joan Koonce Lewis, Associate Professor, The University of Georgia

The Public Interest

Consumers have a special-interest perspective on matters affecting them which often is very different from the public interest. The **public interest** is concerned with generally accepted, socially shared standards and practices pertaining to the welfare of *all* those in the community. Policies, to be in the public interest, must promote the interests of individuals that are collective. As a result, decisions made by government in the public interest should theoretically supersede the concerns of all special-interest groups. In fact, the public interest should serve as a counterweight to special-interest groups seeking exclusive benefits. Thus, the public interest often requires resolving issues among consumers (but not private matters or interest conflicts), various consumer organizations, different businesses, competing unions, several levels of government, and other groups (business managers, local government officials, police officers, church leaders, military personnel, secretaries, postal employees, the poor, the elderly, women, students, and children).

Consequently, the public interest should be concerned with the welfare of all those in the community rather than cater to private matters or interests. The difficult and broad task of serving the public interest involves compelling and competing challenges. Examples include: safeguarding the environment, seeking fairness in taxation, encouraging quality housing, feeding the hungry, saving endangered species, protecting workers from employment hazards, proving housing for the homeless, assuring universal access to health care, and guarding our nation from potential adversaries.

One's Consumer and Public Roles Differ

Consumer roles and public roles for people sometimes differ and can even conflict. **Consumers** are people who acquire goods and services for ultimate consumption or use by a person, family, or household. Consumers go shopping and purchase goods and services in their efforts to accomplish their own economic goals. Ronald H. Smithies, former Director of the National Advertising Review Board, commented that the business of consumers "is that which we all are when we are at home."

Each of us is a member of the public and probably supports the goals of several special-interest groups, such as family, church, neighborhood, community, employer, local government, etc. In such efforts, Americans usually visualize themselves as having **citizen roles**, such as taking primary responsibility for their own affairs, adhering to certain standards of morality and ethics, participating in community affairs, and voting. These are some of our citizen roles which we take as members of a democratic American society.

In an oversimplified manner we are consumers when we cast our **dollar votes** and we are citizens when we cast our **political votes** on other concerns. In our consumer role, spending money counts as a **yes vote**: "Make more of these products please" and "I want to give repeat business to this seller." Not purchasing and/or boycotting counts as a **no vote**: "The product I bought before was inferior," "My previous experience with the seller was not pleasurable," "My conscience will not allow me to buy," and "This particular seller should be boycotted."

Business and the Consumer Interest

Most businesses try hard to meet the needs of consumers by providing fairly priced goods and services when and where desired, otherwise they may wind up without customers and out of business. Turner reminds us that, "business people are fond of saying they are consumers too." They are, says Turner, except in the one area of economic activity "in which they carry out their own business...when they are carrying out their business, the primary responsibility of businessperson is to advance the interest of business. This is not incompatible with advancing the consumer interest," but oftentimes it is in conflict. When forced by government, business is able to disclose standardized information to consumers in a much more meaningful way than when business volunteers some information. Examples include nutritional labeling, written warranties, and Truth in Savings disclosure requirements.

Gronmo suggests that an example of a common interest of businesses and consumers is, "supporting neighborhood stores in their competition with larger companies, which are favored by the concentration tendencies in the distribution system."[14] Also, it is in the consumer interest when companies provide high-quality goods at low prices, which companies do sometimes. (This is why Wal-Mart discount stores have been so successful.) The interests of sellers and consumers similarly overlap when it comes to informational advertising. Another area where businesses and consumers typically agree is on the need for effective business self-regulation.

Businesses are most interested in consumer rights when that interest also clearly benefits business. In general, businesses are willing to help people assert their consumer rights (such as maintaining an efficient complaint-handling system, for example) only when (1) it will not cost too much, (2) the competition is doing it so the business might lose market share if it doesn't do it too, or (3) not doing it will have a negative effect on the "bottom line" of business profits. Moreover, because of fundamental differences in objectives, it is self-evident that the consumer interest is not going to be regularly and actively pursued by American business on its own.

Government's Challenging Public Interest Responsibilities

Government should tend to the interests of all special-interest groups; and that effort should be its charge. In that endeavor, the task of government should be to attempt to reconcile the views of many and make policy determinations in favor of what is perceived by politicians and bureaucrats as the good of all. James Madison stated it another way in *The Federalist Papers* when he wrote that the task of enlightened legislators is to refine the public's views to ascertain the true interests of the country. Inevitably these decisions require compromises by government which depend upon the tenor of the times, the politics of the day, the state of the economy, the strength of arguments offered by the special interest groups, the economic clout of affected groups, and the type of economic/political system in operation. Government must maintain a balance between popular pressures of the day and a larger concept of our national interest.

---

[14]Gronmo, S. (1987), Relationships among consumer interests and other interests: Some implications for consumer policy, *Proceedings of the American Council on Consumer Interests*, 302.

Government's Economic/Political Biases in the United States

Public interest decision making occurs in the real world in what might be described as a **political society** where those making the decisions on behalf of the public interest may interpret that interest with a bit of human bias. One common partiality in the United States is a bias toward supporting competition. Another is a bias toward serving business more than consumers or the general public; this is often called a **free market bias**. Other historical biases include keeping government control and decision making close to the people at the local level, preferring to regulate at the state level instead of at the federal level, and resolving consumer problems with solutions that optimize individual choice, such as warning labels on tobacco products. Biases also vary on the subject of government intervention in the marketplace. The tradition is to prefer non-governmental self-regulatory efforts of businesses to address consumer problems. Another heritage is to seek voluntary solutions rather than mandatory.

Government Making Public Policy Decisions

Government, unfortunately, frequently falls short of effectively promoting the public interest when it tries to do so. For example, policymakers often listen too carefully to the business side of an issue and give them an advantage over the views of unions, consumers, environmentalists, or civil rights activists. In addition, government's politicians often protect the interests of workers (keep jobs in America) rather than protect the concerns of consumers (low prices on comparable imported goods). Politicians have been known to yield to the views of wealthy special-interest groups that make financial contributions to fund elections, rather than consider the ideas of less affluent consumers or consumer organizations. Thus, for a variety of reasons, governments may make a policy determination on any one issue that favors the interest of business and on the next issue a decision may favor organized labor, environmentalists, consumers or another perspective.

It is challenging for a bureaucrat in a regulatory agency to responsibly carry out the public interest while being legally responsible to protect conflicting interests. One of the major challenges faced by agency leaders to correctly identify the consumer interest while carrying out their public interest decision-making. It is important to ascertain the true desires/interests of unions, retirees, poor people, and businesses (both large and small). For example, those working at the U.S. Department of Agriculture have difficulty reconciling the conflicting goals of consumers (good nutrition) and producers (sell more beef), particularly when business interests are pressed upon them more frequently than the interests of consumers.

Government Resolving Public Interest Disputes

Public interest disputes are often about optimizing collective or widely shared benefits for the community as a whole. Citizens pursue various public interest concerns when they demand accountability from their elected representatives, fairer taxes, a cleaner and safer environment, sustained economic growth, protection of endangered species of animals and plants, reduction of outside financial influences on legislators, and more consideration for the economically disadvantaged in society.

Public issues almost always involve the government and its effort to regulate for the good of the people. Most could be called citizenship issues. Resolution of many of these problems and issues by government generally cost substantial sums of money which are paid by the nation's taxpayers. **Public interest concerns** include providing access for citizens to certain goods and services, such as basic health care via the Medicaid program for low-income people, limited health care via the Medicare program for the elderly, and better nutrition via the Food Stamp program for the poor. Other examples are assuring certain acceptable societal standards of safety and quality, such as clean air and safe food, and protecting America's borders from danger.

Public interest issues often arise because of real or perceived market failures or the threat of market failures in which community values have a decisive impact. Government usually becomes involved in public issues to articulate and defend the interests and values of the community threatened.

Interest conflicts often arise between and among different groups, and decisions made in the public interest are often difficult and full of controversy. While government may try to persuade competing interests to a particular position, government has both the authority and responsibility to make final determinations on public interest issues. In effect, when government makes decisions it arbitrates from the perspective of the public interest. Eventually, the public interest is what government decides, however imperfect.

In pursuit of the public interest, government should attend to the needs of all appropriate groups and try to reconcile them. Ultimately, the public good of the people should be protected solely by government. Those who should always represent the public interest (and not special interest groups) include members of the U.S. Congress and the state legislatures, elected local government officials, and the numerous government regulators and bureaucrats serving in the legislative, executive and judicial branches of government.

Government and the Consumer Interest

Consumer interest issues are distinct and are more narrow in focus than public interest issues. The consumer interest tends to center on the economic consuming roles of citizens (rather than their other economic roles) and consumer rights in marketplace transactions. If consumers had their way, they would like a loaf of bread priced at ten cents, but it has been determined by the powers that be in the United States that it is not in the public interest for government to control the supply and demand of bakery goods to heavily subsidize bread prices.

Government has long been interested in protecting consumer interests in selected ways, most fundamentally to prevent fraud and maintain competition. For decades we have had postal inspectors, licensing of trades and professions, antitrust laws, food safety standards, and a variety of product standards. Former Senator Gaylord Nelson once stated that, "Our democratic system of government must lend a helping hand to our consumers in the modern marketplace. Elected representatives of the people must write rules of fair play, and then the government must serve as a referee to make certain that these rules are fairly observed by all."

Over time, a great number of positive actions have been taken by government officials acting in the public interest which have helped consumers make better purchasing decisions, as well as helped them protect and assert consumer rights. Examples include ingredient nutritional labeling of most foods, regulations requiring credit reporting agencies to tell consumers when information in their files has been used to deny them credit, and "lemon laws" to help consumers get their vehicles repaired satisfactorily in a reasonable length of time. By definition, even though occasional government actions may help the consumer interest, government cannot be solely looking out for the consumer interest as the latter is just another special-interest group.

Conflicts between the Public and Consumer Interests Are Usually Caused by Potential Price Increases and/or Threatened Reductions of Consumer Rights

There are frequent conflicts between the public interest and the consumer interest, primarily owing to the strength of today's consumer movement. Major collisions, such as disregarding the consumer view in favor of a business or union perspective, are usually avoided although frictions occur regularly. Conflicts between the public interest and the consumer interest typically arise when the costs of providing increased safety and protection for all consumers is likely to push certain prices up (and that is not in the consumer interest) and/or additional consumer problems might be created by approval of a particular proposal (and most often these are attempts to reduce consumer rights).

Rising prices provide an example of an issue that provides conflict between public and consumer interests. For example, when consumers buy low-priced imported products from third-world countries (such as cotton shirts and blouses) their low-price consumer interest conflicts with the public concern to protect American textile jobs. Other examples include requiring no-fault automobile insurance (which limits the public's ability to sue) and requiring impact resistant doors on automobiles, pickup trucks and vans (which increases purchase costs). Similarly, people frequently face the decision to use inexpensive plastic disposable bottles as a matter of consumer convenience rather than returnable glass containers.

Safety concerns provide another area of potential conflicts between the public and the consumer interest. While many will argue that the consumer interest is to have a 100 percent safe food supply, government acts in the public interest by permitting approved limits of dozens of additives in foods, which are known to cause cancer in animals, because such chemicals increase the harvest. Requiring expensive automatic passive restraint systems for passengers on all new automobiles saves the lives of many consumers, but increases purchase costs for all the public.

Sometimes the Consumer Interest Conflicts with Itself

Sometimes the consumer interest even conflicts with itself. For example, a consumer's desire for choice may conflict with his/her desire for safety when it comes to selecting rotary-style lawn mowers because federal safety regulations have mandated that the design of all safety mechanisms be similar. Mower manufacturers are not free to create new and better mowers to give consumers more choices because they are constrained by the safety requirements. In this illustration, the consumer interest for low prices conflicts with the consumer interest for increased safety since the lawn mower standards elevated prices at least twenty-five percent.

On other occasions the public interest and the consumer interest may coincide. The distributional effects of favoring one group over another for minimal cost is oftentimes a plus for consumers, as well as being in the public interest. This occurs in situations where the public desires to promote the availability of goods and services to certain categories of consumers, such as the elderly, women, children, non-readers, immigrants, low income, and any other disenfranchised consumers at a relatively low unit cost which will be paid for by slightly overcharging the more affluent consumers. Thus, the "haves" in society subsidize the "have nots." For example, while the public-interest goal of requiring banks to cash checks for non-depositors at subsidized prices for poor people may raise prices a little for other consumers (an example of cross-subsidization) when the very small costs of offering such services are passed on to consumers, such action remains within the consumers' interest for equitable access to such things as banking and inexpensive utility rates for all persons. (These concepts are known as *basic banking services* and *lifeline rates*, and are discussed in Chapter 17.)

Consumers Must Look Out for Their Consumer Interests

Consumers themselves must pursue their own consumer-interest objectives because no one else is fundamentally interested in the specific concerns of consumers, and no one else can do it as well as they can. In a narket-oriented capitalistic economy, only one group has as its sole function to consume—consumers. Therefore, consumers should organize to better represent their own interests, to more effectively pursue one perceived set of consumer interests over those of other consumer groups, and to encourage governments to support the consumer interest more often as they act in the public interest. Turner observes that "it is very difficult for an individual or household to do much by themselves, therefore, they must get into groups to demand better prices and quality."[15]

Turner says that "the thrust for participatory democracy is the ideological background of the consumer movement."[16] Deeply rooted in American history, consumerism is like the American revolution in its belief that "power ought to flow from the bottom up (that is, from the people up) rather than from the top down (from the King down)." Thus, long before the point-of-purchase marketplace transaction, sellers need to meet regularly with consumers to provide participatory access for them to make inputs into the corporate decision making process. Those being affected by decisions, consumers, ought to be a part of the process of decision making in corporations and governments. Turner concludes that, "Consumers are to economics what voters are to politics; consumers with rights enhance the wealth of the nation."

---

[15]Turner, J. S. (July 18, 1994). Speech to University of Georgia class in Washington, D.C.
[16]Nasibitt, J. (1982). *Megatrends* (Warner Books), 177.

Businesses and Governments Sometimes Help Consumers

Various actions by businesses and governments greatly help consumers in pursuit of the consumer interest. In fact, enlightened businesspersons and intelligent government leaders frequently take the consumer interest to heart in their deliberations and decisions even though their main purposes are different from consumers.

As illustrations, in the public interest government encourages the formation of cooperatives to serve unprofitable markets, offers subsidized loans to low-income consumers for education, and mandates useful nutritional labeling for food products. The consumer interest is served by government when it prevents the creation of new monopolies, as well as when it promotes health and safety. Government also serves the consumer interest when it writes laws and creates regulatory agencies that help stop frauds, misrepresentations, and marketplace exploitations.

The interests of business and consumers generally overlap when it comes to informational advertising. In a similar manner, companies which install toll-free 800-number telephone hotlines to handle complaints are helping the consumer interest as well as their own profit-interest motivations. The need for business self-regulation is another area where businesses and consumers typically agree. Both groups, for example, are interested in maintaining fair advertising standards and trying to stop businesses from practicing fraud and deception.

How Consumers Pursue Their Interests

In the aggregate, the voices of 265 million consumers are heard in the American economic marketplace in their daily decisions to buy or not to buy. This country has a substantial number of disadvantaged consumers (e.g., the economically poor, young children, non-English speaking, and some elderly people), perhaps comprising 20 percent of the population, who experience varying degrees of difficulty in buying. We also have the great majority of consumers (probably 60 percent) who go about their consuming with a less than perfect understanding of how to find acceptable-quality goods and services at fair or low prices. Consumer advocate Esther Peterson says that many of them "are simply enthralled with the worst that mass marketing and communications has to offer...that sell false glamour, false fears of personal failure, and false choices between ten different kinds of denture cleaners and twenty different antacids."[17]

There are only a relatively small number of consumers who are well informed in many areas of buying, perhaps only 20 percent of the population. They are "a minority who are engaged, educated, enlivened by choices and wise and considered actions."[18] A smaller subset can be called the **cognoscenti** because they are information-seekers who remain informed on events affecting the consumer interest and practice good health and nutrition. A number of people are becoming **aggressive-assertive** consumers, those who are well informed about their consumer rights and who vigorously pursue getting their money's worth in the marketplace. These consumers are the ones most likely to get redress when wronged by businesses because they are savvy, assertive and empowered.

---

[17]Peterson, E. (1994, March 10). Speech to the Consumer Federation of America, Washington, D.C.
[18]Ibid.

Occasionally, large numbers of consumers band together in a coordinated manner to encourage others to boycott a certain product or seller. A **boycott** is an abstinence from using, buying, or dealing to express protest, or to coerce. At times, individual consumers will buy selectively by holding back their dollar votes and refusing to patronize a certain seller or product perhaps because they do not like the quality, prices, service, sales atmosphere, or attitude of personnel. They may wish to evidence their ethical or moral displeasure, perhaps because of labor practices, political beliefs, environmental concerns, or the unconscionability of the goods sold, and/or they want to demand corporate accountability in the marketplace. Such abstentions are personal boycotts. Such boycotts are an established form of non-violent blackmail. The potential lost sales usually is not the motivation for the seller to capitulate;[19] rather it is a fear of controversy and the accompanying negative publicity. Boycotts threaten companies' images and employees' morale, not their pocketbooks. Boycotts give corporations an incentive to be socially responsible, although it takes responsible and involved consumers to mount a boycott. At any point in time, there are more than 60 groups simultaneously participating in 200 or more boycotts. A vocal minority can make a boycott a powerful tool for consumers as they exercise their most sovereign right—to buy or not to buy.

The Challenge of Being an Effective Consumer

It is a challenge to be an effective consumer pursuing the consumer interest. While it is easy to simply "go out and spend money," the real effort comes in obtaining good quality for a fair price. Also, it is sometimes difficult and taxing to take actions to secure, protect, and assert our consumer rights. For example, it takes time and effort to complain to a store manager or to a government agency about a problem. It also takes time and commitment to become actively involved in local, state, and national consumer organizations that try to protect the rights of consumers. Nevertheless, the voices of consumers need to be heard on matters that affect them in the regulatory and political arenas in Washington, in state capitals, and in town meetings across America.

In short, consumers need to be more responsible in pursuing their interests. In doing so, people will improve their consumer education which will help them make better choices. The choices will be better not because anyone says so, rather because, "they do not regret them, and would not do so even if they had better information or understanding."[20]

Joining consumer organizations is one of the best ways to improve one's consumer education because most groups publish a newsletter. In addition, the financial dues paid to a consumer organization helps support the goals of all consumers. It is vitally important for consumers to contribute to consumer organizations so that their interests are protected and exercised on a daily basis in public policy matters.

This active pursuit of the consumer interest often results in positive changes and improvements in the marketplace. Mayer argues that the "ultimate success [of these efforts] depends on how the economic welfare of consumers has been affected." Pursuit of the consumer interest is a personal matter, as individuals interpret and decide what problems, issues, and concerns merit their attention.

---

[19]However, as one critic observed "If just a quarter of customers called and requested cable disconnections, cable companies would fall to their knees and beg forgiveness."

[20]Morgan, J. N. (1985). What is in the consumer's interest? In K. P. Schnittgrund (Ed.), *The Proceedings of the American Council on Consumer Interests* (p. 2).

Top Ten Reasons NOT to Take a Consumer Economics Course*

10. I'm a business major, so I don't need to know anything about consumers.
9. I want to lose money on a regular basis.
8. When my landlord refuses to return my security deposit, that will be okay with me because he deserves it anyway.
7. I don't care if my food contains waste products, if the toys my kids play with could kill them, or if the drugs my doctor prescribes will make me turn green.
6. The thought of taking a class that doesn't require lab reports, integrations, or speaking in front of a group of strangers intimidates me.
5. My mother is going to buy my clothes and food for me until I'm 40.
4. I like having a grade point average below a 1.5, and I wouldn't want to do anything about it.
3. I will be earning a salary in the six figures the year after I graduate, so I don't need to worry about getting a deal on my Lamborghini.
2. With all the scholarships this college has given me during my six years here, they're practically paying me to go to school.
1. College courses aren't supposed to be useful in real life.

*Sheila Stogdale, Churchville, Virginia

No one is suggesting that we each want a professional consumer view, although that is helpful at times. **Consumer advocates** are people who work for nonprofit organizations that seek to influence public policy to the benefit of consumers. They monitor the activities of regulatory agencies and legislatures to ensure that consumer interests are recognized and safeguarded. They conduct research, communicate with legislators, talk with the press, build coalitions, and activate grass-roots networks to support particular consumer-interest positions. Some advocates focus their efforts at the state level, while others specialize on federal government activities.

Who will decide which problems, issues, and proposals have aspects that may negatively or positively affect the interests of consumers? It will not be business or government, since neither has that direct responsibility. The reality is that the consumer interest must be protected by the ones who are ultimately responsible—the consumers themselves, as well as a number of nonprofit consumer-oriented organizations.

Consumer advocate Ralph Nader says that, "there can be no daily democracy without daily citizenship. If we do not exercise our civic rights, who will? If we do not perform our civic duties, who can? The fiber of a just society in the pursuit of happiness is a thinking, active citizenry. That means you!" Consumer advocate James S. Turner adds that consumers cast dollar votes on a daily basis and political votes are made about once a year, yet both are vital to responsible citizenship.

The academic field of **consumer economics** utilizes economic concepts and principles, along with normative analysis, as it makes value judgments about the formulation and evaluation of public policies from the viewpoint of the consumer interest. The standards being applied, products of moral reasoning which differ from person to person, are those rooted in the consumer interest. Thus, many consumer economics instructors and their students are active in pursuing the consumer interest.

Millions of us go about trying to pursue the consumer interest every day in our own, varied ways, sometimes informed and sometimes not. We are just ordinary people who want to get our money's worth while asserting our rights in marketplace transactions and we want to make sure that all consumers are treated equitably. As individual consumers, it is our task and our responsibility to better understand the consumer interest and to seek it!

Review and Summary of Key Terms and Concepts

1.   What is a **consumer**?

2.   List the **fundamental economic activities** performed by consumers.

3.   Distinguish between **consuming** and **utilizing** as economic activities.

4.   Distinguish between **saving** and **investing** as economic activities.

5.   Briefly discuss why consumers are **not sovereign** in the economic marketplace.

6.   What is the **seller-consumer conflict**, and why will it never be resolved?

7.   Briefly summarize a fundamental aspect of the consumer interest using a **price-quality model**.

8.   Define the **consumer interest** and explain the aspects of **acceptable quality** and **fair** or **low prices**.

9.   Briefly explain the concept of **value-for-money** as it relates to the consumer interest.

10.   Explain why consumers make a lot of poor and **inefficient tradeoffs**.

11.   Briefly explain the concept of **equity** as it relates to the consumer interest.

12.   Distinguish between **opportunity rights** and **benefit rights**.

13.   List five **values** that are important when learning about the consumer interest.

14.   Identify two of the eight **consumer rights**.

15.   Summarize the critical role of **information and understanding** in assessing the consumer interest.

16.   Summarize how the consumer interest can be explained correctly using a **value-for-money/equity model**.

17.   What happens to supply and price for consumers when **discrimination** occurs in the economic marketplace?

18.   Explain why the consumer interest is a **special-interest group**.

19. What is meant by **free riding**?

20. Compare and contrast the **public interest** and the **consumer interest**.

21. Give some examples of how business and government sometimes **support** the consumer interest.

22. List some of the **key economic/political biases** in the United States.

23. What are the two primary reasons why **conflicts occur** between the consumer interest and the public interest?

24. Summarize **why consumers themselves** must look out for the consumer interest.

25. How do actions by **businesses and governments** sometimes help consumers?

26. List some ways how consumers **pursue their interests**?

27. What do you think is the major **challenge** of being an effective consumer?

Useful Resources for Consumers

Consumer Federation of America
1424 16th Street, NW, Suite 604
Washington, DC 20036
202-387-6121

Consumers Union
101 Truman Avenue
Yonkers, NY 10703-1057
914-667-9400

National Coalition for Consumer Education
195 Main Street, Suite 200
Madison, NY 07940
201-477-8987

Public Citizen
1600 20th Street, NW
Washington, DC 20009
202-588-1000

"What Do You Think" Questions

1. Why is it vitally important for you and other consumers to **understand and pursue the consumer interest**?

2. Select one of the eight important **consumer rights** and explain why it is important both to you and to other consumers.

3. Explain why the concept of **equity** sometimes requires a paternalistic attitude that encourages protection of certain kinds of consumers.

4. What types of actions do you think American society should take to help consumers make more **efficient marketplace decisions**?

5. The term **acceptable quality** can have many definitions. What do you generally think that word means to you in your marketplace transactions? Also, explain how that definition might change for different products and services you purchase.

6. What kinds of actions can you suggest to sellers that would encourage them to **more often serve the consumer interest**?

Chapter 2

The Consumer Movement Continues to Evolve

OBJECTIVES

After reading this chapter, you should be able to

1. Summarize what the economic marketplace looked like for American consumers during the early periods of the consumer movement, prior to the 1960s.

2. Provide examples of what happened during the consumerism era of the 1960s and 1970s.

3. Summarize the responses of government and business to the consumerism era of the 1970s and 1980s.

4. Give examples of social and economic factors that make consumer movements successful.

5. Provide an overview of the status of today's consumer movement.

6. Discuss the future of the consumer movement, particularly as it will be shaped by the major players in the arena: sellers, governments, consumer organizations, and consumers.

The idea of consumerism is embedded in American history. Many consumers at the turn of the past century somehow passively tolerated tenement housing, unsafe working conditions, unwholesome food, and a host of other consumer problems. Americans in the 1960s rebelled against similar problems and ushered in the decade of consumerism. Today's consumer movement serves as an important means to achieve a just and fair society. The consumer movement aims to challenge the status quo because the latter wants to maintain its advantages in society.

This chapter looks at the changing consumer movement and suggests why the role of the consumer has changed and how it will continue to evolve. The chapter begins with an historical review of the early periods of the consumer movement and the consumerism era of the 1960s and early 1970s. Then the responses of government and business to the surges of interest in the consumer movement are examined. This includes a description of social change as an evolutionary process which provides insight into today's mature and successful consumer movement. The chapter concludes with a review of the roles that the major players in the consumer movement will perform in the future.

The Early Periods of the Consumer Movement

The first three periods of the consumer movement occurred before 1890 (awakening to consumer problems), from the 1890s to 1929 (early consumer movement), and from 1929 through the 1950s (renewed consumer interest).

Awakening to Consumer Problems: Before 1890

Our ancestors lived a highly individualistic life. They wanted freedom and independence and were extremely self-reliant. They were basically self-sustaining, cooperative, and giving. The welfare of consumers depended in part on the honesty and buying skills of the few local shopkeepers. If the shopkeeper was smart enough to purchase good-quality products, then consumers who bought from these shopkeepers at least had access to good products.

The range of products available to consumers was quite small. The products were generally simple in design and were in everyday use. Buyers were faced with few products that were not within their range of experience. Intelligent buyers, therefore, had the expertise to make a reasonable evaluation of most products.

Most goods had no trademarks, and few had brand names. The wise consumer knew the merchandise and tried to avoid shoddy products. However, consumers had almost no protection against merchants who raised prices needlessly, and they could do little to stop frauds, such as misbranding and adulteration. The prevailing consumer motto was **caveat emptor**, meaning "let the buyer beware."

Toward the end of the last century, the effects of a rapidly growing society changed the role of the consumer. Industrialization, along with population growth, brought 40 percent of the population to the cities. A nationwide system of railroads served the economic needs of those who had moved into urban areas, where employment opportunities and local trolley transportation systems thrived.

The ensuing congestion, however, also led to "urban poverty, tenement housing, immigrant ghettos, municipal corruption, hazardous working conditions, sweat shops, child labor and a variety of consumer problems."[1] To fight these problems, people, particularly women, banded together. The numerous reform organizations created were concerned with political change. Newly created unions sought equity for people of the working class. The populists and progressives promoted economic and social change to correct "the imbalances, injustices, and inequities of an economic system that contained too much exploitation of the weaker and poorer by the stronger and richer."[2] Volunteer groups of do-gooders concerned themselves with local issues, such as food adulteration.

Early Consumer Movement: The 1890s through the 1920s

The years from the 1890s through the 1920s were a time when most people in the U.S. still lived on farms in rural areas, and these years can be described as the early consumer movement. This initial movement was an extension of other social movements (labor, cooperatives, and women's groups) which provided the foundations for today's consumer activities. The first Consumers' League was formed in 1891 in New York City. In 1899, the National Consumers League was founded to fight marketplace injustices, and soon branch offices were established in 20 states. During these years, Congress passed over 50 consumer protection laws.

A feeling for the times can be seen in typical newspaper headlines:

STANDARD OIL "TRUST" SUCCEEDS THROUGH BRIBERY, GRAFT, FRAUD, VIOLENCE, AND THE DESTRUCTION OF COMPETITION

AGRICULTURE DEPARTMENT DOCUMENTS 1400 PAGES OF FOOD ADULTERATION

FORMALDEHYDE USED AS FOOD PRESERVATIVE

GROUPS OPPOSE FOOD AND DRUG LEGISLATION, INCLUDING AMERICAN MEDICAL ASSOCIATION

PRESIDENT ROOSEVELT INVESTIGATES FOODS

PURE FOOD AND DRUG LAW PASSES CONGRESS

CHICAGO HOUSEWIVES LEAGUE FORMED TO CHECK SANITARY CONDITIONS IN FOOD STORES

CONGRESS PASSES ANTITRUST LAWS TO PROMOTE COMPETITION

U.S. ENTERS WORLD WAR

Patriotic fever, wartime shortages, and postwar readjustments then diverted much attention from consumer problems. After the war, during the early 1920s, consumer incomes rose sharply. More and newer products appeared for sale, and advertising expenditures, which had been criticized as serving no useful purpose, quickly exceeded $3 billion annually. Buyers were confused by the growing array of products, and it is no

---

[1]Herrmann, R. O. (1970), *The Consumer Movement in Historical Perspective* (Pennsylvania State University, Department of Agricultural Economics and Rural Sociology), 1.

[2]James S. Turner, The consumer interest in the 1990's and beyond: The 1995 ACCI Colston Warne Memorial Lecture, *Consumer Interests Annual*, 41, pp. 1-11.

wonder that such consumer outrage books as *Counterfeit, Not to Be Broadcast, 40,000,000 Guinea Pig Children, The American Chamber of Horrors,* and *100,000,000 Guinea Pigs* became best sellers. The books illustrated dozens of instances of misbranding, mislabeling, and unsafe practices being committed by large, well-respected companies that injured or cheated consumers.

In 1929, Consumers Research was formed by F. J. Schlink, author of the best-selling *Your Money's Worth* (subtitled "A Study in the Waste of the Consumer's Dollar"), and it published *Consumers' Research Magazine.* During these years, a number of product-testing laboratories, some of which were run by department stores and trade associations, were established to provide buying information to the public. The federal Bureau of Standards established a national system of weights and measures.

At that time, **trusts** were combinations of firms that got together to reduce competition and control supplies and/or prices throughout a geographic area or industry. The battle against the trusts established the Federal Trade Commission Act in 1914. The fight for pure food resulted in passage of the Pure Food and Drug Act of 1906. These events along with rising prices and an increasing torrent of advertising all helped make the public aware of their interests as consumers as distinguished from their interests as workers or property owners. The appearance of a consumer consciousness was now well established in American society.

Renewed Consumer Interest: 1929 through the 1950s

A variety of circumstances brought on a renewed interest in consumer issues from 1929 through the 1950s, which was also a time of population migration to the cities. Early on, the Great Depression of the 1930s came. Typical headlines tell about the times:

ONE-THIRD OF LABOR FORCE UNEMPLOYED

BARGAIN SALES OF PRE-DEPRESSION MERCHANDISE

CONSUMERS SHOULD BEWARE OF SHODDY MERCHANDISE

IS ADVERTISING RESPONSIBLE FOR THE WASTEFUL PROLIFERATION OF BRANDS AND COSTING CONSUMERS MORE?

"USE IT UP, WEAR IT OUT, MAKE IT DO, OR DO WITHOUT"—NEW CONSUMER SLOGAN

PICKETING DETROIT HOUSEWIVES FORCE MEAT PRICES TO ROLL BACK 20 PERCENT

EMPLOYEES ON STRIKE AT CONSUMERS' RESEARCH, INC.

NEW TESTING GROUP ORGANIZED—CONSUMERS UNION, INC.

PURE FOOD AND DRUG LAW NOW OUTDATED

NEW SULFA "WONDER DRUG" KILLS NEARLY 100 PEOPLE

Because of the Depression and World War II, demand for consumer goods was almost totally depressed for 15 years from 1930 to 1945. The postwar period of the late 1940s and into the 1950s saw strong economic growth and rising consumer incomes for our primarily blue-collar society. During the 1950s, thousands took advantage of the educational opportunities offered to World War II veterans, which pushed them up the economic ladder and helped gradually transfer the United States into a better educated and increasingly white-collar society. Magazine circulation for the popular buying information magazine *Consumer Reports*, published by Consumers Union, Inc., grew to almost half a million by 1950. The National Association of Consumers, a small consumer interest group, disappeared in a merger with the Council on Consumer Information.

During the 1950s, grass-roots issues were not numerous, but the increased use of installment credit and the buying of new homes and durable products did provide some incentive for including consumer education courses in the schools. Schools increasingly began to teach students the hows and whys of buymanship until the Soviet Union sent up the first satellite, Sputnik, in 1957. This event rapidly turned attention away from such life adjustment courses and the curriculum began to emphasize science and mathematics.

Some consumer issues still caught the headlines, however. In *The Hidden Persuaders*, Vance Packard argued that the public was being manipulated by advertisers. Generally speaking, however, the relative economic prosperity of the 1950s, Senator Joseph McCarthy's campaign against so-called communists, and the growing interest in space and national defense kept things rather quiet on the consumer front.

Consumerism: The 1960s and Early 1970s

By the 1960s, Americans were much more aware of the marketplace. Television made every consumer an expert, because for the first time in history people were constantly exposed to product claims. The decade of the 1960s saw a new social movement evolve in which more economically informed Americans (better than their parents) expressed dissatisfaction with the existing social, economic, and structural systems. Such disharmony helped people develop a greater social conscience, and they demanded social change. As members of an increasingly wealthy industrial society that met most of its people's basic needs, Americans could afford to turn their attention to social concerns, such as race relations, consumer problems, pollution cleanup, product safety, and social justice. Since neither the economic marketplace nor the government was adequately addressing these concerns, American consumers perceived this inattention as a violation of the public trust and demanded action. This has been called the consciousness revolution that recast American values by establishing new social norms.

People became more open to self-criticism regarding social and economic problems, many of which were of deep concern to consumers. Some of the best-selling books were Rachel Carson's *The Silent Spring* (1962, environment), Michael Harrington's *The Other America* (1962, poverty), Jessica Mitford's *The American Way of Death* (1963, funerals), David Caplovitz's *The Poor Pay More* (1963, poverty and credit), Maurine Neuberger's *Smoke Screen: Tobacco and the Public Welfare* (1963, cigarettes), and Richard Harris' *The Real Voice* (1964, drug safety). The nation was becoming more aware of its problems, and this ushered in the loosely organized era of activist consumerism, which lasted until the mid-1970s.

During these years, **consumerism** was a label put on the efforts of a growing number of consumer advocates who questioned the inadequacies of the marketplace and the unwillingness of business and government to deal with important consumer needs and demands. Concerns included: (1) the increasing complexity of products confronting consumers in the marketplace, (2) frustration with the growing specialization of services that were difficult to assess, (3) false advertising, (4) empty warranties, (5) selling that was impersonalized, (6) serious automobile, health, and product safety problems, and (7) stopping government decisions that ignored the viewpoints of consumers.

Consumerism emerged because many people concluded that making money should not be the only objective of the capitalistic economic system. Many Americans began to question the logic of commitments to maximizing economic growth that were crucially important to earlier generations. People demanded justice and fair play in the marketplace, which represented a significant shift in the national value system. Americans began to realize that fulfilling the consumer interest, as suggested by Adam Smith in his 1776 book *The Wealth of Nations*, is the best means to enhance the wealth of the country.

The term **consumer movement** characterizes the organized activities of a loose coalition of groups of people working toward the achievement of a number of related goals which (1) protect consumer rights (such as health and safety), (2) help consumers gain power to control critical factors in their lives (i.e., competent choicemaking and appropriate redress), and (3) limit marketplace abuses. Thus, the consumer movement seeks honest packaging, accurate labeling, truthful advertising, fair pricing, and improved safety standards. An effective consumer movement encourages the competitive economic system of capitalism to reward those companies that produce better products. People involved in the consumer movement come from several areas of society: community, senior citizen, cooperatives, labor unions, foundations, academics, consumer information, consumer advocacy, and consumer affairs professionals in business and government.

Consumer advocate Lee Richardson says that, "the *consumer movement* is what consumer activists do." Stephen Brobeck, Executive Director of the Consumer Federation of America, defines **consumer activists** or **consumer advocates** as "those persons affiliated with nonprofit organizations who seek to influence public policy to the benefit of consumers." Arch W. Troelstrup, former professor of family economics at Stevens College, says of the *consumer movement* that, "It punctures false claims, it spreads knowledge of new quality products, it harnesses science for the service of the buyer." He argues that the consumer movement also helps restore the capacity of the competitive system to reward those companies which are producing better products. "The central aim of the consumer movement," says Troelstrup, "is to help organize the economy in ways that will best serve the consumer interest."

The beginning of the consumer movement of the 1960s probably began with a boycott by a group of housewives in Denver, Colorado, who picketed local supermarkets protesting high prices. With nationwide publicity of this event and others, the consumer movement grew and began to make its strength felt in America. Numerous groups with an interest in consumer concerns began to spring up.

In March 1962, John F. Kennedy presented the first presidential message to Congress directed at consumer concerns. He asked for legislative action and new programs in several areas. The most important aspect of this message, however, was the now famous Consumer Bill of Rights. Kennedy stated that consumers have four rights: (1) the right to safety, (2) the right to be informed, (3) the right to choose, and (4) the right to be heard. This message provided a great surge of interest in consumer concerns.

Consumer problems remained in the news. President Kennedy established a Consumer Advisory Council to assist his Council on Economic Advisors. The thalidomide drug scandal resulted in the birth of over 20,000 deformed babies around the world, although few occurred in the United States. The congressional hearings prior to passage of the Kefauver-Harris Drug Amendments revealed scandalous information about large numbers of ineffective and useless drugs being sold to unsuspecting Americans.

In 1964, President Lyndon B. Johnson created a new White House position, Special Assistant to the President for Consumer Affairs. He appointed Esther Peterson to this post. With White House visibility, consumer concerns became front-page news. Later that year, Johnson sent a consumer message to Congress urging passage of several new laws. These indeed were exciting times for consumers and consumer advocates, and the liberal landslide in the 1964 election gave strength to those calling for reforms. Ralph Nader's call for volunteers to come to Washington to research and become active on consumer issues resulted in hundreds of people joining what *Washington Post* writer William Greider called "**Nader's Raiders**."

The consumerism era brought on a number of events: (1) housewives boycotting supermarkets because of high meat prices, (2) exposés in the form of books, news articles, and radio and television programs, (3) the formation of numerous local consumer-action groups, (4) a flurry of legislative action on national and state levels, (5) scandals concerning fabrics, drugs, food, credit, and product safety, (6) further presidential support by Lyndon B. Johnson and Richard M. Nixon through more consumer messages, (7) introduction of consumer education courses into many schools, (8) an increased media interest in consumer issues as news, (9) Nader's Network of consumer organizations, and (10) a general broadening of support for consumer concerns.

In 1968, the Consumer Federation of America was formed. Its strength came from the nearly 200 other consumer organizations that were members. It lobbied for consumers in Washington, D.C. and pushed for more government intervention in the marketplace. The premise was that consumers needed more than information to make wise decisions; they needed strong voices to speak and leaders to fight for them. These years saw the "ism" in consumerism become appropriate as once-quiet consumers organized and spoke out on a wide spectrum of issues, often on issues of justice and fairness. Active leaders were almost militant in promoting the moral and ethical rights of consumers.

Responses to Consumerism in the 1970s and 1980s

Business and government had different responses to the demands of consumers through the years. In general, however, business tended not to listen, took few positive actions, and typically remained disinterested in consumerism issues. Government listened and took some actions to help consumers.

Business Response

The social consciousness of the early 1960s, rising incomes of consumers, and higher expectations of quality (suggested primarily by advertising) were signs that could have predicted the consumerism of the times. A greater number of Americans had money and wanted quality goods and services. Substantial numbers of Americans had little money but still wanted those same goods and services.

Businesses tried to provide what consumers wanted, but the good quality and low prices were difficult to find. Increasing inflation, beginning in the mid-1960s, and rising unemployment, combined with the louder voices of consumer advocates, finally convinced business that consumerism was a force to be reckoned with.

Who is Ralph Nader, the Nation's Leading Consumer Advocate?

Ralph Nader is America's most famous consumer advocate. To many he is "Saint Ralph" or the consumer's "knight in shining white armor." To others he is a paranoid, overwhelmed with a sense of moral righteousness. He is a crusader, a muckraker and a person of enormous integrity; one who has given up all material possessions in his devoted pursuit to better the lives of consumers. He has made major contributions to American society, particularly in the form of serving as a catalyst to pass laws and regulations to protect and empower consumers.

In 1965, shortly after graduating from Harvard Law School, Ralph Nader wrote a book entitled *Unsafe at Any Speed* that indicted the auto industry for habitually subordinating safety to style and specifically criticized the design safety of the General Motor's Corvair automobile. The book became a best seller only after it was revealed that General Motors had investigated Nader's background in an attempt to discredit both the man and book. The resulting controversy led to an apology by the chairman of the board of General Motors during televised congressional hearings. Ralph Nader became an instant "folk hero," and the public's response prompted passage of the National Traffic and Motor Vehicle Safety Act later that year. Nader deserves credit for getting government to require automakers to install seat belts, air bags, and other safety equipment.

Nader's lawsuit against General Motors gave him the then-large sum of $425,000 in an out-of-court settlement. He used this money to establish several new consumer organizations, such as the Center for the Study of Responsive Law, Public Citizen, and Center for Auto Safety. The money also paid for summer interns to work on various ad hoc task force projects. These people became known as **Nader's Raiders** in part because of the excellent quality of their investigative research which typically resulted in a written report or book followed by changes in government laws and policies. Ralph Nader moved the idea of consumerism (then primarily concerned with bargain shopping and redeeming supermarket cents-off coupons) completely off the women's pages of the newspapers to the front pages.

Nader and his various satellite organizations still combat practices that are hostile to consumer's interests. They conduct quality research and get good press coverage in an effort to force businesses and governments to do more of what is right for consumers. Nader wants America to live up to its democratic ideals—to make the free enterprise system work as it is supposed to—by helping consumers to more effectively participate in the American economic and political systems.

In the early 1960s, the typical business response was "ignore the demands of the consumer activists and they will go away." Fear was the reason. Some business persons said, "Fight the consumerists! Save our free enterprise system!" The food industry reacted violently against Esther Peterson's modest proposal for a truth-in-packaging law, accusing her of being anti-American. Business views about consumer issues were often grudging and negative. Business had to be dragged into the realities of the times. Because of the reactionary attitudes of business, by the mid-sixties the historical business motto of caveat emptor, in existence since the 1500s, had changed to **caveat venditor** "let the seller beware!" Consumers were upset and would not take it anymore!

But some businesses started going along with the demands of consumers, especially when those demands did not cost much money. A few business leaders actually viewed the consumerism movement as an opportunity. Those who did sought the help of both consumers and consumer advocates, knowing that such action would, at the very least, help improve their public relations images and perhaps also result in improved sales.

Still, the overall response of business to consumer demands for change in the 1960s was negative. The typical business response was concisely stated by the editors of *Business Week* in 1969:

Deny everything. Nearly everyone goes through a phase of shock when hallowed business practices are questioned, and this is the automatic response.

Blame wrongdoing on the small marginal companies. In any industry where fragmentation and ease of entry are the rule, the argument is popular that the major companies are blameless, but that the small outfits must cut corners to survive.

Discredit the critics. "Hell," says one congressional staff man, "I've had publishers, worried about circulation sales, conducting an investigation down here peddling stuff on the communist nature of consumerism based on 1942 documents."

Hire a public relations person. A big campaign to modify public opinion is alluring. But as one PR man says, "There's no sense in a PR campaign if you have nothing to say."

Defend the legislation. Trade associations and Washington law firms are specialists in this, and it is often effective, at least for a while. It worked for the tobacco industry in 1965. It also worked in respect to the truth-in-packaging law.

Launch a fact-finding committee to find out whether anything really needs to be improved in the way the company does business. The food industry is deeply involved in this now.

Actually do something, whether you think you are guilty or innocent.[3]

On the positive side, during this time period a growing number of businesses created consumer affairs positions in the corporate structure. Typically, these people worked in the public relations department and were in charge of handling consumer complaints. It all started when Esther Peterson left the Johnson administration to become an in-house consumer advocate on her own terms for Giant Food, with complete freedom to speak out according to her convictions, both publicly and within the company. Giant Food was the only food company that was accessible during the truth-in-packaging controversy.

By the early 1970s, over 1000 regional and national businesses had hired **consumer affairs professionals (CAPs)**, people trained to represent the interests of both consumers and their employing organizations. Further, a significant number of the appointments were for higher-level positions, such as consumer manager and vice president for consumer affairs. During this time, a new professional association was established, the Society of Consumer Affairs Professionals in Business (SOCAP). Collectively, on a national level, the corporate consumer affairs professional, particularly those in positions of high authority, played an important role in getting an increasing number of businesses to respond in a favorable way to consumer demands for change.

Government Response

As consumer problems with price and quality persisted and complaints continued about the disparity between claims and performance, consumers looked for ways to fix

---

[3]Reprinted from the September 6, 1969, issue of *Business Week* by special permission, copyright by McGraw-Hill, Inc.

the systematic poor attitudes of sellers. When the growing dissatisfactions were not met by corporations, consumers took their grievances to government.

Social Change as an Evolutionary Process

Social change has been described as an eight-stage evolutionary process:

1. **Situational evolution**—awareness of the changes starts to dawn slowly on those affected;
2. **Growing frustration**—quiet dissatisfaction slowly develops, but people do not know what to do about it;
3. **The lonely voice**—someone articulates the developing situation and seizes the public attention, which serves to alert "astute managers with an invaluable early warning system for detecting emerging social change";
4. **Dissatisfaction coalesces**—people succeed in giving voice and shape to the growing frustration below the surface that has not yet been focused;
5. **Action/reaction**—public support evolves into a mass movement where demands for change are made, compromises are few, requests for voluntary change are resisted, and obstinacy fuels the demands for change;
6. **Political action**—leaders of the movement organize their followers, who have the votes, to put pressure on politicians for mandated changes, but the latter are supported by the status quo, which results in passage of a watered-down version of the demanded reforms;
7. **Institutionalization**—supporters of the change gradually win institutional acceptance (at the economic, political, and social levels) as responsible leaders are appointed to political office and hired by corporations to administer the programs, and
8. **Incremental change**—"supporters of the new changes work for gradual, incremental improvements that ultimately achieve most of what the mass movement had demanded," demonstrating that the changes are mainstream ideas and part of the national agenda.[1]

[1]Private correspondence from Paul S. Forbes, September 19, 1989. Reprinted with permission.

During the 1960s and early 1970s, the over-arching belief was that informed consumers are essential to the fair and efficient functioning of a free-market economy. Congress chose **affirmative disclosure** (encouraging assertions of accurate information about products and services) as a major technique for regulating business. Local, state, and federal legislation became the primary governmental response to consumer problems. If a problem arose, it seemed logical and not expensive to write a new law or regulation, start a special agency, and/or create a commission to study the matter and make recommendations. Ralph Nader speculated that consumer legislation was likely to be enacted only under one configuration of interests: divided business groups and united consumer groups. Dozens of consumer protection bills were proposed and many were passed, although most were cosmetic gestures to appease constituents.

Many states and localities passed a number of laws and regulations in an effort to protect consumers. Examples include civil and criminal penalties against offenders, injunctions against unethical merchants, licensing of business services (such as television and automobile repairs), mandatory posting of octane ratings for gasoline, prohibition of pyramid sales promotions, banned advertising of any items when sufficient quantities were not readily available, and "little FTC" laws making it unlawful to use fraud, deception, or false pretense in the sale or advertising of merchandise. However, putting new laws on the books is one thing and effective consumer protection is another. Weak and unenforced consumer legislation results in inadequate consumer protection.

The federal legislative rush to protect consumers during the 1960s and early 1970s resulted in more than 500 bills being proposed, many for political reasons only. Less than 30 were made into law, and enforcement was typically weak. Still, Congress had passed laws that confronted all the major problem areas facing consumers: credit, warranties, product safety, cosmetics, medical devices, appliance energy labeling, real estate, drugs, and food. More consumer protection laws were passed between 1965 and 1975 than during the entire period between 1890 and 1965. In addition, three new regulatory agencies also were established: the Consumer Product Safety Commission, the National Highway Traffic Safety Administration, and the Environmental Protection Agency. On the legislative front, the consumerism years saw tremendous progress, especially when compared with earlier years. In addition, the existing government organizations tried to do a better job. By the end of the decade, there were 42 complaint departments in the federal government and more than 225 county and city consumer offices.

What Makes Consumer Movements Successful?

The history of the consumer movement in America provides insights as to why, on occasion, consumer interests seem to rise and fall and then rise again. Six social and economic factors seem associated with interest in consumer problems.

Rising Expectations of Consumers

Interest in consumer issues is so strong that it is now a part of the **American psyche**, the unconscious soul or spirit and behavior of the American population. Consumerism has become part of the social fabric of American life. People today demand and expect refunds for products that don't live up to their expectations. They want "somebody" to fix their problems "right now," and they want a "good buy." Today's consumers demand that business and government pay attention to consumer issues, and lately that includes more tangible concerns about banking, insurance, health care and pensions. Today in the United States, interest in consumer issues is accepted by custom and by law. Many now believe that consumerism is synonymous with "free-market democracy" in that it gives people a voice in the economic and political decisions that affect them as consumers. Informed consumers encourage the competition that disciplines the marketplace.

Scandals and Dramatic Crises

Print media during the 1800s, radio during the 1920s and 1930s, television in the late 1940s and 1950s, and all mass media in the more recent decades have provided a ready outlet for scandals. Scandals, such as price fixing, bribery, adulterated foods, unsafe automobiles, bureaucratic incompetence, and dangerous chemicals, are viewed by consumers as violations of the public trust. These occasional lapses by business serve as a recurring impetus that fuels the consumer movement. Best-selling books and journalistic exposés of political and commercial corruption by investigative reporters quickly gain and hold the attention of Americans. When enough consumers are upset about a particular scandal, they demand corrective action by government officials.

Today, the investigative television shows "60 Minutes" and "20/20" can keep the entire country talking about a story for weeks. The media helps sustain the consumer movement. Important in some scandals are **whistleblowers**,[4] employees in government or business who cry out against injustice by exposing fraud and mismanagement at their place of work at the risk of reprisals by their employers.[5] In a similar way, the efforts of consumer advocates are useful in focusing attention on issues in a credible manner.

Without media attention, scandals and dramatic crises would have little or no impact. Many Americans were shocked and outraged by Upton Sinclair's book *The Jungle*, which exposed the scandalous and unhealthy conditions of the meat-packing plants and led to a new food and drug law. The Chase and Schlink book, *Your Money's Worth*, resulted in the formation of several product-testing organizations. The liquid form of a drug called Elixir Sulfanilamide caused a national crisis when it killed nearly 100 people, and this, in part, resulted in improved drug and food legislation in 1938. Another drug scandal involved thalidomide, which caused birth defects in thousands of babies and led to further drug amendments in the 1960s.

Consumers often have the support of the media in their efforts.[6] Today there are "Action Line" columns in over 100 newspapers in the United States, as well as consumer "Call for Action" lines on 70 radio and television stations. Several hundred newspapers and television and radio stations also employ reporters who uncover unfair business practices and disseminate valuable consumer information to the public.

Ralph Nader's book *Unsafe at Any Speed* did not sell well until the televised congressional hearings disclosed the scandalous investigation of Nader by General Motors. The publicity made him into something of a hero, and he soon became the nation's leading spokesperson for consumers. This also contributed to passage of major automobile safety legislation later that year.

Charismatic People

Certain people have a special quality of personal magnetism or charm and a demonstrated ability to win the devotion of large numbers of people. This **charisma** carries over into their leadership styles.

Throughout each consumer era, a few individuals have inspired others to listen, to think, and to act. People followed Theodore Roosevelt, and when, as President, he called

---

[4]In 1989, Congress passed the Whistleblower Protection Act that protects government employees who claim they have been punished for revealing fraud or waste. Now the government must defend its personnel decisions by proving through clear and convincing evidence that they would have taken the same action against an employee if he or she had not engaged in whistleblowing activity. Wronged whistleblowers can collect attorney fees in court if they win.

[5]In 1994, outside auditors vindicated an investment manager who was fired after accusing his employer, Prudential Insurance Company of America, of inflating the value of two real estate investment funds. The former employee turned down the opportunity to rejoin Prudential. According to a recent study, more than one-third of whistleblowing federal employees suffer retaliation.

[6]However, a major problem with media exposes is that they rarely provide the aroused viewer, listener or reader with information (telephone number and address) on how to learn more about the topic, how to offer assistance, or how to join a group.

for food and drug legislation, the country responded. Schlink's writing led to the formation of Consumers' Research, Inc., which published its findings in a periodical (now called *Consumers' Research Magazine*) to which thousands subscribed. People also responded to the leadership of Colston Warne, who founded *Consumer Reports* magazine in 1936, with a readership of hundreds of thousands. Warne's large physical size added to his charismatic presence when he spoke out supporting the consumer interest to groups around the world. *Consumer Reports* is now the nation's most popular consumer magazine, with a circulation of about 5 million copies monthly.

Vance Packard was a popular author throughout the 1950s, and when he appeared on television talk shows and addressed consumer issues, people really took notice. John F. Kennedy was legendary for his charismatic personality, and his famous Consumer Bill of Rights heralded a new era of consumer interest. Esther Peterson was such a tremendous spokesperson for consumers that pressures were put on President Johnson to remove her. Ralph Nader's charisma from the 1960s continues today as he fights against overpriced automobile insurance.

Active Government Organizations

Federal, state, and local government organizations have much to do with promoting the consumer interest. They have the political power, after all, to propose and/or enforce laws and regulations. Government organizations strengthen the consumer movement by their very presence because they represent an institutionalization of the concept. Once a governmental agency is created, it is difficult to eliminate—thus the constituency (consumers in this instance) is likely to be served forever.

An *active* government organization is one that is vigorously pursuing its mission rather than just existing. Good leadership can make a difference. In the 1890s, for example, Dr. Harvey W. Wiley of the Department of Agriculture got excellent news coverage when he dramatized the food adulteration problem. He created a "poison squad" of 12 men who were fed adulterants common to the diet of most Americans to establish the "influence of food preservatives and artificial colors on digestion and health." None died, although some became ill. The overuse of unsafe and adulterated food was well publicized and led to improved legislation.

During the 1920s, the Federal Trade Commission was responsible for the strong enforcement of the laws that mandated the breakup of business trusts that illegally conspired to fix prices. The importance of antitrust efforts continues as Federal Judge Harold H. Greene recently said that, "if the United States is today a consumer and consumption society, rather than one dominated by cartels with price-fixing abilities, it is largely because of the antitrust laws."

The drug thalidomide deformed over 20,000 children worldwide in the 1960s, but not in the U.S. because the Food and Drug Administration prohibited its sale. The FDA's Dr. Francis Kelsey was most active and vocal in her disapproval of this drug, and she was almost singlehandedly responsible for the refusal to allow thalidomide to be marketed in this country. Strong leadership at the Consumer Product Safety Commission in the 1970s resulted in a prohibition of the sale of flammable sleepwear for children.

At times, both the White House and Congress help sustain the consumer interest. The executive branch has its U.S. Office of Consumer Affairs (USOCA) serve as presidential spokesperson, even though USOCA lacks legislative authority. When the President's Special Assistant for Consumer Affairs, who is head of the USOCA, gives congressional testimony or speaks out on consumer issues, it is usually well publicized. Through the years, Esther Peterson, Betty Furness, Virginia Knauer, Bonnie Guiton (the first African-American in the position), Ann Wallace, Polly Baca (the first Hispanic-American in the position), and Bernice Friedlander have forcefully projected the consumer interest to Congress and government agencies. When congressional committees hold hearings on consumer concerns, these are typically well publicized.

State and local governments actively sustain the consumer interest in a number of ways. In all states, the attorney general represents both consumer and public interests. In most states, the representation consists of a full staff of lawyers and professionals. Since it is usually good politics to be pro-consumer, most attorneys generally support consumer interests. Each state also has a Weights and Measures Department that is charged with the responsibility to safeguard the interests of consumers.

Throughout the country every state has a state office of consumer affairs (OCA) to help consumers in complaint-handling. Most of the time the OCA is under the office of the attorney general, but sometimes it is attached to the office of the governor. Frequent public service announcements to advertise the OCA toll-free complaint hotline and many public appearances by committed government officials go a long way toward supporting consumer interests. Many states also have a consumer services mission in their state insurance and banking departments that offer information, education and complaint-handling. Some have toll-free telephone hotlines.

Some states have employed **state-paid consumer advocates** to actively pursue the consumer interest before its regulatory commissions, such as the state public utility commission (PUC) and the state agriculture department. In this way, the state's concern for the public interest is balanced against the interests of consumers.

Active Private Organizations

A number of private organizations have helped to sustain interest in consumer matters. In 1891, a New York City action group **whitelisted** shops that treated employees fairly. In contrast to **blacklisting** stores that treated employees poorly (by creating a list of persons or organizations that are disapproved or boycotted or suspected of disloyalty), whitelisting encouraged patronage of those businesses that "paid fair minimum wages, had reasonable working hours, and decent sanitary conditions." By 1903, the National Consumer's League (NCL) had 64 branch offices in 20 states. Today's largest consumer action group, the Consumer Federation of America (CFA), represents over 250 national, state, and local pro-consumer organizations, with a combined membership exceeding 50 million people. It actively represents the consumer interest on health, safety and economic issues before governmental policymaking and regulatory bodies and the courts. The Conference of Consumer Organizations (COCO) is a similar but smaller group.

Every state today has a statewide consumer action group; many larger states have multiple organizations. These groups typically charge a small membership fee, such as $10, produce an informative newsletter, and actively lobby in the state legislature and before regulatory agencies. Particularly strong consumer groups exist in California and Ohio. Some cities and even neighborhoods are well organized, too.

Many private complaint-handling and mediation organizations also exist, such as the Major Appliance Consumer Action Panel (MACAP). There also are dozens of Automobile Consumer Action Panels (AUTOCAPs) in cities across the country.

Other privately organized groups include the Ralph Nader's Center for the Study of Responsive Law, a relatively small group of lawyers and technical specialists who work on reform issues, and numerous offshoot organizations (the "Nader Network") to which Nader contributes money, support, and advice but no longer has an active role: Public Citizen, whose 80,000 members support a $7 million budget and a staff of 60 working in several sections (Congress Watch, Health Research Group, Litigation Group, Critical Mass Energy Project, and Buyers Up); U.S. Public Interest Research Group; Clear Water Action; Center for Auto Safety; Pension Rights Center; Center for Science in the Public Interest; Essential Information; National Association for Public Interest Law; Trial Lawyers for Public Justice; National Insurance Consumer Organization; Aviation Consumer Action Project; and Telecommunications Action and Research Center. Altogether these groups employ about 1500 people and serve 2 million members.

Citizen utility boards (CUBs) are funded by member dues to serve as watchdog organizations that intervene in rate cases and legislative hearings on electric, gas and telephone matters. They represent consumer views before public service commissions. CUBs were inspired by Ralph Nader, and they exist in a number of states. The laws governing CUBs require utility companies to send materials soliciting membership in the CUB annually along with customers' utility bills. Such mandated access provides an opportunity for consumer leaders to get their messages out. Wisconsin has 90,000 members who pay annual membership fees of $3 to $100.

One of the most powerful private consumer organizations is Consumers Union (CU), publisher of *Consumer Reports* magazine. The publication is authoritative, respected, and well read by Americans. Consumers Union also has something historically uncommon among consumer groups, and that is money. Although not affluent, its profitable ventures allow CU to donate funds to fledgling consumer organizations to help them succeed. CU also funds advocacy offices in Texas, California, and the nation's capital. Also powerful is the Consumers International, headquartered in Hague, The Netherlands which represents 180 affiliated consumer organizations in approximately 70 countries.

Consumer organizations often work to achieve their goals with occasional help of other organizations. A **coalition** is an alliance, particularly a temporary one, of people or groups to accomplish some single effort that is a jointly held goal of each. Since coalitions have more than one organization involved, it is easier to create public awareness of a concern and/or push for legislation. Consumer groups have found it beneficial to work with other organizations, often with government, labor, and environmental organizations, and sometimes even with traditional opponents, such as businesses, to move toward a particular goal. For example, even though a union might be seeking higher wages which could raise prices and hurt the consumer interest in low prices, a consumer organization and a union might work together to support a law to require public disclosure of prescription drug prices inside drug stores. The National Coalition for Consumer Education is an example of a permanent coalition.

Consumer groups work with unions, chambers of commerce, cooperatives, credit unions, Better Business Bureaus, and businesses. Coalition organizations have included the Credit Union National Association, National Council of Better Business Bureaus, and leading companies such as American Express, Avon Products, and J.C. Penney. The Coalition for Health and Safety is a partnership of consumer, health and insurer groups.

The American Council on Consumer Interests (ACCI), successor to the Council on Consumer Information, is the professional association for about 800 academics in the consumer field. The Michigan-based National Institute for Consumer Education serves educators at all levels. The National Association for Administrators in Consumer Affairs

(NAACA) is an organization of 150 state and local consumer affairs professionals representing consumer protection offices. The Society for Consumer Affairs Professionals in Business (SOCAP) serves a similar function for over 2700 people working in business. The National Coalition for Consumer Education (NCCE) is an association of people from education, business, government, and advocacy organizations.

Poor Economic Conditions

When the economy experiences high unemployment and/or rising prices, consumers feel the pressure. They become acutely interested in what happens to their dollars, they get upset, and they organize. As a result, consumer protection efforts often succeed.

The inflationary period of the early 1900s helped give rise to the union movement. The Depression of the 1930s brought consumer education courses into the schools and forced the federal government to legislate unemployment programs, pass Social Security laws, and establish the Securities and Exchange Commission (SEC). The consumer voice was recognized for the first time by government through the Consumer Advisory Board. Inflation in the 1960s and 1970s helped provide the impetus for passage of consumer legislation, including the Real Estate Settlement Procedures Act, Emergency Petroleum Act, and Motor Vehicle Information and Cost Savings Act. In contrast, the good economic conditions during most of the 1980s did very little to provide an economic climate conducive to increasing consumer protection. More recent years have brought enormous economic pressures on most consumers' budgets because of rapidly increased expenditures for income taxes, social security taxes, installment debt repayments, and health care. Also, a frightening employment situation exists for many.

Today's Consumer Movement is Strong

Today's consumer movement is mature, well-organized, active, effective, and productive. It is primarily concerned with:

1. **Fighting consumer problems** to protect consumers from such things as dangerous and defective products, price gouging, product performance failures, delivery failures, deceptive advertising, dishonored promises and warranties, and frauds and ripoffs.
2. **Strengthening redress systems**, especially for consumers who have access problems in the marketplace (i.e., elderly, children, poor, new immigrants).
3. **Increasing the quantity and quality of objective and useful information** about products and services, as well as safety and environmental issues.
4. **Improving the effectiveness of existing laws and regulations** to protect consumers.
5. **Cultivating strong consumer organizations** to more clearly articulate and champion the consumer interest.
6. **Motivating the vast powers of government** to assist (or at least not block) efforts to improve the way the capitalistic economy works so that it better supports the interests of consumers.

7. **Trying to fix the political system** itself by limiting political action committees (PACs), prohibiting legislators from accepting honoraria, and financing elections with public funds.
8. **Mobilizing and empowering citizens** to effectively participate in our democracy.

Traditional consumer organizations, such as the Consumer Federation of America, National Consumers League, and Consumers Union, are successfully retaining the financial support of consumers. Such groups have found that people want to join consumer organizations that provide tangible benefits, rather than just making them feel good. Thus, consumer groups often offer redress assistance and buying information. The Washington Consumers' Checkbook organization, for example, provides reports on the attributes of service providers in the community, including physicians, television and auto repair dealers, and plumbers.

The causes of consumerism are no longer the exclusive domain of the traditional consumer groups. For example, the 35-million-member American Association of Retired Persons (AARP) advocates improved benefits in areas such as health, telecommunications, and adequate information for women. The 70,000 member Gray Panthers group similarly advocates the interests of older Americans. The AFL/CIO has promoted consumer education among its members for years, as has the National Credit Union Association. Both the Association of Community Organizations for Reform Now and Center for Community Change organize low-income consumers to improve their communities. A number of consumer issues are also vital to the interests of the 160,000 members of the National Organization for Women, as well as the National Association of Attorneys General, which provides a forum for the chief legal officers of 50 states and 5 jurisdictions. As a result, today's consumer movement is fragmented by a plethora of groups supported by a diverse set of constituencies and such variety provides part of the strength and vigor of the consumer movement.

Businesses and consumers are increasingly working together to resolve problems and to seek opportunities for compatible beneficial interest. One method of collaboration is through **consumer advisory panels**. These are corporate-sponsored meetings in which businesspeople meet regularly with consumer leaders, usually activists and academics, to share concerns and explore ways in which the company can better serve consumers. Cooperation has become a mutually satisfactory course of action.

Businesses and governments also confront consumer problems and issues. Many have created a **consumer affairs department**. Whether in the corporation or government agency, most consumer affairs departments are organized to centrally manage consumer complaints. Many have an 800-number telephone service, a consumer/community outreach program, a system to track consumerism issues, and a consumer information and education program. These offices are usually staffed by consumer affairs professionals (CAPs).

Today's consumer movement exists in challenging times. Budget cuts are the extremist conservative's way to "reduce the burden" of government regulation of business. The reality is that the Congress and many state legislatures are attacking and undermining a number of key consumer protections. "The philosophy of Congress seems to be let the buyer beware," says Bernice Friedlander, acting director of the U.S. Office of Consumer Affairs.[7] Budgets are being slashed for state and local consumer protection agencies. Appropriations have been sharply reduced for the federal Consumer Product Safety

---

[7]Ruth Simon, You're losing your consumer rights, *Money*, March 1996, p. 101.

Commission, Environmental Protection Agency, and Federal Trade Commission. The resulting gaps in the consumer protection safety net are not expected to last forever because the major players in the consumer movement—all of them—are fighting back. The desire for a "level playing field" of an honest marketplace has long been shown to be the common interest of sellers, governments, and consumers. Times will change. Public opinion polls consistently show very strong support for consumer issues, especially those related to health, safety, and the environment. Added to that list are current consumer questions about privacy, errors in data files, bias, and fairness. Will Americans see progress on these issues or will we see a lack of outrage among consumers?

The Major Players Influencing the Consumer Movement

The future of the consumer movement will be determined by the major players in the arena: sellers, governments, consumer organizations, and consumers. Many predict that consumerism in the future will once again turn out to be the sellers' best friend because it will help force businesses to improve products, which will simultaneously serve consumers better and make the sellers more competitive in the world marketplace.

Sellers

To profit in the years ahead, sellers will have to assign the highest priority to the things that satisfy consumers—quality goods and services at fair prices, safe and reliable products, ethical advertising and marketing practices, and redress systems to handle consumer problems. Efforts are underway to achieve those ends, especially by retailers who are sometimes accurately described as "the consumers' buying agents." By serving consumers well, business tries to best attend to its enlightened self-interest.

Companies that have successful consumer affairs departments, particularly those which handle complaints, as well as an information and education program to respond to inquiries, are not going to close those operations tomorrow; they will be around as long as there are consumers who buy goods and services. Publications, workshops, school programs, media, and public appearances by corporate officials can effectively promote a company's perspective, as well as consumer education.

Successful corporations will have more professionals working in consumer affairs departments who consider the consumer interest along with the very important profit motive. (Ralph Nader calls these people "consumer advocates in pin-striped suits.") Smart businesses will continue to value working together with consumer advocates and academics to define and resolve consumer concerns. Use of consumer advisory panels helps corporations gain a consumer interest perspective on a variety of emerging key issues, permits an opportunity to monitor important internal units, and improves representation of the consumer viewpoint to top management.

Smart businesses will better measure the bottom-line values that consumer affairs programs contribute to profitability, through systematically evaluating the company's customer service practices, sources of consumer complaints, delivery systems, new products, and overall satisfaction. Sellers also will increasingly consider customer satisfaction to be a critical measure of management performance.

More companies will have their consumer affairs offices report directly to top management. These high-level consumer affairs professionals communicate with consumer advocates, track and resolve complaints, publish information and education materials, and advise management on a range of concerns. A number of Society of Consumer Affairs Professionals in Business (SOCAP) professionals perform advocacy functions, within and outside the firm, in addition to managing complaint-handling and information/education operations. The National Society of Patient Representation and Consumer Affairs operates similarly.

Trade associations will continue to represent the collective self-interest of businesses by promoting a self-regulation industry perspective. Businesses increasingly will come to the conclusion that handling complaints on an industry-wide basis is good for individual businesses, as well as for consumers. The mediation and arbitration programs which remedy consumer complaints will continue to expand. Businesses also will continue to fund a number of pseudo-consumer organizations that promote free-market solutions (only!) to consumer problems, such as Consumer Alert[8] and the American Council for Science and Health.[9] Critics say that these groups are just shills for business. Such groups are tightly bound to a particular philosophy rather than to the genuine interests of consumers.

Governments

The same institutionalization process of improved representation of the consumer interest has occurred at all levels of government. All executive departments and agencies in the federal government have a person designated as a consumer affairs officer who reports to the appropriate cabinet secretary. This effort exists because of a 1979 presidential executive order establishing *Consumer Representation Plans* throughout the executive branch. Each of the over forty offices is charged with being sure that the consumer's point of view is considered when reviewing policies and programs. The extent to which the consumer's voice is heard varies with each agency and each political administration. Government consumer affairs professionals also provide consumers with information and handle complaints. All of the consumer affairs officers meet regularly with the President's Special Assistant for Consumer Affairs as members of the Consumer Affairs Council. This group is responsible for developing consumer programs and coordinating the current Administration's consumer policies. Vice President Al Gore's effort to "reinvent government" includes an executive order of the President asking agencies "to survey their customers to determine their satisfaction with existing services, to post service standards and measure results against them and to provide the means to address customer complaints."[10]

There are also numerous agencies at the federal level that have precise consumer interest responsibilities, such as the National Highway Traffic Safety Administration, Federal Trade Commission, Consumer Product Safety Commission, and Food and Drug Administration. In addition to having a main office in Washington, most of these federal agencies have regional field offices located in major cities. These government efforts will

---

[8]1024 J Street, Room 425, Modesto, CA 95354; 209-524-1738.

[9]1995 Broadway, 16th Floor, New York, NY 10023; 212-362-7044.

[10]Barr, S. (1994, March). Gore puts the hammer down. *The Washington Post*, p. A-17.

remain as long as there are consumers. Most federal agencies also are required to seek the viewpoints of consumers on regulatory proposals. As a result, regulatory hearings are frequently held in major cities in the United States where the public can participate in the government decision-making process.

The nation's Attorneys General remain vigorous in protecting the interests of consumers. There also are nearly four hundred state, county and municipal consumer protection offices, and many handle complaints. Some states also employ a consumer advocate to challenge unwarranted public utility rate increases. Many local governments have established a municipal Office of Consumer Affairs. The National Association for Administrators in Consumer Affairs (NAACA) is an active association serving government professionals. In recent years tight government budgets have forced many consumer watchdog agencies to cutback their efforts. Such action invites a backlash by honest businesses that will demand better policing of the economic marketplace.

The U.S. Congress and state legislatures remain constantly aware and interested in consumer interest concerns. Legislators recognize that consumers are voters, too! Governments tend to not forget consumers because there are a number of consumer interest organizations intent on reminding governments of their responsibilities. While legislators have a tendency to focus on one issue and then go on to the next one, legislative hearings are held almost weekly on proposed legislation affecting consumers. Legislatures also frequently conduct oversight hearings to assess the efforts of regulatory agencies as well as to modify laws and regulations affecting consumers.

The changing economic and political times of today may limit government's abilities and commitment to act on problems facing consumers. Expectations about what government can and should be able to do to help consumers may be lower, but public policy decision making by government will greatly affect the consumer interest.[11]

Consumer Organizations

The consumer organizations in the consumer movement which fight for the consumer interest are constant in number, forceful in strength, and financially stable. They tend to have growing memberships and increasing participation, salable ideas, effective fundraising techniques, and high organizational credibility. There are over three hundred grassroots state and local consumer organizations and about one hundred national organizations focusing on consumer concerns. Many are quite able to aggressively address consumer issues, including such groups as the Consumer Federation of America, National Consumer's League, Public Citizen, the Center for the Study for Responsive Law, and the Center for Auto Safety. The constituents of these organizations, consumers themselves, seem to be quite willing to help finance the efforts.

The newest members joining consumer organizations are the elderly, minority, handicapped and disadvantaged consumers; those characteristically underrepresented in mainstream consumer organizations. Together they supplement the forever supportive middle-income, middle-aged members. One such group is the National African-American Consumer Education Organization. Many consumer organizations, especially those at the national level, have reached a high level of professionalism. Their opinions are often

---

[11]Monnet, D. (1994, August). Consumers in the world markets. *At Home With Consumers*, 15, 6.

consulted by business, government and the media. Professionals and volunteers regularly lobby on consumer issues in the state capitals and in Washington, D.C.

Consumer organizations are quite capable of developing and presenting well-prepared arguments and mobilizing resources and support. They often use the Freedom of Information Act as a tool to obtain information from agencies of the government. When appropriate, consumer groups initiate lawsuits to force government to act promptly, particularly when the Administration seems uninterested in enforcing consumer protection laws and regulations. Consumer groups are increasingly effective in using direct-ballot initiatives to pass pro-consumer legislation.

Consumer organizations continue to have excellent access to the media, which CFA's Stephen Brobeck says is "the greatest strength" of consumer groups.[12] Most are credible with the public and are good at fighting for specific issues that interest their constituencies. In recent years, a number of single-issue consumer groups have been created in areas such as nutrition, automobiles, credit cards, and insurance, in addition to the many vibrant state and local consumer groups. Even the *Wall Street Journal* recognizes the credibility of various consumer organizations when, for example, it stated, "When Consumer Federation of America talks, congressmen listen."

Most consumer organizations have a clear view when pursuing the consumer interest that is not simply an out-of-date anti-business, anti-government or anti-future perspective. Consumer organizations value the opportunity to directly deal with corporations because they see it as an appropriate way to resolve problems without confrontation. Consumer groups that have historical roots with the labor movement often remain "ambivalent when it comes to the interest of consumers at the short-run expense of labor."[13] Taking stands against big labor in favor of consumers risks losing the support of the labor membership.

Consumer groups often form informal coalitions with individual firms, business trade associations or entire industries on questions of consumer policy when a pro-consumer position is supported by a segment of the business community. Advocates for Highway and Auto Safety, for example, includes a number of top consumer activists and insurance company executives. It attempts to "save lives and reduce costs from motor vehicle crashes." The benefits of consumer-business coalitions are enormous.

Stephen Brobeck, executive director of the Consumer Federation of America, says that public support is vital to the future success of consumer organizations. He notes that the support "can be sustained only if two conditions are met: the public must continue to recognize that their interests as consumers are at risk; and they must remain convinced that consumer advocates effectively defend and promote their interests."

Consumers Themselves

Consumer expectations have changed dramatically from thirty or even twenty years ago because better-educated and informed U.S. consumers are more able and willing to articulate their interests. The economy is truly becoming more of a consumer-driven market with each passing year as people increasingly are more active, ask questions, try to find out more, and discuss technical topics with professionals. Today's consumers also

---

[12]Stephen Brobeck (1994, July 18), speech to a University of Georgia summer class in Washington, DC.
[13]McGowan, D. A. (1992, Spring), Gloves off consumer economics. *Advancing the Consumer Interest,* <u>4</u>, 19.

are less compliant and more knowledgeable about where to apply pressure in the marketplace to gain satisfaction. They are their own best advocates in the marketplace. John Naisbitt, author of *Megatrends*, argues that Americans are reclaiming their traditional sense of self-reliance. Naisbitt suggests that, "citizens, workers and consumers are demanding and getting a greater voice in government, business and the marketplace."

Awareness about the consumer interest is undoubtedly the highest in history. Today's consumer interest is no longer being submerged into the broader public interest. Consumers across the country now demand an acceptable quality of goods and services with fair or low prices appropriate for particular levels of quality. In short, they want a good deal for themselves and others.

Consumers today are generally aware that they have certain rights to help them avoid getting ripped off or cheated. They may not be aware about a specific law or regulation that can apply but they "know" there is probably some corporate office or government agency that will help. Consumers in the United States inherently believe both that they have consumer rights and the power to assert them. American consumers live in a society that has permanently imprinted the consumer interest in the mentality of its people, as well as in many of the mechanisms of business and government.

Historian Arthur M. Schlesinger, Jr. says that Americans are moving away from the self-interest "me decade" of the 1980s and are again turning toward public purpose over private interest. He predicts a sharp change in the national mood for the remainder of the decade. Schlesinger observes that, "already there seems to be the start of revulsion against greed and the start of a revival of idealism on college campuses, of community service and a revived concern for social justice."

CONSUMER UPDATE: "GENERATION X" (THE TWENTY-SOMETHINGS) TAKES POLITICAL RESPONSIBILITY

The first major gathering of "**Generation X**" took place two years ago. Dedicated to those born between 1961 and 1981 and as a group labeled as slackers who are pessimistic about the future and underemployed, hundreds of representatives attended the first Youth Leadership Conference in Washington with the theme "Activate the X Votes." Recognizing that the twenty-somethings already have more positive attitudes about equality and civil rights than their parents were taught, the idea is to get what have been called the "apathetic" and "unplugged" who have positive social views into the political system and social activism. Co-Founder of the Lead or Leave organization, Rob Nelson is committed to creating a new constituency of the 75 million to make a difference. The thinking is that one's commitment as a citizen should go beyond voting.

The Future of the Consumer Movement is Bright

The future of consumerism is bright, say C. Glenn Walters and Blaise J. Bergiel, authors of *Consumer Behavior*. They predict that, "the movement is likely to pick up momentum in the next few years." They report that, "(1) consumerism was inevitable, (2) consumerism will be enduring, (3) consumerism will be beneficial, (4) consumerism is pro-marketing, and (5) consumerism can be profitable."[14] Public policy forecasters Graham T. T. Molitor and James Plumb see the United States now entering a period to be characterized "by a huge onslaught of new consumerist legislation and regulation." Helen Nelson, President of Consumer Research Foundation, sees this decade as the "coming of age of the consumer movement."

Michael Pertschuk, co-director of the Advocacy Institute, describes the future this way: "The consumer movement does not stand for excessive regulation or centralized bureaucratic excrescences. Consumer leaders have joined and led regulatory reform efforts. The consumer movement does stand for responsive government intervention in the marketplace: 'the public restraint of private greed.' The consumer movement does not stand for a patronizing 'consumer protection' to protect consumers against their own informed choices. It does stand for free choice among enlightened consumers."[15] Consumer advocate James S. Turner argues that consumerism is not in disagreement with the business interest. He states that, "On the contrary, it shares business' paramount goal: to promote a healthy and efficient economic system—within which both corporations and consumers can thrive."

Boisterous confrontations between sellers and consumers are almost a thing of the past. Rancorous debates on issue after issue are gone. Now, only an occasional well-publicized battle occurs. The future will have more cooperation between sellers and consumers through dialogue, partnerships and coalitions that will result in more satisfied consumers, more profitable businesses, and a more vibrant American economy. Ron Glover, of American Express, observes that, "the bottom-line benefits of cooperation with consumer interest groups...prove that corporate organizations have much to gain from problem-solving with consumer interest groups."

CONSUMER UPDATE: COMMERCIAL TELEVISION IS AN ENEMY

A recent challenge for action was made by Esther Peterson, former Special Assistant for Consumer Affairs to President Lyndon Johnson, who is mad about the enemy of commercial television. She asks, "Why is it okay to be cynical about government, cynical about personal responsibility, cynical about love, but reverent toward the marketing of cars, pain relievers, and just plain junk that is sold daily through television?" She says that, "My choice of enemy is the tyrant television and a social system that leaves children and their incurious parents glassy-eyed before the false promises, its seductive lies and its corrupt fantasy projected on the tube." Peterson argues that a large part of commercial television needs changing.

It is well established now that each side in the seller-consumer conflict knows each other's positions, arguments, and thinking. Now each side tries not to lose the gains already made while still pursuing its own agenda. Where there are overlapping interests, the two work together. There can be no doubt that today's consumer interest concerns are routinely and purposely considered by businesses and governments. The interdependence between sellers and consumers has evolved to the point where all parties recognize that

---

[14]Walters, C. G. & Bergiel, B. J. (1989), *Consumer Behavior* (South-Western), 535.

[15]Pertschuk, M. (1983), The politics of consumer regulation: The public restraint of private greed. In K. P. Schnittgrund (Ed.), *Proceedings of the American Council of Consumer Interests* (pp. 161-162). Columbia, MO: University of Missouri.

neither consumers nor sellers can benefit for long in an environment where informed choice cannot occur. Contributing to this success has been a growing degree of professionalism among business people, government personnel, and consumer advocates. The consumer movement will continue to evolve and bring about a more even balance of power between the interests of consumers and sellers.

Virginia H. Knauer, who held the nation's top consumer affairs post as Special Assistant to Presidents Nixon, Ford, and Reagan, says of the future, "I believe that the modern approach to consumerism—one of partnerships and dialogue instead of confrontation and protest, and one recognizing that, in our increasingly competitive and global marketplace, consumers and businesses share an equal stake in a healthy American economy—means that never again will attention to consumer concerns be just a fleeting marketplace fixation. A growing tide of business and government officials now recognize, once and for all, that the consumer is the final arbiter of marketplace success." James S. Turner calls for a society focused on "demand side economics," that which focuses on the end-user (consumers) and when attended to properly should result in the greatest happiness for all.

Most of the basic consumer issues have been addressed in recent years, yet both the times and issues continue to evolve. While fundamental consumer concerns will always remain the same—such as getting your money's worth, reducing deceptions in advertising and sales, protecting health and safety, and seeking equity for all consumers (including those who are poor and unable to consume)—new problems and issues will arise because of exploding information technology and storage capacity, an increasing interdependence of world problems, and the growing complexity of products and services. A mature and active consumer movement, comprised of consumer organizations, businesses and governments, along with a knowledgeable citizenry, will provide the leadership to help attain, assert, and protect consumer interest concerns in the future. Moreover, the success of the consumer movement of today and tomorrow depends greatly upon the support of the people, and depends upon all those consumers getting concerned and involved.

Review and Summary of Key Terms and Concepts

1. Give some examples of what the **economic marketplace** looked like for American consumers before the year 1890.

2. Illustrate the **kinds of problems** consumers had during the early consumer movement from the 1890s through the 1920s.

3. What were some of the circumstances that led to a renewed interest in the consumer movement **between 1929 and the 1950s**?

4. Provide some illustrations of what happened during the consumerism **era of the 1960s and 1970s**.

5. What did the terms **consumerism, consumer movement** and **consumer advocates** mean during the 1960s and 1970s?

6. Explain why **Ralph Nader** was and remains a leading consumer spokesperson.

7. Summarize the **responses of governments** to the consumerism era of the 1960s.

8. Distinguish between **caveat emptor** and **caveat venditor**.

9. What is meant by the term **affirmative disclosure**, and why did it occur?

10. Summarize what is meant by **"social change is an evolutionary process."**

11. What does **rising expectations of consumers** have to do with making consumer movements successful?

12. Explain how **scandals and dramatic crises** contribute to making consumer movements successful, and include an explanation of **whistleblowers** in your response.

13. How does **charisma** contribute to making consumer movements successful? Give some examples.

14. Identify illustrations of how **active government organizations** contribute to making consumer movements successful, and include an explanation of **state-paid consumer advocates** in your comments.

15. Identify illustrations of how **active private organizations** contribute to making consumer movements successful, and include an explanation of the terms **whitelisting**, **blacklisting**, **citizen utility boards** and **coalition** in your response.

16. List three of the **primary concerns** of today's consumer movement.

17. Distinguish between **consumer advisory panels** and **consumer affairs departments**.

18. What will the most successful **sellers** do in the future in response to consumerism?

19. How will **governments** contribute toward helping to shape the future of the consumer movement?

20. Summarize how **consumer organizations** contribute toward helping to shape the future of the consumer movement.

21. What does Ralph Nader think people need to improve their **power**?

22. How will **consumers** contribute to shaping the future of the consumer movement?

Useful Resources for Consumers

American Council on Consumer Interests
University of Missouri
240 Stanley Hall
Columbia, MO 65211
573-882-3817

Center for Study of Responsive Law
P.O. Box 19367
Washington, DC 20036
202-387-8030

Congress of Consumer Organizations
P.O. Box 158
Newton Center, MA 02159
617-552-8184

National Consumers League
1701 K Street, NW, Suite 1200
Washington, DC 20006
202-835-3323

Public Citizen
2000 P Street, NW
Washington, DC 20036
202-833-3000

Society of Consumer Affairs Professionals in Business
801 North Fairfax Street, Suite 404
Arlington, VA 22314
703-519-3700

U.S. Public Interest Research Group
218 D Street, SE
Washington, DC 20003-1900
202-546-9709

"What Do You Think" Questions

1. Thinking about Ralph Nader's comments on **citizen empowerment**, list some examples of activities that college students might do to help reform and improve American society.

2. Consider **Michael Pertschuk's** description of the consumer movement and offer your views about his perceptions. Is he on target? Why or why not? Also, comment on whether or not you visualize a contrast between the viewpoints of Pertschuk and Virginia Knauer.

3. What do you think about **Esther Peterson's accusations** against commercial television? Is she accurate? Why or why not?

4. Historian **Arthur Schlesinger** predicts a sharp change in the national mood for this decade which will turn away from private interests toward public purposes. Comment on (A) whether you think the mood shift toward idealism will occur, (B) why or why not, and (C) what kind of future you predict for this country.

5. Choose any issue of interest (e.g., abortion, prostitution, overseas economic aid, legalizing drugs) and consider the **eight steps** presented in the text on the topic of social change as an evolutionary force. (A) Where along the eight steps do you believe the issue is now? (B) What do you think must occur for the issue to continue towards change?

6. Your life is already full of consumer experiences, some satisfying and others not so. Thinking about your personal experiences and about society's needs, what are five consumer topics, concerns, issues, or whatever that you believe **need improvement** to make one's life as a consumer better?

Chapter 3

Consumer Rights, Responsibilities and Remedies

OBJECTIVES

After reading this chapter, you should be able to

1. Recognize and understand how to use the legal rights available to consumers.

2. Appreciate the moral rights that consumers possess in the marketplace.

3. Cite some examples of consumer responsibilities that are related to consumer rights and why people often do not complain.

4. Be acquainted with the remedies available to resolve consumer problems and the appropriate procedures to complain effectively.

5. Recognize that the complaining process should follow sequential levels and channels, and what damages to ask for when suing.

6. Recognize when to use a class action lawsuit as well as know the specific ways to break a contract.

7. Understand how to use a small claims court to sue when necessary.

8. Consider using various "techniques of last resort" to fight back and win against ripoffs and frauds.

The American economic marketplace is unquestionably the best in the world. Reasons include the enormous supply of high-quality goods and services, the multitude of choices available, the large number of competitors, the belief and trust in self-regulation instead of heavy government intervention, the emphasis on safety standards for virtually all products and services, and a serious concern for the environment. Another reason the American marketplace is so good is the existence of a strong consumer interest perspective in society—people want to get their money's worth. Plus, when there is a problem with a product or service, the American consumer wants it resolved, and resolved right now!

Americans are fortunate to have a number of legal and moral rights available. Because of budget cutbacks in state, county and city consumer affairs offices, however, most problems have to be solved by consumers themselves. Unfortunately, few Americans know much about or understand how to use their many legal and moral rights in consumer-seller transactions. To be effective advocates of their interests, and to help provide some of the discipline necessary to keep the marketplace honest, consumers must become knowledgeable and empowered.

This chapter accepts that implicit challenge by examining consumers' legal and moral rights as well as the important consumer responsibilities associated with these rights. Some people do not complain, and this void hurts both consumers and sellers; the chapter examines why they do not complain. The last part of the chapter details in step-by-step fashion the remedies available to consumers who seek to correct any wrongs encountered. One appendix is included at the end of the chapter to provide more depth to the subject of rights, responsibilities and remedies: "Writing a Letter of Complaint."

Legal Rights of Consumers

A **right** is an entitlement to something or to be treated n some particular way. Rights of consumers are important because they empower people to protect themselves in the economic marketplace. Consumers have three types of legal rights: (1) **Implied warranties** which arise from common law or by operation of law and need not be specified by the parties,[1] (2) **Express warranties** which arise from contracts (and largely governed in the states by the Uniform Commercial Code and by the federal Magnuson-Moss Warranty Act), and (3) dozens of **statutory rights** which are those provided in written laws and regulations. These are discussed below.

Implied Warranty Rights Are Powerful Legal Rights

A **warranty** or (**guarantee**) is a written or oral assurance by the seller of property that the goods or property is of the quality represented or will be as promised. It generally means that the seller will repair or replace a defective product or service within a specified period of time. A person who purchases a new clothes dryer, buys a stereo system, or pays for auto repairs that later fails to function properly has the right to get the

---

[1]**Common law** is a system of laws originated and developed in England based on court decisions, on the doctrines implicit in those judgments, and on customs and usages, rather than on codified written laws.

problem corrected. If it is not fixed, the consumer has the right to get the product or service replaced or obtain a refund of money paid. When no remedy occurs, the consumer can bring legal action against the seller.

All states have similar warranty laws mandating an implied warranty *every* time goods are sold by merchants to consumers. Thus, the law requires that merchants provide implied warranties when they sell clothing or bicycles or whatever, but a neighbor selling similar goods at a garage sale does not have to provide such warranties. An **implied warranty** is a written or unwritten promise that the manufacturer implicitly asserts that the product is usable and will not fail during normal use. There are two types.

Warranty of Merchantability

The first type of implied warranty is a **warranty of merchantability**, which means that the consumer has a right to expect that the product is reasonably fit for the ordinary purposes for which the goods are expected to be used. This means that the goods should be in proper condition for sale and that they will perform as intended. For example, a vacuum cleaner is expected to function properly and clean dirt from carpets and rugs. It should vacuum, not just sweep, as with electric brooms. Note that in a number of states, courts have ruled that home builders are responsible for any defects in their work, even if there is no written contract or warranty that makes responsibilities clear. Authority for such a ruling comes under the concept of implied warranty of merchantability, and this legal right can be upheld even *after* a written warranty has expired. In 1990, the U.S. Supreme Court ruled that manufacturers could not unreasonably and unconscionably put short time limits on warranties. Thus, if a consumer believes a new product should have a warranty longer than its written warranty, it probably does.

Warranty of Fitness for a Particular Purpose

The second type of implied warranty is **warranty of fitness for a particular purpose**. Here the seller is presumed to know the particular purpose for which a buyer is purchasing the goods *and* knows that the buyer has relied upon the seller's knowledge, skill, and judgment to select and sell appropriate goods. In order for a warranty of fitness for a particular purpose to be created between the seller and the buyer, the seller should have "reason to know" the buyer's purpose for purchasing the product and the buyer must rely on the seller's skill or judgment in selecting the goods.

This important legal right of warranty of fitness for a particular purpose protects consumers who go to buy a product or service from a merchant and trust the advice they receive, buy it, and then suffer because it does not perform as anticipated. For example, Jean Johnson, from Logan, Utah, goes to an electronics store to buy a television antenna and tells the salesperson that she wants to pick up the Salt Lake City stations. After installing it on the roof, she finds that the television works, but the pictures coming from the Salt Lake stations are just not clear. This is a simple case of breach of implied warranty. The store created the contract when Jean relied on the advice of the salesperson, and it is violated because she cannot receive the television picture desired. The store owes her a refund, even if the product has scratches from putting the mast up on the roof.[2]

The same legal rights apply to all types of services. For example, if one is charged $8 for dry cleaning services, it is understood that the soiled clothes should be returned clean. The proprietor has a legal obligation to stand by the quality of the work. If the clothing is not cleaned properly, either they should be processed again or the cost should be refunded. To avoid the warranty of fitness for a particular purpose, some dry cleaners are careful to tell customers that they do not remove "stubborn stains".

Express Warranty Rights are Enforceable

In the area of warranties, express warranties are covered by both statutory and common law. An **express warranty** can be created by written or verbal words or by demonstration as it sets out the specific assurances by the manufacturer or seller.[3] Once created, an express warranty is extremely difficult to destroy. **Written express warranties** are statements that specify the name and address of the warrantor, the product or parts covered, the duration of the warranty, what the warrantor will do, and who will pay for it. Each state has provisions under the Uniform Commercial Code that regulate implied and express warranty rights.

CONSUMER UPDATE:
Do You Really Have to Mail in the Warranty-Registration Card?

Many products come with warranty-registration cards that are to be mailed back to the manufacturer. Most contain irrelevant requests for personal information, such as income, age, and motivations for purchase; facts often used for marketing purposes. Failure to mail in the warranty-registration does not void the warranty. Consumers need only to keep their sales receipt. Many people choose to send in the warranty-registration card, without responding to the personal questions, so they can be notified by the manufacturer about product defects or recalls.

There is a federal statute in the area of warranties also. Sellers who offer warranties on consumer products that cost $15 or more are required to comply with various standards under the Magnuson-Moss Warranty Act. Basically, the federal law demands that a warranty should mean what it says and that the details should be spelled out in easy-to-understand language. The law requires that guarantees be conspicuously designated as either **full** or **limited**. This immediately gives consumers an indication of the degree of warranty coverage provided. The law also encourages the use of an informal dispute

---

[2]McDonald's became the first chain to correctly extend the concept of implied warranties by establishing a formal policy of guaranteeing a free meal for dissatisfied consumers: "If you are not satisfied, we will make it right—or your next meal is on us."

[3]Alperin, H. J. & Chase, R. F. (1986) observe on page 312 in *Consumer Law: Sales Practice and Credit Regulation* (West) that, "a seller creates an express warranty under the Code when he (1) makes any affirmation of fact or promise about the goods, (2) describes the goods, (3) uses a sample of the goods, or (4) uses a model of the goods."

procedure whenever warranty problems arise between sellers and buyers. Consumers who successfully file state or federal lawsuits against warrantors may be awarded their purchase costs, attorney fees, and damages. (Detailed information on consumer rights and remedies under the provisions of the Magnuson-Moss Warranty Act are included in Chapter 5.) As a defense against a warranty claim, a seller may argue that the buyer was given an opportunity for reasonable inspection that was disclaimed by the buyer's inaction.

Those who offer warranties sometimes try to disclaim or repudiate them to make them void. For example, state laws permit a warranty of merchantability to be disclaimed legally if it is done in clear, conspicuous, and specific language. A popular example is when a used automobile is sold **as is**, or with all its faults.

CONSUMER UPDATE:
Unconscionability May Get One Out of a Contract Because
the Seller Took Unfair Advantage of the Consumer

Unconscionability is a legal doctrine having to do with unscrupulousness under which the court may invalidate an agreement, or a portion of it, if it is so one-sided as to be unreasonable. Perhaps the seller took advantage of the consumer's ignorance, inability to read, inability to read English, physical infirmity or some recent personal crisis (i.e., death in the family, accident). Unconscionability implies that the consumer believed that he/she had no choice in the buying situation which resulted in the purchasing terms being so one-sided that they unreasonably favored the seller. Examples of unconscionability might include inflated prices, unfair contractual terms, horribly high interest charges and some rent-to-own contracts.

If the bargaining positions of the seller and the buyer were so unequal that the seller took advantage of the consumer, it might be possible to get out of the contract. If the consumer believes a contract to be unconscionable, the following steps are recommended: (1) notify the seller in writing that the deal was unconscionable, (2) do not make any payments, and (3) return the purchased goods and/or tell service providers that such services are no longer needed. The consumer may be sued, but unconscionability may be an excellent defense.

Lots of Other Legal Rights Also Exist

Dozens of federal, state, and local laws, regulations, and ordinances are available to protect consumers, and many of them will be described in Chapter 5. Below are two key legal rights provided for in illustrative statutory laws: (1) Consumers have the legal right to find out the reason why they are turned down for credit based on information provided by a credit-reporting agency under provisions of the Fair Credit Reporting Act; and (2) Consumers have the right to use an informal dispute procedure when unsatisfied with what a manufacturer does about a product warranty complaint, as provided for in the Magnuson-Moss Warranty Act.

CONSUMER UPDATE:
Rule #1 of Consumer Life—When in Doubt About a Purchase,
Put It on Your Credit Card

Consumers have the legal right not to pay for a cost of disputed purchase made on a credit card when they complain about it to the merchant and the creditor. This right is provided in the Fair Credit Billing Act. Let your credit card company—VISA, MasterCard, American Express, Discover, whatever—help you fight the merchant or unscrupulous scam operator that provided you with an "unsatisfactory purchase" that you charged on your card. Those credit card users who dispute charges have an excellent chance of getting their money back; those who paid with cash or a check may never again see their money. See Chapter 5 for details.

Moral Rights of Consumers Are Legitimate Expectations

In addition to legal rights, consumers have moral rights in the marketplace. **Moral rights** are expectations of consumers that the marketplace will be guided by principles, rules, and standards of good conduct that arise from conscience or a sense of right and wrong. Moral rights are not provided automatically in the marketplace, but they are expected.

General Moral Rights

Some general moral rights include:

- Being treated equitably in the marketplace

- Being treated courteously by salespersons when shopping even though a purchase may not be made

- Being given an opportunity to compare prices and products inside stores without interference

- Being able to buy goods and services with socially acceptable minimum standards of quality

- Being sold products that are safe, both to the consumer and the environment

- Being assured of honesty from merchants in every transaction

- Being assured of a certain degree of privacy

- Being given fair treatment by sellers regardless of economic, political, religious, racial, ethnicity, gender, or youthful appearance

President Kennedy's Consumer Bill of Rights

President John F. Kennedy took the idea of moral rights for consumers a major step forward when he formally proclaimed a "Consumer Bill of Rights" in a speech before the Congress of the United States. The rights as President Kennedy set them down in 1962 are:

- The right to choose

- The right to safety

- The right to be informed

- The right to be heard

All subsequent presidents have confirmed to the nation that consumer rights in America are here to stay.

A List of Consumer Rights for All Americans

The moral concerns of Americans about consumer expectations in marketplace transactions have evolved into today's list of eight important consumer rights:

1. **The right to choice**, by which consumers have the right to be assured, wherever possible, access to a variety of products and services at competitive prices. In those industries in which competition is not workable and government regulation is substituted, consumers have the right to an assurance of satisfactory quality and service at fair prices. Having choices is sometimes more complicated than not having choices, but consumers benefit from choices.

2. **The right to information**, by which consumers have the right to be given accurate and adequate information upon which to make free and intelligent decisions as well as be protected against fraudulent and misleading information, advertising, labeling, and other deceptive marketing practices.

3. **The right to safety**, by which consumers have the right to expect that their health and safety—as well as financial well-being—will be properly and effectively protected in the marketplace.

4. **The right to voice**, by which the interests of consumers will be given full and fair consideration in government policy-making situations and expeditious treatment in its administrative tribunals.[4]

---

[4]The right to complain is guaranteed in the first amendment to the U.S. constitution which provides citizens with freedom of speech.

CONSUMER UPDATE:
Student Consumers Rights to Information
in Academia Are Limited

Student consumers, especially undergraduates and students in technical education programs, generally have few rights in the world of information in academia. In spite of the fact that students pay thousands of dollars in tuition and fees for such educational services, they are often prohibited from obtaining access to vital information. To assess the quality of the academic programs on campus, the nation's 14.7 million student consumers taking post-secondary education courses generally have little more than word-of-mouth information obtained from other students. While that information is useful, it often is not accurate or reliable.

Quality indicators that schools already possess or would find it relatively inexpensive to obtain include: the views of peer institutions on the academic reputation of major or department, quality of instructors, teaching scores for instructors, quality of academic advisors, average class sizes, data on over-enrolled required courses, retention rates for each academic year, graduation rates, percent that go for graduate study, employment rates of graduates (including how many went to work for Burger King and McDonald's), and median salaries of graduates (starting salaries plus figures after 1 and 5 years).

---

5. **The right to redress or remedy**, by which consumers are provided a full and fair hearing in any case of dissatisfaction and wherever possible, the complaint is satisfactorily resolved.

6. **The right to environmental health**, by which consumers may consume in an environmentally sound manner and be protected from the ill effects of pollution of the air, earth, and water that may occur in the performance of everyday marketplace transactions.

7. **The right to service**, by which consumers may expect convenience, courtesy, and responsiveness to consumer needs and problems as well as all steps necessary to ensure that products and services meet the quality and performance levels claimed for them.

8. **The right to consumer education**, by which consumers are provided the right to continuing consumer education without which consumer-citizens cannot enjoy the full benefit of the other enumerated rights.

Responsibilities of Consumers

Along with their rights, consumers also have responsibilities. A consumer right is not worth much unless it is sought after and protected. This reminds us of the definition of the consumer interest, which is concerned with securing, protecting, and asserting consumer rights in marketplace transactions in order that all consumers receive an acceptable quality of goods and services at fair or low prices.

In the broadest sense, therefore, the first responsibility of consumers is to assert (but not abuse) their consumer rights when seeking value for money in marketplace

---

CONSUMER UPDATE:
"Access to Consumer Credit" Should Be a Consumer's Right*

Many consumers take for granted obtaining a credit card, a car loan, or a loan to buy a house. Recent mortgage lending data collected by the federal government seem to indicate, however, that loans may not be reaching all segments of the population equally.

The ability to obtain credit, to borrow money, is often critical to an individual's access to opportunities. For example, obtaining an automobile loan may be necessary in order to purchase a car, which in turn may be necessary to reach a potential workplace. While no federal or state law guarantees that consumers receive credit—some consumers may not be able to obtain credit because of poor creditworthiness, for example-federal law does require that consumers be treated fairly in applying for credit and that they have an equal opportunity to obtain credit.

Without a doubt, access to credit plays a critical role in "making things happen" for consumers. Being able to realize the "American dream" of owning a home is almost always directly tied to the ability to obtain mortgage financing. Home improvement loans allow consumers to improve the quality of their residences and to protect their housing investment for the future. Access to credit through tuition loans often makes the difference in whether individuals can actually pursue their goal of being able to further their educations. And since obtaining a college degree is often tied to better job opportunities, it's clear that the circle of opportunity for consumers often is contingent on the role credit plays in their lives.

Consequently, unfair or unequal treatment of consumers in the credit application and credit granting process can have serious implications for consumers. Government-gathered statistics over the last several years have raised the alert that consumers, particularly minority consumers, are not being treated the same as non-minorities in the credit application and credit granting process. Today, significant resources are being dedicated by the federal government, community and consumer groups, and credit grantors to address concerns about unequal treatment and to remedy any perceived or actual inequities in consumers' gaining access to credit.

*Maureen P. English, Assistant Director, Division of Consumer and Community Affairs, Board of Governors of the Federal Reserve System

---

transactions. A second responsibility is to know what questions to ask and ask them. A third broad responsibility is to complain when not satisfied. Complaining involves three types of activities: (1) switching brands or stores, (2) making a complaint to the seller or manufacturer, and (3) telling others about the unacceptable experience. Listed below are several specific responsibilities that are related to consumer rights.

Regarding *the right to choose*, consumers have the responsibility to

- Understand their personal motivations for buying certain products and services.
- Recognize persuasive selling techniques.
- Compare products for both price and quality.
- Exercise independence of judgment in decision making.
- Avoid buying by habit.
- Choose carefully from whom they buy.
- Practice comparison shopping in an effort to frequently get a **best buy**, which is a product or service that, in the buyer's opinion, represents acceptable quality at a fair or low price for that quality.
- Consider the cost of time and other resources in decision making.

- Continue to buy when products and services are satisfactory.
- Refuse to buy when products and services are unsatisfactory.
- Recognize the ecological consequences of choices.
- Be honest in dealings with sellers.
- Encourage sellers and governments to enhance access to choices for all consumers.
- Make purchases from sellers who support consumer rights.

Regarding *the right to safety*, consumers have the responsibility to

- Use products with reasonable caution and care, and report defects.
- Carefully read product labels and use products as intended.
- Read and follow care and use instructions carefully, and respond to recalls.
- Read and heed any warning labels.
- Question sellers about the safety attributes of products.
- Examine merchandise for safety features before buying.
- Assume personal responsibility for normal precautions when using a product.
- Inform retailers, manufacturers, industry trade organizations, and government agencies when a product does not perform safely.
- Support efforts to improve safety for all consumers.

Regarding *the right to information*, consumers have the responsibility to

- Use available information.
- Seek out accurate information about products and services.
- Read advertisements and promotional materials carefully.
- Analyze and understand performance claims.
- Ask questions of sellers about products and services when complete information is not available.
- Support sellers who make serious efforts to provide useful information to all consumers.

Regarding *the right to voice* (or *to be heard*), consumers have the responsibility to

- Become informed and speak up about issues that affect all types of consumers.
- Seek remedies to consumer problems.
- Seek to right wrongs occurring in the marketplace.
- Assist others in asserting their consumer rights.
- Support efforts to increase the ability of consumers to participate effectively in corporate and government decision making.

CONSUMER UPDATE:
Compliment Whenever Appropriate

In our increasingly complex society, which also seems a bit hurried at times, it is wonderful to find a competent salesperson who willingly gives the time necessary to inform consumers about the diverse aspects of a purchase. When a salesperson does this job effectively, it is clearly appropriate to give a word of thanks.

When possible, give a sincere thank you to the salesperson, and then to the manager, on your way out of the store. Your comment is justified because it was deserved, because management likes very much to hear about employees, because business needs to hear some good news from customers now and then, and because it is your responsibility as a consumer to take special note of excellence in service. Some people offer compliments on the assumption that they will get even better service the next time. Whatever your motivation, try to provide a deserved compliment.

Regarding *the right to redress or remedy*, consumers have the responsibility to

- Know where and how to go about seeking redress.
- Speak up when errors occur, when safety problems are apparent, and when the quality of products or services is inferior.
- Make suggestions for product and service improvements.
- Complain to and compliment sellers as appropriate.
- Seek satisfaction directly from the seller before using other forms of redress.
- Utilize informal dispute mechanisms when available.
- Seek out and utilize third-party complaint-handling procedures where available, such as the state, county, or city office of consumer affairs.
- When appropriate, use the legal system to redress wrongs.
- Support efforts to broaden access to redress mechanisms for all consumers.

Regarding *the right to environmental health*, consumers have the responsibility to

- Become informed about environmental issues.
- Learn the environmental effects of alternative product and service choices.
- Compare products for their effects on the environment.
- Make reasoned and environmentally sound consumption choices.
- Support sellers who practice positive environmental policies.
- Support efforts to stop the use of consumer products that are harmful to the environment and to enhance the availability of goods friendly to the environment.

Regarding the *right to service*, consumers have the responsibility to

- Expect and demand good service.
- Compliment service providers where appropriate.

Regarding *the right to consumer education*, consumers have the responsibility to

- Become more informed about how to get their money's worth in the American economic marketplace.
- Learn how to assert all the consumer rights.
- Become more knowledgeable about the American economic marketplace and the consumer's role in it.
- Learn how to protect and assert the consumer interest.
- Become an educated consumer.
- Support efforts to have more consumer information and education programs accessible to all students and the public.

CONSUMER UPDATE: Public Access to Government Data

Public access to government-held data has become an area of increased attention. The government holds vast amounts of data that relate to consumers lives on a day-to-day basis—such as data dealing with the foods we eat, the medicine we take, the products we use, the cars we drive, and the air we breathe. Significant interest has grown over the last several years in putting that data in the public's hands. Knowing that information is power, that consumers are responsible for their decisions, and that consumers should have access to information in order to make informed choices, government agencies have paid increasing attention to the need to get government-held data into consumers' hands.

In fact, over the last several years representatives across government have come together to discuss how *best* to get information to the public. These meetings—which have come to be known as the "Solomon's Conferences" (taking their name from the location of the first meeting)—have dealt with issues such as:

- In what format(s) should the data be provided (for example, paper format vs. electronic)? Can an electronic format replace paper?
- Is it enough to provide the public with the data the government has collected in just its "raw" form, or should the data be presented to the public with "value-added" capabilities (such as providing reports that analyze the data)?
- Should the public be charged for the data, and, if so, how should the pricing structure be determined? Should non-profit users be charged less than other users?

The debate over *whether* consumers should have access to more government data seems to be over. Now it's a question of *how* to make information readily available to consumers in a way that's easily understood.

*Maureen P. English, Assistant Director, Division of Consumer and Community Affairs, Board of Governors of the Federal Reserve System

Why People Don't Complain

It is impossible for consumers to go through life without experiencing occasional difficulties in marketplace transactions. Research shows that approximately one out of four purchases results in some type of problem. Illustrative problems include faulty products, unsafe products, poor product performance, problems with delivery, being shortchanged at the cash register, errors in credit billing statements, communication failures with sellers, frauds, and ripoffs. Sometimes consumers just change their minds and want to return products. Consumer affairs offices in business and government are receiving more than twice the number of complaints than they did ten years ago.

Even though sellers are generally receptive to complaints, many consumers do not complain. People do not complain because they think complaining will not be worth their time, because they think that complaining will not do any good, and because they do not know how or where to complain. Many consumers do not complain because they believe the benefits of complaining will not exceed the costs.

John Goodman, president of Technical Assistance Research Programs (TARP), has research data on customer dissatisfaction. It shows that about one-third of consumer dissatisfaction with a product or service stems from either unfulfilled expectations or lack of knowledge regarding use. Another one-third stems from company policies and procedures, and a final one-third results from product defects. The percentage of customers experiencing problems with selected products and services who do not complain are 60 percent for high-priced durable goods, 50 percent for medium-priced durable goods, 37 percent for high priced services, and 45 percent for low-priced services.

For small consumer problems that resulted in a loss of a few dollars or a minor inconvenience, only 3 percent of consumers complain, 30 percent return the product, and nearly 70 percent either do nothing or discard the product. Research from the A. C. Nielsen Company shows that of those people who experience major consumer problems, such as a financial loss of about $150 or more, about one-third never complain.

TARP data reveal that the average business does not hear from 96 percent of its unhappy customers. For every complaint received at company headquarters, the average business has another 26 customers with problems, at least 6 of which are serious concerns. Depending on the industry, between 65 and 90 percent of non-complainers do not buy from particular businesses again and they never tell the business why. In sum, every complaint represents dozens of dissatisfied customers.

Many businesses view consumer complaints as a public relations necessity and fail to use complaints to seriously evaluate the effectiveness of their efforts. The data provided by consumers who complain offer businesses the unique opportunity to assess the efficiency of their operations and the quality of their products. Complaining consumers who have had their complaints resolved satisfactorily and quickly tell 6 people. In contrast, those who are not satisfied tell two or three times as many people.

Enlightened business leaders view customer complaints as opportunities in disguise. They invite customer complaints and use complaint data in worthwhile ways, because they see that what consumers think about a company is almost more important than the complaint problems themselves. Depending upon the business, it probably takes 5 to 10 times the cost of properly handling a complaint for a company to go out and find a single new customer. Smart business people know that if they are totally consumer-focused and deliver what customers want, everything else falls into place, i.e., sales, profits, bonuses, happy employees. From the business perspective, **consumer satisfaction** is when a customer's needs, wants, and expectations are met or exceeded, and that satisfaction results in repurchases and loyalty to the seller.

Remedies to Resolve Consumer Problems

While laws exist to protect consumers from frauds and misrepresentations, no laws require merchants to offer refunds, exchanges, or credits on merchandise they sell. Before making purchases, shoppers should inquire about the seller's **return policy**. This is the guiding principle or set of procedures used by sellers that explicitly states the conditions under which products can be returned, exchanged, or credited. Policies are often written on sales receipts and posted inside store premises near the cash register; many states have laws requiring the posting of return policies. Most sellers require that products be returned within a limited time period, in good condition, in the original packaging, with a sales receipt; others are more flexible in their conditions. Some companies may require a restocking charge of up to 15 percent of the price and/or prior authorization before you can return an item.

CONSUMER UPDATE: Young Shoppers Are Discriminated Against

Many stores discriminate against high school and college age consumers. Store employees in expensive stores, especially in malls, seem to believe that every young person wearing jeans and tennis shoes, looking young, sounding a little loud, and carrying a backpack is going to steal everything in sight. Sometimes the discrimination is based on skin color. In 1994, New York City became the first city to prohibit such unfair discrimination. Violators may be reported to the Human Rights Commission.

Teenage Research Unlimited reports that young people spend over $100 billion dollars annually. More often than not, young consumers have money to spend. Many have their parents' credit cards; some have their own. Surveys show that students doing comparison shopping projects in local stores wind up buying the goods 90 percent of the time.

Some merchants are getting smart by providing sensitivity training for their sales personnel. Others remain oblivious that young people actually do have money. More than one young shopper has said, "Whenever I'm carefully watched in a store, I take my business elsewhere." Responsible young shoppers who are unfairly discriminated against complain to store supervisors and mall managers; some write letters to the store owners and to community human rights commissions.

If you buy goods or services that are unsatisfactory and not at the level you expected, ask the seller to take back the goods, if possible, and obtain a refund. If not, ask the seller to reduce the price to accommodate your dissatisfaction. You may ask a seller for a refund or price reduction even if you simply changed your mind. Perhaps you don't like the color after all, or it really doesn't fit the decor of the home, or you spent too much money and need the cash for something else.

Sellers are willing to handle the numerous types of consumer complaints for several reasons: (1) to fulfill the desire to act fairly and honestly in marketplace transactions and maintain a positive reputation, (2) to obtain early warning signals about defects and possible violations of laws, (3) to learn about problems with products or services, so they can be corrected quickly, (4) to avoid bad publicity, particularly from assertive consumers who write letters to third parties (such as government agencies), (5) to reduce third-party liability claims, (6) to keep customers satisfied and loyal (so they will not go to the competition), (7) to increase profits over the long run by making sales to new customers who receive positive word-of-mouth comments from existing customers, and (8) to avoid government regulation and improve relationships with regulators.

Most sellers now realize that doing the job right the first time and effectively handling complaints results in increased consumer satisfaction because these efforts encourage old customers to continue to buy. That kind of reputation also helps bring in new customers.

How to Complain Effectively

Follow these procedures to complain effectively: (1) Pursue your complaint as soon as possible after experiencing dissatisfaction, while events are still fresh in your mind; (2) clearly identify the problem and document it with evidence; (3) if possible, register your complaint with the person responsible for the transaction, otherwise go to that person's boss; (4) explain how you want your complaint resolved (i.e., apology, repair, refund); (5) be courteous and show respect, but be firm and persistent (realizing too that even though you were wronged, there are two sides to every story); (6) be willing to compromise, especially if you will not otherwise benefit; and, (7) be prepared to wait a reasonable amount of time for the responsible person to make a decision on your complaint.

The Complaining Process Should Follow a Sequence

The only way to remedy seller wrongs is for consumers to personally take actions to resolve such matters. Simply put, consumers must complain, and if complaining does not work, they should tell lots of people about their experiences and then consider seeking legal action.

Americans should simply refuse to accept shoddy products or service.[5] When you have a negative marketplace experience, make sure your complaint does the most good. To be an effective complainer, you must first decide on the objective of the complaint. If your objective is to be treated a little better while in a store, just ask to see the person in charge. This may be the store manager or an assistant manager. Simply report the quality of service you received and request that someone more capable be provided so you can spend your money in the store. If your objective is to remedy a wrong, more work is necessary.

Table 3-1 shows the five sequential levels of complaining: (1) to business, (2) to manufacturers, (3) to self-regulatory groups, (4) to consumer action personnel, and (5) to the private-action legal arena. If the problem is an illegal fraud, you should, of course, begin by reporting the crooks to the police. You can follow these channels individually or simultaneously, but usually one should begin the complaint process with the seller.

---

[5]It is often reported in the popular press that the Germans and Japanese would never accept the quality of goods that most Americans do.

Sequential Levels to Bring Your Complaint	Sequential Channels for a Complaint
1. Local business	Salesperson → supervisor → manager/owner
2. Manufacturer	Consumer affairs department → president and/or chief executive officer (CEO)
3. Self-regulatory organizations	Better Business Bureau → county medical societies → consumer action panels (CAPs)
4. Consumer action agencies	Private consumer action groups → media action lines → government agencies
5. Small claims or civil court	Small claims court → civil court

TABLE 3-1   Complaint Procedure—Sequential Levels and Channels

Note that federal agencies, such as the Food and Drug Administration, Consumer Product Safety Commission, and Federal Trade Commission, are not included in this table. These agencies can register consumer complaints, but they do not have the power to resolve individual consumer problems. Complaining to federal government agencies helps them obtain information to take collective actions against sellers.

Complaints about services should follow the same channels. Each type of service provider (i.e., doctors, chiropractors, lawyers, nursing homes, telephone bills, landlords, tax collectors, pre-schools) has an overseeing self-regulatory body and/or government agency. Appropriate addresses and telephone numbers can be obtained by looking in the front pages of the telephone directory and the blue pages listing government agencies.

1. The Local Business

The best approach in complaining is to give the seller every opportunity to right the wrong before taking additional action. For example, a complaint about an unsatisfactory product, such as a faulty Panasonic telephone, should be brought to the attention of the merchant. Take the telephone back and talk to a salesperson. If he or she cannot resolve the problem, simply ask to see the supervisor. If you still get no satisfaction, such as a refund, a substitute product, or a repair, ask to see the manager or owner.

2. The Manufacturer

When a problem with a product cannot be resolved satisfactorily directly with a merchant and/or the difficulty is really with the product itself, you can keep your complaint about the merchant's lack of cooperation within the business self-regulatory scheme by bringing it to the attention of the manufacturer's consumer affairs department.

Some companies, particularly automobile manufacturers, have a consumer affairs department **zone office** to respond to complaints. This is a corporation's decentralized geographic arrangement of consumer affairs office operations throughout the country to handle complaints. Both the zone and central corporate offices of consumer affairs should be equally able to resolve all difficulties.

A growing number of companies, particularly product manufacturers, provide toll-free telephone numbers for consumer inquiries and complaints. When a consumer experiences dissatisfaction at the merchant level, he or she can telephone the company. Addresses and telephone numbers of companies can be found on warranties, owner's instruction manuals, product hang tags, or in the library. Check *Standard and Poor's Registry of Manufacturers* or *Thomas' Registry of Manufacturers*.

CONSUMER UPDATE:
To Accurately Address Complaints, Use the
Consumer's Resource Handbook

The federal government's U.S. Office of Consumer Affairs publishes the *Consumer's Resource Handbook* every year. In addition to offering tips on buying smart, it provides thousands of addresses in a consumer assistance directory format. Included are corporations, national consumer organizations, car manufacturers, Better Business Bureaus, trade associations, government consumer protection offices, aging offices, banking authorities, insurance regulators, securities administrators, utility commissions, vocational and rehabilitation offices, weights and measures offices, selected federal agencies, and military commissary and exchange offices. Single copies are available free by writing: Consumer's Resource Handbook, Consumer Information Center, Pueblo, Colorado 81009.

Should you get no resolution from a senior-level manager in the consumer affairs department (don't take "no" from a low-level person!), then it is time to communicate with the manufacturer's president or chief executive officer (CEO). Simply send a complaint letter addressed to the title "President" or "Chief Executive Officer" and await the response. The chapter appendix explains and illustrates how to write a complaint letter.

3. Self-Regulatory Organizations

The role of self-regulatory organizations is to attempt to resolve disputes between consumers and sellers. Should the particular business, manufacturer, or profession not resolve the consumer complaint, then it's time to use sources of assistance outside the business. These are often called **third-party complaint-handling sources**. For example, county medical societies have judicial committees that handle written complaints, usually concerning overcharging or improper treatment, against member physicians.[6]

One major self-regulatory organization is the Better Business Bureau (BBB), which has offices in 138 communities. The Better Business Bureau typically has four functions:

---

[6]In 1994, the Federal Trade Commission gave the country's medical societies the legal authority to discipline physicians for fee gouging when it occurs with other fraudulent or unprofessional behavior. Medical societies also may publicize such actions.

(1) to provide prepurchase information to the public on such topics as "Tips on Buying a New Car," (2) to handle inquiries (11 million annually) by providing reports to consumers on hundreds of local sellers, (3) to mediate disputes between consumers and businesses by accepting consumer complaints, forwarding them to the business involved, and encouraging settlement between the parties, and (4) to arbitrate disputes between consumers and participating sellers, often automobile manufacturers.

Consumers can obtain a number of useful booklets on consumer topics by visiting a local Better Business Bureau office. Those interested in learning about the reputation of any business in the country need only telephone the local Better Business Bureau where the company is located to obtain an oral report. Consumers wanting to complain about a seller must do so in writing to the BBB, which then mails a copy to the company, allowing 15 days for a response. Most sellers then tell the BBB their side of the story, which the BBB then presents to the consumer for reaction. Often a compromise settlement is reached between the consumer and the company.

Mediation is the process of negotiating to resolve differences by a person who acts as an intermediary agent between two or more conflicting parties. Companies that do not respond to complaints or mediate in bad faith can lose their membership in the Better Business Bureau. Consumers with unresolved problems can still take their complaints to a government consumer protection agency, small-claims court, or an attorney.

Arbitration is a form of adjudication. Here a dispute is resolved by the judgment of an impartial third party who holds a hearing, listens to arguments and evidence presented by both sides, and makes a decision or judgment. In addition to the reputable American Arbitration Association, many industry trade associations are involved in arbitrating consumer disputes. Examples include the New York Stock Exchange, National Association of Securities Dealers (NASD), Chrysler Customer Arbitration Board, and local Better Business Bureaus. Arbitrators are appointed by mutual consent of the parties involved, by provisions in a consumer contract (such as a credit agreement), or according to statutory provisions. The consumer almost never has to pay a fee for arbitration services.

The BBB has entered arbitration contracts with most automobile manufacturers, as well as other companies. Typically, a consumer who has complained to an automobile dealer about some problem usually also complains to the zone or head office of the manufacturer. When disputes still cannot be settled, the consumer can then ask the BBB through its Automobile Consumer Action Panel (AUTOCAP) to step in on the matter. In an arbitration case, the BBB hears the oral arguments of the consumer and the manufacturer and then makes a decision. Typically, the decision is binding on the manufacturer but not binding on the consumer. Thus, a still dissatisfied consumer, if he or she desires, may go further and sue in court or ask a government agency for assistance.

Several industries have established **consumer action panels (CAPs)** to facilitate handling of complaints on an industry-wide basis. These are complaint-handling boards of impartial people, usually sponsored by an industry trade association, whose purpose is to mediate or arbitrate disputes between consumers and manufacturers or dealers. The usual 5 to 11 people who serve on CAPs are executives from a specific industry plus some consumer representatives. When the consumer action panel receives a complaint from a consumer, it asks the manufacturer or dealer to reinvestigate and report back. The typical CAP generally has the arbitration authority to make a decision that is binding on the business, but the consumer can accept or reject it.

Complaining to self-regulatory groups gives them the last opportunity to get the business to resolve the problem. Very often these groups can bring about a solution to a problem because they can be more objective than individual manufacturers or dealers, and such agencies have high success rates in resolving consumers' problems. For example, the car dealer's consumer action panel AUTOCAP resolves over 40 percent of its complaints in favor of car owners. When a problem cannot be handled by the local business, the manufacturer, or a local self-regulatory organization, consumers may contact one of the many consumer action panels or industry trade associations:

Automotive Consumer Action Program
(AUTOCAP)
8400 Westpark Drive
McLean, VA 22102

Better Business Bureau Autoline
Council of Better Business Bureaus
1515 Wilson Boulevard
Arlington, VA 22209

Better Business Bureau National Consumer
Arbitration
Council of Better Business Bureaus
1515 Wilson Boulevard
Arlington, VA 22209

Carpet and Rug Institute
1100 17th Street, NW
Washington, DC 20036

Cemetery Consumer Service Council
P.O. Box 3574
Washington, DC 20007

Direct Marketing Association
Mail Order Action Line
1101 17th Street, NW - Suite 705
Washington, DC 20036

Direct Selling Association
1776 K Street, NW
Washington, DC 20006

Electronic Industries Association
Consumer Electronics Group
2001 Eye Street, NW
Washington, DC 20006

Funeral Service Consumer Action Program
(FSCAP)
11121 West Oklahoma Avenue
Milwaukee, WI 53227

Furniture Industry Consumer Action Panel
(FICAP)
HP-7
High Point, NC 27261

Home Owners Warranty Program (HOW)
2000 L Street, NW
Washington, DC 20036

Household Goods Dispute Settlement
Program
400 Army-Navy Drive
Arlington, VA 22202

International Association for Financial Planning
2 Concourse Parkway, Suite 800
Atlanta, GA 30328

Major Appliance Consumer Action Panel
(MACAP)
20 North Wacker Drive
Chicago, IL 60606

National Advertising Division (NAD)
Council of Better Business Bureaus
845 Third Avenue
New York, NY 10022

4. Consumer Action Agencies

Consumer action agencies are third-party public and private organizations that purposefully and forcefully represent the interests of consumers, often by accepting individual complaints and taking action to resolve such problems. There are three common types of consumer action agencies: (1) media, such as newspapers, radio, and television stations, (2) government, such as state, county and city offices of consumer affairs as well as state attorneys general offices, and (3) private, such as local, state, and national consumer activist organizations.

In many communities the media is actively involved in consumer protection. A number of local newspapers, radio, and television stations have "Action Line" programs whose purpose is to take actions to resolve a variety of problems concerning the public.

Sometimes it is getting a pothole fixed on a busy street; often it is a consumer problem. When a consumer's effort has failed to solve a problem, the action line staff investigates and tries to right the wrong. An example of a media action line is Call for Action. Call for Action is a network of radio and television stations that offer resolution for consumer problems. Call for Action's national office is located at 3400 Idaho Avenue, NW, Suite 101, Washington, DC 20016.

After being contacted by a media action line, many sellers quickly give in to the consumer's position because they fear the possibility of negative publicity. Typically, media staff are quite limited in the number of complaints they can investigate. As a result, they usually select complaints that are representative of the consumers' problems and often a bit sensational.

Government consumer action agencies include various consumer affairs departments and the offices of the attorneys general. Usually the Office of Consumer Affairs (OCA) is a state responsibility operating under the legal authority of the Attorney General's office. Typically, government consumer action agencies run public service announcements on radio and television to solicit consumer problems, and they have toll-free telephone numbers for consumers to obtain complaint forms. Government consumer action agencies are located in the state capital with branch offices in major cities. In some instances, large cities and counties have their own offices of consumer affairs. Telephone numbers for state, county and city government consumer action agencies are listed in the front pages of the telephone book. These organizations have a high success rate in resolving consumer complaints because they can bring civil and criminal actions to enforce the laws and regulations, and they sometimes get fines and money back for consumers.

Private consumer action organizations exist everywhere. Local consumer action groups are just some of the many special-interest organizations trying to achieve their ends, such as helping senior citizens, improving access to low-income housing, and trying to preserve the environment. State and local consumer action organizations are usually well known to the populations they serve, such as the Consumer Education and Protection Association in Philadelphia and the California Consumers Association. At the national level, particularly active private consumer organizations include the Consumer Federation of America, Center for Auto Safety, and National Consumers League.

5. Small Claims and Civil Courts

Seeking remedies through the first four channels in the complaint procedures in Table 3-1 can rectify almost all consumer complaints. If these procedures fail, it is possible that the matter can be pursued in the legal arena. A recent survey by the American Bar Association found that at least 40 percent of consumers confront a non-criminal legal problem every year.

Numerous civil matters are resolved in state and federal courts, and a written record is made of the happenings. Proceedings are completed with the assistance of attorneys, witnesses, a judge, and often a jury. Few people take consumer complaints to an attorney and file suit against a seller in the regular civil court system because it is quite expensive. Attorney fees vary but easily could amount to $500 or even $1,000 to take a simple case to court. Examples of cases that consumers probably should bring to civil court include a breach of contract situation for a $3000 faulty air-conditioning system, a $5000 shoddy remodeling construction job, or a landlord-tenant dispute over $1500 in rent. People with limited incomes can go to legal-aid societies, usually listed in the telephone book under "Legal Aid" or "Legal Services", for less expensive attorney fees.[7]

Use Small Claims Lawsuits to Sue When Necessary

For reasons of cost and convenience, many people choose to use small claims courts to resolve consumer problems. A **small claims court** (or **pro se court**) is one that specializes in adjudicating legal claims involving small amounts of money in a simple and economical manner, with relaxed procedures and rules of incidence, sometimes without the assistance of attorneys. Fully one-fourth of the total civil caseload in the United States is made up of small claims actions. Almost all states have small claims courts, and many courts are open during evening hours as well as weekends. The maximum amount that can be litigated is usually limited to $1200, although a number of states have a jurisdictional limit of $5000 or higher. Nine states permit jury trials.

Costs are kept low, in part, because a written transcript is not kept of the proceedings, although court records are maintained. In most small claims courts, consumers are prohibited from bringing an attorney into the courtroom. The idea is that the consumer can present his or her own legal claim before a judge (or arbitrator) in an informal setting, as some of the more formal legal proceedings are relaxed. The seller-defendant is usually allowed to have an attorney, although they are prohibited in some states. On most military bases and college campuses, free legal assistance is available to offer guidance on small claims cases, as well as other legal issues.

CONSUMER UPDATE:
Rental Car Company Violates Human Rights Law

A 24-year old George Washington University law student successfully sued Hertz Rent A Car in small claims court for not renting a car to her. Pamela Sosne had an excellent driving record. However, rental car companies generally will not rent to people under age twenty-five without a hefty surcharge because statistics show that young people have more accidents than other age groups. Hertz does rent to people ages 21-25, but only if they are employed by a firm that has a contract with them. Sosne was awarded $101 in compensatory damages under the District of Columbia Human Rights Act which prohibits discrimination in the sales of goods or services. The only defense for a company is to show the court that they would be forced out of business unless they discriminated. Many cities have similar laws.

To file a small claims court action, you would go to the courthouse and inquire as to which court hears small claims. A small fee, often $10, is required, along with fees of normally $3 for each court summons or subpoena. A **summons** is a notice issued to a person summoning him or her to report to court as a juror or witness. A **subpoena** is a legal writ requiring appearance of certain items in court. When you complete the necessary forms, it is important to fill out the full legal name of the **defendant** (the person who

---

[7]Arizona's "Quick-Court" consists of conveniently located kiosks resembling automatic teller machines that permit consumers to get free information on a wide array of legal problems, including consumer transactions. The system prints out completed forms, which can then be filed in court.

allegedly committed the wrong act and is the subject of the litigation), and to carefully describe the action with which the lawsuit is concerned. The court will subpoena all necessary witnesses and the defendant for the day of the trial. The legal summons has a motivational effect on many defendants, since about one-quarter of all small claims cases are settled out of court before the hearing date.

The day the case is heard, you, the **plaintiff** (the person who has filed the small claims or civil court case and is suing the defendant), should be well prepared and have a clear understanding of the sequence of events that led up to the claim. Bring all relevant documentation. In most courts, the decision of the judge can be appealed by the loser to a higher court, which results in considerable attorney fees and related costs. Small claims court decisions are won by the plaintiff about three-quarters of the time and are not appealed.

Winning a small claims decision does not mean that you automatically get full satisfaction. Often the judge makes a compromise decision, perhaps ordering a $300 judgment on a $400 claim. Also, it is sometimes difficult to actually collect from the defendant. The small claims court does not act as a collection agency, rather it issues **judgments**. These are judicial decisions and determinations of a court of law, often creating or affirming an obligation, such as a debt.

If you experience difficulty collecting, you can go back to small claims court to ask the judge to order a **writ of execution**, which is a right to exercise a claim against the defendant's property, bank accounts, personal property (such as a motor vehicle), and wage income. Executions on real estate are not allowed. Going to small claims court takes time and energy, so consumers must weigh the potential benefits of going to court against the potential costs.

How Consumers Can Break a Contract

When consumers receive goods that do not conform to the express or implied warranty, they can attempt to remedy the situation or break the contract. Four ways are:

1. **Keep the goods and sue the seller for damages.** Here the consumer asks the court to order the defendant to pay the dollar value of the losses.
2. **Revoke acceptance and seek a return of the purchase price.** Here the consumer returns the goods to the seller and formally communicates a revocation of acceptance to the seller, usually in writing. This is the essence of state **lemon laws** that permit revocation of a new car after it has been repeatedly returned to the shop for a series of unsuccessful repairs. Consumers who return other goods to sellers and revoke acceptance run the risk that the seller will then sue the them for non-performance of the contract, although a well-prepared consumer often wins with a sympathetic judge.
3. **Ask a court to reform the contract.** When a court orders **reformation** it alters or corrects the contract to remove faults or defects; sometimes the court makes the seller actually do what was promised.
4. **Ask a court to rescind the contract.** If granted by a court, an order of **recision** annuls the contract and that puts each party back into the position they were in before the alleged unfair or deceptive practice occurred.

Most consumers do not choose to keep the goods and seek damages. In revocation, the consumer must fulfill a number of prerequisites because minor defects are not acceptable cause and consumers must give sellers an opportunity to cure the difficulty. Revocation must occur within a reasonable amount of time after discovering that a problem with the product substantially impairs the value of the item to the consumer. Given appropriate circumstances, courts do reform and rescind contracts.

Damages to Ask for When Suing

When consumers go to small claims or civil court for a breach of contract or deception lawsuit, they sue for relief and/or damages. To remedy the wrong, consumers ask the judge for assistance. (If a criminal act also has occurred during the unfair or deceptive practice, it is incumbent on the federal, state, county or city to seek civil and criminal penalties.) Damages consumer plaintiffs may seek in court include:

1. **Restitution** is the act of restoring to the rightful owner something that has been taken away, lost, or surrendered, such as money given to the seller.
2. **Compensatory damages** are out-of-pocket losses plus the difference between the consumer's expenses and the value claimed by the seller, such as payment for mental anguish, physical pain and suffering, and various incidental and consequential expenses.
3. **Incidental expenses** are those which result because of minor concomitant circumstances, such as taxi fares.
4. **Consequential expenses** are those costs which the consumer incurs following as an effect, result, or conclusion of the unfair or deceptive trade practice, such as losing a day's wages and attorney's fees.
5. **Punitive damages** are those which aim to penalize or inflict punishment.[8]
6. An **injunction** is a judicial order that commands, directs, orders, or prohibits a party from a specific course of action, such as prohibiting a seller making certain sales or advertising claims.

Use a Class Action Lawsuit When Many Are Wronged

Theoretically, the law protects consumers against frauds and misrepresentations, whether the case involves a Pepsi Cola overcharge of 5 cents, a $20 toaster, or a $20,000 automobile. The obstacles for redress are high for inexpensive items. It is difficult to prove deceit, and legal costs are significant given the expected small payoff. Thus, the pooling of grievances is sometimes allowed by the courts in the case of deceptions and misrepresentations through **class action lawsuits**. These permit representative members of a common class, such as consumers who have been similarly wronged, to seek joint redress of their grievances by suing for damages on behalf of themselves and all those similarly

---

[8]In 1991, the Supreme Court refused to limit punitive damages, thus preserving a powerful tool for consumers to redress wrongs. Limits on punitive damages may be established by legislatures.

CONSUMER UPDATE: Yes! You Can Get Out of Many Contracts*

It is easy to give into the persuasive powers of a salesperson and sign on the dotted line of a contract. Later you may conclude that you should not have obligated yourself. Getting out of a contract depends upon (1) an appropriate federal or state law, and (2) the goodwill of the seller.

Automobile purchases and leases–You usually can cancel if you have not yet taken possession of the vehicle, before the paperwork for the title gets processed at the department of motor vehicles, before you have put more than 5 or 10 miles on it, or before the loan or interest rate have been approved. Auto leases are almost impossible to cancel.

Insurance policies–Most states permit a free cancellation period of 10 days; some allow 30 days to change your mind. Nationwide sellers are usually lenient. Follow correct cancellation procedures described in the fine print of the policy. Thus, you may be able to cancel life, health, disability, and credit insurance policies.

Extended Service Contracts–These contracts almost always have a cancellation clause, typically 15 to 60 days. Most can be canceled later with a nominal service charge.

Various federal and state "cooling-off laws" (described in Chapter 5) that permit cancellation of contracts for health spas, campground contracts, home improvements, and timeshares.

* Some of this material is based on Dan Moreau, "You Signed it. Are You Stuck?" *Kiplinger's Personal Finance Magazine*, October 1993, 53-56.

---

situated. Such lawsuits are usually permitted at the discretion of the state court where commonalities can be clearly shown.

Consumers who successfully file state or federal class action lawsuits may be awarded their purchase costs, attorneys fees, and damages. In addition, consumers injured by a breach of warranty may file a federal class action lawsuit. A class action lawsuit may be filed under the Magnuson-Moss Warranty Act if there are at least 100 named plaintiff-consumers each with a minimum claim of $25, and the total is at least $50,000. Few warranty problems meet all the restrictions necessary for consumers to economically and successfully pursue a class action lawsuit under the provisions of the Magnuson-Moss Act.

Techniques of Last Resort: How to Fight Back—And Win!—Against Ripoffs and Frauds

When you have been deceived or ripped off, you can fight back using these procedures:

1. Review the deception and look for actual illegal actions by the seller. If something illegal occurred, report it to the police, state office of consumer affairs, or state attorney general. Also, think about suing the perpetrator in small claims court. Most people have access to an attorney for free or at low cost. Many college students enjoy the advantage of having a **student attorney** on campus. These persons are lawyers employed by the educational institution to attend to many of the legal interests of the student body. They give advice and guidance on legal issues, and occasionally file suit on behalf of a concern affecting one or more students. Low-income consumers can seek assistance from **legal-aid attorneys** who are available in most communities. When there is a lawyer involved, the complaining consumer has greater leverage when carrying on the fight because an attorney offers the appearance that the consumer is quite serious about the matter.

2. Calculate the numbers to determine the likely value that a seller might settle for to get rid of your complaint and offer them a deal which they very well may accept. Sometimes it is important to obtain a full refund, so you should push for it. In other instances, 100 percent may not be necessary. Therefore, when seeking redress, it is important to know the likely value that a seller might settle for to get rid of your complaint. To begin, know that commissions for door-to-door and telemarketing sales often amount to 1/3 to 1/2 the total price. This is in contrast to 5 to 10 percent for most retail store sales commissions.

To illustrate the calculation, assume the bad transaction cost you $200. The salesperson may have earned $80 commission on the deal, while the cost of the product or service may have amounted to a genuine $70 or so, leaving a gross profit of $50 to the seller. Most sellers are willing to give a complaining consumer the salesperson's commission plus part of the gross profit, perhaps $130 in this example. Consequently, when communicating with a seller, calculate how much you are willing to compromise and figure how much wiggle room the seller probably has to settle the complaint.

Then quietly tell them that it is in their best interest to compromise with you—one individual consumer—because the trouble you are going to cause them will hurt their sales and give them bad publicity. Tell them that for, "X" dollars, you will walk away satisfied. If they don't accept, tell them that you have "all the time in the world" to continue to pursue your rights and that you're going to fight back. Tell them that unless your reasonable demands are met, you will soon take a whole host of actions.

3. Fight back with multiple actions. If the seller remains unwilling to accommodate your interests after you have been polite and forceful, communicate to them that you are prepared to do the following:

- **Write complaint letters** to the Better Business Bureau, Office of Consumer Affairs, and state Attorney General.
- **Sue in small claims court** on the legal basis of **unconscionability** ("it was patently unfair, your honor, and the seller took advantage of me") because a judge can sympathetically rule in favor of one consumer without setting a precedent for all others.
- **Make a big sign and prepare to picket outside the place of business** of the seller or where the seller goes to visit potential customers. Avoid slanderous and libelous words and keep moving (so you do not impede others) and you will break no laws. Before you begin to picket, politely show the seller the sign and ask for a settlement.
- **Prepare a handout on consumer ripoffs** and distribute while picketing. Be careful from a legal perspective not to precisely disparage the seller in a slanderous and libelous manner, and share the handout with all your friends, neighbors and co-workers, too.
- **Offer to give speeches on consumer ripoffs** to any group that will listen.
- **Send your story to media action lines** run by local newspapers and television stations.
- **Send your story to the author of this book**, who will consider running it as a boxed insert in the next edition.

CONSUMER UPDATE:
How to Organize a Boycott

One should use a boycott as a last resort. The *National Boycott News* recommends the following considerations: (1) Consider your target (the industry leader, the worst company, the one most likely to change); (2) Write the company explaining your position and seek a face-to-face meeting with a company official; (3) Should discussions prove fruitless, announce that you are considering a boycott and that you will continue negotiations over a list of demands that you present to the company; (4) Choose which company products to boycott and seek the cooperation of other groups which will support the boycott while sending the company names of boycott co-sponsors; (5) Call a press conference (if possible, at a company site) to distribute your list of demands and use graphic visual aids to help make your points.

Review and Summary of Key Terms and Concepts

1.   What are **rights**, and what do they have to do with **implied warranties** and **express warranties**?

2.   Distinguish among the two types of **implied warranties**: **warranty of merchantability** and **warranty of fitness for a particular purpose**.

3.   How are **express warranties** created, and what is a **written express warranty**?

4.   Explain the meaning of selling a product **as is**.

5.   Give some examples of **moral rights**, and tell how they differ from President Kennedy's **Consumer Bill of Rights**.

6.   Select two of the **consumer rights of all Americans**, and explain what they mean.

7.   Which **student consumer rights** do you think most important? Why?

8.   List some **responsibilities of consumers**.

9.   Why don't people **complain**?

10.   Discuss how many people **complain about certain goods**.

11.   Explain why it is beneficial for consumers and sellers to **get satisfaction**.

12.   Why are **return policies** important, and what are some reasons why **sellers are willing to handle consumer complaints**?

13.   Summarize the **complaining process**.

14. When should a consumer take a problem to a manufacturer's **zone office**?

15. What are **third-party complaint-handling sources**?

16. Distinguish between **mediation** and **arbitration**.

17. What are **consumer action panels**?

18. Explain the term **consumer action agencies**, and give some examples of the different types.

19. Summarize the processes followed in a **small claims court**, and in your response define the terms **summons**, **subpoena**, **judgments**, and **writ of execution**.

20. Explain two ways that consumers might **get out of a contract**.

21. Distinguish among the terms: **restitution** and **compensatory damages**.

22. What are **punitive damages**?

23. What is a **class action lawsuit**, and why is this important to consumers?

24. What two actions in **fighting back** look reasonable to you?

Useful Resources for Consumers

Automotive Consumer Action Program
National Automobile Dealers Association
8400 Westpark Drive
McLean, VA 22102
703-821-7144

National Association of Attorneys General
444 North Capitol Street, Suite 403
Washington, DC 20001
202-628-0435

National Consumer Law Center
11 Beacon Street, NW, Suite 928
Boston, MA 02108
617-523-8010

"What Do You Think" Questions

1. Consider the term **implied warranty rights** and the views of the Supreme Court on the subject. Think of several examples where the concept of implied warranty rights could help consumers and explain why.

2. Which of the **moral rights** of people do you think are most important? Why?

3. Select one of the **consumer rights for all Americans** and tell why it is important to you.

4. Which two **consumer rights** are important to you? What can students at your school do to be certain those rights exist?

5. Do you think **student consumers** are discriminated against in your business community? Offer some concrete ideas on how students might go about changing the attitudes of business owners and their sales personnel on discrimination against students.

6. Think about a recent situation where you or a friend were ripped off in the marketplace. Review the suggestions on **fighting back**, and record some notes to guide your action to try and resolve the situation.

7. Many people fail to **complain** about consumer problems. What types of actions can sellers and government take to help get more consumers complaining?

Appendix Issue 3-A:
Writing a Letter of Complaint

Don't put up with poor treatment by sellers or government agencies. Do not accept being "brushed off" by someone in authority. If you cannot think clearly when someone is pressuring you, go away and take some time to think. Then sit down and make some notes of things to say. Either go back later and complain or write a letter of complaint.

When writing a consumer complaint letter, type the letter on business-size paper and aim your communication at the right person. Sometimes it's the consumer affairs office, sometimes it's the company president or chief executive officer (CEO). A reference section librarian can locate corporate names and addresses. The "Who's Who" books have the home addresses of lots of big name executives.

1. Explain the problem. Be clear and concise in explaining the problem. Be factual, and do not dwell on sensitive issues. Avoid being sarcastic or overly emotional; let them know that you are a reasonable person. Try to say it all in one sentence, and add clarifying statements if needed. Also, tell the story of what you have already done in attempting to resolve the problem.

2. Identify your expectations. Be firm and courteous when requesting (don't demand) what it is that you want the seller to do. Do you want something repaired, a product replaced, or a refund? Give choices, if appropriate.

3. Give persuasive reasons. Sellers are people just like everyone else, and they like to be treated with both intelligence and respect. Give logical reasons why the action you want is, first, the right thing to do and, second, also in the best interest of the seller. If you have been a long-time customer, tell the seller, especially if you intend to buy from that seller in the future.

4. Document your request. No seller is going to do what you want without a little proof, so include appropriate documentation. Sellers want to see such things as a receipt for proof of purchase, a canceled check, a charge slip, or a service invoice. Never send originals because they may become lost. If such documentation is no longer available, just explain why.

5. Use an action close. The way to get action is to ask for it. Therefore, in a positive way, tell what action you will take next should the seller not respond affirmatively within an appropriate time period. Give a reasonable deadline. Include your address and telephone number.

The second complaint letter (and, if necessary, the third, fourth and fifth) should briefly repeat the problem, remind them that they have not yet responded to your letter (or the response was unsatisfactory), tell them you will now complain to third-party agencies, and enclose a photocopy of your previous correspondence.

SAMPLE COMPLAINT LETTER

Your address
Your city, state, and ZIP code
Today's date

Name of person (if known)
Job title
Company name
Street address
City, state, and zip code

Dear Mr. or Ms. last name (or Dear Reader):

I am writing to tell you of my dissatisfaction with (name of product and its serial number or the service performed), which was purchased (tell where and when). The exact problem is that the product (tell the reasons for the complaint, that it no longer functions, is wrong for the task, or whatever). What I have already done to try and resolve the problem is (tell the story of what occurred as well as the actions and statements of particular salespersons or managers).

In order to resolve this problem, I think that you should (state what specific action or actions you believe the seller should take on your behalf).

In all fairness, your company should (give the refund, exchange the product, or whatever) for the following reasons. (Give two or more reasons whenever possible.)

Enclosed are photocopies of (sales receipt, invoice, previous letters, whatever) that support my request for action. Please note (in one specific document) that (focus the reader's attention on a particular item you want them to be sure and see because it supports your position).

I look forward to receiving your reply providing a speedy resolution to this problem, and I will allow three weeks before referring it to the appropriate government consumer protection agency. Please write to me at the above address or contact me by telephone (give both home and work numbers if it would be difficult to locate you during daytime hours).

Sincerely,

Your name

Enclosures (include copies of appropriate documents)

Chapter 4

Ripoffs and Frauds in the Marketplace

OBJECTIVES

After reading this chapter, you should be able to

1. Recognize how ripoffs and frauds work against consumers.

2. Explain why ripoffs and frauds exist in the economic marketplace.

3. Understand what ripoffs and frauds have in common.

4. List general guidelines to help consumers avoid ripoffs and frauds.

5. Recognize that ripoffs are not illegal and that quite a few ripoffs exist.

6. Understand that fraud also exists in the marketplace and that fraud is difficult to prove.

7. Distinguish between puffery and untrue, deceptive and misleading advertising.

8. Recognize that many well-know corporations commit economic fraud.

9. Describe a number of ripoffs and frauds, including some in telemarketing and mail, buying, vehicle sales and repairs, and investments.

It would take an encyclopedia to describe all of the ripoffs, misrepresentations, schemes, scams, and frauds aimed at taking money from consumers. A few new ones are invented every year, too. These exist in all areas of the economic marketplace. Ripoffs and frauds occur in all societies, especially where there is a seemingly inherent motivation among people to take advantage of others in economic transactions. The perpetrator's incentive to seek easy profits is only exceeded by consumers who want to take advantage of a really good deal, or better yet, get something for nothing. The informed consumer must learn about the variety of ripoffs and frauds to avoid the come-ons, hooks, and traps used by unprincipled sellers. Consumers also have dimes and dollars stolen from them everyday through illegal price fixing by large corporations.

This chapter begins by examining how ripoffs and frauds work against consumers and why they exist in the marketplace. Next we overview what ripoffs and frauds have in common. This is followed by a number of guidelines consumers can use to avoid being taken. Importantly, consumers need to understand that ripoffs are not illegal (at least until a judge says something different) and that a number of them exist. Fraud exists in the marketplace as well, and it is very difficult to prove in a court of law. Then we distinguish between puffery and untrue, deceptive, and misleading advertising. After observing that many well-known corporations commit economic fraud, the chapter provides examples of the different unscrupulous practices that exist to cheat consumers out of their money. Additional ripoffs and frauds, primarily dealing with credit and investments, are covered in later chapters.

How Ripoffs and Frauds Work against Consumers

The purpose of business in the capitalistic economic system is quite clear: to make a profit. Theoretically, the goal of business should be to strive to do nothing else but satisfy the consumer, and the reward of profits should come its way. However, not every businessperson believes this. Some lie and cheat. When that occurs, it places honest businesses at a competitive disadvantage because customers looking for a bargain buy from the bad sellers rather than the good ones. Most businesspeople know that such imperfections in the economic marketplace do not provide a "level playing field" among sellers, or between sellers and consumers. As a result, some businesses practice ripoffs, misrepresentations and deceptions against consumers. The result of ripoffs and frauds is that consumers are fooled into putting up money for a good or service of inferior quality that is not a good value, and often is overpriced.

Economic theory suggests that competition is supposed to force dishonest businesses out of operation because consumers will refuse to buy from them and instead buy from honest ones. It stands to reason that if people find out who the honest ones are and buy only from them, the dishonest ones will be eliminated. After all, consumers who were once taken should not fall for the same deception again.

But many of them do. And, dishonest business people have more than 265 million American shoppers as potential customers to choose from, including 2 million military personnel and 14 million students, and, therefore, do not need repeat customers—although the sad fact is that they often get them.

Today, one in six Americans reports being a fraud victim, according to a study by Princeton Survey Research Associates. The breakdown by age: 15 percent of people age

18 to 29, 20 percent of those 30 to 49, 18 percent of those 50 to 64, and 14 percent of those 65 years and older.

Consumers who are susceptible to deceptive schemes usually lack specific knowledge about the product or service, thus they are more vulnerable than others who are more informed. The consumer who is too trusting and does not ask critical questions becomes a victim. Consumers must recognize that the purveyors of schemes and scams are expert at both lying and selling.

Why Ripoffs and Frauds Exist in the Marketplace

Ripoffs and frauds exist in the American marketplace for a number of reasons:

1.   The capitalistic market gives the advantage to sellers, the full-time specialists, in the buyer-seller relationship.

2.   Consumers are not well informed in many areas of buying. We live in a complex economic marketplace where consumers make numerous decisions daily, and they cannot possibly be well informed in all necessary areas of buying. Consumers who are ignorant (lacking in sophistication) about how to shop for best buys, particularly for expensive products and services, will not be able to follow rational rules of comparison shopping.

3.   Left unprotected by government, unsophisticated consumers become a catalyst for unscrupulous business practices because unethical business practices are rewarded with profits.

4.   Some unscrupulous sellers (only a small percentage of the many) aim to deceive and profiteer.

5.   Some sellers, including so-called reputable firms, occasionally try to ripoff consumers.

6.   Consumers are too trusting of sellers.

7.   Consumers lack knowledge about ripoffs and frauds.

8.   Sometimes consumers are greedy, and they have a desire to "get something for nothing" or to "get a lot for a little," such as health and wealth.

9.   Many consumers have a sweepstakes mentality. Part of the reason for this attitude among people is that 34 states have lotteries and lots of consumers expect to win something for nothing. In a recent national survey, 11 percent of the respondents said that the best way to get rich was to play the lottery.

The U.S. Postal Service recently sent out pink-colored "sweepstakes postcards" to 200,000 consumers telling them that, "You are a winner! Congratulations!!" The card then listed "five wonderful prizes." Over 55,000 people called the toll-free number to claim their prize. "Winners" were played a tape recording advising them to be more careful about phony sweepstakes solicitations. This study means that about 30 percent of consumers reply to contest scams. A national survey by Louis Harris indicated that 29 percent of people contacted by the guaranteed prize postcard scheme have responded.

10. Price fixing and other illegal forms of collusion exist to control supply or price, but they are nearly impossible for consumers to recognize. (Only government has the ability to identify and stop price fixing.)

11. Consumers believe false advertising. Most people think that magazines and newspapers will only accept advertisements from reputable sources. The reality is that if newspapers have no good reason to suspect an advertiser, they generally print the ad.

12. The practice of deception is profitable for dishonest sellers because in today's economic marketplace they usually can make a lot of money before the authorities get around to investigating and prosecuting them. Probably only two percent of victims ever complain to the fraudulent sellers. Those sellers generally find it easy to satisfy the complaints of the two percent, and this usually can keep the government regulators at bay for several months to a few years. The unscrupulous sellers continue to profit by fleecing the next 98 percent who do not complain. Making it more difficult, surveys show that fewer than 10 percent of consumers who say they were swindled report the crime to the proper government authorities. Many consumers—especially men—are too ashamed to complain.

13. Only a small percentage of victims complain to government agencies, usually because they are embarrassed.

14. Many scam artists escape by fleeing the boundaries of a state and/or declaring bankruptcy. Crooks often get away with their illegal schemes by fleeing the boundaries of one state and setting up a new business in another state under a different name so they can go on and cheat more victims. Both federal and state penalties against deceptions are primarily civil in nature. When caught, perpetrators sometimes have their bank assets frozen, and such funds are used to make partial refunds to some consumers. When stuck, the scam artist can declare bankruptcy to avoid owing any debts. But rare is the case when a criminal law is broken resulting in the bad guys serving jail time. Typically, perpetrators negotiate a settlement with a government, pay a civil fine, and move on, all the time avoiding criminal prosecution. The average life of scam business is as short as 30 to 90 days.

Since competition does not drive such sellers from the marketplace, society has to depend on the efforts of consumers to first, recognize and avoid such practices, and second, report any observed deceptive practices to the proper government authorities. Moreover, for a variety of reasons, consumers fall prey to sellers who pretend to offer goods and services at competitive prices. Some deceptions are perpetrated by fly-by-night, out-of-town businesses, while others are practiced on consumers by well-known, so-called reputable businesses.

What Do Ripoffs and Frauds Have in Common?

Ripoffs and frauds have some commonalities. Misleading advertising is frequently used to lure consumers into various schemes. People who are often well-educated, affluent, and well-informed are led to believe that they are getting a great bargain, perhaps even getting something for free. Many scams appeal to those who have a need for money. Some frauds make you feel stupid if you do not accept the sure-fire deal they are offering. Scams often promise to realize the consumer's dream of financial security. They also want the consumer to act fast. Crooks prefer the quickest method of payment (so they can get away faster), such as **automatic debit** (a withdrawal) of a checking account, credit card, personal check picked up by courier, or overnight mail of cash.

When consumers are enticed and persuaded (sometimes after being told they are the "guaranteed winner" of a contest) to go to a sales office and listen to a sales pitch, they may be subjected to one or two hours of coercive sales tactics, including false promises, and be pressured into making a major purchase.

Appeals to vanity are common. When consumers balk, the seller lowers the price until it reaches an amount the victim will pay. They pressure the victim to act now, and they refuse to put their offer in writing. They often ask for a cash advance under the pretext of needing the money to pay various non-existent expenses. Shady sellers always tell lies when attempting to separate consumers from their dollars.

General Guidelines to Avoid Ripoffs and Frauds

Here are some guidelines to avoid ripoffs and frauds. Most ripoffs and frauds can be avoided by using common sense and a bit of healthy skepticism.

Be Cautious in Marketplace Dealings

1. Talk to friends and acquaintances to learn about their experiences with particular sellers, products, and services.
2. Buy only from reputable sellers that you know or from those who are recommended by someone you trust.
3. Avoid being too courteous with every salesperson or telephone caller and, instead, hang up the phone and walk away from unwanted solicitations.
4. Stop being so trusting about salespersons, because scam artists lie all the time.
5. Be cautious of "expert" testimonials (endorsements) of a product, because these people are often paid large sums for their statements.
6. Get the names, addresses, and telephone numbers of salespersons and companies.
7. Check out the reputation of the seller by contacting the Better Business Bureau,[1] the State Attorney General's Office, or an Office of Consumer Affairs. Telephone the same agencies in the state of any out-of-town sellers.
8. Research the company in the library by looking them up in business-reference volumes, such as Dun & Bradstreet.
9. Try not to be overly sympathetic to salespersons, especially those that pretend to be "your friend," so you can avoid falling prey to frauds using this tactic.
10. Be wary of purchasing from door-to-door salespersons. Always ask for proper identification and carefully examine it.
11. Be cautious about buying anything over the telephone. It is good advice never to buy over the telephone unless you originated the call or you know the caller.
12. Realize that a flashy professional Internet web site does not guarantee that the sponsor is legitimate.
13. Get verbal promises in writing.
14. Ask telephone solicitors to mail you information rather than discussing it over the telephone.
15. Read and understand sales agreements and contracts before signing. Make sure the terms are the same as those given in the sales presentation, and get a copy of the documents.

---

[1]One scam telemarketing company was caught running a sham better business bureau that consumers could call for information on business opportunity marketers.

16.   Read advertisements and warranties thoroughly, looking for limitations in the small print.
17.   Get an attorney or trusted friend to look over documents and contracts when a substantial amount of money is involved.

Ask Lots of Questions

1.   Ask salespersons to explain advertisements, product operations, warranty terms, and so on.
2.   Ask to see the company's written policies on refunds and exchanges.
3.   Ask to see written warranties and read them. Understand the warranty before buying, such as what it covers, for how long, and who will honor it.
4.   Ask what your legal rights are if you later want to cancel the contract, and get such promises in writing.
5.   Ask the seller to give you time to think before you make up your mind, such as overnight.

Things Never to Do

1.   Never put yourself in situations where you may be set up to be deceived, such as listening to sales pitches on the telephone or going to a motel or a model home to hear a sales presentation.
2.   Never buy on impulse.
3.   Never allow yourself to be persuaded and pressured into hurrying and making a quick decision. Stop and think before buying. Ask yourself the following questions: "Do I really need this?" "Why am I buying this?" "Does something sound a little fishy?" and "Would I be smarter to ask a trusted friend before buying?"
4.   Never take a vehicle home for a one- or two-day tryout because regardless of what the salesperson says, the dealer does not have to take it back should you change your mind.
5.   Never reveal account numbers or partial account numbers of a credit-card, checking account, or social security over the telephone for "identification" or "verification" purposes, unless you initiate the call, have been a satisfied customer of the business in the past, and are certain of the caller's identity.
6.   Never send cash, money orders, or checks to a post office box or anywhere else unless you are positive about the reputation of the company.
7.   Never permit a courier service to come by your home or workplace to pick up cash, money orders, or checks.
8.   Never pay money for a prize.
9.   Never pay money in advance to obtain a loan.
10.   Never pay with cash. Put transactions on a credit card or write a personal check. If you pay with a credit card, you may have the legal right to not pay your credit-card company when you are dissatisfied with poor-quality goods and services purchased from a seller. To cancel a check with a **stop payment order**, you need to telephone your bank before the check is presented there for payment.

Be Informed Before Going Shopping

1. Educate yourself about the product or service you are considering buying and become aware of the likely prices involved. What does it do? What does it not do?
2. Read magazines that contain lots of useful buying information, such as *Consumer Reports*, *Kiplinger's Personal Finance Magazine*, *Money*, *Smart Money*, and *Worth*.
3. While learning about a product you expect to buy, try to make up your mind as much as possible before you actually go shopping.
4. Always try to comparison shop for product features, price, and service at two or more sellers.

Know Your Rights

1. Know your legal rights as a consumer, especially regarding implied warranties, door-to-door rescission, cooling-off periods, charge-back credit regulations, stop-payment check rights, and other remedies to correct wrongs.
2. If you do not like a particular clause in a contract, say so, cross it out, and get the initials of all parties next to the crossed out portion evidencing agreement that the clause is negated.

Be Alert to Signs of Being Ripped Off

1. Be alert to commonly used deceptive practices, such as bait-and-switch advertising.
2. Realize that no legitimate business will ever force you to make a quick decision or send a courier to your home to pick up money; these are not normal business practices.
3. Know that if you have to send money or buy a product, you have not won anything.
4. Realize that high-pressure sales tactics are a strong tipoff that you are the target of a scam.

When in Doubt

1. Realize that nothing is *free*. It is almost impossible to get something for nothing. If the deal sounds too good to be true, it is. Check so-called bargains carefully.
2. Realize that you are more likely to be struck by lightening than be an actual winner of a contest or lottery, therefore, such notification is almost always false.
3. When you think that you might be the target of a ripoff or fraud, ask for advice from an impartial third person. To check the reputation of the seller or caller and to verify claims telephone the Better Business Bureau, State Attorney General's Office, District Attorney's Office, Consumer Fraud section of the Police Department, or an Office of Consumer Affairs.
4. If you want to check the validity of a telemarketing call, ask the caller to mail you printed information. Once received, you can verify it.
5. Once you say "No" to a seller, stick to your position and leave the premises.

6. On important decisions, wait and talk to a trusted friend or impartial advisor.
7. Always try to get a second estimate for expensive repairs, such as on your vehicle or your home.
8. If you must act "right now" to take advantage of a deal, don't because this is a tipoff that you are being scammed.
9. When in doubt about any marketplace transaction, don't!

CONSUMER UPDATE:
Get Your Name Off Mailing Lists and Telemarketing Lists

If desired, write to the Direct Selling Association (Mail Preference Section, P.O. Box 3361, Grand Central Station, 6 East 43rd Street, New York, NY 10017-4609) and ask to have your name removed from computer mailing lists. To get your name removed from telemarketing solicitations write to the Telephone Preference Section at the same address. This takes approximately 3 months.

Ripoffs—and There Are Many—Are *Not* Illegal

Ripoffs are unfair acts of exploitation of consumers in marketplace transactions. Most ripoffs are (believe it or not) legal unless and until they are shown to be frauds. A deal may be legal, but that does not mean it is a good buy. Many ripoffs have consumers paying prices that are too high. Other ripoffs permit little recourse when consumers are caught in an unfavorable situation. While a company's product or service may not be purposefully designed as a ripoff, sometimes the effect on a consumer is exactly that—getting taken advantage of by not getting one's money's worth. Some examples:

*   Paying $6000 for a used car that's really worth only $4000.
*   Signing a contract to "pay a few dollars a month" for a multi-year contract to receive several magazines of marginal interest that you later find out could have been bought at lower prices at a newsstand.
*   Paying $6 a month to lease a push-button telephone from AT&T (instead of buying one for $35).
*   Paying $19.95 for a "special list" of government surplus property that is practically being given away (such as the infamous $44 Jeep), because it is also available free in a publication titled, "Federal Sales Guide", that can be obtained from the General Services Administration.[2]
*   Ordering $49.95 worth of vitamins advertised to "heal cold sores, prevent common colds, reduce hangover symptoms, and increase energy," only to discover that the claims were false.

---

[2]A free copy may be obtained by writing the Consumer Information Center, Pueblo, CO 81009.

- Saying "yes" to a caller asking you to buy light bulbs, trash bags or another household product to benefit disabled persons only to later discover that the price is five to twenty times its value.
- To get your tax refund a little faster, you pay $35 to take out a **refund anticipation loan** from a tax service that files returns electronically. Such rapid refunds have an effective annual interest rate of 80 percent or more.
- Paying $29 for 8 ounces of "Dream Thigh Cream" that is supposed to melt away unsightly fat in days, only to realize that the product does not work.
- Wasting 20 cents per gallon paying for high octane gasoline ($100 a year) when only 5 percent of today's cars require higher octane gas to perform correctly.
- Being persuaded to pay for an extended service contract on a new television, VCR or automobile that pays off less than 2 percent of the time.

Ripoffs against consumers are a bad deal and they are unfair because buyers get little for their money. But, they are not illegal. Ripoffs may be exploitive, unethical, and sometimes unconscionable, but they are generally legal. **Price gouging** is one form of ripoff, and it occurs when a seller charges an exorbitant price in a situation where the buyer has little, if any, option except to pay. For example, consumers staying at a hotel who find that the soda machine down the hall sells Pepsi for $1.25 a can. Having no choice at a sporting event except to pay $4 for popcorn and $3.50 for a drink are similar examples. In essence, the seller who price gouges takes advantage of his market power by exacting large markups. Until a judge says that a particular ripoff or price gouging circumstance is **unconscionable**, such practices are legal.

Negative Option Buying Plans—Ripoffs?

A **negative option plan** is a legal sales agreement between a consumer and a company that periodically delivers merchandise, such as books, compact discs, and videos. The contract obligates the consumer to accept and pay for an item unless he or she notifies the company within a specified time period that a particular item is unwanted. The advertisement may read, "Eight compact discs for $1.00!" When the offer is accepted, the consumer typically agrees to buy additional purchases under the club's negative option plan. If you want the selection offered, you do nothing; it will be shipped to you automatically. If you do not want the selection, you must tell the seller not to send it. The difficulty for consumers occurs when the negative option notice appears at their home address while they are away on vacation, or they simply neglect to return the notice, and it results in them having to pay for goods not wanted. This is known as "stop-us-before-we-mail-you-more-merchandise marketing." Ripoff![3]

A variation of the negative option technique is the **soft-sell** used by some of the nation's best-known companies who offer you either a free trial membership or complimentary copies of magazines. When the trial period is over, they assume that you want the membership or subscription service because you have not contacted them to say that you do not want it to continue. Then they bill you for an entire year. Companies

---

[3]Once you fulfill the commitment to purchase so many items, you can request that you be switched to a positive-option plan. Then you get the catalog but do not have the obligation to return a postcard unless you want to purchase something.

selling long-distance telephone service sometimes use the same sales technique. This is trickery.

Rental Car Insurance—A Ripoff Industry?

Beware of the rental car industry because it is full of ripoffs, particularly in three areas: rental prices, hidden fees, and insurance.

Rental Car Prices that "Take You for a Ride"

Rental car prices are very confusing because the industry likes it that way. In many instances, you can get the best rental car price (even lower than the corporate rate) by ignoring the so-called discounts and telephoning around to make some cost comparisons. Once you have a price quote and reservation in hand, simply show up at the rental car counter of a competitor and ask for a better price. This is known as the **walk-up price**. Try it and you will get a better price or a nicer vehicle, or both.

Hidden Fees

The typical rental car company assesses umpteen fees in the small print of the contract, such as charges for refueling, exceeding mileage limits, returning the vehicle late, city surcharges, airport surcharges, additional driver fees, under-age surcharges, child's car seat fees, bike rack charges, transporting fees to take customers from airports to rental offices, and late fees. These charges may add as much as 40 percent to the overall bill, yet they are never mentioned in the advertised rental rates.

Overpriced, Unneeded Insurance

In addition, rental car companies often use questionable selling techniques to peddle horribly overpriced insurance to consumers that often do not need the coverage. **Rental car insurance** are contracts sold through rental car companies designed to protect the consumer from bills if a rented vehicle is damaged or stolen. Rental car insurance has been called "a classic consumer ripoff" by the U.S. Public Interest Research Group (PIRG) because the coverage sold, sometimes using high-pressure sales techniques, is very expensive ($1.25 to $13.95 per day) and often duplicates the customer's private insurance coverage.

Rental car companies generally sell five types of overpriced insurance to consumers: (1) **Collision-damage waiver (CDW)** pays if your rental car is damaged or stolen (and most drivers know it as collision insurance). This coverage has been banned in New York and Illinois, which wisely restrict the liability of drivers to $100 and $200. And, contrary to impressions received by many consumers, CDW does not cover bodily injury or personal property damage. (2) **Loss of use (LOU) waiver**, sometimes called **loss-damage waiver**, pays the rental car company for each day that the damaged rental car is in the repair shop instead of being rented to someone else. (3) **Personal accident insurance (PAI)** that pays for injuries to the driver or passengers. (4) **Personal effects insurance** or **personal effects coverage (PEC)** that protects against the theft of any personal items left in the vehicle. (5) **Additional liability insurance** which is an umbrella policy that provides up to $1 million for bodily injury and property damage caused to others in an accident.

Each of these insurance coverages run from $1 to $14 a day. Many uninformed consumers wind up paying these exorbitant charges that duplicate the coverage already provided by an employer's insurance (if the rental is for business use), available on their personal automobiles and homes, or provided automatically through credit cards and motor club memberships.

Smart consumers should take the following actions:

1. Telephone your insurance agent and find out if your personal auto policy covers the potential types of losses that are possible when renting a vehicle. Obtain a copy of your insurance policy (with the appropriate section marked by the agent) to show if needed; a copy is required for overseas rentals. Also confirm that your homeowner's (or renter's) insurance policy covers theft of items from rental cars.

2. Telephone your credit-card companies to inquire about their automatic **secondary collision-damage** and **loss-of-use coverage** that provides insurance when a vehicle is rented using their credit card. Some credit-card companies, such as American Express, MasterCard, and Visa, pay for the portion of damage to a wrecked rental car not covered by your personal auto insurance.

3. If your present auto insurance policy does not provide adequate protection, ask your insurance agent to add a **rider** to your policy to cover collision and loss-of-use costs in rental cars. The cost? Only $20 to $30 a *year*—a whole lot cheaper than the rental car companies' daily fees! Also, be certain that you have liability insurance that covers rental cars.

The only people who should consider purchasing insurance coverage sold through rental car companies are consumers without auto insurance, those who are underinsured,[4] foreign visitors, and people who do not want to report a rental-car accident to their own insurance companies.

Credit- and Debit-Card Registration Services—Ripoffs?

In case of lost credit and debit cards, the cardholder should notify debit and credit card companies to avoid legal liability for fraud and misuse. Some firms sell a **card registration service** that registers all the credit- and debit-card numbers of a consumer and arranges for cancellation and replacement of any lost or stolen credit cards. For $25 to $60 a year, you only need to make one telephone call to report all card losses. While this may be a useful service to those consumers who do not keep a record of their credit cards, this is not an efficient purchase decision.[5]

---

[4]Be aware that some personal auto policies do not extend coverage to rental cars when the policyholder is on a business trip, although many such business travelers are covered by an employer's policy.

[5]The Fair Credit Reporting Act (See Chapter 5) limits cardholder's liability to $50 in the event of a fraudulent use, and most creditors waive all costs in the event of fraudulent usage. In addition, every card issuer has a telephone number (most are toll-free) that you can call yourself to report a lost or stolen card and to get a replacement card. Further, almost all renter's and homeowner's insurance policies provide automatic coverage of up to $500 for lost or stolen credit and debit cards.

Health Products—Ripoffs?

Health products are an especially appealing areas for schemes since most people want to be in shape but few want to work to become trim and healthy. As a result, people are quite susceptible to health-related misrepresentations offering quasi-scientific claims like: "Regrow a full head of hair with foreign tonic!" "End arthritis pain with this stylish copper bracelet!" "Scrub away cellulite with ancient ingredient!" "Bleaching cream brightens your skin!" "Spray Slender Mist into your mouth to depress your appetite!" "Weight-loss secret from the Orient!" "Melt fat away while you sleep!" "Miracle cure for cancer!" "Bee pollen formula cures herpes!" Such advertisements ask for money and promise "money-back" guarantees.

Opting for such unproven pills, potions, drinks, gadgets, and programs may waste precious time that could be used for proven remedies and therapies. You can only be sure of four things in health quackery: (1) the product will not do what is promised, (2) your health may be harmed, (3) you will have wasted your money, and (4) you will not get a refund.

Weight-Loss Plans—Ripoffs?

About 50 million Americans will go on a diet this year. While some will succeed in taking off weight, very few—an estimated five percent—will manage to keep all of it off in the long run. The only way to lose weight and keep it off is to eat fewer calories or use more calories. This can be done by eating less food, exercising more, or both. There is no magic bullet to eliminate fat from the system.

Quackery succeeds in this $30 billion industry because there are so many customers who are willing to try some new diet book, pill, cream, or something they think might work. Ideas that do not keep the weight off include diets that focus on one particular food, such as grapefruit; pills, such as starch blockers, advertised as diet aids; electrical muscle stimulators; body wraps, preceded by application of some cream or lotion; and pills and capsules that promise to burn, block, flush or otherwise obliterate fat. Rapid weight-loss programs can jeopardize a dieter's health, as well as one's wallet. Last year General Nutrition Centers, Inc., the largest retailer of nutritional supplements in the U.S. was fined $2.4 million to settle federal allegations about deceptive claims on over 40 products sold in its 1,500 stores. Also last year the Federal Trade Commission (FTC) accused some of the makers of very low liquid-diet programs (New Directions, UWCC Permance Program, HMR Fasting Program) of falsely claiming that their products were risk free; the ads were stopped.

Commercial weight-loss programs, such as Jenny Craig, Nutri-System, and Weight Watchers are not very successful at helping people keep weight off either. A National Institute of Health panel reviewing industry-supplied data found that dropout rates go as high as 80 percent. While many commercial programs help people lose ten percent of their body weight, they all fail over the long term. That's why the Federal Trade Commission recently filed complaints against most of the well known diet program companies for false advertising.

Disclosure is the solution. Weight-loss centers should be required to provide clear and comparable information about a program's cost, length, effectiveness, and safety, as well as the qualifications of the staff. This is a multi-billion dollar industry that offers consumers products and service that do not do what people expect.

CONSUMER UPDATE:
Job-Search Companies—Ripoffs?

Unscrupulous sellers also take advantage of consumers who are seeking employment. Because people may be experiencing difficulty in locating a job, they sometimes turn to private employment agencies. The process works like this: The person completes an application form and signs a contract to register interest in certain types of jobs. The **job-search company** then provides some career counseling, helps improve the person's resume, and tries to locate suitable job positions for which the person can interview. Most headhunters, executive recruiters, management consultants, and outplacement firms are reputable businesses; some are not.

The way some of these companies make money is to charge a fee, often $500, $1000, $2000, or more, for trying to place someone in an employment position. Ads tucked away in classified sections entice consumers by claiming they can open hidden jobs or boasting about secret connections, sometimes with overseas employers. Most of the disreputable firms offer nothing more than sloppily done resumes and outdated lists of corporate contacts. Some firms go through the motions of forwarding your resume in an attempt to help you find a job; others require that you send out your resumes. The small print in the signed contract spells out the limitations, such as printing costs are an extra charge and that the firms do not guarantee clients jobs. The job seeker must pay any remaining fees "when the person accepts a job of his or her choice," no matter how it was found.

The unethical career counselors make big promises about getting job interviews, sometimes even charging a surcharge of 10 percent to guarantee a new job within 6 months; then they do not deliver. Most legitimate employment agencies collect no fees in advance from those looking for work. They only get paid if and when the person finds employment for which the agency arranged an interview. Reputable agencies typically collect their entire fee from the employer, not the new employee. Some states prohibit fees from being paid ahead of time before a job is taken; others prohibit employment firms from collecting fees from employees.

Telephone Company Ripoffs

The telephone business is competitive, but unfortunately for consumers in some corners of the market companies are competing not to offer the lowest rates. Instead, they are offering various telephone services for the highest prices they can charge.

Alternate Operator Services

Alternate operator services (AOS) are a relatively new segment of the telecommunications industry. AOS companies are pushing up the prices of long-distance telephone services for consumers who make credit-card and third-party billing calls. After buying some switching equipment and hiring some operators, these companies lease long-distance lines from the major carriers and enter into contracts with businesses such as hotels, motels, airports, hospitals, and universities to resell standard intrastate and interstate long-distance telephone services. In many cases, the AOS company charges exorbitant prices, often from two to ten times the traditional cost of making a long-distance telephone call through companies such as AT&T, MCI, or U.S. Sprint.[6] This occurs even if you call collect or charge the call to your telephone credit card. The approximately 90 AOS companies share their profits with the owners of the businesses with whom they contract. Today, one in six publicly available phones is an AOS telephone.

If you are ripped off by these charges, you can complain to your local telephone company and refuse to pay the exorbitant amounts charged. The local companies, which are required to do the billing for the AOS companies, can offer credits to complaining customers.

A Federal Communications Commission (FCC) order requires AOS companies in interstate commerce to inform users of the services how much calls will cost. They must put identification on or near the telephone. The FCC also ordered them to not block callers from using other long-distance carriers, if the customer requests. So far, the FCC has chosen not to regulate rates. Consequently, if you are in a motel and are going to make a lot of telephone calls, you might consider making your calls from a public telephone. When in doubt, dial 0 to reach a local telephone company operator or 00 to reach a long-distance operator and ask about the cost of the call.

Coin-Operated and Credit-Card Telephones

Calls placed from the nation's nearly 2 million pay telephones are now deregulated. Owners of premises that have pay telephones receive a commission (usually 15 percent) on the local and long-distance charges that callers ring up. Companies are selling their new telephones and contracts to hotels, motels, airports, truck stops, drugstores, gas stations, universities, hospitals, and prisons. The premise owner's incentive is to choose the telephone equipment that charges the highest rates. The marketplace does not promote competition when the owner of the telephone is not its primary user.

Inside Home Telephone Wire Maintenance

Another telephone company ripoff is the price charged for inside wire maintenance and repairs. Local telephone companies charge between $1 and $2 a month, often lumped into the monthly service amount on your bill. If there is a service problem with the telephone wire inside your home, the telephone company will repair it.

On average, you will need this service once every 15 to 20 years. For every dollar collected by the telephone companies, they keep about 85 cents for profit, thus, the price is astronomical compared to the economic value of the service. About 2/3 of telephone customers have maintenance plans, and about 1/3 of them do not even know that they are paying for the plans.

The state government regulatory agencies presume that this service is competitive and that competition will regulate prices of services offered. In some states, customers must affirmatively act in order not to be billed for inside wire maintenance services. This is called an "**op out plan**."

---

[6]Consumers in most states who need assistance in dealing with their telephone shopping requirements may call the Tele-Consumer Hotline (800-332-1124) for help. Supported by industry and consumer groups, the organization answers questions about phone services and mails consumers fact sheets. For $2, Telecommunications Research and Action Center (202-408-1400) will send you a cost comparison of the major plans; TRAC, P.O. Box 12038, Washington, D.C. 20005.

Some Long-Distance Telephone Calls

Those who frequently make long-distance calls (more than $10 a month) should consider signing up for one of the various "discount" programs advertised by the long-distance telephone companies. Only 30 percent of households have signed on, perhaps because of the confusion associated with the rates and the advertising. The companies often offer cash and free long-distance minutes to switch from one carrier to another. Every year about 16 percent of U.S. households switch telephone companies.[7]

Another alternative is to buy service from a **long-distance reseller**. These are firms that buy long-distance time in bulk from the major carriers and sell those minutes to consumers. You may not recognize these companies as household names, but their prices are low.

The person who makes only a few long-distance telephone calls per month pays the highest rates when compared to others. Historically, low-volume telephone users have had little choice since only heavy users of telephones are given preferential rates. Now they can use **telephone dumb cards** which are low-tech telephone cards that permit the use of a preset number of prepaid telephone minutes at a flat rate per minute. Calls made on a prepaid card are usually lower than dialing zero and using a credit card, but only if you keep calls short (under four minutes) and make them during the day, when standard rates are the highest. Avoid getting ripped off by being aware that prices vary widely, generally from 60 cents per minute all the way down to 10 cents.

CONSUMER UPDATE:
Please Telephone "1-900-RIP-OFF"

The over-the-phone information services industry is growing rapidly. Numerous firms promote services that are desired by somebody out there and accessible by telephone. Most services are outrageously overpriced. People pay money to listen to recordings and/or talk with others about astrology, murder confessions, sex, engine overhauls, Easter bunnies, and chat with well-known people, like baseball player Jose Canseco or the Vatican's Pope. You can even play a round of "Let's Make a Deal". Although not illegal, when the bills get high, family members are dismayed when they discover that someone in their household spent $100 or $400 last month dialing 900- and 976-numbers. One observer wrote of these numbers, "1-900-RIP-OFF."

Insurance (Health, Cancer, and Life)—Ripoffs?

Advertisements in the Sunday newspapers, in various magazines, and on television make fantastic claims about the need for insurance protection against the likelihood of death, cancer, and other dread diseases. Usually a celebrity, movie star, or athlete makes the promotion. And they may get $100,000 or more for one day of taping commercials.

---

[7]The illegal practice of **slamming**, the unauthorized switching of a customer's long-distance telephone service, continues in the industry with more than 3000 annual complaints to the Federal Communications Commission.

All too often these people are pitching nearly worthless health and life insurance policies. Suggestions that, "One out of three people will get cancer" and that "The average hospital stay for cancer victims is 2 months" are pure fabrications. Companies tell such lies to create illusions and fears that they promise to fix. They may claim that, "Cash benefits are paid directly to you" or "No one can be turned down for life insurance." Then they set artificial time limits, such as, "You must apply by October 15!" or, buried in the small print, "No benefits for two years." Mail-order insurance is largely a world of schlock.

The products being advertised are called **supplemental health insurance** and **term life insurance**. The ads mention the initial benefits, such as guaranteeing acceptance and providing $10,000 to $50,000 in life insurance coverage, and then fail to tell crucial details—what several insurance commissioners describe as serious misrepresentations and omissions. The state of Washington has tough advertising standards and has prohibited the broadcast of commercials from many of these companies, arguing that they were "false, deceptive, or misleading advertisements."

This insurance is poorly explained and quite expensive compared with policies sold by local insurance agents. Such advertised policies often contain severe restrictions and limitations on the coverage provided.

Robert Hunter, insurance expert for the Consumer Federation of America, says that most of these life insurance policies pay nothing if the policyholder dies within the first two years. Upon the non-accidental death of a 60-year-old man, these policies generally pay about $1500. To keep the premiums level, the benefits also drop further with age. For example, the policy advertised by one television actor pays only $500 at age 65 and only $350 at age 70. A study by the state of Wisconsin found that only three policyholders in 1000 collect in the first seven years.

These ads continue partly because most state insurance commissioners and legislators are reluctant to write regulations that are strict enough to get them off the air. Compared to standard policies in the industry, such mass-marketed policies are a ripoff—you pay way too much for what you receive. People who have life insurance coverage through their employment or who already have a private policy do not need mail-order policies.

Most advertised health policies duplicate coverage that consumers already have, restrict the conditions for paying a claim, do not pay for preexisting conditions for the first two years the policy is in effect, pay minuscule benefits, and pay nothing until the insured has been in the hospital 14 days. These types of health insurance policies simply do not provide the insurance protection that consumers think they are getting. Such policies are just ripoffs. Further, the purchase of inadequate insurance coverage lulls many consumers into falsely thinking that they are properly insured when, in fact, they are not.

Consumers who have major medical coverage as part of their health insurance plan are adequately covered for illness, including cancer. Major medical coverage can be added to most health insurance policies, if it is not there already, for perhaps another $30 per month.

The National Association of Insurance Commissions (NAIC) reports an industry-wide payout ratio of 37 percent for mail-order health insurance policies. A **payout ratio** is the proportion of premium dollars paid out as benefits to insurance purchasers. That means, industry-wide for these types of policies, for every dollar paid in premiums policyholders only receive 37 cents through claims. This horrible return does not come close to the NAIC payout ratio standard of 65 percent for policies sold directly to consumers and 75 percent for policies sold to groups. Policies with low pay-out ratios are ripoffs. If you need a policy, see a local source for insurance, examine the coverage, get confirmation on the payout ratio (from the state insurance commission, if necessary), read the policy, and compare prices.

A LIST OF PROBABLE RIPOFFS

Ripoff	The Promise Explained	The Reality
Fake Checks	The check made out to you; also stamped "This is not a check"	Can only be used to purchase over-priced products from a catalog
False Gold and Platinum Credlt Cards	$49.95 membership fee for a "similar" card	Can only be used to purchase over-priced products from a catalog
Low-Interest Credit Card	$99 permits you to transfer other credit balances to the low-interest card	If a real Visa or Mastercard is received, the rate will rise later; most often the consumer receives a booklet explaining how to apply for a card
Unordered Merchandise	Company mails something with the hope that receiving party will pay	You may keep anything shipped to you and then you can assess the sender storage fees and charges to return the goods
Phony Bills	Bill comes in the mail, perhaps for a deceased relative	A likely fraud; ask for copy of a signature on order form
Unclaimed Funds	Letter on official-looking stationery saying a "routine audit" has determined that you are owed money; send $35 for processing fees	Only scam artists charge processing fees
Going Out-of-Business Sales	Sign looks legitimate and the store seems full of goods	Lots of poor quality merchandise brought in when liquidating a legitimate business; must be licensed
Home Improvements and Repairs	Promises high-quality work and must have X dollars as a down payment	Unlicensed repairpersons take the money and run; sometimes they just do shoddy work with poor materials
Free Baby Photos	Company offers free baby photos but pressures the consumer to buy expensive photo packages	Take the free photos and pay an inexpensive service charge; skip the package deal
Magazines	Young people sell magazines pretending that they are working their way through school	Either one overpays for the subscription or the "salesperson" disappears with the money (continued)

A LIST OF PROBABLE RIPOFFS

Ripoff	The Promise Explained	The Reality
Vacuum Cleaners, Sewing Machines, Encyclopedias, and Fire Extinguishing Systems	Usually legitimate door-to-door sales of consumer goods	Often horribly overpriced and the merchandise is not needed
Campground Memberships	Consumer signs 25-year lease to use same plot in campground for two weeks every year	Overpriced and not really needed; companies often go bankrupt
Health Club Spas, Weight-Loss Center, Martial Arts Facilities, and Dance Lessons	Consumer signs a contract for a series of services and some success is quickly achieved	Firm often cannot deliver what was promised; many companies go bankrupt
Freezer Meat	Very low advertised price for frozen meat	Meat sold at "hanging weight" before fat is cut off; poor quality meat is substituted when packed
Frozen-Food Freezer Plan	Bulk purchase of meat delivered regularly and it includes purchase of freezer	Freezer is overpriced; quality of food is excellent in the beginning, then declines
Degree Mills	Sell diplomas for a price with an extreme minimum of on-site educational experiences	Such diplomas do not meet the standards of the genuine accrediting associations
Term Papers	Sell term papers on any topic	Poorly written and referenced essays that if turned in to a school will result in disciplinary action
Song Writing and Vanity Publishing	Promise to publish your work and you can expect to make royalties on the sales	Firm collects substantial up-front fee that pays the cost of production; profits never exist
Phony Bank Examiner	Asks for help in identifying teller who is embezzling funds by having consumer make withdrawal from that teller	The receipt from the "bank examiner" is worthless because he really does not work for the bank
Pigeon Drop	Person "finds" money in a bag or envelope and offers to share it with a nearby consumer	After taking "pigeon's" good-faith money to a lawyer's office for safe-keeping, the bag of money is switched; a partner is often used and the lawyer does not exist
Work at Home	Advertisements for huge profits for at-home tasks	Products completed at home often refused by seller; sometimes the "deal" requires consumer to run similar ads to get money from other consumers

Fraud Also Exists in the Marketplace

A **deception** is a form of trickery involving the selling of goods or services to consumers. Efforts to stop consumer deceptions depend greatly on the definition used by the Federal Trade Commission. This is because the Uniform Commercial Code, as well as the deceptive practices acts in many states, accept the federal definition. Historically, the FTC defined **deception** broadly as, "a tendency or capacity to deceive." Using this standard to protect all consumers, the FTC did not have to prove actual deception or definite injury to consumers. Since 1983, the FTC more narrowly defined **deception** as a material "representation, omission, or practice that is likely to mislead the consumer acting reasonably in the circumstances, to the consumer's detriment." **Material information** is information that is important to reasonable consumers and which is likely to affect their choice of a product or service, such as express statements about the product's cost, safety, quality, effectiveness, performance, durability, and warranty protection. This newer definition of deception places an increased burden of proof on consumers and government consumer protection agencies.

Legally, **fraud** (or **deceit**) is a deliberate deception practiced in order to secure an unfair or unlawful gain or advantage where the seller intentionally misleads the buyer. Here the buyer must have relied on the word of the seller as being true. Fraud comes about when a knowing deception causes the consumer to enter into a transaction, and by doing so the consumer suffers a financial loss.

Several elements must be proven to show fraud, and this is why it is so difficult to prove a case of consumer fraud in a court of law:

- false representation,
- knowledge that the facts stated were untrue,
- intention to deceive the victim,
- actual belief on the part of the victim, who is ignorant of the falsity of the representation, that the false representations are true, and
- damages suffered by reliance on the untruths.

A **misrepresentation** is the reporting of something by words or conduct in a mistaken or false manner that is not in accordance with the facts. This includes relevant omissions as well. Someone making a misrepresentation with an intentional false statement of fact—generally made as an inducement to contract—is committing fraud. As noted, however, proving fraud is difficult since it requires the speaker's knowledge of the falsity of the statement and an intent to deceive.

More often what happens in marketplace transactions is that a seller innocently, but mistakenly, represents something to be true that is not. When such negligent, innocent, mistaken, and unintentional false statements are made as an inducement to contract, it generally is considered in common law to be an instance of "constructive fraud." Why? Because such inducements to contract are highly unfair to consumers. Since the difficult burden of proving fraud is upon the consumer and since such proof is difficult to show, consumers can turn to state and local government for help—the office of consumer affairs that has the authority to pursue such cases.

CONSUMER UPDATE:
Classified Advertisements Are Full of Lies

Classified advertisements placed in newspapers and at the back of magazines are almost never investigated for truthfulness by the owner of the publication. As a result, this form of advertising attracts unscrupulous sellers.

Popular scams regularly seen in classified ads include:

- Overseas employment opportunities (you pay an **up-front fee** [also called an advance fee] for a list of names of potential employers who are not hiring)
- Loans for consumers with poor or no credit history (advance fees are charged, and if victim gets a loan it will be at a very high interest rate)
- Earn money by working at home (promoter sells overpriced goods for victim to work on and then does not buy them back when completed)
- Phony education scholarships (victim pays for a worthless outdated book listing scholarships for which he or she will not qualify)

You can be confident of two things when responding to a classified advertisement: (1) the reality will not be the same as what was advertised, and (2) you will not get your money back, even though the promoter "guaranteed" that refunds would be available.

All states have consumer protection acts that protect consumers against deliberate frauds, and some states base their definition on the one used by the Federal Trade Commission. The FTC's standard for deception rests on what a *reasonable consumer* would do, which is a rather narrow perception. Fortunately, most states are more generous in their definition of fraud than the federal government in that they provide that practices are fraudulent if they have a "capacity or tendency to deceive," even if they do not actually deceive. Thus, the state may find practices to be deceptive or unfair "if the ignorant, the unthinking, and the credulous" could be deceived. States with such a broad definition have the power to prohibit marketplace behaviors that are deceptive *or* unfair. Moreover, the broader definition in many jurisdictions helps protect all consumers, as well as particular consumers who might not be shielded under the more narrow standard—e.g. children, the elderly, and those whose first language is not English. States with the broader definition do a better job of protecting consumers than those with a narrow definition.

Untrue, Deceptive, and Misleading Advertising Also Exists

Deceptive practices are considered fraudulent, and are against the law, when the statement, omission, or practice is likely to mislead a consumer. In the area of advertising, for example, the Federal Trade Commission can find that silent omissions are materially deceptive when sellers tell only half truths. The FTC decides advertising deception on a case-by-case basis. In states where the statute more broadly protects consumers from deception, the state attorney general can fight deceptive advertising that escapes the authority of the FTC.

Bait and Switch Advertising Is Illegal

Bait and switch advertising is defined as an alluring but insincere offer to sell a high-quality product or service at a bargain price that the advertiser does not intend or want to sell. This idea is to lure a great number of shoppers and sell them a substitute. The seller then pushes an inferior substitute at an exorbitant price. The bait is the product or service advertised at the apparently low sale price in order to attract the customer into the store. The well-meaning consumer wants to take advantage of the bargain, but the salesperson almost steadfastly refuses to sell the product, for such reasons as..."There aren't any left," "You can't get delivery for 3 months," "Many people who bought it aren't satisfied," and "The product just isn't very good." Instead, the salesperson persuades the customer to buy a similar but more expensive item. This is the switch. Many retailers, such as mattress sellers, use bait and switch tactics. One reason why bait and switch works is that once consumers have experienced the search costs of shopping, they may not bother to look elsewhere.

Do not confuse bait and switch with **trading up**. This is a perfectly proper sales technique where a salesperson encourages a customer to buy a higher-priced item in order for the salesperson to make a bigger sale, earn a larger commission, and/or better fill the customers needs and wants. Sometimes there is a fine line between trading up and bait and switch selling practices.

Puffery Is *Not* Illegal

One must not jump to the conclusion that a fraud has occurred whenever a false statement is made, however. Loose statements and exaggerations concerning the quality, value, or goodness of a product may be considered sales talk or puffery. **Puffing involves exaggerated statements and opinions by a seller as to the quality or value of an item offered for sale that is not made as a representation of fact.** Puffing is not considered fraud in the eyes of the law, since everyone knows a seller will tend to exaggerate a bit. Sellers are allowed some leeway in describing attributes of their products, and such overstatements are typically considered innocent misrepresentations. Statements such as, "This is the finest-quality wool coat money can buy," "This is the most powerful vacuum cleaner made in America," and "There is not a bit of rust on this five-year-old car" should not be taken seriously by consumers.

Economic Frauds of Large Corporations

Economic frauds largely hidden from the public eye steal billions every year. Many are instances of **price fixing**, where competing sellers interfere with market forces to control prices and/or supply. The dollar loss for economic frauds in this country has been estimated by the Commerce Committee of the U.S. Senate to be over $40 billion annually. Some of the world's largest and most respected companies have been caught fixing prices or otherwise behaving in horribly unethical ways. Below are listed a number of illustrations of recent economic frauds perpetrated by large corporations, names you will immediately recognize.

- The Miracle Ear Clarifier (Bausch & Comb) advertised for years that its products "filtered out unwanted background noise." This year it was assessed a $2.75 million civil penalty by the Federal Trade Commission for making deceptive claims.

- The Federal Trade Commission reached a settlement this year with NordicTrack, a major maker of indoor exercise equipment, for making false claims about how much weight one could lose by using its cross-country ski exercise machine.

- Mrs. Fields Cookies, Inc. agreed to settle charges by the FTC that advertising a cookie line as "low fat" was false for two of the cookies in the line. Eskimo Pie settled a similar calorie content false advertising case with the FTC.

- First Brands, Inc., the makers of STP, paid $888,000 last year to settle an FTC complaint that they were making false and unsubstantiated claims for motor oil additives.

- Reader's Digest agreed this year to pay $40 million to settle a lawsuit that claimed a subsidiary bilked schools out of millions of dollars by monopolizing the magazine subscription fundraising business.

- Sears, Roebuck and Company settled charges a couple years ago that it cheated customers by performing shoddy and unnecessary work at its auto repair shops across the nation. The California Department of Consumer Affairs, which originated the investigation, found that Sears oversold auto repair work 90 percent of the time, with unneeded repairs averaging $223 per car. The $15 million settlement with those who filed 15 class action lawsuits requires giving coupons worth $50 to thousands of customers. Sears also has retained an outside group to make unannounced "shopping audits" of its auto centers.

- All brands of infant formula recently came under a price-fixing investigation by the Federal Trade Commission. The three dominant manufacturers have 90 percent of the market. The government argues that they have done little or no competitive advertising and their products have been priced almost identically for a decade.

Telemarketing and Mail Scams

Several types of ripoffs, misrepresentations, and deceptions regularly use mail and telecommunication as ways to reach consumers.

Mail Fraud

The Postal Service reports that the average American gets 250 pieces of junk mail, mostly advertising materials, every year. That amounts to over 40 pounds of catalogs, political flyers, charitable solicitations, sweepstakes packets, magazine subscription offers, coupons, food samples, investment opportunities, and the like. This is five times the amount of junk mail received by consumers in any other country. More than half of all adults in the United States purchase something by mail every year, and millions of them are victims of mail fraud.

Mail fraud, according to the 1872 Postal Service Law, is the use of the mail for "any scheme to defraud, or for obtaining money or property by means of false or fraudulent pretenses." Mail fraud is one of the top five areas of consumer complaints to government agencies.

Mail frauds work because people frequently do not recognize them as deceitful until it is too late. Some people are victims because of that common human weakness, an inability to resist an apparent bargain. Others are victimized because they lack knowledge. Deceptive mail-order schemes often appear to be a good deal, an excellent business opportunity, or a chance to make a quick buck. To avoid mail fraud, the consumer has to know it when he or she sees it. The most familiar tactic in mail fraud is misleading or false advertisements by which the perpetrators use the mails to lure consumers into their scams. Consumers are led to believe that they are getting a really good deal, perhaps something free. The consumer unwittingly puts up money expecting a product of excellent quality, but instead receives something of poor quality and of little or no value.

Lack of physical contact with victims makes identification of mail-order crooks difficult. Also, the geographic distance between the victim and the perpetrators makes apprehension more difficult and expensive. Because of the usual small amount of money that is lost, many consumers are willing to chalk up the loss to experience rather than report it to authorities. Still, the U.S. Postal Service manages to obtain convictions against about 1000 swindlers each year.

Telemarketing to Get Your Money

The U.S. Office of Consumer Affairs reports that over 140,000 telemarketing firms are in operation and that about 10 percent of them deliberately practice fraud. The National Fraud Information Center estimates one-half of all telemarketing calls to consumers' homes are from crooks trying to defraud the public. Solicitors of all kinds telephone more than 18 million Americans every day. According to the Federal Trade Commission, telemarketers focus about two thirds of their calls on the elderly and the general public; they also target investors and small business owners.

The most popular telemarketing frauds are sweepstakes and contests, charitable solicitations (also known as **telefunding**), lotteries for wireless cable and cellular phones, fraudulent investments, business opportunities, precious gems, refund companies, living trusts, timeshares, buying club memberships, water treatment units, travel certificates, and vacations. Telemarketing continues to be one of the top five areas of consumer complaints to government agencies.

Telemarketing is selling a product or service over the telephone. Many worthwhile products are marketed using telecommunications, such as up-to-date financial news, stock quotations, insurance company financial-soundness ratings, legal aid by the minute, sample music cuts, and critiques of latest films.

At the same time, almost anything can be sold by unscrupulous sellers over the telephone, including bad deals on prize offers, penny stocks, office supplies, magazine subscriptions, credit repair, job opportunities, precious metals, travel packages, art, business ventures, cellular telephone lotteries, travel clubs, coupon books, and quasi-charities. The term **telefrauds** describes what unscrupulous telephone salespeople do—use the telephone for non-legitimate sales. Many people describe the proliferation of legitimate and unscrupulous telemarketing techniques as **junk calls**.

Both good and bad telemarketing sellers use 800-numbers and 900-numbers to market goods and services. An **800-number** is a toll-free long-distance telephone line; **888-numbers** now are also toll-free. About 40 percent of all long-distance calls are made to 800-numbers. A **900-number** is a caller-paid long distance service that allow consumers and businesses to access information over the telephone. (Local callers dial **976-numbers** the same way.) The caller pays for telephone numbers with 900 and 976 prefixes. Watch out when responding to advertisements that give an area code that seems unfamiliar because it may be an international number that is long-distance, and the toll charges are likely to be enormous.

One indicted telemarketing promoter was quoted as saying that, "If you ask 100 people any question, at least 3 of them will say 'yes'. With the right pitch, you can sell anything over the telephone." The American Association of Retired Persons estimates that telephone marketing swindlers cheat American consumers out of $40 billion annually. The North American Securities Association reports that consumers lose $1 million an hour to investment scams promoted over the telephone. Senator Richard H. Bryan says that the concept of "reach out and cheat someone" clearly applies to the telemarketing industry.

Many telemarketing scams originate out of **boiler rooms**. This is a place (historically in the basement next to the heating unit) where a number of people use high-pressure telephone sales tactics to sell stock, commodities, petroleum partnerships, unmined gold, re-opened oil wells, land, travel clubs, and other so-called opportunities. The National Fraud Information Center (800-876-7060), coordinated by the National Consumers League, can advise you with information, referral services and assistance should you have questions. One popular telemarketing prize is a "$100 savings certificate," that, rather than being a U.S. Government Series EE savings bond, is a "savings coupon" good towards the purchase of merchandise from a small catalog of overpriced goods.

Sweepstakes

A **sweepstakes** is an advertising or promotional device by which prizes are awarded to participating consumers by chance, with no purchase or entry fee required in order to win. One's chances of winning are determined by the number of participants and the number of prizes to be awarded. Some sweepstakes sponsors, especially those who are marketing products and services, put up all the prize money themselves. Marketers-both legitimate and fraudulent—use sweepstakes because they are extremely effective in generating attention for the sponsoring companies. People should *never* have to order something or pay a fee to enter and win a sweepstakes.

In contrast to a sweepstakes, a **lottery** is a promotional device by which prizes are awarded to members of the public by chance but which requires some form of payment in order to participate. Here the participants' contributions form a fund to be awarded as a prize to the winner or winners. Only states and certain exempt charitable organizations may conduct lotteries; all other lotteries are illegal.

The highly publicized sweepstakes by Publisher's Clearinghouse, Reader's Digest, and American Family Publishers are legitimate, and they also sell lots of magazines. These reputable companies sell magazine subscriptions through direct mail, and a proven way of getting people to return their forms is to run a sweepstakes. Millions enter the contest and some also order magazines. By the way, being named a "finalist" means that you sent in a previous entry; it does not improve your odds. By federal law, competitors in sweepstakes competitions must have an equal chance of winning. This means, for example, regardless of whether or not you purchased magazines through a Publisher's Clearinghouse offer. Also, a sweepstakes sponsor must disclose the odds of winning.

These well known companies do give away all the prizes, although you probably will not win. Publisher's Clearinghouse odds are typical; the chances of winning $1000 to $60,000 are 1 in 122.5 million; you have 1 chance in 12.5 million of winning $500, 1 chance in 4.9 million of winning $100, 1 chance in 2.45 million of winning $50, and 1 chance in 2869 of winning $5. Columbia University statistics professor Herbert Robbins calculated the odds. Comedian David Letterman once accurately joked that, "the odds of winning Publisher's Clearinghouse are about the same as not entering at all."

Some fraudulent operators have been calling consumers telling them that they have won the Reader's Digest Sweepstakes, or another sweepstakes. Then they say that the winnings may not be released until a cash or certified check in the amount of $500, or even $10,000, was sent by overnight courier or wire service to cover shipping, handling, and taxes. The bad guys even send a courier service to the conned consumer's home to pick up the money, which will never be seen again.

A variation of the fraudulent sweepstakes occurs when the winners (or should that be "losers"?) are invited to join a sweepstakes club, perhaps for only $5 a month. The "winners" are promised that the company will use its "special formula" to identify the sweepstakes—that are held monthly—that offer them the greatest odds of winning; then the company signs them up. Victims—often the elderly—are later talked into joining a number of similar clubs. Losses of $1000 to $3000—a month!—are common. Recently, a scam artist had his 42 sweepstakes companies closed by the federal government, but not before he grossed $82 million in just one year.

Prizes and Free Gifts

Nearly all consumers in the United States have received (and probably will again in the future) at least one official-looking "notice" or telephone call stating that they are the "guaranteed winner" of one of the "following four prizes worth thousands of dollars," including a glamorous vacation and a new automobile. Such claims are almost always lies. Prizes and free gifts offered by sellers are simply come-ons. Such sellers simply want to interest consumers in something. Legitimate businesses use these marketing techniques because they work; so do unscrupulous sellers.

Prizes are a popular way to interest consumers into buying home fire-prevention systems, raw land for investment purposes, vacation condominium time shares, home security systems, water treatment systems, vitamins, and a host of other products they are not likely to buy without some persuasive encouragement. Selling such products recovers the promoter's money spent giving away the cheap prizes. (You don't really think any legitimate business can give away a camera worth $149, do you?) Yes, manufacturers can make a 35-mm camera for $5, and semiprecious stones can be put into a setting for $3. Such products are truly cheap, but nothing requires that good-quality prizes must be given away. The truth is that you always win the cheapest prize.

Gifts and prizes are used to get consumers to the telephone or into the showroom so the persuasive sales force can interest them in overpriced products and services. The values of the prizes, such as jewelry, are grossly misrepresented. Discount coupons, for example, instead of being usable at stores on "Mainstreet America," may only be utilized at facilities of the sponsor of the prize promotion.

One of the gambits commonly used by scam telemarketing operators is the guise of marketing research in combination with prizes and awards. The promoters ask you to help their market research by testing a product. To encourage participation, consumers are offered fabulous gifts and prizes with inflated values, either free or at substantial discounts, such as a motor boat or a motorcycle. To receive the merchandise, the consumer is coaxed into paying an up-front "processing fee," "redemption fee," "taxes," or a "shipping-tax-and-handling fee," perhaps $295 to $495. It turns out that the fee is much higher than the value of the product.

Contests

A variety of companies offer premiums and prizes to promote their products to consumers. Such contests are often confused with sweepstakes. Postcards and other mailings are usually used which offer "congratulations" to you as the winner of some prize.

Many contests purposely have very easy, simple solutions. Once the consumer mails in his or her solution, he or she is sent a prize for winning, although it is usually something of low quality and of little value.

Some sewing machine and vacuum machine manufacturers, for example, encourage potential buyers with prizes. They award books, cameras, and jewelry to winners of "easy-to-win" or "everybody-really-wins" contests. To claim a prize, a consumer need only respond correctly to the promoter's question(s), mail in some postal card response, telephone the seller, or visit the sales showroom.

Some telemarketers, but especially the unscrupulous ones, use 900-numbers to market contest offers and sweepstake-like promotions. You, the "lucky winner," might also be told that you are eligible to enter a **tie-breaker contest** where, for an additional fee, you are allowed to compete for a much larger prize. Such telemarketers typically offer a *series* of tie-breaker contests, offering the hope of winning some grand prize. Of course, there is no big prize; but there are huge 900-number bills instead.

Some contest scams require that as a winner all you have to do is to telephone the company's 900-number to collect the prize. Using 900-numbers costs the calling consumer lots of money, often $15 to $60 to simply call up and ask about the prize. To entice people to respond, slick telemarketers sometimes allow victims to call toll-free 800-numbers where they get a recording saying that in order to receive the prize they must call another number, and yes, it is a 900-number.

Other fraudulent contests require that the "winner" pay money up front, often several hundred dollars, to collect the award. Still other scams require that you call a 900-number to "verify," "redeem," or "audit" the existence of your prize. If paid, such verification, redemption, and auditing fees will never be seen again. Such is also the case with the payment of "refundable deposits" and "prepayment of taxes." The price of the call to find out what you have "won" could be $35, $50, or $149. You pay for the call but typically receive nothing. Or, you may be asked to pay a $49 or $299 "shipping and handling fee," perhaps for a fishing boat and later you receive a toy boat.

A variation of the contest scam occurs when one calls to say that "as a credit card holder you have won." The caller then asks for your credit card number for "verification" purposes. If you do give them your number, your next month's credit card bill is likely to reveal substantial unauthorized charges to your account.

Postcards and Letters Saying, "You Definitely Have Won!"

A postcard addressed to you might say, "One of the individuals named below [your name is listed] ... is a guaranteed winner of a $1000 certified check," "A Mercedes Benz Sedan," or "A Hawaiian vacation for two." Others say, "You are one of the first round prize winners in the $5000 Instant Cash Sweepstakes," "You have a one in three chance of winning a third-round prize of $1000," "You have definitely won!" a motor vehicle, a color TV, $10,000 in cash, a dream vacation, a car telephone, or something else. Others ask you to call a telephone number with a 900 area code, where the toll charges can be as much as the company wishes-sometimes $50 or more.

Some telemarketers ask you to call a toll-free 800-number, where you are subject to persuasive suggestions to part with a little time or money, or both. Some companies ask that you only return the postcard indicating your interest; others ask that you enclose a few dollars. The intent is to get the consumer's interest and then sell magazines, cosmetics, an investment opportunity, or another special deal. As disclosed in small print (and sometimes not disclosed at all because they are lying), most entrants will get the minimum prize, inevitably something worth $10 or less. Also, if you mistakenly provide the telemarketers with your credit card number-perhaps as part of a verification process—they are likely to place unauthorized charges on your credit account. Many of these companies also make money selling the names of **sales leads**—those who answer the mailings—to other businesses which may not be legitimate.

CONSUMER UPDATE:
The Gifts and Prizes ... What They *Really* Are

Sellers try hard to convince consumers that the "prize" they have won is worth a lot of money. Consumers are enticed to "send money for shipping and handling" or "come and listen to a one-hour sales presentation with no obligation." In actuality, the prizes and gifts are simply worthless.

- "1/2 Carat Diamond Ring" ... A zirconia stone valued at $10
- "1 Carat Genuine Semi-precious Stone" ... A cheap gemstone valued at $3
- "Big Screen Television" ... A big-screen projection system that reflects a fuzzy picture from your TV screen that is enlarged against a wall, valued at $10
- "$500 Savings Bond" ... A zero-coupon bond of a corporation currently valued at $5 because the company is near bankruptcy and won't be around 30 years later to pay the $500
- "35 Millimeter Camera" ... An all-plastic camera worth about the price of a roll of film
- "Food processor" ... A hand-operated food chopper
- "Stereo system" ... A plastic toy that fits in your hand
- "Genuine Leather-Like Luggage" ... A cheap plastic bag shaped like luggage with metal brackets so weak that they would collapse if a child sat on it
- "Clock" ... Made of cardboard or plastic
- "Vacation cruise" ... You must send in a redemption fee of $295
- "Motorcycle" ... A plastic replica suitable for a very small child
- "Full-size Motor Boat" ... A five-foot inflatable rubber raft powered by a small battery-activated motor

*Carol Ann Walker, Personal Finance Manager/Air Force Aid Officer, Peterson Air Force Base, Colorado

Many Charities Are *Not* What They Claim to Be

About 8 in 10 American households make charitable donations each year, averaging $800 a year. However, the generous American public winds up giving part of that money—actually billions of dollars annually—to fraudulent charities too. Many disreputable companies use a variation of the name of a nationally recognized charity so they sound like credible organizations. When you are considering giving money and you want to avoid unscrupulous organizations, you must learn how to spot fraudulent charity appeals and obtain adequate information about how the charitable group plans to spend your donation. You need to be confident that most of your contribution is going to the charity's programs, not being spent on fundraising and administrative costs (including high salaries for officers).

Americans are a giving people, and unscrupulous charitable solicitation promoters are aware of this fact. Some charities play on feelings of guilt: "Won't you contribute to the starving Africans?" Others just want a token amount because you can afford it: "Won't you contribute just $5 to help?" Often the credentials of such organizations seem legitimate and their names sound familiar. Consumers rarely find out that they have given to a fake charity. All statements and documentation deserve close attention, particularly when the charities are not well known to the consumer. There are outright fraudulent charitable groups preying on the generosity of the American people.

There also are charities that might better be described as **quasi-charities**. These are charities that have not yet been closed down by a government agency, but they appear to be unscrupulous, in part because they spend an excessively high proportion of their income on administrative expenses and fund raising and they give very little money to those really in need. Any charity that spends more than 25 cents out of every dollar of income on fundraising and administrative expenses is suspect.

The major activity of most such quasi-charities is "program services" for public education about cancer, heart disease, orphaned animals, or whatever. They "educate" the public by mailing out additional solicitation letters. That, plus mailing costs, fat salaries, and overhead, eats up most of the money raised. They are greedy self-serving operations. The executive director of one Better Business Bureau states that, "It happens all the time, and unfortunately, there's not much that the law can do."

Legitimate charities sometimes pay exorbitant fees to professional fund raisers—commercial telemarketers—to collect for them. A study by the Connecticut Attorney General says that telemarketer's fees average 70 percent! For example, in a recent year the Marketing Corporation of America raised over $12 million for the March of Dimes, although less than half went to the charity. Reese Brothers raised $2.3 million for Mothers Against Drunk Driving (MADD), but the charity only received $1.2 million. Many commercial telemarketers contract with charities to pay them a flat fee (perhaps $25,000) to use their name for 12 weeks of solicitations during which time they might collect $400,000. Recently it was disclosed that the Marine Toys for Tots Foundation, the fundraising organization for the Marine's Christmas drive, had collected $10 million the previous two years and spent nothing on toys. To be certain that your money goes to the charity and not a fundraising firm, send your check directly to the charity.

It is appropriate for you to ask for a written disclosure of the percentage of your money that will actually be delivered to the primary charitable cause. At least 50 or 60 percent of each dollar ought to go towards the main mission of the charity. Get the disclosure in writing because some telemarketing charities lie telling people that "100 percent of the proceeds go to the XYZ charity," when in fact proceeds means "money after expenses."

Some charities use contests to attract donors in which the participants' contributions create a fund to be awarded as prizes to the winners. The promoters describe the charitable programs, explain the contest game along with the rules and regulations, and ask that the contestant return the entry form with or without a donation. Other fraudulent schemes promise, in exchange of purportedly tax-deductible donations of $1000 or more to a fake charity, to deliver prizes to the participants. Many generous people send in donations.

By necessity, charities have full-time fund-raising specialists who either write, telephone, or knock on the household doors of consumers. Some charities employ outside specialists under contract to raise funds. Toiletries, brooms, candy, and household products are the types of things sold by private companies to consumers on behalf of charitable organizations. Too often the charity benefits very little through such collections.

Recent data from the Philanthropic Advisory Service of the Council of Better Business Bureaus reveal the ten most-asked-about national charities that have the highest fund raising expenses: Vietnow, National Caregiving Foundation, Oblate Missions, Walker Cancer Research Center, Help Hospitalized Veterans, Dakota Indian Foundation, Cancer Fund of America, Retired Enlisted Association, North Shore Animal League, and Marine Toys for Tots Foundation.

The question to ask is, "How much of every dollar collected goes to those for whom it is collected?" To check the legitimacy of a charitable organization contact: (1) a local Better Business Bureau, or (2) the state Office of Consumer Affairs. These groups also can provide addresses of charities to which letters can be sent by consumers seeking financial details. Every charitable organization ought to be willing to provide an annual report on request that describes its purpose, programs, accomplishments, and some financial details. The Council of Better Business Bureaus publishes a *Annual Charity Index* paperback guide that provides snapshots of over 200 of the most-asked-about charities.

Three watchdog groups can provide written reports (sometimes free) on fundraising costs for national charities: (1) The Philanthropic Advisory Service of the Council of Better Business Bureaus (4200 Wilson Blvd., Arlington, VA 22203-1804/703-276-0100), (2) National Charities Information Bureau (19 Union Square West, Dept. FT, New York, NY 10003-3395/212-929-6300), and (3) American Institute of Philanthropy, 4579 Laclede Avenue, Ste. 136, St. Louis, MO 63108 (314-454-3040).

Buying Ripoffs and Scams

Numerous misrepresentations and scams exist to take advantage of consumers who are enticed to spend money trying to improve the efficiency of their buying practices. These ripoffs and scams prey upon people who are consciously trying to buy products and services at low or fair prices. By cautiously looking for what is wrong with such deals you can avoid being victimized.

CONSUMER UPDATE:
Watch Out for Telemarketing Recovery Room Scams!

Consumers who have lost money through prize promotions, merchandise sales, investment swindles, and so-called charity drives often have their names put on a "sucker's list" which is sold to other telemarketers so they can be victimized again. These lists contain an amazing amount of detailed information, including name, address, telephone number, the dollars spent on the scam, and sometimes even a credit card number.

This is called a **recovery fee scam** where they falsely promise that, for a fee or a donation to a specified charity, they will recover the consumer's lost investment money, or the product or prize never received. Typically, the telemarketer will call claiming to represent a government agency or consumer organization and report that the thieves have been caught and that their remaining assets have been frozen. The salesperson then says, "For only $250 (or $1000) in attorney's fees (or a charitable donation), we can 'recover' at least one-half of the money you originally lost, and perhaps all of it." Other promoters state that they already are holding the money for you. After the swindler disappears with the recovery fee, the consumer has been scammed a second time. The promoter's telephone pitch should be rephrased to begin, "Congratulations! You have been selected to lose even more money." This unscrupulous practice is also known as **reloading** or **double-scamming**. Believe it or not, there also is a re-recovery scam where people pretend to be FBI agents (or U.S. attorneys or IRS agents) who ask for fees to cover "taxes" on their recovered money.

Buying Clubs

Promoters of **buying clubs** often use telephone solicitations to entice people to come to their offices. The sales office is usually a suite of motel rooms rented for a few weeks. Consumers are given gifts for being willing to "just listen to an explanation about our exciting membership buying program."

Most of these outfits are nationally based, and they come through communities that have nursing schools, vocational schools, and colleges. They like the concentrations of large numbers of people. Persuasive salespersons talk students and townspeople into signing contracts for $500 or more. For paying this amount, the consumer gets an upgraded gift, such as a stereo or television (which is not worth $500), a catalog showing all the goods available through the buying club (brand-name goods only, since Sears, Penney's, and others refuse to participate), and a toll-free telephone number for placing orders. Once the consumer has signed the contract, they are stuck.[8]

What happens is that you will have problems with high shipping costs, setup charges, nondelivery of merchandise, delays in shipping, unavailability of goods, substitution of goods for out-of-stock items, unavailability of the latest models, difficulties in returning goods, long-term contracts, firms going bankrupt, and warranty service. Many duped consumers plunk down their money failing to realize that they can get the same products for the same or better prices at local discount stores, or through reputable catalog mail-order buying services (such as Unity Buying Club or United Buying Service) that charge annual membership fees of $5 to $15. Not surprisingly, most buying clubs do not

---

[8]Colorado allows purchasers of buying club contracts valued at $100 or more a one-day cooling-off period to rescind the contract. See Chapter 3 for advice on getting out of contracts.

give out their price lists to consumers because it would allow comparison shopping in advance of joining.

Rent-to-Own

Rent-to-own (RTO) businesses exist so that consumers can obtain durable goods (including household goods and vehicles) using a series of short-term rental-purchase agreements. People respond to advertisements that say, "No credit hassle!" "No long-term commitment!" "No down payment!" and "Free service in your home!" There are no down payments or credit checks required. Such goods as televisions, stereos, microwave ovens, washers and dryers, video equipment, refrigerators, automobiles, and furniture can be obtained by making regular payments. This can eventually lead to ownership over a period of time. Each weekly or monthly payment creates a new rental agreement, with the customer having no obligation to continue beyond the present period.

A rent-to-own contract can be compared to a credit contract. If a consumer buys a $400 television set on an 18-month credit contract, he or she might pay $27 a month, or $480 in total. Under an 18-month RTO plan, the consumer could pay $25 a month for many more months, perhaps totaling $1,200 for the *same* television! If rent-to-own payments were considered interest, the effective annual rate in this example would be over 200 percent. Renters who miss a payment may have their goods repossessed; to get them back, they have to begin renting again.

Many RTOs charge exorbitant prices and they are often located in poor inner-city and rural areas. Twenty percent of the customers at the nation's largest rent-to-own company, Rent-A-Center, with 1000+ stores, are unemployed and receiving government aid. If you have a poor credit history or experience difficulty raising the amount of money needed for purchasing, the weekly or monthly payments may seem so low that the terms are attractive. Rent-to-own companies are aggressive collectors of past-due amounts and frequently repossess goods.

Rent-to-own businesses have long been exempt from the state[9] and federal laws governing credit because they offer "rental lease" contracts instead of credit contracts, thus no credit has been extended. (The state of Pennsylvania defines rent-to-own as credit sales, and RTO interest rates there are limited to 18 percent.) RTOs also are usually exempt from provisions in the Uniform Commercial Code, usury laws, and cooling-off laws. Because the renter is making payments that add up to much more than the cost of an item, conceptually, the effect is the same as charging interest.

A California Public Interest Research Group study revealed that RTO contracts often have charges equivalent to 200 to 300 percent interest, instead of the more typical 16 to 24 percent for similar credit purchases in standard retail stores. Critics call this exploitation.

---

[9]Last year a federal judge declared void all rental contracts issued to Thorn EMI's rent-to-own customers after August 1, 1990, and ordered the company to refund all payments made under the contracts because he stated that the contracts violated state usury laws as well as the federal racketeering law.

Coupon Books

You may think you are getting a good deal when you buy a book of coupons purporting to offer excellent values. With **coupon books**, the consumer is offered free merchandise or services or discounted prices on goods and services. The coupon book might cost $39.95 for six discounted restaurant meals in a community or $149.95 for several nights of lodging at various motels. Three problems exist: (1) the coupons often have restrictions as to times and locations which may not be convenient, (2) the coupon book promoters often sell many more than the participating merchants have been led to believe, and later the merchants may be unwilling to honor all the requests, and (3) some of these operations get a few businesses to agree to participate and then lie about the others. As the complaints start to come in, the promoter quickly leaves town to go elsewhere seeking more victims.

Vacation Certificates

Promoters of **vacation certificates** claim that for only $59.95 or perhaps $129.95, you are eligible for, "Three days and two nights of free lodging at excellent hotels in Las Vegas, Miami, New Orleans, or even Hawaii," or any number of other desirable vacation spots. Vacation certificates typically include discount or free coupons for a handful of hotels, selected restaurants, and certain attractions in a resort area. The deal is that you pay lots of dollars for something of very little value, and, because of certain reasons described below, it is likely that you will not be able to use the certificate anyhow. Many consumers, especially young people, falsely believe that these certificates have substantial value. The American Society of Travel Agents reports that of all the travel vouchers sold, only ten percent provided customers with actual vacations.

This scheme is sometimes tied into a legitimate promotion by a local supermarket or department store that is unaware of the minuscule value of the vacation certificates. The big prize winner might receive groceries while the other winners might receive vacation certificates.

To receive a free vacation certificate, you may be required to attend a sales presentation. Sometimes there are age or income conditions, or a requirement that you be accompanied by your spouse, so that you both will be there to sign on the dotted line of a contract.

The lure of a free vacation certificate is often used in advertising to draw people to the seller's sales sites with the goal of selling a specific product or service. Vacation certificates are used by time-share resorts, membership campgrounds, automobile dealers, and solar energy companies as prizes. Some vacation certificate promoters ask for a major credit-card number to validate a complimentary vacation and then illegally charge fees on the consumer's credit-card account.

Winners of vacation certificates sometimes are required to pay a non-refundable processing and handling fee, or a refundable deposit from $50 to $100 to reserve each vacation time request. And, of course, they say, "Yes, we can charge the amount to your credit card!" They promise that the deposit will be returned upon your arrival at the place of lodging or after the vacation is complete. It's not.

Telemarketers sell vacation certificates, too. Here the consumer pays a fee of $50 to $500 to receive a travel certificate that includes round-trip air transportation for one person and lodging for two people for a week in London, Hawaii, or another vacation spot. Once they have the money or credit card number, the victim discovers that oral misrepresentations occurred because they cannot deliver the promised deals. When written materials are sent describing the offer, the writing contradicts what was said on the telephone. (If it is the same, they simply may be lying.) Also, reservations are difficult to confirm, and you must comply with hard-to-meet hidden or expensive conditions. In spite of suggestions to the contrary, refunds do not exist.

Complaints about these deals include: the written information given after the sales presentation is different from what was promised, the available lodging is typically at cheap hotels that have names that sound like the better hotels, the hotel accommodations can only be obtained through the promoter, rooms are available only on a space-available basis, the hotel price is a daily rate based on occupancy of several days, airline reservations are almost impossible to obtain, the cost for the second airfare ticket is over $1000, there are substantial charges for extra fees, and the certificates are limited to use during off-season time periods, with perhaps 80 percent of the year being considered the peak season.

Also, such vacations are not free when you have to pay for part or all of the transportation, meals, drinks, taxes, and miscellaneous expenses. It is virtually impossible to get a refund from one of these promoters because most declare bankruptcy within a year of starting business.

Scholarship Aid

It seems that during times of rising tuition bills, the **scholarship aid** businesses come out of the cracks in the sewer. Advertisements are placed in school newspapers suggesting: "We match at least two scholarships to your abilities!" "Money for college, results guaranteed!" "Scholarships go begging every year because people do not apply!" Many students have received postcards in the mail, perhaps from something called the "National Scholarship Foundation," promising a guaranteed scholarship because of the student's "present academic and financial circumstances." Perhaps saddest of all because these students rarely can afford to waste money, are advertisements which claim, "Guaranteed scholarships for foreign students!"

Tens of thousands of students every year fall for such misrepresentations. How nice it would be if the claims were true, but they are not! The "unclaimed billions" in the advertisements count employee tuition benefits and the money given out in federal grants. Contrary to advertised promises, even the best of these services offer only leads, not money. For the fee of $45, $119, or even $495, the consumer-applicant receives a computer listing of scholarships that are available as of a certain date (when the information was compiled by the promoters). This is nearly useless information. Common experiences include inappropriate leads, application deadlines that have passed, wrong addresses, incorrect telephone numbers, and strict eligibility requirements. One financial aid expert estimates that 9000 students apply for each $1000 award offered through these private-source scholarships.

Spending three or four hours with a high school guidance counselor or a college financial aid officer looking through the school's library of scholarship materials will locate many more and much better quality leads for funds. Also, look in the library for *The College Money Handbook* (Peterson's Guides), *Paying Less for College* (Peterson's), and Robert and Ann Leider's *Don't Miss Out* (Octameron Press). Most commercial scholarship businesses are ripoffs. The worst firms file for bankruptcy; the "best" continue to sell something of little value.

Vehicle Sales and Repairs

Part of the difficulties faced by consumers in the area of automobiles comes from the fact that the American automobile industry is one of the last bastions of **hard selling**, where the customer must be "sold" something by highly persuasive practices. Sometimes these techniques border on misrepresentation. Thus, it is no surprise that used car sales are one of the top five areas of consumer complaints to government agencies. The world of auto sales and repairs remains a market dominated by an attitude of **caveat emptor**—Let the buyer beware!

Fictitious List Prices

A **list price** is the posted amount that consumers are expected to pay for a product or service, and it is often the price suggested by the manufacturer. A truthful list price is found when substantial sales are actually made at that price in a particular market area. A list price on a product in a department store is usually truthful, since it is the actual price that people pay for the product. The list price on the window of a new car in a dealer showroom is pure imagery. Such prices are designed to make consumers believe they are saving money when they purchase an automobile for less than the list price. In fact, only about 3 percent of new car sales are made at list price.

Many used car dealers also post less-than-truthful list prices and then give all customers a discount. A number of states and localities have regulations prohibiting the deceptive practice of false list prices, but it is difficult and expensive for governmental consumer protection agencies to conduct the in-depth investigations necessary to get enough evidence for conviction.

CONSUMER UPDATE:
Subleasing Someone Else's Vehicle Is Risky Business

Some consumers fall for the dangerously expensive subleasing scam. Here a subleasing broker offers to arrange, for a fee, for you to sublease someone else's vehicle. You are supposed to take over the actual owner's loan or lease payments on their vehicle. These contracts are illegal in most states, and they typically violate the terms of the original loan or lease. This means that the lender can repossess the vehicle even after you have made all the payments.

High-Balling the Value of the Trade-in Allowance

High-balling is a technique used by an automobile salesperson who offers a shopper an extra-high trade-in allowance on his or her present car to create interest in a vehicle even though the offer may later be repudiated by the salesperson's manager. The **high ball** is the high trade-in allowance, a price in excess of the used car's real value. The high offer is made in an effort to keep the potential customer in the showroom seriously interested in purchasing a newer automobile.

This is the way the scheme usually works. The buyer desires a new car with a list price of $14,000 and wants to trade in his or her own vehicle worth only $1500. The salesperson offers the buyer an inflated trade-in value of perhaps $3000 toward the new car, and the buyer expects to pay only $11,000 ($14,000 - $3000). The salesperson writes up the contract, gets the person's signature on it, and goes to find the manager, who must okay all sales. The salesperson soon reappears with the manager close behind, shouting at the salesperson and threatening dismissal. The salesperson apologetically explains that the manager would not okay the contract because the trade-in price was mistakenly misquoted. The buyer then ends up buying the new car at a still high net price, say $12,000 (instead of the $11,000 previously bargained amount), and goes home feeling good about the price he or she paid for the car and glad he or she could help the salesperson out of the predicament with the manager. The result of this high-ball sale is that the dealer gains an extra $500 because the buyer gave up $12,000 in cash plus a trade-in car worth $1,500 for something he or she might have easily bought for $13,000 instead of the $14,000 list price with some honest bargaining.

Low-Balling the Price of a New Vehicle

Low-balling is an unscrupulous technique used by a salesperson who offers to sell a shopper a product, such as an automobile, at an unusually low and unrealistic price that will not be honored when the customer actually wants to make the purchase. The suggestion of a low-price deal is made in an effort to keep the potential customer in the showroom and seriously interested in purchasing an automobile. Again, as with high-balling, the salesperson returns with a contract rejected by the sales manager. Then the price rises, after the customer has had his or her heart set on that particular automobile. Many times the customer still goes ahead and buys at a price somewhat higher than it would be with good bargaining.

Automobile Repair Scams

Surveys show that the odds of being cheated in an auto repair is 50-50! This is one of the top five areas of consumer complaints to government agencies.[10] This occurs in part

---

[10]Almost all states have automobile repair laws requiring shops to give consumers a written estimate of anticipated charges, to return parts that were replaced, and to obtain advance permission from the consumer before completing work that was not foreseen when the estimate was made.

CONSUMER UPDATE:
Odometer Fraud Remains a Problem

The U.S. Department of Transportation reports that a high percentage of late-model used cars have odometers that have been turned back. **Odometer fraud** occurs when an odometer is rolled back or disconnected and when incorrect information is given about the accuracy of the odometer reading. The federal Odometer Law requires that the odometer reading be entered on the automobile's title in all states. You should never make a purchase decision solely on the miles shown on the odometer; have a trusted mechanic go over a car prior to purchase.

---

because most people know little about the operational aspects of an automobile, hence they are especially vulnerable to automobile repair deceptions. For example, when a transmission specialist shows a car owner metal filings that purportedly came from the transmission pan, do you know whether the transmission actually needs replacing? If a service station attendant along the interstate highway points out a leak on a shock absorber, does the car really need new shocks? Consumers with automobiles that need repairs usually have more success patronizing businesses that have mechanics certified in specialties by the National Institute for Automotive Excellence, which is an independent voluntary certification program for mechanics.

A frequent auto transmission deception has to do with a common method of checking them, known as, "**RCI,**" or **remove, check, and install**. Consumers wind up paying $75 to $250 in RCI charges and perhaps another $300 to $1000 for transmission repairs. The misrepresentation occurs when the transmission personnel knows the extent of the needed repairs after road testing a car, checking the transmission pan, and conducting an external check of the transmission system. Yet they do not tell the consumer. Instead, they say they cannot give an estimate for repairs until after they do an RCI procedure, which actually is unnecessary. Other recurring problems in this industry include making unnecessary repairs and charging for work not performed.

Investment Swindles

Many consumers are lured into investments that are bad deals for them but great for the salespersons. There are hundreds of business opportunities and investments that are just wrong for particular investors; others are downright swindles. People are talked into these scams and ripoffs by professional salespersons who are armed to the teeth with dazzling statistics, great promises, and impressive references that seem to confirm the illusions they present. These sellers are masters at manipulation, and they are prepared to provide smooth and seemingly logical answers for every objection raised. The professional swindler always offers reassuring comments to smoothly convince consumers to part with their money.

The Investment Swindler's Game

Consumers who invest their money are typically looking to achieve two things: (1) getting as high a return as possible (in interest, dividends and/or a long term appreciation in the value of the investment), and (2) safety. Swindlers attract unsuspecting investors with the promise of an unusually high return.

Investing consumers should be highly skeptical when an investment opportunity emphasizes:

- A very high yield or return
- A quick return
- "Secured principal" is guaranteed
- Approved by the Internal Revenue Service or "IRA approved"
- A "once in a lifetime" opportunity
- Assurances of good locations for vending machines or display racks
- No experience necessary (but send money)
- Promises of an "exclusive territory," or
- The chance to "get in on the ground floor"

Offers for "financial opportunities of a lifetime" are usually exactly that—the consumer's one good chance to lose a lot of money. Most such offers promise high profits for those with little or no business experience. Unfortunately, the investing consumer ends up with the experience, while the promoter earns the high profits.

Among the many scams are those for "investments" in rare coins, art, precious metals, gold and silver contracts, commodities, foreign currencies, off-shore investment funds, "prime" bank notes, oil and gas lease programs, wireless cable television, interactive video and data service television licenses, cellular telephones, specialized mobile radio, invention promotion, Rembrandt prints, land sales, gum ball machines, pay telephones, electronic games, pop corn vending machines, and display racks for greeting cards or compact discs. Worthless collectibles are popular too, such as 1957 Chevy miniatures, china dolls, and painted dishes. Some schemes are employing holy themes, such as offering divinely inspired investment advice.

A **swindler** is an unscrupulous promoter who concocts an investment scheme that has zero possibility of making money for anyone other than the schemer. Swindlers cheat people out of money or property, and many of them are very good at it. Some swindlers are outright crooks. Others start out to be honest people but wind up sacrificing their ethics for the fast buck of an investment scam. Still others start out with legitimate intentions, but when those go sour because of bad design or poor management, they abscond with the investor's money.

The result of all swindles is the same—the investing consumer loses. Consumers lose because their personal greed exceeds their caution and they believe what they want to believe. The sales techniques used by swindlers are effective; they have to be. Swindlers try to convince consumer-investors of several things: (1) the plan will produce large profits, (2) there is low risk, (3) they are confident you are going to make money, and (4) it is urgent that the consumer act right now. The swindler wants to manipulate the consumer's feelings so he or she feels obligated to go through the deal at an early stage, because those who act before thinking carefully become victims.

Investment swindlers reach their victims in the same ways used by legitimate firms—by telephone, direct mail, referrals, advertisements, on-line investment bulletin boards (reached via America Online, CompuServe and Prodigy), and the appearance of being reputable. Investment swindlers often place classified advertisements in newspapers and magazines or run local television and radio commercials; some run large, expensive advertisements in what one would think would be reputable publications, such as *USA Today*. The ads invite the prospective investor to call an 800 number where they hear the sales pitch.

Shady financial people often get started by establishing their trustworthiness with early investors to obtain referrals to others. Some swindlers even join local civic groups, giving the appearance of legitimacy.

Tips on How to Avoid Financial Swindles

To avoid being taken by investment deceptions, the first line of defense is to ask a lot of questions, and ask them until you get satisfactory answers. Unfortunately, most swindlers are adept at evading questions and giving dishonest answers. They also are good at making themselves difficult to investigate. To check out an investment opportunity, write or telephone the local police, Better Business Bureau, financial editor of your local newspaper, Office of Consumer Affairs, state securities administrator, and such self-regulatory agencies as the National Association of Securities Dealers, National Futures Association, and Securities and Exchange Commission (SEC). The SEC receives over 35,000 complaints about investments each year. If you suspect something in an investment offer is not quite right, report it to the appropriate authorities and regulatory agencies.

Follow these suggestions to avoid getting involved in a bad investment:

- Ignore any deal that sounds too good and hang up the telephone on sales calls;
- Never make an investment based on an unsolicited telephone call;
- If an investment promoter seems to able to predict the future, it is a scam;
- Be wary of hot tips, especially from acquaintances and fellow members of church, fraternal and other organizations;
- Make a close and cautious examination of any investment;
- Demand to see a prospectus or risk-disclosure statement that describes the risks involved in an investment;
- Get oral promises in writing;
- Check out the claims and the person making the claims;
- Verify the history of the firm selling the investment;
- If an investment sounds unfamiliar, get the opinion of a trusted financial advisor;
- Don't invest in anything unless you understand it and can see it;
- Find out who is earning commissions and management fees on the deal, as well as how much they amount to; and
- Monitor the progress of any investment you make.

**CONSUMER UPDATE:
Financial Planning Seminars—Ripoffs?**

A growing number of schemes have as their sole purpose to sell overpriced business-type manuals at seminars. It takes most victims of investment schemes weeks or months to realize that they have been ripped off.

People sometimes pay $10 or $20 to attend a half day or whole day seminar at a local motel titled, "Low Down Payment Real Estate" or "Invest for Success" or "Improve the Quality of Your Life." Most meetings are free, although some charge a fee of $10 to $39 to attend.

These seminars are often sponsored by those who run **infomercials** (sometimes called **lie-mercials**) on television or place large advertisements in local newspapers, which always include testimonials from "satisfied" customers. You may even be sent "complimentary tickets" in the mail. Promoters offer these "free seminars" to entice potential customers to attend. As a sales incentive, consumers are given a "rebate check" that may be used to pay part of the cost of any purchase made during the sales presentation. Once in attendance, you will be met by motivational speakers, upbeat loud music, testimonials from the believers, and some shills who are usually the first ones to "buy and sign on the dotted line." When the seminar is over, the promoters move on to the next town. Late Late Show host Tom Snyder describes one real estate infomercial by saying that, "The Dave Del Gotto Cash Flow Method is the one where Dave shows you how the cash flows right from your bank account into Dave's."

The question is after paying out the money-to attend the seminar, for the books, cassettes and videotapes, and perhaps for a membership to receive future counseling or advice, "Does the purchaser get his or her money's worth?" Some will say "Yes," but most, after only a few weeks or months, will reach the opposite conclusion. Instead, they will have paid way too much money for the value received—they've been ripped off.

Ponzi Schemes Are Illegal[11]

The Ponzi scheme is named for Charles A. Ponzi, who defrauded hundreds of people in the 1920s by paying off old "investors" with money coming in from new "investors." A **Ponzi scheme** is an investment scam in which the victims are promised an unusually high rate of return in only a few months and are duped into thinking that they will earn this return for a long time period. The earliest investors actually receive good returns, sometimes with their own money, which when paid attract more investors. In reality, there is no investment because the promoter is using the money taken from the many later investors to pay high returns to the few first investors before absconding with the remaining funds. The major factor in the eventual collapse of a Ponzi scheme is that there is no significant source of income other than from new "investors." The Ponzi swindler may operate his or her scheme for some time before disappearing with all the "investments" or revealing the bad news that the investments all went "sour."

The 40,000 investors who put over $32 million in International Loan Network (ILN) during the early 1990s, with promises of returns of 500 percent or more on real estate

---

[11]Helpful information for this and the following two sections came from: *Pyramid Schemes: Not What They Seem!* (Direct Selling Education Foundation), *Tips on Multi-Level Marketing (How to Tell a Legitimate Opportunity From a Pyramid Scheme)* (Better Business Bureau), and *How to Avoid Ponzi and Pyramid Schemes* (U.S. Securities and Exchange Commission).

deals, lost 90 percent of their money before the SEC froze their assets. They began operations again in 1996.

Typical Ponzi schemes include so-called investments in industrial wine for use in manufacturing salad dressings, and the buying and selling of race horses, collectible art, and precious metals traded in foreign markets. Consumers are led to invest in Ponzi schemes by promises of 30 to 100 percent profits in perhaps only 6 months. As some early investors take out their profits, others are encouraged to leave their profits in the "investment" to accumulate to even greater sums. When too many investors want to take their profits, the promoter disappears with the money.

Pyramid Schemes Are Illegal

Pyramid schemes operate on the fallacious assumption that the so-called investors all can make money by getting others to give money to join the operation. In the "Friends Helping Friends Pyramid" scam, you give the "president" of the pyramid $100 to become a member. Then it is your responsibility to recruit others (friends, relatives, strangers) to join. When you sign two people up and collect their $100 each, you give it to the president and you move up the pyramid. Once you recruit eight members, you become president of a new pyramid. When your recruiters bring in new members, you are $800 richer. This is illegal. Why is illustrated in the following example.

Many pyramid schemes operate by selling "distributorships" to others, say at $1,000 each. Being a distributor gives the person the exclusive right to sell distributorships to other investors for $1,000 each and to sell certain products to the public. Each $1,000 received from selling new distributorships is then split on a 50-50 basis with the promoter. Thus, theoretically, each distributor can recoup his or her initial $1,000 investment by selling only two distributorships.

Month	Participants
1	6
2	36
3	216
4	1,296
5	7,776
6	46,656
7	279,936
8	1,679,616
9	10,077,696
10	60,466,176
11	362,797,056 (far exceeds U.S. population)
12	2,179,782,336
13	13,060,694,016 (more than *double* the world population)

Initially, this appears that this can go on forever with all "investors" making money. Pyramid schemes offer the appeal of quick and enormous profits to the participants. But, since the offer must be made to many people, like a seemingly endless chain, the mathematical progression quickly reaches ridiculous numbers. In fact, the number of "investors" that it takes to keep this scheme going quickly exceeds the population of the world. This is shown in the illustration which assumes that the promoter initially sells distributorships to six persons, each of whom brings in an additional six investors every month.

Lots of "investors" are motivated to participate in pyramid schemes because each new participant pays for the chance to advance to the top to profit from payments of others who might join later. The illustration above also shows why the pyramid scam is so lucrative to the original promoters. Those at the top of the pyramid of "investors" quickly receive a lot of money. The scam works for the promoter because large numbers of people at the bottom of the pyramid pay money to a few people at the top. There is no way the "investors" coming in at the lower levels in a pyramid investment scheme can make any money, and this is why they are illegal. If one joins at level three or four, for example, the odds are almost impossible that an "investor" can ever profit. Since it is mathematically impossible for this "investment" to succeed, it is classically fraudulent.

CONSUMER UPDATE:
The Airplane Pyramid Scheme

One pyramid scheme that has been seen in many communities is "Airplane." Here the promotor explains that there is one pilot, two co-pilots, four crew members, and eight passengers, where the pilot captain is at the apex of a four-tier pyramid. Newcomers pay perhaps a $1000 fee to buy one of the eight passenger seats, shown as empty squares on a diagram. In theory, each pilot collects $8000-eight times his or her original "investment." Every person in the pyramid is responsible for recruiting more people to join the airplane. After all eight passenger spaces have been sold, the pilot leaves the airplane with his or her illegal profits. The two co-pilots then can split the original airplane investment game in half and move up to pilot status, thus creating two airplane games and beginning the process anew. Once again, at the bottom are new passenger seats to be sold at $1000 each. In theory, each of the passengers will eventually move up to a pilot captain's position so they can collect the big money. With this pyramid scheme, it is hard to tell the **scammers** from the **scammees** as they constantly change with new people joining and leaving the airplane.

No matter how it is described, this pyramid stuff always collapses! Plus, victims of pyramid schemes usually do not know where they are in the pyramid or that the odds are heavily stacked against them.

Telltale signs of pyramid investment schemes is that (1) they rely upon new investors to pay returns, commissions, or bonuses, (2) there is a need for an inexhaustible supply of new investors, and (3) there is a conspicuous absence of a product or substantial efforts to make profits through productive work, the sale of the products.

Some pyramid investment schemes are made to look like multi-level marketing businesses. **Multi-level network marketing** is a legitimate sales method that uses a network of independent distributors to sell consumer products and the bulk of income is earned from product sales. In an attempt to avoid prosecution by government agencies, pyramid schemes try to look legitimate. Therefore, many pyramid investment schemes do have a line of products to sell while the promoter claims to be in the business of selling the products to consumers. The products often are things like cosmetics, long-distance telephone service, hair care, vitamins, miracle products, and exotic cures.

The key difference between a multi-level network marketing investment and a pyramid scheme is the illegal investment schemes make their money primarily from the proceeds of new "investors." These are the new recruits to the so-called business. The real motivation in a pyramid investment scheme is to recruit new investors, not to sell products.[12]

Multi-Level Network Marketing Investments Are Legitimate

Multi-level network marketing is a legitimate sales method that uses a network of independent distributors to sell consumer products. Sales are usually made in customers' homes. These are bona fide business opportunities, such as Mary Kay Cosmetics, Amway, Shaklee, and Herbalife.[13]

As a distributor, the investor in a multi-level marketing opportunity is an independent business person, setting working hours, and earning money selling products or services supplied by an established company. In a multi-level business, distributors also have the opportunity to develop and manage their own sales forces by recruiting, training, and supplying others to sell. A distributor's compensation then is based upon fees earned for recruiting others into the business, commissions earned on personal sales, and a percentage of the sales of the recruited sales force. To be legitimate, a multi-level marketing investor must earn the bulk of his or her profits from product sales.

Here is an example of how a multi-level marketing opportunity works. An investor puts up $2000 to buy into and become a dealer of a product line, perhaps some cosmetics or household cleaning items. By going door-to-door, the person investing in this business can sell some products that the public might like and make a little money. The investor is further told that if he or she recruits other persons to invest $2000 each to start up a distributorship, the first investor will receive a $500 bonus for each recruit and a 5- to 10-percent commission on the wholesale value of all the sales of the newer investor-distributors.

Key differences between illegal pyramid schemes and multi-level marketing opportunities are: (1) the bulk of the income in a multi-level marketing business comes from product sales, (2) legitimate companies sell quality products and do repeat business with their customers, (3) start-up fees for legitimate businesses are small, (4) legitimate companies that require inventory purchases will usually repurchase any unsold items, and (5) legitimate companies want to make money with the investor and expand the overall market for the business.

Chain Letters Are Illegal Pyramid Schemes

Chain letters involve the sending of money through the mail with the chance that nothing will be received in turn. These are illegal and they operate on the same fallacious principle as pyramid schemes. As a result, the great majority of participants must lose.

---

[12]The largest "private investment fund" in Russia, known as MMM, collapsed recently as the value of the fund was lowered from $56 to 46 cents. (That is greater than a 100 to 1 drop in value.) This left between 1 and 10 million investors defrauded by what was a pyramid scheme. MMM advertised on Russian television even after repeated government warnings that MMM was a scam.

[13]The 100,000 sales force of NuSkin distributors have been accused by the attorney general of Michigan of being an illegal pyramid franchise.

Typically, a letter from some distant city arrives addressed to you with instructions to send a sum of money (perhaps $2 or $20) to the top name on an enclosed list of perhaps five names. Then you are to eliminate that name, add your own name and address at the bottom of the list, and mail copies of the new list to all the people on it. The appeal is that your name will be added to a multitude of subsequent lists by other people in the chain and you will receive enormous sums of money within a month or so.

Another chain letter scam says, "Earn $19,500 by buying a $5 computer program called Network!, copy it onto floppy disks, and send it on to five people." The letter also says that the five people who receive the copied disk will in turn make five more copies and send them on, and so on, until thousands of people have the program. You will make money because those thousands will send $5 each to the originator of the chain letter. Selling a product, such as a computer disk, is a gimmick to try to avoid the appearance of an illegal pyramid scheme.

The reality of the mathematical progression of numbers tells us that the only people getting rich off this venture are its earliest promoters. Typically, the narrative also falsely claims that, "This is a perfectly legal enterprise!" or "Approved by the Postal Service!" Anyone who participates is not only out the $2, $5, or whatever amount (plus the cost of stamps), but his or her name and address is now clearly recorded, which makes it easier for a government fraud unit to locate should they investigate this particular scam. Chain letters are a violation of the mail fraud statute—up to five years in prison and fines of up to $1000, or both. The government generally goes after the chain letter organizers, not the participants who are the victims.

Referral Rebate Sales Are Illegal Pyramid Schemes

Referral rebate sales are a variation of the illegal pyramid scheme, and it occurs when a buyer is induced to sign a contract with the promise that he or she will receive a rebate or other consideration for each additional customer referred to the seller who later makes a similar purchase. Payment of the consideration is contingent upon a subsequent sale. For example, a buyer might sign a contract to purchase a $1000 stereo system with the promise that $50 will be credited to the $1000 debt for every person that the buyer refers to the seller who purchases the stereo system.

The impossible mathematics of the pyramid scheme is again seen with this variation-referral rebate sales—and that is why they are illegal. Usually exempt from these laws are referrals for real estate, automobile and insurance sales, areas where it is traditional for sellers to pay their customers finder's fees for referrals.

Work-at-Home Scams

Swindlers practice their pathetic motives on people who least need to be ripped off, those unable to work away from their homes because of difficulties in obtaining transportation, or because of health or family responsibilities. Advertisements for work-at-home schemes often appear in the classified sections of newspapers and magazines as well as on matchbook covers. Such "Earn Money at Home" opportunities sound lucrative and easy to do in the privacy of one's home. They promise to purchase the completed items. They promise good incomes, too, but they lie.

CONSUMER UPDATE:
Information Highway Scams

Chain letters, penny stock swindles, unregistered stocks, phony oil leases, fantasy ostrich farms, pyramid schemes, and other get-rich stratagems are on the global computer electronic mail networks, such as Internet, computer bulletin boards, and on-line services. Prodigy's Money Talk bulletin board, CompuServe, and America Online do not screen messages for fraud. Con artists have adapted yesterday's old scams to today's technology. Federal and state government "cybercops" are stopping scams every month, but more and more are popping up. Complaints to the North American Securities Administrators Association, an organization of state regulators, (202-737-0900), will be directed to the correct agency.

Popular work-at-home scams include stuffing envelopes, clipping grocery coupons, putting gift items together, sewing neckties, raising chinchillas (to sell the fur pelts), gilding greeting cards, and home assembly of crafts. Products completed by people working at home are later refused by the promoter because, "They do not meet our quality standards," and the worker is left with lots of worthless items. The purpose of the promoter is to profit by selling the overpriced materials or equipment needed, selling instructions on how to perform the at-home tasks, and (believe it or not!) selling instructions on how to buy classified advertisements to run the same work-at-home scheme.

Review and Summary of Key Terms and Concepts

1.   Give some reasons how ripoffs and frauds **work against consumers**.

2.   List four reasons **why ripoffs and frauds exist** in the marketplace.

3.   Give some examples of what ripoffs and frauds have **in common**.

4.   Offer several **guidelines to avoid ripoffs and frauds**.

5.   Define **ripoffs** and give some examples.

6.   Why are **negative-option buying plans** ripoffs?

7.   Summarize one of the ripoffs present in the **rental car insurance** industry.

8.   How effective are the popular **weight-loss programs** over the long term?

9.   How can a **job-search company** rip a consumer off?

10.   Summarize one of the ripoffs present in the **telephone company industry**.

11.   What is the ripoff problem with the **supplemental health insurance policies**?

12.   Explain the importance of **material information** to the concept of **deception**.

13.   Distinguish between **bait and switch advertising** and **trading up**.

14.   Choose two examples of recent **economic frauds** committed by large corporations and summarize their violations.

15.   What is **mail fraud**, and why does it work?

16.   Explain how **telemarketing** promotions and **telefunding** seem to work.

17.   Distinguish among: **900-numbers, 976-numbers**, and **800-numbers**.

18.   What do **prizes, free gifts, contests**, and **sweepstakes** have in common as schemes?

19.   Explain how to identify fraudulent charities and **quasi-charities**.

20.   Summarize why **buying clubs** are such bad deals.

21.   How does a **rent-to-own business** function?

22.   Why do **coupon books** often turn out poorly for consumers?

23.   Why are **vacation certificates** bad deals for consumers?

24.   What is the common problem with **scholarship aid**?

25.   Distinguish between **hard selling** and **high-balling**.

26.   Summarize how the "**RCI**" approach to transmissions works.

27.   What do most **investment swindlers** promise, so as to entice consumers to give them money?

28.   List three **suggestions on how to avoid getting involved in a bad investment**.

29.   How do **Ponzi** schemes work?

30.   Briefly distinguish between a **pyramid scheme** and a legitimate **multi-level network marketing** business opportunity.

31.   Explain why **chain letters** are illegal.

Useful Resources for Consumers

Alliance Against Fraud in Telemarketing
1701 K Street, NW, Suite 1200
Washington, DC 20006
(202)-835-3323

Call for Action
3400 Idaho Avenue, NW, Suite 101
Washington, DC 20016
(202)-537-0585

Consumer Action (in California)
116 New Montgomery, Suite 233
San Francisco, CA 94105
415-777-9635

Council of Better Business Bureaus, Inc.
4200 Wilson Boulevard
Arlington, VA 22203
(703)-276-0100
http://www.bbb.org/bbb

Federal Trade Commission
http//www.ftc.gov/bcp/scam01.htm

National Fraud Information Center
P.O. Box 65868
Washington, DC 20035
(800)-876-7060http://www.fraud.org

U.S. Postal Service
http://www.usps.gov/websites/depart/inspect/
welcome.htm

"What Do You Think" Questions

1. **Frauds** in the marketplace seem rampant, especially in **telemarketing**. Outline a plan that would greatly reduce such deceptions. In your response, be sure to comment on civil and criminal penalties, as well as the right of free speech.

2. The text has "**A List of Probable Ripoffs**." What commonalities do you see occurring time after time in these various scams?

3. **Rent-to-own businesses** argue that they offer needed products and services in the community. Assume that you agree with that position. Then offer suggestions on how the rent-to-own industry might go about providing deals for consumers that would be perceived as being more equitable.

4. Why do you think **credit repair clinics** are difficult for government regulators to close down? What can the government do about this industry?

Chapter 5

Laws That Help Consumers

OBJECTIVES

After reading this chapter, you should be able to:

1. Understand appropriate provisions of laws and regulations that protect consumers and help them obtain redress.

2. Read several sample complaint letters (found in the chapter appendix).

Uninformed consumers lose in marketplace transactions. They often pay too much for goods and services, purchase products of inferior quality, and sometimes suffer the consequences of unsafe products and illegal discrimination. Informed consumers also find themselves losing in the economic marketplace. The marketplace where consumers meet sellers is difficult and challenging for all. Fortunately, there are a number of federal, state, and local laws and regulations that serve to protect consumers and help them remedy marketplace wrongs. Most of these laws do more than offer disclosure—instead, the laws empower knowledgeable consumers by giving them a legal right to take action. This chapter is placed early in the book to provide a strong focus on the legal protections available to consumers before you read the remaining chapters. It may be read in sequence with the other chapters and/or it may be used as a reference.

This chapter focuses on federal and state laws and regulations, and it offers an occasional reference to local ordinances. It describes about 60 legal protections for consumers in the following areas: sales transactions, vehicles, warranties, housing, and credit/debit transactions. Because of space limitations, this chapter excludes some laws that protect consumers.[1] Also, a number of sample complaint letters can be found in the chapter appendix.

Laws on Sales Transactions

There are over twenty laws and regulations in the area of sales transactions.

Telemarketing Solicitations Regulations of the FCC and FTC

The Federal Communications Commission (FTC) and the Federal Trade Commission (FTC) have issued national regulations to comply with the Telephone Consumer Protection Act of 1991, the Telephone Disclosure and Dispute Resolution Act of 1993, and the 1994 Telemarketing and Consumer Fraud and Abuse Prevention Act, which went into effect January 1, 1996. Enforcement of the laws are given to the Federal Communications Commission, the Federal Trade Commission, the state attorneys general, and consumers themselves.

These rules are designed to help protect consumers against deceptive and abusive telemarketing sales practices. Rules cover unsolicited telemarketing solicitations, "junk fax," and auto-dialer calls. The rules cover most types of telemarketing calls, including calls to pitch goods, services, "sweepstakes," and prize-promotion and investment opportunities. Following are the key provisions of these laws.

1. **Telemarketers are prohibited from calling** you once you have requested to be placed on its **"do not call" list.** The consumer is the only person who can implement the protection. To do so, the consumer must take the trouble to explicitly inform the telemarketer that calls are no longer permitted. It is important to record in writing the date, time, company name, and the caller's name every time a telemarketing call is received. The list is valid for only 12 months, after which the telemarketers may call

---

[1]For example, see E. Thomas Garman (1996), *Ripoffs and Frauds: How to Avoid and How to Get Away*, Revised edition, Dame Publications.

again. Furthermore, the "do not call" list is for individual products being sold, not the entire company's line of products.

Violators are liable for up to $500 in damages per unwanted call and up to $1,500 in damages per willful violation. Consumers may sue telemarketers who break this law in their local small claims court and collect the money. Consumers also may report violations to their state attorney general for action.

Many telemarketers participate in the Direct Marketing Association's "National Do Not Call List," as they have agreed not to telephone consumers who add their names to this list. To sign up, write Telephone Preference Section, Direct Marketing Association, P.O. Box 9014, Farmingdale, NY 11735-9014. If you want to remove your name from most mailing lists to receive less advertising mail, write Mail Preference Service, Direct Marketing Association, P. O. Box 9008, Farmingdale, NY 11735-0998.

2. Calling times are restricted to the hours between 8 a.m. and 9 p.m.

3. Recorded sales pitches to consumers' homes are prohibited, unless the consumer gives permission to, or has a business relationship with, the company.

4. Before they make their sales pitch, telemarketers must "promptly" tell you that it is a sales call, provide the name of the seller, and tell what they are selling. However, telemarketers are allowed to delay telling the purpose until they have established "rapport" with the call recipient.

5. If the pitch is for a sweepstakes or prize promotion, they must tell you how to enter the contest, that no purchase or payment is necessary to enter or win, and the odds of winning. They also are required to tell you any restrictions or conditions of receiving the prize. It is illegal to misrepresent the value or nature of a prize.

6. It is illegal for telemarketers to lie or misrepresent any information. In the area of telemarketing of investments, work-at-home, and business opportunity schemes, for example, it is illegal to lie or misrepresent the facts about the goods or services, the earnings potential, profitability, risk, or liquidity.

7. Before you pay, telemarketers must tell you the total cost of the goods or services, as well as any restrictions on getting or using them, or that a sale is final and nonrefundable.

8. Whoever takes money from your banking account is required to have your verifiable authorization to obtain payment. This is your express permission, such as in writing on paper or audiotape.

9. Before taking money from your bank account, they must tell you that the money will be taken from your account and they must use one of three ways to obtain authorization: (a) written authorization, (b) tape record your authorization, or (c) send you a written confirmation *before* debiting your bank account. If they tape record your voice, the consumer must receive the following information: date of the demand draft, amount of the draft, the payor's name (who gets the money), the number of drafts (if more than one), a telephone number that you can call during normal business hours, and the date that you are giving your oral authorization.

If they obtain your written permission, they must give you all the information required for a tape recorded authorization *and* tell you that in the confirmation notice the refund procedure you can use to dispute the accuracy of the confirmation and receive a refund.

10. It is illegal for consumers to help deceptive telemarketers if they know, or consciously avoid knowing, that the telemarketer is breaking the law.

11. Consumers are not required to pay for credit repair, recovery room, or advance-fee loan/credit services until such services are actually provided. (**Recovery room**

operators who call victims of prior scams and promise to recover their lost money for a fee are prohibited from seeking payment in advance.)

12. The strongest provision of the new regulation, perhaps, is that state law enforcement officers, such as the attorney general, now have the power to prosecute fraudulent telemarketers who operate across state lines by suing in federal courts. State officials are allowed to get nationwide injunctions that will prevent an unscrupulous seller from moving operations to another state. State governments will no longer have to chase fraudulent telemarketers from state to state. Instead, such businesses will be shut down entirely. Fines are $10,000 per violation, and consumers are supposed to receive restitution of losses suffered. The new regulations do not preempt stronger state laws where they exist.

CONSUMER UPDATE:
Terrible Weaknesses Exist in the Telemarketing Regulations

Some weaknesses remain in the FTC's telemarketing sales rules and it is almost impossible for consumers to distinguish between legitimate and fraudulent telephone sales pitches. One weakness is that if the telemarketer chooses to not mention its refund policy as part of its sales offer, such information need not be provided to the consumer. Another weakness is that the telemarketing caller is permitted to avoid telling the purpose of the call until he or she has established rapport with the person called. This leaves too much time for the unscrupulous telemarketers to lure the consumer into a web of deceit.

It is terrible for consumers that the regulations do not prohibit courier pickups of payments. Worse, a telemarketer does not need a person's signature granting permission to withdraw funds from one's bank account (**automatic debiting**) if they get the consumer's express verifiable authorization. Similarly, the law does not prohibit the use of unsigned checks (**demand drafts**) without first getting the same explicit authorization from the consumer.

The continuing problem is that persuasive crooks have an easy time getting thousands of consumers every day to inadvertently agree to allow funds to be withdrawn from their accounts. The Fair Credit Billing Act (examined later in the chapter) gives consumers specific legal rights when paying with credit cards, but the law's protections do *not* apply to checking account withdrawals.

Other moral rights exist for consumers in telemarketing transactions. Consumers have the right to request the telemarketer to mail written information about the investment, charity, product, service, its cost (including yearly cost, such as for magazines), and guarantee. Consumers also have the right to ask whether the caller is a professional telemarketer/fundraiser or a volunteer.

"900-Number" FCC Regulations

The Federal Communications Commission (FCC) issued rules in 1993 to implement part of the Telephone Disclosure and Dispute Resolution Act. Consumers who do not want calls made from their telephones to 900-numbers (pay-per-call services) must be given a block on their telephones. The consumer's local telephone company must list the charges for pay-per-call services separately on the customer's bill.

All pay-per-call services costing more than $2, either on a flat-fee or cost-per-minutes basis, are required to begin with a **preamble**, a message disclosing the price and the identity of the company providing the service. They must sound a warning signal telling the consumer that he or she has only three seconds remaining to hang up before another tone begins that lets the caller know the paid service is beginning. Callers must be permitted to hang up early and not be charged. Services aimed at children under age 12 are prohibited; services directed to 12- to 18-year-olds must state that parental permission is needed to complete the call. Companies must provide a local number or a toll-free line to call with billing questions.

Ads for 900-numbers must meet certain disclosure standards. Advertisements in print or broadcast media are required to provide specific pricing information, consisting of reporting charges for service options callers might select.

Rules for settling disputes are similar to credit card regulations. Billing complaints must be acknowledged in writing within 40 days and resolved within 90 days. The 900-number companies, or their representatives, have 90 days to eliminate the disputed charges or investigate and demand payment. A consumer's credit rating cannot be penalized until the dispute is addressed. Consumers should complain first to their local telephone company because it is authorized to resolve disputes; an oral communication is sufficient notice to initiate a billing review. If requested, the local telephone company will provide a written explanation and copies of any documentary evidence of the consumer indebtedness.

CONSUMER UPDATE:
Fight Back Against Ripoff Telephone Charges

Shockingly large telephone bills can be caused by fraud, ripoffs charges of alternate operator services (AOS) and coin-operated customer-owned telephones (COCOTS), use of 900- and 976-numbers, calls made by unattended children, and long-distance billing errors. Don't put up with such charges. Instead, complain to your local telephone company and ask them to credit your account.

Although the rates of non-traditional telephone companies are generally not regulated, consumers who are ripped off may challenge any and all excessive charges to their local telephone companies. Even though the local telephone company did not cause the problem and is not responsible for its solution, complaining consumers usually get some relief. Local telephone companies are required by law to do the billing for other firms that provide services to their customers. The contract typically states that, "Contested charges by consumers will be charged back to the original service provider." As a result, local telephone companies are inclined to give in to consumer complaints. Ask for a supervisor, if necessary.

Unordered Merchandise Regulations of the Postal Service

Federal regulations of the U.S. Postal Service state that if you receive merchandise in the mail that you did not order, you may consider it as a gift. You are under no legal obligation to pay for it or return it. Postal Service regulations specify that you do not have to pay for unordered merchandise and that it is illegal for the company to bill you for it or send you dunning communications for unordered merchandise. In fact, the only materials that can be mailed to you without your permission are those clearly marked as free samples and merchandise mailed by charitable groups asking for a contribution. Even in these cases, you can consider any merchandise as a gift.

Of course, you cannot keep something like a video cassette recorder inadvertently mailed to your home. You should write or call when such a legitimate shipping error occurs and return it to them providing they pay all costs involved.

If you are sure the merchandise was never ordered, write the sender that you are keeping it as a free gift. You may want to send the letter by certified mail and keep the return receipt and a copy of the letter. Say you are sending a copy of your letter to the Office of Consumer Affairs, and do so. A sample complaint letter is at the end of this chapter.

The unordered merchandise regulations state that you can refuse a shipment that arrives by U.S. mail simply by not opening it and returning it to the post office. By writing "Refuse to accept" on a package and giving it back to the post office, it is returned to the sender at no cost to the consumer.

If you are not certain that you ordered goods that have arrived by U.S. mail, consider sending the company a letter (preferably certified with a return receipt requested) and ask for proof of your order. The small print in sweepstakes promotions often say that you have actually ordered something, like magazine. If you get unordered merchandise by private delivery services, such as UPS or Federal Express, do not accept the shipment. Realize, too, that this unordered merchandise rule offers you no protections. If you have already accepted something from a private delivery service, write the sender a certified letter and get a return receipt. Demand proof of your order. If there is no valid proof, tell the sender that unless the merchandise is picked up within 30 days, you will dispose of it. If you return it, be sure you do so at the sender's expense and get a receipt from the carrier.

Negative Option Mail-Order Rule of the FTC

Books, records, compact discs, videotapes, and other items are often sold through membership in a negative-option club. Typically, the consumer receives an introductory offer, such as three books for $1, if you agree to purchase more items. A **negative option** is a consumer decision-making situation in which the consumer must notify the company that a particular selection is not desired in order to not receive it, because if the company does not receive the negative notification, the consumer will receive the goods according to the previously agreed-to contract.

The Federal Trade Commission (FTC) Negative Option Rule requires that sellers clearly and conspicuously give consumers certain information about the plan in any promotional material. For example, the seller must tell: (1) how many selections you must buy, if any, (2) how and when you can cancel your membership, (3) how to notify the seller when you do not want the selection, and (4) when to return the negative option form to cancel shipment of a selection. The regulation requires that the company give consumers at least 10 days to reject the monthly or periodic selection, based upon the **mailing date** (the date the form must be postmarked to the seller) or the **return date** (the date the form must be received by the seller).

Mail-Order Merchandise Regulations of the FTC

The Federal Trade Commission (FTC) has a trade regulation concerning mail-order merchandise sales. The regulation requires that (1) the buyer should receive any ordered merchandise when the seller promises to deliver it, such as within three weeks, unless the advertisement promises a different shipping time, (2) when no date is mentioned, the seller must ship the merchandise no later than 50 days after receiving the order (evidenced by receiving the payment, charging a credit account, or getting the telephone order), and (3) if the consumer does not receive the ordered merchandise by the 50-day deadline, the order can be canceled and the consumer can get his or her money back. The 50-day clock does not begin until the order is received. At least one part of the transaction must take place through the U.S. mail in order for the rule to apply.

The seller has specific responsibilities if the promised delivery date (or 50-day limit) cannot be met. The seller must communicate to the consumer with an **option notice** the new shipping date. The consumer then has the option to cancel the order and obtain a refund or agree to a new shipping date. If paid by charge or credit card, the seller has one billing cycle to credit the account. A free means of response must be provided, such as a postage-paid postcard or a toll-free telephone number. If the consumer fails to reply and if the delay will be less than 50 days, the company can assume the consumer agrees to the delay. For delays over 50 days, money must be refunded to consumers who have not given their consent to such a delay. Prepaid orders that are canceled must be refunded within 7 days.

If you have received the notice and have agreed to a new shipping date, the company must notify you if it cannot deliver by that date. You once again have the opportunity to respond to the company that you either accept the extended shipping date or want a refund. The company must cancel the order and refund your money if you do not sign and return the second notice.

These regulations cover a number of mail-order situations for consumers, mostly affecting transactions with traditional mail-order firms. However, there are exceptions to the rules: mail-order photo finishing; magazine subscriptions; serial deliveries (such as negative-option plans, as in book and record clubs), except for the initial shipment; mail-order seeds and plants; COD (cash on delivery) orders; and credit orders that are not charged until the goods are shipped. Note that the regulations do cover orders placed by telephone and paid for by mail.

Refunds for orders paid by check, money order, or cash must arrive at the consumer's mailing address within 7 business days of the merchant's receipt of the cancellation. For credit-card orders, the consumer's account must be credited within one billing cycle. The FTC defines a **business day** as Mondays through Saturdays, not Sundays or the Mondays following a national holiday. The mail-order merchandise regulations of the Federal Trade Commission also apply to shopping by telephone, fax and computer.

COD (Cash on Delivery) Rule of the Postal Service

In 1987, rules were issued by the U.S. Postal Service allowing people to pay for COD packages with a check made out to the mailer instead of to the Postal Service. This option enables consumers who experience difficulty with mail-order merchandise to stop payment on a check before it is cashed. Then the buyer will only be out the bank fee for stopping payment on the check.

It is important to recognize that mail frauds have not gone away. Consumers are still allowed to give cash, money orders, and certified checks to the U.S. Postal Service for COD packages sight unseen. In short, now consumers have the right to pay COD charges to the seller or to the Postal Service. Uninformed consumers may not realize that the new U.S. Postal Service regulation exists and, therefore, may not exercise their right.

Door-to-Door Sales Regulations of the FTC

The Federal Trade Commission (FTC) has a trade regulation under the Truth in Lending Law regarding door-to-door sales. It provides a **cooling-off period** which is a time period during which the consumer has the opportunity to reconsider the wisdom of making a door-to-door contract purchase. During the cooling-off period, a consumer may change his or her mind, cancel the contract, and obtain a refund.

The FTC door-to-door regulation applies to sales agreements for $25 or more made in your home or at a location that is not the permanent place of business for the seller. Therefore, consumers can cancel agreements for $25 or more made in motel rooms, restaurants, their homes (including dormitory rooms), and the homes of friends or acquaintances. The rule applies whether the consumer invited the seller into the home or the seller made the arrangement. The cooling-off period also applies when your home is used to secure the loan no matter where the contract was signed.

The FTC regulation does not apply to sales made entirely by mail or telephone, for emergency home repairs, maintenance or repairs on personal property, arts and crafts sold at fairs or other locations (such as shopping malls, civic centers, and schools), for automobiles sold at temporary locations when the seller has at least one permanent place of business, for purchases of insurance, securities, or real estate, or for sales made at the seller's normal place of business.

The FTC regulation states that consumers have the right to cancel most door-to-door contract purchases (both cash or credit transactions) within 3 days of the original purchase. The FTC regulation requires that on door-to-door sales of $25 or more, the salesperson must verbally tell consumers of this right to cancel a contract, give the consumer a written contract, and give the consumer two copies of a "notice of cancellation," that must be in the same language used in the sales presentation.

The law requires that the notice accompanying the contract be dated, show the name and address of the seller, and include the following statement: "You, the buyer, may cancel this transaction at any time prior to midnight of the third business day after the date of this transaction. See the attached notice of cancellation form for an explanation of this right." Consumers have until midnight of the third business day after the contract date to cancel. To do so, the consumer either: (1) dates, signs, and mails the form to the address given for cancellation, being sure to retain one of the detachable copies of the cancellation form and getting the envelope properly canceled with the correct date by the Postal Service, or (2) hand delivers it to the same address. If necessary, consumers can make their own cancellation form letter as long as it provides the same types of information found on the proper cancellation form.

The seller has several responsibilities to perform within 10 days if a consumer cancels a sales agreement: (1) cancel and return any contract papers signed, (2) refund any money and return any trade-in, and (3) tell the consumer how and where the product not desired will be picked up or returned.

Within 20 days, the consumer must make available to the seller the item to be returned, and it should be in the same condition as when it was received. The consumer must pay return shipping charges if he or she agrees to do so. Alternatively, the seller might agree to pick up the item and/or pay for the return shipping expenses.

Door-to-Door Sales Cooling-Off-Period Laws in States

There is no general three day right to cancel all contracts. Most states have their own cooling-off period laws that extend the protections offered in the FTC regulation for door-to-door sales. States often allow consumers to cancel sales contracts made for any amount, including those under $25, if the agreement was made away from the seller's regular place of business, such as in the consumer's home or in a motel suite. The contract must have been for personal or household purposes. Most states provide that such contracts can be canceled by midnight of the third business day (Saturday usually counts as a business day). To cancel, follow the instructions on the cancellation form provided as part of the contract. Most states require notice of contract cancellation in the same language as the oral presentation. Some states have specific statutes that allow cancellation of magazine contracts sold door-to-door.

Cooling-Off Laws for Health Spas, Timeshares, Campground Contracts, Mortgage Refinancing, Etc.

Many consumers are pressured into signing contracts on the spot, in order to take advantage of a one-day-only deal. Most states have specific cooling-off statutes for particular types of contracts no matter where the agreement was signed, in someone's home, in a motel suite, or at the seller's place of business. In general, cooling-off laws permit the consumer to reconsider his or her action and exercise a penalty-free cancellation of an agreement after thinking about the situation for three to fifteen days. There is no need for any justification.

Laws generally require that the consumer receives notification of the right in writing from the seller. A written notification of cancellation, sometimes called "Buyer's Right to Cancel", should be delivered by certified mail, return receipt requested, or by personal delivery, to the address on the contract. If delivered in person, the consumer should have an employee acknowledge in writing receipt of the cancellation. Consumers should always keep a copy of any cancellation notice. Other contracts you can cancel under various state laws include dance lessons, seminar sales, dating services, discount buying clubs, hearing aids, rental housing locators, trade and correspondence schools, foreclosure sales, home repairs, martial arts, condominium sales, and multiple magazine subscriptions.

Consumer Leasing of Automobiles

The Consumer Leasing Act was passed in 1976 to protect consumers who lease automobiles. It covers leases for personal or household use that are longer than four months when the total obligation is less than $25,000. It requires that the leasing company disclose to consumers written information about payments, taxes, title, licensing fee, insurance, warranty, who will pay for maintenance and repairs, and how the purchase price will be calculated if the lease has an option-to-buy provision.

The Federal Reserve Board is currently drafting **Regulation M** that updates present law. It is *hoped* that the proposed regulations will include such disclosures as (1) total gross cost, (2) total amount due at lease signing, (3) vehicle **residual value** (value at the end of the lease), (4) early termination charges, (5) various estimated charges, e.g. financing, taxes, insurance, registration, excessive wear and tear, (6) depreciation, (7) adjusted capitalization cost, and (8) and **annual lease rate (ALR)** which would be roughly equivalent to the annual percentage rate (APR) used in credit transactions. Most of these disclosures are *not* now made.

Airline Delayed Arrivals

Airlines often have delayed arrival times because of inclement weather or mechanical problems. However, the sole legal obligation of an airline company is to place the passenger on its next available flight to that person's destination. There are no government regulations requiring them to pay compensation on delayed flights. If the delay was caused by the airline (perhaps when an airplane sits on a runway waiting for a replacement part), the airline *may* have a policy to provide some compensation. In such instances, the airline company usually will provide vouchers for meals, cash for miscellaneous expenses and taxi costs to and from a motel, the cost of overnight lodging, and sometimes a voucher for travel on a future flight. Usually, only assertive consumers who ask get such compensation.

Airline Bumping Regulations

Department of Transportation (DOT) rules do exist for overbooking problems on oversold flights, but these exclude charter flights and commuter flights with 60 or fewer passengers. If your flight was overbooked and no one volunteers to give up a seat, the last one on is usually the first to get bumped. The U.S. Supreme Court ruled recently that passengers bumped from oversold flights may sue for compensatory (not punitive) damages for actual injuries in a state court.

Should you be **involuntarily bumped**, you are not entitled to reimbursement when the airline is able to get you to your destination by means of any airline within 1 hour of your scheduled arrival time. Beyond 1 hour but less than 2 hours (4 on international flights), assuming you met the airline's check-in requirements, the airline must pay you a cash penalty. The amount must equal the one-way fare to your final destination up to $200. If you are more than 2 hours late, the airline must pay you twice the amount of the ticket up to $400. You also get to keep your original ticket which can be used in the future or for a refund. If your are involuntarily bumped, make sure that the alternate ticket is for a confirmed seat, not standby, because you may get bumped again.

Many airlines provide up to $25 in cash or vouchers for food and miscellaneous expenses—if you ask for them—for those who are involuntarily or voluntarily bumped when a flight is seriously delayed. You probably will have to ask for the benefits. Those who elect to be **voluntarily bumped** (four-fifths of the total) usually receive a voucher for a free domestic round-trip ticket, sometimes some cash, experience a few hours delay at the airport, and continue to their destination on a later flight.[2]

Even though most airlines may compensate consumers with cash for free meals, telephone calls, and other minor necessities in these situations as a gesture of goodwill, you may have to ask for the number and call the consumer affairs office of the airline to get help. Complaints about airline service may be made to the Department of Transportation (202-366-2220).

There are no regulations requiring that airlines assist a consumer if a flight is missed because the passenger was late. For an additional fee of $50, airlines will put late arriving passengers on another flight. Persuasive consumers sometimes get this service for no additional cost.

Airline Regulations on Lost Baggage

When airline baggage is delayed, most airlines will make arrangements to deliver it to you as soon as possible. Typically, no compensation is offered for the inconvenience. When you have been seriously inconvenienced by the baggage delay, and if you ask, you are likely to receive cash to purchase necessary items. Should the airline not provide cash, send your receipts for clothing and whatever (keep photocopies) to the airline's consumer affairs office with your complaint letter requesting reimbursement. No government regulations exist here.

Department of Transportation (DOT) regulations do specify that the airlines have a maximum liability for lost or damaged baggage of $1850 on domestic flights and a maximum of $920 on international flights. However, the regulations do not say what has to be covered. As a result, policies among the airlines vary. Most airlines do not accept any liability for lost computers, cash, jewelry, camera equipment, or similar valuables. When your baggage is seriously delayed or lost, most airlines will voluntarily provide courtesy bags containing toiletries and give you up to $25 in cash or vouchers for miscellaneous expenses.

Pet Lemon Laws

Several states require dog sellers to disclose facts about the animal's health to the purchaser in writing, including health, age, and medical history. California requires sellers to reveal what state the dog came from, whether obtained from a licensed or an unlicensed dealer, its immunization record and health information. New Hampshire requires sellers to show prospective buyers a health certificate for both dogs and cats. Animals usually can be returned within one or two weeks of purchase; animals suffering from congenital disorders may be returned up to a year from the purchase date.

Some states (AR, CA, CT, FL, NH, NY, VT, VA) also have laws that allow consumers to return an unhealthy dog to the seller for a refund, another animal, or

---

[2]No such regulations exist for hotels and motels, even reservations guaranteed with credit cards and confirmation numbers. A breach of contract situation exists when a hotel tries to turn a consumer away who has confirmed reservations, therefore, insist to the manager that he or she book you elsewhere and pay for the room.

payment of veterinary expenses to cure the animal. Consumers are entitled to the cost of veterinary services used to determine the animal's health status or to relieve its suffering. Alternatively, consumers may be entitled to another animal plus some veterinary expenses. Those who want to keep their unhealthy animal are entitled to receive reimbursement for limited and reasonable veterinary expenses.

Weight-Loss Center Laws

Some states and localities have statutes to regulate weight-loss centers. For example, New York City's law requires four steps: (1) commercial weight-loss centers must post a prominent "Weight-Loss Consumer Bill of Rights" sign in rooms where sales presentations are made that inform consumers there may be serious health problems associated with rapid weight-loss, and that only lifestyle changes (such as eating healthful meals and regular physical activity) promote permanent weight-loss, (2) weight-loss centers must hand out the bill of rights to potential clients, (3) centers must disclose the hidden costs of products or laboratory tests that may be part of the program, and (4) weight-loss centers are required to tell dieters the duration of their recommended program.

Rent-to-Own Laws

In an effort to stop consumers from being overcharged, a number of states have passed laws regulating aspects of rent-to-own contracts.[3] In New York, for example, consumers are allowed a 7-day "cure" period to make delinquent payments and/or redeem an item that has been repossessed. This action reinstates the original contract with credit for all previous payments. If partial payment is made along with voluntarily returning the merchandise, the reinstatement time period can be extended up to 180 days.

New York also requires contracts to disclose: (1) the cash price of an item, (2) the price of the rental option, and (3) the total price (a combination of the first two, which cannot be more than 100 percent greater than the cash price). This information must be attached to each displayed item. Amounts assessed for late charges are limited, and consumers are allowed to buy the rented item at any time for the cash price less one-half the total of previous payments. Further, if advertising mentions the possibility of ownership, the total cost of the option must be given. Since many rent-to-own companies operate nationally, there is interest in legislation at the federal level.

Deliveries and Installations Laws

Some states protect consumers from having to wait at home for hour after hour for deliveries and installations that never happen or occur quite late. California, for example, requires a maximum delivery-installation time period of four hours for cable television companies, utilities, and business firms with 25 or more employees.

---

[3]An excellent summary of the problems associated with rent-to-own buying can be found in: Swagler, R. & Baschon, C. (1989). *Advancing the Consumer Interest*, 1, 30-31.

Laws on Vehicles

There are a number of laws and regulations regarding vehicles.

Odometer Fraud Law

Odometer fraud occurs when an odometer is rolled back or disconnected and when incorrect information is given about the accuracy of the odometer reading. The Federal Odometer Law requires that the odometer reading be entered on the vehicle's title in all states. Federal law permits consumers who are wronged by odometer fraud to sue the seller and, if they win, collect $100 in damages, plus attorney's fees.

Motor Vehicle "Buyer's Orders" Laws

Several states have laws designed to stop dealer financing arrangements from being changed after the customer has agreed to a deal. The situation occurs when a purchaser contracts to buy a car, based on assurances that dealer financing will be obtained at a certain percentage rate. Perhaps a week later, after leaving the trade-in car behind, the dealer telephones saying that the financing rate is going to be several points higher, meaning much higher payments. Such contracts are binding in most states. A number of states now require that the sale of a car is not finalized unless the proposed sales contract is approved under the terms agreed to by the purchaser. The consumer can cancel the contract and require any down payment and/or trade-in be returned if anything specified in the contract is changed.

Lemon Laws for New Vehicles

A **lemon law** is a statute designed to assist vehicle purchasers who are experiencing major car defects or severe mechanical difficulties and/or are finding it impossible to get the vehicle repaired satisfactorily in a reasonable length of time. All states have such laws, and such authorities have been upheld by the U.S. Supreme Court.

The term was coined by Connecticut legislator John J. Woodcock III, who first came up with the "lemon law" concept to provide consumers with a remedy to their problems with defective cars. A **lemon** is described by Woodcock for consumers as, "a chronically defective vehicle that defies repair, or ... a vehicle with defects so difficult to diagnose and repair that the consumer becomes immersed in the wear-down process resulting in the new-car buyer throwing in the towel, after absorbing an emotional and financial beating." More than 150,000 consumers every year face problems associated with the purchase of a lemon vehicle.

Most states legally define a **lemon** as a passenger vehicle meant for personal or family use that has been unsuccessfully repaired four or more times for the same problem that substantially impairs the use, value, or safety of the vehicle or the car has been in the repair shop for a cumulative total of 30 days during the first year. Lemon laws offer improved warranty protections to consumers. Report safety problems to the National Highway Traffic Safety Administration at 800-424-9393.

The lemon owner wants to return the car and get his or her money back or get a replacement vehicle because the problem is major and has reduced the use, safety, or value of the vehicle. This procedure is called **revocation of acceptance**. It is instigated by returning the vehicle to the dealer and writing a letter specifying why this action is being taken. This may be difficult for many consumers to accomplish; thus in states without lemon laws most consumers have to hire attorneys and sue in civil court to obtain redress. Some states, such as Virginia, provide that if the consumer wins in court, the consumer's attorney and expert witness fees shall be paid by the manufacturer. Since in many cases returning a vehicle may cause a hardship on consumers, lemon laws do not require lawsuits. In lemon law states, problems with the vehicle must occur within one year or during the length of the warranty period, whichever is shorter.

The typical lemon law provides that if a newly purchased car is in the shop for a total of 30 days during the first year of ownership (or 12,000 miles) or if the same problem is not successfully repaired after three or four attempts, the consumer is entitled to redress. The manufacturer usually has two choices: (1) refund the purchase price, including all collateral expenses (such as title fees, repairs, mileage to and from the dealer, sales taxes, inspections, and vehicle rental) plus money for loss of use of the original car, less a reasonable charge for the miles driven, or (2) replace the vehicle with a comparable model acceptable to the consumer.

Consumers exercising their lemon law rights must first exhaust remedies under a manufacturer's informal dispute settlement procedure before going to court. In these cases, the dealer or manufacturer usually has to pay the prevailing consumer-plaintiff's reasonable attorney fees (if any), expert witness fees, and court costs.

One provision of many lemon laws creates a state recovery fund that enables lemon vehicle buyers to collect court judgments against automobile dealers or salespeople. Even after winning a lawsuit, sometimes the consumer cannot collect because the defendant closes the business and/or leaves town. A state recovery fund typically requires that each dealer and salesperson be assessed $10 to $100 a year to create a fund out of which claims can be paid to consumers.

Used Vehicle Lemon Laws

Lemon laws that cover used vehicles are in effect in Connecticut, the District of Columbia, Massachusetts, Minnesota, New York, and Rhode Island. Each law varies as to the age of the vehicle, its mileage, and cost. The Massachusetts law requires mandatory but limited warranty protection on used vehicles for engines, transmissions, steering mechanisms, and brakes. For used vehicles with less than 40,000 miles at the time of purchase, the warranty period is 90 days or 3,750 miles; vehicles with between 40,000 and 79,999 miles must be warranted for 60 days or 1000 miles; for those with between 80,000 and 124,999, the warranty must be for 30 days or 750 miles. Before a consumer can get a refund, the dealer must be given three repair attempts for the same defect or the car must be out of service for 11 business days. Massachusetts also requires auto dealers to give a consumer a refund should the vehicle fail state safety inspection within 7 days of purchase and if the inspection-related repairs are expected to cost more than 10 percent of the purchase price.

Used Vehicle Lemon Branding Laws

About 34 states require seller to label **lemons**, vehicles with serious defects, that have been repurchased under the requirements of state lemon laws. The laws specify that the title of a vehicle be properly branded with a clear indication that the vehicle was a lemon and that disclosure must be made to consumers at the point of sale.

Vehicle Repair Laws

Unfair and deceptive practices abound in the auto repair industry. As a result, most states have a vehicle repair law designed to protect consumers from unscrupulous merchants. Generally, such laws provide that on request, a consumer must be given a written repair estimate from someone that is going to repair his or her vehicle, unless the business is unwilling to do the repair. Later, if the mechanic or body repair person determines that the repairs are going to cost more than 10 percent above the estimate, the shop must obtain the consumer's permission to go ahead at the higher price. No charges are allowed for unauthorized work.

It is also illegal for repair shops to suggest that certain repairs are necessary or desirable when such is not the case. Finally, a consumer has the right to get back any parts replaced by the repair shop. If covered by a warranty or rebuilding arrangement, the consumer may view the parts, but may not be able to keep them.

Secret Warranty Disclosure Laws for Vehicles

For many years, automobile manufacturers have offered **secret vehicle warranties** to relatively few consumers that provide free repairs or reimbursement of incurred expenses when persistent problems develop beyond the traditional warranty time period. The problems usually affect the vehicle's performance or safety, but are not the subject of a formal recall. Secret warranties offered by auto manufacturers are disclosed in **factory service bulletins** that are sent to dealers authorizing them to make the repairs. In such cases, the dealers, not consumers, are notified. Historically, the dealers have been allowed to offer to make repairs at their discretion, and only those owners who complain the loudest received the free repairs. About 500 secret automobile warranties are in effect at any point in time. Manufacturers sometimes call these efforts **policy adjustments** or **goodwill service**. What is especially bad about secret auto warranties is that not all affected consumers benefit since most owners remain unaware of the manufacturer's policies.

Only a few states (CA, CN, VA, and WS) have secret warranty disclosure laws for automobiles that require the manufacturers and dealers to notify all affected owners when such repairs will be paid for by the manufacturer. These laws typically require auto manufacturers to notify by first-class mail all owners that may be affected by a manufacturer's warranty adjustment program. This includes notifying those owners who have already paid for the relevant repairs; therefore, those consumers may obtain reimbursement. Dealers also must tell consumers who have purchased an extended warranty if a particular repair is covered under such a program; dealers also must tell consumers if future repairs could be covered under an extended warranty. In some states, consumers are allowed to sue and collect damages from any auto manufacturer who violates the secret warranty disclosure law.

Federal Trade Commission Used Car Rule[4]

Each year, Americans spend about $100 billion to buy more than 17 million used cars. If you are buying a used car, the Federal Trade Commission's Used Car Rule may help you.

The rule requires all used car dealers to place a large sticker, called a **buyer's guide**, in the window of each used vehicle they offer for sale. The buyer's guide will state:

- Whether the vehicle comes with a warranty, and if so, what specific warranty protection the dealer will provide.
- Whether the vehicle comes with no warranty ("as is") or with implied warranties only.
- That you should ask to have the car inspected by your own mechanic before you buy.
- That you should get all promises in writing.
- What some of the major problems are that may occur in any car.

Whenever you purchase a used car from a dealer, you should receive the original or an identical copy of the buyer's guide that appeared in the window of the vehicle you bought. The buyer's guide must reflect any changes in warranty coverage that you may have negotiated with the dealer. It also becomes a part of your sales contract and overrides any contrary provisions that may be in that contract.

Dealers are required to post the buyer's guide on all used vehicles, including used automobiles, light-duty vans, and light-duty trucks. A **used vehicle** is one that has been driven more than the distance necessary to deliver a new car to the dealership or to test drive it. Therefore, "demonstrator" cars are covered by the rule. Motorcycles are excluded.

Warranty Information in the Buyer's Guide

A major portion of the buyer's guide gives you new and important information you can use when you select a used car. In the past, lack of information and misunderstanding about warranties frequently were a source of consumer problems. The following section explains the warranty portion of the buyer's guide. The buyer's guide is shown so that you can understand the information that follows.

A. "As is"

About one-half of all used cars sold by dealers come without a warranty, or "**as is**." This means that if you have problems with the car after you buy it, you must pay for any needed repairs yourself. The dealer has no further responsibility for the car once the sale

---

[4]Source: Buying a used car (1985, May). *Facts for consumers*. Federal Trade Commission, Bureau of Consumer Protection, Office of Consumer/Business Education, Washington, D.C.

is complete and you drive off the lot. If the dealer offers a vehicle for sale "as is", without any warranties, the box provided next to the "as is" disclosure will be checked.

B. Implied Warranties Only

Under most state laws, almost every purchase you make from a merchant is covered by an implied warranty, unless the seller tells you in writing that implied warranties do not apply. The most common type of implied warranty is called a **warranty of merchantability**. This means that the seller promises that the product will do what it is supposed to do. For example, a car will run; a toaster will toast.

Another type of implied warranty is the **warranty of fitness for a particular purpose**. This applies when you buy a vehicle on the dealer's advice that it is suitable for a particular use. For example, a dealer who suggests that you buy a specific vehicle for hauling a trailer warrants, in effect, that the vehicle will be suitable for hauling a trailer.

If your vehicle does not come with a written warranty, it is still covered by implied warranties unless the buyer's guide is marked "as is." Several states (Kansas, Maine, Maryland, Massachusetts, Mississippi, New York, Vermont, West Virginia, and the District of Columbia) do not permit "as is" sales. In these states, dealers must sell their vehicles with implied warranties.

If problems arise that are not covered by the written warranty, you should investigate the protection given by implied warranties. Implied warranty coverage varies from state to state. Your state consumer protection office may be able to provide more information about specific implied warranty coverage in your state.

In those states that do not permit "as is" sales by dealers, or if the dealer offers a vehicle with only implied warranties, a disclosure entitled "Implied Warranties Only" will be printed on the buyer's guide in place of the "As Is" disclosure. The box next to this disclosure would be checked if the dealer chooses to sell the car with implied warranties and no written warranty. A copy of the "Implied Warranties Only" disclosure is shown in the following pages.

C. Warranties

If dealers offer a warranty on a used vehicle, they must fill in the warranty portion of the buyer's guide. Examine the warranty carefully *before* you buy to see what is covered and what is not. The warranty that the dealer offers may give you some idea of what the dealer thinks about the condition of the vehicle.

If the dealer makes any promises to repair the vehicle that are not listed on the buyer's guide, ask the dealer to add those promises to both the buyer's guide and the sales contract. The sales contract also must include other specific information about your warranty.

Look for the Following Information on the Buyer's Guide

D. See if the warranty offered is "full" or "limited." A **full warranty** provides the following terms and conditions:

- Warranty service will be provided to anyone who owns the vehicle during the warranty period when a problem is reported. Warranty service will be provided free of charge, including such costs as returning the vehicle or removing and reinstalling a system covered by the warranty, when necessary.

- At your choice, the dealer will provide either a replacement or a full refund if the dealer is unable, after a reasonable number of tries, to repair the vehicle or a system covered by the warranty.
- Warranty service is provided without requiring that you return a warranty registration card.
- No limit is placed on the duration of implied warranties.

If any one of the preceding statements is not true, then the warranty is limited. A full or limited warranty need not cover the entire vehicle. The dealer may specify only certain systems for coverage under a warranty. By giving a **limited warranty**, the dealer is telling you that there are some costs or responsibilities that the dealer will not assume for systems covered by the warranty.

E. Check the percentage of the repair cost that the dealer will pay. For example, "the dealer will pay 100% of the labor and 100% of the parts..."

F. Check which specific systems are covered. The exact systems (such as frame and body, brake system, etc.) covered must be listed. A list of descriptive names for the major systems of an automobile is printed on the back of the buyer's guide.

G. Check the duration of the warranty for each covered system. For example, "30 days or 1000 miles, whichever occurs first."

Unexpired Manufacturer's Warranties

If the used vehicle is still covered under the terms of the manufacturer's original warranty, the dealer may add the following paragraph in the space below the warranty disclosure.

> MANUFACTURER'S WARRANTY STILL APPLIES. The manufacturer's original warranty has not expired on the vehicle. Consult the manufacturer's warranty booklet for details as to warranty coverage, service location, etc. This does not necessarily mean that dealers also offer *their own* warranty in addition to the manufacturer's. If you have any questions about warranty coverage, ask the dealer to let you examine any unexpired warranty on the vehicle.

Other Sections of the Buyer's Guide

There are other important parts of the buyer's guide. These parts are explained below and are also noted on the sample buyer's guide in the accompanying figure.

H. Spoken Promises

A statement appears on the buyer's guide that warns consumers not to rely on spoken promises. Oral promises are difficult, if not impossible, to enforce. Have the dealership put any promises in writing, or do not count on the promise.

This statement also reminds you to keep the buyer's guide after purchasing the vehicle. The buyer's guide will serve as proof of written promises.

I. Service Contracts

When you buy a car, you may be offered a **service contract**. Although often called **extended warranties**, service contracts are not warranties. Warranties are included in the price of the product. Service contracts come separately from the vehicle, at an extra cost. To decide whether you need a service contract, you should consider several factors: whether the warranty already covers the repairs that you would get under the service contract, whether the vehicle is likely to need repairs and their potential costs, how long the service contract is in effect, and the reputation of the dealer offering the service contract.

If a service contract is offered, the dealer will mark the box provided. However, in those states which regulate service contracts under their insurance laws, the dealer is not required to include this disclosure on the buyer's guide. Therefore, if you do not see the disclosure, ask the salesperson about the availability of a service contract.

Remember, when you purchase a service contract within 90 days of buying the vehicle, federal law prohibits the dealer from disclaiming implied warranties on the systems covered in that service contract. For example, if you buy a car "as is," the car normally will not be covered by implied warranties. But if you also buy a service contract covering the engine for 6 months, you automatically get implied warranties on the engine as well, which may give you additional protection even beyond the scope of the service contract.

J. Prepurchase Independent Inspection

The buyer's guide also includes a suggestion that you ask the dealer whether you may have the vehicle inspected by your own mechanic either on or off the premises. An independent inspection lets you find out about the mechanical condition of the vehicle *before* you buy it.

Some dealers will permit you to take the car to an independent mechanic. Others may have good reasons (for example, insurance restrictions) for denying this request.

With the dealer's permission, you can bring an independent mechanic to the used car lot. If you do not already have a mechanic you rely on, ask someone who knows about cars for the names of competent, reputable mechanics. You also can find mechanics through advertisements, car repair establishments, automobile associations, and automobile diagnostic centers in your community.

K. Vehicle Systems

The buyer's guide includes a list of the 14 major systems of an automobile and some of the major problems that may occur in these systems. You may find this list helpful to evaluate the mechanical condition of the vehicle. The list also may be useful when comparing warranties offered on different cars or by different dealers.

L. Dealer Identification and Consumer Complaint Information

On the back of the buyer's guide you will find the name and address of the dealership. In the space below that you will find the name and telephone number of the person at the dealership who should be contacted if any complaints arise after the sale.

BUYER'S GUIDE

H IMPORTANT: Spoken promises are difficult to enforce. Ask the dealer to put all promises in writing. Keep this form.

VEHICLE MAKE _____ MODEL _____ YEAR _____ VIN NUMBER _____

DEALER STOCK NUMBER (Optional) _____

WARRANTIES FOR THIS VEHICLE:

A

☐ **AS IS - NO WARRANTY**

YOU WILL PAY ALL COSTS FOR ANY REPAIRS. The dealer assumes no responsibility for any repairs regardless of any oral statements about the vehicle.

C

☐ **WARRANTY**

E

☐ FULL   ☐ LIMITED WARRANTY: The dealer will pay _____% of the labor and _____% of the parts for the
D   covered systems that fail during the warranty period. Ask the dealer for a copy of the warranty
             document for a full explanation of warranty coverage, exclusions, and the dealer's repair obliga-
             tions. Under state law, "implied warranties" may give you even more rights.

SYSTEMS COVERED: DURATION:

_____   _____
_____   _____
_____   _____
_____**F**_____   _____**G**_____
_____   _____
_____   _____
_____   _____

I ☐ SERVICE CONTRACT. A service contract is available at an extra charge on this vehicle. Ask for details as to coverage, deductible, price, and exclusions. If you buy a service contract within 90 days of the time of sale, state law "implied warranties" may give you additional rights.

J PRE PURCHASE INSPECTION: ASK THE DEALER IF YOU MAY HAVE THIS VEHICLE INSPECTED BY YOUR MECHANIC EITHER ON OR OFF THE LOT.

SEE THE BACK OF THIS FORM for important additional information, including a list of some major defects that may occur in used motor vehicles.

B

☐ **IMPLIED WARRANTIES ONLY**

This means that the dealer does not make any specific promises to fix things that need repair when you buy the vehicle or after the time of sale. But, state law "implied warranties" may give you some rights to have the dealer take care of serious problems that were not apparent when you bought the vehicle.

FIGURE 5-1   A Typical Buyer's Guide

Below is a list of some major defects that may occur in used motor vehicles.

Frame & Body
　Frame-cracks, corrective welds, or rusted through
　Dogtracks—bent or twisted frame

Engine
　Oil leakage, excluding normal seepage
　Cracked block or head
　Belts missing or inoperable
　Knocks or misses related to camshaft lifters
　　and push rods
　Abnormal exhaust discharge

Transmission & Drive Shaft
　Improper fluid level or leakage, excluding normal
　　seepage
　Cracked or damaged case which is visible
　Abnormal noise or vibration caused by faulty
　　transmission or drive shaft
　Improper shifting or functioning in any gear
　Manual clutch slips or chatters

Differential
　Improper fluid level or leakage excluding normal
　　seepage
　Cracked or damaged housing which is visible
　Abnormal noise or vibration caused by faulty
　　differential

Cooling System
　Leakage including radiator
　Improperly functioning water pump

Electrical System
　Battery leakage
　Improperly functioning alternator, generator,
　　battery, or starter

Fuel System
　Visible leakage

Inoperable Accessories
　Gauges or warning devices
　Air conditioner
　Heater & Defroster

Brake System
　Failure warning light broken
　Pedal not firm under pressure (DOT spec.)
　Not enough pedal reserve (DOT spec.)
　Does not stop vehicle in straight line (DOT spec.)
　Hoses damaged
　Drum or rotor too thin (Mfgr. Specs)
　Lining or pad thickness less than 1/32 inch
　Power unit not operating or leaking
　Structural or mechanical parts damaged

Steering System
　Too much free play at steering wheel (DOT
　　specs.)
　Free play in linkage more than 1/4 inch
　Steering gear binds or jams
　Front wheels aligned improperly (DOT specs.)
　Power unit belts cracked or slipping
　Power unit fluid level improper

Suspension System
　Ball joint seals damaged
　Structural parts bent or damaged
　Stabilizer bar disconnected
　Spring broken
　Shock absorber mounting loose
　Rubber bushings damaged or missing
　Radius rod damaged or missing
　Shock absorber leaking or functioning improperly

Tires
　Tread depth less than 2/32 inch
　Sizes mismatched
　Visible damage

Wheels
　Visible cracks, damage or repairs
　Mounting bolts loose or missing

Exhaust System
　Leakage

DEALER

ADDRESS

SEE FOR COMPLAINTS

FIGURE 5-1 (continued)   A Typical Buyer's Guide

Private Sales

If you buy a used car from a private individual (for example, through a classified newspaper ad), the sale is not covered by the rule. Private sellers do not have to use the buyer's guide. In most private sales, the car is sold "as is." Without a written contract with specific repair provisions, the private seller in most states has no further responsibility for the car. If you have a written contract, the seller must live up to the promises stated in the contract. Depending on its age, the car may be covered by a manufacturer's warranty or service contract. Ask the seller to let you examine any unexpired warranty or service contract on the vehicle.

Even without the buyer's guide, when you buy a used vehicle from a private party, you can follow the suggestions given here. For example, refer to the list of potential problems in the buyer's guide. In addition, ask the seller whether you may have the vehicle inspected by your own mechanic. It is important to find out about the mechanical condition of the vehicle before you buy it.

Spanish-Language Sales

If you buy a used car and the sales talk is conducted in Spanish, you are entitled to see and keep a Spanish-language version of the buyer's guide. The Used Car Rule includes a text for the Spanish-language version.

Laws on Warranties

There are a number of laws and regulations on warranties.

Magnuson-Moss Warranty Act

The conflicting viewpoints of consumers and sellers has historically resulted in warranty problems. The concept of warranties that used to give consumers dissatisfaction because of a lack of clarity and deceptions perhaps can best be summed up by the old adage, "The bold print giveth and the fine print taketh away." As a result, governments have written laws to govern warranty situations. The Magnuson-Moss Warranty Act was passed in 1975. It authorized the Federal Trade Commission to write regulations that interpret and implement the law, primarily through an effort to require disclosure of warranty terms. The Magnuson-Moss Warranty Act attempts to restore a sense of fair play in the marketplace by giving consumers an understanding of warranties more equal to that of the sellers.

A **warranty** or (**guarantee**) is an assurance by a seller that the goods or property sold are of the quality represented or will be as promised. Warranties on consumer products are offered by manufacturers as a promotional device to help differentiate one product from its competitors. In fact, whole advertising campaigns are sometimes designed around a product warranty.

The seller sees the warranty as something that limits the firm's liability, since it legally obligates the manufacturer only so far in dealing with buyers who have problems while simultaneously inducing particular expectations on the part of the consumer. For example, a written warranty may specify which remedies are available to consumers with problems and may limit how much the company will pay. An **express warranty** is a written guarantee setting out specific assurances by the manufacturer or seller.

The consumer, however, views warranties in a different light. Many consumers accept warranties uncritically, assuming that the act of offering a warranty suggests that this is a quality product.

Standards for Companies that Offer Warranties

The Magnuson-Moss law and subsequent regulations do not require that a manufacturer offer a guarantee, but if a manufacturer does offer a written warranty, it must comply with various standards. Basically the law demands that a warranty should mean what it says and that the details should be spelled out in easy-to-understand language. Therefore, products claiming a "money-back guarantee," suggesting that they are "fully guaranteed," or promising "satisfaction guaranteed or your money back," should do what is promised. Sellers are prohibited from giving something to consumers with the big print and taking it away with the small print.

Warranties must use clear and simple language to tell the following: (1) the name and address of the warrantor, (2) whether the warranty is given only to the original purchaser, (3) a description of exactly what is warranted and for how long, (4) an indication that a registration card must be returned if that is the warrantor's procedure, (5) the procedure for placing a claim, (6) what the company will do in case of problems, and (7) step-by-step procedures to follow to settle a dispute between the buyer and the seller.

To reduce problems with warranties, the Magnuson-Moss law requires that consumers be able to examine warranty coverage before they make a purchase. Any product that costs $15 or more is covered under the law and must be made available for inspection. Either sellers can print the warranty on the outside of the product package or retailers must post a sign near products that have warranties indicating where in the store a customer can go to examine the warranty.

What Some Confusing Phrases in Warranties Really Mean

The law has improved the opportunity for consumers to understand and practice their warranty rights; however, the language on warranties remains legalistic and perplexing for many. This results in confusion since state laws often offer more protections to consumers than the federal laws. Some examples of typical phrases that appear in current warranties follow:

1. "This warranty gives you specific legal rights, and you may also have other rights which vary from state to state." This means that the consumers' strong implied warranty rights of merchantability and fitness for a particular purpose may be provided for under the laws of the state where you live.

2. "Some states do not allow limitations of incidental or consequential damages, so the above limitations may not apply to you." This also means that the laws of the state where you live may provide more protection.

Many consumers also have trouble understanding such legal concepts as incidental and consequential damages. To illustrate, your warranted vehicle antifreeze may not perform as advertised leading to a frozen engine needing $2000 in consequential repairs. There also could be incidental towing costs to get the vehicle to the repair shop.

3. "This limitation or exclusion may not apply to you." Again, state laws may offer more protection.

4. "Some states do not allow limitations on how long an implied warranty lasts, so the above limitations may not apply to you." Here you need to find out if your state provides any limitations on to how long implied warranty rights last.

Although these phrases are accurate and provide important protection for consumers, they seem to confuse rather than clarify the issues.

In all warranty situations, you have to find out for yourself whether your state laws offer more protection that provided for in the warranty because a lack of uniformity exists among the states. To complicate matters more, written warranties typically take multiple paragraphs to state the limitations of the seller. To assert these rights under state laws (variations of the Uniform Commercial Code), consumers often have to resort to civil lawsuits.

Disclaiming Implied Warranties Is Prohibited Except When Something Is Sold "As Is"

Importantly, the Magnuson-Moss law prohibits warrantors from disclaiming implied warranties unless the product is clearly labeled **"as is"** when sold. This phrase indicates that the product, such as a used vehicle, comes with no warranties, either express or implied. Therefore, when the buyer purchases something marked "as is," he or she assumes full responsibility for determining the condition of a product being purchased. It also releases the seller of all legal claims.

Full and Limited Warranties May Be Offered

The law requires that express guarantees be conspicuously designated as either full or limited, which immediately gives consumers an indication of the type of warranty coverage provided. To meet the federal standards to be a **full warranty**, the warrantor must: (1) remedy a defective product within a reasonable time and without charge in the event of a defect, malfunction, or failure to conform to the warranty, and (2) after a reasonable number of attempts by the warrantor to remedy defects, the warrantor must give the consumer the option of either a refund or replacement without charge. The latter part of this definition is known as a **lemon clause** because it provides recourse to buyers who are stuck with products that seem to be unrepairable. Replacements must be made free of charge, including removal and reinstallation, while warrantors may deduct an amount for depreciation based on actual use when they replace products. In addition, another requirement for full warranties is that the consumer must not have to do anything unreasonable to get warranty service, such as return a heavy product, like a washing machine, to the seller. Full warranties cannot require the return of a warranty registration card either.

The FTC has the authority to define what is a reasonable number of repairs for various products. Consumers with persistent automobile complaints can use the power of lemon clauses for cars with full warranties, as well as state lemon laws to motivate sellers to make proper repairs. It is also important to note that products offering full warranties cannot place limits on the duration of implied warranties; thus a warrantor offering a full warranty is liable for any incidental and consequential damages, such as food, lodging, towing, car rental fees, and food spoilage. Full warranties apply to both the original purchaser and subsequent owners during the warranty period.

Limited warranties are much more widespread because of the severe obligations placed on sellers offering full warranties. A **limited warranty** is any written guarantee that provides less than a full warranty. If any full warranty requirement is not provided in a warranty, the warranty is classified as a limited warranty. For example, a limited warranty may cover parts only, instead of parts and labor, or it may cover repairs only, instead of replacement or refund. Many limited warranties require that the buyer has to return a warranty card to activate the warranty. Nevertheless, many limited warranties provide excellent coverage on consumer products.

Informal Dispute Procedures Are Encouraged

The Magnuson-Moss Warranty Act encourages the use of an **informal dispute procedure** whenever warranty problems arise between sellers and buyers. Such a procedure allows impartial people to review the arguments and evidence of the complaining consumer and the seller in an attempt to resolve the conflict about warranty service. Warrantors are not required to set up such procedures, but when they do, the procedures must meet minimum standards established by the FTC (known as **Rule 703**) and explain the details in their written warranties. When a warrantor has established an informal dispute procedure, the consumer must use it before taking any legal action. Therefore, manufacturers are motivated to set up an informal dispute procedure as an alternative to engaging in costly litigation with consumers with warranty service problems. Rule 703 requires that consumer disputes be settled within a 40-day time period.

Consumers who successfully file state or federal lawsuits against warrantors who do not have an informal dispute procedure may be awarded their purchase costs, attorneys fees, and damages. In addition, consumers injured by a breach of warranty may file a federal class action lawsuit. Few warranty problems meet all the restrictions necessary for consumers to economically and successfully pursue a class action lawsuit under the provisions of the Magnuson-Moss Warranty Act.

The Magnuson-Moss Warranty Act does not preempt the field of state warranty law. Instead, it adds another layer of consumer protection while preserving rights and remedies under state law.

Laws on Housing

There are a number of laws and regulations that exist in the area of housing.

Renter's Security Deposits

Almost all states have laws governing security deposits paid by renters to landlords. Typically, a landlord cannot collect more than one month's rent as a security deposit. That amount must be held in an interest-bearing bank account, and the interest must be paid to the tenant within 30 days of the yearly anniversary date of tenancy. At the end of the tenancy, the landlord may only deduct for unpaid rent and for damages beyond reasonable wear and tear. Security deposits must be returned, noting deductions, within 30 days after the tenancy ends, otherwise the consumer may be entitled to double or triple damages.

Late Possession of the Rental Property

Sometimes consumers experience difficulty in taking possession of rental housing because the landlord cannot deliver the unit. The problem may be that the previous tenant will not move out, or the landlord may find that it will take more time to put the facility into proper condition. Regardless of the reason, this may cost the renter extra money in the form of motel expenses until the move can be made.

In all states, consumers so wronged have the right to sue in an attempt to collect damages from the landlord. He or she should be forced to reimburse the renter for costs of lodging elsewhere, plus any storage expenses. It is easy to win such lawsuits where there is a "damages" clause in the lease contract; such lawsuits will fail if the lease contains a clause that totally absolves the landlord of any liability in such situations. In such cases, the dispute may be resolved by compromises made between the landlord and the tenant.

Habitability of Rental Unit

All states and municipalities provide legal rights to tenants. The habitability of the rental unit must meet some legally prescribed minimum standard, such as running water, functional toilets, heat during the months of fall, winter and spring, and a working stove. In most states, an implied warranty covers the availability of heat and the safety of access areas, such as stairs. Filing a lawsuit against a landlord for nonperformance is permitted in all states. This is usually done in a small claims court (described in Chapter 3), where for a nominal filing fee (perhaps $15) lawsuits up to a certain dollar amount (perhaps $2500) can be pursued without an attorney.

In addition, reporting building-code violations to a local government housing authority is not just cause for eviction or for harassment in the form of a rent increase or utility shutoff. Also, joining a tenant organization is not cause for eviction; tenant organizations aim to improve the bargaining power of tenants.

In many states, tenants may legally make minor repairs themselves and deduct those costs from their next rent payment. This is subject to certain restrictions, such as giving sufficient prior written notification to the landlord.

Interstate Land Sales

The Interstate Land Sales Full Disclosure Act (passed in 1968) is designed to help consumers avoid land sale scams. The law requires developers who are selling (or leasing) 100 or more unimproved lots across state lines to file detailed information about their properties with the Department of Housing and Urban Development. Before signing a contract, the developer is required to show consumers the **property report**, which describes relevant details about the venture. In addition, consumers have a seven-day cooling off period during which they may change their minds (for misrepresentation or any other reason). When considering buying undeveloped land that is exempt from this law, people are advised to be certain that the contract includes a cancellation clause.

Community Reinvestment Act

The Community Reinvestment Act (CRA) requires federal agencies to encourage depository financial institutions to help meet the credit needs of their communities, especially low- and moderate-income neighborhoods. The federal regulatory agencies, such as the Federal Reserve Board, assess the institutions' records of meeting those credit needs by preparing a written evaluation of the institutions along with the assignment of a concluding rating supported with facts. These are disclosed to the public. Lenders must tell inquiring consumers their CRA rating.

Fair Housing Act

Discrimination is acting on the basis of bias or intentional prejudice. It is illegal to discriminate in the financing of housing. Various laws prohibit discrimination on the basis of race, color, religion, national origin, sex, elderliness, parenthood, or handicap.

The Fair Housing Act prohibits discrimination on the basis of race, color, sex, religion, handicap, familial status, or national origin in the financing, sale, or rental of housing. The Fair Housing Act directly prohibits discrimination in mortgage lending. It empowers the Department of Housing and Urban Development and the Attorney General to help assure non-discriminatory practices in all aspects of the housing market. For example, it is illegal to discriminate against families with children when renting or selling a house or apartment. The Justice Department can ask for compensatory monetary damages for persons victimized and assess civil penalties. The maximum civil penalty for a first finding of discrimination is $50,000, and up to $100,000 for a subsequent violation.

Home Mortgage Disclosure Act

The Home Mortgage Disclosure Act (HMDA) requires certain lending institutions to report annually on their mortgage lending practices, including both originations and purchases of home purchases and home improvement loans, as well as applications for such loans. The type of loan, location of the property, race or national origin, gender, and income of the applicant are reported. Such information, which aggregately must be disclosed to the public, can help determine how well institutions are serving the housing credit needs of neighborhoods and communities. Lenders must post a notice of lending availability in their public lobby.

These data also allow others to check on any discrimination in the pattern of lending. Recent data from the Federal Reserve Board reveal that while 11 percent of white people are rejected for home loans, the figure is 24 percent for blacks. These numbers do not prove that discrimination is occurring in housing lending, but they do suggest that discrimination may be happening. Consumers need to be aware of the housing laws that can be used to protect them.

State Housing Discrimination Laws

In addition to the federal regulations prohibiting discrimination, all states have fair housing laws with similar purposes. The typical state law protects against the following acts: (1) refusal to sell or rent or to deal or negotiate with any person, (2) presenting different terms and conditions to different people for buying or renting housing, (3) advertising that housing is available to certain persons, (4) denying housing is available for inspection, sale, or rent when it really is available, (5) **blockbusting**, which is persuasion of owners to sell or rent housing by telling them that priority groups are moving into the neighborhood, (6) denying or making different conditions or terms for home loans by commercial lenders, and (7) **redlining,** which is drawing a red line (or any other color for that matter) around areas of a community and refusing loans to people wanting financing in those areas.

A number of exclusions to federal and state laws usually exist. An exclusion usually occurs when a private individual sells or rents a home without employing a real estate broker, without using discriminatory advertising, and without having sold more than one residence in the past 2 years. The laws also are not applicable to the rental of rooms or units in buildings of not more than four families if the owner lives in one of the units and if no discriminatory advertising is used. Also, religious organizations or private clubs may give preferences to their members in housing.

Laws on Credit

There are a number of laws and regulations in the area of credit.

Limited Liability on Credit Cards

The Fair Credit Reporting Act, passed in 1972, limits the liability for unauthorized use of credit cards, including telephone credit cards, and provides other consumer rights. It results in a maximum liability of $50 per card. This **credit-card liability** occurs only if you receive notification of your potential liability, you accepted the card when it was first mailed to you, the company provided you with a self-addressed form with which to notify them if the card was lost, and the card was used illegally before you notified them of the loss. If you notify the credit-card company within two days of a lost or stolen card, you are not legally responsible for any charges; after that time period you are liable for only $50 in false charges. In addition, there is no time limit for reporting unauthorized charges when someone has illegally used your credit card; however, you must specify in a complaint letter to the credit card company that it is an "unauthorized charge."

Although your financial liability is low, some companies specialize in selling lost credit-card insurance; it is profitable for them and an unnecessary expense for you. Besides, consumers who have renter's or homeowner's insurance typically have coverage that automatically protects them against such losses. Further, as a gesture of goodwill, most companies waive the $50 fee for unauthorized use of credit cards. As might be expected, the credit-card insurance companies generally do not offer such information.

Amendments to the Fair Credit Reporting Act in 1995 require that when information held by a credit bureau plays a role in denying a consumer credit or insurance, he or she must be informed, able to check the file, and make corrections. The Medical Information Bureau (MIB) is the company that collects and maintains information on consumers' credit history, medical conditions, driving records, criminal activity, participation in hazardous sports, and more. Copies of an MIB report are available for $8; call (617)-426-3660 or write MIB, Box 105, Boston, MA 02112.

Electronic Funds Transfer Act

People often make regular **direct deposits**, such as a paycheck, stock dividends, or Social Security benefits, to financial accounts electronically. You also can authorize your financial institution to pay recurring bills in both regular amounts (such as a mortgage or automobile loan) and irregular amounts (such as for electric or telephone bills). The federal Electronic Funds Transfer Act (EFTA) permits you to stop a pre-authorized payment by calling or writing the financial institution, so that your new order is received at least three days before the payment date. Written confirmation of a telephone notice to stop payment may be required by the institution.

The EFTA Applies to Electronic Transfers, Debit Cards, and Credit Cards Used as Debit Cards

All kinds of electronic transfers occur daily for most consumers. Federal and state regulations have been adopted to provide protection for EFT users. (Electronic benefit transfers are currently exempt from the EFT regulations, since most electronic benefits programs are experimental.) The 1978 Electronic Funds Transfer Act is the governing statute and the Federal Reserve Board's "Regulation E" provides the specific guidelines on EFT-card liability. The Electronic Funds Transfer Act affects consumer use of electronic transfers, debit cards, and credit cards used as debit cards.

Rules specify that a valid card can be sent only to a consumer who has requested it. Unsolicited cards can be issued only if the card cannot be used until validated and the user is informed of liability for unauthorized use as well as of other terms and conditions. When you sign up for EFT services, your depository institution must inform you of your rights and responsibilities in a written disclosure statement containing the above information.

Consumers get written receipts when withdrawing money or making deposits with an ATM machine or using a point-of-sale terminal to pay for a purchase. These show the amount of the transfer, the date it was made, and other information. General protection of customers' accounts exists in the form of a periodic statement that financial institutions regularly send out. These show all electronic transfers to and from your account, any fees charged, and the opening and closing balances. EFT users should regularly reconcile the information on their periodic statement with the written receipts.

Correcting EFT Errors on Periodic Statements

Should you find an error in your periodic statement, notify the issuing organization in writing as soon as possible. Correct notification procedures can be found in the disclosure statement. You have 60 days from the date of the statement or receipt error to notify the financial institution, otherwise the institution has no obligation to investigate. Always telephone and follow up with a letter. If the institution needs more than 10 business days to investigate and correct a problem, generally it must return to your account the amount in question while it finishes the investigation (within a required 45 days). If there was an error, the institution must correct it promptly by making the correction final. If there was no error, the institution must explain in writing why it believes there was no error and let you know that it has deducted any amount temporarily credited during the investigation. However, the institution must honor withdrawals against the credited amount for 5 days. You may ask for copies of documents relied on in the investigation and again challenge if a mistake has been made.

Lost EFT Cards

The sooner you report a lost electronic funds transfer (EFT) card, the more likely you will limit your liability if someone uses your card without your permission. Cardholders are liable for only the first $50 of unauthorized use if they notify the issuing company within 2 business days after the loss or theft of their card or code. Between 2 and 60 days, cardholder liability for unauthorized use rises to $500. If you fail to alert the financial institution within 60 days, you risk *unlimited* loss. Thus, you are liable for every dollar stolen in your account, plus your maximum overdraft line-of-overdraft credit. The logic is that if cardholders examine their monthly statements, they will note unauthorized use of the account. These regulations are for specific EFT cards *and* for other cards used to make an electronic funds transfer (such as a Visa credit card). A number of states have laws that provide additional protections for consumers in EFT transactions.

It is difficult for consumers to dispute an item with a merchant (for faulty goods, for example) if the merchant has already been paid by means of EFT. Because the merchant already has the money, the consumer's only recourse to correct or reverse EFT transactions is to ask for a refund.

Automatic-Billing Disputes

As a matter of convenience, many consumers give their credit card or checking account number to vendors so that regular monthly fees may be automatically charged, or debited, to their accounts. If charges come directly out of a checking account, a problem may occur because your money is gone and it is hard to get it back.

DID YOU KNOW?
Your Current Homeowner's/Renter's Insurance May *Already* Cover the Liability for Lost Credit and Debit Cards

Many companies sell specialized liability insurance in a separate policy for an annual premium of $30 to $60. In addition, some firms sell a **card registration service** that will notify all companies where you have debit and credit cards in the event of loss because for a fee of $19 to $49 a year, after they get one telephone call from you. Alternatively, in case of loss, you can notify debit and credit card companies yourself.

It is important to know that homeowner's and renter's insurance policies typically cover the liability for the unauthorized use (usually theft) of both debit and credit cards. If such protection is not in your current policy, the coverage generally can be added to a homeowner's or renter's policy for $10 to $15 a year.

Consumers do have protections from *electronic* debits to their bank accounts under the Automated Clearing House (ACH) rules governing financial institutions. After receiving a statement, consumers have 15 days to tell their bank that the charge was unauthorized. It is then the bank's responsibility to prove the validity of the charge, or reverse the debit. However, there are no protections for consumers for *paper* debits. Alternatively, if you permit charges to a credit card, you have the protections of the Fair Credit Billing Act (discussed below) that allow consumers to dispute an unauthorized charge up to 60 days after it occurred.

Fair Credit Reporting Act

Most credit reporting is done by **credit bureaus**, which compile information about credit applications and forward it to the creditor. A creditor comes under the Fair Credit Reporting Act only when credit information from one firm is forwarded to another and a credit decision is based on that information. The objective of the act is to place certain restrictions on credit-reporting agencies to reduce errors.

Rights Exist If You Are Denied Credit

If you are denied credit because of a poor credit report, the law requires disclosure to you of the name and address of any credit-reporting agency that supplied information about you. You can then request a summary of the contents of your file at the credit-reporting agency without a fee; a cost-free credit report must be requested within 30 days of denial. If you dispute an item, it must be reinvestigated. If the information was in error, it must be corrected. You also may wish to tell your side of the story on a disputed item by adding, in 100 words or less, a **consumer statement** to your credit file (see an example of a "consumer statement" in the chapter appendix). All such information (corrections or your side of the story) must be sent to anyone who received a credit report on you in the previous 6 months.

Even if you have not been denied credit, for a small fee (usually about $5 to $15) you can obtain a copy of your credit bureau file. A credit record may be retained for a period of 7 years for judgments, liens, lawsuits, and other adverse information except for bankruptcies, which may be retained for 10 years.

When you apply for life insurance or employment, a credit bureau is usually paid to compile an **investigative report**. This is a much more detailed report than a regular consumer credit report. It often includes interview comments from neighbors and friends about your lifestyle, morals, character, and reputation. The FCRA requires that you be informed when this kind of report is being compiled.

DID YOU KNOW?
How to Get a Copy of Your Credit Report for Free

Most of the more than 2000 local credit bureaus belong to national groups that have access to credit histories of over 80 million people, such as Equifax (P.O. Box 740256, Atlanta, GA 30374-0256; 800-685-1111), Trans Union (P.O. Box 7000, North Olmsted, OH 44070; 800-851-2674), and TRW Credit Data (P.O. Box 8030, Layton, UT 84041-8030; 800-682-7654. If you have been turned down for credit within the past 60 days because of information in a credit report, you can get a copy of the report free. Otherwise, the cost is about $8. TRW gives consumers a free "complimentary report" once a year, just for the asking. Excellent pro-consumer corporate policy, TRW!

Fair Credit Billing Act

The Fair Credit Billing Act (FCBA) went into effect in 1975 to protect against billing errors and the receipt of unsatisfactory goods and services when consumers use a credit card to pay for purchases, including those made by mail or telephone. It establishes procedures for the prompt correction of all types of errors on open-end credit accounts. It provides safeguards against unsatisfactory purchases and uncooperative merchants. The law also protects a consumer's credit rating while the consumer is settling a dispute. In the past, complaining about a credit card bill often resulted in delays and in harmful information going into a consumer's credit file. Four sample credit complaint letters are in the chapter appendix.

Under the claims and defenses portion of the law, also known as the **charge back** section, consumer's may legally withhold payment for a disputed amount for a number of reasons. Here your credit card company will attempt to "charge back" the disputed amount to the merchant. Consumers may not be responsible for a charge on their credit account if it:
  (1) is in error,
  (2) was not made by a person authorized to use the account, or
  (3) is for goods and services that were not provided or delivered according to agreement, or in other words they were "unsatisfactory."

To exercise your rights,[5] you must notify your credit card company of your problem in writing that you dispute the charge within 60 days of the postmark date of the bill on which the charge appeared, e.g, when it was *mailed to you*. A telephone call to the lender will *not* preserve your rights.

The credit card issuer must investigate such inquiries and respond in writing within two billing cycles. During the time when the company is looking into the problem, consumers are not required to pay the questioned amount or pay any finance charges associated with the disputed amount. These rights do not guarantee consumers a refund, but the law does require that the credit card issuer investigate the matter in their effort to resolve the dispute.

With all challenges to credit card bills, if the credit card issuer turns down the challenge, the consumer still owes the amount of the charge, plus any finance costs that have accumulated (but were suspended until the challenge was resolved). However, any subsequent reports sent to a credit bureau must state that the consumer disputes the charges, and the consumer must be told who receives such reports for the following six months.

The law is limited to credit card purchases for over $50, which have not been paid for, that were made within your home state or within 100 miles of your home (whichever is farther). While this excludes overseas purchases, some U.S. credit card issuers have voluntarily extended the coverage around the world. In practice, most credit card companies allow consumers to contest any disputed amount, regardless of amount or distance from one's home. With telemarketing transactions, a consumer can easily make the case that the purchase occurred inside his or her home. In addition, the seller may have placed advertisements in the local media which, of course, would be within 100 miles of the consumer's home.

If the consumer has already paid the card issuer for a charge before realizing that a problem existed, one's legal leverage has been lost; however, most issuers are willing to work with customers who have been ripped off. Moreover, making payment with a credit card offers consumers much more protection than when paying with cash or a check.

The FCBA also states that bills must be mailed to cardholders at least 14 days before payments are due. Companies are required to send a reminder of their consumer credit rights under the FCBA to all customers twice a year. Another provision requires that retailers who voluntarily give price discounts of up to 5 percent to cash customers must publicly state that information. In this way, cardholders can choose to elect to pay cash and thus avoid the extra costs the merchant imposes on credit accounts.

Consumers Get to Keep $50 of the Disputed Amount if the Credit Card Company Fails to Follow the Rules

Failure of the company to follow all the rules within the proper time limits, the law allows the cardholder to keep the first $50 of the amount in dispute, even if it is money the consumer owes. Alternatively, the consumer may sue for damages resulting from the violation, plus twice the amount of any finance charge (not less than $100 or more than $1,000), plus attorney fees and costs.

---

[5]These rights exist both in the United States and overseas, although in some foreign countries local laws may limit one's FCBA rights.

Reason #1 to Challenge a Credit Bill—Consumers Are Not Liable for the Errors of Others

A consumer has the right to dispute a charge and temporarily withhold payment for that charge while the credit card company investigates for a number of reasons: (1) something you did not buy, (2) something purchased by an unauthorized person, (3) something not properly identified on a bill (i.e., place, description, date), (4) an amount different from the actual purchase price, (5) something not accepted on delivery, (6) something that was not delivered according to agreement (e.g., wrong quantity, incorrect specifications, or unreasonably late), (7) arithmetic errors, (8) failure to reflect a payment or a credit, (9) failure to mail the billing statement to the current address, provided the lender received notice of that address at least 20 days before the end of the billing period, and (10) any item for which a consumer requests additional clarification.

After investigating a challenge, the credit card issuer typically forwards the complaining consumer a photocopy of the signature on the credit slip. The issuer's position often is, "Well, if that is your signature, you still owe us the money, so stop your complaining and pay us what is owed." Consumers should not be taken in by such an attitude and quickly give in and pay the disputed amount. If it is your signature, but there is some genuine problem with the bill, write the card issuer again reaffirming the challenge. This time write to a supervisor at the credit card issuer, being even more explicit with your explanation. A sample complaint letter to a supervisor at a credit card company is shown in the chapter appendix.

Another good reason to challenge an "error" is that the credit card bill was received too late or not received at all. This problem often occurs when people move from one address to another and when the Postal Service loses the mail. In this instance, the consumer simply writes to challenge the finance charges that were incorrectly imposed on the account. Such charges should be credited on the account provided the lender received notice of that new address at least 20 days before the end of the billing period.

If the credit card issuer disagrees with and rejects the challenge, they must tell the consumer why they believe the bill is not in dispute. At this point, the consumer may ask for copies of relevant documents and then refile the complaint (perhaps with more information). Refusal to pay may result in the lender beginning collection procedures, although credit card issuers usually do not begin to send collection letters for 90 days.

Reason #2 to Challenge a Credit Bill—It Appears to be an Unauthorized Charge

If your reason for the challenge is that the charge appears to be unauthorized, the card issuer will forward you a photocopy of the signature on the credit card slip so it can be examined. Should the consumer write back reporting that the signature is not valid, the credit card issuer must give in and accept the challenge as legitimate. That means that the challenged amount will immediately be credited. If the amount involved is substantial, the card issuer's fraud investigative unit will contact the consumer in an effort to obtain additional information that might be useful in investigating and catching the culprit who falsified the signature.

Reason #3 to Challenge a Credit Bill—Unsatisfactory Goods

Examples of unsatisfactory goods and services include: (1) ordered merchandise was not ever delivered to your home, (2) stitching in a new jacket ripped out under normal use, (3) fraudulent emergency auto repairs were made to your vehicle while on an out-of-town trip, (4) you did not enjoy a terrible meal at a restaurant about which you complained to the merchant, and (5) you lost a night's sleep in a noisy motel room where you complained to the night manager to no avail.

Key to successfully winning a dispute is that you *must* make a real attempt to resolve the problem with the merchant. The chapter appendix contains illustrative letters that can be sent to the merchant and the credit card issuer. If you attempt to challenge a credit card bill on the grounds that you are dissatisfied without first, or simultaneously, contacting the merchant in an attempt to resolve the matter, the card issuer will very likely refuse your request and reinstate the charge to your account.

Moreover, consumers may challenge billing errors for defective or deficient products or services. If you use a credit card to purchase goods that are shoddy or damaged, or if you receive poor quality services, the law protects you by giving you certain rights that may be exercised. In addition, the defective nature of the goods or services is a valid defense against any later lawsuit by a credit card issuer.

When Necessary, Consumers Should Write Firm Letters to Merchants and Credit Card Companies

To properly dispute a credit card charge, first, write the merchant to complain and, if appropriate, seek a compromise. Second, write a complaint letter to the credit card company. Provide the credit card company with a chronology and as much documentation as possible, so that they can contact the merchant to try to thrash things out. During that time creditors cannot send **dunning letters** (notices that make insistent demands for repayment) to you or send negative information about your account to a credit bureau without stating additionally that, "Some items are in dispute." Consumers who pay off their bills before realizing a problem exists are *not* entitled to a credit.

When writing, be pleasant but firm, state only the important details, and tell them what you want done. Many consumers wisely charge any and all expenses that might later turn out to be a problem, such as air travel and auto repairs while on trips. For travel expenses, the 60-day period to contest a charge begins from the date of the bill, not the date of travel. Three companies have extended the challenge time for travel charges: Visa voluntarily extended the time period from the date of travel, MasterCard 120 days from the date of the bill, and American Express up to a year.

CONSUMER UPDATE:
Sample Complaint Letters to Resolve Credit Problems

There are five sample letters in the chapter appendix that deal with credit problems. Of those letters, one disputes an item on a credit card bill. The second complains to a merchant requesting credit for an unsatisfactory purchase. The third complains to the credit card issuer to obtain a credit for an unsatisfactory purchase. The fourth complains to a supervisor at a credit card issuer, and it is to be used if the credit card issuer turns down an initial request to dispute an item on a credit card bill. The fifth letter adds to one's credit file information.

Equal Credit Opportunity Act

Discrimination in lending against women, the elderly, and religious and racial minorities resulted in the passage of the Equal Credit Opportunity Act of 1975, which prohibits discrimination in granting credit. Rejecting a credit application due to poor credit history is legal, but rejecting a person on the basis of sex, race, color, age, marital status, religion, national origin, or because the person receives public assistance is not. It also prohibits discrimination because of good faith exercise of any rights under the federal credit laws and regulations. By law, credit applications cannot probe for information that could be used in a biased manner. The Equal Credit Opportunity Act requires creditors to provide to the applicant a written statement, if requested, of the reasons for refusing credit. Should discrimination be proven in court, the lender may be liable for up to $10,000 in fines.

Lenders must use the same criteria to judge applications from single and married persons. A married man or woman applying for credit need not disclose marital status or a spouse's income unless he or she is dependent on that income, in which case it is used as the basis for granting credit. Several states take exception to this, considering any property acquired by either the husband or wife, known as **community property**, as jointly owned and equally shared.

Fair Debt Collection Practices Act

This 1977 legislation was aimed at eliminating abusive, deceptive, and unfair debt collection practices. It applies to third party debt collectors or those who use a name other than their own in collecting consumer debts. Banks, dentists, lawyers, and others who do their own collecting are exempt. **Collection agencies** attempt to make collections of debt from consumers that could not be obtained through the usual procedures of sellers.

Collection agencies are prohibited from harassing debtors, telephoning before 8:00 a.m. or after 9 p.m. on Mondays through Saturdays, making numerous repeated telephone calls during the day, misrepresenting themselves (such as claiming they are attorneys, unless they are) or the purpose of their communication, using profane or abusive language, making threats, making racial or ethnic slurs, or spreading rumors that the debtor is a "deadbeat." Direct contact with debtors' employers or any other third-party with respect to monies owed is prohibited.

Even with these limitations, realize that collection agencies can be irritatingly persistent in collecting past-due accounts. If they are not successful, they take the consumer to court and seek a default judgment as the last resort.

Debtors have the right to request that collectors cease communication, and if debtors are represented by attorneys, all future contact regarding those accounts must be with the attorneys. Should the collector persist, debtors should write a letter and firmly inform the collector to stop. Should harassment continue, the debtor can report the law violations to the Federal Trade Commission, the state attorney general, and the local telephone company.

Fair Credit and Charge Card Disclosure Act

The Fair Credit and Charge Card Disclosure Act of 1988 provides that credit-card issuers must reveal a number of important pricing details before consumers sign up for the credit cards. The law requires any direct-mail credit application or solicitation to reveal: (1) the annual percentage rate (APR) of interest, including the way the rate is calculated and if the rate is variable, (2) the method used to calculate the monthly account balances against which the company applies interest or finance charges, (3) all fees, including annual fees, minimum finance charges, transaction charges, cash-advance fees, late fees, and fees for going over the credit limit, and (4) the length of time of the grace period, if any. Information such as APRs, annual fees, and grace periods must be provided in tabular form. Companies that impose an annual fee must provide disclosures before annual renewal. Card issuers that offer credit insurance must inform customers of any increase in rate or substantial decrease in coverage should the issuer decide to change insurance providers.

This law allows consumers to comparison shop for credit cards. Since research from the Survey Research Center of the University of Michigan indicates that about 35 percent of us shop for the most attractive interest rate on credit cards, a lot of Americans are able to use the information.

DID YOU KNOW?
You Might Be Able to Refuse to Pay the "Punitive Interest Rate" Increase When a Bank Credit Card Company Raises Your Interest Rate

If a bank credit card company raises the interest rate on an existing account (for a legitimate reason or otherwise, a **punitive interest rate**), the consumer has the right in 20 states to reject any commitment to paying the higher rate. To do so, one must notify the card issuer in writing. Various state laws (CA, CO, DE, IL, IA, ME, MD, MO, NE, NH, NY, OK, SC, SD, VT, WS, WY, NJ, PA, WV) allow a bankcard holder to continue to pay off balances under the terms of the original agreement provided that no additional charges are made on the card and the account is closed. Any continued use of the credit card means that the consumer has accepted the new higher terms.

State Laws on Credit Card Disclosures

Several states have laws requiring additional disclosures to credit card customers. In Massachusetts, for example, the law requires that credit-card users who have paid an annual fee who cancel their cards before their membership has expired are eligible for a partial refund. Also, all banks (including out of state) must notify cardholders in Massachusetts one month in advance of assessing an annual fee.

Home Equity Loan Consumer Protection Act

Recent data from the Federal Reserve Board reveal that 12 percent of all homeowners, about 7 1/2 million people, have established some type of home-equity loan. A **home-equity loan** is an open-ended credit plan secured by the borrower's principal residence. Some 40 percent of home-equity loans are used for home improvements, 30 percent are used to repay debts, and the remainder is used for new purchases. Less than 3/4 of 1 percent of such loans are delinquent, and this compares to 2 1/4 to 3 percent for other types of consumer loans. Borrowers can lose their homes if they do not repay their home-equity loans.

The Home Equity Loan Consumer Protection Act of 1988, Regulation Z of the Federal Reserve Board, and a 1994 mortgage disclosure regulation (see below) attempt to curb some of the abuses in the growing home-equity loan market by providing borrowers with more information about the costs of such loans. The regulations prohibit lenders from unilaterally changing the terms of a loan after a contract has been signed. It prohibits lenders from calling in loans before the due date, except in cases of fraud or misrepresentation by the borrower in connection with the loan, failure to meet the payment obligations, or borrower behavior that jeopardizes the value of the home.

Advertisements promoting initially low "teaser" rates must display the current long-term interest rate with equal prominence. Advertisements must include cost information, such as loan fees, the rate used to compute finance charges, and the maximum potential increase in the rate.

For variable-rate home-equity loans, lenders must link their interest rate formula to a public index outside the lender's control. They also must tell applicants the frequency of changes in the annual percentage rate and provide a 15-year historical table showing how the rate and payments would have been affected by changes in the value of the index.

All borrowers must receive detailed information on the home-equity loans along with the credit application before any fees are paid. Lenders have to disclose information on interest rates, fees, interest ceilings, an estimate of fees imposed by third parties, and repayment options, and they must provide an example of a repayment schedule. Should any terms change before the loan is finalized, the consumer has the right to demand a complete refund of all fees paid.

Still legal are variable rates that may fluctuate widely, **balloon loans** in which regular monthly payments are followed by an extremely large lump sum payment of the balance, and **negative amortization** of a loan that allows the unpaid balance to grow rather than diminish. The latter occurs when the repayment amount received by a creditor is less than the amount of interest assessed during a given time period.

Most banks give you a special checkbook to access your home-equity loan. A number of credit-card companies in concert with banking institutions are offering home-equity loans with a credit card that can even be used at ATM machines. Therefore, every time the card is used, part of the equity in the cardholder's home disappears. Home-equity loans allow consumers to charge regular purchases, even impulse items, on their credit account. This service is being offered, in part, because interest on home-equity loans is deductible when calculating personal income taxes while other consumer interest is not. Many consumers are afraid of the temptation of being able to charge things against their homes. After all, misuse of a home-equity loan can put you right out of your home.

Home Ownership and Equity Protection Act

The Home Ownership and Equity Protection Act (HOEPA) of 1994 amends the Truth in Lending Act and aims to eliminate the unscrupulous practice of making predatory loans in the second mortgage market. Many homeowners, especially older, low-income, and minority consumers, have fallen prey to fast-talking salespersons who promise to finance home repairs, consolidate bills, or pay for other important expenses.

The way the scam works is that the financing uses the consumer's home as security for the high-cost, and often unaffordable, loan. As a result, the homeowner winds up spending regular income on high credit repayments. Within a short time period, the is unable to make the monthly payments. Next the person's home is lost through foreclosure or forced sale. Oftentimes, the financial institution that eventually causes the loss of the home is an historically reputable lender that had purchased the credit contract from the firm that originally financed the loan. In the meantime, the shady, high-interest-rate lender has absconded with the equity, often many thousands of dollars, in the home. This is a form of **reverse redlining** where, instead of ignoring neighborhoods of minorities and the poor, unscrupulous lenders intentionally target and victimize consumers in the communities where credit is often difficult to obtain.

The Home Ownership and Equity Protection Act discourages legitimate lenders from making such loans or buying credit contracts from the original holders of the notes. HOEPA also provides new remedies for victims of such unethical practices.

The law creates new regulations for a particular type of closed-end loans. **Closed-end loans** are those with set payment terms, such as 60 monthly payments of $200. (This is in contrast to open-end loans where consumers can tap into a line of credit, like a credit card or a traditional home equity loan.) A loan that uses a person's home for security will meet the requirements of the law and be defined as a **special home-ownership closed-end loan** when one or more triggers occurs: (1) if the annual percentage rate (APR) of the loan is more than 10 percentage points above the yield on certain Treasury securities, and (2) the loan's up-front fees and charges are greater than 8 percent of the total amount of the loan or $400, or more. (Exempt from HOEPA regulations are traditional residential mortgage loans, reverse mortgages, and open-end credit transactions.)

Lenders now must make a great number of disclosures regarding the terms of such loans, and they are prohibited from using certain terms and placing onerous conditions in their contracts.

When violations of the HOEPA law occur, the victims of such high-interest loans have three *years* to cancel the transaction.[6] The borrower, of course, is required to give back the proceeds of the loan to the lender, however, all obligations to pay interest and closing costs are canceled. These claims may be made against the original lender as well as the current holder of the note. This recision right is expected to be a powerful influence in the market and, hopefully, force the reduction or elimination of such home-ownership closed-end loan scams.

---

[6]This right of recision is provided in the Truth in Lending Act, and it extends the historic three-day cooling-off period for some credit transactions.

Summary of Key Terms and Concepts

1. Summarize the FCC/FTC regulations on **telephone solicitations.**

2. Explain how you can **get your name off** telemarketing companies call lists.

3. What are the rules for settling disputes with **900-number companies**?

4. Outline the **unordered merchandise regulations** of the Postal Service.

5. List the key portions of the **negative option mail-order rule** of the Federal Trade Commission.

6. What special responsibilities does the **mail-order seller** have if they expect to be slow in forwarding your merchandise ordered by mail?

7. Summarize the federal *and* state **door-to-door sales regulations**. In your response, define the term **cooling-off period**.

8. What are typical limits on **cooling-off** time periods for consumer purchases for **health spas, timeshares, campground contracts, and mortgage refinancing**?

9. Outline the **airline bumping rules**.

10. Choose one of the following and list the consumer protections available: **airline lost baggage regulations, pet lemon laws, weight-loss center laws**.

11. How does New York state regulate **rent-to-own laws**?

12. Explain the term **lemon**, and the typical benefits of **state lemon laws**.

13. What does the Massachusetts **used car lemon law** do?

14. How do **vehicle repair laws** usually protect consumers?

15. What does a good state law on **secret vehicle warranties** do?

16. Distinguish between **warranty of merchantability** and **warranty of fitness for a particular purpose**.

17. Define the term **service contract**, and give the benefits of a service contract when buying an automobile **"as is."**

18. Distinguish between **full warranty** and **limited warranty**.

19. Under the Magnuson-Moss Warranty Act, explain the topic of **disclaiming implied warranties**.

20. How do **informal dispute procedures** work under the Magnuson-Moss Warranty Act?

21. What are the typical provisions of a state law governing **renter's security deposits**?

22. Define the term **discrimination**, and explain how federal laws are aimed at problems in housing discrimination. In your response, distinguish between **blockbusting** and **redlining**.

23. Tell how consumers have a limited **credit-card liability**.

24. Summarize the protections offered by the **Electronic Funds Transfer Act**.

25. What rights do consumers have in **automatic-billing disputes**?

26. What are your rights if you are **denied credit**?

27. List the consumer benefits of the **Fair Credit Billing Act**, and tell when consumers may properly challenge a charge on their credit bills.

28. What protections are offered under the **Equal Credit Opportunity Act**?

29. Choose one of the following and list the consumer protections: **Fair Debt Collection Practices Act, Fair Credit and Charge Card Disclosure Act, State Laws on Credit Card Disclosures,** and **Home Equity Loan Consumer Protection Act**.

30. Distinguish between **balloon loans** and **negative amortization**.

Useful Resources for Consumers

Consumer Information Center
Pueblo, CO 81009
(719)-948-4000 (publications)
(*Consumer's Resource Handbook* is free)
http://www.gsa.gov/staff/pa/cic/cic.htm

Direct Marketing Association
Corporate Headquarters
6 East 43rd Street
New York, NY 10017

Direct Selling Association
1776 K Street, NW
Washington, DC 20006

Federal Aviation Administration
Office of Consumer Affairs, APA-200
800 Independence Avenue, NW
Washington, DC 20591
(800)-FAA-SURE

Federal Communications Commission
1919 M Street, NW
Washington, DC 20554
(202)-632-7000 (consumer assistance)

Federal Communications Commission
2025 M Street, NW, Room 8210
Washington, DC 20554
(202)-632-7048 (complaints about radio or television)

Federal Trade Commission
6th and Pennsylvania Avenues, NW
Washington, DC 20580
(202)-326-2222 (publications)
(202)-326-3128 (complaints)
http://www/ftc.gov

National Association of Consumer Agency Administrators
1010 Vermont Avenue, NW, Suite 514
Washington, DC 20005
(202)-347-7395

U.S. Department of Transportation
Aviation Consumer Protection Office
C-75
Washington, DC 20590
(202)-366-2220

"What Do You Think" Questions

1. The text lists over twenty laws and regulations on **sales transactions**. How would you describe the themes of the numerous laws? Give reasons why you think there are so many laws.

2. The **Federal Trade Commission Used Car Rule** offers a number of protections for consumers. Considering your knowledge of the buyer-seller relationship in a used car transaction, offer your views on the necessity for such a regulation.

3. The problem of **lemon** automobiles is especially serious for the purchaser. Review the typical provisions of **lemon laws**, and offer your views of the degree of protections provided consumers.

Appendix Issue 5-A
Sample Letters Challenging Credit Card Charges

COMPLAINT LETTER CHALLENGING AN ERROR ON A CREDIT CARD BILL
(Send this letter whenever an error is found on a credit card bill)

Return address
Today's date

Name and address of credit card company

Dear reader (use correct name if known):

RE: Credit Card Charge Account #(put your number here)

I am writing today to complain about a charge that appeared on my recent bill. The amount of (give dollar figure here) that appeared on my bill with a date of (give date here) is in error.

The reason why the amount on me bill is being challenged is that you (made an arithmetic error, failed to reflect a payment or a credit, failed to mail the billing statement to the correct address [provided the company was notified at least 20 days before the end of the billing period], failed to mail the billing statement [and you assume it may have been lost in the mail], it is something that you did not buy, it is something purchased by an unauthorized person, it is something not properly identified on the bill [place, description, date], an amount different from the actual purchase price, it is something not accepted on delivery, it is something that was not delivered according to agreement, an item simply needs clarification, or another good reason). (Explain your side of the situation more fully. If appropriate, explain why you are willing to accept a partial credit rather than a full credit.)

Therefore, I expect that (name of credit card company) will immediately credit my account for the challenged amount (and, if appropriate, remove any interest assessed on that particular charge). (If appropriate, also say that your assume that the credit card company will reinvestigate this transaction and send you a letter reporting the findings.) I fully expect that my credit card account with (name of credit card company) will remain credited in the amount of (put amount here).

Thank you for your cooperation in this matter.

Sincerely,

Your Name

Enclosure

COMPLAINT LETTER TO MERCHANT REQUESTING CREDIT FOR AN UNSATISFACTORY PURCHASE
(Send this letter as soon as credit card bill is received)

Return address
Today's date

Name and address of merchant

Dear reader (use correct name if known):

RE: Credit Card Charge Account #(put your number here)

I am writing today to complain about a charge from (name of merchant) that appeared on my recent (name of credit card company) bill. This bill is in error, and I am asking (name of merchant) to credit my account for (amount of credit desired).

The reason for this request is that (it is something that you did not buy, something purchased by an unauthorized person, something not properly identified on the bill [place, description, date], an amount different from the actual purchase price, something not accepted on delivery, something that was not delivered according to agreement, or another good reason). (Explain your side of the situation more fully. If appropriate, explain why you desire a partial credit rather than a full credit. Also, if true, tell them that you intend on doing business with them again.)

Therefore, I expect that (name of merchant) will credit my credit card account in the amount of (put amount here) as soon as possible. Thank you for your cooperation in this matter.

(This is an optional paragraph that could be placed immediately preceding the one above.) Should (name of company) not credit my account by the next billing cycle, at that time I will file an official complaint to (name of credit card company) under the rights provided consumers by the Fair Credit Billing Act. That law and the contract between (name of merchant *and* the name of the credit card company) both require that my account be immediately credited for the amount challenged while the credit card company investigates the complaint. Since my facts as described above are correct, the law also says that the credit on my account will remain.

Sincerely,

Your Name

**COMPLAINT LETTER TO CREDIT CARD COMPANY ABOUT
AN UNSATISFACTORY PURCHASE
(Send this letter on the same day as the letter to the merchant)**

Return address
Today's date

Name and address of credit card company

Dear reader (use correct name if known):

RE: Credit Card Charge Account #(put your number here)

I am writing today to complain about a charge from (name of merchant) that appeared on my recent bill. The amount of (give dollar figure here) that appeared on my bill with a date of (give date here) is in error. As you can see from the enclosed letter, I have already attempted to get (name of merchant) to credit my account for (amount of credit desired).

The reason why the amount on me bill is being challenged is that (it is something that you did not buy, something purchased by an unauthorized person, something not properly identified on the bill [place, description, date], an amount different from the actual purchase price, something not accepted on delivery, something that was not delivered according to agreement, or another good reason). (Explain your side of the situation more fully. If appropriate, explain why you are willing to accept a partial credit rather than a full credit.)

Therefore, I expect that (name of credit card company) will immediately credit my account for the challenged amount (and, if appropriate, remove any interest assessed on that particular charge). Plus, (name of credit card company) will reinvestigate this transaction with (name of merchant) and send me a letter reporting your findings. I fully expect that my credit card account with (name of credit card company) will remain credited in the amount of (put amount here).

Thank you for your cooperation in this matter.

Sincerely,

Your Name

Enclosure

COMPLAINT LETTER TO SUPERVISOR AT CREDIT CARD COMPANY
(Send this letter if the credit card company turns down your request for a credit)

Return address
Today's date

Name and address of credit card company

Dear supervisor of lower-level employee (at credit card company):

RE: Credit Card Charge Account # (put your number here)

Please see the enclosed letters in reference to an incorrect charge of (put amount here) on my (name of credit card company) account. I have asked the merchant to correct the error and I have asked (name of credit card company) to correct the error. Your (name of credit card company person who signed letter saying that upon completion of their investigation they will not credit your account) has made a mistake in writing to me saying that (name of credit card company) has decided not to properly credit my account for (repeat the reason given in their letter); therefore, I am asking that you take corrective action.

(Give your reason[s], such as simply sending you a photocopy of your correct signature does not invalidate your proper claim of defective/shoddy/deficient product or service.)

Should my account not be credited by the next billing cycle and the amount of the original charge remain on the account, I will then file an official complaint to the Federal Trade Commission under the rights provided consumers by the Fair Credit Billing Act. As you know, that law and the contract between (name of merchant *and* the name of the credit card company) both require that my account be credited for any amount challenged while the credit card company investigates the complaint. I contend that your investigation was insufficient and that the facts of the situation, described in the enclosed letters, are correct. The law says that the credit on my account will remain when the merchant is wrong. If (name of credit card company) fails to follow all the government rules within proper time limits, (name of credit card company) is required by law to credit my account for $50 of the amount in dispute. Alternatively, I can sue (name of credit card company) in the local small claims court asking the court for the credit, plus attorney fees and costs.

Further, (name of credit card company) will not lose a penny on this complaint since all you have to do is process your credit against (name of merchant) as detailed in your contractual agreement with that merchant.

If after reinvestigating this complaint, (name of credit card company) still does not credit my account I will close my account. If I close my account, (name of company) will lose approximately (amount of dollars here based upon last year's total finance charges) from interest charges and (amount of dollars here based on three percent of last year's total purchases) from discounts to retailers for each charge. That means (name of credit card company) will lose (total amount of both figures) if my account is not properly credited.

Therefore, I expect that (name of credit card company) will credit my account for the challenged amount (and, if appropriate, remove any interest assessed on that particular charge).

Thank you very much for your cooperation in this matter.

Sincerely,

Your Name

Enclosures

**EXAMPLE OF A "CONSUMER STATEMENT" TO ADD TO ONE'S
CREDIT REPORT TO TELL
THE CONSUMER'S SIDE OF A DISPUTE
(Up to 200 may be added to one's credit file)**

Return address
Today's date

Name and address of credit bureau (TRW, Equifax, or Transunion)

Dear reader (use correct name if known)

Please add the following consumer statement to my credit file:

"Last year, I co-leased an apartment for one year with a friend. One week before our lease expired, I moved back to my hometown. Prior to my departure, I called the leasing agent for the apartment complex and confirmed that I owed nothing on the lease. However, unbeknownst to me, my former roommate had damaged the apartment in the process of moving out. In addition, he remained in the apartment five days beyond the date of the expiration of the lease. He further chose not to pay the realty agent for those expenses. Six months later, the XYZ Collection Agency notified me that I was responsible for the $300 not paid by my former roommate. I promptly paid them."

After this consumer statement is added to my credit file, please send me a copy of my credit report. Thank you for your cooperation in this matter.

Sincerely,

Your Name

Chapter 6

The Capitalistic American Marketplace

OBJECTIVES

After reading this chapter, you should be able to

1. Give an overview of how the capitalistic American economic system functions.

2. Understand how the U.S. economic system allocates resources

3. Appreciate the key role of government in influencing the U.S. economy, especially through its use of fiscal and monetary policies.

4. Describe the broad social and economic goals of American society.

Many consumers do not understand how the American marketplace functions. It is important for each of us to comprehend how conditions in the socio-political-economic world affect our personal economic opportunities and well-being. We also should know how our own individual behaviors and economic choices will affect the social-political-economic systems.

This chapter is organized to help consumers become more efficient at getting their money's worth and to enable them to fulfill their responsibilities to all consumers in society. Both these goals require a basic knowledge of how the capitalistic American economic system functions and an understanding of the broad social and economic goals of American society. Part of that comprehension requires an appreciation of standards and levels of consumption and living. Consumers need to recognize that these goals are difficult to reach and they are sometimes in conflict with each other. This chapter addresses these economic topics at a fundamental level.

How an Economic System Functions

At its essence, an **economic system**, or **economy**, is an organization for the production and distribution of goods and services. It provides the way for economic decisions to be made. More descriptively, an *economic system* is an organized set of institutions, laws, technologies, traditions, ideas, and popular attitudes that propel production, the management of resources, and the conduct of business. To work effectively, an economic system depends on the cooperative efforts of several components, including businesses, governments at all levels, and millions of consumers. Altogether, these forces determine the answers to the key economic questions:

- **What** kinds of goods and services shall be produced?
- **How** will goods and services be produced?
- **How** much shall be produced?
- **For whom** shall goods and services be produced?

The central economic problem in any economy is how to satisfy unlimited wants with limited resources. **Resources** are things used in the production process, and resources are limited in supply. After all, each country only has so much land, labor, capital, and management expertise. People's wants are unlimited, as well as variable and changing. It is impossible to satisfy all of them with the limited resources available. Therefore, priorities must be established. The field of **economics** is the study of how people and society choose to employ the scarce productive resources among alternative wants to produce various commodities and distribute them for consumption now or in the future. **Economists** analyze the costs and benefits of improving patterns of resource allocation.

The subject matter of economics is divided into positive economics and normative economics. **Positive economics** is concerned with questions of certainty, such as in describing "what is," in a manner somewhat devoid of norms, values, or political overtones. **Normative economics** is concerned with questions of "what ought to be" in a manner that encourages use of value judgments, desirable behaviors, standards or goals, and what is best for society. Economists use scientific, historical, descriptive, and quantitative methods to obtain knowledge. Principles, theories, and policies used to analyze economic behavior frequently come from **models**, which are abstractions of reality.

Societies differ in the ways they organize production and consumption in order to cope with the same basic problems, and find answers to the key economic questions. The economic system established in a country helps decide the best use of that society's resources not just for today, but for future generations as well. There are only two dominant types of economic systems, socialism and capitalism.

Socialism As an Economic System

Socialism is an economic system in which the producers possess both political power and means of producing and distributing goods. Government owns most resources, other than labor. Centralized economic decision making is the norm. Here the politicians answer the key economic questions of *what kinds of goods and services will be produced, how will goods and services be produced, how much shall be produced* and *for whom they should be produced.* Government policy determinations made in a socialistic economic system are often affected by a committee of people (typically elected without other names on the ballots) who decide what they think is best. Money prices do not control supply and demand because central planners make such decisions, and, as a result, rationing of limited amounts and long waiting lines occur.[1]

Many socialistic economic systems around the world are run by the **totalitarian** form of government where one person or party exercises absolute control over all spheres of human life and opposing parties are not permitted to exist. Totalitarian decisions are made to reflect the narrow views of a single person or idealogy. **Communism** is a political party with an idealogy that implies a socialistic economic system and totalitarianism in the political sphere, with individuals subservient to the state. China, Cuba, and North Korea are the only remaining socialistic countries with a communistic perspective.

In a socialist economic system, government is the boss. Under socialism, people believe that government is best able to do the planning and setting of economic goals, deciding what to produce and then selling the products. Expenditures by government (instead of by consumers or businesses) play the dominant role in a socialistic economy, often exceeding 50 percent of domestic spending.[2] In socialistic countries, employment with the government greatly exceeds the private sector.[3]

In the ideal socialistic country, economic justice is achieved when people determine their own needs and take from the common product of society. The socialist Karl Marx's dictum is, "From each according to his ability, to each according to his needs." However, there are few incentives for producers and workers to innovate and economize in a socialistic economic system. Instead, stagnation and regimentation prevail and are usually tolerated by the people.

In recent years, the countries of the former Soviet Union have been trying to move away from socialism and toward capitalism, and it has been horribly difficult. To illustrate, the level of living has always been low in Russia; however, since 1990, economic output in Russia declined 34 percent, consumer spending dropped 38 percent,

---

[1]A **traditional economic system** still exists in many developing nations where long-established customs, religious beliefs and family practices dominate the society's decisions on the key economic questions of *what, how, how much* and *for whom.* These economies generally reject consideration of alternative ideas.

[2]Sweden, recently buffeted by a struggling economy, has begun to trim the benefits of its "welfare state" and reduce its public expenditures, which currently account for nearly 75 percent of all domestic spending.

[3]In the U.S., only 17 percent of employed people work for local, state or federal governments.

and inflation has raged at an annual rate of 300 to 1000 percent. Genuine structural reform may take 20 years or more.

Capitalism As an Economic System

Decisions involving social and economic problems made by each society are made within its own particular economic system. The **American market system**, or **socioeconomic system**, is unique in its market-oriented approach based on the traditions and laws of the United States, which values capitalism in making its decisions on how scarce resources are allocated among alternative uses. Thus, the American economic system achieves the broad economic goals of society in an "American" way. **Capitalism** is an economic system characterized by open competition in a free market, in which the means of production and distribution are privately or corporately owned and development is proportionate to increasing accumulation and reinvestment of profits.

Property Rights

The success of American capitalism hinges on the fact that the United States is a nation of laws and legal systems. Private enterprise is achieved through the legal right of private property. **Property rights** can be defined as the right to use, restrict, or dispose of personal, business property and capital as the owner sees fit. For the most part, property is used by its owners to make a profit.

Private ownership capitalism relies upon a market system to allocate resources, goods and services to their most highly valued uses. Thus, most productive efforts in the U.S. are carried out by privately owned corporations, partnerships, and individual citizens. There are some exceptions, such as city-owned bus lines, state-owned liquor stores, and the federal government-owned Hoover Dam. However, most of the factors of production in our economy are privately owned. The greatest difficulty in exporting capitalism has been the absence of and respect for laws protecting property rights of citizens.

The absence of government ownership is known as **laissez faire**, a French term meaning "leave alone." Under laissez faire, whatever happens in a capitalistic economy is, by definition, the best thing that could have happened. Market forces under laissez faire often bring about the best alternative. The economic decisions on what to produce in a capitalistic economy are made by consumers and profit-seeking entrepreneurs and corporations that decide how and how much to produce.

Profit Motivation

Profit in an accounting sense is payment for the use of resources, generally defined as income minus expenses. It is an advantageous return or gain received on a business undertaking after all operating expenses have been met. In an economic sense, **profit** acts as an incentive for business entrepreneurs to undertake the production of goods and services for the satisfaction of customer demand. The profit earned by a business becomes the property of the owners. The motivation for profit explains why businesses are so inventive and dynamic.

A **normal profit** is what is required by an entrepreneur to remain in business while keeping all factors of production engaged. Economists consider payments to owners, including shareholders, to be costs, or factor payments, just like other normal business expenses. Normal profits represent the opportunity cost of the resources being employed in another use by the entrepreneur. **Excess profits** can also occur. These are profits above those needed to keep all factors of production busily involved in the entrepreneurial effort. It is important to realize that excess profits serve as a motivation for other entrepreneurs to enter the same line of business to compete for profits. The economic question of for whom to produce is made by *prices* and *income* in a capitalistic economy, thus, resources in an economy flow to where profits are highest.

The desire for profit can be either positive or negative. When it is positive, it can have a tremendous effect on one's personal wealth, create jobs in the community, and lead to successful economic development for the country. When it is negative, profit can lead to exploitation of consumers, businesses, and governments, for example, through the illegal dumping of toxic wastes. Profit should be the reward not the goal.

Competition

In the American capitalistic market system, competition is directly related to the profit motive. **Competition** is the rivalry between two or more businesses striving for the same customers or market. Competition encourages the most skilled, the most ambitious, and the most efficient to be effective and rise to the highest levels of economic performance. Economists like to say that competition exists when a number of firms sell the same good, but no one firm is large enough, by itself, to affect the price of the good.

Traditionally, competition has been thought of simply as competition on price. Competing firms try to offer the lowest prices on products consistent with paying for all operating costs and making a normal profit. Today, businesses compete on price as well as other factors, such as product improvements, methods of selling, service, and advertising. Competition is wonderful for consumers as long as it gives them choices among alternatives. Competition is important in the American economy because it ensures the availability of products and services at low costs (which is in the consumer interest) and it helps small businesses enter and thrive in the marketplace.

Adam Smith, the father of neoclassical economics, described the importance of competition in his handbook of economic development entitled *The Wealth of Nations*, published in 1776. He argued that the greatest efficiency in an economy can come from specialization, division of labor, and exchange. Smith contended that government should not interfere in the market. Such noninterference would allow producers to compete freely with one another as if guided and regulated by the **invisible hand** of price competition to produce the greatest quantity of goods at the lowest possible prices. This is in contrast to the **visible hand** of government regulators.

In a competitive market, Smith argues that the producer maximizes profit by being as efficient as possible. This means keeping prices low, improving the product, and selling as much as possible. In this way the producer serves the interests of consumers, as well as those of the producer. In his words, "Consumption is the sole end and purpose of all production; and the interest of the producer ought to be attended to only as far as it is necessary for promoting that of the consumer." Competition is absolutely essential to create the changes in demand and supply that occur. This is why public policy places great attention on maintaining and strengthening competition.

CONSUMER UPDATE: American Capitalism Is *Not* Without Its Defects

No economic system is perfect. There is little doubt that capitalism is harsh on vulnerable consumers and inefficient workers. In a capitalistic economy, the profit motive sometimes encourages companies to cheat consumers, mistreat workers, or ruin the environment. Pope John Paul II recently offered his view of the post-communist world arguing that capitalism can be acceptable only when it has an ethical and moral core.

Stephen J. Brobeck, executive director of the Consumer Federation of America, the nation's largest consumer advocacy organization, says that the following marketplace imperfections exist in all capitalist societies: "Bottlenecks that seriously hinder or prevent competition, predatory marketing practices that restrict competition, insufficient information or inability to process information that hinders effective competition, products containing hidden or delayed adverse health or safety impacts, deceptive or unconscionable sales practices (often directed at the least well-informed and lowest-income groups), and inadequate marketplace pricing of essential but rapidly depleting natural resources."

Capitalism rewards only the most efficient firms. Those businesses which do not cut costs and remain competitive are forced to close. Many jobs are lost. As harsh a description as it may seem, most of those jobs are described by economists as unproductive, otherwise the business would have remained competitive. Change and competition are difficult for businesses, workers and consumers.

Mixed Economic Systems Predominate Today

Most economic systems are not purely socialistic or capitalistic, rather they are mixed. Most often there is a mix of private and public ownership and enterprise, such as in Sweden and the United Kingdom. On a continuum, the United States and Canada are illustrative of somewhat pure capitalism while countries like Cuba and China have extremely socialistic economies. These markets also differ in the extent to which competition or monopoly prevail. Depending upon the culture and politics, each economic system offers individuals different degrees of information, mobility and freedom in the marketplace.

A worldwide trend is occurring toward private property rights, free markets, and the free flow of resources. Countries moving in this economic direction must permit prices to rise on basic items (such as food, clothing, rents and fuel) by cutting economic subsidies, creating banking systems, permitting unprofitable enterprises to fail and go out of business (take bankruptcy), and allowing profitable companies and their shareholders to keep a larger share of the profits.

Allocating Resources in the U.S. Economy

The economic system in the United States takes a variety of resources and allocates them primarily through the price mechanism in its market-driven economy. How this occurs is discussed below.

Ameristroika: The Future of Capitalism?
Managers and Workers Own Part of the Company

A new trend in capitalism is occurring. Instead of having the investors own all the shares of ownership in a corporation, managers and workers own a significant part of the company. Oregon Steel Mills in Portland is an example. In danger of going out of business, Oregon Steel, a manufacturer of high-quality steel pipe for natural gas, started an employee stock ownership plan to try and financially rescue the company. An **employee stock ownership plan (ESOP)** is a method through which employees can own shares of the company they work for which they typically use later for retirement purposes. The shares can be given to the managers and workers and/or purchased by them. In this way, the employees become part owners. ESOPs work by establishing a trust through which employees' funds are invested into company shares. When a company sets up an ESOP, the just-created trust borrows money to buy the company stock it will distribute to the employees over time. Therefore, the company gets a large cash infusion with each ESOP purchase.

At Oregon Steel time clocks were removed and suggestions were welcomed. Workers take 20 percent of the company's pre-tax profits in profit-sharing instead of direct income or raises. Executives have the same arrangement. Thus, employees share in the ownership, as well as in the profits. About 70 percent of the employees who worked for Oregon Steel at the time of its public stock offering in 1988 have stock holdings valued over $100,000. A new employee earning $20,000 would accumulate over $30,000 in stock after 10 years. Rules require that an employee must resign from the company before selling most of his/her stock. Morale is high. Production is up. Quality is excellent. Some say that this is the future for capitalism. In 1994, United Airlines recently reached an agreement to sell majority control to its employees, therefore, United is the largest employee-owned company in America.

"Ameristroika" is what Gar Alperovitz calls this event. He is author of *Rebuilding America* and president of the National Center for Economic Alternatives. **Ameristroika** represents a fundamental restructuring of the American capitalistic economy led by civic-minded entrepreneurs, workers and their labor unions, and supportive local governments which results in employee ownership of business firms. Hundreds of U.S. firms have already moved in this direction. The best-known example, Wierton Steel in Pennsylvania, is 77 percent employee owned. Avis, Inc. is one of the largest worker-owned firms. Such populist institutions may well be the wave of the future.

Types of Resources

As a nation, the United States has limited availability of natural resources (such as coal, oil, and varieties of ore), limited quality of such materials (such as the availability of high-grade ores), and limited technical skills and money for investment in future development. All these things are resources insofar as the economy is concerned. The task of the economic system is to determine the best combinations of the various factors of production to ensure prosperity and well-being for consumers and businesses alike. Consideration must be given to how much is to be produced and for whom. **Production** is the process of creating finished goods by using the factors of production. The four major factors of production are labor, land, capital, and management. Figure 6-1 presents a graphic illustration of the relationship between output and the factors of production.

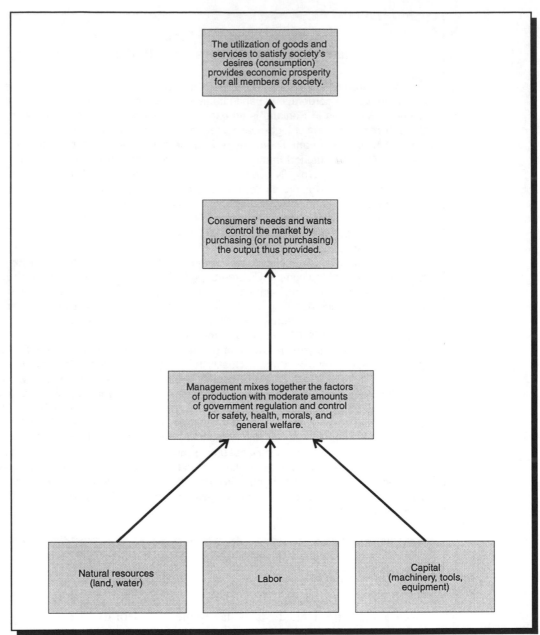

FIGURE 6-1   The Relationship Between Output and the Factors of Production

Resource Availability

The amounts of resources available usually remain reasonably stable or decline over time, but the population keeps growing.[4] Therefore, sooner or later production falls behind

---

[4]According to the United Nations Population Fund, the world's population, 5.7 billion in 1996, is likely to nearly double to 9.5 billion by 2025 and to reach 14 billion before the end of the next century unless birth control use increases dramatically around the world (more than the current 45 percent of women).

population growth. This will result in a lower level of living unless the supply of resources, including substitutes, increases faster than the population grows. This may occur because of advanced technology, the production of synthetic raw materials, the development of new skills, research, the accumulation of **capital** (any form of material wealth used or available for the production of more wealth, such as money), and general initiative and creativity. Of course, some resources are finite, such as coal and oil, whereas others are renewable, such as timber.

For consumers, **resources** are that which families or individuals use to obtain what they want. Such consumer resources include human and nonhuman resources and economic arrangements. **Human resources** are individual energies and abilities, as well as those which can be hired. **Nonhuman resources** include time, durable and nondurable consumer goods, money income, borrowing power, capital, and land. **Economic arrangements** are systems to support the economy, such as marketing and credit. Resources for consumers also include things they do not control, such as schools, parks, streets, and highways.

Effective use of resources can improve **economic well-being**, or the level of living of individuals and families. Thus, families usually are self-motivated to try to identify their strengths and marshal their resources in an attempt to meet the needs of family members successfully.

Important among these resources is **human capital**, which is the sum total of abilities, skills, and knowledge people have that permit them to perform work or services. An economist values human capital by computing the present value of the stream of future earnings from the sale of labor services. Some of the important determinants of human capital value are diet, health, education, on-the-job training, and willingness to migrate among regions, industries, and occupations.

How Resources Are Allocated

Key factors that affect how resources are allocated are supply and demand, the price mechanism, government and large corporations. Scholars have noted that perhaps the major economic event in the twentieth century in the United States has been the creation of large corporate entities. By their existence, corporations have taken on many of the characteristics of governments. The policy decisions that governments and many corporations make create an enormous force in how resources are allocated. For example, the decisions in the 1970s to safeguard the environment have created several new industries concerned with pollution, waste, and related issues.

The supply of and demand for resources are the primary factors that affect the allocation decisions of the market. If a great deal of one resource is needed to make a particular product that is valuable to a society, the allocation of that resource will be diverted away from use in products of lesser value that employ smaller amounts of the resource. For example, the high demand for petroleum in the production of plastics is different from the demand for petroleum for use in kerosene in today's market. The premise of supply and demand is that such buying and selling leads to optimal outcomes.

Consumers continually demand products through their purchases. If a lawnmower of questionable safety is manufactured, consumers can either accept or reject it. If they buy it, they accept it; if not, they reject it. Essentially, the consumer casts an economic vote for or against the product by this action. An **economic vote**, therefore, is the spending or non-spending of dollars for products and services.

AN ECONOMIC FOCUS ON...Standard and Level of Consumption and Living*

The indiscriminate use of the concepts **standard and level of consumption** and **standard and level of living** is prevalent in the spoken word of politicians and writing in popular media as well as academic publications. The concept **standard** refers to the level of material and nonmaterial goods and services that an individual or a group *desires to attain*, whereas the concept **level** refers to the *actual situation that has been achieved* and is being experienced.

Even though early academicians did not clearly distinguish between the concepts standard and level of living, they pointed out the importance of these concepts. Watkins wrote, "the standard of life is the central fact in the dynamics of consumption, and hence is of dominant importance for the theory of economic and social progress".[1] Devine, in stressing the significance of the concept standard of life wrote, "the greatest national asset of any civilized, enlightened, prosperous, and progressive people is the standard of life of its adult population." [2] p. 157. Devine, a sociologist, defined standard of living as, "that spiritual atmosphere, that indefinable force, compounded of income and what we buy with it, ideals and tastes and the environment provided by our fellow, which is something different from any of them, a power to which unconsciously we defer in every choice we make, and which we frequently invoke to sustain arguments or justify general policies." [3]

The economist Ely, however, defined the standard of living somewhat differently as, "the number and character of the wants which a man considers more important than marriage and family constitute his standard of life." [4] Sumner, a social psychologist, defined standard of living as, "the measure of decency and suitability in material comfort (diet, dress, dwelling, etc.) which is traditional and habitual to a subgroup." [5]

It can be seen from the above discussion that early writers defined standard of living differently depending upon their academic orientation. Davis is credited with clearly distinguishing between the concepts standard and level of living. He defined standard of living as "the plane of living which an individual or a group earnestly seeks and strives to attain, to maintain if attained, to preserve if threatened, and to regain if lost." [6]

The **level of living** (or **plane of living**), according to Davis, is composed of several things that a person has currently attained: the level of consumption, working conditions, possessions, freedoms, and atmosphere. **Consumption** includes purchased goods and services as well as having access to and using goods provided by either the public sector or the environment without charge.

Working conditions include hours and intensity of work, regularity of employment and security, health benefits, safety, opportunity for advancement, comfort and beauty of the surrounding environment, and congeniality of personal relationships. **Possessions** include tangible physical stocks of goods, intangible ownership of savings and investments, insurance protection, and developed human resources and connections. **Freedoms** include those related to expression, speech, movement, association, religion, learning, and earning. Atmosphere includes the feelings of being wanted, loved, secure, and experiencing harmony with one's fellows in the home and outside the home.

Note that every variable of these components of the level of living places certain demands upon time and space. These demands may be met or avoided, enjoyed, accepted, or despised.

Linder argues that, "a given pattern of consumption is accompanied by a certain way of living, reflected in the amounts of time that an individual allocates to his various consumption goods." [7] Simply stated, consumption itself requires time. Having relatively little time available for consumption may lead to **simultaneous consumption** (the consumption of more than one item at the same time), **successive consumption** (using the item for a short period of time or not consuming it completely before using another item), and/or using a more expensive version of a commodity. Clearly, time is a scarce commodity which should be taken into consideration when defining the level of living.

Space is another very important factor to consider when examining the level of living of an individual or a group. Both time and space set limits on the choices available in human life and, thus, constitute the spatio-temporal framework within which people interact. The following three situations illustrate the importance of space as limiting factor in maximizing satisfaction. First, a person may possess a good and have the time to use it, yet lack the space necessary for use of the good. Imagine yourself having a tennis racket, balls, and the time to play with your partner. But, because tennis courts are not available, you can not play. In this type of situation, space may be called **limitational space**.

The second situation may exist when the consumer good is available, but because of the simultaneous use of space by other individuals, additional time is required for consumption. In our crowded cities, this situation is prevalent when driving, especially during rush hour. Because other drivers are using the same streets, travel from one point to another may take longer than if fewer drivers were present. In this type of situation, space may be called **interactional space**.

In the third situation, the good is available, time for consumption is available, but space required for consumption is not available at a desirable location. For example, you may go to the theater to watch a play, only to find that the seat you would prefer to have is already taken. So, you select another, less preferred seat. In this case, consumption takes place, but on a lower level of satisfaction than you desired. This situation exemplifies **locational space**.

Given the vital role of time and space in consumption activities, the content of the level of living should not only include consumption, working conditions, possessions, freedoms, atmosphere, but also the resources of time and space.

---

[1]Watkins, G.P. (1915). Welfare as an Economic Quantity (Houghton Mifflin Company), 97.

[2]Devine, E.T. (1915). The Normal Life (Survey Associates), 157.

[3]Ibid, 156.

[4]Ely, R.T. (1923). Outlines of Economics (MacMillan), 378.

[5]Sumner, W.G. (1940). Folkways: A Study of the Sociological Importance of Usage, Manners, Customs, Mores, and Morals (Ginn and Company), 156.

[6]Davis, J.S. (1945). Standards and Content of Living, *American Economic Review*, (35), 10.

[7]Linder, S.B. (1970). The Harried Leisure Class (Columbia University Press), 112.

*Mohamed Abdel-Ghany, Professor, The University of Alabama

The Price Mechanism at Work

Price is the exchange value stated in terms of money. Pricing goods is a complex task. Originally, each seller establishes a price based on a need to first of all survive in the market—to make a profit. Often firms seek to earn a targeted **return on investment (ROI)**. This is the amount of income earned on an investment and it is often expressed as a percentage. Most companies need to earn a ROI of 20 percent or more to be successful and grow. As an illustration, to achieve this goal, and using a cost-based approach, a firm might determine that the total costs of manufacturing and marketing 100,000 compact discs is $500,000; that works out to $5 a unit. If the manufacturer seeks a 20 percent profit, the wholesale price will be $6 ($5 X 120%). A retailer may then price the purchase of 1,000 compact discs at $12, representing a 100 percent markup, knowing that the average markup might eventually fall to 20 or 30 percent because of price reductions, scratched disks, unsold items and the costs of selling the goods (employee salaries, rent, utilities, financing, etc.). Sellers use a variety of pricing strategies in attempting to achieve their marketing goals. As a general rule, it is to the economic benefit of both sellers and consumers alike to allow prices to be established by operation of the free market rather than some government agency or legislation.

As the demand for specific products increases, manufacturers will try to supply more. As these manufacturers use more resources, the market prices of these needed resources will help decide who gets the resources. As a resource in high demand becomes more scarce, the price normally rises. Therefore, higher prices ultimately place a restriction on utilization, and allocation priorities are established. Prices thus reach a point where demand for a resource is roughly equal to supply. Actual prices, however, are also influenced by custom, tradition, competition, and public authority.

As a resource, energy is very important in today's economy because it is a high-priority item. Energy-producing resources in America are at times in good supply and at other times in short supply. To buy these resources (oil, for example) from other countries is sometimes very expensive. Consequently, prices rise for consumers and become too high for many to afford. In such an instance, priorities are established primarily by the prices charged. Conversely, if **buying power** is low (people have little money to spend for a given resource), regardless of availability, that resource will not be heavily used because there is no demand.

Prices in the supply/demand scenario are originally set by sellers. Maynes states that the **price mechanism** is "a system of motivation and error correction."[5] He explains that a rising price signals that a particular seller is performing well, "other things being equal," and more goods should be produced. A price fall indicates the opposite. Sellers are motivated to respond to price signals by their self-interest in profits, higher wages, interest and rent. Further, over time, the market economy is a "system of error correction." A continuing fall in demand for a good, other things being equal, signals that the firm is doing something wrong and that further errors on the part of the firm will lead to financial bankruptcy. Note also that the price signal is a crude device because it communicates failure, but not the causes. The economists' statement "**other things being equal**" comes

---

[5]Maynes, E. S. (1992). *Consumerism* (unpublished paper dated October 23, 1992).

from the latin phrase **ceteris paribus**, meaning everything else is held constant. Such assumptions are crucial to the models economists develop when making hypotheses.

The Circular Flow of Economic Activity

The major actors in the American economy are consumers, producers, and government. Figure 6-2 shows the mechanism by which land, labor, capital, and management resources are allocated among these components of the economic system. The **circular flow** of economic activity is the process by which a society determines the remuneration to the factors of production and by which it distributes income to the various components of the economy. The figure shows how goods and payment for them move among the various sectors of the American economy. Producers depend on individual employees to do the work, individuals depend on producers to employ them, consumers depend on producers to produce goods and services, producers depend on consumers to buy, and government takes in money through taxes and also makes expenditures. The model shows a oversimplified picture of the real world, but it does provide a useful tool to visualize the complications of the economic world in which consumers live.

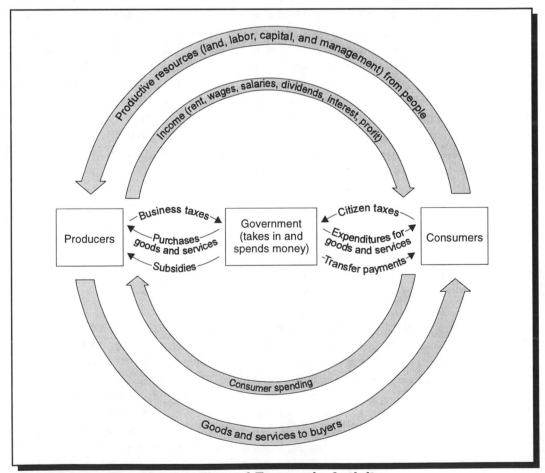

FIGURE 6-2   The Circular Flow of Economic Activity

The Multiplier Effect

Assume for a moment that the government wanted to increase national income by $10 billion so that more people would have jobs which would also increase tax revenues (because employed people pay taxes). To accomplish this goal, would government have to increase its own autonomous spending $10 billion? The answer is "No," and the reason is the multiplier effect. The **multiplier effect** is the dollar change in income produced by a change in expenditures made independent of income. It demonstrates that an increase in one sector of the economy will result in a manyfold increase elsewhere in the economy.

For example, an increase in government spending of $10 billion on **infrastructure** (the basic facilities, equipment and installations needed for the functioning of a society, such as highways, bridges, dams, and water systems) immediately increases the incomes of construction workers by $10 billion. The construction workers spend $8 billion on domestic goods (80 percent) and 1 billion on imported items (10 percent); 1 billion is saved (10 percent). The $8 billion spent (groceries, rent, clothing, etc.) becomes income for another group of workers who then spend 80 percent of their $8 billion on domestic goods ($6.4 billion), while spending $0.8 billion (10 percent) on imported goods and saving $0.8 billion (10 percent). Each round of spending becomes smaller but the overall total effect is quite large.

As one's disposable income rises, consumption and savings rise by a certain proportion. Consumers typically spend 90 percent of any extra income they receive and save 10 percent. The causes of this effect come from the **marginal propensity to consume (MPC)**, the **marginal propensity to import (MPI)** and the **marginal propensity to save (MPS)**. The MPC is the change in consumption as a proportion of change in disposable income; the MPI is the change in consumption due to spending on imported items. The MPS is the change in savings as a proportion of change in disposable income. The **multiplier** (1/MPS + MPI) equals 5 (1/20) when MPS and MPI are both .10. Thus, an initial increase in expenditure of $10 billion results in a total change in the economy of $50 billion.

How the U.S. Government Tries to Manage the Economy

Government plays a vital role in the U.S. economy, especially in its use of fiscal and monetary policies. The Congress uses its taxing and spending policies and the Federal Reserve Board uses its monetary policies to help achieve social and economic goals.

Fiscal Policies: Taxing and Spending

To exist and perform its duties, government must raise taxes and spend money. By taxing and spending, government influences both the patterns of production and consumption. It does this by purchasing goods and services to provide for the public good and by making **transfer payments** for which it does not expect anything in return. For example, government purchases many goods and services, such as roads and school buildings, teachers' salaries, and defense armaments. Other transfer payments include veterans' benefits, welfare payments, and farm subsidies. According to the Office of

Management and Budget and the Joint Committee on Taxation, last year taxpayers spent $51 billion in direct subsidies to business (including $29 billion for agribusiness) and another $53 billion in tax breaks for corporations.

Government also redistributes wealth among the population from the taxpayers through a progressive tax system. In general, governments use both progressive taxes and regressive taxes to raise money. For example, federal income tax is a **progressive tax**, since it is a tax that demands a higher percentage of income as income increases. A state sales tax is an example of a **regressive tax**, since it demands a decreasing proportion of a person's income as income increases. To illustrate, a person earning $50,000 has an easier time paying a sales tax of $24 when purchasing a television set than a person earning $12,000, who has to pay the same $24 tax on the same purchase.

The taxing and spending policies of the federal government affect interest rates, inflation, employment, production, and economic growth. **Inflation** is the value of money in terms of goods and services. As inflation occurs, it reflects rising prices for goods and factors of production, including land, labor, capital, and management. Government tries to control the economy by coordinating its fiscal and monetary policies.

Fiscal policy is the federal government's policy with respect to taxing, spending, and management of the national debt; it is the government's effort to raise taxes and allocate money. Fiscal policy is a powerful tool for influencing the flow of spending and thus for promoting economic growth and stability. To stimulate demand for goods and services, government can lower taxes and/or increase its own spending. Note that when government imposes taxes on citizens and businesses, it lessens the ability of these citizens and businesses to compete or bid for productive resources because they have less money. Lower taxes keep more money in the pockets of consumers and businesses, which they can then use to buy goods and services. Increased government spending causes businesses to expand their production of goods and services to meet the increased demand. Economic expansion and growth are the result. The reverse action is often taken during times of high inflation. Raising taxes and reducing government spending both take money out of circulation. This reduces demand and slows economic growth, which usually lowers inflation.

Monetary Policies: Managing Money and Credit

Monetary policy is the federal government's policy to attempt to manage the supply of money and credit in the economy so as to influence total spending and thus have an effect on general economic stability, consumption, a stable dollar, sustained non-inflationary economic growth, and long-run stability in our international balance of payments. If money is scarce, interest rates go up; lower interest rates encourage economic growth.

In the United States, the Federal Reserve System runs the nation's central banking system. The Federal Reserve System, commonly called the **Fed**, was created in 1913 and is governed by a management group known as the **Board of Governors**. Current laws set three primary goals for the Fed: (1) maximize employment, (2) stabilize prices, and (3) maintain moderate long-term interest rates. The Federal Reserve System is the non-political operating arm of the Federal Reserve Board. The System consists of a seven member Board of Governors with headquarters in Washington, D.C. and twelve Reserve Banks located in major cities throughout the United States. The Fed acts as an independent regulatory agency that influences the amount of money and credit commercial banks utilize.

The Fed performs many banking services. In addition to providing checking accounts for the Treasury, issuing and redeeming government securities, and acting as a fiscal agent for the U.S. government, the Federal Reserve System also moves currency and coin into and out of circulation, collects and processes millions of checks each day, and transfers billions of dollars worth of electronic payments.

The Fed regulates the availability of credit for businesses and consumers by controlling the growth of the **money supply**. This is made up of checkable accounts and cash in the hands of the public (called **M1** by economists); savings accounts, time deposits, and money market and mutual funds (**M2**); and the major monetary instruments used primarily by institutional investors (**M3**). For example, readily available money and liberal financing conditions for housing, automobiles, and other big-ticket items encourage a high rate of economic growth. Control of the money supply is important because if money expands too rapidly, the extra funds cause prices to rise and this stimulates inflation. Alternatively, when the money supply does not keep pace with the economy production, prices fall, production slows and unemployment rises.

The Board of Governors of the Federal Reserve System (Fed) uses three tools to manage money and credit:

1. Reserve Requirements

The Fed sets reserve requirements for its 4000+ member banks. **Member banks** include all federally chartered national banks (3360) and any state-chartered banks that request to be members (978). The **reserve requirement** (or **reserve rate**) is a percentage of total deposits that depository institutions cannot loan out but must maintain every day in the form of vault cash or as deposits with a Federal Reserve bank. The reserve requirement serves as a backup for the deposits of consumers, businesses and governments at member institutions. The reserve requirement is currently 10 percent. Each of the nation's 27,000 depository institutions must take action to maintain the proper reserves on a daily basis. Overall, this is called the **fractional reserve system** because banks keep less than 100 percent of their deposits on hand.

A low reserve rate puts dollars into the banking system that banks can lend and relend again, thus the multiplier effect is quite large with only a 10 percent reserve ratio. Note that the banking system actually *creates money* as each individual bank can lend its excess reserves (up to the balance of the remaining 90 percent of funds deposited) which are then spent, deposited by others and relent again. For example, when you are granted a loan, the money just appears as numbers on your bank statement. The bank creates the money simply by adding the numerals to your account. Recognize that this created money then disappears as you repay the loan because each repayment is taken out of some other personal account.

A high reserve rate requirement has the contracting effect on the economy because it reduces the amount of money available for lending. Changes in the reserve requirement occur infrequently, only when very strong action is warranted. During a time of high inflation, the Fed is likely to raise the reserve requirement to tighten the money supply and the ripples of such a policy multiply many times throughout the economy. Member banks then may be forced to either curtail loans or sell securities, and this should slow demand, which should lower prices on goods and services. Since deposits vary daily and the legally-required reserve requirement must be met every day, when a bank runs short it must borrow needed funds (usually only for overnight) from an approved source. When a bank borrows from another commercial bank which has excess reserves to lend, the interest rate paid is called the **federal funds rate**. (The Fed changes this rate somewhat frequently.) When a bank borrows directly from its regional Federal Reserve bank (this source is called the **discount window**), the interest rate charged is called the discount rate.

2. Open-market Operations

Fine tuning of the money supply is attempted by the Fed when it uses its **open-market operations**. This is the buying and selling of government securities by the Federal Reserve System undertaken to influence the volume of money and credit in the economy. The Fed only buys or sells its own debt instruments: Treasury Bonds, Notes, and Bills. If the Fed wanted to tighten up the money supply, its **Federal Open Market Committee (FOMC)** might direct the **Federal Reserve Bank of New York** (the Fed's trading office) to sell bonds to banks. Money to pay for these bonds flows out of the economy and into the Fed because when the member banks write checks to purchase Treasury securities, they use funds that in effect tie up a larger percentage of bank funds. Since this money is no longer available for lending, such an action decreases the money supply. When the Fed wants to increase the money supply, perhaps to help stimulate the economy out of a **recession** (a period of moderate decline in the national economy characterized by decreasing business activity, falling prices, and unemployment), it does the opposite. Here the Fed purchases Treasury securities back from banks, which makes the member banks more liquid and therefore able to make loans.

3. Discount Rate

The Fed also sets the **discount rate**, which is the interest rate at which the member financial institutions may borrow money, usually for short periods, from a regional Federal Reserve bank. It is called a discount rate because the interest is subtracted up front when the loan is made to a member bank rather than collected later upon repayment. During a time of high inflation, the Fed is likely to set a high discount rate because this discourages borrowing by banks, which then grant fewer loans to consumers and businesses. Alternatively, lowering the discount rate encourages economic growth because the banks would be inclined to borrow more from the Fed and thus lend more. Changes in the Fed's discount rate often pressure other lenders (savings and loan associations, credit unions, consumer finance companies, etc.) to change their interest rates in the same direction. Thus, rates for automobile and housing loans are quickly affected by changes in the discount rate.

Note that the Fed has researched the issue of its impact on the economy and concluded that over the years the **velocity of the money supply**, a measure of the number of times money changes hands in the economy, is 1.6527. Thus, for every $100 the Fed puts into the economy it amounts to $165.27 by the end of the year. Thus, when the Board of Governors of the Federal Reserve System wants to spark up the economy and encourage economic growth, the Federal Reserve System follows a policy of **easy money**. Reserve requirements are low, interest rates are low, and money and credit are readily available. Thus, consumers are encouraged to buy homes, clothing, and automobiles, which stimulates further production of such goods. Companies borrow to expand their businesses and hire more people.

Although this looks good on paper, efforts to manage the economy and encourage economic stability and growth are fairly difficult to control. For example, investors on Wall Street greatly control long-term interest rates, not the Fed. Federal Board Chairman Alan Greenspan also notes that each time long-term interest rates drop one tenth of a percentage point, the U.S. economy receives a stimulus of about $10 billion because lower rates trigger new housing starts, spur business investments and create jobs. Greenspan notes that those rates are controlled by the availability of and investor demand for long-term securities *not* specific monetary actions of the federal government. As another example, if banks are too nervous to lend and businesses are too depressed to borrow, the Fed's efforts to stimulate the economy can quickly falter.

Moreover, the fiscal and monetary tools available to the government are fairly blunt instruments, and there is considerable lag time before effects can be seen and properly measured. Nevertheless, these are the tools available and government does the best it can. The whole idea is to try to reduce the extremes of the economic cycles: rapid inflation and serious recession or depression.

Broad Social and Economic Goals of American Society

Every economic decision is made in light of certain goals. Public-policy decisions made by societies are based on broad social values and goals, while individuals make decisions based on their personal values and goals. A **public policy** is a plan or course of action by a government designed to influence and determine decisions, actions, and other matters concerning or affecting the community or people rather than private affairs or interests.

The United States is firmly committed to a great variety of worthy economic goals: stable prices, a balanced budget, no tax increases, a steadily declining trade deficit, and no cuts in benefits to the elderly, the poor, the sick, or anybody else. Public policy-making can occur in any branch of government—executive, legislative, or judicial. Public policies are shaped by a number of factors, such as the availability of resources, past experiences of the policy-shaping person or group, and the ideas of concerned public officials and activist citizens. (Public policy-making is further discussed in Chapters 9, 10, and 11.)

In its eternal quest to resolve the problem of scarcity and address the key economic questions for its population, each society establishes a number of economic values and goals. The primary economic goals of American society are (1) economic freedom, (2) full employment, (3) price stability, (4) economic growth, (5) economic productivity, (6) economic security, and (7) economic equity or justice.

Society's economic goals are at times in conflict, or at least in substantial tension, with one another. When goals conflict, difficult choices have to be made. Economic goals give society a sense of direction and a benchmark from which to measure progress.

As the American society seeks to achieve these economic goals, it assumes that a problem of scarcity exists, democracy will prevail as the form of government, and capitalism will remain the economic system.

The U.S. *Assumes* Scarcity, Democracy, and Capitalism

The topics of scarcity, democracy and capitalism are examined below. Recognize that these three concepts are at the essence of American society.

Scarcity

To accomplish its economic goals, society must make choices about how to use its available resources. The fundamental economic problem facing all societies is that of **scarcity**, that is, the short supply of productive resources relative to the ever-increasing needs and wants of the people.

Democracy

In the United States, society is conceptually organized as a **democracy**, which is government by the people, exercised either directly or through elected representatives. In a *true* democracy, however, the majority can do whatever it wants, including restrict the freedoms of the minority. The framers of the Constitution of the United States feared a true democracy and instead created a republic to prevent government from imposing forms of tyranny on the citizens. (To verify, check the pledge of allegiance to the flag.) A constitutional government form called a **republic**, such as the one we have in the U.S., provides that the citizens and the government are both subject to certain laws established to protect and enhance—not restrict or deny—citizens' rights to life, liberty, and property. Instead of resorting to violence or threats of violence to make changes, democratic governments submit their ideas and programs to periodic free elections. Laws and representatives rule the U.S., not the people directly.

In a weak democratic form of government, policy decisions are often made in favor of the strong capitalistic interests in the economy, indulging the interests of business. In a strong democracy government, decisions are made by elected representatives who are occasionally accountable to the multiple interests in society (e.g., church, organized labor, physicians, consumers, environmentalists, abortion rights advocates). The United States has a strong representative democratic form of government operating within a capitalistic or free market oriented economic/political system. The accountable government tries to solicit the views of all affected special interest groups. In a democracy like the Republic of the United States, the power in society comes from the bottom up—from the people to the government.

Capitalism

Economic systems vary from country to country because people have different traditions and different ideas about how to use their limited resources. Thus, the people in each society make different choices about how they want their economy to operate.

The economic system in America is called **capitalism**, and it is characterized by open competition in a free market, in which the means of production and distribution are privately or corporately owned with increasing accumulation and reinvestment of profits. In a capitalistic economic system, decisions as to what to produce, how much to produce, whether to produce for the present or the future, and how to distribute production are determined primarily by individuals and businesses.

Primary Goal: Economic Freedom

The first broad social and economic goal of American society is **economic freedom**. Economic freedoms are rights that business, labor, and consumers enjoy in the American economy pertaining to the production, development, and management of material wealth. These freedoms are given to American consumers in the Bill of Rights of the Constitution, along with other rights and freedoms. People are free to make decisions about the use of resources under their control.

People decide for themselves if they want to own property, which job or career they want, whether they want to go on strike for a raise, whether they want to move freely across our land and whether they want to save or spend their money in the marketplace. They make these decisions without being coerced by others. Other economic freedoms include the right of a worker to bargain with his or her employer, to join a union, to go on strike, to change employment, to quit his or her job, or to retire. At the heart of our economic system is citizens making their own decisions, not government.

For businesses, the concept of economic freedom means the opportunity to pursue profits and the absence of unnecessary regulation. Privately owned, profit-seeking businesses can be started anew or changed as market forces demand; this is the right to **private** or **free enterprise**. Economic freedom gives businesspeople, merchants, producers, and manufacturers the right to decide on the nature and method of operation of their businesses, such as when and where to advertise, and how to market their goods and services.

Consumers have freedom of choice in the marketplace—that is, the freedom to buy or the freedom to reject. Consumers have the right to decide what kind of home to live in, what goods to buy, what papers and books to read, and how to manage their towns and cities. Importantly, consumers also have the freedom to make many informed decisions. Each consumer must decide what a purchasing decision means, what it will mean in the short run, and how it will affect others (environmentally and socially) in the long run. Therefore, knowledge is basic to economic freedom.

Colonists believed that the nation could best be served if citizens had the freedom to produce, trade, and consume as they saw fit, with a minimum of regulation by government. This approach of government is called **laissez-faire capitalism** where private businesses are encouraged to operate with a minimum of government restrictions. Thus, we use such terms as **free enterprise**, **private enterprise**, and capitalism to describe the American economic system.

Primary Goal: Economic Efficiency

Another broad social and economic goal of American society is **economic efficiency**. This is the degree to which one makes use of resources to maximize well-being. For consumers, economic efficiency includes getting value for one's money, making the best of one's abilities, and using one's limited time and energy to your best advantage. From the nation's point of view, economic efficiency involves satisfying the wants of millions of people in such a way as to please as many people as possible. If the country is inefficient, it is wasting some of its productive resources. When possible, society should be concerned with using the least amount of resources to obtain a given output; thus, in general, benefits should outweigh costs.

Difficult economic decisions often must be made in the name of economic efficiency because society's economic goals frequently conflict. For example, it is clear that our economy now uses less coal than it did twenty years ago, and that severe unemployment exists in West Virginia's and Kentucky's coal mining communities. The question is whether society should allow private decisions or government actions to determine how to move the productive resource of labor into other jobs. Should the country rely on hunger and desperation to move the workers to new jobs, or should government provide training programs to develop new skills and moving expenses to help people get to areas in need of productive labor? On an individual level, should an accountant earning $20 per hour take a day off work and paint a room in his home or should he hire a painter for $12 per hour to do the job?

The well-being of individuals and families is greatly dependent on their economic efficiency. Each person has certain economic resources that may be measured in terms of income or wealth. The overriding economic objective of a consumer is to use these resources as efficiently as possible to maximize his or her economic well-being. **Economic well-being** equals economic resources times consumer efficiency. **Consumer efficiency** is getting one's money's worth. Consumers who are more efficient with their resources have a higher level of living than others with similar resources.

DID YOU KNOW? Household Incomes in the United States

Household income in the U.S. recently was over $42,000. Of all households, those with incomes over $100,000 amounted to 4.7 percent; those with incomes of less than $25,000 amounted to 38 percent.

Primary Goal: Full Employment

American society also holds **full employment** as another economic and social goal, which suggests that all of an economy's resources, particularly labor, are fully utilized. An unemployment rate of zero cannot occur because there always is some frictional, structural, and cyclical unemployment resulting from such events as plant closings, career changes and worker mobility. The operational measure of full employment is probably in the 4 1/2 to 6 percent unemployment range. The **natural rate of unemployment** is the minimum level to which unemployment can be reduced without stimulating inflation.

The social goal of full employment recognizes the lost output that accompanies high unemployment, the squandering of human resources, and the costs to individuals and families because of economic hardships. From an individual perspective, people not only want to get jobs, but they also want to keep them. From society's perspective, it is vital to keep the productive resources of labor at work.

Recall that the **central economic problem** of any society is that productive resources are scarce relative to the wants of the population. Therefore, it is a colossal waste to allow some of those productive resources to stand idle. Industrialized nations face the harsh trade-off between providing low-wage jobs for millions of their less-skilled workers or leaving those people with no jobs at all because those with inadequate skills live in a world that increasingly demands higher levels of skills.

Primary Goal: Price Stability

Another broad social and economic goal of society is **price stability**. This means that expected changes in the average price level are small enough and gradual enough that they do not materially enter business and household financial decisions. It means the absence of significant inflation or deflation. While reasonable price stability might see prices rising 2 or 3 percent per year, greater increases require consumers, businesses, and governments to make costly adjustments to offset the effects of inflation. Price stability contributes to economic efficiency, in part, by reducing the uncertainties that tend to inhibit investment.

Inflation is revealed as rising prices for goods and factors of production. Inflation is caused by too much demand, sharply increasing costs of products and/or too much money circulating in the economy. **Deflation** is a decrease in the general level of prices. During times of price inflation, most workers' real incomes will go down. **Real income** is money income relative to the prices of goods and services. It is what one's money will actually buy in contrast to the designated value of the money itself. Although the purchasing power of the dollar has declined over the past 50 years, today we have many more dollars in income than in 1944. Because incomes have not kept up with inflation over the past 15 years, the resulting purchasing power of most consumers has remained flat or declined slightly.

One gauge of the amount of inflation is calculated monthly as the government's **consumer price index (CPI)**, which is an index of price changes of hundreds of basic commodities and services. The CPI is frequently and mistakenly called a measures of the cost of living for consumers because it does not reflect the changes in buying or consumption patterns that consumers probably would make to adjust for relative price changes. The CPI assumes the purchase of the same market basket, in the same fixed proportion (or weight) month after month. The CPI always overstates the cost of living because it has an upward bias. Some people benefit from inflation (most homeowners), while others suffer economic harm (those on fixed incomes).

Primary Goal: Economic Growth

One of America's primary social and economic goals is growth. **Economic growth** is a condition of increasing production and consumption in the economy—and hence increasing national income—over the long term. The individual's desire for a better life and the rising aspirations of all the American people shape the direction of our economy. The logical deduction is that we must have greater economic growth if everyone is to get ahead and improve their level of living. A great motivator of economic growth is our interest in continuing to increase our standard of living.

Stages in the Economic Cycle

An **economy** is a system of managing the productive and employment resources of a country, community, or business. Government attempts to regulate the American economy to maintain stable prices (low inflation) and stable levels of employment (low unemployment). The intent is to try and achieve sustained economic growth. An **economic cycle** (sometimes called a **business cycle**) is a wavelike pattern of economic activity that includes four temporary phases that undulate from boom to bust: expansion, recession, depression, and recovery (Figure 6-3).

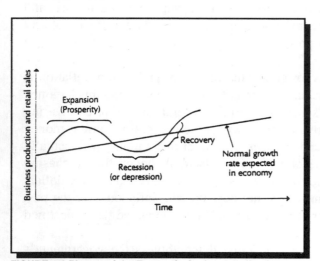

FIGURE 6-3 Phases of the Economic Cycle: A Roller Coaster

The optimal phase of the economic cycle is the **expansion stage**, where production is at high capacity, there is little unemployment, retail sales are high, and inflation and interest rates are low or falling. This makes it easy for consumers to buy homes, cars, and expensive goods on credit; it also encourages businesses to borrow to expand production to meet the increased demand. As the demand for credit increases, short-term interest rates rise because more borrowers want money.

As consumers and businesses purchase more goods, this increase exerts inflationary pressure on prices. Eventually, interest rates and inflation climb high enough to stifle consumer and business borrowing, send stock prices down and choke off the expansion. The result is flat economic growth or even a decline. In such situations, the economy often moves toward a **recession**, generally described as a decline in business activity or a downturn in the economy. Many economists further define a recession as two consecutive quarters of a decline in economic activity.[1]

The phases or stages in the economic cycle are officially defined by the U.S. Department of Commerce's Business Cycle Dating Committee within the National Bureau of Economic Research. Its definition of a **recession** is "a recurring period of decline in total output, income, employment and trade, usually lasting from six months to a year and marked by widespread contractions in many sectors of the economy."[2]

Especially difficult recessions are sometimes characterized as **stagflation** which occurs when the painful combination of slow economic growth and high unemployment simultaneously is confronted with rising inflation. During recessions consumers typically become pessimistic about their future buying plans. The average U.S. recession is an economic decline of 2.2 percent which lasts for 11 months. The decline during the 1990-1991 recession was 1.1 percent; the decline during the 1973-75 recession was nearly 5 percent. The U.S. has had 9 recessions since World War II.

A **depression** is a severe downward phase of the economic cycle where unemployment is very high, prices are very low, purchasing power is sharply decreased, and economic activity has virtually ceased. Depressions do not occur in the American economy anymore (the last one occurred throughout the 1930s and into the early 1940s) because of the existence of so many social and economic safety-net programs, such as insured bank deposits, unemployment benefits and social security. Instead, the U.S. economy now occasionally experiences prolonged periods of sluggish economic growth (such as 1989 through 1991) where it may occasionally experience quarters of very minimal or negative growth. This also can be called a **psychological recession** because very slight economic growth (perhaps 0.5 to 1.5 percent) and persistently high unemployment (6.0 percent or more) can together negate the positive expectations about the future held by consumers and businesses causing them to continue to depress spending which prolongs the negative scenario.[3] Sometimes this pushes the economy back into a technically defined recession.

The slowdown eventually ends and consumers and businesses become more optimistic. The economy moves into the **recovery phase** where levels of production, employment, and retail sales begin to rapidly improve, allowing the overall economy to experience some growth from its previously weakened state. The stock market and new housing starts generally lead the way. To complete the business cycle, the economy moves from the recovery phase into the expansion phase. The whole economic cycle normally takes 3 to 4 years from start to finish.

---

[1] Economist Robert J. Samuelson observes that, "What no one says (but everyone recognizes) is that recessions are a grim sort of industrial policy. They promote efficiency and punish sloppiness."

[2] A **rolling recession** is a term used to describe the fact that while the overall U.S. economy might be enjoying growth there may be one or more geographic regions that are experiencing economic decline. A rolling recession seemingly moves around the country from one geographic region to another.

[3] A psychological recession is partly caused by personal experiences of unemployment and the fear of job insecurity. Other causal factors include an omnipresent communications system that constantly offers large doses of negative information, such as violence on television and in movies, alleged "scandals" on tabloid television, and "action" news about death and mayhem on the streets of life. Americans in recent decades are not and have not been optimistic about the future. Rather, discontent is rampant and many people are anxious about tomorrow.

Growth is measured by economists by finding out how much is produced in a given time period. The government regularly announces the annual rate at which the gross domestic product has grown over the previous **quarter**, a time period of 3 months. **Gross domestic product (GDP)** is a measurement of the goods and services produced within the U.S. (regardless of ownership) over a period of time, such as 1 year, measured in dollars.[6] It excludes earnings on U.S. investments abroad. GDP is the broadest measure of the economic health of the nation as it is composed of the key economic factors of personal consumption, government expenditures, private investment, inventory growth, and trade balance that have occurred within the U.S. borders. The GDP of the United States is expected to be over $6.2 tillion this year.

Revisions in how gross domestic product is caluclated have reduced recent GDP figures slightly. Nowadays, less than a 2 percent annual increase in GDP is considered low growth; more than 3 percent is considered vigorous growth. Economic growth during the 1950s and 1960s averaged 4 percent annually. Since 1990 the economy has been growing just over 2 percent annually. As long as inflation is held to 3 percent or less (by restraint in federal taxing and spending and by tight monetary policies of the Fed), the economy is likely to continue to grow at an annual rate of no more than 2.5 percent.

The GDP, which is reported quarterly, can have a strong effect on government policy because it shows whether the economy is in a recession and whether inflation is out of line. When using GDP as a measure of economic progress, the figure should be corrected for price changes and increases in the population. Since prices usually rise every year in the United States, part of an increase in GDP represents some amount of inflation. As a result, the government develops figures that subtract the effect of inflation from GDP, and the result is known as **real gross domestic product**. The population also increases regularly. Therefore, another key economic figure published by government is the **real per capita gross domestic product**, which is a measure of economic growth on a per-person basis after subtracting the effects of inflation. This is perhaps the most valid measure of economic growth. The U.S. per capita gross domestic product this year is expected to be over $19,600.

The U.S. Department of Commerce publishes an **index of leading economic indicators (LEI)**, which is a measure designed to forecast swings in the economy, such as whether the nation is growing or sliding toward a recession. The LEI is a composite index, reported monthly as a percentage by the Commerce Department, suggesting the future direction of the cyclical economy of the United States. It summarizes 11 components that historically tend to move downward or upward before the economy swings in those directions. Examples are new orders for consumer goods and materials, new business formation, new private housing starts, average weekly claims for initial unemployment insurance, consumer expectations measured by the University of Michigan, and growth of money supply, which taken together generally offer a somewhat reliable prediction about future directions in the economy. A falling index for 3 or more consecutive months is a signal that economic growth will slow in the months ahead, although monthly moves in the index are not nearly as important as the cumulative, long-term trend. These and other economic indicators are used by governments and businesses to help make policy decisions. Since they are so widely reported by the media, such indices also influence consumer buying decisions.

---

[6]The current GDP is misleading since the expenditures associated with prison building, nuclear waster disposal, crime, divorce, timber sales, and natural disasters are considered economic gains. Some argue for a **genuine progress indicator (GPI)** that would subtract growth for negatives.

Monitoring Consumer Attitudes: Indicators of Economic Confidence

Two private organizations report on consumer attitudes toward the economy in an effort to include the human factor in economic matters. The Conference Board, a New York-based organization, and the University of Michigan's Survey Research Center, frequently measures consumer views regarding the health and direction of the economy. Are consumers pessimistic or optimistic about their futures? Researchers want to know how consumers are feeling about their present situations, expectations for the future, and buying intentions. For example, *The Conference Board* tracks in one confidence index (with a sample of 5000) consumers' plans to buy cars, houses, and appliances and take vacations. The *Survey Research Center* reports (with a sample of 500) consumers' expectations about personal finances, business conditions, and buying conditions as it tries to get at the psychological reasoning behind consumers' decisions.

Future directions in economic growth are largely affected by personal perceptions that motivate spending and saving decisions. This, in turn, pushes the economy higher or pulls it down. Since consumer spending accounts for two-thirds of the nation's gross domestic product, such buying intentions are vital. Evidence clearly shows that **optimism** about future economic conditions breeds consumer confidence and a willingness to buy and to acquire debt. Consumers are quite adept at forecasting future economic events—3 to 9 months in advance—such as unemployment, interest rates, inflation, home and vehicle purchases and general business conditions. Such early indicators, especially when they occur for 3 months in succession, give businesses and governments information to help them make better plans and policy decisions.

Primary Goal: Economic Productivity

Perhaps the single most important factor affecting the economic growth of a country is its workers' **economic productivity**, the economic output of an hour of labor. It is the key indicator of a nation's efficiency. Real income and the level of living cannot increase without increases in the productivity of a nation's labor force. People's resources of knowledge and skills must keep expanding. Wages, salaries, interest earnings, and income from other sources divided by the population, known as **per capita income**, was $22,800 last year.

In the United States, labor represents 70 percent of business costs while capital represents the remaining 30 percent. Productivity in the U.S. is held back by fewer technological innovations, low business profits, slowdowns in economic growth, increases in inflation, large numbers of young employees, growing numbers of underskilled workers (including women returning to the paid workforce), and a poorly educated citizenry.[7] Key to improvements in labor productivity are growing resources, high savings rates, declining government deficits, improving labor quality, more technological developments, low energy costs, and productivity incentives. Rising productivity enables businesses to produce more without hiring more workers. International groups rank the U.S. as the most competitive economy in the world.

Productivity increases in the **manufacturing sector** in recent years generally have been less than 2 percent per year while productivity increases in the services sector have been less than 1 percent. The **service sector** economy of the United States—retail stores,

---

[7]According to a four-year long Department of Education report, *Adult Literacy in America*, nearly half of the 191 million Americans over age 15 read and write so poorly that they have difficulty holding down their jobs. Education Secretary Richard Riley commented that, "the vast majority of Americans do not have the skills they need to earn a living in our increasingly technological society and international marketplace."

restaurants, hotels, real estate, banking, accounting, computers, airlines, and utilities—is vital to economic growth. The recent enormous job layoffs in these industries have caused wrenching corporate adjustments in order to create a much higher level of productivity. This implies that the **downsizing** going on—reducing the size of workforces in businesses and governments—does contribute to better productivity. Firms that have grown inefficient or whose products are no longer desirable must give way to new businesses with new products. Fierce competition, layoffs, and bankruptcies are indicators that productivity increases are soon to arrive. Economic productivity in the U.S. surged so much during 1994 and 1995 that the cost of labor declined (**wage compression**), signaling that the economy may continue to grow without serious inflation pressures. As efficiencies continue, the long-term trend toward smaller payrolls is expected to remain.

The U.S. currently has 83 percent of its 120 million workers in the service sector and 17 percent in manufacturing. While some manufacturing jobs have been lost to foreign competition, the greatest reason has been increased productivity in manufacturing. Increasing productivity in the service sector, by using more computers on the job, retraining adult workers, increasing educational requirements for new hires, working at home (telecommuting), and using just-in-time inventory methods, will result in higher real earnings for those workers. Increased productivity permits wages to go up without those increases being eroded by inflationary price increases.

Productivity increases raise the real earnings of workers. Therefore, increasing real productivity is crucial to long-term improvement in the standard of living for any population. Higher productivity enables businesses to increase wages without causing inflation. Without improvements in productivity, young people cannot look forward to a better economic life than their parents.

CONSUMER UPDATE: Wage Inequity in the U.S.

Average wages adjusted for inflation declined during the 1980s, according to an analysis by the National Commission for Unemployment Policy. Only college graduates and those in the top 20 percent of the income distribution gained significantly. Those with marketable skills are moving up while **wage inequality** grows. Wages for those with less-than-average earnings are now actually lower than they were 15 years ago. One reason for the falling income is that the consumer price index overstates the negative effects of inflation. People cope with wage inequality by using credit and putting more family members into the paid labor force.

Primary Goal: Economic Security

Another social and economic goal of American society is **economic security**. This is the desire for protection against the economic risks people face in their lives, such as loss of employment, illness, business bankruptcy, bank failures, poverty, and destitution in old age. Individually, consumers take action to protect themselves by saving money and buying insurance to protect against such events.

To achieve this important goal, labor unions[8] negotiate contracts with employers to provide for job security and pension benefits. Over the years, the middle-class has enhanced its economic security with a multitude of government benefits: Social Security, Medicare, mortgage interest tax deductions, veterans benefits, student loans, farm subsidies, unemployment compensation, roads and bridges, airports and railways, and federally insured bank deposits. Some would call this **middle-class welfare**. One of the big lies in American society is the growth of "big government programs being forced upon unwilling voters" because most federal spending goes for these popular programs.

Some Americans, however, remain in **poverty**. The government's official definition is about $14,800 for a family of four. Last year the number in poverty amounted to 38 million, or 14.5 percent of the population. The poverty rate in 1971 was 12.5 percent.

CONSUMER UPDATE: Tax Equity in the U.S.

According to the most recent tax data available, and reported by the Tax Foundation, the top 1 percent of income earners pay 27 percent of all federal individual income taxes and the top 5 percent pay 45 percent of the burden. The top 10 percent pay 58 percent, the top 25 percent pay 78 percent, and the top 50 percent pay 95 percent of all federal income taxes. The 56 million filers representing the lower half of income earners paid only 5 percent of all federal income taxes collected. The current progressive income taxes rates are 15 percent, 28 percent, 31 percent, 36 percent, and 39.6 percent.

Supporters of income tax reform in the U.S. argue for greater simplicity and fairness. Proposals to change the progressivity of the current income tax, such as a **flat tax**, however, will result in greater inequities. For example, eliminating or reducing the tax on investment income (interest, dividends and capital gains) and inherited wealth would benefit only those who receive such income—the rich.

Primary Goal: Economic Justice

A key social and economic goal of American society is **economic equity** or **economic justice**. Economic justice exists when the benefits and burdens are distributed equitably according to some accepted rule.[9] This involves application of the concepts of fairness and equity (what is right and wrong) to private and public economic decision making. Individually, citizens are willing to do what is good by volunteering, donating to charity, and participating in community efforts to help the needy. Society has a broad goal of economic justice. There is plenty of room for disagreement of specifics, but government has decided to fix the price of electricity because it is fair to establish an equitable minimum employment wage. Government also has decided to provide minimal health care

---

[8]Union membership as a percentage of nonagricultural employment in the U.S. is 15 percent; it is 11 percent of the nation's private-sector work force.

[9]Today about 36 percent of the nation's net worth is held by the wealthiest 1 percent of households; it was about 20 percent in 1975.

for the poor because it is the moral thing to do, and, on the same grounds, redistribute income by taking income from the wealthy[10] and providing for the needy.

On a consumer decision-making level, equity suggests that we should require nutritional labeling on food products to help consumers buy foods that are good for them. Shall we also require that consumers without bank accounts be permitted to cash government checks for minimal cost at banking institutions? How we achieve the goals of fairness in society requires a serious debate of the issues.

Review and Summary of Key Terms and Concepts

1. Define **economic system**, explain how such a system functions in an economy, and identify the **key economic questions** that every society faces.

2. What is the **central economic problem** in any economy?

3. Distinguish among the terms **economics**, **positive economics** and **normative economics**.

4. Summarize the differences between a **socialistic** and a **capitalistic** economic system, being sure to define the terms **totalitarian** and **communism** in your response.

5. What is the **American market system**?

6. Why are **property rights** important to the American market system?

7. Distinguish among **profit** (in an economic sense), **normal profit** and **excess profit**.

8. Discuss the evolving concept of **competition** in a market economy.

9. What are some of the **defects of capitalism**?

10. Briefly explain how **employee stock ownership plans** are beginning to change the essence of capitalism.

11. Comment upon the availability of **resources**, and distinguish between **human resources** and **nonhuman resources**.

12. Distinguish between **economic well-being** and **human capital**.

13. Distinguish between **standard of living** and **level of living**.

14. What is an **economic vote**?

---

[10]During the 1950s, corporations paid 31 percent of the federal government's general tax collections; they now pay only 15 percent.

15. Discuss what is involved in **allocating resources,** focusing upon the **price mechanism**.

16. Summarize how a manufacturer might go about establishing a projected **return on investment**.

17. Summarize the **circular flow** of economic activity and explain how the **multiplier effect** works.

18. Distinguish between one's **marginal propensity to consume, marginal propensity to import** and **marginal propensity to save**.

19. What are **transfer payments**?

20. How do **progressive** and **regressive** taxes differ?

21. Summarize what is meant by the term **monetary policy**.

22. Explain the term **money supply** and its component parts.

23. Explain how **reserve requirements** work and why our banking system is called a **fractional reserve system**.

24. Distinguish between **open-market operations** and using the **discount rate** in influencing monetary policy.

25. Distinguish between **velocity of money** and **easy money**.

26. What is **public policy**, and what are the **broad social and economic goals of American society**?

27. Distinguish between a **true democracy** and a **republic**.

28. Define the term **capitalism**, and tell what spurs economic growth in such an economic system.

29. Give some examples of **economic freedoms**.

30. Distinguish between the broad economic goals of **economic efficiency** and **consumer efficiency**.

31. Describe the **central economic problem** in the context of the economic goal of **full employment**.

32. Explain the term **economic cycle** by using such terms as **expansion, depression, recession** and **recovery**.

33. What is meant by the economic goals of **price stability** and **economic growth**?

34. Distinguish between **gross domestic product** and **real gross domestic product**.

35. Explain how major research organizations monitor **consumer sentiment**, and how the **index of leading economic indicators** works.

36. What does the term **downsizing** have to do with the national social and economic goals of **economic productivity** and **economic security**?

37. Define the term **economic equity**, and give examples of the concept.

Useful Resources for Consumers

Board of Govenors of the Federal Reserve System
20th and C Streets, NW
Washington, DC 20551-0001
202-452-2631

Department of Labor
Office of Consumer Affairs
Washington, DC 20210
202-219-6060

National Labor Relations Board
Office of the Executive Secretary
1099 Fourteenth Street, NW
Washington, DC 20570
202-273-1940

National Institute for Consumer Education
207 Rackham Building
College of Education
Eastern Michigan University
Ypsilanti, MI 48197
313-487-2292

"What Do You Think" Questions

1. In terms of **resource availability**, there are a number of resources available to consumers, including **human**, **nonhuman** and others. Trace through an imaginary day in the life of a family and identify 20 or more examples of such resources.

2. How do you think the concept of the **price mechanism** works in reality? Give some examples.

3. Thinking of the community where you are going to school, give some examples of how the **multiplier effect** works in banking, employment and retail sales.

4. Which two of the **broad social and economic goals** do you believe offer the most potential for conflicts in public policy decisions? Explain your reasoning.

5. What are your thoughts on the tax equity situation in the U.S. today?

Chapter 7

Economic Concepts Critical to Consumer Success

OBJECTIVES

After reading this chapter, you should be able to

1. Explain the concepts of supply, demand, and market equilibrium.

2. Recognize situations where supply and demand do not work.

3. Give examples of income and substitution effects.

4. Summarize how indifference curve and budget line analysis can be used in decisionmaking.

To effectively participate in society, an individual performing the roles of worker, citizen and as a consumer must have an understanding of the economic marketplace. Good personal decisions will result when you are able to visualize the economic effects—both for yourself and for society as a whole—of alternative courses of action. Several economic concepts are important in the process of being able to reason rationally. This critical thinking is required to properly analyze consumer issues as well as alternative proposals to resolve consumer problems. This chapter examines the economic concepts of demand, supply, market equilibrium, when supply and demand do not always work, income and substitution effects, and indifference curve and budget line analysis. One appendix is included at the end of the chapter that provides more depth to the rational decision making: The Life Cycle and Permanent Income Hypothesis.

Demand in a Market Economy

The American marketplace is best described as a **market economy** or a **market-oriented economy**. This is an economy that is guided mostly by decisions made in the private sector, by consumers and businesses. The American economy is characterized by decentralized decision making. In contrast, China, Cuba, and North Korea have government-controlled, centrally-planned economies.

A **market** is an organized situation in which buyers and sellers register their individual economic demands and make their decisions to buy and sell. The express their demands by **economic voting** which is the spending or non-spending of dollars for products and services. If they buy, they accept; if not, they reject. Consumers, businesses and governments cast economic votes for or against all products and services by such actions.

Each market works in the same way. High profits signal other business firms that more should be produced. As more firms enter a market and compete for the same customers, prices drop and, at the same time, supplies go up until a new equilibrium is reached.

In our modern and complex world, there are thousands of markets. Buyers and sellers come together to let supply and demand decide wholesale and retail prices of products, the prices of labor, and the cost of stocks and money. The market system adds up the collective decisions made by millions of buyers and sellers in all the markets and converts them into aggregate forces of supply and demand. The quantities of supply and demand interact with each other and determine the prices of goods and services.

A number of economic concepts affect decision making, including economic voting, demand, elasticity of demand, supply, market equilibrium, farm prices, price fixing, price ceilings, income and substitution effects, opportunity cost, marginal cost, diminishing marginal utility, and cost-benefit analysis.

How Demand Affects Prices

When buyers and sellers meet in a market, they are very interested in price. They want to know how much each is willing to buy or sell at a particular price. When they agree on a price, it is called the **market price**, what a willing and able buyer is willing to pay a willing seller.

Demand (sometimes called **effective demand**) in a general sense is the willingness and ability of consumers to spend money on certain products and services. The **law of demand** suggests that as the price increases, the quantity demanded of goods and services will decrease. Conversely, as the price decreases, the quantity demanded will increase. In short, there is an inverse relationship between price and quantity demanded. Common sense and simple observation tell us that this principle is true.

The concept of demand also can be explained in terms of **substitutability** of products one for another. Usually there are a reasonable number of substitutes for any one product. Thus, an increase in the price of one product tends to make consumers substitute other products for it, and this action tends to constrain price increases. Similarly, a decline in the price of a product will make consumers substitute it for other products.

The Demand Curve Slopes Downward and to the Right

Demand is technically defined in economics as a schedule that shows the various quantities of a product that consumers are willing and able to purchase at each specific price in a set of possible prices during a specific period of time. It is difficult to construct a demand schedule for a specific product in advance because we must know exactly how many units people would actually buy at given prices. Still, we know that people will buy more units of a product at a low price than they will at a high price. Although the quantity of a good tends to vary inversely with price, this does not imply that the variation in the amount sold is always proportionate to the change in price. Demand portrays a series of alternatives that can be set down in tabular form.

Table 7-1 reflects the relationship between the price of apples and the quantity that a consumer would be willing and able to purchase at each of the prices. The consumer typically uses price as a reference point; thus the question is, "What amounts of products will consumers buy at various prices?" By itself, a demand schedule of a single consumer's buying intentions cannot indicate which of the five possible market prices will actually exist for apples because this price depends on both demand and supply.

Price per Pound	Quantity Demanded per Week
$5	10
4	20
3	35
2	55
1	80

TABLE 7-1   A Single Consumer's Hypothetical Demand for Apples

The inverse relationship between the price of a product and the quantity demanded can be illustrated on a graph that charts quantity demanded on the horizontal axis and price on the vertical axis. The five price-quantity possibilities in Table 7-1 are plotted as appropriate points on the two axes in Figure 7-1. Each of these points represents a specific price and the corresponding quantity that an individual consumer is willing and able to pay during a specific time period. We assume that the same inverse relationship exists between all points as between the ones graphed. This allows us to generalize and draw a curve to represent all price-quantity possibilities within the limitations of the graph. The resulting curve is called a **demand curve**, labeled *DD*, which slopes downward and to the right because the relationship it illustrates between price and quantity, is inverse.

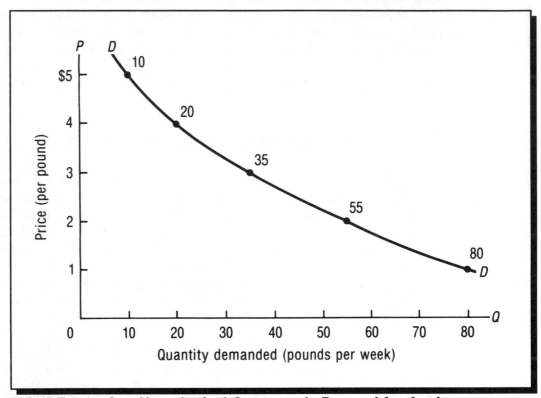

FIGURE 7-1   One Hypothetical Consumer's Demand for Apples

The assumption of competition forces us to make a transition from the illustration of one consumer to that of a large number of buyers in a market. If we sum the demand schedules of each and every consumer at the various prices, we now have a *market* demand curve instead of an *individual* demand curve.

Figure 7-2 illustrates that an increase in demand is reflected as a shift of the demand curve to the right, for example, from *D1D1*, to *D2D2*; the converse occurs with a decrease in demand, resulting in a shift of the demand curve to the left, for example, from *D1D1*, to *D3D3*. A demand schedule may be represented by a curve or a straight line. A change in demand means that there are shifts of the entire demand curve to the right or left.

Notice that one assumption in a demand curve is that price is the most important determinant of the amount of a product purchased by consumers. Thus, economists are fond of saying, **ceteris paribus**, meaning **"other things being equal,"** or everything else held constant. In the real world, however, this is not true. Factors other than price do affect purchases. When **non-price determinants of demand** change, the location of the demand curve shifts to the right or left, as graphed in Figure 7-2 as *D2D2* and *D1D1*, respectively. The non-price determinants of demand include (1) tastes and preferences of consumers, (2) number of consumers in the market, (3) money incomes of consumers, (4) prices of related goods, and (5) expectations of consumers regarding future prices and incomes.

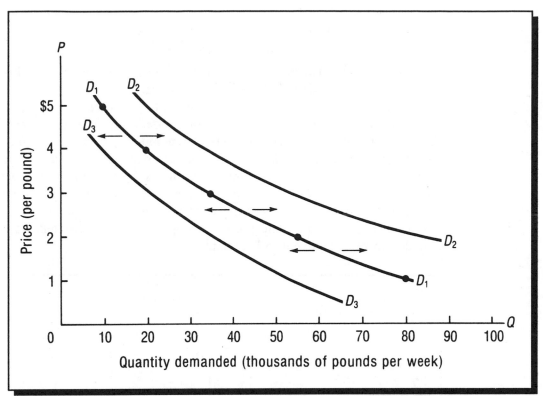

FIGURE 7-2 Many Hypothetical Consumers' Demand for Apples

Demand is Characterized by Its Elasticity

Elasticity is a term that expresses the change in one variable in response to a given change in another variable. This concept is useful to sellers when faced with the problem of determining at which price to offer goods for sale. While it is true that a greater number of sales can be made at lower prices, it is questionable whether greater revenue from the larger sales will offset the reduced revenue from the reduced price. Further, the changes are not proportional. **Price elasticity of demand** is a measure of consumer responsiveness to a change in price. How well a seller fares by raising or lowering prices depends on the degree of price elasticity. The demand for some products is such that consumers are relatively responsive to price changes; the demand for such products is said to be **elastic**. For other products, consumers are relatively unresponsive to price changes. When price changes result in only modest changes in the amount purchased, the demand is said to be **inelastic**.

The **elasticity of demand coefficient** E_d (shown in Equation 7.1) is a measure of the degree of elasticity or inelasticity of a particular section of a curve. It refers to the ratio of the percentage change in price to the percentage change in the quantity of a good that will be purchased as a result of the change in price. To calculate the percentage changes, you actually divide the change in price by the original price and the resulting change in quantity demanded by the original quantity demanded. Demand is inelastic if a given percentage change in price is accompanied by a relatively smaller change in the quantity demanded. Demand is elastic if a given percentage change in price results in a larger percentage change in quantity demanded. The formula for the elasticity of demand coefficient is

$$E_d = \frac{\text{percentage change in quantity demanded}}{\text{percentage change in price}} \qquad \text{(Equation 7.1)}$$

The U.S. Department of Commerce publishes the income sensitivity factors for various products. Examples of measures include an elasticity of 3.0 for pleasure boats, 2.0 for new automobiles, 0.5 for gasoline, and 0.2 for electricity.

Elasticity of demand may range from perfect elasticity to perfect inelasticity, as illustrated in Figure 7-3. **Perfectly elastic demand** may occur for a product for which an infinite number could be sold at a given market price. For example, demand curve *D1D1*, (a straight horizontal line) in Figure 7-3 illustrates the situation of a wheat farmer who is able to sell all of his or her product to the government at a special subsidized price. Consumer goods that tend toward greater elasticity include luxuries, large-expenditure durable goods, and substitute goods. Examples of goods that tend toward inelasticity include groceries and vehicle license plates.

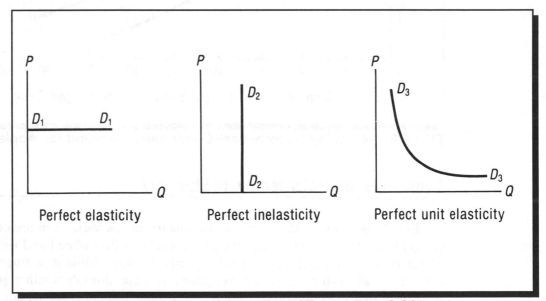

FIGURE 7-3   Demand Curves Showing Different Elasticities

The determinants of elasticity of demand include (1) substitutability (the larger the number of good substitute products available, the greater the elasticity of demand), (2) proportion of income (the products that take a greater bulk of income, that is, expensive goods tend to have a greater elasticity of demand), (3) necessities and luxuries (the demand for necessities tends to be inelastic while the demand for luxuries tends to be elastic), and (4) time (the longer the time period under consideration, the more elastic is the demand for a particular product).

Demand curve *D2D2* (a straight vertical line) in Figure 7-3 is **perfectly inelastic**, indicating that the same quantity of the product will be bought regardless of the price. A change in the price of automobile license plates, for example, results in no change in the quantity demanded. (At some point a rise in price would encourage owners of older automobiles to consider not licensing the vehicles.) Consumer goods that tend toward inelasticity include necessities, small-expenditure perishable goods, and complementary goods.

In the special case of **unit elasticity**, demand curve *D3D3* (a hyperbola) in Figure 7-3, an increase or decrease in price will leave total revenue unchanged, since the loss of revenue occurring because of lower prices is offset by the gain in revenue from the increased sales. Thus, changes in price and quantity are proportional throughout the demand curve, resulting in an elasticity coefficient of exactly 1.0, or unity.

Supply Affects Prices

Total **supply** in a general sense is the maximum amount of a product or service available for sale at a given price. The **law of supply** suggests that as the price goes up, so does the quantity supplied. Conversely, as the price goes down, so does the quantity supplied. For example, if the price of apples is rising, more growers will be interested in planting apple trees in hope of future profits. When prices are declining, supplies also drop because fewer sellers will want to provide that product in the market for little anticipated profits.

The Supply Curve Slopes Upward to the Left

Supply is technically defined in economics as a schedule that shows the various amounts of a product that a producer is willing to supply for sale in the market at each specific price in a set of possible prices during some specific time period. A supply schedule portrays a series of alternative possibilities, as shown in Table 7-2, for a single producer of apples. The farmer uses supply as a reference point, thus the question is, "What prices will be required to induce producers to offer various quantities of apples?"

Price per Pound	Quantity Supplied per Week
$5	60
4	50
3	35
2	20
1	5

TABLE 7-2   An Individual Producer's Hypothetical Supply of Apples

It can be seen clearly in Table 7-2 that there is a direct relationship between price and quantity supplied. As the price rises, so does the quantity supplied; as the price falls, so does the quantity supplied. The law of supply works because producers are willing to provide more of a given product at a high price than they are at a lower price. For the producer, a higher price is an incentive to produce more.

The relationship between price and quantity supplied can be explained on the basis of substitutability. For example, when resources and productive techniques are readily adaptable to producing a variety of products, a farmer will shift his or her resources from other commodities to apples, for example, if the price of that product is rising. This occurs simply because the farmer will earn more money. Realistically, switching from producing one very different product may be quite complex and expensive, but such shifting does occur among different producers.

The concept of supply is graphically presented in Figure 7-4 utilizing the single producer's data from Table 7-2, represented by S1S1. The supply curve slopes upward to the left. Figure 7-5 shows the same single producer's data along with data from hundreds of other hypothetical apple producers to create a *market* supply curve instead of an *individual* supply curve.

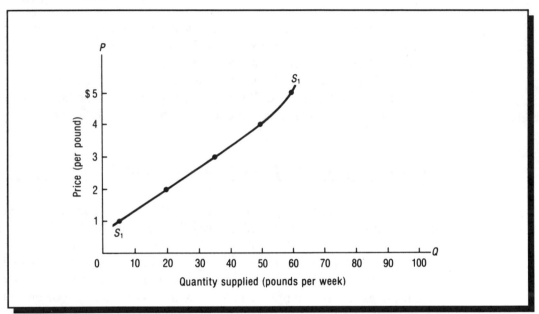

FIGURE 7-4　One Hypothetical Seller's Supply Curve for Apples

Several Non-Price Determinants of Supply Exist

The non-price determinants of supply include (1) techniques of production, (2) prices of resources, (3) prices of other goods, (4) expectations of future prices, (5) number of sellers in the market, and (6) taxes and subsidies. A change in any determinant will cause the supply curve to shift to the right or the left. As illustrated in Figure 7-5, a shift to the right, from *S1S1*, to *S2S2*, represents an increase in supply; a shift to the left, from *S1S1* to *S3S3*, designates a decrease in supply. A change in supply is involved when the entire supply curve shifts. Supply curves are also predicated on the economist's ceteris paribus assumption.

Market Equilibrium Is the Ideal Where Price Meets Supply

When the concepts of supply and demand are brought together, you can visualize how the interaction of consumer buying decisions and producer selling decisions determine the price of a product and the quality that is bought and sold in the market. Table 7-3 shows the market supply and demand for apples assuming a competitive market.

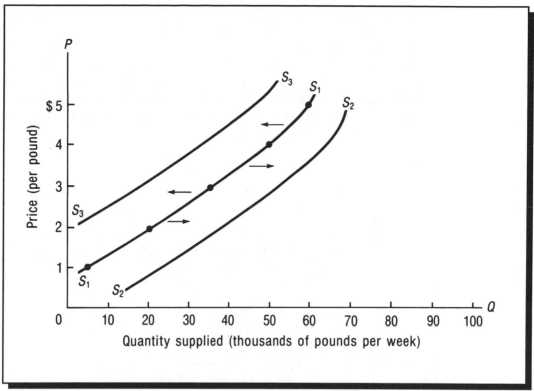

FIGURE 7-5   Supply Curve for Many Sellers of Apples

Total Quantity Supplied per Week (pounds)	Price per Pound	Total Quantity Demanded per Week (pounds)	Surplus (+) or Shortage (-) (pounds)
60,000	$5	10,000	+50,000
50,000	$4	20,000	+30,000
35,000	$3	35,000	0
20,000	$2	55,000	-35,000
5,000	$1	89,000	-84,000

TABLE 7-3   Hypothetical Market Supply of and Demand for Apples

The question to be answered is, "At which price might apples sell in this market?" At a price of $1 per pound, the price of apples is so low that consumer demand is very high. But, the same $1 price is too low to encourage farmers from putting their resources into apple production. The price of $1 cannot persist as the market price because competition among buyers will bid the price up. At a price of $2 per pound, the supply shortage has been reduced but not eliminated. At the other extreme, a price of $5 per pound results in consumers willing to take only 10,000 pounds of the large supply of 60,000 pounds. Thus, the high price encourages farmers to produce apples but discourages consumers from buying (creating an unwanted surplus). At a price of $4 per pound a surplus still exists, and competition among sellers should continue to bid down the price of apples.

Finally, at a price of $3 per pound, and only at this price, does the quantity of apples farmers are willing to produce and able to supply to the market equal the amount of apples consumers are willing to buy. There is neither a shortage nor a surplus at this **equilibrium price** where the price between buyers and sellers is in balance. Differences between supply and demand intentions of sellers and consumers will prompt price changes that will bring their plans together.

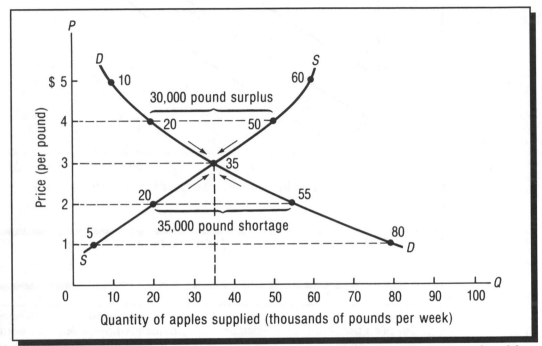

FIGURE 7-6   Equilibrium Price and Quantity for Apples As Determined by Market Demand and Supply

A graphic presentation results in the same conclusion, as shown in Figure 7-6. The intersection of the downward-sloping demand curve *DD* and the upward-sloping supply curve *SS* indicates the equilibrium price and quantity, in this instance $3 per pound and 35,000 pounds. A shortage of apples would occur at below-equilibrium prices. For example, apples priced at $2 would create a 35,000-pound shortage, drive prices up, and in so doing increase the quantity supplied and reduce the quantity demanded until equilibrium is reached. Further, apples priced at $4 per pound would create a 30,000-pound surplus, and in so doing push prices down and thereby increase the quantity demanded and reduce the quantity supplied until equilibrium is reached. At the equilibrium price, there is no burdensome surplus for sellers and no shortages for the consumers.

When Supply and Demand Does Not Work

Under competitive conditions, the number of possible relationships between supply and demand is enormous. For example, demand may increase while supply remains constant, or vice versa. Perhaps demand will increase while supply decreases, or vice versa. Or perhaps demand and supply will increase, but demand will increase more than supply.

In the real world it is extremely difficult, if not impossible, to construct actual demand and supply curves for various goods in the market. Yet we can still reach useful conclusions about what such curves would look like in competitive markets if we construct them. When prices are not at the point of equilibrium, economists study particular markets in an attempt to ascertain why the laws of supply and demand are being violated. The answer lies in the economist's assumption about "other things being equal" because this is rarely the case.

Farm Prices Often Are Not Set by Supply and Demand

If a seller, such as a farmer, wants to set the price different than the market price established by the free forces of competitive supply and demand, the market will have to be rigged or the forces of supply and demand will have to be changed. This is precisely what happens in three instances: (1) when government sets a *parity price* for an agricultural commodity that is higher than the market price, (2) when government sets price ceilings, and (3) when business firms illegally conspire to fix prices that are higher than the market price.

Instability in farm prices occurs, in part, because of short-run business fluctuations, wide variations in foreign demand, natural hazards (such as weather), and the pressure of competition in making adjustments to changing market conditions. Demand for farm products is both price and income inelastic. In an effort to guarantee consistent supplies of the product for consumers, as well as keep farmers in business, government sets prices on many commodities. These are known as **price supports** because government establishes prices that are higher than the equilibrium prices. A **parity price** of a farm commodity is a standard for measuring the purchasing power of that commodity in relation to prices of other goods and services during a definite base period. Since a high guaranteed parity price would result in excessive commodity surpluses (and additional tax dollars going to pay for storage costs), the government parity prices are generally accompanied by production limitations.[1]

Price Ceilings Are Occasionally Imposed by Government

Price ceilings are government-established prices that are lower than equilibrium prices. They upset the rationing function of prices by causing product and resource shortages. Government then typically introduces some sort of bureaucratic rationing

---

[1]The Office of Management and Budget and the Joint Committee on Taxation estimate that total farm subsidies from the federal government last year at $30 billion.

system for products at the controlled prices. Using the argument of equity, a number of prices in the American economy are set by government instead of letting market forces prevail, such as agricultural price supports, the minimum wage, and rent controls found in some communities.

Price Fixing Eliminates the Competitive Forces of Supply and Demand

Instead of having prices set by the forces of supply and demand, some business firms conspire to set high prices. They do this by (1) shrinking supply or (2) controlling the price. They can enjoy the excess profits until an alternative product develops or the government successfully accuses them of collusion in interfering with the free competitive forces of demand and supply. A federal or state court then finds them guilty of illegal **price fixing**.

Income and Substitution Effects

The discussion so far has suggested a logical and common-sense law of demand in that there is an inverse relationship between price and quantity demanded. One complementary explanation suggests that consumers are both able and willing to buy more of the product. The **income effect** suggests that a consumer will buy more of a product, as well as other products, as the price declines in relation to the consumer's income. For example, if you usually buy 1 pound of fish each week at $4 per pound and it declines to $3 per pound, you now have $1 available for buying more fish or another commodity. A decline in price increases the real income of the consumer.

This explanation is incomplete, however, because of the **substitution effect**. This complementary explanation of demand suggests that a lower price for a product increases the relative attractiveness of that product and makes consumers want to buy more of it. In the fish example, as the price drops, the prices of other products remain unchanged, which makes the price of fish even more attractive. Consequently, the lower price will induce the consumer to substitute fish for some of the now less attractive items in the food budget. At the lower price, fish may be substituted for steak, veal, or chicken. The income and substitution effects combine to help make consumers willing and able to buy more of a specific good at a low price than at a higher price.

Opportunity Cost

An **opportunity cost** is the most valuable alternative that must be sacrificed to satisfy a want; it is the thing that we must do without when we decide upon a particular allocation of resources. For example, the opportunity cost of buying a $16 compact disk might be an evening at the movie theater with a friend. Therefore, giving up the movies—the cost of the best alternative—is the opportunity cost involved when you choose to buy the CD. Note that most opportunity-cost decisions are in situations where once you choose an alternative, you cannot select the others.

Knowing the opportunity cost of alternatives allows you to place a value on the resource. Consumers use the principle of opportunity cost either consciously or unconsciously in their decision making. When understood and used consciously, the concept of opportunity costs helps people prioritize their decisions because they must make choices based on the best value that will provide maximum satisfaction among alternative opportunities.

Opportunity costs often involve money amounts, as well as psychic benefits, and these both should be considered carefully in decision making. Further, most opportunity costs involve personal tastes and preferences that are difficult to quantify. However, properly valuing the costs and benefits of alternatives is a key step in rational decision making.

Some opportunity costs may have larger costs than you might think. For example, by paying $10,000 for a motor vehicle, first you lose the dollars paid, then you lose the alternative use for those dollars, and finally you lose the value of another $10,000 (probably $14,000 before taxes) that must be earned to take the place of the dollar paid. When understood and used knowingly, the concept of opportunity costs helps consumers prioritize their decisions because they must make choices based on the best value that will provide maximum satisfaction among alternative opportunities. People often refer to **tradeoffs** when discussing opportunity costs because analyzing the opportunities involves trading one thing for another. In a world of scarcity, a tradeoff involves sacrificing one resource for another.

DID YOU KNOW?
Going to College Has Opportunity Costs

If four years of college tuition and related expenses amount to $40,000, that is not the total cost of going to school. If you could have obtained a job paying $12 an hour and worked 52 weeks a year for 40 hours a week, you would have earned $99,840 ($12 x 40 x 52 x 4 years). Thus, in this example the total real cost of going to college is $139,840.

Marginal Cost

It often is difficult for consumers to maximize their self-interest in marketplace transactions. Recognizing this, most consumers try to optimize their preferences. **Optimizing** is making something, such as a buying decision, as good or as effective as possible. The concept of marginal cost makes some consumer economics decisions more effective.

Utility is the ability of a good or service to satisfy a human want. Utility also is a subjective notion because the utility of a specific product may vary widely from person to person. As a result, utility is not susceptible to precise quantitative measurement. **Marginal cost** is the additional cost of something compared to the additional value received. Sometimes making consumer decisions is difficult enough without having to consider too many variables. The marginal cost concept reminds us to compare only important variables.

For example, two new automobiles are available on a dealership lot in Chicago, Illinois, where Scott Marshall is trying to make a decision. Both cars are the same make and model. One with a sticker price of $13,100 has a moderate number of options. The other with a sticker price of $14,800 has numerous options. It is unnecessary for Scott to consider all the options when comparing both vehicles. The concept of marginal cost says to compare the additional cost, $1,700 in this instance ($14,800 - $13,100), with the cost of the additional options. Scott must only decide if all the additional options are worth $1,700.

AN ECONOMIC FOCUS ON...The Propensity to Consume*

The consumption expenditure of a household is determined mainly by its level of disposable income. It means that consumption expenditure depends on disposable income, so that we can predict how much consumption will be associated with a given level of income.

The relationship between consumption expenditure and income is known as the **consumption function**, or the **propensity to consume**, a name that is associated with the British economist John Maynard Keynes. A consumption function for a hypothetical household is illustrated by the schedule in the first two columns of Table 7-4. The difference between income and consumption is saving, shown in column 3.

The consumption and saving data are graphed in Figure 7-7. Disposable income is measured on the horizontal axis and consumption expenditure on the vertical axis. The 45-degree line is a guideline which indicates that any point on the line is equidistant from the two axes. This means that if a household consumption expenditure lies on this line, it is then equal to the household's income (i.e. the household spends all of its income on consumption).

The consumption function is drawn as a straight line, C, which represents the data in columns 1 and 2 of the table. The intersection of this line with the 45-degree line is the household's **break-even point**, or often called the **point of zero saving** where consumption is exactly equal to income. This point is assumed to occur when disposable income is $200.

To the right of the break-even point the household is consuming less than its income. The difference, saving, is represented by the vertical distance between the consumption line and the 45-degree line. To the left of the break-even point the household is consuming more than its income. The difference, dissaving, is attained by the household either by going into debt or by dipping into past saving.

Given the data in columns 1 and 2, we can calculate two important measures of the relationship of income and consumption. One measure is the **average propensity to consume (APC)**. It is the ratio of consumption to income. It denotes how a household divides its income between consumption and saving. For example, at an income level of $400, the household will spend 80 cents of each dollar or a total of $320, and it will save 20 cents of each dollar or a total of $80. In other words, it will spend 80% of its income, and save 20%. Note that since consumption plus saving equal **income**, then the average propensity to consume (APC), and the **average propensity to save (APS)**, (defined as the ratio of saving to income), must always total 1 at any income level. Columns 4 and 5 in Table 7-4 show the derived APC's and APS's. Graphically, the APC at any point on line C, is measured as the slope of a line from the origin to that point.

The second important measure of the relationship of consumption and income is the **marginal propensity to consume (MPC)**. It indicates the percentage of each additional dollar of disposable income that will be consumed. An MPC of 0.60, as shown in column 6 in Table 7-4, means that 60% of any increase in income will be spent on consumption. The formula for calculating MPC therefore can be represented by:

$$MPC = \frac{\text{change in consumption}}{\text{change in income}}$$

The fraction of each additional dollar of income that does not go into consumption will go into saving and is defined as the **marginal propensity to save (MPS)**. The MPS's corresponding to the changes in income are shown in the last column of Table 7-4. The sum of MPC and MPS must always add to 1. Graphically, the MPC at any point on line C, is measured as the slope of line C. Note, however, if the relationship between income and consumption is represented by a curve rather than a straight line, then the MPC is measured as the slope of a line that is tangent to the point on the curve.

The **consumption function** shown in Figure 7-7 is characterized by a declining APC and a constant MPC. Figure 7-8 shows some other types of conceivable consumption functions. In Figure 7-7, function (1) has a constant MPC that is less than one, and a constant APC. Function (2) has a steadily rising MPC, however it is still less than 1 within the limits shown. The APC falls from T at point A to 1 at point B and thereafter continues to decline until point C, when APC and MPC are equal. Beyond C, MPC exceeds APC, and APC rises. Function (3) has a MPC which declines from a magnitude in excess of 1 to 1 at point d, and thereafter to lower magnitudes. The APC is always higher, declining to 1 at point E, and thereafter continuing to fall. Function (4) has a constant MPC of 1, and APC of less than 1, which rises from zero at point F and approaches 1.

The relationship between marginal and average propensities in general are characterized by the following rules: (1) if marginal is constant and equal to average, average is similarly constant; (2) if marginal is less than average, average is declining; (3) if marginal is greater than average, average is rising; (4) if marginal is rising or declining and at some point equals average, average at that point has reached a maximum or minimum.

It is important to conclude that at any given level of income, the APC relates consumption to income, whereas the MPC relates a **change** in consumption to a change in income. The marginal approach is invaluable in examining consumer behavior toward change.

*Mohamed Abdel-Ghany, Professor, The University of Alabama

Table 7-4. Hypothetical Consumption Function

Disposable Income	Consumption	Saving	APC	APS	MPC	MPS
100	140	-40	1.40	-.40		
200	200	0	1.00	.00	.6	.4
300	260	40	.87	.13	.6	.4
400	320	80	.80	.20	.6	.4
500	380	120	.76	.24	.6	.4

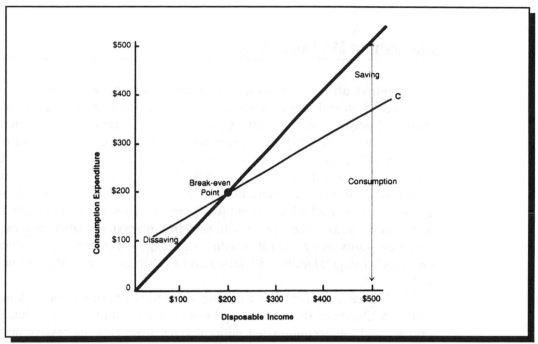

FIGURE 7-7

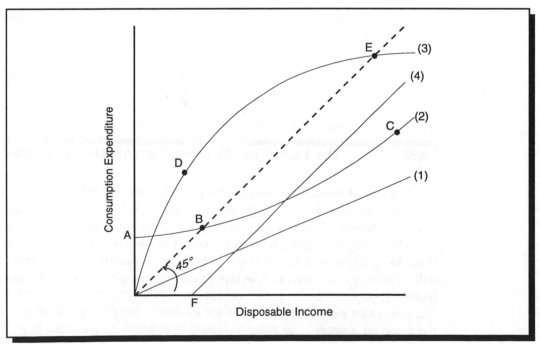

FIGURE 7-8

Diminishing Marginal Utility

Marginal utility refers to the extra utility, or satisfaction, that a consumer obtains from one additional unit of a specific product or service. You might receive a certain amount of satisfaction from eating a piece of candy (utility), and you can obtain a slightly different amount of satisfaction (marginal utility) from eating a second piece of candy.

Although consumer wants are insatiable, wants for specific commodities can be fulfilled. However, the more of a specific product a consumer obtains, the less anxious the consumer is to obtain more units of the same product. You might enjoy eating one bag of popcorn at a ball game, but the desire for a second is less intense; for a third or fourth, very weak. The **law of diminishing marginal utility** suggests that specific consumer wants can be fulfilled with succeeding fewer units of a commodity. Thus, a consumer's marginal utility will decline as he or she acquires additional units of a specific product.

To illustrate, assume that we can measure utility or satisfaction with units called **utils**. Table 7-5 illustrates the relationship between the quantity of a product, such as bags of popcorn, and the accompanying utility derived from each successive unit. It is assumed that diminishing marginal utility sets in with the first number of bags of popcorn purchased. Each successive unit yields less extra utility than the previous one as the consumer's desire for popcorn gets closer to fulfillment. Total utility can be found by totaling the marginal utility figures.

Units of Popcorn	Marginal Utility (utils)	Total Utility (utils)
1	10	10
2	8	18
3	7	25
4	6	31
5	5	36
6	4	40
7	3	43

TABLE 7-5   The Law of Diminishing Marginal Utility (Applied to Popcorn)

The law of diminishing marginal utility suggests that the demand curve for a specific product is downward sloping. If the successive units of a product provide smaller and smaller amounts of marginal, or extra, utility, the consumer will buy additional units of a product only if its price falls. A consumer might buy more popcorn if the price drops from $4 to $3 or even $2 per bag, but because of diminishing marginal utility, he or she will choose not to buy more at this price because giving up more money for popcorn means giving up other goods, which are alternative ways of getting utility. Sellers recognize that because of the principle of diminishing marginal utility, they must lower the price on a product in order to induce consumers to purchase large quantities of the product.

AN ECONOMIC FOCUS ON...Indifference Curve and Budget Line Analysis*

The roots of the **indifference curve analysis**, also known as the **ordinal utility theory**, can be traced back to the work of the Italian economists Vilfredo Pareto.[1] The economists Eugene Slutsky[2], John Hicks, R.G.D. Allen[3], and Harold Hotelling[4] have contributed to the development of the theory that was formalized by John Hicks.

Indifference curve analysis replaced the **marginal utility theory** by assuming that utility is ordinally measurable, rather than cardinally measurable. In other words, the consumer is assumed to be able to order or rank on a scale of preferences all alternative sets of consumption possibilities, rather than be required to assign numbers known as "utils" to measure utility.

Therefore, for any two combinations (or bundles) A and B of goods, a consumer either prefers A to B, B to A, or is indifferent between them. The consumer's preferences also are assumed to be consistent and transitive. If A is preferred to B and B to C, then A is preferred to C.

The consumer's preferences are assumed to express a diminishing **marginal rate of substitution**. It is the rate at which an individual is willing to give up one good in exchange for another good, while maintaining the same level of satisfaction. Finally, it is assumed that more of a good is preferred to less.

Figure 7-9 is an indifference map showing the preference of a consumer for two goods, let us assume oranges and apples. The quantities of the goods are measured along the two axes. Any point on the map represents a specific combination of oranges and apples. The consumer is assumed to be able to rank all of these combinations, indicating with respect to any pair of combinations whether he/she prefers one to the other, or is indifferent.

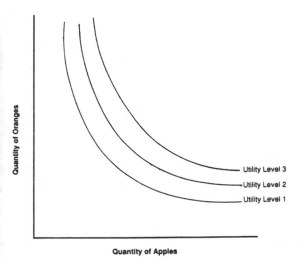

FIGURE 7-9

Any one **indifference curve** shows combinations of oranges and apples yielding the same level of utility to the consumer, while higher or lower levels of utility are represented by indifference curves lying farther

from or closer to the origin, respectively.

Indifference curves have three characteristics which result from the assumptions made earlier. First, indifference curves are concave from above with a downward slope, from the assumption of diminishing rate of marginal substitution.

The second characteristic is that indifference curves cannot intersect (from transitivity and more preferred to less). This characteristic is illustrated in Figure 7-10. In this graph (1) and (2) are indifference curves, and the points A, B, and C represent three different combinations of oranges and apples. C must obviously be preferred to B because it contains more oranges as well as more apples. C and A are equivalent because they lie on the same indifference curve (2). Similarly, A and B are indifferent, since they lie on indifference curve (1). Since C is indifferent to A and A is indifferent to B, therefore C must be indifferent to B (due to the transitivity assumption). However, as previously mentioned, C is preferred to B because it contains more of oranges as well as apples. Hence, we can conclude that indifference curves cannot possibly intersect.

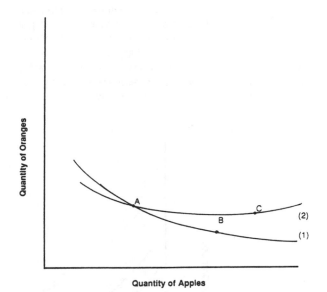

FIGURE 7-10

The third characteristics of indifference curves is that they pass everywhere in the commodity space. For example, an infinite number of indifference curves lie between any two of the indifference curves shown in Figure 7-9.

So far we have presented a picture of the consumer's preferences only. His/her indifference map shows what he/she is willing to do with respect to different combinations of oranges and apples. What the consumer is able to do depends upon the consumer's income and the prices of oranges and apples.

The **budget line** (it may also be called the **opportunity line**) describes the possibilities open to the consumer, given his/her money

(continued)

income and the prices of oranges and apples. We can represent the budget line on an indifference map. Suppose that the consumer budget is $10 (the amount to be spent on oranges and apples), the price of oranges is $2 per pound, and the price of apples is $1 per pound. If the consumer should spend all of the $10 on oranges, he/she would buy 5 pounds of it. Similarly, he/she could purchase 10 pounds of apples if he/she were to spend all of the $10 on apples. The budget line is the straight line connecting these two points. It is shown on Figure 7-11 as line YX. It represents all combinations of oranges and apples that the consumer's budget will allow him/her to purchase.

The slope of the budget line YX is OY/OX. Where OY is the amount of oranges the consumer could purchase with the entire $10. Likewise, OX is the amount of apples the consumer could purchase with the entire $10. Since OY equals the budget/price of oranges, and OX equals the budget/price of apples, then the slope of the budget line equals:

(the budget/price of oranges)/(the budget/price of apples) =
price of apples/price of oranges
which is the rate of relative prices.

Given the consumer's indifference map and his/her budget line, satisfaction is maximized at the point at which the budget line is tangent to an indifference curve. This point is represented by point A in Figure 7-11. It implies the purchase of quantity X_1 of apples and Y_1 of oranges. Note that the combination A is on the highest indifference curve that the consumer's budget line will allow him/her to reach and it is the only combination available to him/her on that indifference curve.

Combinations such as B or C are on a lower indifference curve and as such will not be chosen. Even though combination D is on a higher indifference curve, it lies above the budget line and therefore is unattainable.

At the point of tangency A, the slope of the budget line (Px/Py) is equal to the slope of the indifference curve at that point (marginal rate of substitution of y for x). Thus, the consumer in our example maximizes satisfaction when his/her purchase of oranges and apples is such that the rate at which he/she is willing to give up oranges for apples is just equal to the ratio of the price of apples to the price of oranges.

---

[1]Pareto, Vilfredo (1906). Manuel D'Economic Politique.

[2]Slutsky, E. (1915). Sulla Teoria del Bilancio del Consumatore. *Giornale deli Economist*, LT, 1-16.

[3]Hick, J., & Allen, R.G.D. (1934). A Reconsideration of the Theory of Value. *Economica*, XIV, 52-76, 196-219.

[4]Hotelling, H. (1935, January). Demand Functions with Limited Budgets. *Econometrica*, 66-78.

*Mohamed Abdel-Ghany, Professor, The University of Alabama

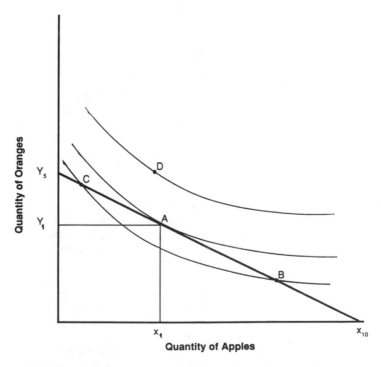

FIGURE 7-11

Review and Summary of Key Terms and Concepts

1.   What is a **market economy** and what role does **economic voting** play?

2.   Distinguish between **demand** in a general sense and **demand** from the perspective of an economist.

3.   Explain and give an example why a **demand curve** slopes downward and to the right.

4.   Give 5 examples of products and services that are said to be relatively **elastic**; give 5 more examples which are **inelastic**.

5.   Distinguish between **supply** in a general sense and **supply** from the perspective of an economist and then define the **law of supply**.

6.   Explain the concept of **equilibrium price** and give three examples from everyday living.

7.   Summarize why **farm prices** are unstable and what many governments do in attempting to resolve the instability, and in your response be sure to define **price supports** and **parity price**.

8.   Distinguish between **price fixing** and **price ceilings**.

9.   What does the **substitution effect** have to do with the **law of demand**?

10.   Distinguish between the terms **marginal utility** and **the law of diminishing marginal utility**.

11.   What are **opportunity costs** and why are they important to consumers?

Useful Resources for Consumers

National Council on Economic Education
1140 Avenue of the Americas
New York, NY 10036
800-338-1192

"What Do You Think" Questions

1. Try to envision the United States exactly as it is minus **property rights** for individuals and describe some ways in which our economic system would be different.

2. There literally are thousands of **markets** for consumers looking to purchase lunch in a restaurant. Think about the concept of **competition** in the immediate geographic area where you live and make two lists: (A) factors that enhance competition, and (B) factors that detract from competition.

3. The laws of **supply** and **demand** work well in an economic system when, in the words of the economists, "**others things are equal**." The world of reality, however, offers many exceptions because of **non-price determinants of demand**. Briefly describe 5 situations where these laws do not function effectively.

4. List examples from everyday life where the **substitution effect** negates the **income effect** in the areas of food, entertainment, and transportation.

Appendix Issue 7-A
The Life Cycle and Permanent Income Hypotheses*

Economists offer two related explanations for human consumptions behavior. The life cycle hypothesis (LCH) and the permanent income hypothesis (PIH) are the two most useful models to understand the savings and spending behaviors of consumers. Even though the two models differ in definitions and in depicting consumer savings behavior, they have essentially similar promises and conclusions. Both models, under the utility framework, view consumers as being rational and informed. Thus, consumers will wisely arrange their whole resources over the life cycle and keep a certain level of consumption stream. The essence is that humans consume based upon their idea of what their long-run or permanent income is expected to be. To maintain a steady rate of consumption, consumers save little when current income is low; savings is higher when current income is higher.

Life Cycle Hypothesis

The **life cycle hypothesis** was proposed by Franco Modigliani and his colleagues during the 1950s. According to this model, as a consumer, you will arrange your life resources in such a way that you would like to enjoy the same level of consumption before and after your retirement. In order to do this, you have to save some money for your retirement when you are working, instead of spending all you earn. When you reach your retirement age, you begin to **dissave** (spending more than earning). If you know how long your life expectancy is going to be, you could figure out how much you should save to keep your level of living unchanged after you stop earning. Since your savings will increase when you start working, and decrease when you stop working, the amount of your savings can be depicted as a hump-shaped line along with your age.

Using a simple formula, you can figure out how much you should save when you know how many years you are going to work and how long you are going to live after retirement. If R = retirement years, W = working years, C = consumption level, Y = annual income, and S = Y - C = annual savings, we have: RC = WS = W(Y-C). It means that the total savings from working should equal the total expenses needed for retirement.

For example, if you have a job with an annual salary of $50,000, and you know you will work for 30 years and live a retired life for 20 years, you can determine that your consumption level must be $30,000. That means if you still want to lead a life at the same level of living after retirement, you have to save $20,000 annually when working. In this example, there are several assumptions: the interest rate is zero; your annual income will remain the same; there is no change in your family compositions, so that the consumption level is unchanged all your life; and you are not going to give money to your children or other people when you die. If necessary, you may relax some of these assumptions and re-estimate your consumption and savings levels.

Permanent Income Hypothesis

In a seminal book published in 1957, Milton Friedman proposed the **permanent income hypothesis**. This model has the similar conclusions as that of the life cycle hypothesis, but uses some different terms. PIH suggests that consumer income can be categorized as permanent income, current income, and transitory income. Approximately, your annual income is **current income**, then the average (there are several ways of figuring it out) of your annual incomes over your earning years is your **permanent income**. The difference between the current income and the permanent income is **transitory income**.

PIH posits that consumers always save and consume a fixed fraction of their permanent income, and save total transitory income. Thus, total savings consists of the sum of a fixed fraction of permanent income and all transitory income. It implies that consumers will leave a large amount of money to their children or other people when they die, which is the major difference between PIH and LCH.

For instance, if you have a job with an annual salary of $50,000 over your earning years, your permanent income will be the same as your current income, $50,000, and your transitory income will be zero. If your saving rate is 20%, you will spend $40,000 and save $10,000 every year. In another case, if you earn $40,000 in the first year, $50,000 in the second year, and $60,000 in the third year, your permanent income is $50,000, and your transitory incomes will be $10,000, 0, and $10,000, respectively. You will still spend $40,000 each year and save the remaining. For example, in the first year, you will save nothing. In the third year, you will save 20% permanent income, and all transitory income. Then, the total savings are $2,000. Here we do not consider retirement years and income from household assets. If these two variables are accounted, the permanent income will be adjusted, but the principle will be the same.

Shortcomings of Models

LCH and PIH are superior to the Keynesian absolute income hypothesis because they can explain why the American long-term saving rate remains almost the same while income has increased sharply and some other macro economic phenomena. However, many empirical studies show that these models cannot satisfactorily explain consumer saving behavior, especially when microeconomic data are used. The fundamental shortcoming of

these two models is that they are based on the assumption that consumers are rational and fully informed. Neither is true in the real world.

Many revisions have been proposed, and among them is a **behavioral version of life-cycle hypothesis (BLH)**. BLH, proposed by Hersh Shefrin and Richard Thaler, acknowledges the limitations of consumers. Basically, the hypothesis holds three assumptions. First, consumers lack self-control, and they look for external instruments to help them to save enough money for retirement needs. Second, consumers have mental accounts in their minds, and they treat these mental accounts differently in terms of saving and consumption. Specifically, these accounts are current income account, asset account, and future income account. Consumers tend to spend all their current income account, but spend nearly nothing from their future income account. The tendency of spending their asset account is somewhere in between the previous two. Third, consumers frame their incomes according to these income sources, which means they have different consumption and saving patterns when incomes come from dissimilar sources.

They are more likely to save income from uncertain sources, such as bonuses, premiums, gifts, or other windfalls, and more likely to spend income from regular sources, such as salaries. BLH seems to take into account some key limitations of human beings, and it addresses behavioral characteristics of consumer savings. Proponents of BLH claim that their hypothesis is a more general one and LCH is a special case of BLH. Since this model is somewhat new, the testing of its validity is just in its beginning stage.

*Jing-jian Xiao, Assistant Professor, University of Rhode Island

Chapter 8

Consumers in the Global Marketplace

OBJECTIVES

After reading this chapter, you should be able to:

1. Summarize five fundamental economic problems facing the world.

2. Explain the key economic concepts important to understanding global trade.

3. Recognize economic problems and challenges facing the United States as it tries to compete in a global economy.

4. Consider whether free trade or managed trade should govern international trade.

5. Realize that there is a movement toward freer trade using regional trade agreements.

6. Understand some aspects of the dark side of marketing to developing countries.

7. Appreciate the breadth of the international consumer movement and the number of vital issues affecting consumers around the world.

Global integration has occurred on a massive scale in recent decades. It has been fostered by cheap and better communications and the development of worldwide markets for trade and finance. Because of the increasing interdependence among national economies, the world is a single economic marketplace. How each country's government deals with the economic issues and how world organizations choose to organize trade and deal with environmental concerns greatly affects the consumer interest. Watching these events with a keen interest, and participating in many of them, is the international consumer movement.

This chapter is for people who wish to better understand the global marketplace and how to pursue the consumer interest when dealing with consumer economic issues. It begins by examining some of the world's fundamental economic problems, such as pollution and overpopulation, problems that are fundamental to every society. It next focuses on the economic problems and challenges facing the United States, such as low savings and big deficits, as it tries to compete in a global economy. Following is an examination from a global perspective of the issues of free trade and industrial policy. This is set in a context of regional trade agreements, such as the North American Free Trade Agreement. The chapter continues with a look at the dark side of marketing to developing countries. The chapter closes with the role and impact of the international consumer movement.

World Economic Problems

The central economic problem facing all societies is the **scarcity** of limited resources to satisfy the unlimited needs and wants of humans. There never seems to be enough to go around for everyone. In a given year, the **resources** available to produce goods (primarily labor, capital and technology) cannot be increased by any great amount and the technology available for production is subject to a limited amount of improvement.

Populations around the world have looked increasingly to government to solve their problems. Thus, it is the task of politicians to deal with scarce resources in an attempt to resolve the **fundamental world economic problems** facing their countries. These fundamental economic problems include providing for the people adequate food, clothing, shelter, medical care, and education. Unfortunately, people often expect more of their governments than the governments are able to deliver. And politicians usually promise more than what is possible.

Economic progress is the solution to resolving such problems. Progress is steady improvement and movement toward a goal as a society or civilization. Education is at the heart of such progress. Each country moves forward at its own rate of growth, and some countries have benefitted more from economic progress than others. The decisions about how to create material well-being, to whom to distribute the benefits and costs, and how to weigh economic growth against other societal values are made in each country by government, businesses and consumers.

Countries moving toward more advanced stages of economic development enjoy many benefits of economic progress. Examples are high levels of living, shorter work weeks, less physically strenuous labor, longer life spans, more productive lives, excellent recreational facilities and choices, access to higher education, new technology, modern medicine, conveniences, high-quality products and more of them, and automation. The industrialized non-communist countries of the world, so-called **first world countries**, such as the United States, United Kingdom, France, and Italy, have benefitted the most from economic progress. First world countries are often called **developed countries**.

Second world countries are the communist and formerly-communist nations of the world which have limited trade and interdependence with other countries. Compared to the first world countries, these countries fare less well in economic development and quality of life. **Third world countries** are underdeveloped or developing countries with little economic wealth and often an emphasis on agriculture and/or mining. Third world countries are also called **developing countries** or **less developed countries (LDCs)**, and they are disadvantaged in such areas as health care, literacy, employment skills, and life expectancy.

Of the world's 5.7 billion people, 4.5 billion live in third world countries, 0.4 billion live in Eastern Europe and the former Soviet Union, and 0.8 billion live in industrialized nations. Five fundamental problems typically exist in second and third world countries: (1) damaging pollution, (2) population growth that strains resources, (3) persistent poverty, (4) excessive military spending, (5) crime, corruption and anarchy, and (6) growing external debt.

Economic Problem: Damaging Pollution

Governments around the world have difficulty raising taxes to pay for cleanup expenses for damage to air, water, and land that often occurs with industrial progress and population growth. People also pay for pollution in terms of forfeited health and well-being. Conserving and replacing remaining natural resources is another costly priority of every nation in the world. In the United States, for example, taxes are collected and paid out of the government's Super Fund to pay for some pollution cleanup efforts.

Economic Problem: Excessive Population Growth

The world faces a difficult challenge in trying to provide food, clothing, and medical care for its people. Since 1974, the world's population has increased 1.5 billion, or 40 percent. More than one-half of the world's population is younger than age 20 years; 45 percent of Africans are under age 15. (In the United States, approximately 28 percent of the population is under age 20.) These young people will be entering their reproductive years in this generation. The world's growing population and accompanying overcrowding causes severe environmental degradation (deforestation and soil erosion), puts extreme pressure on land and water resources (water depletion), and produces people with little expectation of good health, education, or employment.

Population growth in developing countries is dramatically higher than in the industrialized world. The average fertility rate for the world is 3.35 percent each year while the rate for both developed countries and the former Soviet Union countries is 1.91 percent; it is 1.85 in the United States. (The population of the United States at the beginning of this year was 265 million.) The fertility rate in developing countries is 3.78 percent annually—it is 4.58 in Mongolia, 4.62 in Bolivia, 6.10 in Sub-Saharan Africa, 6.71 in Saudi Arabia, 7.16 in Iraq, and 8.50 in Rwanda. This in spite of the fact that almost half of all third-world women use some form of contraception. World population is growing at a rate of 90 million a year, 7.5 million a month, 1.7 million a week, 245,000 a day, 10,000 an hour, or 170 a minute—97 percent are born in developing countries.

A variety of efforts are undertaken by most societies to control population growth in an effort to preserve the quality of life for future generations. One talked-about worldwide economic goal is **zero population growth**. This suggests that for every child born and for every immigrant who enters a country, an equal number dies or leaves the country. A worldwide fertility rate of about 2.11 would accomplish that goal. (The .11 allows for the deaths of children.) Ready access to family-planning services and increased educational opportunities combined with strong political leadership helps lower birth rates and reduce the strain on economic resources.[1]

At current rates, the world's population of 5.7 billion will climb to 8.5 by 2025. The World Bank predicts that 2 billion of the additional 3 billion people will live in countries where the average person earns less than $2 a day. Findings presented at the United Nations' International Conference on Population and Development, held in Cairo, Egypt, revealed that by the year 2050 world population will reach 9.5 billion, placing an enormous strain on political leaders, economic resources and the environment. The result is increased "planetary overcrowding."

Economic Problem: Persistent Poverty

Poverty is the state of being poor where one lacks the means of providing material needs or comforts. According to the World Bank, 1.3 billion people live on less than $1 a day. Two-thirds of the world's population goes to sleep hungry at night.

Millions of people in the world die of malnutrition and hunger-related diseases every year; 40,000 die every day. Poverty is also a cost of economic development because often it is caused by the inequitable distribution of the benefits of change. Governments around the globe must decide how their societies will attempt to lessen the discomfort of poverty by redistributing income. In the United States, government provides an array of transfer payments to those in poverty, such as Social Security, unemployment compensation, Aid to Families with Dependent Children (AFDC), and Medicaid.

Economic Problem: Excessive Military Spending

Military spending by third world countries amounts to over $110 billion annually. A recent report by the United Nations Development Program observed that many of the world's poorest countries spend more on military than on other items. For example, Angola, Chad, Pakistan, Peru, Syria, Uganda, and Zaire spend half as much on education *and* health as on military. If such countries cut back on military spending by perhaps half, that amount would be available for **economic development** (increasing the production and management of material wealth of a country or state through investments in such things as education, infrastructure, and agriculture).

---

[1]China has a 1.2 billion population, and its official policy of "one couple, one child" includes heavy-handed measures ranging from forced abortions to expensive fines.

Economic Problem: Crime, Corruption and Anarchy

The lawlessness and tyranny currently seen in many of the poorer regions of the world are illustrative of what our planet is likely to be more like in the twenty-first century.[2] Slums and shantytowns are proliferating into sprawling villages with surging numbers of young people who have no job opportunities and little hope for a better life. Many turn to crime. Unsafe streets—particularly at night—are teeming with young people committing unprovoked crimes in cities around the world. This occurs in countries like Liberia, Rwanda, and Somalia as well as Pakistan, Brazil, and the former Yugoslavia. Continuing refugee migrations to urban areas contributes to a growing crisis of resource scarcity. Distinctions between crime and war are becoming blurred. For many, says Kaplan, war is a "step up not down."

Extortion by law-enforcement and immigration officials also prevails in most of those capital cities. Indications are that such corruption is increasing. Places with a declining resource base—like Nigeria, Brazil, and Indonesia—are becoming ungovernable as nation states. Language, ethnicity, history, and religion are more likely to define civilizations in the future, rather than today's political borders.

Economic Problem: Growing External Debt

The industrialized countries have made enormous loans to the developing countries in the past, expecting that the principal would be repaid along with regular interest charges. Many loans were made to oil-exporting nations which had been earning great profits because of oil-price increases. The beginnings of the international debt crisis occurred when Mexico stated in 1982 that it was no longer able to repay its debt obligations to foreign creditors. In the years since, about two dozen countries made similar pronouncements. Their **debt service**, amounts required to repay principal and interest, on over $1.5 trillion owed had simply become too overwhelming. Countries like Argentina, Brazil, Chile, Mexico, Nigeria, and the Philippines accumulated debt equal to 25 to 90 percent of their gross domestic products. Their debt service had grown to 20 to 45 percent of the value of exports from these countries.[3] Solutions are still being sought to avoid financial ruin for both creditors and debtors.

International debt problems for individual countries occur for several reasons:

1. large budget deficits fueled by too much government spending;
2. too few taxes on citizens;
3. too much money used for consumer goods rather than investment;
4. closed economies and heavily subsided industries that protect local businesses from international competition;

[2]Robert D. Kaplan (1994), The Coming Anarchy, *The Atlantic Monthly*, pp. 44-76.

[3]Deficit spending by the U.S. federal government throughout the 1980s in combination with a seemingly insatiable consumer appetite for imported goods, reversed the historical position of the United States from being a creditor nation to its current status of being the largest debtor nation in the world, owing over $560 billion to other nations. That debt amounts to about 9 percent of the U.S. gross domestic product. The size of one's economy is a large factor in a country's ability to handle its debt. Still, the U.S. requires a continuous inflow of foreign lending and investment to offset its passion for imports.

5. high inflation exacerbated by printing more and more paper currency;[4]
6. loans made with **variable interest rates**, which rise and fall with current interest rates and inflation;
7. sluggish worldwide economic growth;
8. growing difficulties in earning **hard currencies** to use for repayments (legal tenders that are willingly accepted in international trade, such as dollars, pounds, yen and deutsche marks); and
9. political leadership unwilling to recognize and act upon solutions in a timely manner.

The 1980s and 1990s saw a lot of **debt relief** (or **debt restructuring**). Here governments obtain agreements from lenders to develop new repayment terms that typically extend the term of the loan and permits a grace period when repayments for interest and/or principal are not required. The decade ahead will continue to see rising international debts. Numerous developing countries are strapped with huge debts and they are undertaking government and business reforms both to strengthen their economies and meet their financial obligations. The most common reform in many developing countries is to shift their economic systems away from socialism and toward market-oriented capitalism. This often requires **privatization**, which is the selling of government-owned businesses to private citizens.

Capital Flight Damages the Economies of Less Developed Countries

Affluent business people in developing countries often have access to illicit systems to exchange local-country money for hard currencies. **Capital flight** occurs when wealthy citizens of one country smuggle their cash out to another country that is more likely to be a safe haven for the funds. Safe from runaway inflation and a poor net return, from steep taxes on business profits and from government overthrows where capital can be expropriated. The amounts on deposit in the United States, Switzerland and France are staggering. Mexico, for example, owes over $100 billion yet its citizens have nearly that amount on deposit in foreign banks. Capital flight seriously damages the economies of those countries because, once the funds are shipped abroad, that capital is not available for local economic development.

What Are the Key Economic Concepts Important to Understanding Global Trade?

The purpose of trade is to import; exports are the price a country pays for the imports. There are four economic concepts that are essential to understanding global trade.

---

[4]**Hyperinflation** (an extremely high rate of inflation) in an economy undermines both business and political confidence. Recent annual inflation rates for selected countries include Brazil (1000%+), Ukraine (1,000%+), Russia (300%+), Argentina (300%+), Uganda (300%+), Israel (40%+) and Mexico (25%+).

CONSUMER UPDATE: Developing Countries, Educated People, and Healthy People Make Good Trading Partners and Customers

For over 50 years, most of the industrialized countries have helped developing countries try to improve lives of the people. "Over the past 25 years, infant mortality rates in the developing countries have been cut in half, life expectancy has grown by more than a decade, nutritional levels are up substantially, 1 billion people have clean water who didn't have it before and average real incomes have doubled."[1] Developing countries make good trading partners too, buying approximately $200 billion in U.S. goods. This trade supports 3 million American jobs.

[1] Jessica Mathews, Overdrawn at the Bank, *The Washington Post*, April 29, 1994, A-27.

Pareto Efficiency: Economic Trade Is a "Win-Win" Situation

Economic trade across international boundaries is a necessity because no one country has everything it needs or wants. One country wants something that can be produced with relative ease in another country. Unfortunately, many people falsely assume that international trade is a **zero-sum game** where the wealth of all traders is simply redistributed because the gains of each winner is the other's loss.

In reality, trade is a win-win situation and well-informed people around the world support expanding international trade. If both parties in an economic trade did not intend on gaining, they would not engage in a voluntary exchange. Instead, international trade is based upon the concept of **Pareto efficiency** (or **Pareto optimality**) where both sides to a condition cannot be made better off without reducing the advantage of the other, thus each party in the context must be satisfied. Countries experience mutual benefits and gains from trade until one country reaches the point where it says, "We will give up XYZ just to make you feel better."

Economies of Scale

At the heart of economic trade is the economic concept of **economies of scale**: the cost per unit decreases as the quantity of production increases and all resources are variable. Thus, lower average costs of production occur as the volume of production increases. It is uneconomical to produce 100 aircraft, 1000 television sets or 5000 automobiles, but quite economical to produce many thousands or hundreds of thousands. The task for each country is to find customers at home and elsewhere for all those products.

Absolute Advantage

Countries specialize in making certain goods because of varying combinations of resources and skills. Hence the high-tech countries of United States and Japan are well equipped to produce automobiles and China and Mexico are efficient producers of shoes. An **absolute advantage** occurs when a country has a monopolistic position or if it produces an item at the lowest cost. It is determined by comparing the true costs of producing particular goods in different countries, including the number of hours of labor required and the wages paid for that labor.

Comparative Advantage

Note that while one country, such as the United States, is extremely efficient in terms of hours of labor, absolute advantage is not the critical factor in deciding whether or not to trade. Some countries have an absolute advantage for several products while another country may have no absolute advantages, yet trading opportunities exist because each should seek its comparative advantage. A country has a **comparative advantage** in a good or service if it can supply such with a smaller sacrifice of alternative goods and services than can the rest of the trading world. In international trade it pays a country to trade when it specializes in producing a specific product more efficiently than any others. Moreover, countries should trade what they are good at producing.

To illustrate this point consider this example. A successful president of an accounting firm may possess excellent typing skills, perhaps even better than his or her secretary. Since the secretary may be incapable of managing a large firm, he or she would run the business poorly. Thus, the president has an absolute advantage in both typing and managing. However, the president's time—the comparative advantage—is best spent managing the accounting firm. The secretary has a comparative advantage in typing, since he or she would be ineffective running the business. Therefore, the whole business runs quite efficiently because each works in accordance with his or her comparative advantage.

International trade among countries is based on the principle of comparative advantage. Each country has a comparative advantage in producing some products and they should specialize accordingly. The U.S. Department of Commerce estimates that every $1 billion in exports creates more than 19,000 jobs in the United States.

Challenges Facing the United States in World Trade

Being the largest economy in the world, the United States remains a dominant player in global economics. World trade patterns show that more than half of all international trade, in excess of $1 trillion annually, occurs between **industrialized countries** (Australia, Canada, Japan, New Zealand, United States and all the Western European countries). The leading products being traded around the globe are petroleum,[5] motor vehicles and machinery. The U.S. is a major trading partner for a number of countries. Canada is the U.S.'s best trading partner because it imports so much; the U.S.'s worst trade deficits are with Japan and China. The United States is heavily involved in exports: twenty percent of manufactured goods and thirty percent of farm produce are exported. The U.S. economy "still consumes 90 percent of what it produces and produces 90 percent of what it consumes."[6]

While the U.S. remains the world's largest exporter (12.3 percent; Germany at 11.8 percent, and Japan at 9.3 percent), the five-year-long economic slumps in Europe and Japan have made it difficult for the U.S. to sell goods abroad. Europe's "structural slump" has been brought on by high payroll taxes and tight employment regulations that raise labor costs. Such policies deter the start of new businesses and threatens marginal businesses. The U.S. economy has been growing since the end of 1990.

---

[5]The U.S. currently imports 50 percent of its oil consumption.
[6]Pearlstein, S. (1994, April 3). Trading shots with a wunderkind. *The Washington Post*, p. H-1.

AN ECONOMIC FOCUS: The Consumer Interest in International Trade

It has become a truism that consumers now operate in a global marketplace. From the viewpoint of a citizen of the United States, we not only import a tremendous quantity of goods from countries like Japan, Germany, and China; but "All-American" companies like Gillette, Colgate, IBM, Coca-Cola, Digital Equipment, Dow Chemical, Xerox, and Caterpillar receive more than half of their sales revenue from overseas markets. Because of the growing importance of imports and exports in global economics, it is important for consumers and their representatives to understand where the interests of consumers lie in discussions of free trade and trade restrictions.

The consumer movement, especially in the United States but also elsewhere, has historically attempted to steer clear of involvement in the debate over free trade and protectionism. Because organized labor typically opposes free trade (to save American jobs), consumerists have been caught between two conflicting forces: the consumer interest in lower prices brought about through free trade, and the consumer interest in having strong political allies, in this case organized labor. The consumer movement's low profile on the free trade debate was sustainable when trade issues themselves were thought of as relatively unimportant, technical issues. Today, however, the prominence of trade issues has forced the consumer movement to define the consumer interest vis-a-vis trade issues and reconcile that interest with those of other groups in society, including but not confined to organized labor. In particular, the consumer movement has found itself drawn into discussions about the North American Free Trade Agreement (NAFTA) and the General Agreement on Tariffs and Trade (GATT).

The cornerstone of the argument in favor of free trade is the theory of comparative advantage. The theory, first put into formal terms by economist David Ricardo in 1817, is often misunderstood as merely an argument about the benefits of specialization. It takes no great genius to argue that if farmers in the United States are especially productive when growing potatoes and Mexican farmers are especially productive when growing tomatoes. But what if it were true (which it isn't) that U.S. workers are more productive with respect to every good and service than Mexican workers? Would it make sense for the United States to trade with Mexico at all? The theory of comparative advantage explains why it would.

To simplify matters, imagine a world composed of only the United States and Mexico and producing only two goods--beer and tortilla chips. Imagine further that it takes a U.S. worker one minute to produce a six-pack of beer and two minutes to produce a bag of tortilla chips, while it takes a Mexican worker three minutes to produce a six-pack of beer and four minutes to produce a bag of tortilla chips. Note that U.S. workers are more productive than Mexican workers on both counts.

The key to understanding the theory of comparative advantage is to realize that a country trades *with itself* every time it decides to produce one good rather than another. In our example, every time the United States devotes a minute of worker time to producing tortilla chips, it is giving up two bottles of beer. Thus, the United States should be willing to

trade beer for tortilla chips if it can give up less than two minutes of worker time for each bottle it exports. Conversely, Mexico gives up 1.33 bottles of beer every time it produces a bag of chips; Mexico will gladly trade chips for beer if it can get more than 1.33 bottles for a bag of chips.

Suppose someone proposes an exchange rate of 1.5 bottles of beer for one bag of chips. Will the United States want to deal? Yes, because it costs the U.S. twice as much in worker time (i.e., two bottles of foregone beer production) to produce chips as to produce beer. Will Mexico want to trade under these terms? Yes again because one bag of chips will only yield 1.33 bottles in Mexico but 1.5 bottles in international trade.

Note that the theory of comparative advantage implies an improvement in the standard of living for all parties involved. Referring back to our example, U.S. workers have to work, in the absence of trade, for three minutes to buy a bottle of beer and a bag of chips. With trade, they need only work 2.5 minutes. Similarly, the effort necessary for Mexican workers to afford the same purchase declines from 7 minutes to 6.6 minutes. These differences may seem small, but aggregate them over more workers and more time and you realize the potential benefits of free trade. All of a sudden, the "dismal science" of economics yields a win-win situation.

Despite the impressive lineage and logic of the theory of comparative advantage, there are many parties who view it as too narrow or insensitive to the power differences that exist among trading parties. Consumerists like Ralph Nader have objected to free trade agreements on the grounds that strict consumer protection standards can be challenged as "barriers to trade." If the United States, for example, wants strict limits on pesticide residues on food, this may be challenged by foreign governments as a form of protectionism if American farmers use fewer pesticides than foreign producers. To choose a recent actual example, an American standard requiring tuna to be harvested with minimal threat to dolphins (who become ensnared in tuna nets) was attacked by Mexico and declared an unfair trade barrier under rules of GATT. Positions can be reversed, too, as when Thailand's ban on cigarette advertising was attacked by American cigarette manufacturers on the basis that the ban restricted their ability to compete and therefore constituted a barrier to trade.

After years of quiescence, consumer activists have been rapidly drawn into the debate over free trade and protectionism. Until recently, most consumerists willing to take a public position on international trade issues have downplayed the benefits of free trade and emphasized its potential threats to consumer, environmental, and worker protection standards. But fractures within the consumer movement are beginning to appear. In 1994, Consumers Union, perhaps the most powerful organization in the U.S. consumer movement, endorsed GATT. Ralph Nader responded by accusing Consumers Union of "ignorance, naivete, and co-optation." Clearly, careful and sustained analysis will be required to understand fully the consumer interest in international trade.

*Robert N. Mayer, University of Utah

The economic leadership challenge of the United States is compounded by the enormous amount of excess capacity around the globe to produce most products. The excess has been estimated at 30 percent, and that factor remains at the core of persistently high unemployment figures for a number of countries, including the other industrialized countries.

The Growing U.S. National Debt

The United States today is a far different country, economically, than it was only 15 years ago. The excessive government spending of the 1980s, mostly on consumption instead of investment, has left the nation seriously damaged. The United States has a large **national debt**. It is over $5 trillion, up from $1 trillion when President Jimmy Carter left office. About $800 billion of that amount is owed to foreign countries. The national debt grows because of our refusal to live within our national means.

The federal government's huge **budget deficits** (annual expenditures in excess of revenue) suck up a large portion of the country's capital leaving little to fund normal business growth.[7] Budgets bloated by excessive debt result in a choiceless society, where politicians no longer have the capacity to make the hard decisions and tradeoffs on questions of public policy, resulting in a social climate that encourages avoidance of realities and responsibilities. Since the Clinton Administration was elected in 1992, the amount of the federal budget deficit has been substantially reduced every year. While the deficits have been declining—and most people applaud efforts to reduce the deficit—the total debt is still growing. It will be $6 trillion by the year 2000.

Why the National Debt Will Get Much Larger, No Matter What the Politicians Say

No matter what the politicians say, it is going to get much worse. There are two reasons. First, the full financial obligations of the federal government are at least three times as large as the politicians have been telling us. Other liabilities of the government exist because certain financial outlays and commitments are excluded from both the federal budget and the deficit. They include (1) many **off-budget agencies**, such as the Pension Benefit Guarantee Corporation and the Federal Financing Bank; (2) **government-sponsored enterprises** that perform credit functions and are now privately owned, such as the Farm Credit Administration; and (3) **guaranteed mortgages and loans** where the government insures or guarantees payment of the principal and interest. (The guarantees for the savings and loan/banking crisis of the 1980s will cost taxpayers $500 billion when it is eventually paid for in 30 years.)

Second, the balanced budget debate is predicated on the false assumption that beginning in some future year, such as 2002, tax revenue will be equivalent to planned expenditures. The reality is that the so-called budgeted "cost savings" evaporate in 2002 while the expenses are planned to sharply increase. Third, the **surplus** money in certain trust funds, principally Social Security, goes for normal government expenses leaving promissory notes in the trust fund. Moreover, the politicians have "cooked the books" by classifying so many expenditures and liabilities as **"off budget"** and denying the reality

---

[7]The federal government's budget would be *in balance* if it did not have to pay interest on the national debt.

of pending increases in planned expenditures. These actions give taxpayers false information.

Satirsit P. J. O'Rourke says that, "The problem isn't a Congress that won't cut spending or a president who won't raise taxes. The problem is an American public with a bottomless sense of entitlement to federal money."[8]

Future Generations Will Pay More Taxes

Unless there are net benefits from today's expenditures that are shifted to the future (in the form of investments), tomorrow's generations will have to cough up more tax dollars to pay the interest charges on the increased debt. In essence, future generations will experience a lower level of living because they will be paying higher taxes for today's government spending. Consumers should save more now in anticipation of higher taxes in the future. A large national debt also redistributes income away from low-income people because tax money must be used to pay bondholders.

High Skills *or* Low Wages: America's Choice

A recent report sponsored by the National Center on Education and the Economy observes that America became a great industrial power because of mass education and mass production. Recent years have seen numbers of developing countries realizing the same. Since wages in developing countries are lower than the U.S. (Taiwan's manufacturing wage is 1/5 that of the United States' and Mexico's is 1/9), we can no longer compete with high-wage manufacturing jobs and make the same products.

The only way for Americans to keep high wages is to create high skills. Yet a report by the Labor Department's Commission on Achieving Necessary Skills estimates that 60 percent of all 21- to 25-year-olds lack the reading and writing skills needed in today's workplace; only 10 percent have appropriate math skills. These reports argue that we must forget mass education and mass production and instead seek quality education and quality production. That probably means apprenticeship programs, national testing standards for public schools and more employer training. The jobs in the economy of today and tomorrow require post-high school education for the entire workforce. President Bill Clinton supports these ideas.

Getting Americans to Invest More

Mortimer B. Zuckerman, publisher of *U.S. News and World Report*, observes that experts are baffled about how to reconcile the interests of individual countries with the global economy, how to encourage economic growth with little inflation, and how to help former bureaucratically controlled command economic systems to capitalistic market-driven economies without causing hyperinflation and political turmoil. A challenge for the U.S. is to stimulate the global economy, but it is complicated by the large trade surpluses of Pacific Rim countries, especially Japan, that siphon off employment elsewhere, including the United States. A nation's **balance of trade** is the total value of its imports less its exports. Because of excessive imports over the past decade, the U.S. has an

---

[8]O'Rourke, P. J. (1991), *Parliment of Whores*, Vintage Books.

enormous and growing **trade deficit**. This is the total amount a country owes to other countries because it imports more than it exports. In 1980, the U.S. was the world's largest creditor with other countries owing us $270 billion. Today, the U.S. is the world's largest debtor as we owe over $800 billion.

A long-term solution to these challenges is to take actions to turn this country's priorities around to better focus on increasing productive investments, not consumption. **Investment** is spending intended to promote future production by adding to the stock of capital goods, such as equipment, machinery and technology. Examples of **social investments** include investments in work skills and education, infrastructure, and research and development. Investment, not consumption, is the key economic catalyst for economic growth.

The United States' 50-year emphasis on **consumer consumption** (spend, lend, borrow, and speculate) may be difficult to turn around toward a new focus on investment.[9] Incentives to save and invest are likely to be required. For example, the current system of penalizing savings and investments with income taxes on interest, dividends and corporate income may have to be changed. To succeed in a competitive global economy, U.S. public policy must be shifted toward investing more into its people because they are undereducated and underachieving.

DID YOU KNOW? The United States Saves *Less* Than It Invests

Americans consistently save less than they invest. When a nation invests more than its savings can pay for, the source of funds must be from another country that saves more than it invests domestically. When the U.S. borrows money from Japan and other lending countries to meet its internal investment needs, "the surplus must be balanced by a matching trade deficit."[1] Conversely, Japan must have a trade surplus to match its capital lending. How to fix the problem in the U.S.? Slim down America's enormous federal budget deficit (to reduce the reliance on private savings) and increase the savings of U.S. consumers (which means less immediate consumption and the money can be used for investment).

[1]John M. Berry, U.S. Savings Rate Is a Key Piece in Trade Deficit Puzzle," *The Washington Post*, February 17, 1994. B-1.

Which Way Should a Nation Go: Free Trade or Industrial Policy?

Economist Adam Smith wrote in 1776 that, "If a foreign country can supply us with a commodity cheaper than we ourselves can make it, better buy it from them with some part of the produce of our own industry, employed in a way in which we have some advantage." More recently another commentator observed that, "Trade policy should be above all about protecting consumer interests, preserving their access to the world's supply of goods and services at the lowest possible prices."[10]

---

[9]Private consumption in the U.S. accounts for 87 percent of GDP compared with 72 percent for Germany and 66 percent for Japan.

[10]Corcoran, T. (1994, August 3). Canada clear winner in wheat deal. *The Globe and Mail*, p. B2.

The interest of consumers around the world is centered in low prices, good quality and lots of choices, and these factors are enhanced through the reduction of trade restraints. Import barriers that protect business or labor interests *within a particular country* punish consumers with higher prices *within* that country.

Free trade is considered free or open when goods and services can move into markets without restrictions and prices are determined by supply and demand. When goods are traded between two countries without taxes, it is described as **duty free** trade. While the idea of freely traded goods across international borders is appealing, the political realities of each nation results in them placing restrictions on international trade. Many countries have explicit or implicit forms of industrial policy aimed at protecting certain businesses, farmers, and labor groups. As a result, trade disputes occur between and among countries.

Benefits of Free Trade

It is well established that economic growth is essential for improving the well-being of people. Free trade means greater exports, faster economic growth, and better jobs for each trading partner.[11] Increased trade provides the economies of the global community with a healthier, well-nourished, well-educated and better-skilled labor force. Communities of such able people are the best foundation for future economic growth.

If free trade were allowed to operate among all nations, the principles of comparative advantage would cause economic resources within each country to be shifted to the production of goods for which comparative advantages existed. Benefits of free trade would include lower prices for consumers, greater choices of goods, increased world-wide employment, and efficient allocation of international resources.

Barriers to Free Trade

In spite of the benefits of free trade, each national government is generally much more interested in the well-being of its citizens than the peoples of the world. This is especially true in economic trade. Therefore, for a host of political (mostly profit-protecting) reasons, nations erect barriers to free trade. Some barriers are illegal in the U.S., such as bribery and corrupt government officials, but acceptable in many other countries, and these exist as barriers to success for the U.S. in trade abroad. Most **barriers to free trade** are legal restrictions on imported goods in the form of tariffs, quotas, embargoes, health and safety standards, foreign-exchange controls, and/or dumping.

A **tariff** (or **import duty**) is a tax on imported goods (even though no similar tax is applied to identical goods produced domestically), and it is designed to make imported goods more expensive to the domestic consumers. Average tariffs in the U.S. are 5 percent. Higher tariffs exist on imported orange juice (40%), brooms (42%) and flashlights (25%). Fewer products will be imported if they must be sold at a higher price, thus giving an advantage to domestic producers. A **quota** (or **import quota**) is a government limit on the quantity (often a proportional share or maximum amount) of a certain good that can be legally imported into a particular country during a given time period. An **embargo**

---

[11]Exporting firms in the U.S. pay 10 percent more in wages and benefits.

AN ECONOMIC FOCUS ON... How the Supply of and Demand for Labor Affects Wage Rates in Developing Countries*

Many American-owned firms have established labor-intensive manufacturing facilities in developing countries, such as Mexico. Ten years ago, over half of Mexico's 400 largest industries were foreign owned. Today, General Motors is one of Mexico's largest employers.

The low cost of labor is one of the major reasons for U.S. firms moving manufacturing facilities to developing countries. Such foreign ventures by U.S. firms emerged in the 1960s and continues today. U.S. tax and foreign policies encourage U.S. firms to invest in Mexico and other developing countries in order (1) to provide people in those countries with employment and (2) to give the American firms the advantages of lower wage rates. The U.S. firms offer developing countries key factors of production, such as capital, technology and managerial skills, that permit the utilization of an existing labor factor that is relatively abundant and is either underemployed and/or unemployed.

Basic labor economics explains how supply of and demand for labor affect wage rates in developing countries. The concept of supply explains the lack of suitable employees in the United States when examining the behavior of both workers and potential workers in the U.S. For purposes of illustration, assume that U.S. workers have decided to work in a specific occupation and that all jobs in that particular occupation are quite similar, thus comparable. In choosing an employer, these employees then only need to consider the wages that various employers are offering. As a result, relevant U.S. firms would offer competitive wages. No firm would offer a wage higher than competing firms because it would be paying more than necessary to attract a suitable number and quality of employees. If the U.S. firm pays less than competitive wages, as is the case for those U.S companies inclined to move to Mexico, potential employees will seek employment with the firm paying higher wages. This then leaves the lower-paying U.S. firm without a sufficient supply of labor. A firm may attract desired employees at a lower than average pay only if it offered noncomparable jobs, i.e., with more pleasant working conditions, longer paid vacations, etc. This is simply not the case for the firms that have found it advantageous to move their operations to Mexico.

The availability of potential employees in Mexico stems from the depressed economic conditions of the country. "Sopping up excess labor via economic expansion will, for the first few years, be akin to trying to wipe a flooded basement with a paper towel."[1] Because the existing labor force in Mexico is largely underemployed and/or unemployed, the number of entrants to the Mexican labor force has and is expected to continue to greatly exceed departures. Therefore, the number of potential employees is actually greater than the number of jobs available. Due to such an oversupply of labor, employers can offer a minimal wage and still attract the quality and number of employees desired. For example, in a recent year, the average hourly compensation for workers in the United States was over $14 while it was less than $2.50 in Mexico. Such lower wages easily offset the slightly lower productivity rates of the U.S. manufacturing firms located in Mexico. At such low labor costs, U.S. employers in Mexico are willing to employ more workers than they would in the United States, thus becoming almost as productive as similar firms in the United States. Such savings in wages also allows employers to pay to transport their products back to the U.S. and to other markets around the world while still offering them for sale at competitive prices.

Companies in the United States are increasingly establishing operations in Mexico and other developing countries to reduce costs and improve their competitive edge in pricing in the global market. The low cost of labor is incentive enough to encourage many such ventures.[2]

---

[1] Carlton, J. (1992, September 24). The Lure of Cheap Labor: U.S. Companies Pour into Mexico Drawn Primarily by One Factor: Low Wages. *The Wall Street Journal*, p. R16.

[2] Rather than moving abroad, some U.S. manufacturing facilities (particularly women's garment manufacturers) employ **sweatshop labor** within the borders of the United States, factories that pay less than the minimum wage, ignore federal wage and safety standards, and require 60-hour workweeks. See *U.S. News & World Report*, November 22, 1993, for more details, including "...as many as half of all women's garments are produced in whole or in part by..." U.S. factories.

*Tamra Minor, Assistant to the Vice President, The Ohio State University (or **trade embargo**) are efforts to bring a complete halt to trading with a particular product. While tariffs and quotas are designed to protect economic markets, embargoes are generally imposed for political reasons. **Health and safety** standards serve to guard the public health by requiring that certain products meet specific standards, and these are sometimes used to keep foreign competitors out of domestic markets.

Foreign-exchange controls are restrictions on amounts of foreign currencies that can be legally purchased or sold. When importers are restricted from obtaining foreign currency, they are limited from using that currency to purchase goods to import. A **currency devaluation** is a purposeful decrease in the value of a nation's currency relative to the values of currencies of other countries. This increases the costs of imported goods and decreases the cost of domestically produced goods for foreign purchasers. **Buy-domestic policies** are procurement procedures requiring that governments purchase only from local producers. It is the sometimes popular "Buy American" slogan made into law in the U.S. and abroad. Many countries have these policies covering their own locally produced goods; so do many U.S. states. **Subsidies** are government payments, in the form of cash, tax reductions, low-interest loans, low-cost insurance, government-industry partnership, and/or government-sponsored research, to encourage exports.

Those who favor restrictions on international trade to reduce foreign competition against domestic goods and services believe in **protectionism**.[12] Protectionists argue for trade restrictions to protect the health of consumers (from supposedly dangerous or unhealthy goods), to defend new or weak industries, to safeguard national security (perhaps by keeping certain technology out of the hands of potential enemies), to improve a nation's balance of payments, and to retaliate against another country's trade restrictions. Protectionism can reach the point of a **trade war** where a state of conflict is carried on between nations as each attempts to retaliate against the other's barriers to international trade.

The world learned during the 1930s that the Great Depression was partially due to the protectionist attitudes of the United States and its trading partners during those years. The Smoot-Hawley Tariff Act of 1930 placed U.S. import tariffs on thousands of products, averaging 60 percent, ostensibly to "raise the incomes of U.S. workers." The nations of the world retaliated with their own tariffs and within four years world trade dropped 70 percent. Incomes and prices dropped similarly. In 1934, the Reciprocal Trade Agreements Act became law commencing the decline of tariffs. Beginning in 1947, the General Agreement on Trade and Tariffs (GATT) began the effort towards free trade among nations. Today, tariffs on imports average about 5 percent.

The Institute for International Economics (IIE) reports that barriers to imports "cost American consumers $70 billion a year, or about $1,000 for the average family."[13] The IIE authors further calculate that of the $70 billion, $16 billion goes to the federal government in tariff revenue and $43 billion goes to producers and shareholders in 21 U.S. industries (who can boost their share of the American market and raise prices without serious competition). Four billion goes to 190,000 U.S. blue-collar workers, who get to keep their jobs because of protectionism. Perhaps shocking is the cost to consumers

---

[12]An example of a trade barrier is the 1920 Jones Act that requires trade between domestic ports within the United States must be on U.S. owned ships that were built in the U.S., fly the U.S. flag, and employ only U.S. workers. That boosts shipping costs, so consumers pay higher prices.

[13]Hufbauer, G. C. & Elliott, K. A. (1994, January), *Measuring the Costs of Protection in the United States* (Washington: Institute for International Economics), p. 3.

in higher prices—it amounts to $170,000 a year for each job saved, six times the annual pay of those workers.[14]

Dumping Is an Unfair Trade Practice

Dumping is the practice of selling identical goods in foreign countries for less than the price charged domestically, or for less than the price of production. Countries dump goods to damage foreign competition, to drive rival firms out of a foreign market, to secure a foothold in a particular foreign market, to preserve jobs at home, and sometimes to earn foreign currency, especially hard currency. One famous case was when Sony was selling its television sets in the United States for less than $200 while charging Japanese consumers over $300 for the same model. More recently, Japan was caught dumping computer chips into the U.S. market.

Cartels Are Created to Overcharge All Customers

A **cartel** is a group of firms that formally agree to coordinate their production and pricing decisions in a manner that maximizes joint profits. This is done by controlling and limiting production as well as fixing prices. Cartels are illegal in the United States because they in effect act as a monopoly.

Over twenty years ago, the **Organization of Petroleum Exporting Countries (OPEC)** cartel shocked the world with the first of two sharp increases in oil prices. The second shock saw OPEC raise prices eightfold. The once powerful 12-country cartel still exists but it is no longer able to keep all of its members in line. In recent years, every time OPEC sets quotas individual countries quietly violate the agreement by going ahead and producing and charging what they please. To increase their incomes, individual countries find they can increase their income through increased sales of oil, surreptitiously cheating, and simultaneously watch all their cartel friends voluntarily restrain supply.

As a result, world oil production is rising and prices remain competitive, in part because a number of oil-producing countries do not belong to OPEC. A cartel must firmly control supply to manipulate prices. International cartels still exist in coffee and diamonds.

Industrial Policy—A New Paradigm for the U.S.

Forty years ago the United States was unquestionably the world's economic leader. Times and markets changed and today the U.S. has tough competitors in Europe and Southeast Asia. America's trade policies are currently undergoing reexamination and change because the status quo is unsustainable. Part of the reasoning is that no major U.S. firm now makes compact disc players, VCRs, camcorders or radios. Americans know intuitively that the nation declined when the U.S. lost its consumer electronics industry.

---

[14]Rowen, H. (1994, January 13). The high price of protected jobs. *The Washington Post*, p. A-27.

While it was in the consumer interest to buy Japanese VCRs and automobiles (high quality, low prices), the broader national public interest was to "Buy American," or to help change U.S. priorities to build better quality products.

The U.S. has entered an era of having an explicit **industrial policy**. Here the government plays a growing role in coordinating a strategic plan of policies aimed at protecting and developing selected domestic industries. An industrial policy redirects the invisible hand of the free competitive market by having the visible hand of government give a push to particular economic activities. It does this by asking strategically sophisticated competitors to pursue government- and business-established national industrial goals. The claim is that government must help direct the nation's industrial policy because one cannot trust the future to the invisible hand of the competitive market.

A European example is the Airbus consortium, which with massive financial infusions from four European governments (Great Britain, France, Germany and Spain) over the past decade, has captured one-third of the world market for large commercial jets. Another example is Japan's Ministry of Industry and Trade (MITI) which has vigorously pursued an industrial policy for over 30 years. Japan's MITI in combination with its Ministry of Finance's policies to stimulate capital formulation and investment have made the country an economic powerhouse. Capital gains taxes range from zero to 5 percent, and most forms of consumer savings are not taxed at all. Japan's productivity growth over the past 30 years has been 5 percent every year. MITI is currently developing the New Information Processing Technologies project, a planned 10-year effort to develop innovations in advanced computers. Dozens of Japanese firms are expected to participate.

President Bill Clinton's approach to international economics is clearly one of active government involvement and pragmatism. One of Clinton's first presidential acts was to create a new National Economic Council in the White House to coordinate economic policy. His chief economist, Laura D'Andrea Tyson, pursues Clinton's policy about the importance of monitoring the economic health of our nation's critical industries and establishing affirmative action programs to protect and nurture them. Clinton wants to steer federal research funding toward those industries and use trade restrictions and sanctions to keep foreign competitors from unfairly competing against these industries.

To illustrate, President Clinton announced a several hundred million dollar plan for a government-industry research program to develop super-fuel-efficient automobiles (not gasoline powered) by the year 2003, and he excluded the Japanese companies that produce almost 30 percent of the vehicles sold in the United States. Clinton also met with leaders of the computer and telecommunications industries to announce the new policy of removing export controls on high-tech exports. Clinton promises to fight foreign subsidies with American subsidies.

This decade appears to mark the beginning of a major shift in long-term economic policy of the United States—from the free trade of market forces to a greater reliance on industrial policy. In contrast to previous administrations, the Clinton Administration appears willing to have some tough fights with Japan, China and other countries. It is one thing for a nation to have an industrial policy and another to have the judgment and commitment of resources to make it work.[15]

---

[15]One aspect of U.S. trade policy is called **Super 301**, a stepped-up version of section 301 of the Trade Reform Act re-activated by President Clinton. It provides that the U.S. develop and publish an annual list of countries that have unfair trade practices. Publication puts political pressure on the countries listed and on their political leaders to take some action.

One aspect of this new international economic trade policy, already implicitly practiced among a number of countries (and in some places explicitly), is called **managed trade** (or **results-based trade**). This is an open use of government policy to intervene in the market and arrange country-to-country deals arranging precise splits of import markets. The result will be tacit government agreements on acceptable levels of trade surpluses and deficits. For example, Japan would be permitted to sell X number of vehicles in the United States when the U.S. is permitted to sell Y pounds of rice in Japan. Clinton's "results oriented" confrontational rhetoric is aimed at getting trade agreements in specific industries. Barriers to the Japanese market add as much as 40 percent to the price of U.S. imports sold there and 30 percent to cars sold in France.

The U.S. now seems to be moving toward a more explicit industrial policy. The most successful U.S. industrial policies would include the Homestead Act, land grant colleges, the Civilian Conservation Corps, the Agricultural Extension Service, and the G.I. Bill.

A current example of U.S. industrial policy is Sematech, a microelectronics consortium of 11 U.S. semi-conductor firms. Half its funding comes from the Defense Department. U.S. taxpayer money also is going to back corporate efforts to build battery-powered automobiles and to develop high-speed computing and communications technology. The Pentagon is spending $500 million for production subsidies so American companies can attempt to capture 15 percent of the world market for flat-panel electronic displays; the Japanese now have 95 percent share. Dozens of federal and state programs are helping certain American manufacturers.

The worst industrial policy subsidizes failing industries and companies, seeking to preserve employment. The next worst is for government to spend too much money on ventures with little potential payoff, such as the $100 million robotic arm for the planned space station. One clear risk is from massive price increases from so-called protected industries. Another risk of managed trade occurs in the form of protests from other countries that want special bilateral agreements. Such accords, a form of quotas (with ceilings and minimums sure to follow), make international trade neither free nor well managed.

Being mindful of the risks, the United States seems to be moving forward on creating a more explicit industrial policy, and it is beginning to visualize international trade issues as an integral part of the nation's economic future. Because of inflated price, managed trade is against the consumer interest; however, such trade *may* be in the public interest of the United States as well as other countries.

Regional Trade Agreements and the World Trade Organization

All this talk about industrial policy flies in the face of what Americans have long maintained as our fundamental position: free trade. Ideally, with free trade each competitor should be innovative and responsive to market demands and improve quality to a point above that of the competition. This ideal is rewarded and reinforced with free trade as consumers and businesses can buy at low prices.

The threat of economic stagnation serves to motivate countries to negotiate trade agreements with other countries and a number of regional trade agreements have been developed. A **regional trade agreement** is an effort by an economic community of countries to greatly reduce tariffs to encourage economic trade among the member nations. An **economic community** is an organization of nations formed to promote free trade among themselves and to create common economic policies. Names of regional trade agreements in the news are the European Union (EU), Latin American Free Trade Association (LAFTA), Southern Africa Development Community, Association of Southeast Asian Nations (ASEAN), and the North American Free Trade Agreement (NAFTA). The nations of Latin America and South America along with the United States and Canada are expected to form the American Free Trade Agreement (AFTA).

A commonality among developing countries is an extremely low gross domestic product. As a result, second and third world countries generally visualize economic development as a way to improve the well-being of their peoples. Thus, they usually seek **equitable trade relations** with other countries so as to enable the poorer countries to develop, over time, the capacity to compete on a more equal basis in international markets. Key in such trade agreements is to not undermine the achievement of domestic self-reliance in the production of food.

North American Free Trade Agreement

The North American Free Trade Agreement went into effect in 1994. It establishes a framework for reducing trade barriers and increasing business investment throughout North America—the U.S., Canada and Mexico. Politics aside, NAFTA is working. One of the biggest benefits has been to commit Mexico, which had a closed economy only a few years earlier, to free trade and participation in the international community. Despite Mexico's recent economic currency crisis and devaluation, the NAFTA pact prohibited Mexico from imposing the same 35 percent tariffs on U.S. and Canadian goods that it has put on more than 500 products from other countries.

Mexico now purchases more U.S. products than any other nation except Canada and Japan. Mexico's exports are soaring, enabling the country to cut its balance of payments. Exports from the U.S. to Mexico are above pre-NAFTA levels. Contrary to Ross Perot's prediction of a "giant sucking sound" disaster of the loss of hundreds of thousands of American jobs, it never came about. In ten years, most Americans will view NAFTA as a beneficial arrangement with two important neighbors.

The U.S. Exports "Its Values" Around the World

American exports its values primarily through music, Hollywood films, old television reruns, magazines, theme parks, and advertisements. Such exports provide a substantial balance of payments surplus for the United States. Respect for copyright protection around the globe is essential to the success of this type of international trade.

Critics argue that American images control the whole world. They claim that the cultural identity of nations and of individuals is at risk. Some countries, France and Canada in particular, have established barriers ostensibly to keep some of the American culture out. These include restrictions on who can own media and regulations that a certain percentage of films be domestically produced.

European Union

In recent years, the European Union (EU), formerly known as the European Community, European Economic Community, and European Common Market, took additional steps toward an economic merger that began decades earlier. The **euro**, Europe's new single currency, is expected to go into use by 1999. The EU, headquartered in Brussels, is in the process of removing customs, tariffs, and non-tariff barriers among the major European countries with the aim of creating a "single market" for the purchase and sale of goods and services. The stated objective is to remove trade barriers and administrative restrictions to the free movement of goods, services, people and money within the community. This loose confederation will create a market equivalent to that of the United States, although the total population involved will be larger. This population is now about 355 million persons. It is hoped that a pan-European approach will spur an economic growth rate in Europe in excess of 3 percent and create increases in service industries such as tourism and computer software. The EU is expected to expand from 15 to perhaps 20 countries, if other countries vote to join.

Full economic unification of the member nations of the EU and elimination of all trade barriers is occurring slowly. Some efforts of the European countries to coordinate policy, such as in government-established interest rates, have failed miserably. Harmonization of rules and regulations will clearly facilitate free circulation of goods and services among the European nations. Decisions will be communitywide rather than national and will be made through the European Parliament, a supranational body serving as a weak central government.

Such a single economic bloc in Europe will have economic power to rival that of the United States and Japan. Some Americans fear that such unification is a threat to free trade and that the creation of "Fortress Europe" will result in a substantial loss of trade for American companies. European countries, it is argued, will turn to each other first for the purchase and sale of goods and services. The creation of a North American Free Trade Association was, in part, a response to this concern. Others argue that such a unified market will be easier for American firms to make sales.

Consumer viewpoints are considered at the EU through its Consumer Policy Service (a government unit that seeks environmental and consumer protections) and the Consumers' Consultative Council (that includes members of national consumer organizations, the disabled, and senior citizens).

Perhaps the biggest gain for consumers everywhere will be that products will be held to a common standard, which will eliminate costly delays at the borders. Uniformity and standardization will help consumers in many ways. Examples of consistency should include "European product guarantees," after sales service, cross-border complaint resolution,[16] rules on the use of food additives, policies on food labeling, uniform approaches to microbiological food safety and food additives, and harmonization of motor vehicle testing and equipment.

On the other hand, the consumer interest may be affected negatively in a number of ways. If the EU develops protectionist tendencies and chooses not to trade fairly with the United States, fewer goods and services, at higher prices, will be available to both American and European consumers.

---

[16]Williamson, I. (1994, June). European Community addresses consumer problems. *Mobius*, 13, 35.

Governments in the United States and Europe will battle over a number of issues in trade areas such as food exports, telecommunications, automobiles, textiles, computers, public telephone switches, television programming, insurance, and banking. Consumers also will lose if European governments continue to heavily subsidize a number of companies and products including Japanese and Italian automobiles, Spanish and Portuguese produce, and the airplane maker Airbus. The biggest loss to consumers will probably be a much greater concentration of the market. It is likely that there will be a tendency to permit less rivalry among companies that have the potential to compete with American and Japanese firms, even though this approach will have a negative impact on European consumers. The pattern of unchecked economic power will be familiar: subsidizing products and services to increase market share, reduce consumer choices and raise prices. Although there are many potential public benefits to the economic integration of European countries, it remains to be seen whether or not the interests of consumers—European and elsewhere—will be adequately protected.

The World Trade Organization

All trade around the globe today is overseen by the worldwide organization called the **World Trade Organization (WTO)**, formerly called the **General Agreement on Trade and Tariffs (GATT)**. The WTO, which began as a treaty, is now an institution headquartered in Geneva, Switzerland. WTO strives to eliminate quotas on manufactured goods and other barriers to international trade. WTO member countries represent more than 90 percent of world trade, although WTO rules oversee less than 8 percent of the value of world trade.

The WTO aims to lower world tariffs; cut agricultural and steel subsidies; protect copyrights, patents and other intellectual properties; and open previously closed markets. The impact of lowering tariffs is predicted to add $200 billion to world trade over the next 10 years. It also referees global commerce by attempting to settle disagreements among the 120 countries using WTO rules.

The WTO, like its predecessor GATT, has the power to settle disputes on international trade by enforcing rules, and it encourages parties to reach solutions on their own. When a panel issues a final ruling that determines that a country has violated GATT, it is binding. The offender is supposed to correct its behavior or pay damages, although negotiation over the terms of the sanctions is permitted. The WTO has no independent enforcement power other than expressing approval of retaliatory actions taken by the "injured" nation. In effect, the WTO sets the rules for trade wars.

The first WTO ruling found that certain U.S. clean-air regulations unfairly discriminated against foreign gasoline.[17] The U.S. has filed a complaint against Canada for unfairly discriminating against U.S. magazines.

---

[17]Under the old GATT rules, the U.S. lost 80 percent of the cases filed against it.

The International Consumer Movement

Citizens around the globe are concerned about how economic development and international trade policies affect consumers, how to obtain protection against products harmful to health and the environment, how to deal with health and safety problems, how to be part of the decisions that are made in corporate board rooms that affect well-being, and how to reduce disparities in income and consumption among consumers. Rhoda H. Karpatkin, executive director of Consumers Union of the United States, says that, "as the marketing of consumer products has crossed national boundaries, consumer protection and advocacy must be international as well. National boundaries must not be permitted to become artificial limits to the moral obligations of producers and sellers."

The international consumer movement is based on the fundamental concerns of consumers that people everywhere have basic rights. Five basic consumer rights have been identified: (1) the right to satisfaction of basic needs, (2) the right to redress, (3) the right to consumer education, and (4) the right to a healthy environment. These rights help consumers pursue their interests in efficiency and equity. March 15 is celebrated throughout the world as Consumer Rights Day.

Because consumer needs around the world are universally identical, ordinary people everywhere are getting excited about consumer issues and becoming involved as agents of change. Consumers in both developed and developing countries, people with courage and ideas, are coming forward and influencing the economic market.

Some of the recent changes in the economies of the world, suggest Swagler,[18] affect the worldwide consumer movement. These include: (1) **technological changes** which have caused restructuring of businesses in the communications industry and new products created with biotechnology, (2) **the emergence of the information age** which has increased the need for information but restricted its access largely to affluent consumers, (3) **globalization of the economy** which has raised the cost of information and decreased the level of corporate accountability, (4) **deregulation** which has raised the costs of information search for consumers, and (5) **environmental concerns** which have focused attention upon deterioration of resources and high levels of consumption by a few.

Consumers International

Consumers International (CI) was established in 1960 by Colston Warne (who founded *Consumer Reports* magazine) with leaders from the United States, the United Kingdom, Australia, the Netherlands, and Belgium. It was originally called the International Organization of Consumers Unions. CI was created by relatively affluent societies primarily to promote cooperation in the testing and information work of independent organizations, CI has three goals: to support its members, to expand the consumer movement, and to represent consumers' interests on the international level. Its broad aim is to promote social justice and fairness in the marketplace.

---

[18]Swagler, R. (1993). The coming resurgence of the consumer movement: Prospects and potential. In T. Mauldin (Ed.), *Proceedings of the American Council on Consumer Interests* (pp. 230-34). Columbia, MO: University of Missouri.

To accomplish these ends, CI encourages initiatives in areas of the world where the consumer movement is relatively new. Consumers International "stimulates research and action on international issues, such as pharmaceuticals, pesticides, tobacco, and baby foods; facilitates comparative testing of consumer goods and services; and advocates the consumer case at international forums and elsewhere."

CI Is a Strong Voice for Consumers

CI is a growing and forceful voice on international consumer issues representing 170 large and small consumer associations in 58 countries in every stage of economic development and on every continent in the world. In developing countries, the government infrastructure that provides for consumer protection is often ineffective and/or inattentive to consumer problems. CI is headquartered in The Hague, Netherlands, and it has a regional office for Asia and the Pacific in Penang, Malaysia, one for Latin America and the Caribbean in Montevideo, Uruguay, and a regional office for Africa in Harare, Zimbabwe. CI acts as an information source and clearinghouse, with a number of regular publications.

CI Seeks Social Justice and Fairness

CI's primary concern is to promote social justice and fairness in market transactions. The organization says that there are eight consumer rights: basic needs, safety, information, choice, representation, redress, consumer education, and a healthy environment. The right to basic needs includes food, housing, and health care. CI also focuses on improper marketing practices and the worldwide trade in hazardous products. One of CI's goals is "to cause so much concern that anti-consumer marketing practices will be corrected by the sellers or regulated by the appropriate international bodies and national governments."

Consumers in Developing Countries Are at Risk to the "Dark Side" of Marketing[19]

Consumers in developing countries, particularly the urban and rural poor, usually have very limited discretionary income and little formal education, yet they are often subject to sophisticated sales pressures. Consumers in poorer countries have an "exceptionally high degree of risk to be faced when trying to make prudent consumer decisions. The risk arises from a lack of standards, predatory practices of certain sellers, food adulteration, etc. Information is scarce and therefore extremely valuable."[20] Can you imagine the buyer-seller relationship between limited literacy consumers in developing countries with no background in efficient buying trying to make knowledgeable purchase decisions for processed foods, beauty aids, and over-the-counter drugs?

The global market offers many opportunities for some of the worst aspects of capitalism: profiteering, selling of unsafe products, and a general disregard of any

---

[19]This section was written by Robert R. Kerton, Professor of Economics, University of Waterloo.

[20]Kerton, R. R. (1983). International Consumer Policies. In K. P. Goebel (Ed.), *Proceedings of the American Council on Consumer Interests* (p. 139). Columbia, MO: University of Missouri. See also R. R. Kerton (1990), *Double Standards: Consumer and Worker Protection* (Ottawa, Canada: The North-South Institute).

generally accepted standards of consumer protection. Such selling is often from the industrialized countries (the **north**) to consumers in the developing countries (the **south**). The results of some of the marketing of products to consumers in developing countries include misinformation about the products, endangerment of consumers, unnecessary injuries and deaths, suffering, neglect, exploitation, cynicism, distrust, and fear.

Following are some illustrations of the dark side of marketing to consumers in developing countries: the export of banned or restricted agricultural pesticides and chemicals (polycholorinated biphenyls or PCB's, DDT, aldrin, dieldrin, and paraquat) and other outlawed products; shipping abroad (dumping) nuclear, toxic and medical wastes; mislabeling (birth control pills); selling ineffective drugs; not identifying and labeling the known side effects of prescription drugs; selling dangerous pharmaceuticals (thalidomide for tension and clioquinol for diarrhea); testing dangerous technologies (Depo-Provera for birth control); exploitively marketing inappropriate breast-milk substitutes; permitting unsafe manufacturing facilities (Bhopal); and selling unsafe products (asbestos).

Why do such things happen? The slogan "buyer beware" remains the rule in the developing world, and typically there are few, if any, consumer protection agencies to prevent these difficulties or to help consumers seek redress. Also, a framework of self-regulatory market institutions often does not exist.

What can be done? Economists argue that the important point is to arrange affairs so that the producer, and ultimately the consumer, bears the full cost of producing any good or service. If this is not done, the hazards show up as acid rain or as shiploads of toxic waste cruising the seas in search of ill-informed victims in a country without effective standards.

Small improvements are being made to reduce the export of toxic wastes and dangerous pharmaceuticals. Consumer leaders from 42 African countries met in 1996 and issued the Harare Guidelines asking for each of their countries to support the U.N. Guidelines for Consumer Protection. It is not clear, however, that the poorest countries can provide the minimal resources since a WHO study found that only 5 of 11 developing country had fully functioning pharmaceutical testing labs capable of detecting hazardous products.

The waste on useless or dangerous products has a direct effect on health and well-being. It seems doubly tragic to waste scarce foreign exchange on such products when effective—and sometimes low-cost—alternatives are available.

Realize that environmentally preferred choices often cost a little more than traditional products; thus, consumers must confront the same short-run, long-range choices that society faces. When products are eventually priced to reflect the full costs of production—including environmental degradation—almost all environmentally damaging products will be priced higher than those that are environmentally friendly. The purchases made by consumers can either add to environmental degradation or become part of the several solutions being used by society as a whole.

The idea is for consumers to "think globally and act locally." Those who are concerned about issues like inappropriate global marketing of infant milk formula, unsafe pharmaceutical products, banned pesticides, and toxic wastes perhaps ought to not be called just consumer advocates or environmentalists because they are acting in the role of concerned planetary citizens. People, says Esther Peterson, are enlarging their definition of the consumer interest to include responsible and involved citizenship focusing on ethical concerns about a "fair, safe, and healthy world."

Transnational Companies

Consumers International tries to bring a meaningful balance to the marketplace, primarily through sharing of consumer problems and solutions across international borders. The founders of CI saw the need to develop countervailing powers aimed at protecting consumers from the negative aspects of the global market expansion of goods between countries and the super-powerful transnational corporations. A **transnational company (TNC)** is a profit-seeking organization that operates in more than one country, and although organized under the laws of its home country, it has few ties to a specific nation or region. Over 35,000 TNCs operate in every economic sector and they control 70 percent of all international trade. TNCs pursue their private profit interests in a global marketplace, but are not accountable to any authority that matches their geographic reach or represents the many interests, including consumer interests, that they affect. They are not accountable in part because governments are often indifferent or impotent to consumer concerns when the views of such wealthy firms are being presented. A common accusation is that such corporations are exploitative in that they extract substantial levels of profit from developing countries.

Transnational companies are often criticized for using established marketing methods not intended to differentiate between markets, such as occurred when the Nestle Company expanded its market for dry infant formula by selling it in many African countries. Advertising sought to convince mothers that it was highly desirable to substitute infant formula for breast feeding. Free samples were distributed, often by sales personnel dressed to look like nurses. Unfortunately, the poor, primitive regions where the Nestle's product was marketed quickly became associated with unusually high levels of infant disease and death. Often mothers only had access to polluted water, or they diluted the infant formula to the point where they were unintentionally malnourishing their children. Thousands died needless deaths.

Consumers International United Nations' Authorities

As an accredited nongovernmental agency, CI has the right to appear before agencies of the United Nations (UN) and argue its point of view on proposals. The UN is involved in social and economic issues, as well as peace-keeping, since its charter states that it has a role "in achieving international cooperation in solving international problems of an economic, social, cultural, or humanitarian character." CI attempts to persuade the UN to establish principles of decency and justice which, hopefully, all nations can be persuaded to recognize.

International Codes for Proper Corporate Behavior

The first global consumer protection code of conduct is *The International Code for the Marketing of Breastmilk Substitutes*, and it was passed by the World Health Assembly on May 21, 1981. This international consumer victory is designed to promote the use of a natural and superior product—breast milk—over dry infant formulas. On December 17, 1982, the United Nations General Assembly voted overwhelmingly for international action to help overcome the dumping of hazardous products on the world market by establishing a central list of such products, which is called the *U.N. Consolidated List of Products.*

Global codes have been drafted to put an end to alleged unethical and harmful practices in third world countries by the pharmaceutical and pesticide industries, but they have not yet been passed by the United Nations.

AN ECONOMIC FOCUS: China's Consumer Movement*

China started its economic reform and open-door economic policies in the late 1970s. Since then, the market economy has been growing and the Chinese people are becoming consumers in a real sense. Because of the economic growth and western lifestyle exposure, Chinese people's expectation for consumption has risen rapidly along with the increase of their incomes. They are facing more choices of consumer goods and services. However, their consumer knowledge is not growing as fast as their income and expectations. They are confused, embarrassed, and even cheated in the marketplace. Many consumer problems now exist and have drawn public attention.

Because too many consumer problems and a number of serious tragedies would hurt the stability of the society and the continuation of economic and political reform, a consumer movement led by the government has been launched. The government is the initiator, promoter, and implementor of several consumer protection campaigns. One major effort by government to protect consumers is to create a nationwide network of consumer protection. In 1983, China's first government consumer protection agency was founded in a county near Beijing. A year later, another government agency was founded in a big city, Guanzhou, which is near Hong Kong and in an area where special **open-door economic policies** are granted. These are Chinese government policies that permit and encourage a certain amount of free enterprise.

The China Consumer Association, a national government consumer protection organization, was founded three months later in Beijing. By late 1988, China Consumer Association had 1,170 county and city branches including the two that were founded before the national headquarters. These provincial and city consumer agencies have similar functions as those of state and local consumer agencies in the U.S. But there is no American counterpart to match the China Consumer Association as it is a national government consumer protection agency. In September of 1987, China Consumer Association joined IOCU.

The China Consumer Association and its branches have the following characteristics. First, the staff members come directly from other government regulatory agencies. For instance, the staff members of the national headquarters are from China National Administration of Industry and Commerce that regulates advertising and trademarks, China Commodity Inspection Bureau that regulates the quality of imported goods, and China Standards Bureau that has authority to issue consumer goods standards. Second, the agencies always invite high-ranking officials as their honorary presidents, an efficient way to request operational funds and get things done effectively. Third, the agencies often have well-known experts or scholars to be their advisors, and these advisors serve on a voluntary basis. Fourth, the operational funds are provided by government at corresponding levels, even though the funds are usually inadequate. Fifth, complaint handling and random market inspections are the major functions of these agencies.

China's consumer movement is still in its early stage. Even today, no private organization of active consumers exits.

*Jing-jian Xiao, Associate Professor, University of Rhode Island

---

United Nations Guidelines on Consumer Protection

The international consumer movement, in short, is trying to bring more rational consumer protection standards into existence around the world. The *United Nations Guidelines on Consumer Protection* were passed by the General Assembly in 1985. The guidelines serve as a rallying cry for consumer organizations in countries with weak consumer protection and a guide for governments that want to enact suitable legislation.

The guidelines are based on the following tenets which are already well accepted in the industrialized nations: "that products should be safe and not of inferior quality to that which they purport to be; that restrictive business practices which negatively affect consumers' economic interests should be regulated; that consumers are entitled to the information required to make rational choices and to the kind of consumer education necessary to that end; and that there should be effective and speedy redress procedures for legitimate complaints." Moreover, the UN guidelines are designed to give protection against fraudulent, deceptive, unfair, and dangerous goods.

The guidelines stress the importance of maintaining competition to provide consumers with the widest choice of products and services at the lowest cost. In addition, there is a section that deals with international cooperation to address corporate problems. These include exporting of banned and hazardous products, such as TRIS (the cancer-causing flame-retardant treatment used on children's sleepwear) and some pesticides.

Implementation of these measures and principles must be assessed in view of the conditions prevailing in each country because, as suggested by the United Nations Economic and Social Council Secretariat, "the primary responsibility for consumer protection rests with each state." Therefore, each government must adopt its own consumer protection policies.

The Future of the International Consumer Movement

The international consumer movement is a reality, and it is growing. International consumer groups are advocating the consumer viewpoint on a number of emerging issues, such as destruction of the ozone layer, biotechnological developments, and third world debt. A number of organizations are dealing with the problems of globalization of the marketplace. Consumer Interpol was set up because of concern over the export of products banned or restricted in their countries of origin. It monitors and reports on global trade in hazardous products, wastes, and technologies. The organization provides information through an international warning system comprised of 105 correspondents in 47 countries so that when one group wins a battle and manages to keep a dangerous product out of one country, that same product does not quickly reemerge someplace else.

CI sponsored creation of the Hazardous Technology Working Group following the Bhopal (India) disaster and coordinates the International Coalition for Justice in Bhopal. CI also founded the Action Group to Halt Advertising and Sponsorship of Tobacco (AGHAST), the worldwide Consumers Educators Network, which shares information and teaching resources, and the Book Publishers Network, which provides technical support to consumer organizations engaged in book publishing. Increasingly international consumer organizations are forming coalitions with groups from churches, unions, feminist organizations, and professional associations.

Consumers International supports and participates as a partner in three major international networks. Health Action International (HAI) is a global network of 120 consumer and other organizations that works to further the safe, rational, and economic use of pharmaceutical products. The Pesticide Action Network (PAN) aims to raise awareness of the proliferation of hazardous pesticides and unethical marketing practices. It also promotes workable alternatives to pesticide-dependent agriculture. The International Baby Food Action Network (IBFAN) links more than 100 groups in 64 countries working toward better health and nutrition for children through promotion of breast-feeding and the elimination of commercial infant foods. It coordinated the first global consumer boycott, which was against Nestles.[21]

The number of consumer organizations around the world is growing. For example, India has 27 consumer groups, Brazil has 62, Thailand has 71, the Philippines have 4, Nigeria has 3, and Pakistan has 1. Bangladesh and Indonesia have been characterized as having some of the most active groups in the developing world. Some consumer organizations are private consumer testing agencies that compare products; others conduct product testing with government subsidies. Some are standards associations, consumer activist groups, community action organizations, and professional associations. Consumer organizations in the international consumer movement benefit from a common exchange of experience, research, and ideas.

Esther Peterson commented on the necessity for effective international consumer protection: "It takes time. It comes piece by piece, slowly, painfully, and only after excruciating battles among our own politicians and economic interests, and often only after consumer tragedies of great sadness.... Consumerism must seek to bring the issues to the forefront—to bring about solutions that not only will prevent old tragedies from recurring but new ones from developing." Mrs. Peterson calls for a greater supply of new "professionals who will move our efforts forward—professionals who will contribute to our efforts for what I like to call a 'better, safer, happier world.'"[22]

Review and Summary of Key Terms and Concepts

1. Briefly discuss the idea of **progress** in societies and economic growth.

2. Distinguish among the terms **first world countries**, **second world countries**, **third world countries**, and **developing countries**.

3. Give some examples of how the **population growth** is straining resources.

4. Explain the idea of **zero population growth** in a discussion of how **pollution** and **population growth** affect the economic resources of a country.

5. Why are **poverty** and **excessive military spending** considered world economic problems?

6. Provide an overview of the problem of **growing international debt** in the context of **equitable trade relations** between the **developing countries** and the **industrialized countries**, and explain the following terms in your discussion: **debt service**, **variable interest**, **hyperinflation**, **debt relief**, and **capital flight**.

7. What do the concepts of **economies of scale** and **absolute advantage** have to do with a country's international trade?

---

[21]The consumer boycott of Nestle's products began anew in 1988 because of the company's nonacceptance in full of the World Health Organization's (WHO's) Code on the Marketing of Infant Formula.

[22]Peterson, E. (1988). International Consumer Guidelines. In K. P. Schnittgrund (Ed.), *Proceedings of the American Council on Consumer Interests* (pp. 308-309). University of Missouri.

8. Explain the idea of international trade not being a **zero-sum** game, but in an environment of **Pareto efficiency**. In your response, be sure to explain the concept of **comparative advantage**.

9. Summarize why the United States is having difficulty providing leadership in **world trade**.

10. Explain how the U.S. **saves** less than it invests.

11. Many argue that **investment** (not **consumption**), including **social investments**, is the solution to improving the U.S. **balance of trade** (by reducing **trade deficits**) in an effort to achieve improved long-term economic growth. Summarize that argument when explaining those terms.

12. What are the pluses and minuses of **free trade**, and explain the terms **protectionist** and **trade war** in your response.

13. Choose and explain two **barriers to free trade: tariffs, quotas, embargoes, foreign-exchange controls, currency devaluations, buy-domestic policies** and **subsidies**.

14. Explain what is required for a **cartel** to operate successfully.

15. Summarize why the United States may be embarking on the economic path of **industrial policy**, and explain the idea of **managed trade** in your response.

16. What are **regional trade agreements** and list what participating nations hope to accomplish by joining them.

17. Describe what **WTO** is trying to accomplish.

18. What has **NAFTA** accomplished so far?

19. Summarize what the **European Union** has been trying to accomplish over the years.

20. List some examples of the **dark side** of marketing to consumers in developing countries.

21. Summarize what are the major concerns of the **international consumer movement**.

22. What does **justice** and **fairness** have to do with **transnational companies**?

23. Explain why consumers in **developing nations** are especially at risk.

24. In a general way, what are the United Nations **Guidelines on Consumer Protection** trying to accomplish?

Useful Resources for Consumers

American Council on Consumer Interests
International Newsletter
http://chd.syr.edu/chd/ACCI.html

Consumers for World Trade
2000 L Street, NW, Suite 200
Washington, DC 20036
202-785-4835

Consumers International
24 Highbury Crescent
London N5 1RX
United Kingdom
Tele: 44-171-226-6663
Fax: 44-171-354-0607
consint@dircon.co.uk

"What Do You Think" Questions

1. The terms **first world countries** and **third world countries** are relative to each other. Given that relativity likely will always exist, what responsibilities do you think the **industrial societies** should have toward the **developing nations**?

2. If you could wave a magic wand for but a day, which one of the five **fundamental world problems** would you eliminate on earth? Explain why.

3. Are you optimistic or pessimistic about the future of the United States as a **leading world economy**. Explain why.

4. Several perspectives have been offered about the aims of international consumerism. Review them in an effort to take from them what you need to make your own definition of **international consumerism**.

5. So far, the organized **consumer movement of China** is represented almost solely by government. This is a far different approach than followed by the United States. What positives and negatives might you predict should the U.S. government take a larger role in consumer protection in this country?

Chapter 9

Government Regulation of Economic Interests

OBJECTIVES

After reading this chapter, you should be able to

1. Recognize the important role of business as the engine of the economy in American society.

2. Understand the value of self-regulation of business practices.

3. Explain several reasons why governments regulate economic interests.

4. Describe how government promotes fair competition in the marketplace, including its use of antitrust laws.

5. Identify the four primary antitrust tools that government uses to promote competition.

The economic role of business in the United States today is twofold: to seek profits and to do so in a socially responsible manner. This is largely accomplished by businesses themselves in the form of effective self-regulation. While there are numerous successful efforts of self-regulation, government also regulates business interests. It does this with a view toward promoting the public interest. Here the common good is to keep the marketplace functioning well to serve the interests of both businesses and consumers. The role of government in the economic marketplace can best be understood by appreciating the historical culture of regulation in the United States. Government remains involved in economic matters through its efforts to promote fair competition in the marketplace, and it does this through its antitrust laws.

This chapter begins with an examination of the important role of business as the engine of the American economy. Next we review the self-regulatory role of business in society because this is fundamental to a successful consumer-oriented marketplace. Vital to one's perceptions about government is a understanding of the several reasons why governments regulate economic interests. **Regulations** are enactments and applications of principles, rules, laws, and adjudicative actions to control or govern behavior. This chapter also examines the promotion of fair competition in the marketplace, which is a key government responsibility. It also overviews the federal government's major antitrust laws and closes with a description of the four primary antitrust tools government uses to promote fair competition.

The Economic Role of Business in Society

It is natural to think of **producers** as growers of wheat or apples or manufacturers of automobiles or television sets. However, barber shops and beauty shops, as well as insurance companies, banks, and restaurants also produce something consumers buy—services. Therefore, all are producers in an economic sense because they create goods and services. At the same time, we commonly refer to all of these producers as **businesses**. In every instance, such businesses represent the organized efforts of individuals to produce and sell goods and services that society desires.

Why Businesses Operate As They Do

The primary purpose of a business is the maximization of profits to increase the wealth of owners. **Profit** is the difference between revenue and cost. Any profits earned by a business become the property of its owners. In reality, profit rewards success. An **entrepreneur** is one who organizes, owns, operates, and assumes the risks for a business venture. In order to earn profits, entrepreneurs start businesses to provide a supply of goods and services to meet demands of consumers and perhaps other businesses. Businesses often focus on maximizing short-term profits, but they must constantly reinvest and remain competitive in order to stay in business long term.

To be successful in our market economy, businesses must (1) specialize in providing a limited number of goods and services, (2) be aware of consumer demand, (3) apply the productive resources of labor, land, money, tools, and equipment to the production of goods and services, and (4) be free to apply those resources to meet the consumer demand.

The main task of business is to make a profit. The desire to increase profits leads a firm to produce particular goods and services, to shift from one combination of factors of production to another, to cut costs, and to improve services. If a business does poorly, it will become unable to pay its debts and may seek protection from the bankruptcy court. Under Chapter 11 of the Federal Bankruptcy Code, a business can request protection from creditors while the firm attempts to realign its business affairs. Should this court-guided effort fail, the firm may be sold to another business or declare **bankruptcy**. Bankruptcy occurs when a debtor is judged legally insolvent and whose remaining property is administered for his creditors or distributed among them.

American businesspersons often say that they prefer an economic environment that is left to operate freely, without government intervention. This concept of a hands-off policy toward business is called **laissez-faire**. In reality, however, businesses often prefer some government regulation instead of having to face the harsh realities of competition, where it might be difficult to make a profit or even remain in business. For example, many in the interstate trucking industry and the airline industry prefer to have government regulate the rates that can be charged and the routes that can be taken. While both industries were deregulated to a degree during the 1980s, the competitive environment resulted in many business bankruptcies and increased demands for re-regulation.[1]

Social Responsibilities of Business

Business is not an independent, self-sustaining mechanism operating in its own world; it functions as one part of the social system of society. Because of this participation in the social system, the values, ideas, and beliefs of society in general have a great impact on business. In America, businesses generally pursue the profit motive in a socially responsible and ethical manner. **Ethics** in this context are societal standards of right and wrong behavior. Ethics involves societal perspectives on right and wrong, as well as one's personal views. In business, ethics forms the foundation for what kind of organization is operated. It is hoped that these include values like fairness, balance, candor, and decency. Society suffers when businesses do not exercise self-restraint and good judgment.

Responsibility to the larger community is part and parcel of the ethical behavior of business. Poor business ethics derives only short-term profits, while over the longer term, such skimping on quality or service hurts the organization. Good ethics results in good business. **Corporate social responsibility** means exhibiting moral and ethical values when making business decisions and actions, especially in the areas of economics, law, and philanthropy. Consumers today are increasingly demanding that corporations behave more responsibly and demonstrate genuine concerns about integrity, safety, health, quality of work, and treatment of people. Among the issues are environmental pollution, dumping of hazardous wastes, offensive television programming, testing on animals, hazardous products, employment conditions, and investment in South Africa. A growing number of consumers include consideration of these issues in their personal definitions of quality. Business must no longer just perform successfully in the marketplace; it must demonstrate socially responsible behavior.

---

[1]The increased competition for trucking in the 1980s resulted in a tripling of companies (from 18,000 to 45,000) and a savings of $30 billion in transportation costs over the previous decade.

The Malcolm Baldrige National Quality Award

The quest for excellence in business is emphasized by the **Malcolm Baldrige National Quality Award**, a partnership effort of the private sector and government. Up to two awards may be given in each of three eligibility categories: manufacturing companies, service companies, and small businesses. The core values and concepts underlying the awards criteria are: customer-driven quality, consumer-oriented leadership, demand for continuous improvement, increasing employee participation and development, fast and flexible responses to customers, systems that emphasize quality and prevention, strong future orientation and commitment, management based upon reliable facts, internal and external partnerships, and demonstrated corporate responsibility and citizenship.

Winners typically publicize and advertise receipt of the government award, named after a former U.S. Secretary of Commerce. Recent winners include AT&T Universal Card Services, Ritz-Carlton Hotel Company, and Granite Rock Company. Information on the successful quality strategies of winning companies is shared with hundreds of thousands of firms and government agencies. The overall aim is to motivate other organizations to undertake their own quality improvement programs.

Self-Regulation Is Essential to Good Business Practices

In an effort to avoid government regulation as well as promote good business practices, businesses increasingly have considered **self-regulation**. This is a willingness of businesses to regulate themselves by privately creating codes of practice and setting standards for products and services in an industry, publishing them, and then enforcing them. For example, the furniture industry established flammability standards for upholstery fabrics to prevent fires caused by smokers, which had been a serious problem. The mattress industry also voluntarily established similar standards. The television broadcaster NBC receives 50,000 commercial submissions every year, and the self-regulatory efforts of NBC result in 25 percent of those ads being challenged for substantiation; 10 percent require revisions of some kind. Industry prefers to be guided by private self-regulatory groups instead of being directed by the federal government or the laws of 50 different states.

Effective self-regulation requires an awareness of a problem, recognition of its seriousness, and requisite motivation to take action. The concept of self-regulation assumes the need for regulation. Just the threat of legislation in itself often brings changes in self-regulation that benefit consumers. While there is a legitimate role for self-regulation, government, not business, is responsible for law enforcement. The concept of self-regulation raises the question of what the government ought to do versus what the business or industry ought to do. Still, if government went away, business would want strong and visible self-regulation to nurture confidence in industry and society.

Purposes of Self-Regulation

Self-regulation demonstrates the ability of business to respond to the needs of consumers without government intervention. Self-regulation also seeks to correct abuses by certain businesses in the marketplace, and industries that are strongly self-regulated generally are successful in warding off strict government regulations and maintaining a good image. Speed, informality, and modest cost are important benefits of a self-regulatory system. Consumers gain from self-regulation by having increased confidence in the marketplace and by saving tax dollars that might otherwise be expended by government regulatory agencies.

The purposes of self-regulation are self-serving. Douglas Blanke, director of consumer policy for the Minnesota Attorney General's Office, states that self-regulation's bad image is due, in part, from **occupational** (and **professional**) **licensing boards** which generally are terribly self-serving and protective of their self-interests. These boards are government-sanctioned entities, exempt from antitrust laws. They are created to set standards for and promote each occupation or profession. As examples, self-serving physicians insist that others not be permitted to prescribe drugs; opticians and optometrists get laws passed to keep their profits high; plumbers get rules passed to keep others out of their business; and lawyers protect their own. Blanke argues that self-regulation should take an affirmative role to instill confidence in an industry. To illustrate, in a settlement reached by the state Attorney General with a Minneapolis new-car dealer, the dealer contributed to a Better Business Bureau account which was used to create guidelines for auto advertising and fund a monitoring effort to police future ads.

The interest of the business community in self-regulation is commendable, as well as crucial to the effective operation of the American economy. Government would find it impossible to regulate businesses without the existing positive climate of self-regulation throughout the business community. The self-regulating efforts of the business community set the pace for all businesses in America. This accountability function helps ensure quality in the marketplace.

Examples of Self-Regulation

Some form of self-regulation is in effect in almost all industries. Following are four illustrations of the kinds of self-regulation in the United States.

Chambers of Commerce

In almost every community in America there is a Chamber of Commerce. The primary task of each local Chamber of Commerce is to promote economic activity in its geographic area because a growing economy creates employment opportunities and raises the tax base so local government can provide more and better quality services to its citizens. Chambers of Commerce usually engage in efforts to support ethical business operations, consequently reducing fraudulent business practices, but their strength lies in encouraging new businesses to open.

Better Business Bureaus

Another example of self-regulation is the Better Business Bureau (BBB), and most large communities have one. This is the oldest and most well-known business self-regulatory organization. Obviously, business cannot thrive in a market where many businesses practice deception. Thus, the BBB promotes ethical standards by vigorously supporting good businesses and publicizing the names of businesses that do not comply with their standards. The BBB raises funds by selling memberships to ethical businesses that support these standards.

The nation's 138 BBBs collect information and maintain files on businesses in their communities, identifying which businesses have unsatisfactory complaint records. While not all businesses are members of the BBB, those which are must agree to uphold ethical standards or they are forced to forego membership. While BBBs cannot order refunds or put companies out of business, they do mediate disputes and warn consumers to stay away from companies with poor reputations.

With their excellent knowledge of local businesses, it is no surprise that perhaps the most important function of the BBB is to provide information about companies to consumers *before* they spend their money. **Prepurchase inquiries** at the BBB about the quality of individual businesses total more than 11 million each year. Another 2.3 million people ask the BBB for assistance in resolving problems. Better Business Bureaus also publicize fraudulent schemes occurring in their area.

Standards-Setting Organizations

There are more than 400 **standards-setting organizations** in the United States, such as trade associations, professional and technical organizations, testing laboratories, and laboratories concerned exclusively with standards. The American Society for Testing and Materials (ASTM) and the American National Standards Institute (ANSI) deal exclusively in developing standards for industry for materials, products, systems, and services. Trade associations, such as the Aerospace Industries Association, the American Petroleum Institute, and the Electronic Industries Association also write standards. For example, the American Gas Association (AGA) directs the development of standards for gas-related residential and industrial products that help sellers manufacture better products. Voluntary standards are set by professional and technical associations like the American Society of Mechanical Engineers and the Society of Automotive Engineers. Testing laboratories such as Underwriters Laboratories (UL) also establish voluntary uniform and quality standards to provide some perceived benefits to product users.

Advertising Self-Regulation

The American Association of Advertising Agencies has established and published ethical standards for its trade association members. As a result, individual companies usually establish their own guidelines for their advertisements. Sometimes their standards are higher than those of the industry as a whole. Thus, any advertising by that company must meet its own self-imposed standards.

The entire industry enforces its advertising standards through its self-regulatory National Advertising Review Board (NARB), made up of people from the advertising industry and the public. Operationally, the NARB works alongside the National

Advertising Division (NAD) of the Council of Better Business Bureaus (CBBB). The NAD professional staff investigates more than 140 complaints annually about possible breaches of truth and accuracy in national advertising. Its task is to determine the truth of the claims in question. If adequate substantiation cannot be found, NAD requests the advertiser to modify or discontinue the claims. The NAD initiates investigations, determines the issues, collects and evaluates data, and negotiates settlements. If a resolution cannot be reached, appeals can be made to a five-member panel of the NARB. Cases are kept confidential until resolved, and no fines are imposed. In a typical year, about 70 percent of the advertising challenges are brought by competing advertisers, about 20 percent are initiated by NAD staff, and 10 percent are brought by local Better Business Bureaus, consumers, and other sources. The NARB's Children's Advertising Review Unit (CARU) has about 90 inquiries every year.

If necessary, the advertiser is asked for **advertising substantiation**. This is a request that an advertiser verify and give substance to the objective claims about its products to show that it has a reasonable basis for the claims made. Should the NAD find an absence of adequate documentation, it first requests that the advertiser change the advertisements; it cannot order changes. Second, the NAD will ask the NARB to review the facts and also rule against the advertiser. Should the company still refuse to change the advertising, the refusal is publicized by the NARB and the case information is forwarded to the appropriate government regulatory agency for action, typically the Federal Trade Commission (FTC). Critics complain that by the time the NAD gets around to making decisions on a deceptive ad, it has probably been replaced. Almost 100 percent of all advertisers have cooperated with these self-regulatory efforts.

Other Trade Associations

Thousands of **trade associations** exist that represent the interests of particular occupations or industries. While each is interested in promoting and protecting its own special interest, as it should, many trade associations also are effective supporters of self-regulation that often benefits consumers.

Why Governments Regulate

Governments exist to carry out the will of the people in a particular society. The fundamental purposes of government are to control individual action, safeguard individual and national rights, and promote the general welfare in accordance with the principles decreed to be legitimate. At its most fundamental level, the existence of government is necessary to provide **net community benefits**. This is done by protecting property rights, permitting commerce, and setting an appropriate economic framework for markets to operate. Government's central dilemma is to persuade people to forego or limit anticipated private gain on behalf of actually realizable gains to themselves and to the general welfare. Governments are responsible for taking care of all the problems that the marketplace leaves behind and undone, and these are generally the most difficult to solve.

To **govern** means to choose. Therefore, the act of **governing** is budgeting, and making decisions about how much, and on what, to spend. When government regulates, society itself is making a decision through its bureaucracy to promote certain public or community interest goals. The debate about the role of government in society is not about

CONSUMER UPDATE: Baumol's Disease Explains Why Government Takes on So Many Jobs

Economist William J. Baumol of New York University, has postulated that while productivity has increased in most parts of the manufacturing economy over the years, it has deteriorated in some labor-intensive services because such occupations "require a high level of personal input." Such endeavors as health care, education, legal services, child care, and restaurant and repair services take time and people, and it is nearly impossible to generate substantive productivity increases because many processes simply cannot be speeded up.

Because of this "cost disease of personal services," prices rise faster than the costs of other goods and services in the economy that can and do become more productive, assuming, of course, that such service providers are paid incomes at today's contemporary level of living. When afflicted services are vital to society, they migrate to or get dumped on the public sector. This is called **Baumol's disease** or **cost disease**.

Additional examples include police and fire protection, postal services, sanitation services, welfare, and the performing arts. Without subsidization from the public treasury, such services would disappear. The continuation of such services causes the costs of government to rise.

Most of the high-tech aspects of what Baumol calls the "stagnant services" are not labor—saving devices and they do not lower expenses, rather they increase costs. This stagnancy in productivity—inherent to many jobs in the public sector—is a significant factor in the rising cost of government services. But most taxpayers do not understand the principle; instead many simply illogically argue to "cut excessive government spending." Baumol's prediction for the future is that, by the year 2040, "health care and education will consume more than 60 percent of the American gross domestic product."

Costs in personal services can be effectively managed, but only if they are understood. Baumol observes that as long as productivity in society is increasing as a whole, it is okay to have some sectors lagging. The genuine challenge though, says Baumol, is to get "the public to recognize the difference between the reality and the illusion in the behavior of costs."

more government versus less government; rather it is about what kind of government. Politics has to do with making not-so-easy decisions, and very often it is about making tradeoffs. Moreover, government regulation is a product of good intentions.

Governments institute regulations in the economy to serve particular social goals, priorities, and public-policy purposes. **Public policy** refers to governmental plans and actions affecting a large segment of the citizenry that are taken to promote the general public interest. When government regulates economic markets, it is saying that market forces are inadequate to fully realize certain goals. Government intervenes in a market with regulations when marketplace forces do not promote the common good and where market failures occur. This conveys the hidden message that the American capitalistic marketplace generally succeeds.

Some people have the misperception that it is the government that creates jobs. It is more accurate to state that government spending—putting money in the hands of government agencies, consumers and businesses—for them to spend creates demand. Businesses that offer goods and services to meet such demands then create jobs while in pursuit of profits.

CONSUMER UPDATE: Some Things That Government Does Right!

With the rhetorical rage against so-called "big, bloated, unaccountable government" by certain politicians and social commentators, it is useful to focus on some things that government does right. Some examples and related facts follow:[1]

- Forty years of U.S. spending won the Cold War.
- The U.S. tax burden is the lowest among all industrialized countries.
- Government spending in the U.S. is the lowest in the industrialized world.
- The U.S. annual budget deficit is the second lowest in the world.
- If it were not for the budget deficits run up during the Reagan and Bush years, the U.S. would have a budget surplus right now.
- The number of people in the federal workforce is the smallest (2 million) since 1962. (State and local government employ over 15 million workers.)
- The poverty rate today is 20 percent less than thirty years ago.
- The rate of poverty among the elderly dropped from 30 to 12 percent since 1965.
- Seniors in the U.S. have the best health care in the world.
- Americans over age 65 have the highest life expectancy than seniors anywhere.
- Since passage of the first Clean Air Act (in 1970), air pollution has dropped by a quarter while the U.S. economy expanded by more than 85 percent and the population grew by 28 percent.
- The Federal Housing Administration has helped 23 million Americans buy their homes and another 14 million bought with help from the Veterans Administration.
- The U.S. Food and Drug Administration has the best record, compared to other industrialized countries, for preventing unsafe drugs from reaching consumers.

---

[1]Most of these illustrations are discussed in James Carville (1996), *We're Right, They're Wrong* (Simon & Schuster).

Governments Attempt to Create External Benefits

People of the world always have expected their governments to regulate to protect them against health and safety threats and in more recent years, to protect against environmental dangers as well. Realize that free economic markets provide little incentive for companies not to pollute the environment. Just the opposite motivation occurs because polluters do not have to pay anyone for the privilege of dirtying the water or air. Thus, we have the basis for environmental regulations.

In a perfectly competitive market, all costs associated with a transaction between a buyer and a seller would be captured in the selling price. However, in the real and imperfect world, external issues (**externalities**) arise from market imperfections and often require government action. Both positive and negative externalities exist that result from the selfish interests of business firms. **External costs** are those costs passed onto the community as a result of a market transaction. For example, a company that emits fumes into the air is creating negative externalities from its operations. As output rises, the firm is able to pass some of its costs of operating onto the community in the form of emissions into the atmosphere that lower the quality of community life. Since there is no economic incentive for the firm to stop passing along these costs, it is in the public interest for government to take action. Clean air, therefore, becomes a public good, and government intervenes in the form of a tax or a fine on the company's private benefits to compensate the community. On other occasions, government might force the company to employ costly technology to reduce the air pollution or it might order an outright ban of the practice.

External benefits are those gains captured as a result of private transactions and passed on to the community. The likelihood of external benefits often provides the major justification for government rather than private action. For example, local shipping companies would never be sufficiently inclined to pay for erecting and maintaining a lighthouse to warn of a treacherous shoal on a body of water because their costs would outweigh their benefits. In addition, international shipping companies would simply enjoy the advantage of being free-riders. This market-failure situation can be remedied by government intervention to create external benefits. Government could put a tax on all the ships, tax goods being carried by ships, arrange an international authority to build lighthouses, or use some other method. Shippers would benefit from a lighthouse by having greater reliability of shipping and reduced insurance rates, while the community might enjoy more land use, as well as additional employment opportunities. Only a public authority has the power to create such external benefits. Note also that government remedies produce higher government operating costs, with both external costs and external benefits.

Government, in general, hesitates to regulate, instead preferring the self-regulatory efforts of businesses and unrestricted freedom of choice of consumers. Government in the United States usually does not intervene in the marketplace until self-regulatory market forces prove ineffective or inadequate. When necessary, however, government does step in to redress problems. As former Federal Trade Commissioner Mary Gardner Jones observes, what society depends on "is for the community to police itself. But in order for a community to police itself, you have to have effective sanctions." Consumer advocate James S. Turner says that, "government regulation should be a supplement, not an alternative, to an effective consumer marketplace."

The direct costs of regulations incurred by businesses are passed on to consumers and other taxpayers through the prices of the regulated industry's products and services. Tax revenues must be collected to pay for the government effort to pass, as well as enforce regulations.

Governments Encourage or Discourage Certain Behaviors

In pursuit of the public interest, governments attempt to encourage or discourage certain private behaviors in two ways:

First, because they can tax and spend, government can divert production resources such as money, away from use in the private sector of the economy to the public sector to encourage certain behaviors. The existence of free public schools encourages more education, for example. Government spending on construction programs is another illustration.

Second, government can intervene directly into the free market by establishing rules and regulations that restrict the market in some attempt to enhance the public good. For example, having building codes helps assure safe housing and increases the marketability of such dwellings.

When Is it Desirable for Government to Control the Market?

There are two instances when it is desirable for government to step in and control the market rather than protect and promote competition. The first occurs when events have substantial negative externalities or spillover costs that affect other parts of the economy. Automobiles, for example, operate properly and get good mileage even when they are polluting. Government intervenes in the marketplace by requiring pollution-control devices.

The second instance where it is desirable for government to control some aspect of the market occurs in relation to natural monopolies. When a government has determined that it may be more efficient to have one capital-intensive firm supply a product or service rather than several competing firms, it allows such natural monopolies to operate under exclusive government franchises. Public utilities are **natural monopolies** in the United States. These are private industries offering services whose prices are set with the approval or direction of a public service commission acting on behalf of government.

Utility Companies Are Regulated by Government

One of overarching conceptual beliefs in the United States is that competition should control markets. In the instance of utilities, however, the economies of scale in some businesses, such as electricity and water, argue that it would be foolishly expensive for government to encourage competition that would waste economic resources. Who would want to have two or even three transmission systems with sets of wires going down alleyways and running into every home for the same purpose? Instead, government allows natural monopolies to exist in utilities. There are about 180 major electric utility companies.

To protect the public interest in the results of competition in utilities—good quality services and fair prices—the government creates regulatory agencies to carefully monitor the utilities businesses. A **public utility** is a private business organization subject to government regulation that provides an essential service or commodity, such as water, electricity, transportation, or communications to the public. When only one company provides the utility service, government correctly expects great economies of scale in production, since fixed costs generally do not vary with output. The idea is to pass these economies on to utility customers. Government carefully regulates the industries of transportation, communications, electricity, and gas services.

Public Utility Commissions Regulate Utility Companies

When the government allows a natural monopoly to exist, it sets up a **public utility commission (PUC)** to help ensure that prices are fair and that services are adequate. A PUC is an organized government agency whose primary task is to oversee the economic affairs of utility companies in an effort to assure the fair pricing and quality of such services. In these regulated industries, government usually allows privately owned monopolies to operate subject to a fair and reasonable **rate-of-return regulation** in which rates (for telephones, electricity, gas, etc.) are based on a company recovering its expenses, as well as an established, allowable, but not guaranteed profit margin. Instead of strict rate-of-return stipulations, governments increasingly are regulating utilities by permitting **price caps**, which set ceilings on prices charged to customers and give companies the opportunity to earn above a specified rate of return. The additional earnings are subject to sharing provisions so that customers and companies share in the efficiency gains. In addition, government monitors both the financial performance of the companies and the quality of the service they provide. Moving to more **incentive-based** forms of regulation allows the competitive forces in the marketplace (there are some competitors for many common carrier services) assume more of the burden of regulation. Such regulatory modernization limits price increases without restricting earnings while simultaneously promoting the availability of competitive alternatives.

In rate hearings, government regulators are in the conflicting position of trying to fix low rates for users (consumers, businesses, and other governments) while also judging the adequacy of the rates to provide a fair return to utility company investors. Setting prices for the services of public utilities is a complex process because it often calls for a determination of the value of the assets owned by the utility company, the nature and amount of operating costs, the establishment of a level of rates, the designation of specific rates, and the identification of the public interest. This is why over the past decade most states have established **consumer counsels**, sometimes called **state utility consumer advocates**, to adequately represent the consumer viewpoint in the decision-making process before public utility commissions. About 150 of these consumer counsels belong to the National Association of State Utility Consumer Advocates.

Enormous criticism has been directed at the cable television industry since it was decontrolled in 1984 as a result of the Cable Communications Policy Act. The 8,600 member company industry has been described as an unregulated monopoly because they deny choice and subject buyers to inflated prices.[2] Companies have long been accused of not listening to the public's wishes on programming, as well as overcharging customers. Rates nationally average over $26 a month for basic service (plus nearly $10 more for premium services), with arbitrary increases much higher than the rate of inflation coming every year. Many are looking forward to fuller competition in the cable television business where other firms could offer "cable" services to peoples homes via telephone, cable, satellite, microwave, long-distance, and fiber optics.

Will Deregulation of Power Utility Companies Hurt Consumers?

A 1992 federal law tries to break the power of large utility monopolies by encouraging a limited form of competition in the electric power industry. It allows independent utility companies to sell bulk supplies of electricity to utilities over other utilities' transmission lines. The idea is to have market-driven auctions where the lowest-cost producers of electricity could sell to customers anywhere. In 1996, the Federal Energy Regulatory Commission issued rules that facilitate increased competition. Someday consumers may be able to change electricity suppliers just as easily as they can switch long-distance telephone companies. The pressure to have competition comes from the large users of electricity, primarily manufacturers. Consumer advocates worry that if larger use customers get price reductions, will the power companies raise the rates (or not pass on cost reductions) of smaller users, such as consumers. Another concern is that the coal-fired plants in the midwest that produce electricity the cheapest (5 to 7 cents per kilowatt hour) could increase their output at the expense of increased air pollution.

---

[2]A lack of competition exists in the cellular-phone business as each of the nation's 734 cellular geographic districts has at most two licensed carriers, and even then prices are almost identical.

AN ECONOMIC FOCUS ON...Large-Scale Production and Price Regulation*

Industries such as electric power, gas, water, railroading, local street transportation, cable television, and telephone and telegraph communication are characterized by substantial economies of scale. The high level of investment in capital facilities (such as power generators, railroad tracks and terminals, gas transmission lines) means that average total costs will decline over a wide range of output. Therefore, one large firm would be able to produce a given quantity less costly than several small competing firms.

So consumers must rely for an essential service of a monopolist which, without regulation, might charge unreasonable prices. Legislatures have therefore established state and federal regulatory commissions to control prices of such services in return for protecting these firms from competition by granting them franchises to operate.

Due to the economies of scale, the market demand curve, also the **average revenue (AR)** curve, cuts marginal cost curve at a point to the left of the marginal-cost-average-total-cost intersection as depicted in Figure 9-1. The unregulated firm (monopolist) would produce the quantity Q_m and charge consumers the price P_m. Because in this situation the price exceeds average total cost, the monopolist realizes a substantial economic profit which contributes to income inequality in the society. The price also exceeds marginal cost, indicating a substantial under allocation of resources to this service.

The quantity and the price that would prevail under perfect competition, where the marginal cost equals price (average revenue) is represented by Q_c

and P_c in Figure 9-1. But charging this price would lead to losses for the firm since marginal cost is below average total cost.

The price that the commission would permit the firm to charge consumers is P_r. This price allows the firm to cover costs including the opportunity cost of capital (normal profits). The firm will produce the quantity Q_r at this price.

It is clear that price regulation can simultaneously reduce price, increase quantity, and reduce the economic profits of monopolies. However, government traditional price regulation falls short of being a satisfactory substitute for competition because it allows for inefficiencies to exist. If a firm is allowed to charge a price that is below the profit-maximizing one, it would be in its best interest to exaggerate its reported cost, if it can. There is also a chance that an inefficient management can allow costs to creep up higher than necessary, and then request the commission to grant higher rates. If higher rates are granted, then the firm will be able to earn the normal return on these unnecessary costs.

It can be concluded then, if price to the consumer is to be fair, not only should profits of the regulated monopolies be reasonable but operating costs should be held at a minimum. It is the public responsibility of commissions to only allow necessary and legitimate costs.

*Mohamed Abdel-Ghany, Professor, The University of Alabama

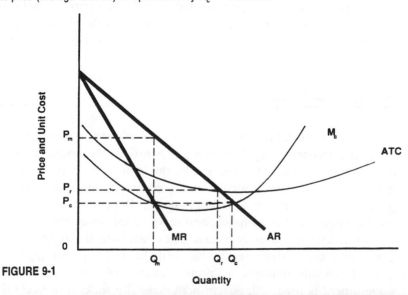

FIGURE 9-1

The Historical Culture of Government Regulation in the U.S.

Two characteristics of American culture dominate the regulatory environment: separation of powers and being a nation of laws.

Separation of Powers

The act or process of governing in the United States at the federal level is broadly divided according to the U.S. Constitution into three branches: executive, legislative, and judicial. Each branch of government serves as a countervailing power against the others. The **executive branch** consists of the President, the White House staff, several executive agencies (such as the Office of Management and Budget, the U.S. Trade Representative, and the Council on Economic Advisors), and members of the Cabinet who represent such departments as Treasury, Justice, Agriculture, Commerce, and Health and Human Resources. The **judicial branch** consists of the legal tribunals of the United States, which includes the U.S. Supreme Court, the U.S. Court of International Trade, the U.S. Tax Court, the U.S. Courts of Appeals, and the U.S. District Courts. The **legislative branch** consists of the U.S. Senate and the U.S. House of Representatives.

In the opening paragraphs of the Declaration of Independence, the founders of this country made it clear that they wanted a separation of powers in government to preserve the concepts that government always derives its "just power from the consent of the governed" and that if government does a poor job, the people maintain the right "to alter or to abolish it." Thus, a number of checks and balances exist between and among the three branches of government as they perform their functions. The President has a check on Congress through the veto power. Congress checks the executive and judicial branches in its "power of the purse," right to confirm appointments, and impeachment. Each house of Congress checks the other in that both houses must consent to legislation. Congress also performs an oversight function as it reviews the efforts of regulatory agencies. Both the President and Congress are subject to the power of the federal courts.

A Nation of Laws

Because the United States is a nation of laws, governments in America cannot act without appropriate legal authority. Therefore, the power to govern is derived from a constitution, statutory laws passed by the legislature, regulations issued by administrative agencies, and decisions made by the courts. When laws and regulations are violated, government can investigate and prosecute. Depending on the statutes violated, penalties can be either civil or criminal, and in some instances both.

Civil law is the body of law that deals with the rights of private citizens, such as consumers and businesspersons, as distinguished from criminal law. To prove liability in a civil lawsuit requires a "preponderance of evidence." In civil cases where the government is involved, government generally seeks to remedy the wrong, and in many instances, government asks the courts to fine the individual or company involved.

Criminal law deals with crime and punishment. Proof in criminal actions requires "proof beyond a reasonable doubt," and violators are subject to imprisonment by government. Judicial court decisions, or **doctrines**, are important authoritative sources for interpretations of statutes.

In criminal situations, a judge can order the defendant to jail. In civil situations, a judge can order the defendant to perform certain tasks or refrain from doing certain things. A judge also can order civil **compensatory damages**, which are monetary amounts assessed against a defendant to make up, offset, or reimburse the financial costs (expenses, losses, and pain and suffering that might have accompanied those losses) alleged by the plaintiff. **Punitive damages**, which are monetary amounts assessed against a defendant with the intent to inflict punishment for wrongdoing, may also be ordered. In 1993, the U.S. Supreme Court reaffirmed the role of punitive damages designed to deter sellers from misconduct that might otherwise generate a profit.

How Government Promotes Fair Competition

One of government's primary tasks began with its involvement in economic matters in order to promote fair competition and to ensure public well-being and safety. Overall **economic well-being** is the level of living of individuals and families or the public. Antitrust laws are aimed at protecting and preserving competition, and the roots of American antitrust laws can be traced to early British common-law court decisions encouraging freer access to certain trades and occupations. Our antitrust laws are designed to allow consumers to choose from among a variety of goods and services at a variety of prices. This is the hallmark of a free-enterprise market economy. Accordingly, antitrust laws should be most strongly supported by the business community.

Free and open competition benefits consumers by ensuring lower prices and new and improved products. In a freely competitive market, each competing business tries to attract customers by cutting prices and/or increasing the quality of its product or service.

The reality of the world is that pure or perfect competition does not exist. We have an imperfectly competitive marketplace. Economies of scale and technology give the advantage to the largest and most efficient firms. American society wants competition because we value it as an ideal.

We worry that when only a few firms dominate an industry, they might set higher prices than would exist if things were more competitive. We also do not want any natural or artificial barriers to entry into a business or industry because those who restrict entry are likely to unfairly control prices. As former Senator Warren Magnuson once stated, "All each industry seeks is a fair advantage over its rivals."

Effects of Little or No Competition—Economic Fraud

An unregulated economic marketplace discriminates against both the public and the honest businesses, notes consumer advocate Carol Tucker Foreman. When competitors agree to fix prices, rig bids, limit output,[3] allocate customers by dividing business among them, or make other anti-competitive arrangements that provide no benefits to consumers, economic fraud occurs. These are examples of **price fixing** which occurs when competing companies attempt to interfere with market forces of supply and/or prices so they might profiteer. Instead of competition holding down prices, in these instances prices are illegally fixed to increase the profits of participating firms. The prices that result when competitors band together in these ways are artificially high. This happens because the businesses are falsely holding themselves out as competitors despite their quiet agreement not to compete. Less competition also means fewer product choices for consumers.

Anticompetitive practices that might be unlawful if undertaken by private business are immune from attack if they are governmental action. All the county government commissioners can get together in an area and agree to fix identical prices for camping fees, for example, but movie theater owners cannot. Also, governments sometimes enter into contracts with businesses that result in extremely high, noncompetitive prices. For example, you cannot buy a fairly priced meal at most large airports because local governments often get a piece of the sale of every meal.

Government Sometimes Prohibits Competition

Government also controls the marketplace for old-fashioned historical and political reasons. Local government, for example, keeps prices unnecessarily high by limiting the number of taxicabs in New York City and lots of other communities. In Wisconsin, there are "minimum markup laws" for products such as gasoline, which *require* sellers to mark up the price at least six percent over wholesale. Arkansas prohibits selling below cost. In California, there are "relevant market area" regulations that reduce competition by permitting, for example, an existing Ford auto dealership to protest the opening of another Ford dealership too close by. In most states, one is prohibited from opening a hospital and competing with existing hospitals until one obtains a "certificate of need" from the government. In New York, they take that one step further by "decertifying" hospital beds that otherwise would bring in increased competition.

The federal government's program of agricultural marketing orders permits grower's cartels to restrict supplies to keep profits high for the sellers. That is the reason every now and then you see television news focus on farmers feeding "excess" milk to hogs and squashing "excess" oranges at the city dump. These programs are operated through agricultural cooperatives that are permitted to legally conspire to fix prices. Even peanut butter is subject to crop production quotas.

The powerful agriculture lobby was successful in getting Congress to pass a law prohibiting the Federal Trade Commission from even studying agriculture marketing orders. The Capper-Volstead Act restricts the FTC's efforts to bring antitrust challenges in the farming industry. The influential insurance industry similarly got the McCarran-Ferguson Act passed which prohibits the federal government from studying or regulating that industry. The powerful special interests are afraid of what might be discovered. Clearly, these are not practices designed to provide consumers with low prices.

---

[3]In 1994, the Federal Trade Commission won its challenge against Detroit-area automobile dealer who for years had conspired to restrict their hours of operation. For the first time in many years, you can shop for a new car in Detroit on Saturdays and Sundays.

Circumstances and reasons are always unique, but the Congress and the courts have exempted a number of businesses from antitrust laws. Examples include natural monopolies, fishing organizations, agricultural cooperatives, labor unions, export trade associations, insurance companies (which are regulated by states), newspaper joint operating arrangements, professional baseball,[4] and the joint export activities of American companies. Other industries have partial exemptions: banking, communications, learned professions, natural gas transmission, professional sports, securities and commodity exchanges, airlines, railroads, and shipping.

Former Senator Howard H. Metzenbaum says that the U.S. Congress is not antitrust oriented for three reasons: (1) members are tainted by money received from political action committees (PACs), (2) powerful business lobbies are against strengthening antitrust laws, and (3) consumers have not strongly indicated that they want more competition and better prices.

Government Gets Businesses to Sign Consent Agreements

To stop price fixing, as well as any other unfair or deceptive trade practices, the appropriate government agency conducts an investigation. In the area of antitrust, for example, if an investigation shows that a violation exists, the Federal Trade Commission files a lawsuit against the alleged offender(s) and seeks a trial. The FTC frequently settles the case out of court with a **consent agreement** (also called a **consent decree**). This is a negotiated agreement between the respondents and the government. The business agrees that it will refrain from engaging in the particular practice to which the commission objects and it further promises not to do something like that in the future. When a business signs a consent agreement, it is not an admission of prior wrongdoing. Sometimes a consent agreement includes a **cease and desist order**. This is a legal order from a court that requires the business to stop some particular act or practice and not do it in the future.

Should the alleged improper practice continue in the future, the FTC has an easy time demonstrating violation of the consent decree. Here the firm will be found in **contempt of court** and fined. Contempt of court occurs when a person or firm deliberately violates an order of the court or refuses to perform as ordered by a judge. In effect, cease and desist orders define unfair and deceptive trade practices with the specificity of individual cases.

The majority of antitrust cases are initiated by the federal government and are settled in out-of-court agreements or decrees between the parties. Judges must approve of all settlements, and in each case a consent decree is filed with the court indicating that the firm agrees to its terms. In a small number of instances, one firm sues another for an antitrust violation, as was the case when Pennzoil sued Texaco and was awarded $6 billion in damages.

---

[4]Baseball's antitrust exemption comes from a Supreme Court decision in 1922 that baseball did not engage in interstate commerce. Since this clearly is a false assertion, the U.S. Congress may overturn the exemption with a new law.

Government Laws That Promote Fair Competition

The public view of "big business" is not positive. People have been suspicious since the trusts and monopolies of the late 19th century. A **monopoly** (or **pure monopoly**) means that there is a single seller of a good or service for which there are no close substitutes. When a monopoly exists, the firm purposefully restricts output and increases prices. The prices are higher than they would be if competition were present in the marketplace. Bigness, however, does not necessarily mean power to monopolize supply and prices. Such power depends upon the position of the firm in the market in which it operates.

The federal government promotes fair competition with its **antitrust laws**. These are statutes concerned with government regulation of virtually any anti-competitive business practices involving abuse of economic power. Anti-competitive abuses can occur from trusts, cartels, monopolies, price discrimination, collusion, and deceptive and unfair business practices. The word **trust** comes from a business practice in the late 1800s in which several companies combined their assets into a common legal ownership and then attempted to minimize or eliminate competition. A **cartel** is a combination of independent firms formed to regulate production, pricing, and marketing of goods by controlling and limiting production in an effort to maintain or increase prices and profits.

The antitrust laws are aimed at preserving industrial market organization and maintaining firm conduct in the public interest. The goal is to prevent giant corporations from acting unfairly to dominate smaller rivals, as well as to prevent attempts to fix prices, carve up markets, or commit other anti-competitive acts. To illustrate, **predatory pricing** is defined by the U.S. Supreme Court as "pricing below an appropriate measure of cost for the purpose of eliminating competitors in the short run and reducing competition in the long run." For example, predatory pricing occurs when a price-cutting firm is willing to hold its new low prices for perhaps 3 to 5 years (with allowances for changes in costs) in an effort to drive out the competition. Recognize also that each state has its own antitrust laws to combat marketplace abuses and protect competitors, small businesses, farmers, and consumers.

There are several major federal antitrust laws: the Sherman Antitrust Act, the Clayton Act, the Federal Trade Commission Act, the Robinson-Patman Act, the Cellar-Kefauver Act, and the Hart-Scott-Rodino Act. Antitrust lawsuits can be brought by the U.S. Department of Justice, the Federal Trade Commission, and state attorneys general, as well as by private persons and companies.

Sherman Antitrust Act

The Sherman Antitrust Act, passed in 1890, declared illegal "every contract, combination in the form of trust or otherwise, or conspiracy, in restraint of trade or commerce among the several States, or with foreign nations." In 1911, the U.S. Supreme Court inserted the word unreasonable before contract. Thus, the law prohibits monopolization and other joint or concerted actions that attempt to unreasonably restrain trade and commerce with the threat of civil fines and criminal penalties.

A monopolist has the ability to set the price by altering supply. This is in contrast to a situation where there is pure competition. In the American economy, there is almost always *some* competition; thus pure monopolies are more an abstraction than a reality. (The same can be said for pure competition.) Monopolistic power in the American economy today means that a business has the power to raise prices above competitive levels. It typically occurs when an organization has exclusive control over a commercial activity, such as the production or selling of a commodity or service, and it has the power to fix prices unilaterally because it has no effective competition. Monopolies may arise from a number of sources, such as economies of scale, restrictions on entry into certain industries, control of raw materials, exclusive patent or copyright ownership, and because of the use of various types of competitive tactics.

When a monopoly exists, the forces of supply and demand cannot determine production and price. Instead, the monopoly decides on the supply and the price for its own gain. Monopolists attempt to erect and maintain barriers to the entry of other firms into an industry.

Monopolization violates the Sherman Antitrust Act and is defined according to the *Grinnel* decision of the U.S. Supreme Court as "the willful acquisition or maintenance of monopoly power in a relevant market as opposed to growth as a consequence of superior product, business acumen, or historical accident." The **monopoly power** of a firm refers to the extent of its control over the supply of the good that is produced by the industry of which it is a part. Being a monopoly is *not* illegal, but acts of monopolization are.

An **oligopoly** is a market condition in which the bulk of production is accounted for by the output of a few dominant firms with the effect that the actions of any one firm will materially affect price and hence have a measurable impact on competitors. Because of the limited number of firms, each firm must consider the reaction of rivals in matters relating to output and price. Price competition in oligopolistic industries is often minimal, such as among the six national airlines that control more than 90 percent of the market.[5] If they are not competing in your city, you are very likely paying excessively high prices. Government deregulation of the airline industry in the 1980s permitted the creation of a large number of "local" monopolies, particularly for passengers who originate or terminate flights at "hub airports" in the nation's 50 largest markets. "Flyers pay 22 percent more to fly out of U.S. airports with little competition,"[6] says the U.S. General Accounting Office.

In order to determine the degree of monopoly power in certain markets, we use concentration ratios. A **concentration ratio** is the percentage of industry sales in an industry produced by the four leading firms in that industry. One can suspect a substantial degree of monopoly power when the four-firm concentration ratio reaches 70 percent. Table 9-1 provides an indication of the concentration in production in selected industries compiled by the U.S. Department of Commerce. From the data it is clear that the common market structure in a substantial portion of the American market for selected goods and services can be characterized as **imperfect competition**. Much of the economy is dominated by concentrated corporate power.

Monopolistic competition is a related noncompetitive market situation. Under monopolistic competition, a number of firms produce similar, but differentiated, goods. Product differentiation usually gives each firm a limited degree of control over prices, such as the situation with coffee growers. Pricing under noncompetitive situations is likely to be higher than it would be under conditions of pure competition.

Despite the American cultural belief in and support of competition, the antitrust laws have not been successful in stopping the trend toward economic concentration in industry.

---

[5]Airline prices have more than doubled over the past fifteen years, after adjustments for inflation.

[6]Schmit, J. (1993, August 5). Hub Fares Higher. *USA Today*, p. B-2.

	Percent of Industry			
Industry	**Four Largest Firms**	**Eight Largest Firms**	**Twenty Largest Firms**	**Fifty Largest Firms**
Book Publishing	23	38	62	77
Mobile Homes	35	50	70	88
Cigarettes	39	57	80	98
Carpets and Rugs	40	53	76	91
Small Arms	43	66	89	96
Creamery Butter	49	78	98	100
Meat Packing Plants	50	66	79	88
Cutlery	56	69	87	98
Flour and Other Grain Mill Products	56	68	83	95
Distilled Liquor, Except Brandy	62	82	97	100
Lawn and Garden Equipment	62	79	98	99
Roasted Coffee	66	75	89	96
Aircraft	79	93	99	99+
Household Refrigerators and Freezers	82	98	100	100
Hard Surface Floor Coverings	83	99	100	100
Motor Vehicles and Car Bodies	84	91	99	99
Greeting Cards	84	88	95	99
Cereal Breakfast Foods	85	98	99+	100
Electric Lamps	86	94	98	99+
Chewing and Smoking Tobacco	87	98	99+	100
Vegetable Oil Mills	89	97	99	100
Malt Beverages	90	98	100	100

Source: *1992 Census of Manufacturers: Concentration Ratios in Manufacturing* (Washington, D.C.: U.S. Department of Commerce, Bureau of the Census), 1996.

TABLE 9-1   Concentration in Selected Industries

Oligopolies and monopolies are deemed illegal under the Sherman Antitrust Act when they "unreasonably restrain trade." The antitrust policy question is whether the government should pursue anticompetitive corporate *behaviors* or anti-concentration *events*. Thus, the issue of breaking up oligopolistic industries becomes a political debate as well as an economic discussion. While the Sherman Antitrust Act does not prevent monopolies and oligopolies, it does make them illegal.

Some economists suggest that it is not necessary to have all the conditions of perfect competition in the economy for the best interest of American consumers. Rather, they argue, the country can do just fine with **workable competition**. Economists Thomas J. Hailstones and Michael J. Brennan say that this is "a condition in which there is a reasonably large number of firms in an industry, there is no formal or tacit agreement among the firms regarding output or price, new firms are free to enter the industry without serious impediment or disadvantage, and no one firm is large or powerful enough to coerce other firms." While the term workable competition might be descriptive, its application becomes wholly judgmental.

What are serious impediments to entry? What is a reasonably large number of firms? To illustrate, how would you describe the competitiveness of the automobile and steel industries in the United States?

The U.S. Supreme Court has held that violations of the Sherman Antitrust Act occur when the behavior "unreasonably restrains competition." Two approaches are used to assess such behavior. **Per se actions** are those that are intrinsically illegal because they always have a negative effect on competition and can never be justified or excused. The government has a number of per se rules. **Rule of reason** is behavior not classified as illegal, per se, but "unreasonable" agreements to restrain trade are illegal. It requires an inquiry into the actual competitive effects of the defendant's actions, as well as any justifications that the defendant may advance. In recent years, the trend in court decisions has been away from per se rules in favor of rule of reason analysis of alleged violations.

Violations of the Sherman Antitrust Act may give rise to both criminal and civil penalties. Individuals demonstrating criminal intent in their anticompetitive behavior may be fined up to $100,000 per violation and/or be imprisoned for up to 3 years. Corporations may be fined up to $1 million per violation.

Clayton Act

Reputed dissatisfaction with the Sherman Antitrust Act led Congress to pass the Clayton Act in 1914. It was designed to prevent monopolies by catching early stage practices that were thought to lead to monopolies, such as corporate mergers and acquisitions, price discrimination, tying agreements, and interlocking directorships. **Interlocking directorships** exist in large competing corporations where one person serves as a director of two or more corporations (other than banks or common carriers because they are exempt) and the elimination of competition by agreement between those corporations would violate any of the antitrust laws.

The potential for the exercise and abuse of market power multiplies as an increasingly higher proportion of sales becomes concentrated in the hands of a smaller number of sellers. For example, in the livestock slaughter industry, a number of mergers has resulted in a smaller number of packers. Fewer packers means fewer buyers of cattle. With less competition for livestock, cattle sellers may wind up receiving lower prices than would prevail in a more competitive situation. In addition, the opportunity for abuse exists because the larger packing companies might reap excess profits by charging wholesalers and retailers higher prices. Consumers ultimately wind up having to pay the unnecessarily high prices. The Clayton Act is designed to remedy the situation when businesses act to substantially lessen competition or to create monopolies in any line of commerce. It is a statute with only civil penalties, although private plaintiffs can sue for treble damages or injunctive relief. The Clayton Act prohibits price discrimination, as well as exclusive dealing and tying agreements, particularly those involving commodities, that substantially lessen competition. These **tying arrangements** are illegal restraints of trade because they require a buyer to purchase a second and perhaps unwanted item if a first item is purchased. For example, it is illegal to demand that a business buy only one specific type of computer paper if it wants to purchase a particular brand of computer printer.

The following are types of antitrust violations that are illegal because they represent joint restraints on trade by attempting to interfere with market forces and control prices:

1. **Horizontal division of markets** occurs when there are agreements among competing firms to divide up the available market by assigning one another certain exclusive territories or certain customers.
2. **Vertical restraint on distribution** occurs when various buyer/seller relationships, such as between a manufacturer and a retailer or between a supplier and a manufacturer, place restrictions on selling, such as agreeing not to sell outside a geographic territory, or agreeing not to sell to unfranchised dealers within another dealer's assigned territory. Manufacturers and retailers may not coerce each other into complying with a supply or pricing agreement.
3. **Group boycotts** and **concerted refusals to deal** occur when there are agreements among two or more sellers with price-fixing intent to refuse to deal with others, or to deal with others only on certain terms and conditions, or to coerce suppliers or customers not to deal with one of their competitors.
4. **Tying agreements** occur when a seller refuses to sell a buyer a product (the *tying* product) unless the buyer also agrees to purchase a different product (the *tied* product) from the seller.
5. **Reciprocal dealing agreements** occur when a buyer attempts to exploit its strong purchasing power by conditioning its purchases from a supplier on reciprocal purchases of some product or service offered for sale by the buyer.
6. **Exclusive dealing agreements** (also called a **requirements contract**) occur when buyers of a particular product or service are required to purchase exclusively from a particular seller.
7. **Joint ventures** occur when the combined efforts of two or more businesses to accomplish a lawful objective, such as joint research and development projects, restrain competition to the extent that the benefits of the venture to society are reasonably offset by the cost of the restraints to trade.[7]

Also prohibited by the Clayton Act are mergers or acquisitions that are likely to lessen competition. A **merger** is the acquisition of one company by another resulting in a union of two or more commercial interests or corporations. Most mergers occur for reasons such as ridding a company of inept management, improving efficiency, meeting changes in market demand, responding to foreign competition, and taking advantage of tax laws. A **horizontal merger** results from bringing under one control a number of companies engaged in the sale of the same or similar products. Mergers among firms competing in the same product and geographic markets have traditionally been subject to the most thorough government scrutiny because they result in an increase in concentration in a relevant market.

A **vertical merger** results from bringing under one control a number of companies that had, or could have had, a supplier-customer relationship, because they may have previously engaged in different steps in manufacturing or marketing a product. These mergers are also examined and occasionally challenged by government. A **conglomerate merger** results from bringing under one control a number of companies belonging to quite unrelated industries. In effect, conglomerates integrate across industries. They occur when two firms merge that are not in direct competition with each other because they compete in different product or geographic markets. Such mergers are rarely challenged except when certain factors exist, such as potentials for reciprocity, for eliminating potential competition, and for giving the acquired firm an unfair advantage over its competitors.

---

[7]Some joint ventures, especially for overseas sales, are permitted by special laws passed by Congress.

Generally, the judgment of the court is that a restraint of trade occurring through a merger must be undue *and* unreasonable before it is held illegal. Mere bigness is not proof of a violation. Thus, corporations with hundreds of thousands of employees, millions of stockholders, and billions of dollars in assets and annual sales are not automatically deemed illegal. From time to time, the Justice Department and the Federal Trade Commission jointly issue guidelines and criteria employed in deciding whether to challenge particular mergers, thus establishing enforcement standards to illustrate how permissive government will be toward mergers. The current guidelines use the **Herfindahl Index,** which is based on individual companies' market shares, to test whether a merger will reduce competitiveness in a particular market.

Federal Trade Commission Act

Congress passed the Federal Trade Commission Act in 1914 to combat unfair methods of competition because it felt that failure of the Sherman Antitrust Act was partially attributable to the institutions entrusted with its enforcement: the Justice Department and the courts. The law created a new government agency, the Federal Trade Commission (FTC), a bipartisan commission of five presidential appointees, confirmed by the Senate for staggered terms, to become a continuous, aggressive, and effective organization designed to study and prevent the practices that lead to monopolies. The law declared that unfair competition should be unlawful. In 1938, Congress passed the Wheeler-Lea amendment to add a ban on "unfair or deceptive practices," which therefore underscored the FTC's efforts to turn its attention to unfair and deceptive consumer practices that disadvantaged honest competitors.

The Federal Trade Commission Act prohibits unfair methods, acts, and practices that lessen competition in interstate commerce. The law provides that the prohibitions can be interpreted and enforced through administrative proceedings by the FTC, subject to review by the courts.

As amended, **Section 5** of the act uses sweeping language that empowers the FTC to "prevent unfair methods of competition and unfair or deceptive acts or practices in or affecting commerce."[8] This section allows the FTC to prohibit existing, incipient, and potential practices.

Section 5 was amended in 1973 by the Trans-Alaska Pipeline Authorization Act, which gave the FTC authority to (1) directly enforce its own subpoenas, (2) seek preliminary injunctive relief, (3) represent itself in civil actions instead of being represented by the Justice Department, and (4) require most large corporations to report profit on a "line of business" basis. Also, the FTC enforces a great number of antitrust and consumer laws, including provisions of the Magnuson-Moss Warranty Act, the Wool Products Labeling Act, the Truth in Lending Act, and the Fair Packaging and Labeling Act.

---

[8]The concept of unfairness is one whose precise meaning is not immediately obvious, particularly since neither the original law nor the Wheeler-Lea Trade Commission Act amendments ever defined it in specific terms, instead allowing the courts and the FTC to offer interpretations. In 1980, the Federal Trade Commission issued a policy statement in an attempt to synthesize the elements of a violation: "**Unfairness** would be found if an act or practice causes injury that is (1) substantial, (2) not outweighed by countervailing benefits to consumers or competition, and (3) not reasonably avoidable by the injured consumers."

Consumer Update: The "Dishonor Roll" of Unfair Competitors

Recent illustrations of companies who the government has charged with unfair competitive practices include:

- **Sara Lee**—The Justice Department fined the company $3.1 million for knowingly failing to notify the government when it acquired the assets of its largest competitor in the shoe polish business.
- **Delta, United Airlines, American Airlines, US Air, Northwest Airlines,** and **TWA**—Agreed to a $458 million price-fixing settlement for overcharging 4 million consumers through a computerized ticking system.
- **Liquid Carbonic**—Four carbon dioxide suppliers (which manufacture more than three-fourths of the nation's bulk supply), including Liquid Carbonic, paid $55 million in civil fines for rigging bids for over 30 years.
- **Reebok**—All fifty states won a $9.5 million class-action lawsuit alleging price-fixing as the company prohibited retailers from selling its products below certain levels.
- **San Jose New-Car Dealers**—The FTC got a group of 47 new-car dealers in California that conspired to cancel 52 pages of advertising in retaliation for an article in the "Drive" section of the paper that advised consumers on how to buy a new car.
- **Merck, Pfizer, SmithKline Beecham, Searle, Schering-Plough, American Home Products,** and **Glaxco**—Fifteen U.S. drug manufacturers, including those listed, have agreed to a $600 million price-fixing settlement brought in a lawsuit by 40,000 retail pharmacies.
- **Reuters America** and **Federal News Service Group**—The FTC has secured an agreement from the two largest sellers of news transcripts that they will no longer divide markets or fix resale prices.
- **Toys R Us**—The Federal Trade Commission currently alleges that the company used its marketing power to keep rivals from getting certain popular toys.

Robinson-Patman Act

The 1936 Robinson-Patman Act (technically an amendment to the Clayton Act) is commonly referred to as the "**chain store act**" because it prohibits price cutting of commodities by large firms designed to eliminate competition from small firms. It is illegal for companies engaged in interstate commerce to grant discounts for the same commodities to large firms, such as chain stores, without granting similar discounts to smaller independent stores when the selling costs do not vary between the two. The law does permit selling at different prices when costs are based on different methods or quantities involved in the manufacture, sale, or delivery of the products. To prove a price-discrimination case, a market analysis must be conducted which shows that actual competitive injury has occurred or that the seller engaged in a significant and sustained local price discrimination with the intention of punishing a competitor. However, a discriminatory price may be lawful when it is charged in good faith to meet (not beat) an equally low price of a competitor.

Cellar-Kefauver Act

The 1950 Cellar-Kefauver Act is an effort to maintain competition. It amends section 7 of the Clayton Act, specifically prohibiting the acquisition of one firm's stock by another when the end result would be to lessen competition or create a monopoly. Mergers are also illegal if there is a trend toward concentration in an industry.

Hart-Scott-Rodino FTC Improvements Act

The 1976 Hart-Scott-Rodino Act requires pre-merger notifications. It provides that all persons and businesses considering a merger of significant size (one party to the transaction has assets or net sales of $100 million or more and the other has assets or net sales of $10 million or more) are required to notify the Antitrust Division of the Justice Department, as well as the Federal Trade Commission. The law establishes a waiting period before certain acquisitions or tender offers may be consummated. After careful economic analysis, the government is supposed to challenge any merger that is likely to substantially lessen competition and increase prices to consumers.

Parens patriae is a legal concept permitted under this law that allows a state attorney general to bring civil actions in federal court on behalf of the people of his or her state to secure monetary relief for price fixing and anticompetitive business practices. A unanimous Supreme Court ruled in 1990 that state attorneys general can obtain court orders to undo illegal corporate mergers.

Four Primary Antitrust Tools That Government Uses to Promote Competition

Government uses four primary antitrust tools to promote fair competition.

1. Empowered individuals. Section 4 of the Clayton Act gives private individuals the right to enforce the antitrust provisions of the Sherman Antitrust Act and the Clayton Act. Persons injured may recover treble damages plus costs and attorney's fees from the defendants. The damages can include lost profits and increased costs of doing business resulting from the violation, and this amount is then tripled before being assessed.

2. Break up large firms. A second antitrust tool government uses is to break up firms that have become so large that they dominate an entire industry. Thus, companies may be forced to divide into several smaller corporations in order to create more competition. The government uses three types of orders in these situations: (A) **divestiture**, which requires a defendant to sell the stock or assets of acquired companies, (B) **divorcement**, which requires a defendant to sever a relationship by ridding itself of a functional level of operations (such as an oil refinery being forced to sell its competitive retail outlets), refrain from particular conduct in the future, and cancel existing contracts,[9] and (C) **dissolution**, which requires a defendant to liquidate its assets and go out of business.

3. Prevent mergers. A third antitrust tool used by government is to prevent mergers that would have a negative effect on competition. This is the focus of the Clayton Act.

4. Take legal action against price fixing. A fourth antitrust tool is for the government to take legal action (civil and/or criminal) in cases of price fixing.

---

[9]A decade-long study by Citizen Action revealed that major oil companies in California, where big oil companies own the majority of gasoline outlets, charge consumers 5 to 10 cents more than in other states.

There are two different types of price fixing. First, **horizontal price fixing** occurs when competitors make direct agreements about the quantity of goods that will be produced, offered for sale, or bought. In one case, an agreement by major oil refiners to purchase and store the excess production of small independent refiners was found to be illegal because the purpose of the agreement was to affect the market price for gasoline by artificially limiting the available supply. Second, **vertical price fixing** occurs when manufacturers make express or implied agreements with their customers obligating them to resell at a price dictated by the manufacturer. One FTC study concluded that vertical price fixing inflates prices 10 to 23 percent. Manufacturers can lawfully state a "suggested retail price" but not fix it by agreement. Few sellers are caught making such agreements.[10] Instead, some manufacturers have chosen to intimidate retailers by cutting off sales.[11] Another example of vertical price fixing is **retail price maintenance laws**, which used to exist in most states until struck down by the U.S. Supreme Court. Today a number of manufacturers (mostly of clothing, prescription drugs, cosmetics, and appliances) want to stop price competition at the retail level by getting the U.S. Congress to pass a "retail price maintenance law" that would establish "minimum prices" and prohibit retailers (discount stores in particular) from selling products below those low prices. Supporters of this anticompetitive concept duplicitously call their proposed legislation a "fair trade" law.

Review and Summary of Key Terms and Concepts

1. What do the following terms mean: **businesses**, **profit**, and **entrepreneur**?

2. Give some examples of the **social responsibilities** of business.

3. Briefly discuss the concept **self-regulation** as being essential to good business practices in the United States.

4. Distinguish between **standards-setting organizations** and **trade associations**.

5. Briefly describe the process of **advertising substantiation** as practiced by the national advertising industry.

6. Summarize why **governments regulate**.

7. Explain the concept of **Baumol's Disease**.

---

[10]The Virginia Alcoholic Beverage Control (ABC) board was sued by wine retailer Herbert Haft forcing them to permit his Total Beverage Corporation the right to seek cheaper prices from any wholesaler he prefers. ABC interpretation of the Virginia Wine Franchise Act requires retailers to purchase only from a designated wholesaler, which often resulted in high costs (plus high profits for the wholesalers) being passed onto consumers. In 1994, an appeals court overruled the ABC board finding for Haft and consumers.

[11]Sony jumped all over retailers in the Washington, D.C. area in 1993 by threatening to cut off deliveries of its products if they put prices of Sony products in the regional publication *Checkbook Bargains*, a magazine that tells consumers where to get the best prices of expensive items. Price-fixing laws are not entirely clear on advertising matters, although to most consumers if price advertising is restricted it is the same as illegally restricting prices. This is why you sometimes see advertisements saying, "Call for best price" or "Call for package deals."

8. Describe the concepts of **external costs** and **external benefits** in explaining why governments regulate economic interests.

9. Distinguish between **rate-of-return regulation** and **price cap regulation**.

10. Explain the existence of **state utility consumer advocates** when **natural monopolies** already have **public utility commissions** to represent the public interest.

11. What can a consumer conclude about the **large-scale production and price regulation**?

12. Provide an overview of the historical culture of government regulation in the United States, and include the concepts of the words **democracy, separation of powers**, and **nation of laws** in your response.

13. What concerns does the American public have about when **few firms dominate an industry**?

14. Summarize the effects of **little or no competition**.

15. Give some examples of when **government prohibits competition**.

16. How does government go about promoting **fair competition**?

17. Summarize the essence of the **Sherman Antitrust Act**.

18. Distinguish among the following terms: **pure monopoly, monopoly, oligopoly, monopolistic competition, workable competition** and a **concentration ratio**.

19. Distinguish between **per se actions** and **rule of reason** as approaches to violations of antitrust laws.

20. Summarize the essence of the **Clayton Act**, being sure to define **interlocking directorships** and **tying arrangements** in your response.

21. Define three of the following types of **antitrust violations: horizontal division of markets, vertical restraint on distribution, group boycotts, tying agreements, reciprocal dealing agreements, exclusive dealing agreements**, and **joint ventures**.

22. Distinguish among the following terms: **merger, horizontal merger, vertical merger**, and **conglomerate merger**.

23. What does the **Federal Trade Commission Act** do, and what does the **Robinson-Patman Act** do? Explain **unfairness** in your response.

24. What is the essence of the **Hart-Scott-Rodino FTC Improvements Act**, and in your response explain the concept of **parens patriae**.

25. List the four primary **antitrust tools** used by government.

26. Distinguish between **horizontal price fixing** and **vertical price fixing**.

Useful Resources for Consumers

Council on Economic Priories
30 Irving Place
New York, NY 10003
212-420-1133

National Advertising Division
Council of the Better Business Bureaus
845 Third Avenue
New York, NY 10022
212-754-1320

National Association of State Utility Consumer Advocates
1133 15th Street, NW, Suite 575
Washington, DC 20005
202-727-3908

"What Do You Think" Questions

1. Imagine a **market-driven economy** in which businesses did not practice effective **self-regulation**. What would the economic marketplace look like in those circumstances? In your response, be sure to comment on the **role of government**, the **quality of life** for citizens, and the **consumer interest**.

2. Creating **external benefits** are a vital function of government. List ten examples of external benefits important to you.

3. Examine the list of a number of **things that government does right** and select two that are important to you. Tell why you think it was important for government to expend national effort on those topics.

4. Governments seek to achieve particular **social goals**. Given the list of six **government goals**, the achievement of which affects the **consumer interest** in a positive manner, why can't government alone be responsible for looking out for the consumer interest? (You may need to briefly review Chapter 1 to fully respond to this question.)

5. Would just having knowledge about the numerous federal **antitrust laws** prevent businesses from doing harm to consumers? Why or why not?

Chapter 10

Government Regulation of Consumer Interests

OBJECTIVES

After reading this chapter, you should be able to

1. Explain the value, importance, and role of special-interest groups in affecting governmental decision making.

2. Explain how the governments regulate the marketplace to benefit consumers.

3. Understand the powers of the Federal Trade Commission.

4. Discuss the pluses and minuses of governments using benefit-cost analysis to make decisions to help protect consumers.

5. Understanding some of the pluses and minuses of economic deregulation to consumers.

A national consensus now exists that products should be safe, the environment should be protected, and that the government should oversee businesses to assure a better economic marketplace. Significant government commitments have occurred over the past thirty years to regulate the economic marketplace to benefit consumers. Consumers are now an important special-interest group in American society. In seeking to counterbalance the power of sellers in the marketplace, consumers have regularly sought assistance from government. A myriad of laws and regulations now exists. Understanding the effects of government regulation on the consumers is vital to citizens concerned about protecting their interests.

This chapter begins with an examination of the role of special-interest groups, including consumers. Since government takes so many actions to regulate the consumer interest, the chapter also overviews efforts of federal, state and local governments to regulate the economic marketplace to benefit consumers. Then the powers of the Federal Trade Commission, the nation's premier federal consumer protection agency, are explained. Next, the benefits and costs of government regulation are analyzed. Finally, the popular concept of deregulation is examined in view of pluses and minuses for consumers.

U.S. Government Goals and the Consumer Interest

The U.S. government seeks to achieve a number of social and economic goals that specifically pertain to consumer satisfaction in the marketplace.

Goal: A Free and Competitive Economic Marketplace

Government regulates aspects of the American economy in an effort to achieve the deeply held American goal to restrict undue concentrations of economic power. Hence, we have a number of federal and state antitrust laws. Theoretically, competition in every industry in America and throughout the economy has two virtues: (1) competition stimulates initiative and productive energy, and (2) competition results in minimum prices to consumers. Americans value competition because, as Professor Donna Iams of the University of Arizona states, "it has been shown (not assumed) that the absence of competition in the market will result in consumers not only paying higher prices, but also having less (or no) choice and experiencing a loss of consumer sovereignty in that product market."

Goal: To Promote Public Well-being and Safety

A major function of government is to promote public well-being and safety. Numerous government regulations exist to help in this endeavor: pure food and drug laws, product safety standards, environmental standards, industrial safety standards, consumer protection regulations, equal opportunity laws, and fair labor practices laws. A variety of federal, state, and local government agencies administer appropriate laws and regulations in these areas. At the federal level, such agencies exist as the Food and Drug Administration, the Consumer Product Safety Commission, the National Highway Traffic

Safety Administration, the Department of Agriculture, the National Institute of Standards and Technology in the Department of Commerce, the Office of Consumer Affairs, and the Environmental Protection Agency. State and local governments usually have departments for food and agriculture, weights and measures, labor practices, and consumer affairs.

Goal: To Demand Adequate Information for Consumers

Government urges a competitive market by regulating the provision of adequate information to consumers. Good examples include care labels attached to clothing and nutritional labels on processed foods. With such information, consumers can make better decisions. The government itself sometimes provides consumers with such information. Pamphlets provided by the U.S. Department of Agriculture's Cooperative Extension Service are examples.

Goal: To Set Uniform Standards

Another way government encourages fair markets is by setting uniform standards. For example, food products such as catsup, mayonnaise, and mustard must be manufactured according to minimum content standards, and lawn mowers must be built to meet certain safety standards.

Goal: To Protect Consumers from Economic Frauds

Government also tries to promote a fair marketplace by protecting consumers from economic frauds. If frauds against consumers are allowed to continue, two bad things occur: (1) they disadvantage consumers, and (2) they give an unfair advantage to particular sellers.

Fraud is a deliberate deception practiced in order to secure an unfair or unlawful gain or advantage where the seller intentionally misleads the buyer. Most deceptive practices are considered fraudulent and are against the law. Another matter entirely is that of consumer **ripoffs**. These are unfair acts of exploitation in the marketplace, most often the charging of high prices and/or permitting no recourse for consumers caught in unfavorable situations. Selling a used car worth $4000 for $6000 is a ripoff; persuading someone to purchase $60 worth of unneeded magazines is not illegal; encouraging a person to "buy now because the price may go up tomorrow"—even when the seller knows the price is not scheduled to rise—is a traditional and broadly accepted sales pitch. Ripoffs against consumers are unfair because you get little for your money, but they are not illegal. Immoral perhaps, but not illegal. Most consumer protection laws and regulations, including fraud statutes, are preventive in nature; they generally afford recourse only after a substantial loss has occurred.

Goal: To Provide Sources of Redress

Competition is also promoted when government helps consumers get **redress**. This means to set right, to remedy, or to rectify. A more fair and competitive marketplace is ensured when companies that make dishonest claims or sell faulty products are forced by government to settle the complaints of consumers fairly. A **consumer complaint** is an allegation by or on behalf of an individual, group of individuals, or other entity that a particular act or practice is unfair or deceptive or is in violation of a law or regulation.

CONSUMER UPDATE:
Recent Government Efforts to Protect Consumers

- **Shell Oil Company** and **Hoechst Celanese Corporation**—A $950 class action lawsuit forces the companies to reimburse homeowners for property damage from polybutylene water pipes that burst or leaked.
- **Egglands Best**—The FTC (in addition to several states) charges the company with false and misleading advertising that its eggs cause no increase in serum cholesterol.
- **Budget Rent A Car**—Paid $75,000 to settle FTC allegations that the company deceptively failed to disclose potential charges for the cost of auto repairs imposed on consumers who had purchased their loss damage waiver insurance.
- **Mrs. Fields**—Settled FTC charges that advertising and promotional materials touting a cookie line as "low fat" were false and misleading.
- **Ruta Lee**—Settled FTC complaints that on Home Shopping Club programming she made unsubstantiated claims for three vitamin sprays and a stop-smoking spray.
- **American Institute for Research and Development**—FTC alleges that the company has been running a deceptive invention-promotion scheme for 20 years.

Consumers Often Gain When Government Regulates to Pursue the Public Interest

In the public interest, but in the name of consumer protection, government attempts to prevent various objectionable practices where competitive forces may not be sufficient to protect buyers. In such instances, government promotes a rebalancing of the bargaining power between buyers and sellers. For example, credit laws require disclosure of interest rate and other cost information to help buyers make more informed choices in the marketplace. In a similar manner, government creates regulations when consumers are unable to adequately evaluate products, such as minimum standards for homeowner's insurance, long-term health care policies, prescription drugs, and food safety. Sellers are also prohibited by law from inserting particularly unscrupulous, excessively one-sided clauses in contracts, which can be described as **unconscionable**.

Government also creates regulations because markets cannot possibly offer the full range of choices that an informed public needs. In theory, for example, consumers should be able to decide how far apart they want the slats in a baby crib, or whether they want to pay an extra $5 to fly on an airplane with a special safety device, or if they want to eat a vegetable that has been sprayed with a cancer-causing chemical that might cause 5 cancers per million people. In reality, it would be horribly expensive, if not impossible, to provide sufficient information to consumers that would allow them to make intelligent choices on such matters. Thus, we have public health and safety regulations.

Governments often go about the regulatory process first by suggesting that businesses voluntarily provide useful information for consumers. Should this not work, government usually increases its efforts to regulate the specific kinds of information provided by businesses. If the public interest is still not being satisfied, i.e., market failure is occurring, government simply tells the businesses what to do or not to do. This is how regulators often go about resolving consumer problems.

The Role of Special-Interest Groups

A **special-interest group** is a group of persons that attempts to influence the statutory, regulatory, economic, and political decisions of government as it appeals for special consideration for its particular concerns. The members of such groups usually have a common bond, such as occupation, industry, or interest. Sometimes they have professional staff working in the state capitals and in Washington, D.C. to look out for their interests.

Special-interest groups are a vital ingredient in the economy because they do have an effect on governmental decision making. They fund research studies, organize communications from people with similar views on topics, influence decision makers, and keep their special-interest members alerted to happenings that might affect them. When people complain about special-interest groups being too powerful, they usually are complaining about money buying too much access to the political process.

Lobbyists Are Important to Effective Government

Lobbyists are people who attempt to influence legislators and regulators to take a desired action, typically in favor of a special interest. They try to communicate the special interests of their group to government officials who might make decisions favorable or unfavorable to their constituency, whether it be tobacco, sugar, medicine, banking, or dairy farming. A **special-interest group** is any person or group that wants to be treated differently than the rest of the people by the government. More than 33,000 lobbyists are registered with the U.S. Senate, over 330 for each Senator.

The U.S. Supreme Court in the *Noerr* decision did not prohibit two or more persons from associating together for the legitimate purpose of trying to persuade government to take (or not take) particular actions that may be harmful to competitors. Thus, the lobbying actions of trade associations and other organizations are legal. Lobbying, therefore, is a constitutionally guaranteed process.

It is important for special-interest groups to have their views represented in government decision making because each has special concerns. After all affected groups have presented their views, elected officials and other government officials must consider what is best for all concerned. Decisions should always serve the public interest.

The U.S. sugar beet growers are naturally interested in staying in business. For this reason, they work to restrict the amount of sugar that can be imported. Lobbyists for the

American Medical Association would be interested in stopping any effort to place restrictions on physicians' fees, such as in Medicare or Medicaid programs. Similarly, a regulated Bell Telephone Company would be interested in encouraging legislation to continue its monopolistic position in the industry, as well as to permit it to compete with other companies in areas where they are presently prohibited (such as equipment manufacture and generation of information for transmission).

Lobbying is a useful input to the decisions made by government, because the people and companies most affected by such decisions provide a clear voice on how they might be affected. An important part of a special interest's influence may be to help finance campaign costs. **Political action committees (PACs)** are lobbying organizations that collect funds to support particular candidates. The best-funded PACs are those started by corporations that solicit money from employees. Millions of dollars are then given to candidates who, when elected, may remember the source of their campaign funds. Campaign contributions do "buy access" to the politicians. Spending time and money getting to know legislators is important to lobbyists so they will have access when the time comes to earnestly talk about an issue. Businesses and business political action committees enjoy a certain degree of power over politicians, primarily through their money, expertise, and control of information.

There is nothing bad about the concept of lobbying, although the general public does have a negative impression of the process, probably because of the millions of dollars in PAC money, some of which is handed out on the floor of the Congress. Satirist P. J. O'Rourke observes that, "When buying and selling are controlled by legislation, the first things to be bought and sold are legislators."

Political Action Committees Make Big Contributions

Congress continues to find it difficult to tighten the laws governing how campaign money is raised and spent on elections. Reelection rates remain well above 90 percent. The political action committees that gave the most money to U.S. House members over the past decade included the National Association of Realtors, the American Medical Association, the National Education Association, the International Brotherhood of Teamsters, and the United Auto Workers.

While personal contributions to political action committees are limited in amount, currently $10,000 to a candidate, contributors can make unlimited donations to **soft money political action committees**. These are PACs that have "no consultation" with the campaign. Contributions can be made to the accounts established by state political parties (not federal) which similarly avoid the federally mandated limits for political contributions. Examples include "Presidential Dinner" and various accounts established by the Republican National Committee and the Democratic National Committee. The biggest soft money contributors over the past decade include Archer Daniels Midland, American Financial Corporation, Atlantic Richfield, United Steelworkers of America, and National Education Association. Watching politicians raise millions and millions of dollars from wealthy individuals for every campaign contributes to their unsavory image. Only when legislators stop having to raise thousands of dollars every day will they be freed from the stigma of corruption.

Many special-interest groups have lobbyists. Local governments (e.g., counties, townships, cities) often create groups to look out for their interests in the state legislature. Similarly, state governments have lobbyists working in Washington to protect their interests, since the federal government sometimes tries to usurp their rights and impose new programs on the states.

Consumers Also Have Lobbying Organizations

Consumers also have lobbying organizations, and the following are some of many that have offices located in Washington. The National Consumers League (NCL), the nation's oldest consumer organization, promotes the interests of consumers and workers and has 2000 organization and individual members. The Consumer Federation of America (CFA) is a federation of 240 national, state, and local consumer organizations that advances pro-consumer policy before the U.S. Congress, the executive branch, federal regulatory agencies, and the courts. Consumers Union of the United States publishes *Consumer Reports*, an informative testing magazine subscribed to by 5 million consumers, and it lobbies on national and state consumer issues. U.S. Public Interest Research Group is a group of professionals that focuses on issues of concern to public interest research groups (PIRGs), organizations existing in several states that were inspired by Ralph Nader. Bankcard Holders of America has 100,000 members, and it educates consumers on the wise use of credit and testifies on consumer-credit issues before federal and state legislative and regulatory bodies.

Public Voice for Food and Health Policy sponsors a yearly food policy conference with the supermarket industry and lobbies on food and health issues. Public Citizen is an organization with 80,000 members that works for consumer justice and citizen empowerment, particularly on consumer and environmental issues. Congress Watch is funded by Public Citizen and is the legislative advocacy arm of that organization. Common Cause is a nonpartisan organization primarily interested in accountability and reform in public affairs. The Center for the Study of Responsive Law is an organization inspired by Ralph Nader that frequently litigates against the federal government on behalf of the consumer interest and financially supports a network of public and consumer interest organizations, such as Bank Watch.

The National Coalition for Consumer Education (NCCE), based in New Jersey, is a countrywide network of individuals interested in promoting consumer education and an awareness of important consumer issues. The National Institute for Consumer Education (NICE) acts as a clearinghouse for consumer education. The Michigan-based group lobbies on the need for consumer education in the schools. The International Organization of Consumers Unions (IOCU), through its central office in The Netherlands, promotes cooperation among consumer organizations around the world in the areas of consumer education, information, protection, research, and testing.

People who work professionally in the consumer affairs field include corporate consumer affairs representatives, consumer reporters, government consumer affairs officials, and consumer academics. While each has somewhat different goals, they all try to represent both the consumer interest as well as their special-interest organization.

"Neg-Reg": A New Form of Regulation

A relatively new form of regulation is being increasingly used in the United States. **Neg-Reg** is a term describing a form of regulatory negotiation. After much study, in 1982 the Administrative Conference of the United States approved regulatory negotiation at the federal level. Neg-reg was codified in the Negotiated Rulemaking Act of 1990.

Under neg-reg, the participants to a regulatory proposal—government regulators, business lobbyists, consumer spokespersons, whomever—get together face-to-face as a committee which is broadly representative of all concerned parties and work with a skilled mediator. They work in public meetings (unlike more traditional rule writing) to try to develop a compromise satisfactory to all, including the regulatory agency. The final agreement often includes promises to refrain from filing lawsuits to stop the compromise from becoming reality. Once agreed upon—and this is often a short-term process—the proposed rule or regulation is published in the *Federal Register* for comments as per usual procedures. Critics can still go to court should they desire, but most do not because courts tend not to intervene on limited grounds. Also, litigation is costly and time consuming.

Neg-reg avoids some of the biggest regulatory pitfalls: delay, bickering, politicizing the issue, and impasse. About 55 proposals have used the process. The Environmental Protection Agency is the biggest neg-reg practitioner.

A dangerous new form of anti-consumer "partnership" in rulemaking recently occurred in the Republican Congress when business lobbyists were allowed to conduct briefings for congressional staff while regulatory reform legislation was being drafted. The lobbyists offered suggested specific language changes during the congressional staff meetings while no other persons were allowed to participate. A congressional ethics committee is investigating.

How Government Regulates to Benefit Consumers

Consumer protection, according to Sylvia Lane, is the prevention of physical or economic disadvantage or damage to the buyers and/or users of goods and services for personal or household use.[1] Accordingly, consumer protection is a public good and can only be brought about in optimal conditions by government actions. Thus, all government consumer protection is paternalistic.

Regulation of the marketplace—including many aspects of the consumer interest—is a fundamental responsibility of government. General economic and legal policies on regulating the U.S. marketplace are determined by the legislative, executive and judicial decisions of federal, state and local governments. The actual responsibility for carrying out the policies is given to administrative agencies of the executive branch. Each agency then decides which problems within its domain are most important and goes about regulating them.

Administrative Agencies: The "Fourth" Branch of Government

Administrative agencies are governmental bodies other than courts or legislatures that have the legal power to take actions affecting the rights of private individuals and organizations. Administrative agencies are created by enabling legislation specifying the

---

[1]As cited in Pestoff, V. A. (1988). Exit, Voice, and Collective Action in Swedish Consumer Policy, *Journal of Consumer Policy*, 11, 1-27.

name, composition, and powers of the agency. For example, the U.S. Congress has created both the Federal Trade Commission and Consumer Product Safety Commission and has delegated certain powers to those agencies. Also, most state and local legislators have created a number of administrative agencies, such as public utility commissions, banking and insurance departments, and weights and measures offices. These agencies act as the "fourth branch of government" and as such are subject to providing the basic constitutional guarantees of due process, equal protection, and freedom of speech. The enabling legislation for each agency (such as the 1914 Federal Trade Commission Act) contains fairly specific guidelines and standards limiting the exercise of agency discretion.

Legislatures are concerned with broad solutions to problems, and they pass laws to accomplish society's goals. Then regulatory power is delegated to administrative agencies because the legislature does not have the high level of expertise nor the amount of time required to deal with the many technical matters. The legislature, be it the U.S. Congress or a state General Assembly, performs an **oversight function** by occasionally holding hearings and reviewing the quality of efforts of each agency. Also, it is normal that laws and regulations are sometimes revised and amended as legislators and regulators respond to the various interest groups in society.

Because the U.S. Constitution establishes a separation of powers doctrine, the federal government is responsible for certain activities (such as national defense) and the states are responsible for other interests (such as education). In the area of commerce or trade, the responsibilities of regulation are also divided. The **commerce clause** of the Constitution provides the power for Congress to pass consumer protection laws, since it authorizes the federal government to regulate interstate commerce and prohibits states from passing laws that seriously hamper interstate or foreign trade. As a result, the federal government traditionally steps in to regulate **interstate commerce** (trade across state boundaries) rather than **intrastate commerce** (trade within state boundaries). In today's enormous and complex marketplace, sales of most goods go across state lines and affect interstate commerce. Consequently, many activities that are purely intrastate can be regulated to some extent by the federal government, particularly when such trade has a *substantial effect* on interstate commerce.

The **supremacy clause** of the Constitution makes federal law the law of the land unless Congress says otherwise. Thus, federal laws are supreme over conflicting state enactments. This ensures that when Congress does pass legislation or regulatory agencies make rules, such legislation and rules preempt or supersede conflicting state laws. This renders the states powerless to act except in ways directly mandated by the federal government. This is also called the doctrine of **preemption**. Consequently, the federal government has the major role in determining how consumer protection responsibilities are divided between the federal and state governments. In so doing, the federal government generally maintains a cooperative attitude with the states as it seeks to set minimum national consumer protection standards. Federal administrative agencies have the same power.

If Congress does not have legislation in a particular area or field of regulation, then states are free to pass laws, assuming that they do not unduly burden interstate commerce. The commerce clause of the Constitution allows the federal government to strike down various state laws when they conflict with each other and place a burden on interstate commerce. Key to the commerce clause is the necessity to keep the state borders open to commerce. In general, courts are reluctant to strike down state and local consumer protection laws and regulations that serve a legitimate state purpose and protect the consumer unless the burdens on interstate commerce are excessive. However, the commerce clause often discourages states from passing more stringent laws than the federal government. An opponent of a particular consumer protection effort would seek to pass a carefully worded federal law with weak standards because it would preempt any stronger state laws. (This is the approach followed by supporters of a federal product liability law, discussed in Chapter 16.)

Executive (Dependent) and Independent Agencies

Over 80 federal regulatory agencies exist. They are headed either by a single administrator or by a **collegial group**, which is a form of administration where authority is shared among colleagues, often five to seven commissioners.

Most regulatory agencies are considered to be **executive (dependent) agencies**, which means that their power resides within the executive office or within the executive departments. At the federal government level, administrative agencies reside within the Executive Office of the President; at the state level, such agencies reside within the office of the governor. Such a location suggests that the regulatory agency is extremely dependent on the executive branch of government, relying on the executive office for its operational philosophy and budget. Examples at the federal level include the Office of Management and Budget (OMB), the Department of Energy (DOE), the National Highway Traffic and Safety Administration (NHTSA), the U.S. Office of Consumer Affairs (USOCA), the Food and Drug Administration (FDA), and a state Department of Agriculture. Such agency heads are appointed by and serve at the pleasure of the President.

Other regulatory agencies are called **independent agencies**. These are politically autonomous agencies that are basically self-governing, since they are accountable directly to the legislature and are somewhat free from the influence, guidance, and control of the executive branch of government. The need for regulatory independence is great because the powers of independent agencies are great. Although the leadership positions of independent agencies at the federal level are appointed by the President, typically the terms are arranged in alternating and overlapping time periods so that one President cannot appoint an entire board. The terms of office are usually 5 to 7 years. Administrators must be approved by Congress, and no more than a simple majority may be from one political party.

Independent agencies are open to some executive influence because members of the President's staff frequently attempt to persuade administrators to adopt the President's position on key matters. Examples of independent agencies include the Consumer Product Safety Commission, the Federal Trade Commission, the Board of Governors of the Federal Reserve System, the U.S. Postal Service, the Securities and Exchange Commission, and a state public utility commission.

Powers of Regulatory Agencies

Each regulatory agency exists and operates according to the enabling legal mandate of a specific statutory law. The agency administers the particular powers given under the statute that created the agency, as well as any authorities provided in other statutes. For example, the Federal Trade Commission administers the Federal Trade Commission Act, the Magnuson-Moss Warranty Act, and several other laws.

Regulatory agencies generally have one, two, or three broad discretionary powers: investigative, quasi-legislative, and quasi-judicial powers.

Investigative Power

Investigative power means the legal ability to gain information about private practices and activities that will permit detection and prosecution of regulatory violations. The two most important and most intrusive investigatory powers are subpoenas and search and seizure orders. **Subpoenas** are legal orders that can compel unwilling witnesses to appear and testify at agency hearings and can compel the production of most types of documentary evidence, such as office memoranda and accounting records. **Search and seizure orders** are legal orders that permit lawful entry of private property, such as a home, an office, or a factory, in an attempt to gather information. For example, both the Internal Revenue Service and Food and Drug Administration have the legal authority to seek the truth about fraudulent claims, perhaps on tax deductions or prescription drug testing.

Quasi-legislative Power: Rulemaking Authority

Quasi-legislative power means the authority to make rules and regulations to carry out an agency's primary legal mandates. A **rule** is defined by the federal Administrative Procedure Act (APA) as "an agency statement of general or particular applicability and future effect designed to complement, interpret, or prescribe law or policy." Agency actions must be taken in accordance with the constraints of the APA, passed in 1946 in an attempt to standardize federal agency procedures. All federal agency rules, whether they are procedural, interpretative, or legislative, are compiled and published in the *Code of Federal Regulations*. Similar standards and guidelines exist in all states.

A **trade regulation rule** is a legally written declaration that has the force and effect of law covering entire industries throughout the country that defines with greater specificity the acts and practices that the agency considers appropriate. For example, in its concern about unfair or deceptive practices, the Federal Trade Commission has a trade regulation rule requiring that all gasoline retailers post octane ratings on gas pumps. Thus, an agency with quasi-legislative powers acts like a legislative body. Using such powers granted by the Congress, the regulatory agency can regulate business practices. For example, the National Highway Traffic and Safety Administration (NHTSA) operates under its original legal mandate of 1966, and since then it has issued more than 100 safety rules and regulations for vehicles. Some results of NHTSA regulations include the requirements that automobile windshields be made of safety glass and that new cars have a third brake light in the rear window.

Informal Rulemaking

Note that rules can sometimes be written by agencies based on their interpretation of existing law, although rule-making efforts are typically made through explicit statutory law. Rule-making by various agencies can be done informally or formally by administrative agencies, depending on their enabling legislation. **Informal rule-making** involves publication of the proposed regulation in the *Federal Register* of a "Notice of Proposed Rule-Making," which provides reasons for the action, as well as a time and place for proceedings to be held by the agency. This is followed by a comment period, during which interested parties can submit their views, and then by publication of the final rule in the *Federal Register*. Occasionally, *all* proposed federal regulations are put into a compendium called *Unified Agenda of Federal Regulations*, published in the *Federal Register*.

Formal Rulemaking

After an investigation, the FTC staff may find evidence of unfair or deceptive practices in an entire industry and recommend that the Commission begin a **formal rulemaking proceeding.** If the recommendation is accepted, a "Notice of Proposed Rulemaking" is published in the *Federal Register* stating the time and place of the hearings, the issues to be considered, and instructions to groups or individuals who want to participate. Throughout the rulemaking proceeding, the public will have opportunities to attend the hearings and file written comments. The Commission will consider these comments along with the entire rulemaking record—the hearing testimony, the staff reports, and the Presiding Officer's report—before deciding whether to accept, reject, or modify the proposed rule.

This is sometimes called **on-the-record rule-making** for two reasons: (1) because the process provides procedures designed to afford interested parties greater opportunities to make their views known than that afforded by informal rule-making, and (2) the Commission's final rule must be based upon the information contained in the record. Formal rule-making has the appearances of a trial, and it is not unusual for a case to drag on for 5 or 10 years before a rule becomes effective. An FTC rule may be challenged in any of the U.S. Courts of Appeals.

Quasi-Judicial Power

Violators of most consumer protection laws, rules, or regulations may suffer one or two penalties: civil penalties and/or court-ordered redress for economic injuries. Forms of redress include recision or reformation of contracts, refund of money, return of property, or the payment of compensatory damages. Few consumer protection statutes call for criminal sanctions.

Quasi-judicial (or **adjudicatory**) **power** is the authority of a regulatory agency to bring charges and prosecute if it suspects that its laws, rules, or regulations have been violated, and to hear civil and criminal cases for legal and equitable relief. The agency can render a judicial decision on such matters as well. Most regulatory agencies have quasi-judicial powers because they are needed to prosecute violators.

The administrative adjudicatory process normally begins with a complaint filed by the agency against a respondent, typically a business. The respondent is entitled to a formal hearing before the agency, at which the respondent may be cross-examined, may be represented by legal counsel, may confront and cross-examine witnesses, and may present evidence of his or her own. No juries are used in administrative proceedings, and the case is usually heard by an agency employee called an **administrative law judge (ALJ)** who legally is charged with the responsibility to be impartial and act in an independent manner during all proceedings. Administrative law judges are usually separated organizationally from an agency's investigative and prosecutorial functions. After hearing the evidence, the administrative law judge renders a decision stating his or her findings of fact and conclusions of law and imposes whatever penalty deemed appropriate within the parameters established by enabling legislation (such as a fine or a cease and desist order). Appeals are reviewed by the top administrator or commissioners of the administrative agency.

For example, the National Highway Traffic and Safety Administration (NHTSA) remains alert to instances of unsafe vehicles and has a telephone hotline to receive complaints. NHTSA has the power to investigate such cases and seek corrective action from manufacturers when appropriate. It also can prosecute, if necessary, willful violations of its regulations. Should a NHTSA administrative law judge assess a fine on an automobile manufacturer, for example, for building unsafe vehicles, that manufacturer can appeal the decision to the head of the agency. After review, should the agency head still decide against the manufacturer, the case can be formally appealed to the traditional court system. Federal cases go to federal courts and state cases may be appealed to state courts.

Note that the Federal Trade Commission is the government's key organization designed to keep the American marketplace free and fair. In 1986, the U.S. Supreme Court broadened the power of the FTC by allowing it to regulate anticompetitive practices that are not covered specifically in the various antitrust statutes. The FTC can write regulations intended to carry out the meaning of the Federal Trade Commission Act, and it can assess civil penalties. At the state level, the attorney general is the chief legal officer, and that person often works in conjunction with the state Office of Consumer Affairs when enforcing consumer protection statutes and regulations.

Some Regulatory Agencies Have the Powers of All Three Branches of Government

Note that agencies with both quasi-judicial and quasi-legislative power have the authorities of all three branches of government. Such an agency can write its own regulations that have the force and effect of law, investigate problems and possible violations of the agency's legal statutes and regulations, bring charges against, and prosecute alleged violators, and adjudicate individual cases by conducting a hearing where an administrative law judge decides on the guilt or innocence of the person or company involved, as well as assess damages and criminal penalties. Such agencies also serve as an "appeals court," because a losing defendant can appeal a judgment to the agency's commissioners or administrator.

If that judgment is still negative, the case may be appealed outside the regulatory framework directly to the appropriate U.S. District Court or U.S. Court of Appeals or appropriate state court. The loser generally has the right to judicial review. Other affected parties may or may not have such a right depending on their **standing to sue**, that is, whether or not they are an aggrieved party whose interests have been substantially affected in the challenged action. In general, the courts are unlikely to overrule an agency decision unless the agency has grossly erred in its interpretation of a statute or failed to follow proper procedures.

How States and Local Governments Protect Consumers

While numerous consumer protection regulations are crucial responsibilities of the federal government, important regulatory powers and obligations are accepted by state and local governments. Each of the nation's 50 states has its own constitution based on

---

Consumers Sometimes Lack "Standing" to Sue

The U.S. Supreme Court's *Illinois Brick Company* decision prohibits consumers from suing price fixers in federal court unless they are *directly* affected. Thus, only the direct purchaser, such as the middleman or wholesaler, affected by a manufacturer's price fixing can sue. The U.S. Supreme Court in 1989 upheld *state* antitrust laws allowing those indirectly injured by illegal price fixing, such as consumers, to sue for damages in state courts.

---

democratic principles that are consistent with the U.S. Constitution and guides the governance of citizens. Many powers are reserved in the U.S. Constitution for the federal government, including coining money, regulating commerce with foreign nations, maintaining uniform laws on bankruptcies, establishing post offices, and providing for the national defense. Other powers are reserved to the states, such as traffic safety, weights and measures, regulation of utility rates, inspection of meat plants and restaurants, regulation of consumer sales and contracts, and licensing and registration of a number of trades and professions. Each state constitution gives it inherent police powers to regulate for the health, safety, welfare, and morals of its citizens, and this is the source of state and local consumer protection laws and regulations.

Although states have wide latitude in the direction of their regulatory efforts, note that in situations where state laws and regulations conflict with those at the federal level, the latter usually prevail. State enforcement of laws and regulations supplements that at the federal level, and since states are closer to the consumer problems, they often provide more effective consumer protection.

All states have similar types of laws governing business and consumer transactions. One group of statutes is called the **Uniform Commercial Code (UCC)**, and it regulates most legal contracts. All states also have a set of statutes designed to prevent unfair and deceptive sales practices applicable to consumer transactions. The latter laws are similar to the federal statutes enforced by the Federal Trade Commission, which prohibit "unfair competition and unfair or deceptive acts or practices." Most such state laws empower a state agency, usually the attorney general's office, to enforce provisions of the statute by conducting investigations, commencing actions for civil penalties, seeking injunctions, ordering consumer redress, and issuing rules. An **injunction** is a court order issued by a judge ordering a person or firm not to do a certain act.

States Follow One of Four Legal Approaches

State consumer protection laws follow one of four approaches. First, the strongest and most common statute is a **"little FTC act"** modeled on the **Uniform Trade Practices and Consumer Protection Law**. Such laws broadly prohibit unfair methods of competition and unfair or deceptive acts or practices, and generally empower both the attorney general and individual consumers with the right to sue violators. Second, most other state statutes are modeled after the **Uniform Deceptive Trade Practices Act,** which more narrowly prohibits 11 specific deceptive trade practices and forbids "any other conduct which similarly creates a likelihood of confusion or misunderstanding." This act typically does not give special powers to the attorney general, and limits consumer remedies to injunctions.

CONSUMER UPDATE:
State Laws Limit the Sale of Contact Lens

Four states (CA, NM, NE, and VA) have state laws that prohibit the sale of replacement contact lenses as merchandise being sold from a retail business other than one operated by a physician, an optometrist, or an optician. In the other 46 states, consumers can purchase contact lens from supermarkets, drugstores, and mail-order outlets.[1] The price runs about $120 to $130 in the states prohibiting competition and less than $80 from alternative retail providers in the other states. Most wearers of soft contact lens need replacements every six months or so.

The question is, "Are the four states in the forefront of protecting the health of consumers or are they restricting competition unnecessarily?" Under the Parker doctrine, the Supreme Court held that if there is enough state involvement in a business or profession, those businesses and professions are immune from federal antitrust laws for federalism reasons.

Sixteen states (AL, AZ, CO, DE, FL, ME, NE, NJ, NY, NC, OH, OR, SD, TX, VT, and VA) require optometrists to hand over prescriptions to consumers after they have been fitted with a first pair of lenses. This permits comparison shopping.

---

[1] The largest firm is Lens Express (800-666-5367).

Third, several states have **consumer fraud acts** that focus on consumer issues as they prohibit deceptive or unconscionable acts or practices and frauds, but do not prohibit unfair competition. Fourth, a few states have a **uniform consumer sales practices act**, which applies only to consumer transactions as it prohibits deceptive and unconscionable practices. In most states, the consumer protection statute specifies that the court look to Federal Trade Commission cases and regulations for guidance in interpreting the state statutes.

Typical Legal Provisions in All States

Typically, state laws protect consumers against unfair and deceptive acts or practices, unfair methods of competition, and unconscionable acts and practices. **Unconscionability** is a legal doctrine having to do with unscrupulousness under which the court may invalidate an agreement, or a portion of it, if it is so one-sided as to be unreasonable. The essence of unconscionability is to prevent oppression and unfair surprise, particularly in unfair contracts and inflated prices. For example, a Connecticut court voided a contract where a consumer agreed under a "rent to own" contract to pay $1268 for a television set that sold at retail for $499. (This topic is examined in Chapter 3.) States with "little FTC acts" add a powerful tool in consumer protection because they permit consumers themselves, in effect, to become "private" attorneys general. In some states, consumer-plaintiffs are awarded attorneys fees in successful lawsuits.

State Attorneys General and Consumer Problems

The decade of the 1980s witnessed a retreat by the federal government from the dominant role it established in consumer protection during the 1960s and 1970s. During the 1980s, both the U.S. Congress and Federal Trade Commission took a less proactive role in consumer issues because the Reagan administration attempted to reduce the role of the federal government in the economy. Critics suggest that during the Reagan-Bush years the posture of the federal government was to let consumers protect themselves in the marketplace. President Bill Clinton has revitalized the federal government's responsibility to consumers.

During the 1980s, the states stepped into the void left by the federal government and these efforts advanced the interests of consumers greatly. In particular, many state laws to protect consumers were strengthened. In addition, numerous state attorney generals have been vigorously filing lawsuits to protect consumer-citizens. For example, over 40 states passed "lemon laws" to protect new car buyers who purchase vehicles that cannot be repaired satisfactorily. Also, when the Federal Trade Commission did not take action, the Texas attorney general sued Kraft for misleading advertising of Cheese Whiz because Kraft called it "real cheese." Several states, including California and New York, sued McDonald's for falsely advertising the high-caloric Chicken McNuggets as a "lean meal." The primary informal coordinating mechanism for state enforcement authorities is the National Association of Attorneys General (NAAG).

Office of Consumer Affairs

Each state has executive, legislative, and judicial branches of government. In addition, certain powers are reserved for the state government, while others are given to local governments, such as counties, cities, and municipalities. In the area of consumer protection, for example, each state typically has a state office of consumer affairs (OCA) in the executive branch, located either in the attorney general's office or in the governor's office, to handle inquiries and complaints about possible violations of state laws. Most OCAs have a telephone hotline to receive complaints. In descending order, the most common complaints to OCAs usually involve automobile sales, automobile service and repair, mail order, and credit.

In addition to a central Office of Consumer Affairs in the capital city, many states also have a network of OCAs located throughout the state. At the local level, a number of individual cities and counties have their own OCA units that respond to violations of local statutes and regulations, as well as state laws. Most OCAs have the legal authority to investigate complaints and subpoena records and testimony.

Weights and Measures Offices

Almost everything consumers purchase is sold by weight and measures like volume, length, and count. In fact, government regulation of weights and measures was probably the first form of consumer protection many hundreds of years ago. **Weights and measures offices** work to protect consumers, businesses, and manufacturers from deceptive and unfair practices. They are generally located in state agriculture departments and consumer protection agencies. Each state has a weights and measures laboratory and staff to check the accuracy of equipment used in the marketplace, such as for gasoline, propane gas, and grocery store scanners. A **seal**, a device to prove authenticity, is usually put on the equipment to attest to the correctness of the accuracy, legal weight, quality or another standard.

Most states have representatives from the public who serve on various regulatory boards and commissions, such as the insurance, banking, and utility commissions and a beautician's licensing board. These are often called **public members** or **consumer watchdogs**. Such representatives are charged with presenting the consumer's voice on these industry-dominated boards and commissions, although concerns are often expressed as to whether or not the "public" members actually represent the public.

Deregulation and the Consumer Interest

Government in the United States has been seriously involved in economic regulation since establishment of the Interstate Commerce Commission in 1886. Over the following decades, government regulation of economic activities expanded, particularly during the Great Depression of the 1930s. Industries that became heavily regulated by government include electricity, gas, telephone service, trucking, railroads, buses, banking, and broadcast media.

The Backlash against Regulation

In the late 1970s, a number of forces came together to suggest that government regulations had gone too far. Consumers were bored, irritated, and sometimes enraged with child-proof aspirin bottles that adults had difficulty opening, automobile seat belts that were uncomfortable, and that the food product of the week that was going to "cause them cancer." The popular jokes was that the government was becoming our "national nanny." Factors such as inflation, changing demographics, and advancing technology also contributed to criticisms of government regulation.

Critics thought there was simply too much government regulation that was stifling individuals, the economy, and society as a whole. Other critics said that there was too much regulation without any sense of the consequences and little or no consideration given to the economic and other adverse impacts of the regulations. Also, excessive and inefficient regulation fuels inflation by adding costs and decreasing productivity. One executive observed that excessive regulation "slows growth in production and employment, impedes innovation and technological advancement, limits capital formation, reduces incentives for capital investment, and weakens the ability of U.S. companies to compete with foreign producers." Yet, at a time when most businesspeople were loudly protesting against government regulations, many of their number found that specific rules were to the advantage of their companies and they vigorously lobbied to maintain them. In 1978, Congress started deregulating in earnest by passing a number of new laws. The effort to deregulate is a movement toward a government policy of laissez-faire.

AN ECONOMIC FOCUS ON...The State Lottery: Monopoly and the Consumer Interest*

Prior to 1964, lotteries had been illegal for more than half a century. That year New Hampshire began the resurgence of lotteries as a legal form of gaming. Today, two-thirds of the states have **state-sponsored lotteries**. These are games of chance in which consumers buy instant scratch (daily winners), numbers (bets made on an unpredictable numeral), or lotto tickets (large jackpot that grows until there is a winner) for a low per unit price. Lotteries are visualized as an easy way to add to state revenues. A citizen referendum or legislative action is required to approve a lottery. Revenues are usually earmarked to fund priority needs (i.e., education, senior programs, capital projects), used to hold the line on tax increases, and/or used as a method to keep dollars at home (if neighboring states' lotteries were drawing home state dollars). A lottery is often viewed as a voluntary tax.

A state lottery is a monopoly. The state is the sole seller of the product (tickets) and has exclusive control over the product, its sale, and prizes awarded. The state operates the lotteries, does advertising and promotion, collects revenues, and appoints or elects the oversight board that reports to the state. Compare this to the public's popular perception of a monopoly, that of a public utility that is sole supplier of electricity or natural gas. A public utility has its own management, reports to stockholders, is scrutinized by a state public utility commission, and is open to questions by consumers if product delivery is not dependable, safe, or reasonably priced. Thus, many consumer safeguards are granted in the case of an essential good, such as energy produced by a monopoly. However, similar protections are not available to consumers who voluntarily purchase state lottery monopoly services.

In a lottery, the consumer buys a ticket from the state through a third-party vendor who is paid on the basis of the state's commission schedule. Both consumer and vendor must accept the state's rules to participate. A consumer's favorite game may change if the lottery officials decide revenue generation would be enhanced through a different package or a different product. New rules of sale may be imposed on vendors and consumers on a take-it-or-leave-it basis.

When the idea of consumer rights is applied to a state lottery, one could ask: What rights (to choice, to safety, to be informed, to be heard) do consumers have in most state lotteries?

As with any monopoly, *choice* is limited—the only lottery in town is the state's. Yes, other gaming opportunities exist but one cannot get a lottery ticket from a competitor. So the choice is to either accept the odds and pay-out offered by the state or not play.

Safety takes on a perspective different from the usual view of security from danger. In a state lottery, a consumer risks his or her dollars for very low odds at pay-out levels that are smaller than any other traditional type of gaming (i.e., slot machines, blackjack).

Another consumer right is to be *informed*. In lottery advertisements, how often are losers depicted? How many times has an advertisement stated that 98 percent of the tickets are losers? Have you ever seen an advertisement that indicates how many dollars (or percentage of gross revenues) are spent to operate and promote the lottery? How often is it made clear that the jackpot is paid out over 20 or more years and due to inflation loses actual purchasing power the whole time? Have you ever seen an advertisement reporting that the state is not paying out the full multi-million amount, but is instead purchasing an annuity for the winner that costs only a fraction of the stated prize amount?

Even if this information were available, would consumers understand it? Perhaps most important, does the state want consumers to understand crucial information about how a lottery functions? The answer is "no" because the objective of a state lottery is to maximize revenues and therefore ticket sales, not inform consumers. It is useful to ask: If consumers knew and understood how a lottery really works, what effect would this have on ticket sales?

Two consistent research findings are that lotteries are a regressive form of taxation and that revenues do not increase expenditures for the intended purpose. For example, if lottery revenues are earmarked for education, the lottery dollars replace rather than augment other funding. This occurs despite original purposes stated in the lottery referenda and/or campaigns to win support for the lottery.

As to being *heard*, citizens can appear before a utility commission to question services or rates. Similar hearings for lotteries generally do not exist. It is doubtful that lottery administrations are interested in consumer opinion about the different products other than those which sell more. Recognizing the vulnerability of some people to become compulsive gamblers, a few states have hotlines (funded with lottery money) that provide information and referrals related to overconsumption.

As a monopoly, are lotteries in the consumer interest? Would the consumer interest be better served if competition existed? Would the state's interest be better served with competition? Does the value of a voluntary tax, often labelled painless, outweigh the principles of competition? So far, the state's purpose of revenue generation has overshadowed attention to consumer rights. Lotteries are not in the consumer interest.

*Carole J. Makela, Professor, Colorado State University

The Concept of Deregulation

Deregulation is a catch-all term meaning increased competition, and it means different things to different people. To many it means to leave a market alone; to others it means removing restraints to competition. To some it means that firms are able to set prices based on market demand. To others it means lower costs and prices. To some it means getting the government off the backs of businesses through wholesale elimination of regulations. To still others it means increased problems for the public because no one is protecting their interests. Moreover, deregulation means that the public should rely primarily on competition and market forces to regulate the economy and the business firms within it.

Deregulation is often seen as anti-consumer and pro-business. Mark N. Cooper, research director of the Consumer Federation of America, observes that the fundamental elements of a deregulated market are "equal access, divestiture, local distribution companies aggressively working the competitive market, vigorous antitrust enforcement, and the removal of barriers to entry into the market."[2]

The effect of deregulation is the removal or reduction of the regulatory authority and active ties of government in an effort to perfect our present economic mechanisms. Techniques to deregulate include: (1) identifying and publicizing burdensome and inefficient laws and regulations, (2) amending or repealing laws and regulations, (3) **privatizing**, which involves relinquishing government control and turning responsibilities over to business, (4) reducing the budgets and the staffs of regulatory agencies, (5) imposing strict benefit-cost analysis reviews of proposed regulations, (6) imposing **sunset laws**, which are laws that provide for required periodic review and sometimes termination of laws and agencies unless their existence can be justified, and (7) appointing deregulatory-minded people to run the regulatory agencies.

For the most part, the process of deregulation has substantially increased the level of competition, lowered prices, and created more alternatives. For example, instead of earning interest rates on savings accounts established by the government, consumers like earning market interest rates. However, the effects of deregulation vary widely, sometimes hurt consumers, and often are anticompetitive. Experience also has shown that while deregulation may initially bring lower prices because of competition—and this is what sold the public on the idea in the first place—the resulting price war sometimes produces company bankruptcies. The industry shakeout that follows may bring increased concentration and leave prices as high or higher than before deregulation, such as has occurred in the airline industry. The negative effects of deregulation include discriminating against low-income consumers with higher prices, such as has occurred in the banking industry. Rural consumers are also forced to pay more as happened after the airline deregulation and is now occurring with local telephone company deregulation.

Increased choices for consumers because of deregulation have brought increased complexity. For example, many people are struggling with telephone bills from three companies, two different sets of telephone Yellow Pages, varying restrictions on airline tickets, and terms such as IRA, NOW account, and adjustable-rate mortgages. Also, it is very difficult to obtain reliable facts and prepurchase information about the costs and conditions of complex services, such as airline travel restrictions and effective interest

---

[2]Howell, J. W. (1983). Legislating Regulatory Reform (Council of Better Business Bureaus), p. 8.

rates on credit and savings accounts. Furthermore, deregulation has brought more risk into consumers' lives as old-line traditional companies, such as banks, airlines, telephone companies, and insurance companies either go bankrupt or get merged out of existence. In many instances, consumers do not even understand the implicit risks they are assuming.

Deregulation Has Critics, But It Will Continue

Critics of deregulation, such as Hobart Rowen of *The Washington Post*, observes that, "Some forms of economic regulation are necessary to protect the public interest in a way that Adam Smith cannot."[3] However, changing times and the Republican Congress are resulting in "defacto deregulation." This occurs when regulators lack the resources to fulfill their legal mandates, when regulators lack the money to enforce rules or conduct inspections, when regulators are very interested in compromising with the industries they regulate, and when regulators are ordered by Congress to undue or reverse some of their longstanding policies.

Regulation for the sake of regulation is an exercise in futility that inhibits innovation, competition, and economic growth. Regulations must be shaped not only by good intentions, but also by both technological and market imperatives, as well as adequate evidence that society's goals are being achieved.

We should recognize that regulatory structures cannot remain static. But, excess should not be rewarded either. The extremists who favor deregulation want sweeping changes in the way regulations are adopted and to cap the costs of regulation. One "slash and burn" proposal given strong support by the Republican Congress was to prohibit all new regulatory proposals from being adopted unless the cost of compliance with existing regulations was reduced by a similar amount. That would have halted the regulatory process, even for proposals that most everyone would agree would be in the national interest. "The public has tried deregulation and finds a great deal to dislike about it," says Consumer Federation of America's Mark Cooper.

Support remains strongest for environmental, health, and safety regulation. As the pendulum swings back and forth from deregulation toward reregulation, consumers will see stepped-up enforcement of existing rules and an increased willingness of government to intervene in the market to correct abuses. Congress often takes its lead from the states, and many recent efforts have been going on at the state level to better protect consumers.

The Powers of the Federal Trade Commission

The Federal Trade Commission (FTC) is the foremost federal consumer protection agency. It is responsible for preventing deceptive practices, false advertising, and unfair competition in the marketplace. It administers laws and regulations governing advertising, credit transactions, product warranties, and packaging and labeling.

Founded in 1914, it has a budget of over $80 million and a staff of 1400 to carry out its statutory duties. The FTC is directed by five commissioners appointed by the President

---

[3]Rowen, H. (1988, October 16). Airline Deregulation at 10: Did the Theory Fail? *The Washington Post*, p. H-10.

CONSUMER UPDATE:
Did Airline Deregulation Fail?

Deregulation has brought about an initial reduction in air fares, but after adjustments for inflation prices are higher today than 15 years ago. Further, airline pricing discriminates in favor of people using the heavily traveled routes. Prices are much higher for those going to and coming from small communities, if such communities have any flights at all. Many more people are flying today than a decade ago, and this has added to problems of congestion and concerns about safety, flight delays, mistreatment of customers, and lost luggage. Critics are calling for at least some government reregulation. Proponents of deregulation, including economist Murray Weidenbaum, argue that all economic reform must have transitional costs.[1]

[1]Weidenbaum, M. (December, 1987). The Benefits of Deregulation (Washington University Center for the Study of American Business), Contemporary Issue Series 25, 11.

---

for 7-year terms. Terms of office are staggered. Although the FTC does not investigate and take action to resolve individual complaints, it investigates and prosecutes when it receives a large number of complaints and/or suspects that substantial harm is occurring.

The FTC has a wide array of legal devices for ensuring compliance with statutes it administers. It seeks to ensure voluntary compliance whenever possible through **advisory opinions**, which are official FTC responses to inquiries by private parties, **industry guides**, which are FTC interpretations of the laws it administers, and trade regulation rules.

Quasi-Judicial Powers

When the FTC suspects a law or regulation has been violated, they have the quasi-judicial power to investigate, prosecute, and later make a final determination on the matter in an adjudicative proceeding before an FTC administrative law judge. Should the initial investigation show promise, a formal investigation is launched. Should the business not be willing to surrender any needed records, the FTC can use its subpoena power to require the respondent to surrender any needed records. The subpoena is a key investigative tool of the judiciary.

If the investigation of a business shows that a violation exists, the FTC frequently settles the case with a consent agreement or consent decree. When a business signs the agreement, it is not an admission of wrongdoing. Rather it is a promise by the firm and an agreement between the firm and the FTC that the firm will not do something specific in the future. Consent agreements always describe the practices that must not occur. Should the illegal practice continue in the future, the FTC has an easy time demonstrating violation of the consent agreement, in which case the firm will be found in contempt of court and fined.

Consent agreements can be very powerful tools in ensuring a fair marketplace. In some instances, the agreement might require the business to refund money to consumers or rescind or change contracts. Before consent agreements are final, however, the terms of the proposed agreement are published in the public record for comment by any interested party for 60 days. The final order, modified if needed, is then issued by the FTC. Settling cases with consent agreements saves the FTC the time and effort of having to fully prosecute cases. It also gets questionable practices stopped rather quickly. When a case is not settled with a voluntary consent agreement, a formal complaint of violation is issued by the FTC. In effect, the FTC prosecutes the case. A hearing is held before an administrative law judge who works for the FTC. Testimony and other evidence are presented in this court of law, and the judge hands down a decision that either the complaint be dismissed or that a formal cease and desist order be entered and then enforced with a consent decree.

The initial decision of an administrative law judge can be appealed to the five FTC commissioners, who can sustain, reverse, or amend the decision. The case can be further appealed through our federal court system to the U.S. Court of Appeals and, if necessary, to the U.S. Supreme Court. Once the decision is made to utilize the regular judicial system, the case may continue for many years.

In instances of false advertising, the FTC judge often determines that a specific consent decree be ordered, such as one demanding an affirmative disclosure, corrective advertising, or a multiple-product order. **Affirmative disclosure orders** require firms to do something in the future, such as provide additional disclosures of specific key facts in future ads when they include the particular claims that were found to be deceptive. For example, the FTC required that the makers of Geritol disclose that the product "will be of no benefit" for a great majority of persons who suffer from tiredness whenever they run ads making such claims about tiredness symptoms. Affirmative disclosures are designed to help consumers form accurate perceptions about product characteristics and values, as well as health and safety risks.

Since affirmative disclosure orders come into effect only when future advertising claims involve previous claims that were found to be deceptive, such orders are of little value when the advertiser omits the previous claims. Thus, Geritol can claim to cure "iron deficiency anemia" without having to disclose anything else. Accordingly, some advertisers are forced by the FTC to run **corrective advertising**. This is a remedial concept requiring advertisers to spend a certain amount of money buying advertising to correct false impressions created by past advertisements. Thus, corrective advertising disclaims previous false advertising claims. This requirement sometimes occurs when the FTC investigates and finds that a company had practiced deceptive advertising. Before corrective advertisements can be run, the FTC must approve them. The intent of corrective advertising is to deprive the business of the gains obtained by unfair methods and to deter false advertising in the future.

Multiple-product orders are formal FTC consent decrees that require that all future advertising about all the products sold by a firm, not just the product that was falsely advertised, carry affirmative or corrective statements. This rarely-used power is designed to deter firms that have a history of false advertising from doing so in the future, particularly those who sell a multitude of products and a variety of product lines.

Quasi-Legislative Powers

The FTC can issue trade regulations that cover entire industries. The FTC occasionally issues trade regulations to prevent unfair and deceptive practices rather than going after businesses on a case-by-case basis. For example, instead of trying to prosecute each funeral home that uses deceptive labeling practices one at a time, the FTC issued its "funeral rule" in 1984. This regulation was designed to stop unscrupulous funeral directors who misrepresented state and local legal requirements regarding embalming, and overcharged for products and services. Handicapped by grief, consumers often made poor decisions in the absence of adequate information. The regulation requires that funeral directors provide information about prices and services over the telephone and, if requested, in writing to consumers who request such information. Thus, consumers can now easily compare casket prices and funeral services when arranging a funeral. In 1980 the U.S. Congress restricted the FTC's authority to issue trade regulations in the area of advertising based on the concept of unfairness. However, the FTC still is able to attack individual instances of unfair advertising through its adjudicative proceedings. It is still able to enact trade regulations aimed at deceptive advertising.

Benefits and Costs of Government Regulation

Laws and regulations to help consumers typically are concerned with (1) **protecting consumers from the health and safety aspects of products** that they are unable to correctly evaluate, such as prescription drugs, toy safety, wholesale meat, deceptive advertising, automobile bumpers, crib safety, and food additives, (2) **protecting consumers from unfair treatment**, such as the opportunity for equal credit, avoiding harassment for unpaid debts, provision of basic banking services to the economically disadvantaged, assistance with warranty complaints, price fixing, and availability of small claims courts, or (3) **promoting the availability of more adequate information** to consumers to help them make comparisons, such as fair packaging and labeling of food products, gasohol labeling, nutritional labeling, and costs of credit.

The positive impacts of most consumer protection laws and regulations include reduced suffering, the protection of lives, more parity, better choices, increased physical well-being, and economic savings. However, the magnitude of these benefits has rarely been estimated or carefully assessed. The idea of benefit-cost analysis evolved from attempts to measure the efficiency of public policy initiatives.

Benefit-Cost Analysis Is a Tool

Consumers appear to be indifferent toward the large sums of money government spends to protect health and safety, even though these costs are paid through higher prices. Business and government have different perspectives. Historically, the approach taken in government regulation was simple: government issued executive orders and passed laws and regulations when leaders *thought* important problems existed that could be alleviated or resolved by issuing rules and/or spending money. Sometimes private remedies were created, but historically the government strategy was to "throw laws and money at problems." Thus, governments passed legislation in such areas as food, drugs, clothing, cosmetics, medical devices, credit, automobiles, warranties, housing, investments, and product safety.

Four difficulties arose from this approach to regulation. First, government typically spent increasing amounts of money on the problems every year. Second, no one was sure how effective the laws and regulations really were. Third, regulations were designed to place the burdens of compliance primarily upon companies while minimizing responsibilities of consumers. Fourth, the negative aspects of the regulation were usually overlooked, including the costs of achieving the regulatory goal, because of the presumed good the regulations were doing. Only in recent years has concern about **unfunded mandates** (regulatory costs imposed on lower levels of government) become an issue.

Benefit-cost analysis (or **cost-benefit analysis**) is a technique of comparing the costs and benefits of risk reduction when one chooses a decision, policy, or action that yields the highest net benefit, given limited time and money. The **net benefit** is the total of all the benefits of a course of action less all the costs. Government began to increasingly use benefit-cost analysis in the early 1980s when, under executive order of the President, all executive branch agencies were prohibited from issuing either proposed or final orders without prior approval by the Office of Management and Budget (OMB). Reasons included an interest in cutting government costs and a belief that in some instances government had intruded too much into private affairs. There was a growing interest in achieving regulatory balance because many believed that there was **overregulation**, which occurs when the social and dollar costs of a law or regulation exceed its benefits.

The President's Office of Management and Budget has centralized control over the regulatory processes of government because OMB must be notified of all regulatory policies, goals, and objectives, as well as of all significant regulatory actions underway or planned. Another source of its power is that agency administrators do not want to upset OMB staff because OMB oversees the initial budgetary requests for all agencies. Before OMB will approve a regulation, the proposing agency must demonstrate that the societal benefits outweigh the costs of the proposal. However, under President Clinton, OMB no longer has veto power over every item. No matter who prepares a benefit-cost analysis it can be controversial, because the outcomes of the calculations are manipulated in every study by making assumptions about what may or may not count as costs and benefits.

The Many Costs of Government Regulation

Government has found that much social regulation, including consumer protection efforts, is not inexpensive. This is partly because regulators historically have not had to seriously consider the costs of achieving legislative and regulatory goals. The immediate and direct costs of a government regulation include many expenses. Government must hold hearings to decide if a law or regulation is truly needed. Then there are expenses to write the regulation, staff an appropriate agency to implement it, perhaps set standards, publicize the information, collect enforcement data, and prosecute those who fail to comply with the regulation. Resources for the Future, a Washington-based non-profit organization that specializes in the economics of regulation calculates the current cost to make and enforce the rule of social regulation—including consumer safety and health, job safety, energy use, and the environment—at approximately $12.6 billion a year.[4]

There are also indirect costs of achieving regulatory goals. First, and perhaps most important, is that regulations to help consumers often reduce freedom of choice for both consumers and sellers by restricting individual liberties. Some consumers, for example, might want to choose an automobile without some of its safety features, such as a passive restraint system or strong auto bumpers, or they might like to buy a child's crib that does not have the bars placed so close together. Consumption decisions in these areas—the

---

[4]John M. Berry (January 20, 1995), Rising Cost of Rules Leads to a Rising Tide Against Them, *The Washington Post*, pp. D-9+.

right to choose—are not left to consumers because manufacturers must either build these products to government regulatory specifications or be in violation of the law. Another indirect cost of regulations is that they often lead to increased costs in the production, manufacture, and distribution of goods and services. All consumers have to pay higher product costs for consumer laws and regulations because the expenses are passed on to the buyers.

How Government Uses Cost-Benefit Analysis

In order to judge the merits of a proposed law or regulation, government is increasingly using benefit-cost analysis to help in the decision making. However, this is an imprecise science that requires many assumptions about applying dollar costs to certain events.

On the cost side of the equation, for example, how much does it truly cost to put safety belts in all automobiles? Does one have to consider the expenses of engineering, as well as the use of buildings and land? What about the alternative costs if the engineering efforts were used elsewhere by the manufacturers? On the benefit side, how much is a saved life worth? Is a child's life worth more than a parent's? What about the benefits of a reduction in serious injuries? Government agencies and special-interest groups have economists, mathematicians, and other specialists to conduct benefit-cost research studies and make their judgments about various regulatory proposals.

Perhaps not surprisingly, measuring risks and determining the acceptability of risks are normative political efforts. Government must carefully review the methodology and biases in such studies (including its own) and use that information, as well as other factors in decision making. Benefit-cost analysis should be just one of many tools utilized by government in making decisions about the value of new consumer protection proposals, or defending or strengthening current efforts.

Regulating with Specification and Performance Standards

Many government regulations on behalf of consumers have to do with establishing product standards. Government has options as to the type of standard to utilize. For example, assume that the federal government is considering strengthening its standard for automobile bumpers. The proposal might be to require bumpers to withstand impacts of up to 5 miles an hour rather than the current 2-1/2 miles per hour.

One factor in the decision is whether government will issue specification standards or performance standards. **Specification** (or **design**) **standards** are quantitative and qualitative measures of comparison that specify technically and precisely how something will function when it is attained by manufacturers and other sellers. For example, the bumper could be required to be made of a prescribed size and quantity of specific metals and plastic materials of certain grades and weights and be attached to the automobile chassis with particular sized bolts. **Performance standards** are quantitative and qualitative measures of comparison that specify the criteria in terms of outputs of objectively measured units, such as content, strength, and other performance characteristics. For example, the bumper could be required to suffer no more than a 20-degree indentation in a 5 mile per hour frontal impact with a stationary barrier. Sellers tend to prefer performance standards over specification standards because they are less restrictive and they encourage competitive and efficient designs to reach the same goals.

A question faced by government is whether the regulation will be absolute or conditional. An **absolute standard** is not limited by restrictions or exceptions and thus has a single level of acceptability. For example, any automobiles failing to meet the bumper standard could be labeled unsafe and could not be sold. A **conditional standard** is a qualified statement allowing for contingencies when certain conditions exist regarding the user of the product or its application. For example, if 85 percent of a sample of automobile bumpers pass the 5 mile per hour test, all bumpers from that manufacturer are presumed to have met the standard.

Another question facing government regulators is whether particular standards be voluntary or required. Trade associations can only set voluntary standards. Government has a great number of guidelines for voluntary standards, as well as mandatory standards. When government relies too heavily on voluntary standards, critics suggest that there is a tendency for business to go into "slow motion."

Sources of Regulatory Inadequacy

Regulations are intrusions into the private marketplace; they are disruptive. Yet government must establish rules and regulations to meet the demands of consumers and sellers for a better and safer marketplace. This is part of the price we pay for a civilized society. We all want good regulations too.

However, there are several factors that result in regulatory inadequacy. We must realize that when a legislative body writes a new law addressing a consumer problem, it purposefully keeps the language broad to allow flexibility in resolving the problem. Implementation of the law is then delegated to a regulatory agency that often must write specific regulations interpreting the legal mandate.

As a result, one difficulty with the regulatory process is that often the laws and regulations themselves are inadequately written to properly address the problems. This usually results because business typically takes rigid positions and opposes constraining regulations, while opposing groups, usually environmentalists and consumers, often take equally extreme and adversarial views. Opponents also try to weaken proposals that cannot be blocked and are likely to become official public policy. The resulting consensus position that evolves requires compromises from all sides, and this has seriously weakened many consumer protection laws and regulations.

The political and legal processes are also quite responsive to appeals from special-interest groups desiring to delay implementation of regulations. For example, although the government issued a regulation requiring passive restraints in automobiles in 1970, it took 20 years to begin to see action. Another difficulty is that consumers may not trust the regulatory agency to actually protect their interests.

The legislature to some extent maintains an oversight function, since it requires government agency administrators to speak at congressional hearings to review progress in implementing regulatory laws. Crucial to good regulatory performance is constant pressure from Congress and the public.

Since legislators and regulators are humans, they cannot foresee all the possible effects of proposed laws and regulations. Government decision makers might be bright and dedicated, but they cannot anticipate everything, and as a consequence, many regulations are amended not long after they are written.

The abilities and prejudices of the bureaucratic leaders administering an agency are always a factor in regulatory successes and failures. Some leaders have considerable expertise in the areas they regulate; some are appointees possessing only management skills. Most regulators are subject to political influences. Some have divided loyalties because they desire employment, or reemployment, in the industry they regulate after completing government service.

Most government agencies have fragmented responsibilities because they enforce a number of executive orders, laws, and regulations, often sharing responsibility with other agencies. There also is a tendency among regulators to remain rigid in their beliefs and to keep on doing what they always have done rather than to innovatively consider new approaches to resolving consumer problems.

Some government agencies are headed by a single administrator who may therefore lack access to alternative views and information in decision making. Other agencies are headed by a collegial group, which is a form of administration where authority is shared among colleagues. A criticism of the collegial approach is that it is often too slow in making decisions.

Finally, another source of regulatory inadequacy is that government has limited resources. It can spend only so much time and money to address consumer problems.

Review and Summary of Key Terms and Concepts

1. What two **virtues** does the U.S. government goal of a free and competitive marketplace have?

2. Give two examples of **recent government efforts** to protect consumers.

3. What do the terms **special-interest groups** and **lobbying** mean, and why are they vital to effective government? In your response, explain the concept of **political action committees**.

4. List a few of the **consumer lobbying organizations** and identify the focus of their lobbying efforts.

5. Define **negotiated regulation** and give two benefits of the process.

6. Why are **administrative agencies** involved in the regulatory process?

7. How does a legislature perform its **oversight function**?

8. What is meant by the **commerce clause** of the U.S. Constitution?

9. Distinguish between **interstate** and **intrastate commerce**.

10. Explain how the **supremacy** and the **commerce clauses** of the U.S. Constitution can come together and decrease consumer protection.

11. Distinguish between **executive (dependent) agencies** and **independent agencies**.

12. Distinguish between the regulatory **investigative powers** of **subpoenas** and **search and seizure orders**.

13. Explain what **quasi-legislative power** means. In your response, explain the terms **rule** and **trade regulation rule**.

14. Distinguish between **formal rule-making** and **informal rule-making**.

15. Explain what **quasi-judicial** power means. In your response, comment upon the role of an **administrative law judge** and the fact that some regulatory agencies have the powers of all three branches of government.

16. What is meant by having the **standing to sue**?

17. Distinguish broadly between the **Uniform Commercial Code** and consumer protection statutes to prevent unfair and deceptive practices.

18. Summarize the essence of the popular legal approach to providing state consumer protection, the **little FTC act**.

19. What is meant by the term **unconscionability**?

20. Summarize the role of state **attorneys general** in consumer protection.

21. Distinguish between the efforts of state **offices of consumer affairs** and **consumer watchdogs**.

22. Summarize the reasons for the **backlash against regulation**, and explain the concept of **deregulation**.

23. Give three examples of **techniques** of deregulation.

24. Compare and contrast **affirmative disclosure orders**, **corrective advertising** and **multiple-product orders**.

25. Explain the idea behind **benefit-cost analysis**, including **net benefit**, in the context of overregulation.

26. List some indirect **costs of government regulation**.

27. Explain why it is difficult to **compare benefits and costs** of proposed laws and regulations.

28. Distinguish between **specification standards** and **performance standards**.

29. Distinguish between **absolute standards** and **conditional standards**.

30. List five sources of **regulatory inadequacy**.

Useful Resources for Consumers

Common Cause
2030 M Street, NW
Washington, DC 20036
202-833-1200

Public Citizen Litigation Group
2000 P Street, NW
Washington, DC 20036
202-785-3704

"What Do You Think" Questions

1. If the nation did not have **special-interest groups** lobbying legislators and regulators, who would represent the interests of business? Of consumers? Of other governments? Briefly describe that kind of society.

2. Considering all the problems and challenges facing consumers, select one area of interest and describe a proposed federal statute to protect consumers which, using the **supremacy clause**, would improve the quality of life.

3. Should **independent agencies** be required to yield to the direction of the executive branch of government? Cite examples in your discussion of why or why not.

4. Succinctly describe what consumer life would be like if all **government agencies** were banned from existence, leaving only the legislatures to run government.

5. Realizing that it is fairly easy to come up with the "right answer" when performing a **benefit-cost analysis**, choose a consumer problem you would like to see remedied and assign madeup prices to variables on both the benefit and cost sides so that the answer comes out in favor of a proposal to protect consumers.

Chapter 11

How to Analyze Consumer Issues

OBJECTIVES

After reading this chapter, you should be able to

1. Illustrate how policymaking in the United States occurs within a system of power clusters or issue networks.

2. Describe how one's economic ideology and political beliefs affect one's understanding of consumer issues.

3. Explain which types of consumer protection proposals would receive the most and the least support in the United States.

4. Understand how to analyze and resolve consumer issues.

5. Discuss a number of issues that would strengthen the balance of power between consumers and sellers.

Issues of interest to consumers are in the headlines of newspapers and magazines every day. An examination of today's consumer issues constitutes the remainder of this book. This chapter provides an introduction to the breadth of current concerns involved in the consumer interest, with more details on the issues presented in subsequent chapters. Crucial to being able to effectively analyze the major issues of the day is to have a well-informed citizenry with the skills to participate in the public policy decision making process.

This chapter begins with a description of how policymaking in the United States occurs. Next is an examination of economic ideology and political beliefs as they affect one's understanding of consumer issues. It is emphasized that consumers need to understand their own personal perceptions as they interpret consumer issues. In this way, an individual better understands why others might be opposed to his or her position and how he or she might be more successful in pursuing specific consumer interest proposals. (An added benefit of understanding is that people find meaning by associating with others who share the same values.) This is followed by an analysis of which consumer protection proposals are likely to receive support and which will be opposed. The next section examines how to analyze and resolve consumer issues, both for yourself personally and for society. The chapter closes with a discussion of several issues that might help balance the power between consumers and sellers. One appendix is included at the end of the chapter on Proposed Consumer Protection Legislation and Regulations.

Policymaking in the United States

Policymaking in the United States is characterized not by warring ideologies of conservatives versus liberals or Republicans against Democrats, but rather by coalitions of people and organizations interested in the issues. The politics of public policy-making, including consumer protection proposals, are usually the politics of moderation and accommodation rather than prolonged and strained battles between groups with opposing views. Economic belief systems and general ideologies are taken into account in reaching resolutions to problems and issues.

Power Clusters

Public policy in the United States is made within a system of power clusters.[1] The term **power clusters** was coined by Daniel M. Ogden, Jr., who argues that a number of participants are involved in most policy shaping.[2] Power clusters are small circles of semiautonomous participants interested in broad, interrelated subject fields, such as agriculture, in which the government plays an active role. These circles operate

---

[1]The key source for this discussion was Ogden, D. M., Jr. (1972). Outdoor Recreation Policy and Politics. In Downs, A., Kneese, A. V., Ogden, D. M., and Perloff, H. S. (Eds.), *The Political Economy of Environmental Control*, (Institute of Business and Economic Research, University of California), 98-103. The literature is dated from a 1964 book in which Douglas Cater described "subgovernments" that shape public policy. See Cater, D. (1964). *Power in Washington* (Vintage), and Freeman, J. L. (1965). *The Political Process* (Random House).

[2]The substance of this discussion is from Ogden, D. M. Jr. (undated). How National Policy is Made, unpublished paper, 143-171.

independently of all other clusters to identify policy issues, shape policy alternatives, propose new legislation, and implement policy. Each power cluster includes government administrative agencies, legislative committees, special-interest groups, professionals, volunteers, and an attentive public. Some people call power clusters **issue networks**,[3] where there are a large number of participants with quite variable degrees of commitment or of dependence on others in their environment. People constantly move in and out of such networks. They do not dominate a program, since no one group controls the politics and issues. Moreover, power clusters and issue networks are communications networks established by the participants in each field of public policy.

Major power clusters exist in all categories of domestic and foreign policy, such as defense, education, natural resources, communications, transportation, justice and law enforcement, urban affairs, health, welfare, commerce, banking, finance, and consumerism. Many clusters have sub-clusters that deal with more specific subjects. For example, the natural resources power cluster has subclusters concerned with water, air, forests, minerals, recreation, and energy policy. Each cluster has a large contingent of active special-interest organizations, some of which are **public policy specialists**. These professionals work in academic settings, public interest organizations, private consulting firms, law firms, and in professional and trade associations.

Attentive Public and Latent Public

An **attentive public** is one that pays attention to one area of public policy, usually because they earn a living in the area and want to advance both economically and socially. The attentive public group reads, listens, has opinions, and talks selectively about the issues of the power cluster. Such a group can easily be aroused over a major controversy and may get actively involved in an organized interest group.

A **latent public** also exists. This is group has interests that are affected by a specific power cluster but generally perceives that its policies, if changed, would not affect them adversely. Individuals are usually active in only one power cluster throughout their lives. A major switch in policy that may adversely affect the latent public can stimulate them to interfere in the power cluster's decision making to protect their own interests. For example, citizens not normally aroused by consumer interest concerns wrote millions of letters, attended public meetings, and put great pressure on the federal government to ban the chemical additive Alar that was used on apples after becoming aware of its cancer-causing potentialities. Recent E. coli food poisoning scares resulted in an awakened public interest. Similar concerns by the latent public occurred after presidential candidate Ross Perot convinced them of the dangers of the rising national debt.

The latent public is difficult to keep aroused, however. A weakness of the latent American public, especially on consumer issues, is that their attention span is about three days. Author Richard Condon argues that television permits the public to be entertained by politics instead of participating in it.

---

[3]Heclo, H. (1980). Issue Networks and the Executive Establishment. In A. King (Ed.), *The New American Political System* (American Enterprise Institute), 87-124.

CONSUMER UPDATE:
Anger and Cynicism About the Ugliness About
the American Political Process

A recent poll by Times Mirror Center has found that Americans believe that the U.S. has become an "increasingly bitter, frustrated, cynical, and selfish place" over the last several years.[1] "Politics" has become a pejorative term.

Writer Pete Hamill observes that civility "is being swept away by a poisonous flood tide of negation, sectarianism, self-pity, confrontation, vulgarity, and flat-out, old-fashioned hatred. Politics is an ice jam of accusation and obstruction, the hardest vulgarians honored for their cynicism, its good men fleeing to tend to private gardens."[2] Hamill says that, public discourse has turned into "all heat and no illumination."

People are tired of partisan and personal conflicts among politicians that are shrill and nasty. They are saddened with a broken political system in which the voices of reason are, in the words of retired Senator Sam Nunn, "drowned out by the extremes in both parties who are usually wrong, but never in doubt."

People are increasingly upset with "politics as usual" where gridlock is the norm. People want to be treated intelligently by politicians and media. People want to be challenged to think about the issues and the alternatives, instead of being force fed an often flatulent quasi-political debate in a time where political eloquence (i.e., persuasion) has coarsened. People are no longer apathetic, they are angry.

---

[1]Cannon, A. (1994, September 21). Bitter Americans Just Don't Seem to Trust or Give a Darn. *Roanoke Times & World-News*, p. A-1.

[2]Hamill, P. (1994, December). End Game, *Esquire*, p. 86. This is a brilliantly insightful article on the future of politics and society.

How Public Policy Is Shaped

Public policy is shaped by interaction among the affected parties: (1) the identified executive government agencies, (2) the legislative committees, and (3) the organized special-interest groups. The three parties are sometimes collectively called the *iron triangle* because they are the most active participants in making public policy.

Many different people make input to public policy, so that decisions that reconcile policy goals and judgments are the product of multiple interactions among people in the public and private sectors. Policy decisions, therefore, are a result of intense interactions by those parties who will be most affected by actions. Changes go on continuously.

All clusters are bipartisan or nonpartisan because they are organized to shape policy, not win elections. Issues that concern political parties are broader, intercluster topics such as talks on spending programs that may affect the outcome of elections. Partisanship does not focus on policy-making, rather it focuses on office-seeking and office-holding. Research suggests that only about 40 percent off the roll call votes in Congress are identifiably partisan. Further, the political parties average about 60 percent loyalty from their members on partisan votes.

Power Cluster Behaviors

Power clusters exhibit five patterns of behavior that shape the policymaking process: (1) they maintain close personal and institutional ties, (2) key participants, driven by their need to be effective, are active participants in the power cluster, (3) power cluster participants try to work out differences among themselves to reach acceptable policy agreements before bills are sent to the legislature, (4) each cluster usually has deep-seated and well-established internal, often philosophical, conflicts among competing interests, and (5) each power cluster, although it is an informal communications network, develops its own internal power structure.

The power cluster system has evolved naturally in the United States because of the concept of separation of powers. At the federal level, the members of Congress are quite independent. In addition, government is open to participation by organized groups in the policy-making process. Power clusters ensure that policy-making retains continuity and stability, without disruption through changes in political power. Because they are decentralized, power clusters can resist presidential and gubernatorial direction; they are accountable to no one because they are informal networks.

The power clusters also promote professionalism and efficiency. Further, each power cluster retains ties to the nation's universities, which can provide a constant source of new professional recruits for its functions in society. Successful leaders must understand the power cluster system and know how to work with it.

The Effects of Economic Ideology and Political Beliefs

An **issue** is a public or social concern which, because of its salience or the degree of its impact, attracts the attention and interest of many people, organizations and public policymakers for discussion, debate, or dispute. Most, but not all, consumer protection issues and proposals are controversial. The major reason for the controversy is that the American people differ in their perceptions of economic reality; they do not agree on how the economy really works or how its performance might be improved. When several people look at the American marketplace, each may see different things. One's perception of truth about the competitiveness of the market, the role of consumers, and how consumer problems can best be remedied is dependent on one's economic ideology.

An **economic ideology** is a set of beliefs and attitudes about the American economic marketplace and the proper roles of business, government, and consumers in that market. Briefly put, an **ideology** is a simplified picture of the world, a coherent perspective that justifies personal decisions and actions. People pick and choose, for ideological reasons, which problems and issues to confront, and which to ignore. **Beliefs** are mental acceptances of or convictions about the truth or actuality of something. Being in the eye of the beholder, beliefs can be true or false.

The attitudes Americans have toward consumer protection proposals vary because of their economic ideologies and their political perspectives. To get a consumer protection proposal successfully accepted first requires an understanding of the economic belief systems of all parties involved in decision making. One's perceptions of economic reality often reveal motivations for or against various proposals.

Stephen Brobeck, executive director of the Consumer Federation of America, says, "one key to working with consumer advocates is to identify mutual or complementary interests. For any corporation that is committed not merely to short-term profitability but to long-term growth, this common ground exists. Business and consumer groups share many of the same objectives—products that work and that consumers want, informed buyers who understand the value of these products, and a means of redress when things go wrong."[4]

It is helpful to know the likely views and arguments of supporters and opponents of a particular proposal. The more knowledgeable one is about the views of another, the more likely it is that effective dialogue can occur between them. The sponsor of a consumer protection proposal must look for possible areas of agreement for specific aspects of the concept among supporters and opponents. Then the sponsor builds support for the idea among affected groups, compromises with opponents where necessary, and shapes a final proposal that the majority can support. Consumer protection efforts are subject to a variety of forces, including conflicting political interests, opposing ideas, economic recession, budget constraints, and the economic ideology of the political administration in power.

There are three predominant economic belief systems in America: (1) neoclassical, (2) managerial, and (3) reformist.[5] Each has its own set of beliefs about the structure of our economy, about how the companies in the United States behave, and about the effects of that behavior on consumers. In addition, each ideology includes beliefs about the best ways to remedy consumer problems and whether certain things are in fact consumer concerns. People tend to hold one set of rather consistent economic beliefs, however, on any given issue people are apt to blend ideologies. The perspectives of people change over time, as well. Table 11-1 summarizes the basic views of the three economic belief systems.[6]

The Neoclassical Belief System

The **neoclassical belief system** holds that our economy is basically a free enterprise competitive system that favors market mechanisms to achieve society's goals. Neoclassicists see the market as not controlled by monopolies and oligopolies but governed by large number of firms vigorously competing based primarily on price. Competitors will watch each other, and if one firm slips up, the judicial system is there to reprimand the offender. Antitrust laws and regulatory agencies are necessary, but basically business should regulate itself. Neoclassicists also want to look carefully at the costs and benefits of any proposals to regulate.

---

[4]Fernstrom, M. M. (1989). *Financial Institutions and the Public Interest: Forging Joint Ventures*. New York: American Express (p. 34).

[5]The essence of this discussion has evolved from Christner, A. M. (1989). Protecting Consumers with Prepurchase Information: Four Economic Ideological Views, *Proceedings of the American Council on Consumer Interests* (University of Missouri), 268-275; Herrmann, R. O. (September-October, 1977). Relating Economic Ideologies to Consumer Protection: A Suggested Unit in Consumer Education, *Business Education World*, 13-15; Mayer, R. N. (1989). *The Consumer Movement: Guardians of the Marketplace* (Wayne Publishers); and Monsen, J. R., Jr. (1963). *Modern American Capitalism: Ideologies and Issues* (Houghton Mifflin).

[6]A fourth economic ideology exists but is not discussed here. Professor Ann Christner describes the **radical reformist** position as one that believes "the market system is inherently flawed and should be replaced by a more equitable mechanism." Ralph Nader is considered to be a radical reformist in economic ideology.

	Reformist	Managerial	Neoclassical
How competitive is our economy?	Dominated by monopolies and oligopolies	Highly competitive, even though it is dominated by large firms	Highly competitive
How do firms compete with each other?	Advertising, minor differences in product design, and services	Prices, product features, advertising, services	Prices
What keeps the behavior of individual firms in line?	Nothing except firm's desire for security and stable growth	Competition of other firms for customers, managers' sense of responsibility to workers, shareholders, consumers	Competition of other firms for customers
How are consumers characterized?	Consumers are relatively powerless; their wants and needs are manipulated by advertising and other techniques and they buy goods of questionable value	Decisions are usually rational, but due to laziness, apathy, or ignorance, consumers do not always make the best decisions	Shoppers are intelligent; all choices are rational, made in the consumer's self-interest, and have satisfactory results
What is the role of consumers in the economy?	They are important buyers in the marketplace whose decisions are manipulated by advertising and other techniques	They are a big influence in the economy, and their buying decisions can be manipulated by advertising	They guide the market by casting their "dollar votes" for products and services they prefer
What kinds of problems do consumers have?	A variety of problems arising from unchecked corporate power: excessive prices, unsafe products, difficulty in obtaining redress	Misleading advertising, difficulties in obtaining redress	Fraud and deception, unsafe products
How can these consumer problems best be remedied?	Government regulation	Business self-regulation, improved systems of complaint handling	Legal action by individual consumer affected
What should be the role of government in regulating the economy?	Antitrust action and strengthened government regulation	Removing barriers to competition, maintaining a high level of economic activity	Minimal, so as not to interfere with competition

TABLE 11-1   Three Primary Economic Belief Systems

The neoclassicists believe that the role of consumers is that of intelligent shoppers who are aware of their choices and who are basically immune to manipulation by advertising and other forms of persuasion. Consumers are already informed when they act in their self-interest by casting their targeted "dollar votes" for the products and services they really need. Their power over the marketplace is called **consumer sovereignty**, because the consumer ultimately decides which products and services society will produce and consume.

The neoclassicist believes that there are few consumer problems other than frauds, deceptions, and unsafe products. It is assumed that consumers seek and process only as much information as they desire or are able to handle. Losses from poor choices are assumed to be minimal. The way to resolve these consumer problems is through individual lawsuits by those affected. Government controls and regulations are considered ineffective, unwanted, and an interference with the free competitive marketplace. Neoclassicists would prefer that informed buyers gather and use information for personal buying decisions because this encourages price competition and quality products. Individual rights and freedom of choice are paramount in weighing the costs and benefits of any proposal to resolve consumer problems.

Consumer-supported government proposals to require passive restraint systems, such as driver-side air bags, and open dating on perishable products to indicate freshness for food products, would be opposed. Mandatory information disclosure laws would be considered superfluous. This is so because the neoclassicist believes that the self-correcting forces of the marketplace will offer such devices or information when the public dollars demand it. Neoclassicists suggest that the additional costs of mandatory programs represent a hidden tax on products so labeled. Advocates of the neoclassical belief system include Nobel Prize-winning economist Milton Friedman, Washington University economics professor Murray Weidenbaum, former President Ronald Reagan, and a number of conservative business persons and politicians.

The Managerial Belief System

The **managerial belief system** emphasizes the key role of the professional manager in today's corporations, and it holds that the best protection for consumers comes from corporate competition and the corporate manager's sense of responsibility. Crucial to this system of thinking is the belief that corporate managers serve responsibly (almost as trustees) and in the interest of workers, shareholders, and consumers. The corporate manager is presumed to possess a high degree of social conscience that helps protect consumers.

While managerialists recognize that the economy is dominated by large corporations, they further believe that competition is based on many things other than price. Of great importance is the recognition that advertising does affect consumers by stimulating demand, which in turn ensures a high level of overall economic activity.

Managerialists see the primary role of government as helping to maintain a high level of economic growth. They recognize that some government actions are needed to protect consumers; thus they are against misleading advertising. Managerialists would not support proposed government regulations to require national no-fault auto insurance or strengthening automobile bumper standards, but they would rely on the judgment of corporate managers to determine if and when consumers really wanted these types of remedies for consumer problems. Further, business should be self-regulatory and government should work toward removing barriers to competition. Some of the biggest supporters of the managerial belief system are the editors of *Fortune* and *Forbes* magazines.

The Reformist Belief System

The **reformist belief system** has its roots in the progressive tradition of the turn of the century and the liberal reform movement of the 1960s. Proponents are interested in progressive and gradual changes, rather than radical changes in political and social situations. The economy is perceived as being dominated by monopolies and shared monopolies. Corporations work with little competition to serve their own ends, which are profits for the shareholders, security, and continued growth. Economist John Kenneth Galbraith has elaborated on this reformist belief system and has labeled such corporations as the **planning system**, which exercises great control over consumers and governments. The remainder of the economy is viewed by Galbraith in much the same way as by the neoclassicists; he calls the remaining small firms, which are quite competitive, the **market system**. Reformists are concerned about the fairness of the marketplace, particularly as the market affects vulnerable consumers, such as the elderly, children, and the undereducated. Reformists are also concerned with the market's imperfections, and they seek to fix the flaws in the system.

Consumers are not viewed as the dominant force in the economy, since advertising effectively shapes their values and beliefs to accommodate the needs of the planning system. Consumer problems arise from unchecked corporate power. These problems include excessive prices, unsafe products, and difficulty in seeking redress. Reformists want to force businesses to use objective advertising information instead of subjective persuasions. They want government intervention to standardize and simplify information formats for products and services, to prevent misleading information, and to set standards for a number of products and services. These standards would reduce the need for consumers to judge safety and effectiveness for many buying decisions.

Supporters of the reformist perspective include the Consumer Federation of America, Consumers Union, and the National Consumers League. Consumer advocate Ralph Nader's perception of the economy is based on this belief system. Many of the proposals to resolve consumer problems that are suggested by his and other consumer organizations come from the reformist belief system. Nader and his followers prescribe stronger antitrust actions and strict government regulation of corporate activities in order to discourage irresponsible actions (such as pollution), to encourage responsible actions (such as making safer products), and to provide much more access to information so that consumers can act more intelligently in the marketplace. Reformists want government-funded comparative consumer information made available with no commercial influence, perhaps to be dispensed through computer vending machines in shopping malls. Reformists suggest that consumers need government protection because of the complexities and technologies in the marketplace today.

Galbraith perceives the economy much as Nader does but offers different solutions to the problems. Antitrust action, he says, is of little value, since a government cannot proclaim half of the economic system illegal. Instead, Galbraith suggests price controls as one method of controlling the power of large firms. Further, government must break the grip of the planning system, with Congress being a much stronger representative of the public interest. Otherwise, attempts to regulate such immense corporate power will be blunted and, as Galbraith believes often happens now, actually serve the needs of the planning system.

Political Belief Systems

The economic belief systems of consumers are definitely affected by their political beliefs and their ideology. In the broadest sense, a **political ideology** is a person's set of attitudes and beliefs about freedom, equality, humankind, and the desired role of government. A person's political ideology also refers to their view of the world, an image of the relationship of people to their government, and how power is used in society.[7]

CONSUMER UPDATE:
Citizen Participation Is on the Upswing

According to a three-year research project by consumer advocate Ralph Nader, student activism is on the rise. Maryland was the first state to require its students to perform community service as a condition for graduation. This is consistent with the growing recognition of citizens that they have an obligation to the U.S. that goes beyond voting and paying taxes; people increasingly want to give a portion of their lives to others. President Bill Clinton's National Service Program is based on this premise.

A study by People for the American Way, chaired by Hillary Rodham Clinton, concluded that much more emphasis should be placed on teaching young people in schools how to become more fully involved citizens. The study of **civics**, the branch of political science dealing with civic affairs, is being revitalized. Increased consumer understandings of active citizens strengthens their abilities to make decisive judgments in both the consumer and the public interest.

Conservatism

Two broad and hazy perspectives dominate political thinking in the United States: conservatism and liberalism.[8] The political spectrum is described as conservative-liberal, right-left, and capitalist-socialist. Supporters of **conservatism** believe in limited government—except in national defense—and have faith in encouraging personal achievement. They do not believe in drastic change. The two cardinal beliefs of conservatives are private-property rights and free enterprise. Conservatives embrace self-help, empowerment, free markets, and, except for abortion rights, decentralized individual choice. Conservatives distrust government and want it out of the way, except when it is absolutely necessary.

Conservatives place great faith in the private sector of the economy rather than relying on government, supporting the old Jeffersonian belief that "government governs best when it governs least." They consider social justice to be essentially an economic question. Conservatives believe that if private enterprise is not creating rising living standards, providing access to health care, and offering ways out of poverty, then the market economy is not at fault. Further, "the solution, or even parts of it, can never, ever come

---

[7]Research shows that less than a third of Americans have anything more than a rudimentary understanding of what it means to be politically conservative or liberal. Only about one-half of all adults know which party controls Congress.

[8]Two other idealogies supported by significant but small portions of the American population are socialism and libertarianism. **Socialism** seeks public ownership of the means of production, public jobs for all who want to work, and increased taxes on the wealthy. **Libertarianism** cherishes individual liberty, and preaches opposition to government and an end to just about all its programs.

from government."[9] Conservatives believe that people should accept as "natural" whatever the capitalistic market offers.

Conservatives believe that government action, if taken at all, should be taken at the lowest possible level, preferring local and state decisions to action by the federal government. Conservatives want to protect the status quo—most yearn for yesterday when things were better. By its very nature, conservatism cannot offer fundamental alternatives to the current directions in society other than to slow down undesirable developments. Historically, conservatives have seldom favored civil rights and affirmative action programs, suggesting instead that, people should be encouraged to be more tolerant and helpful to others.[10] Being believers in the market economy, conservatives support tenant ownership of public housing, choice in schooling, and incentives for welfare recipients to work. Conservatives believe in individuals working harder to make things better.

Liberalism is not a dirty word, as many Republican politicians in the U.S. would have us all believe. Liberals are historically the most mainstream of republican governments (lower case "r") around the globe. Hundreds of years ago, they invented the popular phrase "liberal democracy." Liberal ideals are embodied in all the constitutions of the world's democracies: the rule of law, separation of powers, personal and economic freedom, secular government."[11] Early in the 20th century in the U.S., liberals were known as **progressives**.

Liberalism

Liberalism involves a belief that government should be used to bring about justice and equality of opportunity. The word "liberal" is translated from Greek as "a free man" as opposed to a slave. It implies freedom of thought, freedom from conventional beliefs, and the right of others to think differently than oneself. Liberals believe that democratic governments are fundamentally important in the solution of a nation's collective problems. They believe that government can help liberate people.

Liberals wish to preserve the rights of individuals. While liberals want to retain private property rights and support free enterprise, they also are willing to have government intervene to help right the defects in the capitalistic market-oriented economic system. Liberals realize that a market economy has tremendous advantages for the nation, but that capitalism needs rules and regulations. Liberals believe that individuals need some security for living in and accepting the risks of life in the economic turmoil of a capitalistic society. The believe that government is the most effective way to improve society.

Liberals figure that government programs are needed even though they sometimes cause a loss of liberties. They believe that, "government's highest purpose is to strengthen the capacities of individuals to achieve self-reliance and to nurture the country's rich network of civic organizations that are independent of both the state and the marketplace."[12] They particularly support government efforts to aid the poor and help the unemployed.

---

[9]E. J. Dionne, Jr. (February 4, 1996), The Liberal Revival, *The Washington Post*, pp. C-1+.

[10]Richard E. Neustadt, author of *Presidential Power and the Modern Presidents*, argues that polarization on the issues of race, rights and taxes was critical to building the conservative majority in the 1980s. He suggests that the conservative coalition fell apart as former President George Bush presented a "gentler and kinder" stance to many traditional Democratic constituencies which backfired because the polarization declined. Senator Daniel Patrick Moynihan suggests that a key aspect of the polarization issue is that "class, not race" is a fundamental problem.

[11]Gugliotta, G. (1994, May 17). A Liberal Dose of Liberalism Comes to Washington. *The Washington Post*, p. A-15.

[12]Ibid.

Liberals are concerned about improving the adequacy of health care, eliminating unsafe products, and improving access to education and affordable housing. As a result, liberals are often viewed as being compassionate. Liberals want to challenge the status quo and change it—they yearn for a better world. Historically, liberals have supported civil rights, women's rights, gay rights, affirmative action programs, progressive taxation, the right to unionize, and regulatory efforts that protect the environment and the health and safety of workers and consumers.

Congressman James Leach of Iowa says that liberals are accused of seeking freedom from personal responsibility by transferring inconvenient family and social problems to state bureaucracies. At the same time, modern-day conservatives are criticized for seeking freedom from government (and seeking deregulation) without accepting personal responsibility for social imperatives. *U.S. News & World Report* observes that, "The left wants more private solutions and responsibility and neither side sees much virtue in the other's arguments."[13]

Political Party Beliefs

Data obtained by the Center for Political Studies at the University of Michigan show that voters in the 1992 elections described themselves politically in the following ways: liberal, 8 percent; tend towards liberal, 8 percent; moderate, 25 percent; tend towards conservative, 14 percent; conservative, 12 percent; and don't know or no preference, 33 percent. Data from pollster Peter D. Hart Research Associates reveals that in 1993 American voters reported their political party interests: Democrat, 43 percent; Republican, 31 percent; independent, 26 percent. Surveys by the American Council on Education note that the number of college freshmen calling themselves politically liberal is at the highest level in 20 years, 26 percent. The number calling themselves conservative, 20 percent, continues to decline. Most remain middle-of-the-road, 54 percent.

The annual national study of college freshmen conducted by the University of California reveals that the percentage of students who consider it "important to keep up with politics" is 29 percent, half what it was a generation ago. Those who say they "discuss politics" is only 15 percent. Thirty-four percent, the highest percentage ever, believe that an "individual can have an effect on the course of events." The study also found that a growing number of first-year college students have as a life goal to "develop a meaningful philosophy of life" (45 percent) rather than "be very well off financially" (55 percent). Another study showed that 42 percent of young adults, age 16 to 29, read newspapers daily or almost every day.

Lawrence Chickering, founder of the Institute for Contemporary Studies, believes that American society needs to move away from an obsession with rights and toward a discussion of our obligations. He writes in *Beyond Left and Right: Breaking the Political Stalemate* that, "Without the glue of a common framework to discern what is right or wrong, our society will continue to fragment."

While times and political parties change, over the years most of the people in today's Republican party are somewhat conservative and most of those in the Democratic party are more liberal. Often because of geographic traditions there are liberal Republicans and conservative Democrats as well. Most voters express themselves through the two major parties because the differences are worth arguing about. People's politics are a reflection of who they are, what they hope for, and what they value.

Recent data from the Consumer Federation of America reveal how members of Congress voted on selected important consumer issues. Senate Democrats voted with consumers 77 percent of the time compared to 9 percent for Republicans. In the House,

---

[13]Neglecting Children and Parents (1994, April 25). *U.S. News & World Report*, p. 10.

CONSUMER UPDATE:
Communitarian: A Political Ideology between
Conservativism and Liberalism

The term **communitarian** identifies a new movement in American society, founded by a group of former liberals and conservatives. It is a moderate ideology, or a rationality, somewhat between conservativism and liberalism, particularly on individual rights and responsibilities. It strongly supports the teaching of values and shared moral principles in schools. At its heart, communitarian believes that there is much more to being a human being than the simple pursuit of narrow self-interest. Life requires a civil society, and preserving the freedoms that Americans enjoy will require the cooperative efforts of many.

George Washington University's Professor Amitai Etzioni founded the movement on the belief that the cultural shift during 1980s to excessive individualism, the quest for personal gratification, and excessive consumerism has been hurting families and the society. Etzioni's *The Spirit of Community* is a manifesto for the cause. Communitarians believe that people are each other's keepers. Communitarians offer a blueprint for a collective society rather than simply just a return to individual responsibility. Supporters argue that the political debate should focus less on entitlements and rights and more on obligations and responsibilities.

Some of the beliefs of communitarians include: taking driver's licenses away from students who drop out of school, kicking people out of housing projects when caught with guns or drugs, applying anti-loitering ordinances to get drug dealers off the streets, having spot tests to identify drunken drivers, requiring voluntary national service, place time-limits on welfare payments to single mothers, guaranteeing child-support payments, reform of divorce laws to protect children's interests, provide fringe benefits to part-time workers, elimination of the tax penalty for married couples, and require public funding of campaigns.

The question remains as to whether or not this new paradigm, communitarians, can move into the political mainstream. Note, though, that some thoughts of the communitarians sound much like President Bill Clinton's views. This also is much in line with Hillary Rodham Clinton's comments on the "politics of meaning," building a society that supports caring relationships, social responsibility and ethical living. The Clintons seek to create incentives for social and ecological responsibility.

Democrats voted with consumers 74 percent of the time compared to 12 percent for the Republicans. Republicans are overwhelmingly anti-consumer in their voting.

The Republican party argues that concentration of power in the national government should be avoided because state and local governments, which are closer to the people, should be assigned the first tasks of governing. Conversely, the Democratic party holds that a strong national government is needed to deal with today's complex problems, which are often too costly for state and local governments to undertake.

Democrats desire federal regulations for consistency throughout the country and to ensure an expanding level of economic activity. Republicans believe (almost religiously) that unfettered free enterprise is the force needed for economic growth and it should be regulated as little as possible; Democrats are less trusting of business. Republicans believe that labor and management are able to bargain from equal positions of strength, and that government should intervene only when public welfare is involved. Democrats hold that government should help out labor because it is at a disadvantage in dealing with management.

Politicians in the United States, instead of working together across the liberal and conservative ideologies to resolve problems, often choose to frame their arguments from the more narrow (some say trivial) partisan perspectives of party ideology. This promotes polarization of the electorate and endless arguments over **"false issues"** of family, values,

---

CONSUMER UPDATE:
P. J. O'Rourke on Democrats and Republicans

Commentator P. J. O'Rourke says that, "Democrats are also the party of government activism, the party that says government can make you richer, smarter, taller, and get the chickenweed out of your lawn. Republicans are the party that says government doesn't work, and then they get elected and prove it."[1]

---

[1]O'Rourke, P. J. (1991), *Parliament of Whores* (New York: Vintage Books), p. 19.

---

feminism, work, neighborhood, virtue, children, crime, welfare, quotas, and the death penalty. Such issues turn politics into abstract and phony moralizing. Voters want real solutions to the basic problems of society, not "entertaining debates" on false choices. Real problems include dealing with stagnant incomes, vanishing health insurance, unaffordable child care, aging parents, unemployed offspring, crumbling infrastructure, unavailable housing, inadequate education, helping the working poor, and making both home ownership and a college education more available.[14]

There is always a tension in our society because it is based on firmly held ethical and religious beliefs and, at the same time, it protects as a fundamental right diversity of perspective. Liberals and conservatives personify this tension. This is the genius of the constitutional system. Writer Reinhold Niebhur once observed that the temper and integrity with which the political fight is waged are more important for the health of our American society than the outcome of any issue. Congressman Philip R. Sharp reminds us that, "Congress is not a convent; it is not a tea party. It is the public arena where we battle over ideals and scrap over funding; where we champion just causes and represent regional interests. It is not always pretty or pleasant. It is this system of representation that best assures that the people will control our government."

Support for Consumer Protection Proposals

Recognize that each individual consumer has but a small economic stake in each consumer protection proposal. For example, an improved unit-pricing food label, when used, might only save each consumer a dollar or two per year. However, the consumer interest concerns of value for money *and* equity for all consumers can soon mobilize considerable forces of volunteers. Consumers realize that, as individual people, they do not have the expertise, time, or willingness to deal with sellers on a one-to-one basis to obtain value for money and equity. Therefore, they are willing to support consumer protection proposals put forth by consumer and public interest organizations.

Support for consumer protection proposals varies given the diverse opinions held by the American people, who perceive reality and react according to one of the three dominant economic belief systems. The widest support would likely go to proposals that would optimize consumer choice by improving "the opportunity for the effective exercise

---

[14]For more information on this discussion, see Dionne, E. J., Jr. (1991). *Why Americans Hate Politics* (Simon & Schuster).

What Are Your Economic and Political Belief Systems?

1. **My *economic ideology* can best be described as:**
   Reformist   Managerialist   Neoclassist

2. ***Two* of the characteristics of the economic ideology in which I believe that I like are:**
   A.
   B.

3. **My *political ideology* can best be described as:**
   Liberalism   Conservatism

4. ***Two* of the characteristics of the political ideology (liberalism or conservatism) that I like are:**
   A.
   B.

5. **If I were to join *one* of the two dominant *political parties*, I would probably select:**
   Democrat   Republican

6. ***Two* of the characteristics of the political party (Democrat or Republican) that I like are:**
   A.
   B.

---

of individual responsibility,"[15] such as nutritional labeling and health warnings. Support for making product information available is strong provided that the effort is low in cost, reaches many consumers, comes primarily from business, and involves a minimum of government involvement. Information, by itself, encourages competition and more and better products, which is a goal valued by all three belief systems.

Antitrust proposals would receive the least support. Despite their belief in competitive markets, the neoclassicists would fear any kind of government intrusion and oppose even limited interventions to increase competition. Ralph Nader would favor antitrust enforcement, but Galbraith would prefer price controls. Those of the managerial belief system would oppose antitrust efforts if they would reduce the effectiveness of the corporate manager. Proposals for safety-related concerns would receive mixed support. Reformists support efforts to reduce safety hazards, but those holding to the managerial and the neoclassicist belief systems would not agree with extensive government involvement, preferring first to rely on industry self-regulation.

Consumer advocates usually have a reformist viewpoint. They prefer laws and regulations at the federal level to be effective nationally, rather than passing laws one state at a time. Businesspeople typically have a neoclassical or managerial viewpoint, and they often prefer to be regulated at the state level, since they usually get more flexibility there. Consumer advocates are often biased against corporations, believing that when businesses aggressively pursue profit maximization, the consumer viewpoint often becomes lost. While true, reality also shows that businesses pursue many policies that are either neutral or beneficial to consumers. Consumer advocates defend the use of class action lawsuits

---

[15]Kroll, R. J. and Stampfl, R. W. (1986). Orientations Toward Consumerism: A Test of a Two-dimensional Theory. *Journal of Consumer Affairs*, 20, 218.

and punitive penalties against corporate misbehavior. Businesses object to such powers because they believe them to be too costly.

Consumer advocates are effective at pointing out how to save consumers money in the marketplace; how to prevent thousands of product-related deaths, injuries, and illnesses through health and safety regulations; and how to help ensure fairness in the marketplace through various interventions and disclosure requirements. Neoclassicists and managerialists are usually strong supporters of deregulation. They are also effective at pointing out that the costs of many consumer policy proposals far outweigh any potential benefits.

Analyzing and Resolving Consumer Issues

The process of analyzing and resolving consumer issues generally involves constructive thinking, purposeful analytic thinking, preparation of alternative solutions, government action in the resolution of alternatives, and finally, the discovery of mutually satisfactory solutions.

Constructive Thinking

Constructive thinking is necessary in the resolution of consumer issues.[16] If conditions are ideal, the parties to a civilized argument or discussion in a democratic environment understand what questions they are arguing about, possess some relevant facts, accept facts demonstrated by others, and recognize a point where they should gather more facts. They would disagree about (1) which facts are the most important, (2) the significance of each fact, and/or (3) how the facts are related to one another.

When resolving consumer issues, it must be realistically recognized that some parties to an argument are uninformed, of dull mentality, or under the influence of a strong emotional bias. In such instances, persuasion to an acceptable resolution is more difficult and sometimes impossible. Thus, a crucial first step in successfully resolving consumer issues is to attempt to understand the emotional beliefs and attitudes, economic and political belief systems, and logic of the persons who hold opposing views. In this manner, one can begin to determine ways of thinking-feeling and translate the emotive-evaluative statements made by others. Willing people can then take appropriate steps toward resolving their differences. Then, persuasion depends primarily upon finding common values. To persuade someone to a viewpoint, one must link the new viewpoint with another value or argument shared by both.

Purposeful Analytical Thinking

Analytical thinking (or **analysis**) is an attempt to clarify and simplify a problem or issue using discipline and direction. The purpose of analytical thinking is to determine

---

[16]The logic for this section on constructive thinking is taken from Garey, D. B. (1957). *Putting Words in Their Places* (Scott, Foresman), Chapters 10-23.

CONSUMER UPDATE:
How to Initially Analyze a Consumer Problem

1. Specify the issue or problem that negatively affects consumers.

2. Which consumer right(s) does this problem or issue affect? List.

3. Explain how this problem or issue negatively affects each consumer right.

4. For each listed right, suggest alternative(s) to improve the status quo.

5. Which of the suggested alternatives might be most acceptable to the interests of consumers, governments, and businesses? Why?

---

precisely what a proposition means. A **proposition** is a plan, scheme, or proposal to resolve a problem or issue. Analytical thinking does not tell upon which side truth rests, rather it identifies the questions fundamental to the eventual resolution of a problem or issue. A model to analyze consumer problems is shown below.

Analytical thinking requires a description of the status quo. This could include the nature of the alleged problem or issue and its seriousness, as well as a review of existing relevant laws and regulations. Analysis also requires recognition of what is causing the problem or issue to be discussed. What is the origin and history of the proposition? What is the current controversy that makes this an issue? Why is this issue or problem critical at this time? Realistic interpretations of the causes are important because these may reveal appropriate lines for successful argument later.

Vital to the process of analysis is defining terms, including both stipulated and reported definitions. The resulting in-depth background understanding of the subject also should provide a sufficient amount of evidence to support later arguments. It is imperative to differentiate between something perceived as an initial issue or problem and the ultimate issue or problem, because the latter is more important to an appropriate final resolution.

Analytical thinking also reveals that those groups involved in consumer issues tend to try to protect or maximize their own personal interests or what they think is the public interest. Groups try to protect their interests and advance only those policies which they think will benefit society or themselves. Purposeful analytical thinking requires that one constantly ask how much each group or its program will gain or lose from government action or inaction and how much time and effort each group should expend lobbying on the issue. Disagreements often surround concerns about choice, fairness, safety, competitive markets, right to information, benefit-cost analysis, and assigning responsibility for action.

Since it is easier to defeat a proposal than it is to carefully shepherd a new idea into fruition, one should critically analyze each stage of the policy development when promoting a consumer protection proposal. The early stage of how the problem or issue is originally shaped may be as critical to later success as the later stage of what groups to involve in the formulation of the policy. Similar careful attention must be given to the stages of policy adoption, policy implementation, and policy evaluation.

At all stages, it is vital to frame the debate of an issue in the proper (and most favorable) terms. Business might want to say, "How clean and wholesome do you want your chicken?" and "How much are you prepared to spend?" Meanwhile, consumers should try to keep the focus on "Do you want clean and wholesome chicken or unsafe chicken?"

Participants in support of consumer protection proposals must clarify their goals or objectives and rank them. They should then list all possible solutions while investigating the likelihood of achieving each. After considering each alternative, they should then choose an approach that will achieve the consequences most closely matching their goals.

Preparing Alternative Solutions

In preparing the analysis of a proposed solution to a consumer problem or issue, (1) it must be shown that the present situation includes at least one important deficiency or harm; (2) it must be shown that the proposed approach to resolution would be superior to the status quo; (3) it must be shown that deficiency or harm exists in the status quo; (4) the principles of the planned resolution must be described and, if possible, demonstrated; and (5) finally, it must be demonstrated that the proposal will actually resolve the alleged problems in the future and result in certain advantages.

A useful method of analysis is the **deductive approach**. Here the procedure is to list the main issues and all the subpoints for each fundamental argument. Alternatively, one can list affirmative and negative arguments (factual, rational, emotional, logical, or whatever) in two columns and then identify the points of agreement and disagreement. Properly constructed, the deductive approach results in fully describing all the critical aspects on both sides of an issue.

Most disputes about consumer issues are conducted democratically, in the rough and tumble of open debate in the political commotion and uproar of a robust representative democracy. Each side to a debate is interested in maximizing its position and will compromise only when necessary. Typically, there is an initial difference of opinion on what the outcome or resolution should be. Thus, the mindset begins with more for one side of the issue, meaning less for the other. The task then becomes one of reaching resolution without the stronger party compelling a solution that imposes a loss on the other because the weaker party will break off negotiations in such circumstances.

In order for an acceptable resolution to be reached between private parties, both must benefit. What is necessary for resolution between private parties is that the benefits of agreement equal or exceed the costs of not agreeing.

When there are only private parties involved in resolving an issue, the resolution choices are (1) compromise, (2) one side wins while the other side loses, or (3) deadlock. While the first alternative, compromise, may be desirable, the likelihood of the other two alternatives is greater.

Since parties involved in resolving issues, particularly consumer issues, often vary in strength, they may never reach a compromise because the stronger one either defeats the weaker or a compromise is forced by the stronger with more benefits going to the stronger. For example, strong business lobbies often defeat proposals by consumer groups for effective and easily understandable grade labeling on food products, such as an A, B, C, D system. Accordingly, many consumer issues remain unresolved between business and consumer groups because of the likelihood of suboptimal resolution alternatives. In fact, these can be described as market-failure situations.

**CONSUMER UPDATE: How to Successfully
Move a Consumer Issue Forward***

The goal in working on consumer issues is to improve the lives of consumers. You have to be there during the legislative, regulatory, and policy making discussions or someone else will make consumer decisions for you in your absence. Their views may well be different from yours. To be successful, advocates of the consumer interest should (1) set idealistic goals, and (2) push for genuine progress toward the goals.

To do so, advocates of the consumer interest should: (1) adopt effective tactics (or stand by and get marginalized in the process), (2) use appropriate rhetoric (because inappropriate statements and negative personalizations will dissuade today's opponents from supporting your position on the next issue), (3) avoid attributing bad motives to your opponents (for the same reasons), and (4) put your issue into the context of the popular issues of the day, such as the proposal "helps reduce health care costs" or "helps increase productivity." The overall key to influencing government while you are working on the issue is to develop and offer a well-reasoned analysis of how government and the other participants can successfully obtain progress.

*Mark Silbergeld, Director, Consumers Union Washington Office

---

Government Action in Resolving Alternatives

Public issues are subtlety different from private issues. Government gets involved in the resolution of numerous consumer problems and issues for two reasons: (1) because it desires to ensure outcomes that will protect the public interest, and (2) because it often perceives that government can improve the outcome of many resolutions. Moreover, government intervenes in the generation of alternative solutions for many consumer problems and issues on the justification that there will be **net public benefits**. When government is involved in resolving consumer problems and issues, it must induce others—consumers, laborers, businesses, and other nations—to forego or limit anticipated private gain and instead accept realistic gains to themselves and to society in general.

A rational strategy for both business and consumer interest groups is to analyze how to get government support and deny it to others. When government refuses to become seriously involved in resolving a consumer issue, the private parties are left to try to reach a compromise situation, realizing that a good compromise might not ever be reached.

The extent and degree of government involvement depends on the particulars of each issue and the values of the public (i.e., consumers, manufacturers, retailers, labor, etc.) about what would constitute a reasonable, just, and equitable compromise alternative. Government can ensure outcomes that will protect the public interest, not just serve the interests of consumers over business, for example, and at the same time improve the quality of the compromise. Thus, active government involvement in the resolution of consumer issues has the potential to improve the efficiency of market forces.

How to Lobby the Government Decision Making Process

Attempting to influence the outcome of a legislative or regulatory decision is a time-honored tradition in all societies. In a representative democracy, lobbying is a constitutional right of every citizen. Lobbying is the most fundamental way a person can exercise his or her constitutional right to speak out and petition government. A lobbyist's job is to educate public policy decision makers about an issue and obtain commitments to support one position or another. Lobbyists who receive compensation to influence legislation generally must register with the legislature being lobbied; citizens who simply try to influence the process usually need not register.

The Legislative Process

The political culture and procedures of each of the 50 state legislatures and the U.S. Congress varies, and successful lobbying requires knowledge of the processes. Legislatures typically meet once or twice a year. Legislators are elected by the people in the district where they live, and part of a legislator's responsibilities is to accurately reflect the views of those citizens. Most of the work of legislatures is done through their committees, and the chairs of those committees are powerful members of the legislature.

Recognize that it is far easier to defeat a proposal than to carefully shepherd it to success because there are so many opportunities for opponents to have access to the political process. The measure of success to corporate lobbyists, the monied interests, is how many times the legislative process was thwarted. At the national level, over 6,000 bills are introduced every year. Procedurally, after a bill has been introduced by a member of the legislature, often by an influential legislator, it is assigned to a committee where consideration of the proposal begins as a subcommittee or committee hears its merits. Testimony may or may not be considered. Knowledge of the relative power and biases of each member of the committee is crucial to the lobbying process to get the bill successfully reported out of committee.

The bill then may or may not be debated by the whole house. Amendments may or may not be offered (or even permitted) at this point. Many legislatures then require a second reading and then a third reading to put the bill to a final vote. When a bill passes the first house, it goes onto the second house (if one exists). Here the proposal goes through the same process all over. Amendments made in the second house must also be approved by the first house before the bill goes to the governor (or the president at the federal level). Differences are generally worked out by a conference committee, composed of powerful legislators, and substantial changes are often made at this point. The governor (or the president at the national level) affects the political process by signing or vetoing the bill. A legislature usually needs a two-thirds vote to override the veto and make the bill law.

Know Your Lawmakers

Fortunately, a mountain of public information is available about each legislator. Getting to know where a legislator is "coming from" is vital to the lobbying process because each legislator inevitably votes in his or her enlightened self-interest. Each person's political and economic ideologies can be surmised by reviewing factors such as a legislator's voting record, political party affiliation, employment history, financial interests, business dealings, campaign contributors, and a socio-economic description of the district being represented. Remember that a legislator's position on any single issue will be motivated by a mixture of objectives, some internal and external, but almost always by the interest in being re-elected. Often the most important factor for a legislator in determining how to vote is knowledge of how his or her constituents feel about it. When talking with your legislator, personalize the issue. Emphasize how it affect the lives of your family and friends.

Know Your Issue

The quality of the arguments put forth in support of and against a proposal have much to do with legislative success or failure. Try to emphasize solutions that will not cost the government money. Virtually all the pro and con arguments surrounding a proposal must be considered carefully. Key sources of information for a lobbyist include the staff of legislators and committees, regulatory agencies, and trade associations. Remember that legislators always need solid, rational reasons to support a particular position. A good lobbyist needs to know the arguments of opponents quite well so such points can be honestly, accurately, and objectively projected, and then refuted and downplayed when appropriate. Legislators are generally in need of background information about issues. If you become the expert and have the most information to offer, leaders will rely upon you as a resource.

Lobbying can take the form of personal contact with legislators and their staffs (no more than 30 minutes at a time), mobilization of large numbers of organized citizens, "grassroots" support from a particular constituency, coalitions of groups, involvement of public officials, support of affected private individuals and groups, arousing the public, and fractionalizing and manipulating the opponents. Multiple approaches are common. Most proposals are defeated, considering that well over 90 percent of all bills never pass.

Successful lobbying requires being ready to adapt, negotiate and compromise. Few good proposals pass the first time around, and an effort requiring 5 to 10 years for a bill to pass is typical. Commitment to an issue over a long time is vital to success.

Resolution of Consumer Issues Through Cooperation

Communication and cooperation move debates of consumer issues toward negotiated resolutions using a model of cooperation rather than confrontation. The evolution of a consumer issue is shown in Figure 11-1. Meredith M. Layer, former senior vice president for public responsibility of the American Express Company, says that such an approach to resolution "is about developing new techniques for gaining insight into consumer attitudes and expectations, and avoiding unnecessary confusion, complaints, and conflict." Smart corporations are finding that it is to their advantage to intervene early in the issue-resolution process so that mutual interests with others can be identified and dealt with appropriately. Increasingly, corporations and consumer leaders are working together in resolving consumer issues.

Cooperation requires building relationships among consumer advocates, academics, government personnel, and businesspersons. The process demands trust and understanding

FIGURE 11-1 The Evolution of a Consumer Issue

between those on opposing sides of issues. It requires creative collaboration where people seek to build respect for each other instead of identifying winners and losers. To succeed you should look for a resolution that all parties can agree to and promote that option.

The participants who cooperatively come together to try to resolve consumer issues may have divergent views at the outset, but they must be willing to listen to other perspectives. The intent should be to discover ways to work together so that all parties are sitting together facing the problem instead of facing each other. This requires clarifying areas of disagreement in non-argumentative ways and initially looking for areas of agreement, no matter how small. This approach develops inclusive relationships that are built on trust. The result is thinking together to resolve problems and issues. Recognition of positive work should go to the politicians because they have a stake in the issue; politicians also need to feel psychologically committed. Success is judged on how the economic welfare of consumers has been improved.

Issues That Would Strengthen the Balance of Power Between Consumers and Sellers

More than 100 consumer issues are examined in this book. While many consumer issues have been dealt with in the past with varying degrees of success, other issues remain and more will arise with changing societal conditions and expectations. This section lists and discusses a number of consumer issues that are aimed at strengthening the balance of power between consumers and sellers.

1. Fully Fund Regulatory Agencies

Most regulatory agencies are given a broad legal mandate, but not enough funds to accomplish their goals. While some agencies could use an expansion of their powers, the budget cuts of the past 15 years has cut deeply into their effectiveness. Almost all agencies need increased funding and additional personnel to properly carry out their legal mandates to protect consumers.

2. Encourage Public Participation in Regulatory Proceedings

Too often in regulatory proceedings on both the federal and state levels there is little input from consumers on issues of concern to them. The interests of consumers are just not heard. Why is this? A study of the appointment calendars of the more than 50 regulatory agency heads at the federal level shows that they have 10 times as many meetings with industry representatives as they have with consumer representatives. Similarly, in adjudicatory proceedings, the input from the business community is many times more than that offered by consumer spokespersons. Clearly, there are not enough spokespersons in the consumer interest field.

The public needs improved representation and access to government officials. Consumer interest organizations want legislation that will permit broader participation and representation of consumers and owners of small businesses. These are the groups that normally cannot afford to participate in agency and court proceedings, therefore, they are the voices that are most often not heard in such regulatory actions. What is needed is reimbursement for reasonable attorney and expert witness fees, plus related expenses to ensure that regulators hear a point of view that normally would not be represented.

3. Create Financial Consumer Associations

Common sense, as well as research, suggests that the views of consumers are infrequently heard in financial policy decisions. Industry is always well represented. **Financial consumer associations (FCAs)** are an idea proposed by Representatives Charles Schumer and Joseph Kennedy. FCAs are envisioned as federally chartered, volunteer, member-supported citizen empowerment groups charged with a responsibility to inject a consumer perspective into the financial aspects of policy decisions. FCAs are designed after **Citizen Utility Boards (CUBs)** which have had considerable success in various states. CUBs are funded by member dues to serve as watchdog organizations that intervene in rate cases and legislative hearings on electric, gas and telephone matters.

FCAs would have to be established by law because of their system of funding. The law governing FCAs would require banking institutions to periodically place a notice in customer's statements inviting people to join. Such mandated access provides an opportunity for consumer leaders to get their messages out and ask for a $10 membership fee. A national board of volunteers, elected by the members, would set policy. FCAs would represent consumers' interests before Congress, state legislatures, and federal and state regulatory agencies.

4. Encourage Corrective Advertising

Corrective advertising is a concept that the consumer interest suggests should be widely used by regulatory agencies such as the Federal Trade Commission (FTC). The FTC has the power, which it seldom uses, to include in a consent decree with a business a requirement that it run advertising to correct any false impressions left in the public's mind by previous advertising. The intent is to tell the truth and thus restore the competitive situation to what it was before the advertisements were originally run. Profile Bread, in a classic example, explained in a corrective ad that the reason why Profile Bread has fewer calories as stated in previous advertisements is because it was sliced thinner. In another classic case, Listerine was ordered by the FTC in a decision that was upheld by the U.S Supreme Court to run ads saying that "contrary to prior advertising, Listerine will not help prevent colds or sore throats or lessen their severity."

Corrective advertising is remedial in concept, and it is meant to take away the unfair advantage that an advertiser may have gained by running unfair advertisements. Corrective advertising will not serve as a deterrent to future deception unless it is used more widely.

5. Broaden the Use of Mediation and Arbitration

It is very important for consumers who have complaints about products and services to get their concerns resolved in a timely manner. People with a consumer problem usually turn first to the merchant for **mediation**, obtaining a compromise between a consumer and a seller. If satisfaction is not obtained, the consumer can turn for help to the Better Business Bureau, to an industry trade association, or to a government consumer protection agency.

Throughout the process of trying to resolve consumer problems, there should be numerous opportunities for mediation and arbitration. **Arbitration** is a method of having a dispute between two or more parties resolved by the judgment of an impartial person who is knowledgeable in the area of controversy.

The consumer interest argues that all businesses should have written complaint handling procedures available to the public and that all communities should have arbitration courts to resolve differences between sellers and consumers. These could be newly created neighborhood arbitration courts or the more traditional small claims courts, Better Business Bureaus, and consumer action panels.

6. Expand Consumer Education

The need for consumer education classes in schools is so obvious that it is difficult to imagine why the subject is not required instruction everywhere. Fewer than a dozen states require that consumer education be made available to students, but rarely is it taught to all students. The nation's schools have as their major objective to give students a general education, along with enough skills and abilities that when they graduate they can get jobs and make a contribution to society. Today's schools do not emphasize living skills. They ostensibly prepare students to go on for higher education or to get jobs, but they do not seem to prepare students to live life. Hans B. Thorelli once observed that, "We need more consumer *education*—and notably for the underprivileged. Without education there is no motivation or receptivity, indeed, no basis for informed consumership."[17]

Consumers have to live in the capitalistic American economic marketplace; no other option exists. We also realize that our market economy does not function perfectly and, further, that it never will. In the meantime, consumers every day are faced with a marketplace that contains anti-competitive practices and a whole host of deceptions and misrepresentations. Consumers continue to make poor buying decisions based on insufficient and sometimes inaccurate information. The U.S. marketplace, therefore, makes it hard for consumers to get their money's worth. Ralph Nader observes that, "We don't grow up civic--we grow up corporate. In the schools, we learn how to sell...We don't learn anything about how to be a skilled consumer or skilled citizen."[18]

A better-educated citizenry, in terms of consumer information and issues, can greatly help all consumers live a better quality of life. Consumers must be educated to understand market conditions that can affect them negatively, to know how to go about effectively buying within the American marketplace, and appreciate the mechanisms to help them change the market while securing, protecting, and asserting their consumer rights. Pro-

---

[17]Thorelli, H. B. (1971, November). Concentration of Information Power Among Consumers. *Journal of Marketing Research, 8*, 432.

[18]Nye, P. (1993, January/February). Interview with Ralph Nader: Looking into the 21st Century. *Public Citizen*, p. 19.

active consumer-citizens are needed to help make the American marketplace function more effectively for consumers.

A succinct and widely accepted definition of consumer education has evolved from efforts of the National Institute for Consumer Education: "**Consumer education** is the process of gaining the knowledge and skills needed in managing consumer resources and taking actions to influence the factors which affect consumer decisions." Historically consumer education has focused on providing information; instead, perhaps it should be a catalyst for citizen empowerment.

Consumers Flunk Consumer Education Test

A recent comprehensive test on the nation's consumer knowledge revealed serious inadequacies. Developed by consumer experts, administered by the Educational Testing Service (ETS), and funded by the TRW Foundation, the findings revealed that consumers correctly know only 54 percent of the questions about everyday consumption items. Since it was a four-item multiple-choice exam, guessing should have provided everyone with a score of 25 percent. Fifty-four percent is low!

The test covered the consumption areas of banking, insurance, housing, food, product safety, and durable goods, and it was given to over 1100 people nationwide. The subject areas where consumers scored the poorest were housing purchases, checking/saving, food purchases, and life insurance.

Examples of missed questions include: the annual percentage rate is the best index of the cost of a loan (37% correct), who real estate agents legally represent (33% correct), the decreasing importance of life insurance as one grows older (26% correct), and what agency issues information of auto recalls (17% correct). Those in their twenties scored much lower than those in their forties and fifties. One observer commented on the findings that, "The people show a fierce determination to remain dumb as a post."

Review and Summary of Key Terms and Concepts

1. Briefly summarize the concept of **power clusters** and provide examples of their behaviors. In your response, include explanations of an **attentive public** and a **latent public**.

2. Comment on the anger in the body politic and how people are turning to **civics** as an outlet.

3. Distinguish among the following: **ideology**, **economic ideology**, and **political ideology**.

4. Summarize the key aspects of the **neoclassical belief system**, and include in your response comments on **consumer sovereignty**.

5. What primary differences exist between the **managerial belief system** and the **neoclassical belief system**?

6. Briefly summarize the **reformist belief system**, being sure to explain **the planning system** and **the market system**.

7. Compare and contrast the beliefs of the major **political ideologies, conservatism** and **liberalism**.

8. Summarize the beliefs of **communitarianism**.

9. Which kinds of **consumer protection proposals** would receive the most support? The least?

10. Distinguish between **constructive thinking** and **analytical thinking**.

11. List the five steps to **initially analyze** a problem.

12. Offer some guidelines on preparing **alternative solutions** to resolve problems and on moving a consumer issue forward.

13. Explain why **government** gets into policy debates and what it can add to the **problem resolution process**.

14. List some guidelines on how to **lobby** the legislature.

15. Compare the strengths of resolving consumer issues through **confrontation** or **cooperation**.

16. Give examples of **issues** that might help to **strengthen the balance the power** of consumers with sellers.

17. Distinguish between a **financial consumer association** and **citizen utility boards**.

18. Summarize the idea of **corrective advertising**.

19. Distinguish between **mediation** and **arbitration**.

20. Why is **consumer education** important?

Useful Resource for Consumers

Consumer World is a mega Internet site that includes over 900 sources of information—http://www.consumerworld.org

Consumer Action
1730 Rhode Island Avenue, NW, Ste. 403
Washington, DC 20036
202-775-1580

Public Citizen Congress Watch
215 Pennsylvania Avenue, S.E.
Washington, DC 20003
202-546-4996

"What Do You Think" Questions

1.   From your experience, what do you think is a powerful **power cluster** in the United States? Identify ten organizations and key people in that **issue network**. Think from perspectives of local, state and national.

2.   What is your **economic belief system**? Looking a Table 11-1, identify two characteristics of that belief system that you really agree with, and explain why you hold those views.

3.   Describe yourself as a **liberal** or a **conservative** (a middle-of-the-road choice is not available in this exercise). Then identify the three most important characteristics of that **political ideology** that you really agree with, and explain why you hold those views.

4.   Select any issue of importance to you, not necessarily consumer related, for which a **problem** exists. Review the **model for analyzing a consumer problem** and offer brief comments on each step in that sequence.

Appendix Issue 11-A:
Proposed Consumer Protection Legislation and Regulations

The significant proposed consumer protection legislation and regulations are shown in Table 11A-1 below. One could easily analyze which measures have the support or opposition of persons holding the different economic belief systems.

Year Passed	Law or Regulation	Major Provisions
Proposed	Consumer Protection Against Price-Fixing Act	To reverse Supreme Court anti-trust law rulings and strictly prohibit vertical price fixing, particularly stopping manufacturers from ordering discount stores to set higher prices
Proposed	Retail Competition Enforcement Act	To promote price competition and make price fixing less burdensome to prove
Proposed	Airline Competition Enhancement Act	To give the FTC authority to oversee the industry and encourage competition
Proposed	Ground Transportation Consumer Protection Act	To block airport from charging gross-receipts fees for off-airport car rental companies and set standards for any fees
Proposed	Financial Consumer Associations	To permit federally-chartered membership organizations to inject a consumer perspective into aspects of financial decisions made by government policy makers
Proposed	Consumer Protection Agency	To provide for a formal consolidation of existing federal consumer offices and to allow advocates to present the positions of the consumer interest in federal decision making; includes authority to appeal cases to the courts
Proposed	Class Action Lawsuit Act	To facilitate joint redress through the courts when groups of consumers have common problems
Proposed	Public Participation Act	To provide funds to reimburse costs and expenses of persons testifying before regulatory agencies, such as consumers and owners of small businesses
Proposed	Investment Advisor Regulation Act	To force financial planners to disclose fully to clients how they are compensated
Proposed	Reform of Credit Reporting Practices	To make it easier for consumers to get access to their credit reports and to correct errors
Proposed	Product Liability "Reform"	To decrease the protections offer by strong state product liability laws in existence in most states by limiting the ability of consumer to sue for damages—an anti-consumer bill
Proposed	National Lemon Law	To decrease the protections offered by strong state lemon laws in existence in over 40 states—an anti-consumer bill
Proposed	Truth-in-Investment Return Act	To require all forms of investments to make full disclosure of rate of return information and provide comparable data on yields

Year Passed	Law or Regulation	Major Provisions
Proposed	Repeal of Rule of 78s	To prohibit the use of the Rule of 78s in all consumer loan transactions
Proposed	Reform of McCarran-Ferguson Act	To repeal some of the anti-trust exemptions granted the insurance industry under the McCarran-Ferguson Act
Proposed	National No-Fault Automobile Insurance Act	To set minimum standards for a comprehensive automobile insurance program in which an accident victim's personal injury expenses are paid by his or her own insurance company, regardless of who is at fault

TABLE 11A-1   Proposed Consumer Protection Legislation and Regulations

Chapter 12

Decision Making in Today's Complex Society

OBJECTIVES

After reading this chapter, you should be able to

1. Give several reasons why decision making is more difficult for today's consumers than it was 20 or 30 years ago.

2. Understand the Geistfeld Model of Consumer Choice.

3. Appreciate how to be a pro-environmental consumer.

4. Recognize and describe misleading and deceptive advertising, including ads directed at children.

Today's consumers can be described (to borrow a phrase) as "harried consumers." They are overwhelmed with choices, challenged with new technologies, flooded with information (and much of it is very good and useful), and live in a time when crass commercialism[1] and private materialism have become society's dominant value system, perhaps even its ideology. Consumers today have a weak understanding of sellers' persuasive marketing techniques and thus fall prey to many bad deals and ripoffs. Consumers frequently fail to prioritize among their many needs and wants, and they often fail to make rational buying decisions.

This chapter begins by identifying many reasons why decision making is more difficult for today's consumers than it was 20 or 30 years ago. It thoroughly explains the Geistfeld Model of Consumer Choice is then presented. Following is a section on how to be a pro-environmental consumer. The chapter concludes with a look at deceptive and misleading advertising, including a discussion of television advertising aimed at children.

Reasons Why Decision Making Is Getting More Difficult

Consumption decisions are more difficult than they were 20 or 30 years ago. A typical **consumer decision** occurs as a consumer selects, from among alternatives or preferences, a good or service in a marketplace transaction. Consumers generally try to make good decisions. To do so, each decision is made according to the consumer's values and attitudes in the context of the availability and price of choices at the time.

Economists use the term **rational self-interest** to describe how people make choices. At the individual level, most consumer decisions are undertaken egoistically in a reasonable effort to maximize utility. **Utility** is each person's subjective measure of something's usefulness. The utility of a good or service is its ability to satisfy a human want. While utility is only the ability to satisfy, the actual satisfaction occurs only when goods having utility are used, which destroys some of their ability to satisfy further. A reduction of utility occurs that presumably increases human welfare.

The Consumer Search for Value

Total customer value "is the bundle of benefits customers expect from a given product or service.[2] Consumers search for value in their purchasing decisions. Erik de Gier[3], Research Director for *Consumentenbond* in the Netherlands, suggests that the determinants of total customer value are product value, service value, personnel value, image value, monetary price, time cost, energy cost, and psychic cost. These are the factors that contribute to or detract from consumer satisfaction.

---

[1]**Commercialism** is defined by Michael Jacobson in his book, *Marketing Madness* (Westview Press, 1995), as "the ubiquitous product marketing that leads to a preoccupation with individual consumption to the detriment of oneself and society."

[2]Kotler, P.H. (1994), *Marketing Management: Analysis, Planning, Implementation, and Control*, Prentice Hall, 37-38.

[3]de Gier, Erick (1996), The informed consumer: The believability of research-based ratings, paper presented to the American Council on Consumer Interests.

Consumer Dissatisfaction Occurs

Consumer dissatisfaction in marketplace transactions occurs for a number of reasons, suggests Swedish professor Sloveig Wikstrom:[4] (1) when the number of products increases, the likelihood of unsuccessful transactions increases, (2) when the growing complexity of goods and services makes assessment more difficult, (3) when the number of varieties can become almost overwhelming, (4) when consumers are overconfident that the government is protecting them, (5) when people are busier and have less time, (6) and when increased education and advertising raise consumers' expectations.

Consumers also become frustrated, annoyed, and even dissatisfied when the products and services they purchase do not perform as anticipated and fail to meet their reasonable expectations about performance, durability, safety, and quality in general. **Buyer's remorse** is the term given to a consumer's mistaken expectations about a product, and it occurs when buyers regret their purchases.

The Number and Complexity of Products Is Increasing

The processes of searching and decision making have become more complicated because of the proliferation and diversity of products, technological advances, product complexity, and changes in retail market structures. For example, because the government ordered the breakup of the telephone industry through divestiture, consumers must select among long-distance carriers, choose a number of service features from the local operating company, decide to buy or rent equipment, determine how best to handle repair bills, and decipher detailed bills. Thus, an information overload problem exists for consumers buying telephone services.

Challenges also confront today's consumers in banking and credit. Automated teller machines, direct deposits of paychecks, electronic payment of bills, and home banking are just some of the financial transaction choices available today. Money market deposit accounts, adjustable-rate mortgage loans, home equity credit-line loans, variable-rate bank credit cards, and interest-free checking also are options. These alternatives were unheard of 20 years ago, and similar multitudes of new alternatives are available in nearly every area of consumer expenditure—housing, clothing, transportation, health care, insurance, investments, and so on.

Consumer markets today are larger and more complex than ever before, resulting in an enormous number of products from which to choose. Over 2500 new products are introduced every year, and even though 90 percent survive less than 3 years, this still creates a crowded marketplace. There are over 600 models of new vehicles in the marketplace. It is a sign of a healthy, democratic, capitalistic society to have a great number of products and services to choose from, but such diversity simultaneously provides confusion for consumers.

---

[4]Wikstom, S. (1981). Consumer Dissatisfaction; Scope and Policy Implications. *Studies in the Economics and Organization of Action* (discussion paper of the Department of Business Administration, University of Lund, Sweden), 1-10.

CONSUMER UPDATE:
Why Markets Sometimes Have Only Lousy Choices Available

Adverse selection occurs in many markets. This happens when unobserved qualities are misvalued because of a lack of information. Some examples follow. In the used vehicle market, high-quality vehicles are usually traded to dealers leaving only low-quality vehicles for sale by nondealers. Thus, consumers shopping for used vehicles find a great number of poor-quality vehicles.   In the auto insurance market, the majority of people who purchase insurance are good drivers. As the cost of insurance rises, the good drivers reduce their coverage while poor drivers maintain their coverage, and soon only high-riskiest drivers are in the market to buy insurance. Effective consumer decision making in the retail mattress industry market is frustrated by the purposeful lack of standardization by the manufacturers.

To Cope With the Challenging Marketplace, Many Consumers Blindly Follow Rules of Thumb

Many consumers react to marketplace complexities in their decision making by following **rules of thumb**. These are useful principles that have wide application but are not intended to be strictly accurate. Consumers use various rules of thumb to reduce search costs. Brenda Cude[5] notes some examples of rules of thumb about quality that many consumers use: "buying brand name goods" (actually a poor predictor), "using seals of approval" (sometimes helpful), "buying top-of-the-line merchandise" (better quality, but one also gets unnecessary product features), and "buying high-priced goods" (true for some goods, but false for others). A rule of thumb about price is that "larger sizes are better buys," however, this is often invalid.

Consumer Make Many Irrational Marketplace Decisions

Silber observes that humans have "inherent information processing limits and inabilities to estimate probabilities accurately."[6] It seems that human cognitive limitations sometimes affect decision making negatively. Silber explains that consumers often do not maximize their best interests because irrationality "may be reasonable where the decision-making task is overwhelming." One explanation for the behavior is that the greater the stress and the perceived risk in a decision making situation, the more frustrated and anxious some consumers become. Here many consumers act "reasonably" by not searching for information.

Much human behavior is irrational, including consumer decision making. All people must accept their personal limits as humans and move on. The emotional, non-logical, instinctive side of human nature is probably the normal way of doing things; analytical effort in decision making often is not the dominant manner when thinking, feeling, and

---

[5]For an excellent discussion of this topic, see Cude, B. J. (1990). Students Learn by Doing: Teaching About Rules of Thumb. *Advancing the Consumer Interest*, 2, 19-25.

[6]Silber, N. I. (1990, Spring), Observing Reasonable Consumers: Cognitive Psychology, Consumer Behavior and Consumer Law. *Loyola Consumer Law Reporter*, 2, 70.

acting. This is why much advertising is emotional rather than rational. People make many illogical decisions. Fortunately, not every irrational consumer decision is genuinely stupid.

Researchers are coming to the conclusion that even in purchases of functional products, most consumers are swayed primarily by how a product appeals to their emotions and cultural values instead of its rational factors, such as durability or ease of use. University of Wisconsin researcher Esther Thurson suggests that most people have very little conscious involvement with the things they buy. Thurson observes that, "making consumers feel something is much more important than convincing them that a product is better." It seems that every consumer product purchased satisfies a set of human emotional needs that may be more important to purchasers than the functional needs that the product serves.

Consumers (Irrationally) Often Ignore the Discount Rate

Decision making is tough enough without having to consider the effects over the long term. However, consumers waste money when the time value of money is ignored. The correct consumer finance decision is, when possible, to spend a little more up front to save a lot more money in the future.

For example, energy efficiency labels adorn many large appliances and show consumers which brands operate more efficiently. To illustrate, visualize product A selling for $600, which costs $25 to operate annually, and product B selling for $500, which costs $75 to operate annually. The better choice is simple: pay $100 extra for product A and recoup the $100 from lower operating costs in just a few years.

Unfortunately, many consumers consistently make the wrong choice, both in terms of value for money and disutility for the community at large. Why? Economists and psychologists have not figured it out yet, but some of the reason appears to be an inability of many people to accept the wisdom of discount rates, even when it is explained to them.

The **discount rate** is a measure of the value of a dollar today compared to one received some time in the future. In spite of the simplicity of mathematically applying the impact of inflation and interest earned (perhaps 7 percent combined) to the choices and deriving the correct answer, many people set unreasonably high discount rates for choices they face. They often set irrationally high rates that never could be actually earned. Consumers often make the wrong value-for-money decision even when they discount the choices by 20, 30 or even 100 percent. Seems like many people believe that a bird in the hand is worth two in the bush, even when it is a poor choice.

Information Processing for Consumers Is Difficult, But It Has Very High Potential Payoffs

Consumers are bombarded with volumes of technical information that is difficult to process. Without the advice of experts to guide them, consumers today have difficulty in even understanding which product attributes contribute to quality, desirability, safety, and good performance. Therefore, consumers increasingly rely on the informed judgments of others, particularly product-rating magazines, to help them in decision making. Reliable translators and processors of information include such publications as *Consumer Reports*, *Kiplinger's Personal Finance Magazine*, and *Money*. The difficulty of effective choicemaking forces most consumers to optimize their preferences by ranking them, often from the best to worst. Final selection then is based on the optimal choice for the individual or family. **Optimizing** is making something as good or as effective as possible.

After reviewing the research literature, author James H. Snider calculated that the average American spends nine percent of his or her nonworking, nonsleeping time gathering information for consumer decision making. That includes time spent watching television advertising, and Snider calculates that it amounts to four hours of time for every $100 spent. He also estimates that poorly informed decision making results in consumer confusion and frustration that adds 20 percent to the cost of every purchasing decision people make.

When the searching and decision making of consumers are effective, the products bought fit consumers' wants and the products are obtained with relatively small expenditures of time, effort, and money. Poor consumer search and decision making mean that consumers spend more, in both money and time, yet satisfy fewer requirements.

Snider concludes that the availability of perfect information, which would enable cost-effective decisions to be made, would save consumers 20 percent or permit selections that gave 20 percent more value.[7] Cornell professor E. Scott Maynes calls such positive results **consumer payoffs**; "gains obtained through effective purchasing via lower prices, better quality, or both."[8]

CONSUMER UPDATE:
Yes, the Poor Are Disadvantaged in the Marketplace

Economically poor consumers do pay more in the marketplace. Many factors cause disadvantaged consumers to do more poorly than the remainder of society in the economic marketplace. There are a number of consumer problems associated with values, attitudes and lifestyles of the poor. Sporadic income causes some to buy more than they can afford and to use credit, even for essentials like food. Poor people are less likely to read newspapers and generally do not seek much product information. They take on too much debt, often spending 70 percent of take-home pay on necessities. Somehow, discretionary spending also remains high. Many spend 50 percent of their incomes on housing costs alone; most do not save. Insurance is usually not purchased in amounts needed for adequate protection. The markets in which they shop do not enhance efficient choices. Some merchants use exploitative selling techniques. Many discriminate on the basis of race, ethnicity or appearance. Both ghetto and rural poor have a restricted shopping area while availability of transportation to more efficient shopping areas and the time to do so are often limited.

Many consumers today are able to evaluate, select, purchase, and service many products by using computers in their homes and using Internet services. Society is moving toward an information and telecommunications infrastructure that permits easy access to high-quality marketplace information for consumers. That also means everyone in the nation must in the future become computer literate to be effective shoppers. Then all consumers will have the availability of independent and trusted information sources that will empower them to more effectively participate in marketplace decisions. (Currently,

---

[7]Snider, J. H. (1993, January-February). Consumers in the Information Age. *The Futurist*, 15-19.
[8]Maynes, E. S. (1976). *Decision-making for Consumers* (p. 18). New York: Macmillan.

30 percent of all homes have a computer and half of all workers use a computer at their place of employment.)

Today's marketplace requires more and better-quality consumer information and education programs. To make rational consumer decisions increasingly requires consumers who are willing and able to spend considerable amounts of time, money, and effort searching and deciding.

Price Discrimination Exists and Is Taken Advantage of by Informed Consumers

The 1990s have ushered in the decade of good prices for consumers. Price has pushed aside the previously important factors of selection, convenience, and ambience in the marketplace. Sellers are willing to deal. **Price discrimination**, says Maynes, occurs when "a single seller charges different customers different prices for the same product."[9] Examples include discounts on motels for senior citizens, weekday (or evening only) supermarket specials, frequent-flyer clubs, rebates, free delivery services, upgrades of a product or service, and cents-off coupons.[10] Here the seller discriminates against one type of buyer in favor of another with the goal to charge each consumer the highest price that each is willing to pay.

Individual consumers who are able and willing to seek the lower price/higher quality deals actually do pay less than others. Winning the lower prices may take considerable time, effort, and energy, but for some consumers it's worth it—better prices and/or better quality. Other consumers just pay more.

Any instance of price bargaining, also called **haggling**, is price discrimination because some consumers do better than others. To win in the price discrimination battle, just ask for a better price or better quality for the same price. For example, when making reservations for a hotel or auto rental, simply ask for a better rate; chances are you will get it. Wise consumers realize that the price of almost any product can be bargained lower, especially on goods valued over $200. To be successful, be assertive and speak to a person in charge, such as a manager instead of a clerk, and speak quietly when you make an offer. Be prepared to walk away, too.

Time Is Limited for Decision Making

Adding to our burden of rational decision making is that most of us have limited time because we are very busy people. Lifestyles for many Americans are busier than they were a generation ago, particularly for those who have only a little time left at the end of a long working day. The growing numbers of dual-earner households, especially those with children, often lament their hurried lifestyles. Partly as a result, new products and

---

[9]The thoughts for the basis of this section are those of E. Scott Maynes, Professor Emeritus, Cornell University. See in particular Maynes, E. S. (1990). Price Discrimination: Lessons for Consumers. *Advancing the Consumer Interest*, 2, 22-27.

[10]A related concept is **product discrimination**. Maynes defines this as when "a single seller offers different variants of the same product to different customers for the same price." For example, a hotel upgrades a room for a special customer but charges the standard price.

DID YOU KNOW? Price Discrimination:
Some Frequent-Buyer Program Deals Are a Good Deal

"Earn miles while you drive, fly, sleep, shop, eat, talk, breathe..." "Use ABC credit card and get a rebate of 1 to 5 percent." "Use DEF telephone service and get 4,000 free air miles!" "Earn air miles at GHI hotel." "Accrue 700 shopping points at JKL store to earn a $25 gift certificate." "Join LMN retail book club and get up to 10 percent off on all purchases." "Purchase $15 in OPQ fast food and earn a free video rental."

These offers are examples of price discrimination. **Frequent-buyer programs** are intended to develop customer loyalty to the seller and they often are associated with the use of a particular credit card. Such discounts can be offered to consumers only as long as the deals cover their variable costs and lots of other consumers pay the regular higher prices.

Interested consumers need to compare the genuine value of each price/quality offer of a frequent-buyer program along with the costs required to participate, such as an annual fees and a certain interest rate on credit card. Frequent-buyer programs deals may be appropriate for some consumers, especially those who read and analyze the changing rules, those who calculate the economic fundamentals, credit card customers who pay their balances in full each month, those who have the extra time available to use or collect, people of moderate or low incomes whose opportunity costs are low, and consumers who are extraordinarily devoted to a particular seller's products.

---

services that use time more efficiently generally sell well. A *Wall Street Journal* survey revealed that the microwave was the American consumer's favorite household product, and they rated it "second in importance to their lives, just behind the smoke alarm."

To gain information to make effective choices, consumers must search for it, and that usually takes time, energy, and money. Search costs sometimes include health and happiness sacrifices as well. The increased opportunity costs of time expended tends to decrease comparison shopping efforts, particularly among higher-income consumers.

Searching? Comparison Shopping? Maybe, Maybe Not

In spite of the fact that the national motto of the U.S. apparently is "Shop until you drop," not all people spend hours and hours looking for product information. Some hate to shop.

Another motto is "Work, spend, work, spend." Many people today work and commute so many hours that they don't have time to shop. As a result, a number of consumers do not compare, but instead say, "I want that," and often act on their emotions. Others, after shopping for 1 or 2 hours in a mall, get stressed, exhausted, and even annoyed because they are exhausted after concentrating so hard when searching and making comparisons and choices. Thus, people limit their searches for information. Eleanor May, a University of Virginia professor, notes that, "looking is down and buying has gone up" because consumers are buying with less shopping.

Subjective expected utility (SEU) theory submits that a consumer's decision to engage in a specific behavior is dependent on the marginal rewards and costs that are expected from the behavior. Thus, the more you think you will benefit from comparison shopping (i.e., getting a good buy, increasing the purchasing power of one's income, enjoying the tax-free savings), the more likely you are to devote scarce time and energy to such tasks.

Many people do not comparison shop, even for expensive purchases, because they assume that the marginal benefits of comparison shopping will not exceed the marginal costs. Research on the topic of information search suggests that searching lowers the price paid by consumers up to a point, but after that, searching becomes unproductive.

Some Shop for "*Good* Buys" Instead of "*Best* Buys"

An alternative shopping model exists for some consumers.[11] Here price becomes the dominant force in decision making. The consumer's goals are to develop a sense for an acceptable level of quality or performance and to establish trigger prices for when a product might be a good buy. Consumers regularly monitor (search) the shopping environment maintaining familiarity with product variants and prices for a set of acceptable brands, while eliminating unsatisfactory brands and products. When a seller substantially lowers the price on an acceptable product, that action may trigger a purchase. This system eliminates the need to comparison shop in the traditional sense, taking a purposeful effort to compare models, product features, sellers, warranties, and prices. Using the **price-sensitive model**, consumers are satisfied getting good buys, instead of best buys.

Lifestyles and Values Affect Decision Making, Including Those That Are Politically Correct

Our values and goals also get mixed into the choice-making equation along with our personal lifestyles, particular customs and ceremonies, and how much money we are willing to spend. A **lifestyle** is a way of life or style of living that reflects the attitudes and values of an individual or group. It is typically reflected by the sum of the spending decisions made by a consumer. One's lifestyle is often measured by a person's activities, interests, and opinions. When people shop, they confront their values by simultaneously facing and deciding on environmental questions ("Will the disposal of this product be harmful to the environment?"), health and safety questions ("Does this food have dangerous properties?"), and social responsibility questions ("Has the manufacturer been a socially responsible employer in developing countries?").

Responding to pressures from the unions and consumers, Wal-Mart, Sears, and other sellers have changed some of their marketing activities. For example, both Sears and Levi Strauss and Company have new policies to make sure that goods sold in their stores are not made by prison labor, such as on the Chinese mainland. Wal-Mart stopped selling a jacket whose label showed an American flag, implying "Made in the U.S.A.," that actually was manufactured (and labeled so) in Bangladesh.

More and more consumers are telling U.S. sellers that while they seek low prices in marketplace transactions, their personal definitions of quality include fair treatment of labor. Sellers in the United States are increasingly avoiding foreign suppliers that have been cited for poor or non-existent health, safety and environmental standards. Collectively, these additional buying criteria can be described as being **politically correct**.

---

[11]Carsky, M. L., Dickenson, R. A. & Smith, M. F. (1996), Toward Consumer Efficiency: A Model for Improved Buymanship, *Journal of Consumer Affairs*, 29:2, 442-459.

CONSUMER UPDATE:
Do Consumers Value "Style" or "Substance"?

It can be argued that today's consumers are only interested in buying style. Author Stuart Ewen observes that in packaging, furnishings, dress, and architecture, style has replaced substance. He states that, "**style** is the symbolic leap away from the constraints of mere subsistence." Sellers recognize that consumers are deeply interested in buying style and image more than reality. Ewen suggests that this is not all bad, but that it encourages consumers to buy images rather than substantive value. This is one reason why advertising is often not aimed at what the product or service will do, but rather at illusions, such as sex appeal, wealth, prestige, and beauty.

Author Lewis H. Lapman argues that, "we are a nation of dreamers captivated by the power of metaphor..." and that "material acquisitions matter much less than the states of being that they supposedly announce and contain. It isn't the thing itself that's important but what the thing represents...Products bestow health, long life, status, sexual prowess, intelligence, national security, happiness and peace of mind; all the blessings that devout Christians expect from the hand of God...The collections of goods and services testify not only to social status but also to an individual's worth as a human being."

The Geistfeld Model of Consumer Choice[12]

This section provides a model of consumer choice that helps explain the factors that determine optimal consumer purchase decisions. An **optimal consumer purchase decision** is a personal judgment about a purchase of a good or service that is the most favorable or desirable at the time the decision is made.

Economics is a helpful tool to understand the problems encountered by consumers when making purchase decisions. The simple model developed here focuses on two decision-making components that interact to determine optimal consumer purchase decisions: (1) indifference curves which reflect the amount of satisfaction consumers receive from a purchase decision, and (2) the budget constraint which reflects the reality that consumers make optimal purchase decisions in a world of limited resources. These factors come together through a process in which consumers attempt to make optimal purchases which maximize their satisfaction subject to income and the prices of goods and services. This is followed by a discussion of the information needs of consumers.

Indifference Curves

An **indifference curve** is comprised of combinations of goods and services providing a constant level of satisfaction to a consumer. An indifference curve is shown on an **indifference map** which is that portion in the positive quadrant of a graph that indicates the consumer's preferences among all combinations of goods and services. The farther an indifference curve is from the origin of the graph, the more the combinations of goods along that curve are preferred. An indifference map shows only what a consumer is

---

[12]This entire section was written by Loren V. Geistfeld, Professor, The Ohio State University.

willing to buy; it does not show what one is able to purchase. A single indifference curve represents a consumer's **willingness to trade** one good for another such that satisfaction is constant. In other words, a consumer finds equally satisfactory all combinations of goods along a particular indifference curve. In Figure 12-1 the consumer is indifferent between the apple-banana combinations described by A, B, C and D. This happens because the consumer receives the same amount of satisfaction from each of these combinations making it impossible for the consumer to say that one is better than another. There are several indifference curves in Figure 12-1. As you move up and to the right, each curve denotes a higher level of satisfaction.

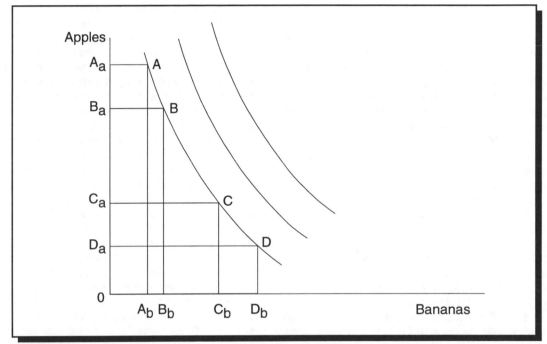

FIGURE 12-1

The "saucer" shape of the indifference curves has important implications. With "saucer shaped" indifference curves, movement along a curve indicates a consumer is less willing to substitute one good for another. This is why indifference curves reflect personal trade-off or the *willingness* to trade. The technical term for this phenomenon is diminishing marginal rate of substitution. This means that if you start with a bundle, a combination of apples and bananas, where you have many apples and few bananas, you are willing to give up a large number of apples to get a few more bananas. Bundle A in Figure 12-1 illustrates the situation in which a consumer starts with many apples and few bananas. If the consumer is to be enticed to move to bundle B, a large number of apples (A_a - B_a) is given up for a few more bananas (B_b - A_b). A consumer starting with bundle C reflecting few apples and many bananas moves to bundle D. By design the number of apples given up in the A-B move is the same as the number of apples given up in the C-D move. In the C-D move the consumer gives up (C_a - D_a) apples while gaining (D_b - C_b) bananas which is greater than the additional number of bananas needed to hold satisfaction constant in the A-B move. The reason for the difference is that in the A-B move the consumer has so many apples that they are boring to eat, while bananas are few in number making them interesting to eat. The consumer is willing to swap many boring

AN ECONOMIC FOCUS ON...
Information Search in the Buying Process*

Information is a necessary ingredient in a consumer's buying process. Sometimes consumers seem to know where to buy and what to buy without any information search, especially when making repeated purchases. The reasons are twofold: (1) they may already know the information they need, or (2) they do not think an external search is worth doing. The first reason indicates the consumer's internal search and the second displays the result of cost-benefit analysis of information search. Thus, information search is an essential step in a consumer's buying process.

Information needs in the buying process can be categorized as price-related and quality-related. If quality is given, consumers tend to search for the lowest price in the market. However, consumers often terminate the search before they find the best buy because their search is limited by their money, time, energy, and/or psychic resources. Consumers will stop the search when they perceive that the marginal search cost exceeds the marginal benefit. If a consumer wants to buy a used car, he or she may visit several car dealers, examine regional auto pricing guides known locally as *Yellow Book* or *Blue Book*, or read newspaper's classified sections. These actions are examples of external information search and involve money costs (books and newspapers, transportation expenses), and time and energy costs (visiting and talking with dealers, reading books and newspapers). The consumer may have to deal with dealer's tricks and persuasion, which involves psychic costs. The buyer may omit some of these actions to make the purchase decision sooner. The extent to which external information is searched depends on the buyer's perception that how much money to spend, how much time to take, how hard to search, and how assertive to be are worth the benefit of the search.

Businesses with price advantages have incentives to provide their price information for consumers. In some comparative advertisements, the sponsor's prices are contrasted with their competitor's prices. Consumers can make use of this kind of information and reduce search costs, such as money, energy, and time costs.

The situation becomes more complicated for consumers when product qualities vary. Due to the diversity of quality and asymmetry of information, poor quality products are encouraged to stay in the market and quality products tend to be pushed out of the market. Let's consider the used car purchase again. In the market, used car sellers want to sell their cars. Some of these cars are good, called "plums", and some others are bad, called "lemons." Sellers usually have better knowledge of their own cars than buyers, and this situation is called **asymmetric information**. Each plum is worth, say $2,000, and each lemon, $1,000. Because consumers cannot distinguish between plums and lemons, they would like to pay only an expected value of these used cars, say $1,500 when the numbers of plums and lemons are the same. This situation will encourage lemon sellers to sell cars, and discourage plum sellers. If a seller sells both plums and lemons, (s)he tends to cheat consumers by claiming lemon cars as plum cars. Thus, because of asymmetric information and diverse qualities, consumers tend to lose in marketplace transactions.

Quality cheating is somewhat limited by some market mechanisms. If the business believes its short-run profit from cheating will negatively affect its long-term profit, the business may choose to be honest with consumers. In addition, to be more competitive and profitable, producers of quality products tend to signal their quality features to consumers.

Signals have several forms. (1) Warranty is one of them. Producers of quality products would like to provide warranties for consumers to enhance consumer's confidence in these products. Producers of poor quality products cannot afford to do this. (2) Advertisements addressing product's unique features or quality characteristics are another form. Sponsors of puffery ads cannot last forever since the dishonest quality claims can be detected after product purchases, and negative word-of-mouth and publicity will spread among consumers. (3) Reputation is a third form. Sellers with a good reputation tend not to cheat since its cost is too high compared to the benefit of cheating. Sellers with a good reputation can charge consumers premium prices because of their reputation. If sellers with a good reputation cheat and are discovered, they will lose their profits from premium prices. Signals from quality product producers and sellers give consumer hints in effectively searching for information and making smart purchase decisions.

The consumer information environment can be improved by increasing benefits or decreasing costs of information search, as suggested by J. Edward Russo, professor at Cornell University. Government can play an important role in helping consumers get access to useful information. A strict liability system will push producers to offer sufficient information on appropriate use of products and to decrease the probability of accidents and tragedies. Regulations on fraudulent and deceptive marketing behavior will suppress the occurrence of questionable quality claims and misleading sale announcements. Setting quality standards will give consumers confidence in product quality at a minimum level. Requirements of clear and understandable information on packaging and labeling will decrease consumer's comprehension and computation costs.

Third parties, such as consumer groups, independent testing organizations, media institutions, and schools also may be helpful in the consumer information search process. Efforts by third parties may decrease consumer's compiling costs, perhaps by offering price comparisons of retail stores and quality indexes of movies or restaurants. Third parties may decrease a consumer's comprehension costs by offering straightforward and understandable information and/or educational programs for complex products or services. Such efforts may decrease a consumer's computation costs by figuring out and presenting healthy nutritional quotients, monthly payments of a long-term mortgage loan, or the annuity amount after retirement. Third parties may also increase the benefit of a consumer's use of information, by providing new information that consumers are unaware of, by reminding consumers of some existing information, or by altering consumer's attitudes about some existing information.

*Jing-jian Xiao, Associate Professor, University of Rhode Island apples for a few interesting bananas. The C-D move is one in which bananas are boring because a consumer has many of them, while apples are fun to eat since a consumer has few of them. In this situation a consumer needs a large bunch of boring bananas to compensate for giving up a few interesting apples. Remember that satisfaction is constant through all of these substitutions.

Budget Constraint

The **budget constraint** describes the relationship between the amount of money one can (or is willing to) spend and the prices of items to be purchased. What one can spend *constrains* or limits what can be purchased. For example, if you go to a store with $10 in your pocket, you are *constrained* to spend no more than $10 while in the store.

When consumers are constrained as to how much they can spend, the prices of goods and services reflect a consumer's **ability to trade** one good for another. Suppose you have $1 to spend on candy and gum costs $.25 while candy bars cost $.50. If the entire $1 is spent on gum, you can buy four packages. The only way you can buy a candy bar is to *trade* two packages of gum for one candy bar. The fact that you need to trade two packages of gum for one candy bar is determined by the prices of gum and candy bars and the desire to spend $1 on candy.

A **budget line** is a line on an indifference map showing all the combinations of goods that can be purchased with a certain level of income. It reflects the reality that consumers' income levels or budgets limit the amounts they can purchase. Putting the budget line on an indifference map indicates the single combination of goods that the consumer is both willing and able to buy. In Figure 12-2, the straight budget line (ab) represents the budget constraint or the combinations of apples and bananas, given their respective prices, that are available to a consumer when spending everything on apples and bananas. Point "a", which is on the vertical axis, represents the number of apples which a consumer can buy if everything is spent to buy apples, while "b", which is on the horizontal axis, represents the number of bananas which a consumer can buy if everything is spent on bananas. Moving along the budget constraint from F to G illustrates the **ability to trade** apples for bananas. The prices of apples and bananas are such that if (F_a - G_a) apples are given up, (G_b - F_b) bananas can be purchased.

Optimal Purchases: Maximizing Satisfaction

Maximizing satisfaction from a purchase involves a consumer's ability to trade (budget constraint) and willingness to trade (indifference curve).[13] The optimal (or satisfaction maximizing) purchase is where the ability to trade and the willingness to trade are the same.

A way to understand why satisfaction is maximized when ability and willingness to trade are the same is to examine what happens when they are not the same. In Figure 12-3 if a consumer starts with bundle R and gives up (R_a - S_a) apples, what happens with respect to willingness to trade and ability to trade? Bundle S is on the same indifference

---

[13]Willingness to trade is also called **personal trade-off** and ability to trade is also called **market trade-off**.

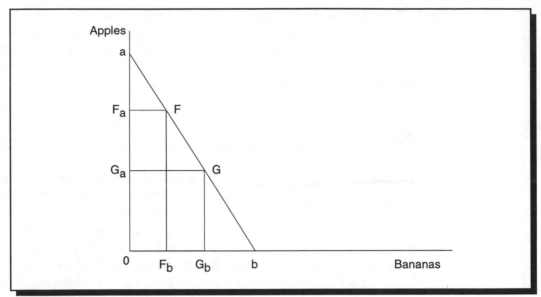

FIGURE 12-2

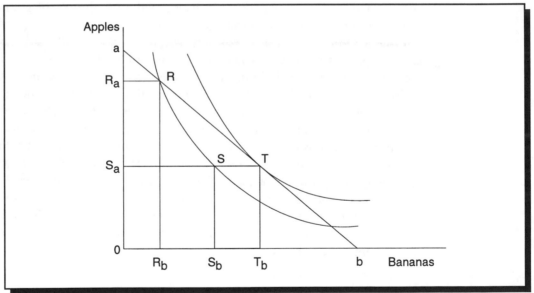

FIGURE 12-3

curve as bundle R indicating satisfaction is constant between the two bundles. This suggests the consumer is willing to trade $(R_a - S_a)$ apples for $(S_b - R_b)$ bananas since satisfaction is constant. However, what happens with respect to the ability to trade? If the consumer sells $(R_a - S_a)$ apples, sufficient money is made available to purchase $(T_b - R_b)$ additional bananas. $(T_b - R_b)$ is greater than the number of bananas needed to keep the level of satisfaction constant by $(T_b - S_b)$ bananas. Since the ability to trade apples for bananas allows the consumer to get more bananas than is needed to hold satisfaction constant, the level of satisfaction can be increased by acquiring a different bundle than reflected by bundle R. In essence, *willingness to trade* moves the consumer to bundle S but *ability to trade* allows a move to bundle T. Since willingness and ability to trade are not the same, the consumer can realize a greater level of satisfaction by going from bundle R to bundle T which is associated with a higher indifference curve.

Inadequate Information and Purchase Decisions

Before discussing specific consumer information needs, it is important to illustrate the result of making a purchase decision with faulty information. This is done by using the consumer choice model described above. Suppose a consumer has a misperception concerning the price of a good. This results in a perceived budget constraint which is different from the actual budget constraint. If a consumer *perceives* the price of bananas to be such that the line ab_2 is perceived to be the budget constraint (Figure 12-4), the consumer will believe that W_a apples and W_b bananas will maximize satisfaction. However, the *actual* price of bananas is higher than the *perceived* price. This results in the actual budget constraint being the line ab_1. Maximizing satisfaction with respect to the actual budget constraint results in a different bundle of apples and bananas than when the consumer attempts to maximize satisfaction with respect to the perceived budget constraint. To illustrate the problem of incorrect perception (inaccurate information), assume the consumer first buys apples and then bananas. The consumer purchases what is believed to be the optimal number of apples, W_a. Given this number of apples, the consumer will start purchasing bananas with the intention of getting W_b. However, once the consumer has purchased V_b bananas all available income has been spent. In other words, the consumer ends up with bundle V rather than bundle W. The consumer thought that indifference curve I was the maximum level of satisfaction, but indifference curve II is the level of satisfaction actually realized. If the consumer had been responding to the actual (or correct) price for bananas, satisfaction would have been maximized at bundle X. In this instance the consumer suffers a loss in satisfaction due to ignorance. This is reflected by the difference in satisfaction levels between indifference curve II where the consumer actually ended up and indifference curve III where the consumer would have been with correct price information.

Consumers Need Two Types of Information

The above discussion suggests consumers need two types of information to maximize satisfaction. The first type of information relates to the accurate perception of the budget constraint. The second information type relates to accurate perception of one's indifference curves.

First Need—Budget Constraint Information

There are two types of **budget constraint information**: income and prices. Consumers who overestimate income will attempt to attain a level of satisfaction that is impossible to reach. When consumers underestimate income, they will not purchase enough of a good resulting in a lower than optimal level of satisfaction. Income information problems are most likely to arise for consumers who are self-employed, seasonal workers, or on commissions. These consumers face a situation in which the amount and flow of income can be quite variable making it difficult to know what it

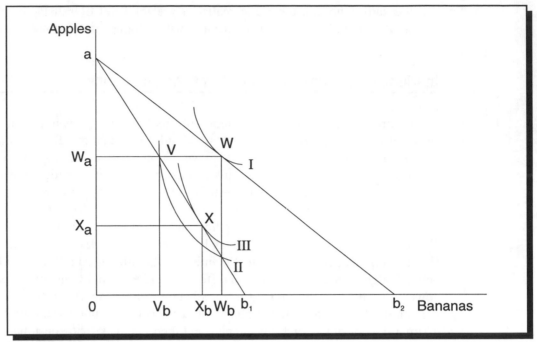

FIGURE 12-4

actually is. In general, income information is the least serious of consumer information problems.

Price ignorance arises when prices of goods vary across sellers and over time making it impossible for consumers to always know all prices. At a given point in time different sellers may charge different prices for the same good or service. Over different points in time prices may change suggesting today's price information may have no bearing on prices tomorrow.

Why do prices vary from *one seller to another*? One reason is that different sellers face *different costs*. A seller who purchases a good at a lower price than other sellers or who has a more efficient operation, can sell at a lower price than a seller not facing these conditions. A second reason is that sellers use different *pricing schemes*. This means that the methods used by sellers to determine selling price are not the same across all sellers. Price variability is also affected by sellers providing services beyond the actual good purchased. Sellers provide service contracts, extended guarantees, "free" credit, "free" delivery, "free" installation, "free" alterations, etc. As more of these *seller services* are provided, selling price will tend to increase.

As noted earlier, prices also vary *over time*. One example is *seasonal variation* in prices. Seasonal price variation is not uniform across all sellers and is most effective where the seller has a "captive" market. Consider what happens in resort areas between the off-season and the on-season.

The *exit and entry of sellers* also causes price variability. A high price seller may leave the market and be replaced by a low price seller. This makes one's sense of price range out of date.

"Full price" can be used to illustrate the price information problem. There are two conceptualizations of full price. The first is **full price** as item price plus *search* costs. This approach recognizes that time and effort spent on information search is not "free." There are several types of search costs that should be recognized.[14] First, *direct money costs* are those out-of-pocket expenses directly associated with the search activity. Second, *direct non-money costs* are costs directly associated with a search that do not cost actual dollars. Third, *indirect money costs* reflect dollars one gives up because of engaging in search. Fourth, *indirect non-money costs* reflect what one gives up other than money because of engaging in search. The inclusion of search costs makes price less obvious since search costs vary across individuals and the various elements of search are not always easily recognized.

The second conceptualization is **full price** as item price plus *use* costs. This is often used with appliances or automobiles. This approach takes operating costs, maintenance costs and depreciation into consideration making the price of a good more than just what is paid to the retailer when it is purchased. Use costs can vary greatly across models. This gives rise to a situation in which an item with a high "store price" may have a relatively low "full price" since its use costs are low.

Second Need—Indifference Curve Information

An important aspect of indifference curve related information is that a consumer must be aware of needs or wants. If a consumer is unaware of needs or wants, purchase decisions do not reflect what is "truly" desired by a consumer.

Society considers some individuals to be incapable of determining "true" needs and wants. Children are not allowed to only eat candy. Speeders receive tickets even though they have a "need" to drive fast. Burglars are punished even though they "need" something inside of a home.

"True" preferences can be distorted. One form of distortion arises when consumers make purchase decisions based on the perceived responses of other consumers. Three such distortions are noted here: the bandwagon effect, the snob effect, and the Veblen effect.[15] The **bandwagon effect** reflects social conformity or social emulation. It arises when consumers *purchase a good or service because others are purchasing it*. The **snob effect** is a social rejection effect. It arises when a consumer *refuses to purchase a good or service because other consumers have purchased it*. The **conspicuous consumption effect**, which is often called the Veblen effect, arises when consumers *purchase a good or service because it bears a high price and purchase visibly demonstrates a consumer's ability to purchase an expensive item*. An element common to these effects is that the consumer responds to the reactions and responses of others. This creates a situation in which purchase decisions may be made in response to something other than one's "true" preferences.

Even in those situations where consumers clearly perceive "true" needs and wants, consumers need much information to make informed decisions. To begin, consumers must be aware of all products or services which meet a particular need or want.[16] To achieve this two questions need to be answered. First, what product set meets the need or want in question? Is the relevant set composed of subcompact automobiles or luxury automobiles? Both are not included since they fulfill quite different functions. Second, what brand/model combinations make up the desired product set? Is the set composed of

---

[14]Maynes, E. S. (1976). *Decision-making for Consumers* (pp.19-20). New York: Macmillan.

[15]Leibenstein, H. (1976). *Beyond Economic Man* (Chapter 4). Boston, MA: Harvard University Press).

[16]Maynes, E. S. (1976). *Decision-making for Consumers* (pp.79-82). New York: Macmillan.

Taurus and Integra models or is a Continental Mark VIII also included? Clearly the product set does not include the Continental product since the Taurus and Integra are included. Lack of awareness of a total product set may give rise to a suboptimal decision—the consumer purchases an Escort when a Neon would have better met his or her needs.

Once the product set has been identified, a consumer must assess the extent to which each particular brand/model combinations meet specific needs. This is essentially a question of assessing quality. First, what product characteristics meet the specific need? Second, how important is each characteristic to meeting the need? Third, to what extent does a brand/model possess the desired characteristics?

Information is not equally available on all goods and services.[17] **Experience goods** are those for which characteristic information is not available until after the good has been purchased and used. **Search goods** are those for which information on characteristics is available prior to using the good. **Credence goods** are goods where a consumer is unable to assess quality even after use. This usually applies to services requiring a high level of expertise to provide. Many goods involve elements related to all three information types—consumers can look-up EPA gas mileage rating for an automobile (search), they may learn through use that actual gas mileage is quite different from the EPA rating (experience), and when the car breaks down and needs to be repaired, they often do not know whether the $900 transmission was needed as long as the problem ceases to exist (credence).

A Concluding Comment on Consumer Choice

This section provided a framework to help understand the importance of being an informed consumer. Uninformed consumers make optimal purchase decisions through luck. Informed consumers make optimal purchase decisions through careful planning and decision making. However, the amount and complexity of information needed to make fully informed decisions can be overwhelming. Consumer education and consumer policy provide an environment conducive to reducing consumer ignorance. However, even in a "friendly" environment consumers must search for information to facilitate optimal purchase decision making.

Understanding How to Be a Pro-environmental Consumer

To greatly reduce environmental pollution and stop degradation of the environment immediately, consumers would have to dramatically change their lives. They would have to stop using many things, such as automobiles, that make life quite civilized. Most people do not wish to give up these conveniences. Fortunately, pollution can be reduced in many ways. Business and government can work to lessen the amount of pollution caused by automobiles and factories. Government can pass laws and regulations to require businesses and consumers to cut down on certain polluting activities.

---

[17]Eastwood, D. B. (1985). *The Economics of Consumer Behavior* (pp. 166-168). New York: Allyn and Bacon.

CONSUMER UPDATE:
On the Difference Between an Environmentalist
and a Consumer Advocate

Environmentalists do not care who gets to fish for halibut in the Alaska Gulf, the owners of large fishing boats or small ones; they simply want to reduce overfishing to protect the species. Consumer advocates want ample supplies of quality fish at low prices (for themselves and others). Therefore, consumer advocates do not want the big boaters to put the small boaters out of business because they know that reduced competition will quickly reduce the quantity of fish available and push up prices. In this particular case, as in many others, people are both environmentalists and consumer advocates.

A **pro-environmental consumer** takes into consideration the environmental impact of his or her decisions in marketplace transactions. Pro-active consumers can take actions to personally reduce environmental degradation. Many negative consequences to environmental problems can be reduced by learning to "look before leaping" when making consumer decisions. Once informed, consumers can then choose and apply technologies and choices in such ways as to minimize stress on the environment.

Many Consumers Use Environmental Factors in Decision Making

Eight out of ten Americans today call themselves environmentalists and report that they consider environmental factors in their purchasing decisions. Yet, a recent article in *The Wall Street Journal* indicated that fewer than one-half of adults report that during the past six months they have actually purchased an item based upon the environmental reputation of the product or the manufacturer. Examples of pro-environmental consumer decisions include: refusing to purchase plastic styrofoam cups and plates, disposable diapers, products in non-recyclable packaging, and non-rechargeable batteries—that is, refusing unless recycling depositories are nearby.

Consumers everywhere are increasingly concerned about which companies treat them fairly and which companies treat the ecology fairly. Consumers today still seek their self-interest in efficiency and getting their money's worth; however, more than half of all consumers report in surveys that they also have expanded their definition of "quality" to include considering how their decisions impact the environment. Thus, a growing number of consumers are refusing to buy certain products, and they occasionally boycott products and sellers based on environmental reasons. Four out of five consumers are willing to pay more when products meet standards of quality on issues of safety, healthiness, and the environment.

Environmental problems facing consumers around the world today include: (1) climatic changes that may result from the possible depletion of the ozone layer, (2) the exhaustion of world resources, such as fossil fuels and certain species of plants and animals, (3) the safe disposal of garbage and hazardous wastes, (4) water waste, inadequacy, and contamination, (5) the impact of acid rain on lakes and forests, (6) the storage and disposal of radioactive waste, (7) the presence of toxic residues in food, and (8) smog over urban areas. These problems represent areas of concern that growing numbers of consumers consider when making decisions in marketplace transactions.

CONSUMER UPDATE:
Coalition for Environmentally Responsible Economies

Many businesses are pro-environment, too. One key effort is the **Coalition for Environmentally Responsible Economies (CERES)**. (It is pronounced seer-eez). Also known as the **Valdez Principles** because that incident inspired the effort, CERES promotes corporate environmental responsibility, beyond that established in law, on a world-wide basis. The principal thrust of CERES has been to inform the socially concerned investment community about corporate behaviors. Over the long run, investors can help see to it that corporate ecological and public-health disasters are minimal and that technologies and systems to stop environmental degradation are developed. One short-term result of CERES has been that a growing number of progressive companies now compete for customers based on consumer concerns about price, quality, service, *and* environment.

CERES encourages the idea of **environmental auditing**, corporations reviewing their activities to determine how well they measure up to a set of standards. Corporations that voluntarily sign on and abide by the principles hire independent outsiders to make such a review, and conduct annual audits. The ten areas of the CERES principles are: protection of the biosphere, sustainable use of natural resources, reduction and disposal of waste, wise use of energy, risk reduction, marketing of safe products and services, damage compensation, disclosure, environmental directors and managers, and assessment and annual review. Adherence to the principles argues for a long-term corporate commitment to continually update practices, in light of technology changes and new developments in science. Over 50 corporations, small and large, have signed on to the principles since they began in 1990. In 1993, Sun Company, an oil giant, became the first Fortune-500 company to endorse the CERES principles.

A key challenge for consumers is to obtain sufficient information to be able to judge how their decisions will affect particular environmental problems. It is an extremely challenging task, even for professional environmentalists, to take all the appropriate factors into account and come up with the best environmental position on a certain product. The answer is subject to later change as well. Illustrative are the continuing controversies over diapers (disposable or cloth?) and paper or plastic shopping bags (the answer is not decisive). Yet, surveys show that almost 90 percent of consumers would like to buy environmentally responsible products, if they could find them. In general, consumers living in developed countries, such as the United States, find it difficult to obtain sufficient valid and reliable information to make environmentally sound buying decisions; it is even harder for consumers living in developing countries to make such decisions.[18]

Consumers Sometimes are "Free Riders" When It Comes to Pollution[19]

To an economist, pollution has its roots in a specific set of circumstances often referred to as market failure. **Market failure** occurs when the competitive marketplace

---

[18]*The Green Buyer's Car Guide*, a 200-page book that ranks every model of car and truck available for sale in the U.S., is available from Public Citizen, 2000 P Street, NW, Washington, DC 20036.

[19]This section was written by Raymond E. Forgue, Associate Professor, University of Kentucky.

fails to provide a maximization of utility for consumers as a whole commensurate with the ability of firms to make a fair rate of return. In general, market failure entails either the underproduction of public goods or the overproduction of public bads.

Public Goods

A **public good** is any product or service for which persons outside a private marketplace transaction benefit from the transaction, cannot be excluded from the benefits of the transaction, and for which there is no mechanism to obtain payment for these benefits. The benefits are often referred to as **positive externalities** and the person outside the transaction who receives them is a **free rider**. For example, your neighbors might wish to put up a sodium-vapor light in his yard for safety. This would be a private transaction between your neighbor and the light provider. Yet, you will benefit if the light can't be restricted from shining on to your property, as well. Nor could the neighbor charge you for the light you receive because you can simply refuse to pay. Of course, neighbors could band together to provide safety lighting services and share the cost. However, there is a natural incentive to free ride, especially if the free riders suspect that the light will be put up even if they fail to participate. The impact of free riders may be such that those willing to pay would fail to raise enough money to provide the street light even though the benefits to all far outweigh the costs to all. That is why local governments are often in the street light business. They have the power to provide the service and spread the cost via taxes over the entire group receiving the benefits.

Public Bads

Public bads operate in a similar but opposite way. A **public bad** is any product or service for which persons outside a private marketplace transaction are harmed by the transaction, cannot reasonably avoid the harm, and have difficulty forcing those causing it to reimburse them for the harm caused. The harm is often referred to as a **negative externality**. However, the person receiving the harm is not the free rider. Instead, the free rider is the person who receives the benefits from the transaction. In essence, some of the costs of providing the benefits are placed on the party(ies) outside the transaction.

Pollution is a good example of a public bad. Let's say your neighbor decides to open a landfill on his property and then sells landfill services to individuals who wish to dispose of garbage. As his neighbor, you might suffer negative effects from this transaction between your neighbor and his customers. Your air might be fouled with noxious odors or the water in the area might be contaminated from runoff from the landfill.

Pollution is basically a situation where someone outside a transaction bears some of the costs of the transaction. Competitive pressures will keep firms looking for ways to cut costs, and pollution is certainly a way to cut costs (by shifting them to someone else). So who is the free rider here? Your first response might be to point to the polluter or, in our example, the neighbor with the landfill. Obviously, they are causing the pollution. But, it is their customers who are receiving the benefits of the landfill by having a place to dump their garbage. Where does their responsibility lie? Should they not pay the full cost of the benefits they receive?

There are five ways to decrease the intensity of negative externalities, such as pollution:

1. Put a cost on the party responsible for causing the externalities. With a pollution tax, polluters must pay a tax that (ideally) is commensurate with the harm caused by the pollution. The tax should be passed on to the customers of the polluter since (ideally) the price of a product should fully cover costs of production.

2. Write a law to expand property rights. Here the expanded property rights would be for those folks who live down wind, down stream, and next door to pollution source. The expanded property rights would allow them to assert (possibly through a lawsuit) that they are being harmed, and force some type of reimbursement. The threat of paying those reimbursements would provide an incentive for polluters to clean up their act.

3. Create a law to restrict the behavior causing the negative externality. This could be enforced by existing federal and state pollution control authorities.

4. Create a market to reduce the externality. Government presently has some laws that give value to "low polluting production facilities." These **pollution-permit rights** may be sold to high polluting companies.

5. Transfer the social costs of the externality into private costs. Some laws exist that require that pollution damages of one firm to be the legal cost of other companies in the business.

In all these scenarios, the costs of pollution taxes and actions taken to avoid lawsuits would be passed on to the customers of polluters. The irony in all this is that we all are the customers. We use landfills. We buy products made in a polluting way. We also are the victims of pollution.

For years, businesses have been saying that pollution controls will add to the price of products and services, and economists have agreed. Such a statement should not be viewed solely as a polluters' attempt to avoid reduced profits. They are a statement of reality. People who buy products and services made in a polluting way are free riders receiving the benefits and not paying the full costs of production—production that is harmful to those external to the marketplace transaction.

A Decision Making Matrix for Pro-Environmental Consumers

Key considerations in marketplace transactions include consuming resources in short supply, using resources efficiently, and considering the effects on environmental degradation. To address these concerns, there are four guiding questions for pro-environmental consumers: (1) Does it reduce waste? (2) Are the containers and products reusable? (3) Are the products and packaging recyclable? and (4) Do the available choices make you want to respond (positively or negatively) to products in the marketplace?

---

[20]Some of these ideas are from Jing-jian Xiao's writings.

CONSUMER UPDATE:
What's Happening with Green Labeling?

Businesses, motivated by conscience and competition, have responded to the consumer's clamor for recycled facial tissue, toilet paper, unbleached coffee filters and reusable canvas grocery bags. Part of the response has been **green labeling, an attempt to provide guidelines to shoppers indicating how environmentally friendly a product is.** Such labeling is voluntary. Many sellers have jumped on the eco-bandwagon and have been describing products on labels and in advertising with green terminology, such as "CFC Free," "ozone friendly," "biodegradable," "compostable," and "recyclable." Some products also carry the independent "seal of approval" of an environmentally conscious organization, such as **Green Seal**; their label (used on 35 products so far) is a blue globe emblazoned with a green check. The Center for Auto Safety recently created a **Green Cars Rating System** to provide information about cars.

In 1992, the Federal Trade Commission issued its "Guides for the Use of Environmental Marketing Claims," that sets some very specific and commonsense standards for commonly used green terminology. As guidelines, without the force and effect of law, they do not preempt state or local laws or regulations. They provide insight into how the FTC will apply its current statutes banning deception. The FTC has announced that it will levy fines against those who continue to make unsubstantiated or misleading environmental claims. Expectations are that consumers will have more confidence in environmental claims and marketers will be encouraged to produce and promote products that are less harmful to the environment.

Does It Reduce Waste?[21]

In an average life of 75 years, a U.S. consumer will produce 52 tons of garbage.[22] That is about 4 pounds of garbage a day. To be a pro-environmental consumer requires a reduction in waste created by consumers in marketplace transactions. In essence, the message is stop wasting. In addition to buying fewer products, techniques to reduce solid waste include buying products and packages that: (1) are consumable (water soluble packets for laundry detergent), (2) are returnable (glass soft drink bottles), (3) are refillable (liquid kitchen soap), (4) are reusable (plastic containers that can be used for storage), (5) extend the useful life of products, so it will not have to be replaced, (6) are packaged in containers that are recyclable, (7) are packaged with a pro-environment perspective, and (8) are not excessively packaged.

Are the Containers and Products Reusable?

Reuse of containers and products reduces unnecessary consumption of resources. Examples include: (1) buying reusable items, when possible, instead of disposables (such as rechargeable batteries); (2) buying products in reusable canvas or string shopping bags, instead of paper or plastic bags; (3) maximizing use of products by selling or donating goods to others, and (4) avoiding single-use items, like plastic razors, cameras, oven cleansing pads, foil baking pans, and disposable diapers.

---

[21]The logic for the arrangement of this heading and some of the content comes from the "Four Rs of Environmental Shopping" (reduce, reuse, recycle, and respond), contained in an excellent set of teaching materials, *Consumer Environmental Education Packet*, 10 units for $30, available from Brenda Cude, University of Illinois, 528 Beview Hall, 905 South Goodwin, Urbana, IL 61801.

[22]Bauers, S. (1990, January 17). Study: Save Earth; Have Fewer Children, *Philadelphia Inquirer*, p. 1.

CONSUMER UPDATE: Progress on CFCs and the Ozone Layer

Chlorofluorocarbons (CFCs) are synthetic chemical substances widely used as refrigerants, plastic foamers (such as in foam cushions, insulation, cups, and egg cartons), aerosol propellants, and computer-chip solvents because they are relatively nontoxic, nonflammable, and do not decompose near ground level. It is estimated that over 100 million refrigerators and 100 million car air-conditioners use freon, the popular name for CFCs. The level of chemicals in the Arctic stratosphere has been found to be 50 times what was expected, and experiments have demonstrated that human activities are the cause.

Industrialized countries now consume as much as 90 percent of the world ozone-depleting substances. The U.S. and 22 other countries signed the Montreal Protocol in 1987, agreeing to no longer produce ozone-eating chemicals commonly used in air conditioners, refrigerators, spray propellants, and fire extinguishers by the end of 1996. As legal production came to a halt in the U.S., a thriving black market came into being to smuggle freon into the United States from Russia, India, and China.

A multilateral fund has been established in the World Bank to help developing countries deal with the cost problem of switching to safe substitutes over the next decade. The developing countries need technical guidance and resources to phase out these harmful substances quickly. Unfortunately, China and India, both large users of CFCs, have yet to agree to limit their usage.

Research has shown that the amount of ozone-destroying CFCs in the atmosphere has nearly leveled off over the past six years. For the first time ever, scientists last year detected an overall decline in the amount of ozone-destroying chemicals in the air. As consumers around the world replace their old appliances with new ones that are ozone friendly, the ozone hole over the South Pole may begin to close, starting in perhaps ten years. Scientists estimate that if all CFCs were immediately banned around the globe, it still would take two centuries for nature to repair the current damage.

Are the Products and Packaging Recyclable?

Recycling is the re-use of materials formerly discarded. It benefits society by reducing the potential volume of solid waste to be disposed of and by slowing the depletion of many mineral resources. As a society, packaging (i.e., cans, bottles, cartons) in the United States uses 50 percent of this country's paper, 75 percent of its glass, 40 percent of its aluminum, and 30 percent of its plastics.[23] Recycling products and packaging allows those materials to be reused in the formation of other goods. Assuming recycling depositories are readily available, items fairly easy for consumers to recycle include newspapers, plastic and glass containers, aluminum cans, scrap tires, automobile batteries, and used motor oil. The marketplace now has available fleece sweaters and other clothing made out of recycled soda bottles.[24] Less than 15 percent of the nation's solid waste is recycled. Government has provided incentives to encourage recycling. Also key to the consumer's role is to purchase products and packaging that use recycled materials, whenever possible. Appropriate environmental symbols are in Figure 12-5.

---

[23]Travis, J. (1990). *Global Wellness Inventory* (p. 6). Mill Valley, CA: Wellness Associates.
[24]Hamilton, M. M. (1994, April 12). Soda-bottle Chic. *The Washington Post*, p. A-1.

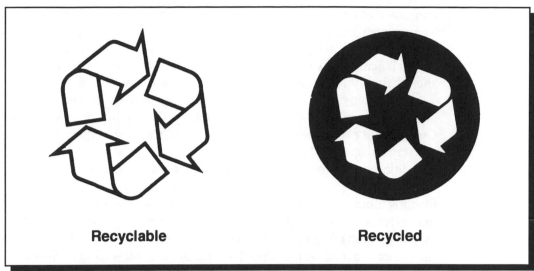

| Recyclable | Recycled |

FIGURE 12-5 Symbols for Recycled and Recyclable

CONSUMER UPDATE: What's Happening With the Greenhouse Effect?

The **greenhouse effect** is the sequence of events where heat energy from the sun is trapped in the earth's atmosphere by ozone, water vapor, and carbon dioxide. The widely held perception is that increased production of manmade pollution gases, especially carbon dioxide from the burning of coal, oil, and natural gas, is trapping solar heat in the lower ozone atmosphere. This acts like panes of glass in a greenhouse, preventing it from escaping back into space, which is raising the temperature of the earth. The 1995 year was the warmest on the planet since recordkeeping began 130 years ago.

In the nation's leading state in the fight against pollution, southern California's regional government and smog-control agencies recommend strong actions to combat the environmental smog problem and bring it into compliance with federal air-quality standards by 2007. Plans include requiring governments and businesses with 15 or more vehicles to switch to cleaner-burning fuels, such as methanol, immediately or as soon as engines become available. Plans also include banning the sale of new barbecue grills that require starter fluid, prohibiting the sale of fast-wearing bias-ply tires, and prohibiting certain chemical formulas used in underarm deodorants. By 2003, 10 percent of the cars and trucks sold in California (and several other states in the northeast) must emit zero pollution. These **zero-emission vehicles (ZEV** for short) are expected to be electric powered.

In the coming years, the EPA and the U.S Congress are expected to consider and act on options, including working with other countries to deal with factors associated with this predicted warming trend. Examples of possible actions include requirements that cars average 50 miles per gallon, homes be insulated to cut heating requirements by 90 percent, users of fossil fuels be heavily taxed, millions of new trees be planted, and elimination of CFCs.

Do the Available Choices Make You Want to Respond (Positively or Negatively) to the Products in the Marketplace?

It is still easy to find examples in the marketplace of products that are excessively packaged. For example, most chewing gum manufacturers use six layers of paper to wrap gum. Many products exist that are harmful to the environment. To be a pro-environmental consumer requires that a consumer become more informed about environmental issues. The product itself may be convenient, but harmful to the environment; the ingredients may be unsafe; the packaging may be overdone. Responsible consumers need to learn what choices are available, too. When alternatives are available in the marketplace, one should simply refuse to purchase goods and services that are not pro-environment.

When only bad choices exist, you can respond to that marketplace failure by communicating your displeasure by telling the retailer and writing the manufacturer. Compliment companies that subscribe to the CERES principles, and if they do not support the standards, ask, "Why not?"

Citizen-consumers who cast their dollar votes for environmentally friendly products are telling the marketplace to do more. So, support environmentally conscious manufacturers and sellers by purchasing their products. Buy products and patronize stores that offer a choice of plastic or paper shopping bags, accept materials for recycling, minimize prepackaging, offer some selections in bulk, use recycled packaging, do not misuse environmental terms (such as "green" and "recyclable") when such descriptions are inaccurate, and recycle their own shipping materials and wastes.

Advertising and Consumers

Advertising is the action of attracting public attention to a product or business, especially to proclaim its qualities or advantages. Advertisements are units of persuasion. In today's marketplace, advertising is essential in communicating to consumers information about the numerous products and services available for sale, such as the name of the product, the manufacturer, size and shape, color and variety, purpose and features, cost (including discounts), and where one can buy the product.

The major purpose of advertising is to familiarize consumers with particular products and services. At its best, advertising provides useful and reliable buying information to consumers to assist in their decision making. At its worst, advertising distorts the decision-making process by manipulating consumers, appealing to their emotions and creating imagery without substance, and sometimes providing false or misleading information that causes confusion and encourages consumers to make poor choices.

More than $1000 per person is spent each year by sellers advertising products and services in the United States. For example, in a recent year, Chrysler Corporation spent $283 on advertising for each vehicle sold, while Volkswagen spent $717. Research indicates that a family that watches television an average of 6 hours a day will see about 500 advertisements a week and 25,000 commercials a year; the average high school graduate has spent 12,000 hours in classrooms and watched 20,000 hours of television. The Center for the Study of Commercialism calculates that the average American will devote almost three years (!) of life watching TV commercials. Advertising, the most obvious form of commercialism, pays for all the expenses of commercial television and accounts for more than 70 percent of newspaper revenues. Twenty percent of all air time on commercial television consists of advertising.

CONSUMER UPDATE:
Which Consumer Products Have the Largest Advertising Expenses?

Data from the Federal Trade Commission reveals that eight industries spend more than ten percent of each sale's dollar for media advertising: proprietary drugs (20.2 percent); perfumes, cosmetics, and other toilet preparations (14.6 percent); flavoring extracts and syrups (13.8 percent); cutlery (12.9 percent); cereal breakfast foods (11.4 percent); pet foods (11.0 percent); distilled liquor (11.0 percent); and periodicals (10.3 percent). Total selling expenses other than media advertising expenses are substantial for many consumer products: photocopying equipment (53.4 percent); proprietary drugs (35.6 percent); bread, cake, and related products (31.8 percent); perfumes, cosmetics and other toilet preparations (30.5 percent); flavoring extracts and syrups (27.9 percent); bottled and canned soft drinks (25.7 percent); typewriters and office machines (25.4 percent); ophthalmic goods (24.4 percent); hosiery (24.3 percent); and calculating and accounting machines (24.0 percent).

Source: Data from Statistical Report: *Annual Line of Business Report*, Federal Trade Commission, Report of the Bureau of Economics, Washington, April 1985, pp. 17-18. These remain the latest data available.

Advertisements bombard us every waking hour of the day, whether we are walking, driving, riding a bus, reading a magazine or newspaper, watching television,[25] putting money in a parking meter, utilizing a public restroom, or simply enjoying a movie.[26] Advertisements fill our ears with sounds and constantly cross our field of vision. We hear and see ads on radio, television, billboards, magazines, newspapers, direct mail, and other places. It seems like there is no place we can turn without being sold something.

Ads help us understand complex issues. By evaluating the information provided, people form opinions about the products or services advertised. Advertising helps consumers become aware of certain brand names and stores. Some ads entertain us; others sometimes insult us. They can tug at our hearts, and they can provide useful information. It is a long-held belief that advertisements have an undeniable impact on what and where consumers buy.

How Advertising Is Regulated

While most advertisements are true and present the favorable aspects of a product, they generally provide incomplete information. Many advertisements contain half-truths, some provide misinformation, and others are simply deceptive.

Advertisements for products and services are subject to self-regulation, such as the Council of Better Business Bureaus' "Code of Advertising," as well as the laws and regulations of federal, state and local governments. Historically the Federal Trade Commission has regulated advertising on a case-by-case basis and with industry-wide trade regulations, but both approaches have proved extremely slow. Today the FTC

---

[25]In the U.S., more homes have televisions than telephones or indoor plumbing.

[26]The Center for the Study of Commercialism has asked the Federal Trade Commission to require film makers to tell patrons when movies contain paid "product placements," such as having an actor on screen drink a Coke instead of a Pepsi. Their reasoning is that consumers are being advertised to without being told. Address: Center for the Study of Commercialism, 1875 Connecticut Avenue, NW, Suite 300, Washington, DC 20009-5728 (202-332-9110).

depends upon voluntary guidelines, such as those issued for environmental claims, and strong backup by state attorneys general. While the FTC weakened its definitions of "unfairness" and "deception" during the 1980s, the states remained vigorous in protecting consumers.

Political advertisements are subject to no regulation of any kind and are generally thought to be protected as free speech under the First Amendment.[27] Commercial ads can be compared to absolute standards of truth and accuracy, but political advertising does not have a similar standard.

Types of Truth and Exaggeration in Advertising

There are four types of truth in advertising: (1) literal truth, (2) true impression, (3) discernible exaggeration, and (4) false impression.[28]

1. Literal truth advertising is that which can be objectively supported by the facts. If an electric shaver claims to "cut closer than a blade," isn't it logical for consumers to expect that the manufacturer would have ample test results available to the public evidencing this fact? Many consumers say they like literal truth advertisements because they provide useful information.

2. True impression advertising is that which is literally true but which creates a false impression. A Tylenol headache remedy advertisement may claim that the product "contains twice as much pain reliever," and it actually may contain double the standard amount of the analgesic, but this does not mean that the product will be twice as effective. An Ultrabrite toothpaste commercial claims that the product cleans teeth while also creating the false impression that usage will improve one's sex appeal.

An **endorsement** (or **testimonial**) is any advertising message that consumers are likely to believe reflects the opinions, beliefs, findings, or experience of a party other than the sponsoring advertiser. This includes verbal statements, demonstrations, or depictions of the name, signature, likeness, or other identifying personal characteristics of an individual or the name or seal of an organization.

Endorsements in media are a form of true impression advertising. They leave the sometimes false impression that the endorser (usually a famous athlete or movie star) actually compared many products before recommending one, that use of the product gave the endorser the ability or skills that he or she possesses, and that the endorser is not receiving money to promote the product. While such statements may be literally true, they are intended by the advertiser to create very strong and positive impressions that may be false.

The FTC advertising guidelines require that endorsements always reflect the honest opinions, findings, beliefs, or experiences of the endorser; that the endorser continues to subscribe to the views presented; and that, if asked, the advertiser can substantiate the

---

[27]Unscrupulous political advertising techniques, such as reliance on innuendo, half-truths, fear-mongering (including racism), negative assaults, distortions, and outright falsehoods, are protected against government regulation by the First Amendment. Such ads reflect the U.S. tradition of rhetorical excess in politics and the failure of politicians to interest the voters into a dialogue on proposals to deal with the serious challenges in society. Meanwhile, advertising remains the messenger of a faulty political process.

[28]Greyser, S. A. (1972, March-April). Advertising: Attacks and Counterattacks. *Harvard Business Review*, 50, 26-28.

endorsement. Further, when payment or promise of compensation might materially affect the credibility of the endorsement, that connection must be disclosed.

Comparative claim advertising also leaves false impressions in that the advertiser sometimes unfairly compares product features with those of competing brands. A Ford automobile advertisement claiming "a luxurious interior like the Mercedes-Benz" and "a smoother ride than a Porsche" may invite the false impression that the automobile provides all the features of the Mercedes or Porsche rather than the selected few. A similar false impression occurs when Coca-Cola claims "that 2 million families that drink Pepsi switched to Diet Coke last year" because the ad fails to mention that Coke lost the same number of drinkers to its competitors.[29]

3. Discernible exaggeration advertising is that which is so far from the literal truth that no consumer is going to be deceived. Advertising statements such as "The finest money can buy" and "The best product on the market today" are seen by consumers as obvious exaggerations. Similarly, a television advertisement that shows a washing machine that grows to ten feet in height obviously is exaggerating, yet the manufacturer may succeed in communicating by exaggeration that this product is bigger and better than the competition.

4. False impression advertising is that which either deliberately or unintentionally creates a false impression in the mind of the consumer. A classic example is the Wonder Bread advertisement which years ago suggested that by eating their nutritious bread a child could "grow bigger and stronger during the 'Wonder Years'—ages 1 through 12--the years that your child grows to ninety percent of his adult height." The federal government charged that this commercial was giving the misleading and false impression that Wonder Bread was nutritionally unique when compared to other breads. False impression advertising is the *only* type considered illegal by federal, state, and local governments.

Types of Advertisements: Informational and Puffery

Most commercial advertising can be classified as either informational or puffery. Unfortunately for consumers, most are puffery advertisements.

Informational Advertisements

An **informational advertisement** provides specific, understandable, relevant, and verifiable claims about the characteristics or qualities a product or service possesses, such as product features, prices, and where to buy. Consumers see many informative ads about prices, products, and availability, such as supermarkets advertising their prices, movie theaters giving the starting times for films, and new sellers, announcing that they are open for business. Such advertisements lessen the time consumers have to spend searching for information and provide consumers with options that lead to more competition and greater satisfaction.

---

[29]Consumers Union, publisher of *Consumer Reports* testing magazine, has a strict noncommercialization policy that, "Neither the ratings nor the reports may be used in advertising for any other commercial purpose." Courts have consistently upheld that policy and enjoined sellers from running advertisements that cite CU's research findings.

Puffery Advertisements

A **puffery advertisement** makes unsupported, subjective favorable opinions and exaggerated statements that supply little or no constructive information about the attributes or value of the product or service. Puffery advertisements intend to persuade, not inform. The words *better*, *best*, *greatest*, and *finest* are typically employed. Puffery ads encourage consumers to buy for reasons other than empirical evidence. People view puffery advertisements "through a filter of protective skepticism," says *Advertising Age*.

The four common types of puffery advertisements are testimonial, institutional, emotional, and comparative ads.

1. Testimonial advertisements are a form of puffery ad that always provide a positive recommendation about a product or service. For example, if a famous baseball player wears a certain type of underwear, you should too. Testimonials are also made by typical consumers, as well as "presumed experts," and the basic message is "Trust the advice I'm giving you about this product or service."

2. Institutional advertisements try to associate the product or service with images, ideas, and institutions that are both familiar and valued by most Americans. For example, Chrysler's automobile ads almost always are associated with the red, white, and blue colors of our national flag.

3. Emotional advertisements are also puffery ads in that they try to persuade consumers to buy because the product or service purportedly satisfies a psychological desire. Emotional ads play on a consumer's inner feelings of guilt, fear, or vanity while trying to make the consumers feel dissatisfied, insecure, or plain miserable, unless he or she buys the product or service advertised. How many people buy American Express Traveler's Cheques because they see commercials where Karl Malden illustrates how traveling consumers lose all their money to thieves?

4. Comparative advertisements are puffery ads in that they provide comparisons with similar products that purposefully show one or two of the advantages of the advertised product while omitting, disguising, or minimizing any bad aspects. Positive comparative ads, for example, show Ford automobiles riding as quietly as a Mercedes-Benz. A negative comparative ad might show a Chevrolet truck coming fully equipped while suggesting that a similarly equipped Toyota charges an extra $550 for that same package of features.

Misleading Advertising Negativelly Affects Decision Making

Advertising is very important in the American economy. Consumers would be terribly uninformed about various products and services if it were not for advertising. We would not even know about the existence of many products and services if it were not for advertisers spending money to tell us.

Much advertising can be described as misleading because it includes misrepresentations. This comes about in part because consumers and advertisers often differ when it comes to their perceptions of truth. A New York advertising research firm, Video Storyboard Tests, finds that about 30 percent of all consumers describe advertising as misleading. This erodes public confidence in the messenger of advertising. One form of advertising that is frequently misleading is **infomercials**, program-length advertisements for products and services.

CONSUMER UPDATE:
Is Advertising Prescription Drugs Directly to Consumers Misleading?

Historically the initial information consumers receive about prescription drugs has come from their physicians. That has changed with today's direct advertising of the products to consumers. Current Food and Drug Administration regulations prohibit advertisements for prescription drugs to mention the trade name of the product when advertising directly to consumers. Upjohn Company, for example, which pioneered the anti-baldness drug Rogaine, includes a toll-free number in its ads that men can call to be referred to a physician who can prescribe the treatment.

Drug advertising promises are excellent at creating false impressions, and in the case of Rogaine, the impression left is that people with baldness can easily reverse their situation. False advertising of over-the-counter stomach acid blockers was stopped by a federal judge, but when commercial success is so dependent upon advertising and promotion other OTC products are sure to run new ads that mislead consumers.

Deceptive Advertising Is Illegal, but Not Until a Government Agency Says So

Deceptive advertisements are proclamations of quality or advantages that consciously and deliberately attempt to deceive and mislead consumers who are likely to rely on the misleading statements of the seller. This is beyond puffery. A **deception** is a form of trickery involving the selling of goods or services to consumers.

One important task of the federal government's Federal Trade Commission is to prevent advertising that has the "tendency and the capacity to deceive." The criteria used by the FTC to determine whether or not an advertisement is deceptive includes its tendency to mislead or deceive, its actual truthfulness, whether the ad as a whole is misleading because it omits important facts, and when an ad has two meanings and one is false or misleading. The FTC declares a **deceptive act** or a **deceptive practice** an action that is likely to mislead the consumer acting reasonably in the circumstances, to the consumer's detriment. To prove an advertisement is deceptive, the FTC must show that the advertiser did not, before the ad was run, have evidence that proved the truth of each interpretation that could be placed on the claim by a nontrivial minority of consumers.[30] The state attorneys general police deceptive advertising under authority of state consumer protection laws, which are often stronger than the Federal Trade Commission's regulations. In one instance, states are pre-empted from regulating advertising. In 1992 the Supreme Court ruled that the law deregulating the airline industry requires that only the federal government has the authority to police deceptive advertising of airlines.

---

[30]The FTC won its first consumer-refund settlement for deceptive advertising in the toy industry in 1996 when it found Remco Toys' "Steel Tec" toy helicopters couldn't fly and their toy motorcycles didn't move on their own.

Several advertising practices are commonly considered deceptive. Making just about any type of false claim is illegal, such as false price comparisons, false retail store price comparisons, and false manufacturer's retail list prices. FTC regulations require that an advertised price reduction or discount be based on fact, not fiction. In addition, when demanded by the FTC an advertiser must substantiate advertising claims with facts.

Another illegal practice is **bait and switch advertising**, where the consumer is lured into the store with a low price and talked into buying something much more expensive. Advertised specials are actually supposed to exist in the stores that run such ads, although retailers avoid the legality by citing limited quantities and giving **rain checks**, which give consumers the right to buy the same product at a later date for the same price. Free gifts are considered deceptive should the seller immediately recover the cost of the free merchandise. It also occurs when the seller fails to reveal all the conditions and obligations placed on the consumer.

"Advertising Dollars"—A Form of Censorship That Attacks the Consumer Interest

The power of advertising dollars, private economic interests, is increasingly coming into conflict with a vital interest of consumers—the right to information. What is watched on television and read in newspapers is often regulated—actually censored—by advertisers. This unethical practice occurs when the media is pressured by advertisers to report, not report, or to tailor certain stories or topics.[31]

A growing number of broadcasters and newspaper editors are afraid to upset a large advertiser so they avoid doing certain investigative stories and/or tone down deserved criticisms. Reporters have been fired for being too aggressive. Auto dealerships in particular are quick to pull ads from a local newspaper or television station; sometimes several advertisers boycott media who run tough stories. For example, articles on "how to buy" and "how to bargain" for autos almost cannot be found in some local markets. Stories on car-dealer trickery (odometer rollbacks, bait and switch, etc.) seemingly rarely reach the public in local markets anymore; local names are not named. Cases exist where newspapers have refused to run ads for discount auto-buying services, so as not to offend local auto dealers. Management from newspapers and broadcasters respond that they have no choice because they don't want to carry material that is insulting to their advertisers, otherwise, they will have no revenue.

Under the First Amendment to the U.S. Constitution, the press is supposed to be free. Auto advertising can make up 20 to 40 percent of the income for a local broadcaster or newspaper, so the motivation for self-censorship is apparent. When media buckles under to advertising pressure and stops doing auto stories or does so only sporadically, consumers lose opportunities to learn more about the products and the sellers. Such actions threaten the consumer interest. One observer claims that, "advertisers pose an even greater threat than politicians to press freedom."[32] More publicity about this problem will inform the public and help strengthen the resolve of station managers and editors to stand more strongly for First Amendment rights and against the pressures of censorship by

---

[31]For decades the media was virtually silent about the dangers of cigarette smoking, long after the negative effects were known, obviously in an effort to protect advertising revenues from tobacco industry.

[32]Snoddy, Raymond (1994, March 15), The threat from advertisers, *Financial Times*, 9.

advertisers. Some voluntary guidelines to govern the practice of media censorship by advertisers are needed.

Television Advertising Directed at Children

According to a report by the House Committee on Energy and Commerce, children today spend more time watching television than they do in school. The average youngster watches 26 to 40 hours of television per week or over 25,000 commercials each year. A large proportion of the advertisements are for expensive toys, candy, highly-sugared cereals and soft drinks, fast food of little nutritional value, and expensive clothing. Teenagers see an estimated 100,000 alcohol advertisements before they reach drinking age. The National Assessment of Educational Progress calls this "a diet calculated to reduce minds (and bodies) to mush."[33]

Arguments for Marketing to Children

Supporters of marketing to children via television advertising say that: (1) limiting advertisements goes against the constitutional right to freedom of speech (for individuals, as well as advertisers), (2) children and parents have a right of "free-choice" to watch what they want, (3) advertising provides useful information on new products, (4) quality programming exists because of advertising, (5) it costs taxpayers to oversee the government effort, (6) self-imposed regulations can be more stringent, (7) it is not an appropriate role of government to censor certain programs or tell parents what their children should watch, and (8) children become better consumers by viewing commercials. Television advertising to children probably will continue in the U.S. because it is quite profitable to many interest groups.

Arguments against Marketing to Children

Children tend to be trusting, and they are inclined to believe what adults say is true. Lacking the maturity of an adult, children are easy targets for marketers. Child advocates argue that this segment of consumers is the most vulnerable and helpless and advertising aimed at them is inherently unfair.

Child advocates argue that: (1) children lack the maturity and knowledge needed to understand and evaluate television advertising, (2) many have difficulty distinguishing between programming and commercials, especially product-based programs and cartoons, (3) **subtle merchandising** continues, the not-so-obvious toy lines written into the plots of animated shows, and (4) children have difficulty discerning ads from programming when a **program-length show** also advertises toys featured as a character focus in the show.

Critics argue that advertising to children promotes violence, advocates anti-intellectualism, encourages food choices of little or no nutritional value, results in obesity

---

[33]And Books, Please, Are for Reading. (1992, June 26). *Roanoke Times & World-News*, p. A8.

and high cholesterol levels,[34] stimulates excessive materialism, fosters family conflicts as children increasingly demand advertised goods, promotes a distorted and surreal view of life portrayed on television that shows that human problems can be solved by buying and utilizing the advertised products, and hinders the development of moral and ethical values in children.[35] In a recent year, federal spending for **public television broadcasting** (the channel without commercial advertising) was $1 per person in the United States, $17 in Japan, $32 in Canada, and $38 in Great Britain.

Government Regulation of Advertising to Children Has Been Weak

Since the early 1970s, and without success, Action for Children's Television (now defunct) and other organizations petitioned the Federal Communications Commission (FCC) to ban all television advertising directed at children, including program-length, toy-oriented shows, and sometimes described as **toy-mercials**, where it is hard to tell the "show" from the "advertisements." Today, toy manufacturers continue to pay TV stations (by purchasing commercials for the shows) to air animated children's programs that are based upon the companies' toys.

The FCC imposed weak restrictions in 1974, less stringent than self-imposed broadcasting industry standards. The Federal Trade Commission entered the controversy in 1978 under the premise that advertising to children is unfair and deceptive. Before the FTC could formally act, Congress removed their authority over such advertising. The free market atmosphere of the 1980s saw repeal of all guidelines under the FCC argument that, "market forces and not government should determine the programs children see."[36]

For years, the Council of Better Business Bureau's Children's Advertising Review Unit (CARU) has had standards for fairness and accuracy which has singled out specific ads that were troublesome. Seeing little progress, Congress passed the Children's Television Act (CTA) of 1990 which began to be implemented in 1992. It requires commercial broadcasters to limit the duration of advertising in children's programming to no more than 10.5 minutes per hour on weekends and 12 minutes per hour on weekdays. The law also requires that the FCC, when renewing a broadcaster's application for license renewal (done every 5 years), consider how well the licensee has served the specific public service obligations for the "educational and informational" needs of children less than 16 years of age in its overall programming. Finally, in 1996, the FCC ordered the nation's 1050 broadcast television stations (1) to offer at least three hours per week of educational programs, and (2) to submit to the FCC the programs they believe meet their obligations to young viewers. Perhaps one day sitcoms and cartoons (e.g., "The Jetsons," "G.I. Joe," and "UltraForce") will not pass the FCC's scrutiny for children's programming.

---

[34]An April 1996 study in *Archives of Pediatric and Adolescent Medicine* shows that the prevalence of overweight among children who watch 0 to 2 hours of television daily is 12 percent; more than 2 to 3 hours is 23 percent; more than 3 to 4 hours is 28 percent; more than 4 to 5 hours is 30 percent; more than 5 hours is 33 percent.

[35]Commercial-free public television programming for children is designed to impart knowledge, values and ethics.

[36]Barry, K. (1983, February 12). FCC Won't Force Child Programs. *The Boston Globe*, p. 35.

Needed: A More Knowledgeable Media Consumer

Rather that asking that media become "more socially responsible," an unlikely event, consumers, especially parents of young children, need to become educated about both the benefits and detriments of media. The New Mexico Media Literacy Project observes that, "Many other examples of corporate greed and irresponsible programming exist; hence we seriously doubt that corporate intentions will even overcome their primary motive—profit." Media literacy builds awareness that, "unsupervised media consumption is habitual and reduces the ability and potential of children to learn, especially the very young." Consumers everywhere need to better understand the persuasive messages provided in media and learn to make wiser choices.

CONSUMER UPDATE:
Television Advertising in Schools Gets Low Marks

Channel One is an innovative but controversial program from Whittle Communications that gives telecommunications equipment to school districts in exchange for permission to air 10 minutes of news and 2 minutes of commercials a day in the middle and high schools. That amounts to the equivalent of six full days during the school year watching Channel One. *Consumer Reports* calls such in-school commercialism "a perversion of education."

The first part of a three-year study by the independent Institute for Social Research revealed that Channel One viewers got only one more question correct on a current events test than non-viewers. More than 40 percent found Channel One equal in value to other material in school. Teachers remain enthusiastic, and only 6 percent had strong reservations. Many people believe quite strongly that schools should be a haven from commercialism. The controversy about Channel One continues as Whittle Communications signs up more schools; 12,000 of the nation's 30,000 middle and high schools already receive Channel One.

Non-commercial television programming for children also exists in the schools. About twenty television cable companies have a non-profit venture, Cable in the Classroom, that provides schools with free educational programming and study materials. Participants include Arts & Entertainment, Black Entertainment Television, and C-Span. The programming is commercial-free. The Public Broadcasting Service (PBS) has offered children's television programming for many years, including such exemplary programs as Sesame Street, Nova, and The Civil War.

Review and Summary of Key Terms and Concepts

1. List some reasons why **consumer decisions** are getting more difficult to make.

2. Summarize the mistake(s) consumers often make with the **discount rate**.

3. Discuss the related ideas of **subject expected utility**, **optimizing** and **consumer payoffs**.

4. Explain **price discrimination**.

5. How do **lifestyles** and **values** sometimes affect consumer **decision making**?

6. Discuss how **information search** affects **satisfaction**. In your response, explain the concept of **adverse selection**.

7. Give some **signals of quality** in the information search process.

8. Summarize how **indifference curves** work.

9. What is meant by **budget constraint**?

10. What is meant by **utility maximization**.

11. What two kinds of **information needs** are necessary for consumer choice?

12. What are **environmentalists** and what do they believe?

13. How can concerns about the environment differ from the perspective of a **consumer** and as a member of the **public**.

14. What does it mean to be a **pro-environmental consumer**? Also, give some examples of pro-environmental actions taken by consumers in marketplace transactions.

15. What is **green labeling**?

16. What are the four parts to the **decision-making matrix** for pro-environmental consumers?

17. Summarize the process of how **chlorofluorocarbons (CFCs)** affect the ozone layer.

18. Discuss the purpose of **advertising**.

19. Distinguish between an **informative advertisement** and a **puffery advertisement**.

20. Explain two of the four types of **puffery advertisements**: **testimonials, institutional ads, emotional advertisements**, and **comparative ads**.

21. Distinguish between **discernible exaggeration** and **false impression** advertising.

22. Distinguish among: **false impression advertising, deception, deceptive act**, and **deceptive advertisements**.

23. What are the differences between **bait and switch advertising** and **rain checks**?

24. Summarize the problem of **consumer information** and **censorship**.

25. List some of the problems that child advocates see with **advertising aimed at children**.

26. Distinguish between the **life cycle hypothesis** and the **permanent income hypothesis**.

Useful Resources for Consumers

Accuracy in Media
1275 K Street, NW
Washington, DC 20005
202-371-6710

Consumer Information Center
P.O. Box 100
Pueblo, CO 81002
gsa.gov/staff/pa/cic/cic.htm
A catalog of 275 free and low-cost federal publications of consumer interest; the text of all the publications is on the Internet.

Environmental Defense Fund
257 Park Avenue South
New York, NY 10010
212-505-2100

Friends of the Earth
218 D Street, SE
Washington, DC 20003
202-544-2600

Greenpeace, U.S.A.
1436 U Street, NW
Washington, DC 20009
202-462-1177

New Mexico Media Literacy Project
6400 Wyoming Blvd., NE
Albuquerque, NM 87109
505-828-3264

"What Do You Think" Questions

1. Do you think that **poor consumers** really pay more in the economic marketplace? Give examples in defending your conclusion.

2. Do you think Americans value **style** over **substance**? In your response, provide several examples of style over substance.

3. Evaluate an advertisement for a commercial product that was objectionable to you. Tell what was misleading, confusing, ridiculous, disgusting, or otherwise objectionable about the message.

4. Deconstruct a television advertisement in the way suggested by the New Mexico Media Literacy Project. Identify the following: (a) the real time visual images, (b) the emotions the music arouses, (c) the subliminal or near subliminal messages, (d) the emotions transferred to the thing being sold, (e) the "techno-events" (e.g., graphics, framming) in the message, (f) the "pseudo" logic of the message, (g) the intended effects for the target audience, (h) the unintended effects of values reinforced by many repetitions of the ad, and (i) the big strategy of the ad.

5. From your experience, describe two examples each of the four types of **puffery advertisements**: **testimonials**, **institutional ads**, **emotional advertisements**, and **comparative ads**.

Chapter 13

The Planned Buying Process

OBJECTIVES

After reading this chapter, you should be able to

1. Recognize the general buying behaviors of consumers: habit buying, impulse buying, and conspicuous consumption.

2. Appreciate the purposes and processes of planned buying.

3. Interpret the value of sources of buying information for consumers.

4. Understand the planned-buying steps of defining the problem and identifying personal values and goals.

5. Illustrate the planned-buying steps of identifying possible alternatives, comparing costs and benefits, and negotiating.

6. Explain the planned-buying steps of selecting the best alternative and accepting and evaluating your action.

Consumers consider many factors when choosing a product, such as performance, style, convenience, durability, price, and impact on health, safety and the environment. In vehicle buying, which is the focus of this chapter, consumers are now conditioned to wait for the rebates, the discounts, and the sales. This is confirmed by a *Worth* magazine survey reporting that about half of us are "always looking for a bargain." To get a really good deal, especially on expensive purchases, consumers need for follow a careful buying process, called planned buying.

The planned buying process includes defining the problem, identifying personal values and goals, identifying possible alternatives, comparing costs and benefits, negotiating, selecting the best alternative, and accepting and evaluating the action. Planned buying is a learned skill and it takes time and effort to perform. The expectation is that after reading this chapter, you will understand enough to be able to overcome the worst aspects of these challenges and learn to make effective personal buying decisions. Each of these areas of concern is addressed and illustrated in this chapter. Following a description of the general buying behaviors of consumers, this chapter provides an illustration of planned buying using the example of buying an automobile.

General Buying Behaviors of Consumers

For the purpose of analyzing and better understanding the approaches people use in decision making, this section divides buying behaviors into three categories: habit buying, impulse buying, and conspicuous consumption.

Habit Buying

A **habit** is a constant, almost unconscious inclination to perform an act, acquired through its frequent retention. Many consumer purchases are made on the basis of habit, including purchases made for customs and ceremonies. People get into the habit of buying a certain product, perhaps one brand of chewing gum or one particular make of automobile, or shopping at a certain store, or eating in the same restaurant, or always paying the same amount on their outstanding credit-card balance. These become programmed decisions of established routines and commitments. Habits are helpful in the sense that they allow or permit time for other decision making that may require considerable time and thought. Followed blindly, however, habits keep consumers from comparing and considering other alternatives.

Impulse Buying

Impulse buying is unplanned, spur-of-the-moment buying of unnecessary products and services. Usually the consumer is already in the seller's place of business, where he or she sees something he or she likes, and he or she just buys it. Merchants exploit impulse-buying behavior by displaying inexpensive items near the checkout counter and developing special signs and displays to encourage spending.

Impulse buying is sometimes a good idea, particularly if a desired item is on sale or the consumer sees something that may have been forgotten before. For example, people often buy on impulse when they are shopping in grocery stores as they see and purchase items that are not on their shopping lists. Others buy on impulse what they see advertised on home shopping television programs. **Home shopping** is a method of enabling consumers to purchase goods and services by means of an electronic device, such as a television screen and key pad, telephone, or home computer.

One of the latest forms of impulse buying is through interactive television shows that encourage consumers to participate in various programs by dialing a local 976 number (the cost of which might be highly overpriced, by the way) and punching in responses on a Touch-Tone telephone. The simple act of buying something on impulse also makes some people feel good.

There is a limit to how much anyone can afford to spend on impulse purchases. Getting carried away on impulse may not leave enough money for the purchase of needed goods and services. Overdoing impulse buying, particularly with the help of credit cards, also can lead to serious financial difficulties. Asking yourself "Why am I buying this?" and "Can I afford this?" helps curb impulse spending, as does making a shopping list and keeping to it.

Conspicuous Consumption

Conspicuous consumption is a person's desire to consume goods and services more for their ability to impress others and demonstrate social status than for their intrinsic value. Years ago the economist Thorstein Veblen coined the term conspicuous consumption to illustrate the transitory pleasure that some types of consumption provided. He suggested that one's happiness with a particular good or service was greatly determined by the number and quality of goods had by others. It seems that one's imagination attributes greater value to objects when they belong to someone else. If you have more than your neighbor, you are happy; if not, you are unhappy. Conspicuous consumption is fed by emulation and the media so consumers want to replace old goods before they wear out and buy new things whether they are needed or not. This is satisfying for many people, but in many cases buying what other people have gives people far less pleasure than anticipated.

For example, Janey Emering of Chicago, Illinois had been driving her automobile for a few years when one day her next door neighbor brought home a brand new car. Janey went over to visit and enviously admired the shiny paint and beautiful interior. By the next day, Janey's view of her old reliable vehicle had begun to change, and within two weeks she had purchased a new car that was even more expensive than the one her neighbor bought.

Many Americans practice conspicuous consumption and feel envious when they believe that they do not measure up in areas that are self-defining—those areas which are important to how they view themselves as people. For many, not measuring up to some standard of material things (such as big homes, living in a prestigious development, fancy cars, stylish clothes, jewelry, etc.) threatens their self-worth. A New York psychiatrist,

Theodore Issac Rubin, says that for many Americans, money and its symbols "have become a basis of self-acceptance."[1]

This type of buying behavior leads people to buy things in an effort to "keep up with the Joneses." It makes them victims of materialism and yuppyism. Conspicuous consumption sometimes leads to overspending as individuals and families spend to demonstrate their self-worth to themselves and to society. The bad news about conspicuous consumption is that just when you pull even with the Joneses, they spurt ahead—so the cycle continues. Such chronic envy can lead to false thoughts of perceived character shortcomings where people tell themselves that they are "failures" and "not good enough to live the good life." Left unresolved, such envy can lead to anxiety and depression, which can negatively affect relationships with others. Unfortunately, conspicuous consumption is a lifelong process that never comes to resolution, unless personal values are confronted and changed.

Research by Kjell Gronhaug and Paul S. Trapp in *The Journal of Consumer Marketing* suggests that social class is "a crucial determinant in consumer behavior...in that consumers associate brands of products and services with specific social classes."[2] Thus, the researchers conclude, perceptions of social class may influence acceptance and purchase of particular brands.

People with a high regard for individuality generally are not conspicuous consumers. Conspicuous consumers who are trying to change can begin with working on self-bolstering by thinking about their good qualities, selectively ignoring some of the things they are lusting after, and improving their feelings of self-reliance by not getting angry about the perceived unfairness of life. Some individuals practice *non*conspicuous consumption by purchasing relatively inexpensive things, such as driving old vehicles and often wearing old sneakers. Both conspicuous and nonconspicuous consumers can be happy in their purchase decisions if they understand the value judgments they are making.

The "Me Generation" or the "Gimme Generation" is a term that also describes many Americans. Perhaps you have seen the bumper sticker that says "I Shop, Therefore, I Am." Author Lewis H. Lapman observes that "many of us can no longer afford what our fathers could—a house, an education for our children—but an enormous percentage of us can afford practically anything else, and we buy it. What is more, we have made the very act of pursuing it almost an end in itself."[3]

Stanley Lebergott argues in *Pursuing Happiness: American Consumers in the Twentieth Century* that the vast amounts of materialistic spending are not evidence of self-indulgence, rather they are indicative of a successful capitalistic society. Instead of laboring all day with one's hands, Americans today are reaping the benefits of the "sum of things hoped for" not just the "evidence of things seen." Increased efficiency at work and labor-saving devices at home have given consumers greater leisure time and multitudes of ways to use it. Lebergott says that Americans work in order to consume because consumption expands the experience of life; in other words, it helps create human happiness.

---

[1]Lawhon, C., (1989, March 10). The Envy Monster. *The Washington Post*, p. C-5.

[2]Gronhaug, K. & Trapp, P. S. (1986, March). Social Class and Consumer Behavior. *Journal of Consumer Marketing*, 29. 78.

[3]Lapman, L. H., (1988, May 13). The Gimme Generation: How We Got This Way. *The Wall Street Journal Reports*. Sec. 3.

CONSUMER UPDATE: American Materialism

Over the past 30 years, American society has evolved to where **materialism** has become an ethic. This is the doctrine that physical well-being and worldly possessions constitute the greatest good and highest value in life. Materialism involves the need for instant gratification, and occasional compulsive spending. Here consumers twist personal wants into needs and buy products and services on credit, even if they cannot afford the monthly payments. Such behavior can cause serious financial, personal, and marital problems.

In today's American society, many people define themselves with what they own. Their self-esteem is tied to material dependency. Bruce A. Baldwin's article in *US Air Magazine* (April 1991) offers a number of suggestions on how to turn away from materialism.

Planned Buying for Important Purchases

Planned buying is a rational decision making process of buying goods and services where one analytically determines which alternative is a priority by examining the marginal costs and marginal benefits involved. Typically, these purchase decisions involve an extensive external information search. Consumers who make planned, rational buying decisions reduce the uncertainty and risk associated with purchases. Bad marketplace decisions are made for three reasons: (1) lack of information, (2) inability to process information, and (3) lack of time to gather or process information.[4] These difficulties can be overcome with planned buying.

Consumer Behavior authors J. F. Engel and R. D. Blackwell observe that the planned buying process occurs most often with high-involvement goods, which are those whose characteristics include high purchase cost, high ongoing operation and maintenance costs, and technological complexity. G. L. Stigler argues in the *Journal of Political Economy* that the optimal amount of search for consumers to undertake is that for which the marginal benefits of search are equal to the marginal costs. Since the benefits depend, in part, on the cost of the good to be purchased, the higher the cost of the good, the higher is the potential savings from search behavior. University of Rhode Island consumer economics professor Anne M. Christner further observes that people should consider a rational approach to buying, and rely on the advise of experts "in the case of very complicated goods (such as automobiles and computers) and abstract services (such as insurance and investments)."[5]

The basic decision making model of planned buying includes several steps that are discussed below.

1. Define the problem. Clearly identify the problem in light of your values and goals. What are your main concerns? What are you trying to accomplish? What are your needs?

---

[4]Hanna, S. (1989). Optimization for Family Resource Management. In D. E. Wendell (Ed.), *Proceedings of the 18th Annual Southeastern Regional Family Economics/Home Management Conference* (p. 57). Lexington, KY: University of Kentucky.

[5]Christner, A. M. (1989). Protecting Consumers with Prepurchase Information: Four Economic Ideological Views. In M. Carsky (Ed.), *Proceedings of the American Council on Consumer Interests* (p. 271). Columbia, MO: University of Missouri.

For example, if you think you want to buy an automobile, the first clarifying question is "Why?" Do you simply want basic transportation to get you back and forth to work, or do you need something more comfortable and dependable for long trips. Understanding the main issues in making the decision helps you clearly define the problem in terms of your personal values.

2. Identify your values and goals. The task is to establish priorities among your needs and wants. To do so, most people ask, "Will this fit my budget?" After that, the following question is usually, "How much can I get for my money?" Basically, this step involves determining whether you can satisfy all your needs, as well as all your wants, or satisfy all your needs but only some of your wants.

3. Identify the possible alternatives. With most planned buying decisions, you already have some background information on the product alternatives, usually gained from experience, perhaps from friends, from the media, or from previous visits to sellers. The task is to collect information and learn about the topic. You especially need information on the criteria or product characteristics that are important in evaluating a product or service. When you are spending a substantial amount of money, it is wise to obtain ample information to effect a good decision. It may be appropriate in your preshopping research to go to the library and visit some stores to collect information.

4. Compare the benefits and costs. It is important to examine the pluses and minuses for each alternative considered. **Evaluation** is the activity of identifying alternative solutions to a problem and determining the relative merits of each. The evaluation effort may be an informal ordering of information done mentally, and such a process is sufficient for most purchases.

To evaluate, you must select proper criteria, which then become the basis for comparing preference alternatives. You must decide which evaluative criteria or product characteristics are important to you. For example, perhaps you are considering the purchase of a room air-conditioner and *Consumer Reports* magazine downgrades one particular model because it does not dehumidify the air as well as other models. If you live in Denver or Phoenix, where it is dry, that factor is of little or no importance; if you live in Houston, it may be of great importance.

Examples of criteria often considered important are safety, convenience, performance, price, design, styling, dependability, durability, warranty, efficiency, economy, materials, service, brand, store image, location, availability of credit, repair services, delivery, and maintenance. Sometimes color is important too.

In this step you are really **comparison shopping**. This is the process of collecting and comparing information on products and services, including library and field data on price, brand, warranty, financing, and other services offered by retailers, to find what you think is the best buy. A **best buy** is a product or service that, in your opinion, represents acceptable quality at a fair or low price. The **quality** of an item, such as a product, brand, seller, or combination of these factors, consists of "the extent to which the specimen provides the service characteristics that the individual consumer desires."[6]

During this step you are trying to compare the alternatives based on the evaluative criteria you are using, and this may include product features, warranties, service contracts, and financing options. This step requires that you become knowledgeable on the topic. This effort is also known as the process of **alternative evaluation**, which is the identification of each course of action and its comparison with others, which may offer a solution to some recognized problem.

---

[6]Maynes, E. S. (1976), *Decision-Making for Consumers* (New York: MacMillan), 52.

To effectively comparison shop, you also must decide which criteria are more important than others in satisfying your physical and psychological needs. Often people place a great deal of weight on one criterion, which makes decision making easier. Still, there are no hard and fast rules, because consumers use numerous methods to evaluate preferences. When you choose a best buy for yourself, the choice is subjective and personal. When you make the choice of a particular level of quality, you do so because you anticipate that you will be satisfied with your selection.

5. Negotiate. Negotiating is the process of conferring with a seller in order to come to terms and reach an agreement on price, as well as to agree regarding other aspects of the deal. Many consumers are hesitant and uncomfortable about **bargaining** or **haggling** when buying appliances, electronic goods, and vehicles, but sellers expect to bargain on price. With inexpensive products, little if any negotiating occurs. Much negotiating goes on for more expensive products and services. Here there will be offers and counteroffers until there is agreement on the final terms.

6. Select the best alternative. The task is to decide which product or service is best for you given your values and goals. This step allows you to rank the preferences for choice. A **consumer decision** is the mental process of selecting the most desirable alternative from among the choices available. If a person logically decides on the basis of known facts, it becomes a rational, correct, and normal consumer decision at the time of the purchase. It can be argued that a consumer could change his or her mind later, as new facts become available, but at the time of the decision, the consumer's determination was rational.

A decision could also be unreasonable. It is determined by how the decision was made, not whether it is correct or not. Four conditions may exist that allow consumers to make incorrect purchase decisions: (1) the decision may be based on incorrect assumptions; (2) the facts upon which the decision is based may be insufficient; (3) the facts may be incorrect; and (4) the consumer's judgment may not be sound. Nevertheless, even some incorrect decisions are made rationally when consumers decide logically based on known facts.

Even if the search process has been extensive, there are typically gaps in what the consumer knows. As a result, consumers use judgment to assign weights to information, rank various criteria according to importance, and bring together a variety of points to a cohesive pattern permitting a decision.

7. Accept and evaluate your action. The rational consumer reflects on important decisions after a period of weeks or months. The intent is not to check the results of the decision to be sure, to doubt the decision, or to be irritated that a few dollars might have been saved by doing something else. Rather, the task is to reaffirm the wisdom of utilizing the process that resulted in your decision and to use any valuable recollections in future decision making opportunities.

Sources of Buying Information for Consumers

Consumers have a variety of sources of buying information. Useful information may come from past buying experiences, as well as friends and relatives. A barrage of information is available through advertising, but most of it is biased and aimed at persuading you to spend your money.

Consumers need sufficient buying information to help them make effective decisions. They need to acquire information up to the point where the marginal costs of finding additional useful, usually objective, information does not outweigh the marginal benefits of collecting it. **Objective information** is knowledge that is presented in a factual or objective manner and is accurate, complete, understandable, and up to date. Consumers need two types of objective information: (1) information to determine what evaluative criteria others believe are important when making a selection, and (2) how much importance they personally should give to each criterion.

The following sources of objective buying information are examined: consumer testing magazines, consumer-oriented magazines, seals and certification programs, mass media, government agencies, Better Business Bureaus, and point-of-purchase sources.

Source: Consumer Testing Magazines

People who are interested in buying a product but are not sure which brand or model to look for in the marketplace often seek help from unbiased consumer testing magazines. *Consumer Reports* (CR) magazine is the single most sought after source for objective and reliable buying data.

Consumer Reports accepts no commercial advertising, accepts no free samples from manufacturers for testing, and instead uses anonymous shoppers to purchase samples from retail stores. CR is responsible only to its subscribers and members. CR conducts extensive comparative testing of products and publishes the findings. *Consumer Reports* often goes to court to prevent use of its test ratings in advertisements. CR also releases summaries of its results for use on radio and television. CR tests all kinds of consumer products, such as irons, televisions, air-conditioners, automobiles, air fresheners, frozen TV dinners, and computers.

Consumer Reports tries to do what average consumers' would do when evaluating products. First, CR establishes the evaluative criteria used in rating each product along with an explanation of their importance. For example, if CR is testing irons, it is of some importance to have temperature settings that are accurate and easy to read, as well as settings to permit proper ironing of wash-and-wear fabrics, cottons, and wools. Second, CR puts a certain weight on each of the evaluative criteria considered. For example, the accuracy of the temperature readings may be of less importance than how well the iron performs.

Consumer Reports classifies products into three categories: acceptable, conditionally acceptable, and not acceptable. Products in each category are listed in the magazine in descending order of estimated overall quality. Consumers generally only want to purchase items that are rated acceptable because the other two ratings are quite negative. Products are rated not acceptable when there is some type of safety hazard, such as an automobile turning over too easily during road testing. The conditionally acceptable rating is used when products have a problem but it can be overcome with special precautions or a simple modification. Sometimes *Consumer Reports* finds a product in the acceptable category that is clearly superior to the others tested and it is "check-rated" as a best buy with an appropriate marking. Armed with this type of buying information, consumers can apply their own weights to evaluative criteria, narrow their choices, and shop in their local marketplace to examine products, compare price and other factors, and make their decisions.

A long-time competing consumer publication, *Consumers Research Magazine,* has a monthly circulation of less than 30,000 and no longer conducts product tests. With its limited budget, *Consumers Research Magazine* reports what it considers to be reliable information about products, services, and a number of other consumer-related topics.

Consumer Reports magazine also conducts research on consumer and public interest issues, such as water safety, life insurance, health food advertising, and small claims courts. Subscribers to *Consumer Reports* are extremely satisfied with the buying information provided because the publication has one of the highest renewal rates in the industry. What people pay for the subscription is recovered many times over by being more informed, which allows them to buy better-quality products, lower-priced products, or both. Computer owners can subscribe to a computerized, on-line (via a modem) shopping and information center service called Prodigy, offered by Sears and IBM that permits state-of-the-art home shopping and product comparisons of brands accessing nearly 400 different information systems, including *Consumer Reports*. Nintendo and AT&T have formed a partnership to develop another information service to offer home shopping, banking, travel information, airline reservations, and stock quotation and purchasing services.

Source: Consumer-Oriented Magazines

There are a number of magazines that appeal to special interests of consumers, such as skiing, photography, boating, personal finance, golf, and automobiles. Popular consumer-oriented magazines include *Kiplinger's Personal Finance Magazine, Money, Consumer Digest, Better Homes and Gardens, Car and Driver, High Fidelity, Personal Computing, Automobile Mechanics, Golf Digest,* and *Stereo Review*. Some of these publications provide a consumer perspective on a variety of money-management, financial planning, product care, and maintenance topics. Some also contain valuable information on consumer products, even though there are serious limitations about the objectivity and reliability of the information.

The magazines usually discuss brands in their articles but do not comparatively rate them. They do not provide details on testing procedures or explain how the ratings were developed. Ratings are often based on personal judgments and limited-use tests instead of extensive laboratory tests. It is not uncommon to see an article evaluating products in a consumer-oriented magazine, an editorial about the products, and advertisements for the same products in the same issue. On the plus side for consumers is that the articles are usually well written and especially easy to understand. Articles often point out important evaluative criteria consumers can use to judge the quality of products. They are also up to date.

Source: Seals and Certification Program Information

Many organizations are concerned with the quality of particular consumer products and test them. Successful products then are awarded a seal of approval or another form of certification by the appropriate group.

Safety seals are certifications of approval by independent testing organizations given to products that meet their minimum standards of safety and performance. If the organization sets high standards, its seals serve as useful guides for consumers. Five valuable safety seals are Underwriters Laboratories (UL), the American Standards Association (ASA), the American Gas Association (AGA), the National Association of Furniturers Seal of Integrity (NAFSI), and the Association of Home Appliance Manufacturers (AHAM). As an aside, consumers should realize that the UL seal applies only to the electrical part of the appliance to which it is attached, usually the cord (see Figure 13-1).

CONSUMER UPDATE:
Are Brand Names Indicators of Quality?

Consumers judge quality in a lot of ways, and one useful technique is the brand name on the product or service. **Manufacturers' brands** (also known as **brand names**) are products and services that have a trademark or distinctive name identifying the manufacturer or dealer and are heavily advertised. Nationally advertised products such as Coke, McDonalds, Jordache, and IBM are brand names. These products are usually labeled "made by..." While the name is not a guarantee of quality, the company has already invested considerable sums of money into its reputation and has an interest in maintaining that image with products and services of a consistent grade of quality. Two additional pluses for brand name products are that they may offer the best product warranties and they may be repaired at the largest number of authorized facilities.

Store brands (also known as **private brands**) are products and services sold only by a particular retailer, chain, or dealer and are labeled accordingly. Products such as Sears Kenmore appliances are well-known quality products sold to the public. Most store-brand products are manufactured by someone other than the seller and are made to the seller's specifications; thus, labels usually read "made for..." or "distributed by..." Store brands often offer good quality at reasonable costs because the reputation of the seller is well known and because advertising costs are somewhat lower than for manufacturers' brands.

Generic brands (also called **no-frills brands**) are lower-quality products sold without a well-known brand name on the label (although most generic products do have names) and sold at substantial savings compared to manufacturers' brand and store-brand products. The name of the manufacturer, packer, or distributor is on the package. Generic-brand products, such as cola drinks, grape jelly, canned fruits, paper towels, cosmetics, and cigarettes, are commonly sold in grocery stores. The lower prices are due to the usually lower (but still for many very suitable) quality, less expensive ingredients, simpler packaging, limited number of sizes, and little or no advertising costs.

Magazine seals and **retailer seals** are certifications of approval given to products and services that, in the judgment of the organization, meet whatever standards the organization has established. Most such seals provide meaningless buying information to consumers. Some magazines, rather than test products, just give approval to any product that advertises on its pages. The seals of retailers are simply a form of advertising that attempts to convey a quality image to consumers, whether deserved or not.

The best-known magazine seals are given by *Good Housekeeping* and *Parents* magazines, and the popularity of these seals shows that they are an effective technique to sell products. The seals provide limited assurances by the magazines that the manufacturers, not the magazines, will provide a replacement or refund for products purchased and found to be defective, although *Good Housekeeping* does offer a limited warranty for products advertised in its magazine. Such guarantees are already provided consumers through the implied warranty laws in all states.

Seal		Where It Can Be Found	What It Means
	Underwriters Laboratories, Inc.	On appliances, equipment, and materials that could be hazardous and products used to detect or extinguish fires	Products have passed original laboratory tests and periodic factory tests and examination, in accordance with U.S. standards for safety.
	American Gas Association	On gas accessories or appliances such as ranges, heaters, clothes dryers	Products certified by the AGA must conform to the standards of the American National Standards Institute for safety and design.
	Good Housekeeping Seal	On most products advertised in *Good Housekeeping* magazine (exceptions include advertisements for such products and services as insurance, real estate, and transportation facilities, among others)	This is a limited warranty, *not* a seal of approval. Products proved defective will be replaced or money refunded by *Good Housekeeping* magazine.
	Canadian Standards Association	On appliances, equipment, and general products that could be potentially dangerous	Products have passed CSA tests and periodic factory inspections in accordance with CSA Standards for Safety.

Sources: Seals reproduced courtesy of the Underwriters Laboratories. Inc.; American Gas Association: *Good Housekeeping* magazine; and Canadian Standards Association. Text used by permission of Money Management Institute of Household International.

FIGURE 13-1 Major U.S. And Canadian Product Seals of Approval

Critics of magazine seals observe that even though the magazines' staffs sometimes do conduct tests before approving products, the only products that qualify for the seals are those which advertise in the magazines. The testing procedures and standards are rarely made public. These magazines have not disclosed the number of cases where refunds or replacements were made to consumers, which effectively removes all accountability to consumers.

Source: Mass Media

Consumer problems are given wide attention in mass media sources, such as television, radio, newspapers, and general-interest magazines. The public is often interested in consumer issues, and these are the subject of feature stories, action columns, and how-to-do-it series. Easy-to-explain topics are popular, such as product safety, complaining effectively, and how to buy particular products; evaluative criteria are occasionally mentioned. More complex issues, such as anticompetitive mergers and price fixing, are generally avoided.

Source: Government Agency Information

Governments at all levels accept the responsibility to provide the public with a certain amount of consumer information. Government publications typically do not name brands or rate products and services, but instead focus on key criteria that consumers can use to judge quality.

Several helpful federal government agencies are described in Chapter 5. Writing the Consumer information Center (Pueblo, CO 81009) will get you a free copy of *Consumer Information*, a catalog that lists 275 available booklets from over 30 federal agencies on a wide variety of consumer information topics.

There is also a Federal Information Center (FIC) that is available only by telephone, and the toll-free number is listed in the government section in the telephone book. The FIC helps consumers find information they want and directs them to the correct federal, state, or local government agency to solve consumer problems.

Source: Facts from Better Business Bureaus

Better Business Bureaus (BBBs) are organizations located in 138 communities that collect information and maintain files on businesses in their communities, and they help consumers identify which businesses have unsatisfactory complaint records. BBBs do not rate individual businesses or tell consumers where to buy, rather they provide useful information to let the consumer judge whether or not to buy from a particular business.

The information service provided by the Better Business Bureau works in the following manner. Assume that Juanita Hernandez, of San Jose, California, is interested in buying a used Toyota. Juanita looks in the newspaper advertisements and in the Yellow Pages, and determines that there are four sellers located not too far from her home that handle Toyota automobiles. Being a wise consumer, Juanita telephones the local Better Business Bureau to inquire about the reputation of each seller. The BBB will tell her the number of years they have maintained files; whether or not they have received recent complaints about the firms, and the nature of those complaints; whether or not the sellers have responded to any complaints forwarded to them by the BBB, and the disposition of those complaints; recent government actions against the firms; and information about any questionable advertising and selling practices used by the sellers.

Source: Point-of-Purchase Information

Point-of-purchase information is practical or technical knowledge printed on the package or product label, or displayed nearby, that discloses, instructs, or warns consumers about products for sale. It is readily available information designed to help the consumer make a decision.

Product labels are very helpful sources of buying information. Various laws usually require that consumer product labels provide the brand name; the generic or common name; the name and address of the manufacturer, packer, or distributor; and the quantity of the contents. Most labels provide more than the minimum amount of information. For example, food products usually list the ingredients, as well as instructions on use; clothing product labels tell about care and use; over-the-counter drug labels suggest appropriate dosage amounts; household cleaning fluids have warnings associated with the products' use; household appliances have nearby signs instructing customers where to go in the store to examine product warranties; and energy use labels are found on refrigerators, freezers, air-conditioners, clothes washers, and other products.

Defining the Problem

Planned buying begins by trying to clearly identify the problem in light of one's values and goals. Questions include: What are your main concerns? What are you trying to accomplish? What are your needs? Understanding the main issues in making a decision helps you clearly define the problem in terms of your personal values.

To illustrate, assume that Bonnie Sidwell of Ypsilanti, Michigan, is interested in buying an automobile. Bonnie recently started a new job about ten miles out of town and requires very dependable transportation for the daily 20-mile drive. Public transportation is not available, and carpooling will not be an option because her work hours are somewhat variable. Bonnie has been driving her mother's old car, which now must be returned so her younger sister can have it. Bonnie would like a new automobile instead of another used one because she anticipates using it for long drives to the mountains when she goes camping during vacations and long weekends, although an almost new car would be okay.[7] She wants something that is large enough to hold her camping equipment but that gets good gas mileage. Bonnie has about $1700 in savings, and she must finance the purchase, as do 70 percent of 10 new car buyers. Bonnie expects to keep the new car about as long as the average consumer, over 8 years.

---

[7]About 30 million used cars and trucks are sold annually, compared to 10 million new ones.

Identifying Personal Values and Goals

The second step in planned buying is to establish priorities among needs and wants. Questions to ask: "Will this fit my budget?" and "How much can I get for my money?" This step involves determining whether you can get all your needs and wants satisfied or whether you can have all your needs satisfied but only some of your wants.

Can Bonnie Afford to Buy an Automobile?

With only $1700 as a down payment, Bonnie wonders whether or not she can finance an automobile purchase given her limited budget. She makes a salary of $27,500, but after withholding for taxes, retirement savings, insurance premiums, and union dues, she takes home $18,000, or $1500 per month. Table 13-1 shows Bonnie's expenses for last month.

Budget Item	Spent Last Month	Possible Cutback Amount
Food	$180	-$20
Rent (Bonnie's share)	300	
Electricity (Bonnie's share)	70	
Telephone	85	-15
Cable television (Bonnie's share)	20	
Credit payment on television	30	
Clothing	60	-20
Gasoline	80	
Automobile maintenance/repairs	30	
Doctor/dentist	30	
Entertainment/recreation	80	-15
Vacations/long weekends	80	
Gifts and contributions	40	
Beautician	30	
Automobile insurance	175	
Life insurance	60	-60
Savings	60	-20
Miscellaneous	90	-20
TOTAL	$1500	-$170

TABLE 13-1   Possible Cutbacks in Bonnie's Monthly Expenses

Even though her $1500 income is totally committed, as illustrated in Table 13-1, Bonnie made notations where there were possibilities of making cutbacks in her expenses in an effort to see if she could afford to finance an automobile. (Automobile financing is discussed in Chapter 17.) Bonnie came up with a total of $170 in possible cutbacks, and this was only because she could drop the private life insurance policy she purchased last year, since her new employer provides subsidized life insurance as a fringe benefit.

Bonnie really did not like all the choices she had made in her budgeted expenses. She figured that the only area with any flexibility was the $175 paid for automobile insurance, since it was for 6 months of coverage. After telephoning her insurance agent, she estimated that the automobile insurance premium for a not-very-expensive new car would be about $900, or $75 a month. So instead of paying out $175 for insurance every 6 months, as in Table 13-1, Bonnie will have to pay $75 a month. The net effect is a higher total for insurance premiums and an additional $100 a month available to spend on an automobile. Bonnie determined that by making the various cutbacks she could budget $270 ($170 + $100) a month for car payments.

After thinking it over some more, Bonnie decided not to cut back $20 a month on savings because she needed the money to pay her night class tuition and for a vacation next summer. Thus, Bonnie determined that she would have $250 ($270 - $20) available each month to spend on financing an automobile.

How Much Can Bonnie Get for Her Money?

Bonnie likes Geos, Nissans, Plymouths, Fords, and Hondas. After thinking about the probable costs of these cars, she figured that she could decide to fulfill her needs by purchasing an inexpensive new Plymouth or Honda. Or, she could fulfill her needs *and* her wants by buying a used Nissan, Ford, or Geo. Her alternatives are to make more cutbacks in her budget, to work overtime, to get a part-time job, or to buy a cheaper or used car.

Bonnie made a list of her needs and wants to help identify her values and goals in this decision-making process. Her worksheet is shown in Figure 13-2. Bonnie found, to her surprise, that there were several features she did not consider as needs and her wants were not as numerous as she had thought.

Bonnie telephoned her bank and her credit union for more information. She wanted to know how much car she could expect to get with her $1700 down payment money and a maximum of $250 a month. Since interest rates to finance automobiles were about 10 percent at both lenders, they provided the following information: $12,000 would cost her $250.80 per month for 5 years, $10,000 would cost $250.90 for 4 years, and $8000 would cost $256.48 for 3 years. Because she wanted a car without rust when it was paid for, Bonnie decided not to finance for more than 3 years. This meant she could not buy an automobile for more than $9700 ($8000 in borrowed funds plus her $1700 in savings).

Next, Bonnie visited the local lenders and asked to look at their books that showed the values of used automobiles.[8] Her bank showed her a recent copy of the *Red Book*, while her credit union showed her copies of the *Black Book* and the *Blue Book*. These are weekly, biweekly, or monthly reports published by independent organizations, such as the National Automobile Dealers Association (NADA), that show the average wholesale and retail prices for various automobiles, depending on the condition of the vehicle, mileage, options, and other factors. After reviewing the materials, Bonnie determined that she could afford a 4- or 5-year-old expensive car with lots of options or a 2-year-old less expensive model, because most of them had retail prices less than $10,000. Her other option was to buy a less expensive new car with the few options that she wanted.

---

[8]The average age of used automobiles in the U.S. is 8 years; 1 in 4 cars is at least 12 years old.

Needs	Automobile Feature	Wants	Don't Care
✓	Power steering		
	Tinted windows	✓	
	Automatic windows	✓	
✓	Automatic transmission		
	Leather seats		✓
✓	AM-FM Radio		
	Cassette player	✓	
	Super sound system		✓
	Telescope and tilt steering wheel		✓
	Automatic light dimmer		✓
	Air conditioning	✓	
✓	Whitewall tires		
	Four-wheel drive		✓

FIGURE 13-2 Wants and Needs Worksheet (for Bonnie Sidwell)

Identifying Possible Alternatives

With most planned-buying decisions, you already have some background information on the topic, usually gained from experience, perhaps obtained from friends, the media, or previous visits to sellers. The third step in planned buying is to collect information and learn about the topic.

You especially need information on the product characteristics that are important in evaluating a product or service. These represent the criteria you will use to evaluate different factors. When you are spending a substantial amount of money, it is wise to obtain sufficient information to effect a good decision. Thus, it may be appropriate in your preshopping research to go to the library and visit some stores to collect information.

Over the next few weeks, Bonnie went **window shopping** for both new and used automobiles. This is the process of conducting preshopping research to gather information about products and services that might be purchased at a later time. Since Bonnie told her friends and coworkers that she was interested in buying a car, they gave her advice on models to avoid, as well as which ones they liked, and why. Bonnie went to the library for information and she visited some automobile dealers, where she asked a lot of questions. Most dealers gave her informational brochures from the manufacturers. She took several new and used automobiles for test drives and gained a lot from the experiences. One model, for example, was uncomfortable to ride in because the driver's seat just could not be properly adjusted to fit her body.

Shrewdly, Bonnie did not carry her checkbook with her so that she might not weaken to sales pressure and be persuaded to buy before she completed her efforts. Also, she had heard about **push money** (or **spiff**) and did not want to fall victim to such pressure. This is a special cash incentive, not a regular commission, offered to salespersons by the manufacturer, dealer, or business owner to sell particular products, usually because that merchandise is selling slowly, or because the profit is especially large. Push money can really motivate salespersons to sell one product over another, and the consumer generally never realizes why the product features of one item are discussed so heavily over another. Navy financial educator Dean Brassington reminds shoppers that, "At the lot, you're going against a pro who sells more cars in a month than most people buy in a lifetime."

DID YOU KNOW?
Repair Cost Estimates Available at New-Car Dealers

The National Highway Traffic Safety Commission (NHTSA) has prepared booklets that contain information that rate vehicles based on their repair-cost histories and the likely impact on collision insurance. NHTSA regulations require new-car dealers to make the information available to shoppers.

In the library, Bonnie found some excellent publications with information on automobiles. The annual April issue of *Consumer Reports* is devoted solely to the buying of new and used automobiles, and it includes articles on how to negotiate the best price. An example of the type of useful Ratings published by *Consumer Reports* (for 27-inch televisions in this instance) is given in Figure 13-3. *Consumer Reports* articles include details on the methodology of the testing project, as well as criteria for the Ratings. The *Consumer Reports Buying Guide Issue* includes comparative information and Ratings on used cars too. Other valuable consumer-related publications on automobiles include *Car and Driver, Motor Trend, Road & Track Magazine,* and *Edmund's New Car Prices. Kiplinger's Personal Finance Magazine* also has a useful annual buying guide issue.

CONSUMER UPDATE: Safety Ratings on Automobiles

The National Highway Traffic Safety Commission requires that safety information be listed on new-car sales stickers. The figures are the results of the government's crash safety tests. Five stars are given for the safest rating; one star for the lowest.

Comparing Costs and Benefits

It is important to examine the pluses and minuses for each alternative considered. You must decide what evaluative criteria and product characteristics are important to you. Examples of criteria often considered important are safety, convenience, performance, price, operating costs, design, styling, time use, ecology, privacy, dependability, durability, service, warranty, and service maintenance.

Ratings 27-inch TV sets
& Recommendations

Overview *Listed primarily in order of picture quality*

Brand and model	Price	Overall score (0–100: P F G VG E)	Picture	Sound	Reception: Cable	Reception: Antenna	Ease of use
JVC AV-27BM6	$500		Excellent	Very good	Excellent	Good	Very good
RCA F27702SB	590		Excellent	Good	Fair	Good	Good
Samsung TXC2715	350		Excellent	Fair	Fair	Good	Very good
GE 27GT618	400		Excellent	Poor	Good	Very good	Good
Sharp 27G-S60	350		Excellent	Poor	Good	Good	Very good
Toshiba CF27E50	500		Very good	Very good	Good	Fair	Very good
Zenith SR2773DT	490		Very good	Excellent	Excellent	Fair	Very good
Sony KV-27V10	550		Very good	Very good	Very good	Good	Good
RCA F27674BC	500		Excellent	Poor	Very good	Good	Good
Sanyo AVM-2755	340		Very good	Good	Fair	Good	Good
Magnavox TP2782	500		Good	Very good	Excellent	Good	Very good
Panasonic CT-27G30	600		Very good	Very good	Fair	Fair	Good
Sony KV-27S10	500		Good	Very good	Very good	Good	Good
Magnavox TP2792	600		Fair	Very good	Excellent	Good	Very good
Mitsubishi CS-27205	550		Good	Very good	Very good	Good	Good
Hitachi 27CX5B	500		Fair	Good	Good	Very good	Good

The tests behind the Ratings

Picture quality is given greatest weight. A viewing panel compared side-by-side images from a pristine broadcast signal, judging clarity and accuracy of colors. **Sound** quality reflects the accuracy of the built-in speakers. The best models rival the fidelity of an inexpensive stereo. **Ease of use** reflects judgments about how easy the remote control and on-screen menus were to use. **Cable reception** is based on lab tests of how well the sets rejected signals from adjacent cable channels. The best sets showed no noticeable interference; the worst, visual "noise" or slight ghosting of channels. **Antenna reception** reflects the ability to receive noise-free off-the-air broadcasts. Throughout, **price** is a national average, based on a price survey.

Excellent · Very good · Good · Fair · Poor

Source: "Ratings: 27-inch TVs" Copyright 1996 by Consumers Union of U.S., Inc., Yonkers, NY 10703-1057. Reprinted by permission from CONSUMER REPORTS, March 1996. Although this material originally appeared in CONSUMER REPORTS, the resulting conclusions presented are those of the author and are not sanctioned or endorsed in any way by Consumers Union, the publisher of CONSUMER REPORTS.

FIGURE 13-3 Consumer Reports Ratings for VCRs

In this step you are really **comparison shopping**. This is the process of collecting and comparing information on products and services, including library and field data on price, brand, warranty, financing, leasing, and other services offered by sellers, to find what you think is the best buy. A **best buy** is a product or service that, in your opinion, represents acceptable quality at a fair or low price for that level of quality. During this step you are trying to compare the alternatives based on the evaluative criteria you are using, and this may include product features, warranties, service contracts, and financing options. To do this you also must decide which criteria are more important than others.

The search for information was extremely beneficial for Bonnie. By talking to friends, going to the library, and returning to visit some of the automobile dealers, she learned a lot about what models and features to avoid and why, as well as about what was important to her. She also learned about dealer service and reputation, warranties, rebates, and financing options offered by the sellers.

Rebates are refunds occasionally available on new cars and other products offered as an incentive by the manufacturer and sometimes the dealer to encourage sale of particular models. They are a deduction from an amount to be paid or the return of part of an amount given in payment. Rebates may result in a lower net price for a specific vehicle. However, making the best decision is often confusing and difficult because rebates are often offered in conjunction with special option packages and various financing plans. **Option packages** are automobile manufacturer incentive packages that offer popular, and sometimes less popular, options at a lower price than normal, in an effort to get buyers to spend money on extras. Sometimes you must choose either the rebate on an in-stock or unpopular vehicle or the reduced-rate financing. (A boxed insert later in this chapter shows how to calculate which is better, a rebate or a low-interest loan.)

CONSUMER UPDATE:
Automobile Bumpers Remain Weak

Over ten years ago, the National Highway Traffic Safety Administration rolled back the federal vehicle standards for car bumpers in the interest of reducing manufacturing costs and increasing gas mileage. The previous standard required that cars be equipped with bumpers that prevented all damage to any exterior part of the automobile and the bumper itself in collisions up to 5 miles per hour into a wall or 10 miles per hour into another car. *Public Citizen* reports that low-speed accidents account for over $4 billion in costs per year, which largely could be avoided if cars had 5-mile-per-hour bumpers. A five-mile an hour impact, such as bumping a rear bumper into a parking lot lightpost, typically causes damage amounting to $1000 to $3000.

Warranties

Warranties (or **guarantees**) are assurances by the seller of property that the goods or property are of the quality represented or will be as promised, that the product will perform as represented, provide true value, and be free from hidden defects or limitations. Warranties on consumer products are offered by manufacturers as a promotional device to help differentiate one product from its competitors.

Also, the seller sees the warranty as something that limits the firm's liability, since it legally obligates the manufacturer only so far in dealing with buyers who have problems by setting time limits, making exceptions to lists of parts covered, and allowing the manufacturer to be its own judge of warranty claims, while simultaneously inducing particular expectations on the part of the consumer. For example, a written warranty may specify which remedies are available to consumers with problems and may limit how much the company will pay.

How Consumers View Warranties

Consumers view warranties differently. Most trust the salesperson's description of the warranty terms associated with a product. Many consumers accept warranties uncritically, assuming that the act of offering a warranty suggests that this is a quality product. Few consumers read written warranties until they are needed. (Details on consumer rights and remedies are provided in Chapter 4.) Good warranties offer peace of mind to consumers when they purchase expensive products, such as automobiles, electronic equipment, and appliances.

Warranties and "Secret Warranties"

Different types of warranties are offered by sellers. First, there are **implied warranties**. These written or unwritten promises give consumers important legal rights that sometimes are stronger than those offered in most written warranties because they give consumers the legal right to expect that products and services are fit for the ordinary purposes for which they are sold.

The second type of warranty offered by sellers is an **express warranty**, which is a written guarantee setting out specific assurances by the manufacturer or seller. This is usually a written statement indicating the name and address of the warrantor, the product or parts covered, the duration of the warranty, and specifically what the warrantor will do and who will pay for it. (More details on implied and express warranties are provided in Chapter 4.) It is estimated that auto manufacturers spend between $500 (General Motors) and $850 (Chrysler) annually per vehicle for warranty repairs.[9]

The third type of warranty that sellers, particularly automobile manufacturers, offer on vehicles is a **secret warranty**. This is a form of extended protection for free repairs or reimbursement of incurred expenses sometimes provided by product manufacturers when persistent problems develop beyond the traditional warranty time period. The problems usually affect the vehicle's performance or safety, but they are not the subject of a formal recall. Secret warranties offered by automobile manufacturers are disclosed in **factory service bulletins** that are sent to dealers authorizing them to offer free repairs or reimbursement of costs to consumers experiencing specific problems. In such cases, the dealers, not consumers, are notified who then offer to make repairs at their discretion. About 500 secret warranties are in effect at any point in time, reports the Center for Auto Safety. Manufacturers typically call these efforts **policy adjustments** or **good-will service**.

Secret warranties arise when dealers report a large number of specific complaints and the manufacturer determines the difficulty to be caused by a design or assembly problem. There are an estimated 30 million secret warranties on cars and light trucks (for example, engine, transmission, and rust problems). The manufacturer pays for the repairs only to consumers who complain and ask about such coverage. As part of previous legal settlements, both Ford and General Motors must make the bulletins available to the public. (Concerned vehicle owners can telephone Ford at 800-241-FORD and General Motors at 800-551-4123.)

The people who find out about secret warranty programs are aggressive, persistent and/or lucky consumers who complain to dealers. Virginia, Connecticut, and Wisconsin recently passed Secret Warranty Disclosure laws that require auto manufacturers to notify

---

[9]Maynard, M. and D. Henry (1996, October 24), Warranty Cost Issue Hurts Chrysler, *USA Today*, 3-B.

CONSUMER UPDATE:
How Much Does It Cost to Drive?

According to the American Automobile Association, those who drive 15,000 miles will pay an average of $3,200 to own and operate a car, excluding the cost of depreciation and loan payments on the principal.

Average Operating Costs	
Gas and oil	$ 840
Maintenance	420
Tires	180

Ownership Costs	
Insurance	
Comprehensive	144
Collision	275
Liability	426
License, registration and taxes	215
Financing: 48 months at 9%	718
Total Cost	**$3,218**

---

consumers of post-warranty adjustment programs within 90 days of adopting an adjustment program. Manufacturers also are required to reimburse consumers who have previously obtained repairs on their own. Secret warranty programs are not in the consumer interest since the great majority of wronged consumers are ripped off because they are excluded from participation.

If you suspect a program exists with your non-Ford or non-GM vehicle, consider sending a self-addressed, stamped business envelope with 50 cents postage to the Center for Auto Safety (2001 S Street, NW, Suite 410, Washington, DC 20009). Include details on the make, model, and year of your car and the specific problem being experienced, and the center will send you appropriate details. Information on secret warranties is published in the center's newsletter *Lemon Times*, which is mailed to all members. Membership is $15 a year.

Service Contracts/Extended Warranties Are Bad Deals

A **service contract** (also called an **extended warranty** or a **maintenance agreement**) is an agreement separate from and not part of the basis of a sale of products and services to make repairs on defective or malfunctioning products. A service contract is an agreement between the buyer of a product and the contract seller (a dealer, manufacturer, or independent insurance company), to whom the buyer has paid a fee, to provide free or nearly free maintenance or repair (or both) to certain components of the product for some specified time period. A service contract is purchased separately from the purchase of the product, often automobiles, electronics, and appliances. Nearly two-thirds of all consumer electronics products are sold with service contracts, even though it makes little economic sense to insure against risks that can, if necessary, be paid for out of current income or savings.

Service contracts are very profitable contracts sold to consumers by dealers. William Sliney, president of the Service Contract Industry Council, reports that profit margins for dealers are fantastic. For every $100 service contract sold, the store keeps $80 to $96. Service contracts are commonly called "extended warranties," even though they are purchase contracts and not warranties. Warranties are included in the price of a product, while the price of service contracts is normally added to the purchase price.

Service contracts are a form of insurance and are marketed in much the same manner. Before buying a service contract, consumers should first check the terms of the warranty since service contracts often duplicate a product's warranty coverage. It is important to recognize that service contracts do not offer the same legal rights as warranties.

The cost of a service contract typically is either paid in a lump sum or may require monthly payments by the purchaser. For example, a 25-inch television selling for $700 could have a service contract that promises to fix anything free, including parts and labor, for the first two years of ownership after the warranty expires. Such a contract could cost $72 a year, or $6 a month. On a new or almost new automobile, the cost could amount to $700 or more for a 3-year service contract.

Service contracts allow consumers to prepay for any service required. Based on massive amounts of repair information, the sellers of service contracts determine with great precision how many repairs each product will need in the future. Reliable products are not likely to need repair during the warranty period. For example, Component Guard, a large service-contract company, states that only 7 percent of the 45 million VCRs need servicing in the first year of ownership (when they are still under warranty!) and only 43 percent need servicing within 5 years; the average repair cost is $95.

Stores often make more money selling service contracts than they make selling the products themselves. Service contracts are so profitable that sellers often telephone consumers about the time the manufacturer's warranty is up suggesting that an extended service contract be purchased.

One interesting service contract is offered by the American Express Company. It is offered solely to American Express cardholders at no additional cost above the annual membership fee. The plan has two parts: (1) a *purchase protection plan* that provides up to $50,000 in insurance coverage for card purchases against loss, theft, or accidental damage for 90 days from the date of purchase (the coverage is in excess of other applicable homeowner's or automobile insurance coverage of the cardholder), and (2) a *buyer's assurance protection plan* that doubles the free repair period of a manufacturer's warranty automatically, up to an extra year, on virtually all card purchases in the United States with manufacturer's warranties of five years or less (except motorized vehicles).

Similar service contracts are being offered by other credit card companies, and even by some banks on checking accounts. The terms of such deals can be changed at any time. If these service contracts can be offered to consumers for "free," you can bet the real cost is not very much.

Retailers sometimes sell their own service contracts, but because of a lack of service facilities, they typically purchase service contracts at wholesale from companies that specialize in repair services and resell them to customers. Thus, consumers may have to take their broken appliances to somewhere other than where they were purchased to obtain repairs.

According to a *Wall Street Journal* article, court documents revealed that a typical Nissan automobile extended service warranty cost the consumer $795. Of that amount, $131 goes for insurance coverage that actually pays for repairs under the contract, Nissan gets $60, the warranty company gets $38, and $11 goes for membership in an automobile club. The remaining $555 goes to the dealer. That is a 70 percent profit ($555 - $795) earned on taking the few minutes persuading the customer and sending the signed contract to the insurance company. On the other hand, if you are the kind of person a "black cloud" of bad luck seems to hang over where unfortunate things happen to you often, a service contract might be an excellent purchase.

The great majority of people who purchase a service contract do not receive its full benefits. About 15 percent of people who purchase major appliances and electronics products buy a service contract for peace of mind in case the product breaks down, but it is almost always unwise economically. *Kiplinger's Personal Finance Magazine* reports that, "the evidence suggests that few people recoup in repair savings what they spend on a service contract." In 1996, they reported that, "80 percent of service contracts...go unused. They often duplicate the warranty. And if the company goes out of business, your contract may be worthless."

Should you be thinking about buying a service contract, consider these questions: When does the contract begin? Do the provisions duplicate warranty coverage? Does the contract include labor? Where can the repairs be done? Are shipping charges included? Or, in the case of a service contract on a vehicle, are costs for towing and a rental car paid for? Can you get a refund if you later decide to cancel? Is the contract transferable if you later sell the product? Is the repairer directly paid or do you have to wait to be reimbursed? What is the arbitration process if there is a disagreement? What happens if the company goes out of business? (This business has plenty of bankruptcies.) Is this additional coverage worth the price paid? Finally, because product manufacturers are aware of their obligations under implied warranty laws, many will repair merchandise past the warranty period free of charge, especially for consumers who are aggressive in complaining.

Leasing Is a Good Choice for Some Consumers

Leasing is a contract granting use of property during a specified period in exchange for specified rent. Car leasing is growing in popularity as an alternative to financing. People are increasingly swayed toward leasing because of leasing's small down payments and acceptable monthly costs. With a lease you are, in effect, renting the car for 3, 4, 5, or more years with the title remaining with the lease grantor. Approximately 25 to 30 percent of retail new-car customers lease.

The down payment is usually small, less than $500. Sometimes there is no down payment. Your monthly payments are based on the price of the car minus its projected resale value at the end of the time period (known as the **residual value**). That figure is divided by the number of months in the contract. Monthly lease payments are lower than monthly loan repayments for equivalent time periods. The reasons is that with a lease you are not paying for the car's entire cost, because at the end of the lease the consumer does not own the car. The lease payment covers the car's **depreciation** (the reduction in the car's value), financing of that amount, sales tax, dealer's expenses, and profit. Sometimes automobile insurance and a service contract are also included in the monthly payment.

You can obtain an open-end lease or a closed-end lease. An **open-end lease** is a leasing arrangement in which the consumer must pay any difference between the projected resale value of the car and its true market value at the end of the lease period. With all leases, you are expected to return the car in good shape and have averaged under 15,000 miles a year. Otherwise, extra costs may be assessed.

In contrast, at the completion of a closed-end lease, the consumer walks away free and clear. A **closed-end lease** is a leasing arrangement in which there is no charge if the true market value of the leased vehicle is lower than the projected resale value at the end of the lease period. The monthly payment for a closed-end lease (the industry standard) is higher than that for an open-end lease. With either of these lease arrangements you may purchase the car for its resale value at the end of the leasing period.

Substantial penalties are also made if you terminate a lease early, during the higher-depreciation years. For example, fees are assessed for early termination if you want to trade it in on another vehicle, as well as if the car is stolen or destroyed. The Consumer Leasing Act is a federal law designed to provide disclosure of all relevant facts pertaining to a lease situation before the consumer signs the contract.

Consumers with no money for a down payment and those who plan on keeping the vehicle for four years or less should consider leasing. If you sell a car sooner than four years, you might not get out of it what you owe. Others who should consider leasing are those who do not want to tie up an amount for a down payment and those who do not like putting their money into depreciating assets, such as cars.

It is difficult, even for accountants, to correctly compare leasing with buying because sellers hide essential information for consumers to use to make a good decision. The federal government is currently in the process of writing new regulations for vehicle leasing (see Chapter 5). Until all lease sellers are required to provide similar information, people interested in leasing need to shop at honest, reputable businesses that will not hesitate to disclose the proper information (including the genuine capitalization cost) necessary for consumers to negotiate a fair deal and understand their obligations under a lease.

Financing Options

When comparison shopping for a car with the knowledge that you are going to finance the purchase, you may have the opportunity to choose between seller financing and borrowing from a conventional lender, such as a bank or credit union. Sometimes seller financing is offered by the automobile manufacturers through their dealers. It may be possible to take advantage of a special low interest rate when you use such **seller financing**. However, you may have a higher monthly payment because of restrictions on the time period of the loan, since special rates are usually only available for financing over 1, 2, or 3 years. Most low-interest specials run concurrently with some type of rebate plan for people who pay cash, or arrange their own financing. You might be able to get a slightly higher interest-rate loan for a longer period through your bank, or credit union, and use the rebate as compensation over and above the extra finance charges.

Many banks have experienced a decrease in demand for automobile loans because of the popularity of automobile leases. In response, they have developed balloon automobile loans. With a **balloon automobile loan**, the buyer takes title to the car, and the last monthly payment is equal to the projected resale value of the vehicle at the end of the loan period. This has the effect of lowering the other monthly payments in order to make them more competitive with the amount of each month's lease payments. When the final balloon payment is due, you have three options: (1) pay the balloon payment and keep the car, (2) return the car to the lender, or (3) sell the car and pay the balloon payment with the proceeds.

CONSUMER UPDATE:
Which Deal Is Better: The Auto Dealer's Cash Rebate
or a Low Interest Rate?

When purchasing a vehicle, you may be faced with having to compare an offer of a low interest rate or a cash rebate. The comparison may seem even more difficult when you arrange your own financing. Here is how to find the better deal.

Suppose an auto dealer offers 4.79 percent financing for 3 years with a $906 finance charge, or you can receive a $1500 rebate if you pay cash or arrange your own financing. Assume that the price of the vehicle before the rebate is $14,000, that you can make a $2000 down payment, and that you can get a 9.5 percent loan on your own.

To compare the two offers fairly, you must add the opportunity-cost value of the rebate to the finance charge of the dealer financing. Then compare the **annual percentage rate** for each using Formula 13.1 where

Y = number of payment periods in 1 *year*
F = *finance* charge in dollars
D = *debt* (amount borrowed)
P = total number of scheduled *payments*

$$APR = \frac{Y(95P + 9)F}{12(P(P + 1)(4D + F)}$$

Steps to follow:

1. Determine the dollar amount of the rebate ($1500 in this example).
2. Add it to the finance charge (dollar cost of credit) for the dealer financing ($906 in this example).
3. Use the following APR formula to calculate an adjusted APR for the dealer financing (12.9 percent in this example).
4. Compare the result (12.9 percent in this example) to the APR that you arranged on your own (9.5 percent in this example). The lower of the two is the better deal.

$$
\begin{aligned}
APR &= \frac{12[(95 \times 36) + 9](\$906 + \$1500)}{(12 \times 36)(36 + 1)[(4 \times \$12,000) + (\$906 + \$1500)]} \quad \text{(Formula 13.1)} \\
&= \frac{56,184}{444,000} \\
&= 12.9 \text{ percent}
\end{aligned}
$$

The financing arranged on your own is more attractive. In fact, any loan you arrange that carries an APR lower than 12.9 percent compares favorably with the dealer-arranged financing in this example.

Choosing Priorities

To assist her in decision making, Bonnie constructed a chart to prioritize her choices in terms of her values, as shown in Table 13-2. She first listed which criteria were really important to her, and then she ranked them.

Bonnie skipped leasing because she simply wanted to own her car, not lease it. She plans on telephoning her bank and credit union again to check on their financing options. She also thought about extended warranties and concluded that they were a waste of money. She figures that since the vehicle has a warranty, any problems that occur will be covered. Should she have problems later on, she can take the product back for repair without a service contract and simply pay for anything herself. Besides, the manufacturer's warranties are for lengthy periods, so the cars must be pretty dependable. Bonnie easily found fuel-economy information in consumer magazines, including independent testing by *Consumer Reports* and by the Environmental Protection Agency

(EPA). The EPA comparative fuel efficiency information also is provided on the window sticker of new cars, and in *EPA Guides* that are provided free through automobile dealers.

Bonnie's Criteria	Bonnie's Ranking
Low price	1
Dependability	2
Safety	3
Comfort	4
Warranty	5
Design	6
Fuel economy	7
Performance	8
Service department reputation	9
Seller financing	10

TABLE 13-2   Bonnie's Priorities on What Is Important to Her

Bonnie's comparison-shopping efforts resulted in her locating two good used cars and three new automobiles. In comparing the costs and benefits, she focused on what factors were important to her. As shown in Table 13-2, Bonnie decided that price, dependability, safety, and comfort were the four most important factors. All the cars were affordable, since they were priced below $10,000, so Bonnie reflected on dependability and safety. Although she really liked the used cars, Bonnie decided to eliminate them from her alternatives because she believed that the new cars would be more dependable. So after much thinking, she narrowed her choices to the three new automobiles.

Criteria	Car 1	Car 2	Car 3
Price	A	A	A
Dependability*	A -	B +	B
Safety*	B +	A	A
Comfort	A	A	B

*Bonnie's impressions gained from *Consumer Reports* ratings of same model car for previous years.

TABLE 13-3   Bonnie's Final Ratings Based on Her Criteria

To help in her decision making, Bonnie made a chart and rated each of the new cars on her most important criteria, as shown in Table 13-3. This process quickly helped Bonnie eliminate one of the three cars (car 3), so Bonnie's final choice was narrowed to two new automobiles. She thought that either of the two cars would provide excellent transportation and comfort. Now Bonnie thought she was ready to negotiate for the better deal.

Negotiating

Negotiating is the process of conferring with a seller in order to reach an agreement on price, as well as other aspects of the deal. Much negotiating goes on for expensive products and services. Here there will be offers and counteroffers until there is agreement on the final terms.

The Goal of Negotiation

To succeed in a negotiation, it is important to maintain a posture of being knowledgeable and having control. The salesperson will try to convince you to buy on his or her terms. Chances are that the salesperson will tell you during the bargaining process that the price you are offering amounts to "stealing the car." Don't believe it, because no one ever, ever, ever buys underpriced cars from a dealer. (Some go bankrupt because of high operating expenses, not for selling cars at prices that are too low.) You must be prepared to say, "No," and buy elsewhere if the terms are not satisfactory. Otherwise, the advantage will be the seller's. Your best strategy when shopping for a car is being willing *not* to buy one from that dealer that day.

The lowest price a consumer can hope to expect to pay for a new automobile is $150 to $200 over the dealer's cost. The best bargaining philosophy is to negotiate upward from the dealer's cost of the product, not to negotiate downward from any sticker prices. The task for the consumer is to correctly figure out how much the dealer paid for the vehicle, and confidently make an appropriate offer. Since the dealer wants to sell at a higher price than $150 over cost whenever possible, the dealer is likely to first argue that a shopper's cost figures are wrong, and then reject any offer close to that amount, unless he or she is convinced the consumer will go elsewhere to make the purchase.

CONSUMER UPDATE:
False Vehicle Price Advertising

Advertised vehicle prices often do not accurately reflect truth because the dealership is given a rebate by the manufacturer after the vehicle has been sold. This is called a **holdback**. It is sometimes listed on the customer's invoice, but in a confusing manner, and consumers rarely understand what it means. Holdback is typically around 3 percent of the manufacturer's suggested retail price, but it can be 5 percent or more.

Another example of false price advertising occurs when a used car dealer illegally promotes a vehicle as **"executive driven,"** implying that it might have been driven by a top executive when, in many cases, the vehicle was bought at auction or from a rental company.

In some states, advertising a used vehicle for $100 over cost violates the law when there are additional charges to the consumer, such as preparation, destination, and document fees. A number of states have a law that requires any invoice cited in a advertisement be made available by the vehicle dealer for customer inspection. Sometimes state statutes prohibit vehicle dealer ads from using the words *at cost, below cost, invoice price, wholesale, factory sale,* and *dealer rebates* because of deceptive practices.

The Process of Negotiation

Bonnie knew that research shows that women consistently pay more for the same vehicle as men. To avoid that discrimination, Bonnie started the process of negotiation by first ascertaining the invoice price. The **invoice price** is the manufacturer's initial charge to the dealer. It is higher than the actual price finally paid by the dealer because the dealer later receives rebates, allowances, discounts, and incentive awards from the manufacturer. The invoice price does include the manufacturer's delivery charges.

The **base price** or **base cost** is the cost of the car without options, but including standard equipment, factory warranty, and freight. This information is printed on the sticker price. The **sticker price** is the automobile **manufacturer's suggested retail price (MSRP)**, including the base cost and certain manufacturer-installed options on the vehicle, and the manufacturer's transportation charges. Federal regulations require that the sticker price be on a label affixed to the car window of newly manufactured vehicles.

While visiting automobile dealers earlier, Bonnie also learned that the sticker price of new cars is apparently just the beginning price, since some dealers affix another sticker of their own to the MSRP—the **dealer sticker price**. This pricing information is euphemistically called the **adjusted market value (AMV)** or **additional dealer markup (ADM)**. This is a popular technique of raising the dealer's profit margin on new cars by adding substantial charges to the sticker price for such things as "pre-delivery inspection," "dealer preparation," "undercoating," "protective finish," or simply "ADM" to cover any additional costs the dealer might add on. Today's cars come with rust-resistant construction that makes after-market undercoating unnecessary and paint sealants that don't need expensive special waxing. You can apply fabric treatments in 10 minutes yourself with a $10 can of Scotchguard. There is no valid reason to buy any of these things. Some automobile dealers also charge extra ostensibly to pay for advertising costs billed to the dealer by the manufacturer, which they call **national dealer advertising (NDA)**. The price the dealer is really asking for the automobile is the **full invoice price**, and it is shown as the total amount on the dealer sticker price on the car window.

While the MSRP or sticker price includes ample markup for the dealer to make a handsome profit, fewer than 10 percent of all buyers pay that price and instead pay more. An automobile dealer must maintain a reasonable profit margin on vehicles sold or go out of business, and most are doing well. **Profit margin** (or **margin**) is the difference between the net cost of a product obtained from a manufacturer, such as an automobile, and the dealer's price to the consumer.

To illustrate, the sticker price for one of Bonnie's alternatives was $9144, and next to it was attached a smaller "price summary" with the following additional figures: $350 for dealer preparation, $300 for undercoating, $400 for shipping, $400 for ADM, and $200 for NDA for a subtotal of $1650 for a grand total of $10,794.

Markup for dealers varies among vehicles, options, and special manufacturer incentives. Experts agree that, in general, dealer markup ranges from 10 to 35 percent of the base price of the car. It is about $800 on subcompacts, $1200 on compacts, $1800 on intermediates, $2400 on standards, $3000 on luxury cars, and $3600 or more on specialty automobiles. For example, on the one vehicle that interested Bonnie the base price was $8100 plus $1044 for the options, yielding a sticker price of $9144. So, she estimates that the dealer paid the manufacturer $7300 ($8100 - $800), plus, specific amounts for each option. Markups on options range from 20 to 50 percent.

Manufacturers frequently have incentives to "push" certain models, and they offer dealers (not consumers) rebates, perhaps of $200 or more for each car sold during a

---

CONSUMER UPDATE:
Hagglers Get the Best Car Deals

Haggling is bargaining, dickering, and arguing in an attempt to come to terms. Haggling over auto prices and options has long been an American tradition, although many are uncomfortable with the pastime. Confronted with poor sales, a number of dealers are converting to **one-price shopping**. Here prices are supposed to be nonnegotiable and fair, with no haggling allowed. How much a consumer gains depends upon how much one is willing to pay to eliminate haggling with sales personnel. In reality, however, consumers can negotiate. A CNW Marketing study of one-price shopping car dealerships found that "if you asked for a discount, you got it."[1] CNW Marketing concludes that it appears that one-price auto dealers set a price about "2 or 3 percent higher than the average negotiated price at the conventional dealerships." Consumers who want to pay the lowest price possible should avoid one-price shopping.

---

[1]Simison, R. L. and R. Templin (1994, October 12), Hagglers Get Best Car Deals, *The Wall Street Journal*, B-1.

---

specific time period. Bonnie figures that the dealer will have a net cost of $7300 or maybe even $200 less for the car that interests her because it is currently being heavily advertised on television by the manufacturer. This is a good figure with which Bonnie can begin negotiating.

Bonnie's dealer has an "additional dealer markup" of $1650, so there is lots of room for discussion about the final price. Each of the ADM items should be seriously questioned, and every figure is definitely negotiable. For example, ADM and dealer preparation are simply pure-profit figures for the dealer. The same quality undercoating, perhaps even better, can be purchased elsewhere for $175, that is assuming it is even needed at all.

Rebates are also sometimes offered to consumers by manufacturers as incentives to encourage them to purchase certain makes and models that are not selling well. Consumers appreciate such rebates, but generally they should be ignored when trying to determine the dealer's cost. Sometimes a dealer will argue that the cost for a particular rebate is being shared by both the manufacturer and the dealer, and if that is actually the case, the dealer's true cost must include his or her part of the rebate. Look for a **factory-direct rebate**, which comes straight from the manufacturer, not one involving the dealer. Rebates typically only apply to cars in stock, so if the car you want is not on the lot, you are out of luck.

Consumer Reports "recommends against accepting any items on a separate dealer sticker. If the dealer says he will not sell the car without these added charges, we suggest you shop elsewhere. We suggest you shop more than one dealer for the best price."

Determining the Price You Want to Pay

In order to do an effective job estimating dealer cost for a vehicle, as well as various options, you may consult automobile guides sold in bookstores and newsstands. Good sources of accurate price information may be obtained from the December issue of *Kiplinger's Personal Finance Magazine* as well as *Edmund's New Car Prices* and *Edmund's Import Car Prices* (http:www.edmunds.com), because each publishes dealer costs and suggested retail prices.

CONSUMER UPDATE:
Searching for a Used Vehicle
on the Information Highway

At a Digital World Conference, Kaleida Labs Inc. demonstrated a prototype system on buying a used car. Using "Auto Finder" a consumer finds a multi-media application permitting choices on class of vehicle and model year. The screen shows a photograph of the selected vehicle and some details, such as mileage and estimated service costs. Next the consumer rummages through "classified ads" pausing to view photographs and other specific information needed to buy. The program even calculates distances from the consumer's home to the sellers. Soon "Auto Finder" will be on-line.

The Home Shopping Network purchase of the on-line Internet Shopping has the potential to create a full-service shopping mall on everyone's computer screen. QVC is also launching an on-line shopping program. America Online is considering the possibilities.

Automobile Brokers and Buying Services

Automobile brokers and buying services exist to help consumers get the best price on new and used vehicles.

Auto Brokers Provide Price Information

Instead of doing all the research on prices and comparison shopping yourself, you could contact an **automobile broker**. This is a profit-making firm specializing in providing detailed price information on automobiles for consumers for a fee. For $10 to $30, a firm will provide a computer printout of the sticker price and dealer costs for the base car and all available options for any particular make and model automobile that interests a consumer. Such information is available from Nationwide Auto Brokers, 17517 West Ten Mile Road, Southfield, MI 48075 (800-521-7257) and Consumer Reports Auto Price Service, P.O. Box 8005, Novi, MI 48050 (313-347-5810). Other firms in the discount pricing business include AutoAdvisor, Automobile Consumer Services, Autovantage, Carchoice, Car Price Network, Century 21, Consumers Car Club, Personal Motor Service, PriceCosto, Sam's Club, United Auto Group, and USA Auto Acquisition Services.

Used vehicle information is available, too. *Consumer Reports* offers price and information search services for used vehicles with a variable fee charged to your telephone bill. Consumer Reports Used Car Price Service (1-900-446-9500) costs about $8.50 for a typical 5-minute call. Alternatively, you can buy an NADA price book at most bookstores for about $5. If available in your community, budget-conscious consumers can shop for a used vehicle at Autonation, CarMax, or Driver's Mart Worldwide, which are national used-vehicle superstore chains where the average profit is only $300 per used vehicle.

A Buying Service Does All the Haggling For You

Alternatively, once you know what type of vehicle you want, you may choose to use a **buying service**. This is a company that charges a fee to arrange discount purchases for buyers of new cars. The price paid for the automobile is usually a few hundred dollars over what the car cost the dealer. With foreign makes, the guaranteed price is a certain discounted percentage off the sticker price. (Amway Auto Network says that the average automobile sells for $875 over the base invoice price.) Skilled hagglers may be able to beat the price, but some people find it convenient to pay a buying service to avoid the time and effort in comparison shopping. Procedures vary, but typically consumers pay an initial fee of $50 to $100 and are referred to nearby participating automobile dealers who have agreed to charge specific discount prices. Buying service companies also stand behind the consumer should the dealer try to renege on prices or services promised.

Well-known buying services include a number of American Automobile Association (AAA) affiliates (see telephone directory); Nationwide Auto Brokers (cited above); Amway Auto Network, 7575 East Fulton Road, Ada, MI 49355 (800-544-7167); United Buying Service (check the telephone directory for an independent office near you, or with your employer to see whether or not your company is associated with them); and USAA Buying Services, USAA Building, 9800 Fredericksburg Road, San Antonio, TX 78288 (800-531-8905). For $150, CarBargains buying service (800-475-7283) will locate five dealers in your geographic area who within two weeks will bid against one another for the best price for the make and model of your choice. You then take the quote sheet to the sales manager at the dealership who has already agreed to the price. With both automobile brokers and buying services, you usually must handle your own financing.

Selecting the Best Alternative

The task is to decide which product or service is best for you given your values and goals. It is sometimes easy when you have "new car fever" to give in, and accept a persuasive and good-sounding deal being offered by a salesperson inside a dealer's showroom. This may not be the best place to make a decision because of pressures to buy that may be applied by the seller, and/or by your own desire to get the process over with. It is better to wait until you get home to make the decision. There you can retrace the steps in the buying process, making sure that your decision is based on good information and a good understanding of your values and goals. Then you can return to the dealer's showroom and sign the necessary papers. In short, the wise consumer waits, thinks, compares, reflects, and then decides.

To put that new car in front of her home, Bonnie needs to be concerned about selecting the better of her two remaining alternatives. Her final two choices were evaluated quite similarly, so Bonnie's decision was based primarily on price, as shown in Table 13-4. The dealer for car 1 wanted $10,794 for everything originally. The dealer for car 2 wanted $11,480, which included $8410 for the car, $1300 for the same options, and $1770 for additional dealer markup. The dealer for car 1 did not want to negotiate the base price of the car, but he was willing to come down on the options and do the undercoating for a decent price. The dealer for car 2 did drop his price on the car, but he refused to come down much on the options or the undercoating. The willingness of the dealer selling car 1 to negotiate made Bonnie's decision easier, and she chose car 1. The car fit her needs and wants, and it was fairly priced. Bonnie made her down payment of $1700 and financed the balance at a low interest rate for three years through her credit union.

Car and Options	Price	Quoted Final Price
Car 1 base price	$ 8,100	$8,100
Car 1 options	1,044	800
Car 1 ADM	1,650	300
TOTAL	$10,794	$9,200
Car 2 base price	8,410	7,900
Car 2 options	1,300	1,120
Car 2 ADM	1,770	740
TOTAL	$11,480	$9,760

TABLE 13-4   Bonnie's Final Selection

The confusing array of numbers shows how difficult it is sometimes to even know when you have a good deal. For this reason, many consumers spend the money and order a computer printout from one of the automobile broker firms before they go shopping. Still, Bonnie thought she had adequate information to make a good decision, so she made it.

Accepting and Evaluating the Decision

The rational consumer reflects on important decisions after a period of weeks or months. The intent is not to doubt the decision, or be irritated that a few dollars might have been saved by doing something else. Rather, the task is to reaffirm the wisdom of utilizing the process that resulted in the decision and to use any valuable recollections in future decision-making opportunities.

Over the next few months, Bonnie seemed to recognize every car on the road that was the same model as hers. She liked her car and enjoyed it. Occasionally, she saw dealer advertisements for the same model with a price a hundred dollars or so less than the amount she paid, but it did not bother her in the least. She had learned in shopping that dealers can lower their prices on three things: the base cost, the cost of options, and the price of additional dealer markup. She knew she did well in negotiating and paid a fair price for the automobile.

Bonnie was confidently looking forward to making other expensive purchases, such as some exercise equipment and a compact disc music system, so she could put to practice some of the experience she gained from going through the steps of rational decision making in buying her car. Bonnie especially enjoyed collecting information and establishing her own criteria with which to compare products. Moreover, Bonnie discovered in this planned buying endeavor that not only did she learn a lot, but she also enjoys her automobile more because of the experience.

CONSUMER UPDATE: Average Life Spans of Appliances (in Years)*

Freezers	21
Refrigerators	19
Ranges/Ovens	19
Dryers	18.5
Room Air Conditioners	15
Washing Machines	15
Vacuum Cleaners	10
Dishwashers	10
Microwave Ovens	10
Color TV sets	8
Stereo Receivers	8
Toasters	8
Camcorders	7
CD Players	7
Personal Computers	6

*Sources: *Appliance Magazine* and the U.S. Department of Energy

Review and Summary of Key Terms and Concepts

1. What is **planned buying**?

2. What are the three reasons why consumers make **bad decisions**?

3. Distinguish between **habit buying** and **impulse buying**, and indicate reasons why habit buying is useful to consumers.

4. Explain the idea of **conspicuous consumption**.

5. What do the terms **comparison shopping**, **best buy**, and **quality** mean in the context of **planned buying**?

6. Identify some **sources of buying information** for consumers, especially those that are fairly objective.

7. Summarize the value of **safety seals** and **seals of approval** to consumers.

8. Distinguish among: **brand names**, **store brands**, and **generic brands**.

9. What do publications like **Red Book**, **Black Book**, and **Blue Book** contain that is helpful for used automobile shoppers?

10. Define the term **window shopping**, and explain why it is important for the automobile shopper.

11. What is **comparison shopping**, and what is a **best buy**?

12. What are **rebates**, and why do sellers use them?

13. Distinguish between an **implied warranty** and an **express warranty**.

14. What are **secret warranties**, and how do they work?

15. Explain the idea behind **service contracts**, both from the perspective of the seller and the consumer.

16. Distinguish between an **open-end** and a **closed-end lease**.

17. Explain how a **balloon automobile loan** operates.

18. Make up a mathematical example that demonstrates Formula 13.1, taking the vehicle manufacturer's **cash rebate** or a **low-interest deal**.

19. Define and explain the term **holdback**.

20. Distinguish between the **invoice price** and the **dealer sticker price**.

21. Distinguish between using a **buying service** to purchase a new automobile and going to a dealer that has **one-price shopping**.

Useful Resources for Consumers

Center for Auto Safety
2001 S Street, NW, Suite 410
Washington, DC 20009
202-328-7700

High Point Convention & Visitors Bureau
Box 2273
High Point, NC 27261
910-884-5255
Brochures and maps are available to scores of local furniture outlet stores that are located near High Point (where two-thirds of the furniture in the U.S. is manufactured); shipping is quite inexpensive.

National Highway Traffic Safety Administration
Owner-reported problems and manufacturer service bulletins
http://www.nhtsa.dot.gov/nsa/nsasearch.shtml

"What Do You Think" Questions

1. From your life experiences, list two or three **best buys**. Explain why each of those purchases was a best buy.

2. **Secret warranties** give one class of consumers, the aggressive complainers, an advantage over other consumers. Do you think that manufacturers should be permitted to offer such policy adjustments? Why or why not? Also, do you think that laws should be passed to require secret warranty disclosures to all consumers? Why or why not?

3. When **choosing priorities** such as Bonnie did in her car buying process, how would you rate the several factors that she used (dependability, safety, etc.) if you were purchasing an automobile? Rank them on a one to ten scale. Explain why you listed your top two factors as most important.

Chapter 14

Food Issues

OBJECTIVES

After reading this chapter, you should be able to

1. Recognize what factors are associated with good eating habits.

2. Recognize several questionable food selling practices that are deceptive because they result in increased prices.

3. Understand that a number of anti-competitive practices exist in the food industry.

4. Distinguish among the agencies and laws in the area of food.

5. Respond to the question, "Does Everything Cause Cancer?"

6. Illustrate how consumers can easily get confused and ripped off when food shopping.

Americans like to eat. However, about half of all Americans are **malnourished** in that they get too little or too much of certain **nutrients**. A nutrient is something, usually a food substance, that promotes growth or development. Americans also have problems with **obesity**, a form of malnourishment where one is 20 percent or more above a healthy weight for their sex, height, and frame. The U.S. Department of Health and Human Services reports that 34 percent of the adult population is obese (nearly 1/2 of women of African American and Mexican American ancestry); they face an increased risk of heart disease, diabetes, and other chronic ailments. Even though many Americans are preoccupied with buying food, eating it, and dieting (at any point in time, almost half of adult women and one-quarter of adult men are attempting to lose weight), it seems that most do not know much about proper eating habits and/or simply do not care. Because consumers do not have perfect knowledge, they spend excessive money on inferior food. The economic marketplace is causes part of these problems, and as a result, consumers have difficulty getting what they need and want when they go food shopping.

This chapter is aimed at helping you better understand the food issues affecting consumers and how you can deal with them. It begins by examining factors associated with good eating habits. Next it overviews of some questionable food selling practices. This is followed by a description of some anti-competitive practices in the food industry and an overview of the agencies and laws designed to protect consumers. The chapter concludes with a discussion of the question, "Does Everything Cause Cancer?," and a review of the ways consumers get confused when shopping for food.

American Eating Habits

For most of us, breakfast is a nutritional flop. About 20 percent of us do not eat any breakfast at all. Many of those who do eat breakfast enjoy cereal with milk. Numerous consumers, particularly children, have fallen prey to misleading advertising claims by cereal manufacturers. A breakfast composed of cereal may provide some useful nutritional benefits (such as the calcium in the milk), however, the great majority of breakfast cereals offers little in the way of nutrition. Other breakfast foods, such as bacon, eggs, toast, and orange juice, may appear to be nutritionally superior, but often also contain too many calories, additives, and fats.

Many children learn poor eating habits in schools because many school-lunch programs use too much food high in fat. The U.S. Department of Agriculture's Assistant Secretary of Agriculture for Food and Consumer Services, Ellen Haas, is concerned that the National School Lunch Program that feeds 25 million children daily in 92,000 schools, encourages unhealthy eating of too many fats. A USDA study found that the percentage of calories from fat for a week in the nation's school lunches is 38 percent; the recommendation is 30 percent.

Americans, as well as children, have problems eating healthy meals Hurried mothers, fathers, and children, particularly in dual-income families, are often guilty of skipping meals. Teenagers and young adults often omit breakfast. Research studies show that after going all night without food, a good breakfast provides the necessary fuel for people to operate effectively during the morning hours. Such an attitude toward food adds to a stressful lifestyle. Consumers are likely to snack a lot rather than relax, eat a proper meal, and really enjoy the food. Many Americans do not take a sensible approach to food intake, even though it is important for leading a long and healthy life.

CONSUMER UPDATE:
Why Learn About Food and Health?

Some question why consumer educators and health advocates insist upon educating people about food and health. There are two reasons. First, you need to know enough to make informed choices in personal decision making. Second, you may wish to participate in changing public policy in food and health.

In the area of public policy, for example, the Center for Science in the Public Interest (CSPI) is calling for a change in this nation's public health policies. They are encouraging government to make good nutrition and the prevention of diet-related diseases (heart disease, diabetes, stroke, and cancer) cornerstones of policy. CSPI wants the government to: (1) promote information that helps people eat healthy diets, including low-fat and vegetarian diets, (2) have the U.S. Surgeon General publish an annual report on nutrition, (3) encourage physicians to prescribe very-low-fat diets for heart patients, (4) motivate broadcasters to promote good nutrition for children, and (5) require that medical facilities serve lower-fat, lower-salt meals.

Calorie Intake

Your body's primary job is to keep your heart and other vital organs operating. Necessary tasks include keeping you breathing, maintaining normal body temperature, giving you the strength to get out of bed in the morning and get through a normal day, and seeing to it that you have enough extra power to cope with any hard physical or mental stresses. All these tasks require energy, which you get from foods that contain calories. A **calorie** is a measure of the energy, or heat, produced by consuming food.

Since nearly everything we eat contains some calories, most of us are able to perform our daily chores. Foods give the energy the body needs throughout the day, and even during the night when we are sleeping. Different foods have various amounts of calories, or energy value. Sweet, greasy, or concentrated foods often have high calorie counts, while watery, bulky, or coarse foods usually have lower ones.

The number of calories a person needs each day differs with sex, height, weight, age, individual metabolism, and physical activity. Any calories not used are stored in the body as fat. As a rule, if you consume fewer calories of food than you burn, you lose weight. Each decrease in consumption of about 3500 calories should cause a weight loss of one pound. The only long-term way to lose weight is through a combination of calorie reduction and physical exercise.

Many consumers are so physically inactive that their bodies do not utilize all the food energy in their diets. Over the past seven years, the average weight of young Americans jumped 10 pounds. See Figure 14-1 for ideal weight guidelines.

The Poor Quality of American Diets

Obvious signs of nutritional deficiency are not apparent in the American public. This is probably because most diets, no matter how poor, still provide enough of the needed nutrients to prevent deficiency diseases. The result, however, is a population that is

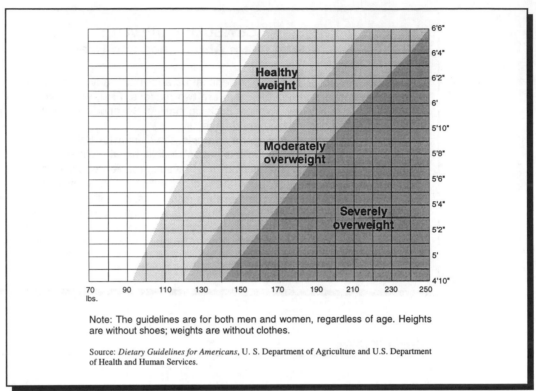

FIGURE 14-1 Ideal Weight Guidelines

slightly overweight. Forty percent of adults are **overweight**, i.e., at least 10 percent over their recommended weight range. Also, the American population neither feels as well nor lives as long as one might expect. The effects of poor dietary habits vary from few noticeable effects to severe difficulties. Health problems from **malnutrition** (poor nutrition often because of an insufficient or poorly balanced diet) include poorer health, obesity, mental stress, physical deficiencies, and increased susceptibility to diseases.

Scientific Evidence Links Diet to Disease

After tracking caloric intake for more than 20 years, the United States Department of Agriculture (USDA) reports that Americans are consuming more food per capita than ever before. The U.S. Surgeon General has reported that five of the top ten causes of death are substantially linked to diet. Obesity contributes to a number of serious health disorders, including hypertension, diabetes, gallstones, osteoarthritis (because the excess weight puts excessive pressure on the joints), and heart disease. Concisely stated, "Hearts are either assaulted by such poisons as animal-based cholesterol or protected by fruits, vegetables and grains."[1] One in four men in the United States dies of a heart attack or a stroke before age 65.

Cancer has been linked to diet also. Dr. Paul A. Marks, director of the Cancer Research Center at Columbia University, reports that one-half of the fatal cancers in

---

[1]McCarthy, C. (1994, April 2). Low Fat Comes to the White House. *The Washington Post*, p. A-17.

CONSUMER UPDATE:
Advertising Foods to Kids

Various national surveys show that young children have a high level of nutritional awareness. But, like their parents, the so-called knowledge is ignored when making food choices. Reasons include regular experiences with: (1) high-fat and high-sodium school lunches, and family meals that often do not meet standards for healthy eating, (2) advertisements for processed foods aimed at children that promote unhealthy choices, (3) packaging that entices children to purchase foods of little nutritional value, and (4) excessive television watching, which uses fewer calories than lying in bed and reduces opportunities for physical activities. As a result, children eat a lot of **junk food**, fast foods or prepackaged snack foods of low nutritional value.

Food companies can and do make health claims in advertising that are prohibited in food labeling. The Food and Drug Administration (FDA) regulates food labels. Under a less stringent set of rules, the Federal Trade Commission (FTC) governs advertising, largely on a case-by-case basis. In 1994, the FTC issued guidelines when advertising health claims.

A report by the Center for Science in the Public Interest listed the best processed foods for children in 19 categories. Reasonable choices were available in most food categories, such as cereals, french fries, pizza, soup, and cheese. Not a single product was recommended in the categories of cookies, fast-food meals, frozen desserts, granola bars, and hot dogs. Foods were not recommended if they contained excessive amounts of fat, saturated fat, cholesterol, sodium, or added sugar, and too few good nutrients.

---

women and one-third in men may be attributed in part to dietary habits. Foods high in fat appear to increase cancer risks, while those high in fiber content appear to reduce them. Fibrous foods include whole grains, cereals, vegetables, and fruits.

Good Nutrition and Good Health

It seems that many Americans are slowly eating themselves to death. We are making ourselves the victims of overconsumption and malnutrition at the same time. Too many of us are functioning far from our peak physical and mental capacities, and too many of us are also prone to illness. Simultaneously, Americans are concerned about health hazards in food. Surveys by the FDA reveal that 75 percent of all consumers are concerned about pesticides in foods, 60 percent are concerned about fats and cholesterol, and 30 percent are concerned about food additives. A growing number of people shop at health and natural food stores.

Good health is a primary factor in our happiness and our ability to work productively. Good nutrition is part of preventive medicine; it helps maintain healthy bodies and protects them against chronic diseases. Consumers who eat nutritiously can expect to enjoy vitality, energy, and a higher quality of life. Suggestions to achieve better health are to eat a nutritious breakfast, get regular exercise, diet wisely, and choose better snacks. A registered dietitian can give advice on ways to tailor a nutritious eating plan for individual needs.

CONSUMER UPDATE:
The Poor Pay More for Food

The Select Committee on Hunger in the U.S. House of Representatives reports that despite the extensive network of federal programs for the poor, the vast majority of beneficiaries remain in poverty, unable to afford an adequate diet. That includes the ten percent of all Americans who receive food stamps. Committee conclusions included evidence that the poor have more restricted access to food stores than the nonpoor because most are not within walking distance of a supermarket. The poor have more limited choices because they often frequent small stores, called **bodegas**, which are tiny grocery shops that don't stock fresh meat or fish, and sell unrefrigerated eggs and lettuce. The few number of supermarkets in poor areas are cramped, usually offering only one-third the physical space available in supermarkets in middle-class neighborhoods.

For these reasons, the poor are forced to pay higher prices for food. How much higher? A study of food prices in impoverished inner-city neighborhoods in New York City by the Community Resource Center found that poor people spent 13 to 25 percent more on groceries than their suburban counterparts. A 20-city study commissioned by Public Voice for Food and Health Policy found that small corner stores were charging as much as 40 percent more.

The Importance of Low-Fat Eating to Good Health

The U.S. Surgeon General's *Report on Nutrition and Health* observes that, "there can no longer be any doubt about the link between diet and disease." It cites saturated fat and dietary cholesterol as the "most pervasive villains in the American diet." Of the 2.1 million Americans who died in a recent year, diet was associated with the cause of death in at least two-thirds of them. The report concludes that, "If you do not smoke or drink excessively, your choice of diet can influence your long-term health prospects more than any other action you might take." The Department of Health and Human Services, headed by Donna E. Shalala, reports that diet-related diseases kill as many Americans as does smoking—over 400,000 annually!

The total amount of saturated fat that one consumes has a greater effect on raising blood cholesterol levels than one's intake of dietary cholesterol. **Saturated fats** are those that are solid at room temperature, such as butter, beef fat, and coconut and palm oils (found in some baked goods and coffee creamers). **Unsaturated fats** are those that are liquid at room temperature, such as corn, safflower and some other vegetable oils.

Fats are necessary in the diet, but too much can cause problems. For most Americans, approximately 40 percent of the daily caloric intake is from fat. Current recommendations are to limit fat to 30 percent or less of total caloric intake.

The body handles fat in three ways: (1) burns it up to produce energy, (2) stores it in tissues, or (3) deposits it in the form of cholesterol along the walls of the arteries (the blood vessels that carry oxygen and food throughout the body).

Cholesterol is a fatlike substance produced by all animals, including humans, that serves as a building block of cells, vitamins, and hormones. Cholesterol is present in all parts of the body, including muscles, brain, nervous system, and liver. High fat levels are clearly associated with many cardiovascular diseases, most particularly heart problems. For example, a recent study found that having *one* fatty meal puts the blood into a state of hypercoagulation within six or seven hours, raising the risk of a heart-blocking blood clot.

CONSUMER UPDATE:
Blood Cholesterol Levels

Cholesterol is a type of fat, a lipid. Pure cholesterol is an odorless substance that you cannot taste or see in the foods you eat. The human body uses cholesterol for a variety of body functions, including making essential body substances, such as cell walls and hormones. Cholesterol is transported in the body through the bloodstream.

There are two types of cholesterol. **Serum cholesterol** is produced by the body for certain functions as described above. The body produces a certain amount of cholesterol regardless of whether a person consumes any dietary cholesterol. **Dietary cholesterol** is found only in foods of animal origin, such as meats, eggs and dairy products.

The average person produces two to four times as much cholesterol in the liver each day than is typically consumed in foods. If your body produces too much cholesterol, odds increase that some will collect in the walls of the blood vessels. You have no control over how much cholesterol your body produces naturally but you can control the amount of cholesterol you eat. Current recommendations are to consume less than 300 milligrams of dietary cholesterol daily.

Cholesterol is a waxy substance in the blood that does not mix with water. Therefore, to carry it in the blood, the body wraps it in protein. This combination is called a **lipoprotein**. Since blood is the medium which carries cholesterol throughout the body, it is called blood or serum cholesterol.

Cholesterol is comprised of component parts. **High-density lipoproteins (HDLs)** have a substantial amount of protein and transport cholesterol to the liver where it is processed and removed from the body; these are the "good" lipoproteins. The "bad" lipoproteins are the **low-density lipoproteins (LDLs)**. Low-density means that these transporters are mostly composed of fat, and they are low in density compared to proteins. Fatty lipoproteins float more easily on the surface of blood. LDLs carry most of the cholesterol in the blood, and can deposit it in the arteries causing heart disease.

Once a blood specimen is obtained, blood cholesterol level is measured in a laboratory. The National Cholesterol Education Project has established standards (milligrams per deciliter) for desirable levels of cholesterol: under 200 total cholesterol, under 160 LDL, and over 35 HDL. About 57 percent of American adults have blood cholesterol levels above 200; more than one-third of the U.S. population has high or borderline-high cholesterol levels. Five to ten percent have HDL concentrations below 35 mg per deciliter, placing them at moderate or high risk for heart disease.

William Castelli, director of the 40+ year-old Framingham Heart Study, observes that four out of five people on earth have blood cholesterol levels of under 150, and they do not get heart attacks. Those above 150 do get heart attacks. A forty-year long study by Johns Hopkins researchers have found that men in their twenties with high cholesterol levels are more likely to develop heart disease and die from it. People with high cholesterol levels are encouraged to lose weight, improve their diet, and exercise. Having an elevated blood cholesterol level is one of the four main controllable factors leading to coronary heart disease. The other three controllable factors are exercise, high blood pressure, and cigarette smoking.

Having good health—and low cholesterol—is as much a hereditary gift as it is an achievement. The malady of a high blood cholesterol level sometimes occurs because of one's genes, which cannot be controlled. All persons with high cholesterol levels should seek the advice of professionals, such as a physician or registered dietitian, because high cholesterol levels are known to cause hardened, narrow arteries, that pinch off blood circulation and eventually cause a heart attack or stroke. Proper diet and drugs can improve cholesterol levels.

Clearly, it is important for better long-term health to cut down on fat intake. Many organizations agree with this recommendation, including the Senate Select Committee on Nutrition and Human Needs, American Heart Association, National Cancer Institute, Department of Health and Human Services, Department of Agriculture, and the National Research Council of the National Academy of Sciences. Note the phrase *cut down*; it does not say cut out.

Some consumers are irrationally distorting the fat message by trying to eliminate it altogether. Others erroneously equate low-fat and no-fat foods with zero calories. Looking at the labeling will reveal some high-sugar, no-fat products to actually be high-calorie foods—those that cause weight gain.

The USDA says that Americans—who spend 44 percent of their food dollars eating out—presently consume 34 percent of their calories as fat. The aim should be to reduce fat consumption to 30 percent or less, which is about a 25 percent reduction from current levels. Some progress is being made. Interest in healthy diets has increased the number of vegetarians in the United States to 12 million, and a growing number are of student age. A recent survey of teenagers found the 35 percent of the girls and 18 percent of the boys though being veggie was "in." In the past five years, consumption of plant-based foods has far exceeded animal products. A more health conscious population has increased its consumption of fruits and vegetables, even though people still eat too many sugars and fats. More food producers are selling good-tasting healthier foods, especially low-fat products.[2] Restaurants are adding delicious low-fat items to their menus too.

CONSUMER UPDATE: Most Theater Popcorn Is Unhealthy

The Center for Science in the Public Interest reports that if cooked in coconut oil (a saturated fat that has been shown to raise blood cholesterol levels), a medium container of buttered popcorn has 71 grams of fat—more than a day's worth of artery-clogging fat! Popcorn with canola oil is not very healthy either, in spite of those misleading signs in movie theaters that state, "Now Popping With Canola Oil. Low in Saturated Fats. No Cholesterol." Shortenings—what those theaters are *really* cooking in—have lots of partially hydrogenated fats and are still 100% fat. Consumers who want healthy popcorn eat air-popped popcorn; ask the theater for some. **Air-popped popcorn** is almost a "free-food," something dieters can eat lots of without taking in very many calories.

Some Americans Are Trying to Improve Their Diets

Surveys show that Americans are becoming better informed about cholesterol and the values of having a good diet. Many people are changing their attitudes toward cholesterol and good health. Unfortunately, however, data reveals that these concerns are not resulting in enough changes in eating habits. Researchers conclude that people "think" they are improving their food habits, but most are not.

Eating Healthy Isn't Difficult[3]

We have heard that we are what we eat. More than that, what we eat now will have an influence on our quality of life both now and as we age. The science of nutrition is a relatively young one, and knowledge is growing rapidly regarding the effect our food choices can have on our health. Many questions remain for nutrition scientists to answer, but one link between diet and health has been proven indisputably, and that is the association between excess consumption of dietary fat and certain diseases. On a short-

---

[2]A regular hot dog contains about 16 grams of fat; the Healthy Choice brand of low-fat hot dogs contains 1½ grams of fat per hot dog.

[3]This section was written by Lucy S. Garman, M.S., R.D.

term basis, eating too much fat can make you feel sluggish and contribute to a weight gain; future effects can be more serious, such as the development of heart disease, diabetes, and some cancers.

Healthy low-fat meals can be purchased or prepared with little disruption to one's lifestyle. For example, try substituting less saturated oils, such as olive and canola for butter or shortening in cooking, and use margarine that is softer or more liquid and thus less saturated as a spread and also for cooking. Removing excess fats when preparing food is not difficult, and often results in a tastier meal. For example, allowing homemade spaghetti sauce or soup to cool overnight in the refrigerator enables much of the fat which rises to the surface to be easily removed.

Other ways to reduce fat intake include using reduced-fat salad dressing, enjoying a bagel instead of a glazed donut, trimming fat from beef, choosing lean meats, eating no more than six ounces of meat per day, consuming poultry without its skin, drinking skim milk, buying tuna canned in water, and snacking on fruits, popcorn without butter, and pretzels. When eating out, try grilled chicken or fish, lean roast beef, vegetables atop a mound of steamed (not fried) rice, and pasta with a tomato-based sauce.

A few small changes in diet can add up to big changes in health. Books with low-fat menus and recipes can be found in stores everywhere. Many reduced-fat and fat-free products are on the market; however, it should be noted that these products are not calorie-free, and can still contribute to weight gain. Excess body weight in itself can contribute to health problems. A word of caution, however. Food is meant to be *enjoyed*, and the addition of a limited amount of fats to a meal can make food more palatable. The line between watching what you eat and becoming "fat phobic" can be a fine one.

Nutritional Labeling and Education Act

Passage of the Nutritional Labeling and Education Act (NLEA) in 1990, the most sweeping change for the food industry in the twentieth century, is an aggressive attempt by government to help consumers eat better. Research shows that NLEA already has helped 89 percent of Americans to improve their understanding of nutrition and dietary intake. The new food labeling requirements are designed both to inform and educate consumers by offering consumers detailed information in the food label so that consumers will be take an active and responsible role in protecting their health by being better able to compare food products and to plan healthy diets. NLEA requires nutrition labeling for most foods (except meat and poultry) and authorizes the use of nutrient content claims and suitable FDA-approved health claims. More than 300,000 products are affected. NLEA is jointly administered by the Food and Drug Administration and the U.S. Department of Agriculture. The U.S. Department of Agriculture's regulations closely parallel the FDA's. Highlights include:

- Nutritional labeling for almost all foods.
- Information on the amount per serving of saturated fat, cholesterol, dietary fiber, and other nutrients.
- Nutrient reference values, expressed as Percent of Daily Value, that can help consumers see how a food fits into an overall daily diet.
- Uniform definitions for terms that describe a food's nutrient content, such as "light," "low fat," and "high fiber."
- Claims about the relationship between a nutrient and a disease (such as fat and cancer) are be regulated.

- Serving sizes are standardized, in both common household and metric measures.
- Total percentage of juice in juice drinks must be declared.
- Voluntary nutrition information on many raw foods, and if compliance is insufficient, the NLEA allows the regulations to be mandatory.

Exceptions to NLEA include restaurant foods and ready-to-eat foods, among others. Packages with less than 12 square inches available for labeling are also exempt, but they must provide an address or telephone number where such information may be obtained.

Food labels are headed with the title, "Nutrition Facts." Mandatory components include: total calories, calories from fat, total fat, saturated fat, cholesterol, sodium, total carbohydrate, dietary fiber, sugars, protein, vitamin A, vitamin C, calcium, and iron. The order in which these nutrients appear reflects the priority of current dietary guidelines. Numerous other components may be listed voluntarily. However, if a nutritional claim is made about the optional components, or if a food is fortified or enriched with them, nutritional information about these components becomes mandatory. A sample label that meets the regulations is shown in Figure 14-2.

1. Shows standardized descriptions of serving sizes

2. Translates fats into calories

3. Shows how much of one day's recommended allotment of a nutrient one serving will provide based on a 2000-calorie diet

4. Lists nutrients that are most important to health

5. Shows daily values for 2000 and 2500 calorie diets.

6. Tells the number of calories per gram of fat, carbohydrates, and protein

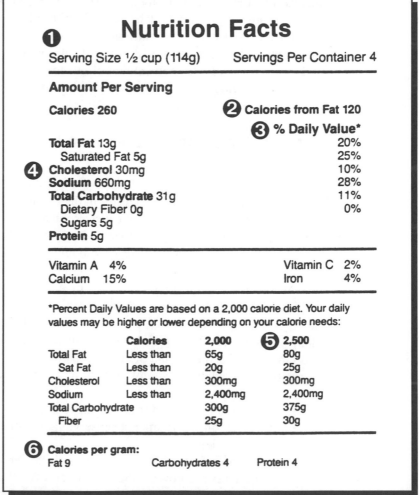

FIGURE 14-2 Sample Food Label

The NLEA requires on food labels what are called **Daily Values (DVs)**, a set of dietary references that apply to fat, saturated fat, cholesterol, carbohydrate, protein, fiber, sodium, and potassium. DVs serve as a basis for the percent of the Daily Value of each nutrient for a serving that the food provides. They are reference values to help consumers gain a perspective on what their overall dietary intake ought to be. The need for each nutrient varies according to age, gender, and physical size. The DV labeling information is based upon a 2,000 calorie diet.[4]

Definitions are now available for such terms as free, low, lean, extra lean, high, good source, reduced, less, light, more, fresh, and healthy. NLEA also requires that many FDA-certified color additives be labeled to help people with allergies avoid them. The Nutrition Labeling and Education Act supersedes many of the older regulatory provisions pertaining to nutritional labeling, diet-food labeling, standardized food identities, and the Fair Packaging and Labeling Act.

Consumers now can tell by glancing at a food label when there is a large amount of fat in a processed food, such as in breakfast cereals. Quaker 100% Natural Cereal, for example, has 6 grams of fat, meaning that 54 percent of the total 140 calories in a serving (before milk is added) come from fat. FDA Commissioner David A. Kessler says consumers can be guided by the "5-20" rule: a product that has 5 percent or less of the "daily value" of fat can be considered a "low-fat food," while any single food that supplies 20 percent or more of one's daily value should be considered "high fat."[5] Sixty-five grams of fat per day probably is the upper limit for most men, 50 would be a better number; maximums for women should be lower. However, all fat intake is variable according to individual calorie needs.

USDA's Food Guide Pyramid

The U.S. Department of Agriculture has published a Food Guide Pyramid to support its latest dietary guidelines. This is an effort to help Americans make trade-offs in their food choices and develop healthier diets. As illustrated in Figure 14-3, the pyramid shows what and how much people should eat from each food group. The emphasis is on consuming different proportions of food categories rather than specific foods themselves. It is one's entire diet that is important. Variety, moderation, and proportions are keys to healthy eating.

Questionable Food Selling Practices

There are a number of selling practices used by relatively few stores that are questionable because they are misleading and often result in increased prices.

---

[4]Although they will not show up on labels, the government's **Reference Daily Intakes (RDIs)** serve as a basis for calculating the daily reference values. The RDIs, which replace the term "U.S. RDAs" (Recommended Daily Allowances), are reference values for vitamins, minerals and protein.

[5]Calculations by *Consumer Reports* reveal that McDonald's, Hardee's and Burger King "no-egg" breakfasts, which include some sausage, average 59 percent of the calories coming from fat.

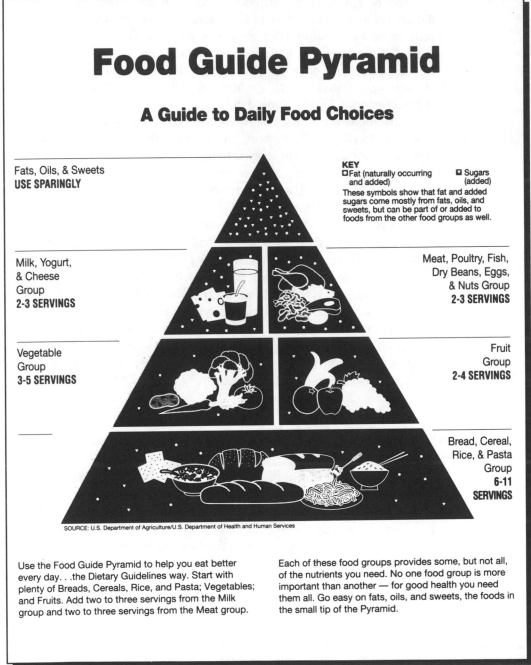

Food Guide Pyramid

A Guide to Daily Food Choices

Fats, Oils, & Sweets
USE SPARINGLY

KEY
☐Fat (naturally occurring   ◪ Sugars
   and added)   (added)
These symbols show that fat and added
sugars come mostly from fats, oils, and
sweets, but can be part of or added to
foods from the other food groups as well.

Milk, Yogurt,
& Cheese
Group
2-3 SERVINGS

Meat, Poultry, Fish,
Dry Beans, Eggs,
& Nuts Group
2-3 SERVINGS

Vegetable
Group
3-5 SERVINGS

Fruit
Group
2-4 SERVINGS

Bread, Cereal,
Rice, & Pasta
Group
**6-11
SERVINGS**

SOURCE: U.S. Department of Agriculture/U.S. Department of Health and Human Services

Use the Food Guide Pyramid to help you eat better every day. . .the Dietary Guidelines way. Start with plenty of Breads, Cereals, Rice, and Pasta; Vegetables; and Fruits. Add two to three servings from the Milk group and two to three servings from the Meat group.

Each of these food groups provides some, but not all, of the nutrients you need. No one food group is more important than another — for good health you need them all. Go easy on fats, oils, and sweets, the foods in the small tip of the Pyramid.

FIGURE 14-3 USDA Food Guide Pyramid

Price Manipulation. Some stores try to draw consumers in by advertising specials while raising the prices for other items. In some stores, selected prices are raised between 5 and 7 p.m. (to catch workers shopping on the way home) and then lowered. In addition, although reliable research evidence is difficult to come by, it is alleged that some stores raise their prices when customers' welfare checks are scheduled to arrive.

Frequent Scanning Errors. Complaints about supermarket errors at the checkout counter are on the rise. Electronic scanners that emit a shimmery red filament across the products also make errors. *Money* magazine reports that at stores with the laser-beamed electronic scanning devices (about 30 percent of all stores), mistakes are made about 10 percent of the time, and the errors are usually in the favor of the supermarket. Errors account for about 1/2 of supermarket profits.

Cents-Off Food Coupons. More than 3/4 of shoppers redeem coupons. Cents-off food coupons are a marketing device designed to encourage purchase of specific products. This is accomplished by having a redeemable value printed on the face of the coupon, averaging 50 cents. While coupon redeemers save money, critics charge that coupons are wasteful, expensive, and time consuming. Each year over 300 billion coupons are printed (1200 for every man, woman and child in the United States), redeemed, stored by retailers (at 8 cents each), and processed.

Games, Sweepstakes, and Trading Stamps. It has been calculated that games, sweepstakes, and trading stamps cost the consumer from 1/2 cent to 3 1/2 cents for every dollar spent at the grocery store. Sperry & Hutchison, the nation's largest trading stamp company, now has an electronic Green Stamp to encourage patronage. Consumers pass a wallet-size plastic card through a scanner as it credits the purchase amount. The credits are later redeemed for gifts from the S&H catalog. When they work, such promotional devices are good marketing techniques for the stores. If sales increase proportionately, costs are covered by the increased profits. All shoppers pay for promotions that do not work by paying higher prices.

Packaging Costs. The cost of packaging adds greatly to grocery prices, amounting to about 8.5 percent of the food dollar. Manufacturers use color and interesting packaging to catch the eye of the grocery shopper, but surveys show that a great majority of people agree that there is too much unnecessary fancy packaging.

Misleading Labeling. Occasionally, the federal government helps companies mislabel food products. The USDA permits the label "fresh" chicken to be used for a chicken that that has never been chilled below 26 degrees, while "hard chilled" to mean birds frozen between zero and 26 degrees Fahrenheit, and "frozen" to mean a bird that has been kept at 0 degrees Fahrenheit or below.

Products that Offer Less for the Money. Food manufacturers are constantly reducing their product's weight or volume without lowering prices. Recent downsizing has been done by StarKist tuna fish, Knorr soup, Lipton instant tea, Kellogg NutriGrain, and Brim coffee. While not illegal, this practice surreptitiously tricks consumers into paying more without realizing it.

Anti-Competitive Practices in the Food Industry

Like some other segments of the American economy, the food industry does not offer consumers the benefits of a fully competitive marketplace. Some examples of anti-competitive practices follow.

Calendar Marketing Agreements Squeeze Out Competitors

In the United States, the soft-drink business is a $50 billion a year industry. Consumers drink about 50 gallons of soda per person each year. Coca-Cola Company and Pepsico have taken steps to increase their profits and reduce choices for American consumers through special **calendar marketing agreements**. These are contracts where, in exchange for quarterly payments or rebates from the local soft-drink bottling companies, the food supermarkets agree to feature only one brand of soft drink for certain weeks during the year. These agreements result in extensive advertising, the best in-store displays, and often the lowest prices. Since a soft-drink bottler can profit with extremely low prices only when a considerable sales volume exists, with calendar marketing agreements, Coke and Pepsi can lower prices while off-brands cannot.

Coke bottlers get an agreement for 26 weeks and Pepsi bottlers get an agreement for the other 26 weeks. The result is that supermarkets then cannot display or advertise other brands. Sometimes Coke and Pepsi skip a few weeks, like during January and February, when all soft-drink sales are poor. Royal Crown executives call these **lock-out agreements** because they monopolize the calendar. Recently, some independent bottlers in North Carolina filed suit against local Coke and Pepsi bottlers; three cases were settled out of court and the Coke bottler lost the civil lawsuit. Calendar marketing agreements exist among local bottlers and supermarkets throughout the country. The question remains, "When will concerned state Attorneys General take on this problem?"

Allocation Agreements for Shelf Space

Allocation agreements also exist, often in combination with calendar marketing agreements. Here food stores and soft-drink companies sign contracts to allocate shelf space on an annual or quarterly basis based upon sales from the previous time period. The result is that the biggest sellers (Coke and Pepsi) get more space the next time. The effect of these agreements is to squeeze out the competitors, both literally and figuratively.

Agricultural Marketing Orders

The federal government's system of **agricultural marketing orders** permits grower cartels to restrict supplies to keep profits high for the sellers. That is why every now and then you see television news focus on farmers feeding so-called excess milk to hogs and squashing so-called non-standard oranges at the city dump. The program is run through agricultural cooperatives. The cooperatives have a great deal of political power because the 50+ year-old agricultural marketing order program continues to legally conspire to fix prices and practice predatory trade practices.

The Federal Trade Commission is prohibited by law from even studying agricultural marketing orders. Also, the Capper-Volstead Act restricts the FTC's efforts to bring antitrust challenges in the farming industry. The special interests are afraid of what might be discovered. Such government-controlled practices are not designed to provide consumers with low prices. In 1993, U.S. District Judge Gerhard A. Gesell permitted a suspension of the California-Arizona Navel Orange Market Order, lifting the restrictions during the November-April growing season. Other agricultural marketing order programs continue.

Economic Concentration in the Meatpacking Industry

Four companies control about three-fourths of the meatpacking industry (IBP, ConAgra, Cargill, and National Beef). That is up from 40 percent a decade ago. Critics complain that the big companies can drive the little ones out of business. This is accomplished by big companies (especially those that operate non-union plants) paying farmers too much for cattle and purposely selling meat too cheaply. Such predatory pricing eliminates competition. In the short run, it is good for consumers to have lower prices. In the long run, as competition disappears, consumers will have to pay whatever prices the producers determine.

Agencies and Specialized Laws Protecting Food Consumers

Since 1906, when the first federal food and drug law was enacted, the government has had an important role in helping consumers. Subsequent amendments and new legislation have made foods even more wholesome and safe.

U.S. Department of Agriculture

The U.S. Department of Agriculture enforces laws and regulations concerning meat and poultry products, including the Meat Inspection Act (1906), Wholesome Meat Act (1967), Wholesome Poultry Products Act (1968), and Nutrition Labeling and Education Act (1990). The Meat Inspection Act prohibits the sale of any processed meat product if the labeling is false or misleading, or if any inferiority has been concealed in any manner. The USDA's Food Safety and Inspection Service (FSIS) inspects meat and poultry for sanitation, accurate labeling, and correct use of chemical additives. Products that pass inspection are given appropriate USDA inspection marks. Those which fail are either reprocessed to satisfy inspection standards or are destroyed. In addition, the USDA monitors packing and processing plants for disease-causing bacteria and signs of pesticide residues.

The USDA has established a new system of bacteria identification in meat and poultry products known as **Hazard Analysis and Critical Control Points (HACCP)**. The USDA recently issued its requirement that "safe-handling instruction" labeling be attached to all raw meat products.

The USDA also has a voluntary grading service that provides buyers with consistent standards of quality. The department has established grade standards for meat, poultry, dairy products, eggs, fruit, and vegetables. Grading is voluntary and not related to safety.

The USDA has an inherent conflict of interest because it is responsible for increasing the demand for beef, pork, eggs, and dairy products (which may contain high amounts of fat) while also being responsible for informing and educating the public about proper nutrition. In a recent year, the USDA spent $21 million for nutrition education. It spent $60 million promoting agricultural products through the USDA's government-sponsored trade associations: Cattlemen's Beef Promotion and Research Board, National Pork Board, Egg Board, and the National Dairy Promotion and Research Board.

> **CONSUMER UPDATE:**
> **Consumer Concerns About Food Safety**
>
> Food purchased in the United States is the safest in the world. In recent years, however, consumers have had reasons for concern. Since 1986, the government has allowed the meat industry to become more self-regulating, with the result that the number of food-borne illnesses has increased while the number of government inspections has declined.
>
> The Center for Disease Control and Prevention estimates that more than 80 million foodborne illnesses occur every year, primarily from **salmonella**, **listeria**, **campylobacter**, and other organisms in food. These result in fever, vomiting, and diarrhea, and contribute to approximately 9,000 deaths annually. Critics observe that existing inspection programs have proven to be inadequate in detecting bacterial contamination. Infection with the virulent E. coli bacteria (estimated at 20,000 annually) may mean death, so it is wise (especially for meat eaters) to pay attention to the advice to properly handle and adequately cook food. Proper cooking kills most bacteria that cause foodborne illness.

The Food and Drug Administration

The Food and Drug Administration (FDA) is responsible for ensuring the purity and safety of the nation's food supply (other than meat and poultry products, which are regulated by the USDA). They also oversee the safety of drugs, cosmetics, medical devices,[6] and the truthful, informative labeling of such products so that they are safe for human use. The FDA, headed by David A. Kessler, regulates veterinary products, such as pet food, cattle feed, animal drugs, and radiological devices, such as microwaves, tanning booths, and television sets. It shares regulation of pesticides with the Environmental Protection Agency (EPA). The FDA has broad control over the safety, purity, and wholesomeness of processed foods. Also, the FDA regulates prescription and over-the-counter drugs.

In the food area, the FDA issues Current Good Manufacturing Practice Regulations, which set requirements for sanitation, inspection of materials and finished products, and other quality controls. It also issues FDA Food Standards, which set standards of identity specifications for many food products.

When the FDA discovers unsanitary, unsafe, adulterated, or mislabeled products that cause deaths, injuries, or adverse reactions, they conduct an investigation. The FDA says that a food is **adulterated** if it bears or contains any poisonous or deleterious substance which may render it injurious to health. A product is **misbranded** if its labeling is false or misleading, if it is offered for sale under the name of another food, and if it is an imitation of another food, unless its label bears the word imitation.

After investigating, the FDA can use one of four authorities: (1) suggest a **voluntary recall**, which is a firm's removal or correction of a marketed product when that product violates the laws enforced by the FDA; (2) **seizure**, which is forcibly taking into custody goods deemed in violation of a law (and such goods are usually destroyed); (3) an

---

[6]The FDA proposed rules to take effect in 1994 that would permit regulation of medical device manufacturers, such as heart valves and pacemakers, during both the design and production process. This followed FDA research revealing that nearly half the medical device recalls were due to flaws in design.

injunction, which is a legal order of the court enjoining, restraining, or prohibiting a party from a specific course of action to prevent an unfair business practice. In the case of the FDA, the order would be to stop offending articles from being sold in interstate commerce; and (4) **prosecution**, which is charging the company and its officials with violations of applicable civil and criminal statutes. The Clinton Administration has sharply increased the budget for the FDA, especially for its research and investigative staff.

CONSUMER UPDATE:
Food Biotechnology: A Brave New World

Developments in biotechnology are causing the FDA to think twice about genetically engineered products (such as potatoes that ward off pests) coming to the marketplace. A *Flavr-Savr* tomato produced by Calgene Corporation looks and feels like an ordinary tomato, but the gene that allows tomatoes to quickly go soft and mushy has been blocked. Is a tomato that doesn't spoil an entirely new product that needs extensive safety testing (because it is a drug), or is it just another hybrid vegetable variety? Even though the FDA does not now require genetically altered foods to undergo a full-scale safety review, Calgene requested one. In 1994, the tomato was approved by the FDA as safe for consumers. Other genetically altered products on the market include tomatoes, squash, potato, and soybean.

Genetic engineers can produce the following menu, as cited by the National Wildlife Federation: Appetizer-tomato juice with flounder gene; Entree-blackened catfish with trout gene; Dessert-rice pudding with pea gene; and Beverage-milk from bovine growth hormone-supplemented cows.

The FDA also approved a genetically engineered hormone that increases milk productivity of cows; the milk is not required to be labeled any differently than traditional milk. The FDA position is that food products created through recombinant DNA technology will raise no new or unique safety issues. The FDA will not require premarket approval of such products or require that foods enhanced by genetic engineering be labeled as such. New nutrients and ingredients will be treated the same as a new sweetener or preservative. Moreover, the federal government does not presume a lack of safety for biotech food products.

The Food Additives Amendment

A **food additive** is a substance directly or indirectly added in small amounts to foods during processing, production, or packaging to improve, strengthen, or otherwise alter it. Food additives are used to maintain or improve nutritional quality, to preserve freshness, to reduce food waste, to enhance the attractiveness of foods, and to provide essential aids in processing and preparing foods. Some additives are vitamins and minerals that perhaps are needed in a person's diet, or they may be added back to a food because they have been removed in processing. Other substances are added to make the food look or taste better. For example, *Simplesse* is an additive used as a fat substitute in such products as ice cream and salad dressing. *Olean* (the brand name for *Olestra*), another fake fat, is controversial because of its possible side effects of "abdominal cramping and loose stools" as well as a tendency to inhibit the absorption of some vitamins and nutrients. Additives, including pesticides, are widely used because society is willing to accept their risks in return for a high quality, inexpensive, and physically attractive food supply.

One example of a food additive results from **radiation ionization** (or **food irradiation**), which uses gamma or electron ionizing radiation to destroy insects and bacteria that can cause spoilage and disease. The process disinfects such foods as cereal grains, fresh fruits and vegetables and extends their shelf life. Chicken, turkey, game hens, and beef have been approved by the USDA (and by 30 other countries) for radiation treatment to reduce bacteria, such as salmonella. The USDA has approved a poultry disinfection method called TSP to kill salmonella. When a food is exposed to radiation ionization, chemical compounds not otherwise found in the food are created, called **radiolytic products**. A few states prohibit or severely limit preservation by radiation because of questions about safety.

Food additives found to be unsafe can be banned by the FDA in various foods, drugs, and cosmetics, by the USDA in meat and poultry, or, in some cases, by the Environmental Protection Agency (EPA). There have been no studies showing any radiation effects whatsoever; food does not become "radioactive."

Intentional and Incidental Additives

Controversy about the hundreds of food additives being used in processed foods led to the passage of the **Food Additives Amendment** in 1958. The law requires proof of the safety of any new chemical additive before it can be marketed. A core principle of the law is the requirement that additives be evaluated on the basis of their safety without any consideration of their benefits.

There are nearly 3000 food additives that are classified as **intentional additives**, that is, those substances which are purposefully and directly put into foods. Over 90 percent of intentional food additives are common flavoring substances and herbs and spices, such as salt, pepper, sugar, corn syrup, and citric acid. **Incidental** (or **unavoidable**) **additives** are substances that become part of the food product unintentionally and indirectly. For example, pesticide residues may remain on farm products and substances may migrate from the packing material into a food. Two potent carcinogens that are incidental additives are mercury in fish and aflatoxin in some corn and peanuts. Other contaminants classified as unavoidable include such things as hairs, feathers, excreta, urine, insect fragments, molds, decomposition, dirt, sand, rocks, and other extraneous matter, the incidence of which should be lowered by good harvesting, storing, and manufacturing practices.

The last group of incidental additives is regulated by FDA **action levels**, which are government-set standards for the maximum unavoidable contamination of various food products. Incidental additives number about 10,000. Action levels are informal standards not issued through regulations, and they have no binding effect. They are merely prosecutorial guidelines.

Legal Limits of Filth

The FDA has what are known as **food filth tolerances**. These are publicly available information specifications of tolerance for many incidental additives to various food products. Technically, the FDA prohibits any food from being sold to humans that contains any filth or putrid or decomposed substances. In reality, this is impossible. Occasionally, little mice and insects simply get into the food supply.

Some examples of filth include legally permitted amounts of insect fragments, rat hairs, bacteria, insect larvae, rodent excreta, worms, decomposed matter, and sticks and stones. For example, the maximum filth allowance for chocolate is "150 insect fragments and 4 rat hairs per half pound." Canned and frozen blackberries and raspberries are allowed "an average of 10 insects and insect larvae per pound." Peanut butter allowances permit an "average of 225 insect fragments or 9 rodent hairs per pound."

The GRAS List

The Food Additives Amendment also established the **generally recognized as safe (GRAS) list**. This is a government-approved list of more than 600 substances that have been used for years and are considered safe by experts in the field as long as they are used as they were originally intended and with good manufacturing practices. Products on the GRAS list do not meet the FDA's clearance standards for safety as required for all legally defined food additives, but they are still considered safe for use in foods. The substances on the GRAS list range from salt and sugar to monosodium glutamate (MSG). This grandfathering clause allows provisional listing of established substances and empowers the head of the FDA to extend the listing. Even though items on the GRAS list are constantly being reevaluated by the FDA for safety, existence of the list proves the adage that old risks are treated more leniently than new risks because they are more costly to regulate.

Sulfites

Sulfites are a group of sulfur-based chemicals on the GRAS list that have been used for years as food additives. A **sulfite** is a preservative or antioxidant that reduces food spoilage by bacteria. It also reduces food discoloration during preparation, storage, or distribution. With sulfites, such food products as potatoes, mushrooms, and shrimp appear whiter and lettuce will not wilt or brown as quickly.

This valuable additive also causes severe health risks such as hives and shock in certain individuals, including about 100,000 asthmatics and others with allergies. Sulfites have been implicated in at least a dozen deaths. The FDA has banned sulfites from raw fruits and vegetables, except potatoes.

Consumer advocates contend that labeling products that contain sulfites is not enough. They want sulfites banned from all foods in restaurants[7] and supermarkets, as well as from prescription drugs. The National Academy of Sciences has recommended that restaurants be required to identify ingredient and nutritional elements in the dishes served.

FDA rules require that if a packaged food has more than 10 parts per million of sulfites, it must identify the sulfite on the label. Examples include: sulfur dioxide, sodium sulfite, sodium and potassium bisulfite, and sodium and potassium metabisulfite. The regulation further requires that prescription drugs containing sulfites provide a warning statement to consumers to that effect. Also, all alcoholic beverages containing sulfites, mainly wines, must indicate such on the label.

---

[7]On a related issue, in 1993, the Food and Drug Administration began proceedings to require nutrition and health claims on restaurant menus to meet standardized requirements and be supported by "a reasonable basis" of evidence.

CONSUMER UPDATE:
FDA Begins Seafood Inspection Program

Most illnesses that occur from seafood are preventable. The FDA currently inspects the nation's 3800 seafood processors about once every four years. The Food and Drug Administration began a program in 1995 to require all seafood processors to implement a quality control program. The new system continues inspections and sampling, but adds a layer of preventive controls. It will not depend upon visual inspection, which is viewed as largely ineffective.

The FDA's **Hazard Analysis Critical Control Point (HACCP)** identifies possible hazards and institutes rigorous quality controls at the most vulnerable places in the seafood systems. HACCP uses microbiology detection techniques, combined with production standards, to identify, monitor, and avoid contamination. Standards exist on such things as the maximum time fish may remain on a loading dock, the temperature of the room where filleting occurs, and the adequacy of pasteurization processes. Processors and importers are required to keep detailed records on every step of handling seafood. An annual drop of 60,000 cases of food poisoning is anticipated. For the first time in history, it is expected that the United States is able to assure the safety of fish and shellfish.

The Miller Pesticide Chemicals Amendment

The Miller Pesticide Chemicals Amendment of 1954 provides the legal authority to establish specific maximum amounts of pesticide residues that are allowed to remain on agricultural products. A **pesticide** is a chemical used to kill pests, especially insects and weeds, to prevent damage and destruction of agricultural crops. Since being created in 1972, the Environmental Protection Agency (EPA) has had primary authority over pesticides. The EPA and the USDA have jointly established enforceable residue **tolerance levels** based on the toxicity of each pesticide (even though not all have been tested by the EPA). These are the maximum legally allowed pesticide residues on foods for more than 600 chemicals, including 300 pesticides. Of these, 73 are known carcinogens that cause tumors in laboratory animals that were fed large dosages for extended periods of time. Many more pesticides have not been thoroughly tested for carcinogens or other chronic health effects. A 1993 National Academy of Science report concluded that infants and children are particularly susceptible to health risks from pesticide residues.

The EPA is generally bound by law to balance the health costs of pesticides against their benefits to the food supply. The USDA tests pesticides itself or delegates the job to other nationally recognized groups, and finally decides on a safe level for human consumption. Both the USDA and FDA monitor inspections of harvested crops by regularly examining such things as samples of soil, silt, runoff, water, fish, and plant life. This law is one reason why the chemical DDT is no longer widely used to spray agricultural products.

The EPA is responsible for setting pesticide residue limits on raw foods. The standard for public health is to ensure an adequate, wholesome, and economical food supply. Historically, once a carcinogenic substance was found, the EPA set the **legal residue level** 100 times lower to allow an extra margin of safety. The EPA does not have a **zero-tolerance level standard** which would accept no risks whatsoever. Historically, it licensed pesticides for use both on raw produce and in processed foods when they posed only a **negligible risk** of causing cancer, which meant increasing chances of cancer by no more than 1 in 1 million over 70 years of life. This negligible risk policy was struck down by the Supreme Court in 1993, and the effects of the decision are discussed below.

The Delaney Clause

The Delaney Clause (named after a former member of Congress) appears in three laws in the Food and Drug Administration regulatory system: the Food Additives Amendments, the Color Additive Amendments, and the Animal Drug Amendments. The clause specifically prohibits the purposeful addition of any **carcinogens** to food. These are substances that have been found to induce cancer in humans or animals. When any food being tested with laboratory animals is suspected of being a carcinogen, regardless of its arguable benefits, the substance is banned. This is known as a **zero-risk standard**. For example, both Red Dye No. 2, a food coloring, and cyclamates, a sweetening additive, were banned a number of years ago. The process of testing a substance to see if it causes cancer takes about two years and costs about $2 million. The Delaney Clause precludes the FDA from approving as safe any food additive found to induce cancer in man or when administered to experimental animals by ingestion or other appropriate test.

A recent Supreme Court ruling supports the Delaney Clause. It stated that, "If pesticides in processed foods induce cancer in humans and animals, they render the food adulterated and must be prohibited."[8] Bills are pending in Congress to legalize the formerly used negligible risk policy (which would eliminate the Delaney Clause) and to give the EPA and FDA more discretion in matters of carcinogenic substances. Pesticide registrants would have to prove that residues on food would pose "a reasonable certainty of no harm" to the consuming public. The administrator of the EPA, Carol M. Browner, supports the proposed changes.

Saccharin and Aspartame—Sugar Substitutes

Saccharin is a widely used sweetener found to be carcinogenic. While the FDA was preparing to ban the additive under its legal authority, Congress passed a specific law creating a moratorium on the ban of this product making it temporarily exempt from the Delaney Clause in response to a large public outcry.[9] This extends the use of saccharin, presumably by diabetics and others with health problems, while further research is being conducted. In the meantime, products that contain saccharin must be labeled: "Use of this product may be hazardous to your health. This product contains saccharin, which has been determined to cause cancer in laboratory animals."

The availability of the additive *aspartame* (Nutrasweet and Equal), which is 180 times as sweet as sugar, may result in the eventual banning of saccharin. Aspartame is a combination of two naturally occurring amino acids. Although aspartame is controversial, it has not been found to be carcinogenic. Aspartame consumption in the United States averages about 14 pounds per person annually, and the FDA considers the product

---

[8]Weisskopf, M. (1992, July 7). Court Curbs Carcinogenic Pesticide Use. *The Washington Post*, p. A-1+.

[9]Top officials of the company that makes Sweet 'N Low (Cumberland Packing Company) plead guilty last year to funneling more than $224,000 in illegal campaign contributions to persuade politicians in an effort to encourage them not to ban saccharin, the sugar substitute's key ingredient. Among the recipients were Robert J. Dole and Alfonse M. D'Amato.

generally safe for most people. The additive *acesulfame*, being marketed as Sunette, was recently approved by the FDA for use as a tabletop sweetener and as an ingredient in chewing gum, dry drink mixes, gelatins, puddings, nondairy creamers, and tablets and packets. It differs chemically from aspartame and saccharin. *Brazzein*, 2000 times sweeter than sugar, has just been developed by the University of Wisconsin-Madison.

Nitrites—Preservatives

Food preservatives are a number of natural substances and chemical additives that tend to preserve or are capable of preserving food products. For example, sodium nitrite inhibits the growth of poisonous botulism bacteria in bacon, hot dogs, and luncheon meat, and it also adds a specific flavor to these foods. When combined with secondary amines in the body, the nitrites produce something called **nitrosamines**, which are carcinogenic. The FDA has insisted on lowering the amount of nitrites allowed in food products even though nitrites are not carcinogenic by themselves, and it is continuing to run further tests on nitrites.

Benefits and Costs of the Delaney Clause

Critics of the Delaney Clause, and of other laws limiting food additives, argue about the benefits and costs of a totally risk-free food supply versus accepting some degree of minimal risk. Factors to consider include opportunity costs of greater health risks, higher food prices, shorter storage times, and changed appearance of some foods. It is important to observe though, as Public Citizen's William B. Schultz says, "Congress chose to eliminate carcinogens in easy places, namely for unimportant additives that are intentionally added to food."[10] Schultz says more additives need to be banned.

The Color Additive Amendments

The 1960 Color Additive Amendments required reevaluation of all color additives, including those previously thought to be safe. The law demands that all food additives be shown to be safe before being used in foods. The FDA is to set limits on the amounts of color that can be used in foods, drugs, and cosmetics. Further, no color can be used to conceal any inferiority of a product, since this might deceive consumers. The chemical food colors Red Nos. 2, 8, 9, and 19, as well as Orange No. 17, were banned under this law in recent years. Red No. 3 and Yellow No. 5 remain controversial food colors that are still undergoing testing.

Under the Delaney Clause, any color additive shown to cause cancer in either animals or humans is automatically considered unsafe and, therefore, must be banned by the FDA. The color additives industry is challenging the Delaney Clause using the concept of negligible risk, or specifically the **de minimis** policy. This is a legal argument that means the law does not concern itself with trifling matters. Use of a de minimis policy by the FDA means that small risks should be ignored by the regulators because the number of

---

[10]Schultz, W. B. (1989, July). Speech to Virginia Tech's 6th biennial "Consumer Issues in Washington" class.

people who will die from carcinogens in food is few. Thus, the marginal benefits of use outweigh the costs. Instead of balancing the benefits and costs, the industry wants the regulators to make a de minimis judgment to accept that certain additives will cause perhaps 1 in 10,000 cancers, thus establishing a floor below which government action is not required. The San Francisco appeals court rejected the de minimis concept, although the public-policy argument continues.

Assessing Consumer Risks: Does Everything Cause Cancer?

It seems like a year does not go by without someone saying that the food we eat, the air we breathe, the water we drink, and the drugs we use cause cancer. While it is important to recognize that the government is trying to protect consumers from products with inherent dangers, Dr. Alvan R. Feinstein, professor of clinical epidemiology at Yale University, suggests that we also should realize that people are clearly more afraid than they need to be about the risks they encounter in their daily lives.

The FDA, Energy Department, and Environmental Protection Agency are alarmed about the public uproar over possible environmental hazards. The question is whether or not our current risk-assessment methods are reliable enough to help consumers make informed decisions about what to eat and where to live, work, and play. Consumers need to be able to define the risks and make clear choices, especially about such perils as radon, dioxin, pesticides, food additives, and radiation.

EPA attorney Edward Gray says that rigid enforcement of the Delaney Clause in a narrow sense for pesticides in processed foods "forces you to make stupid decisions and scientifically untenable regulatory positions because it fails to allow you to distinguish between a serious risk and a piddling risk. It doesn't allow you to get rid of the bad chemicals and leave the less bad ones in their place."[11]

Environmentalists who fear the cumulative effects of pesticides in the food supply want to return to the zero-risk standard of the Delaney Clause for all pesticide residues in raw and processed foods. Others want assurances that for each new chemical that is approved, others will be eliminated. National Resources Defense Council (NRDC) attorney Janet Hathaway says, "The only benefit is to the makers of new pesticides. The public health is not going to benefit."[12] Environmental and consumer advocates suggest that we are a nation of 265 million human guinea pigs.

Such conflicting messages about risks—both negative and positive—contain a lot of technical information, and they are compressed for consumers on the television news. This can lead to misunderstanding, confusion, and distrust. The National Resources Defense Council observes that, "there is a great lack of public confidence in the government's willingness to protect public health."[13]

People process information about risks differently, with the result that consumers' fears grow out of proportion to the actual risks. Examples of irrational behavior include:

---

[11]Weisskopf, M. (1988. October 24). New Pesticide Policy Leaves Residue of Questions. *The Washington Post*, p. A-11.

[12]Ibid.

[13]Seabrook, C. (1989, September 8). It's Always Something (Or is it?). *Roanoke Times & World-News*, p. B-3.

refusing to fly on an airplane, sun bathing all summer long, smoking cigarettes, and eating too much fat every day.

Simply providing information about risks, such as biotechnology products, "is not the solution to this complex problem. As much attention must be paid to consumer perception of risk as to scientific variables. Ignoring consumer concerns, or worse yet, labeling them as irrational and discounting them, is guaranteed to create hostility and will ultimately stand in the way of successful product acceptance."[14] This hurts both seller and consumers. Thus, it is in the interests of both sellers and consumers that, "we have strong regulatory powers to ensure that consumers once again feel confident in delegating risk assessment to the regulators."[15]

Research and a Risk-Free Society

It is important to recognize that the government continues to make efforts to reduce risks to humans, but that a risk-free society is impossible to obtain. Besides, such a society, if possible, would be intolerably expensive. Accordingly, government is forced by various laws and regulations to weigh dangers to health against economic costs.

R. David Pittle, Technical Director for *Consumer Reports*, reminds us that most substances do not cause cancer, no matter how high the dose. Of the many thousands of substances in use such as food additives, pesticides, and chemicals, only a relatively small number have been shown to cause cancer. However, when millions of consumers are exposed to small doses of carcinogenic chemicals, the risk of an increase in cancer cases rises sharply because of the cumulative effects. Plus, human cancer may not manifest itself for many years after the exposure. Thus, it is prudent and ethical for the government to continue to take appropriate actions to protect the public from environmental pollutants, pesticides, and food additives.

Research Conducted on Animals

Regulatory decisions are based on human tests when such data exist, but quite often such information is not available. Evidence on carcinogens often comes from animal testing that is widely used and accepted by the scientific community. Small animals, such as rats and mice, are commonly used to find out if certain substances cause cancer. Research has determined that all substances found to cause cancer in animals also cause cancer in humans. Thus, animal research is critical to assessing the safety of many products. However, animal testing also is not without controversy.

In laboratory experiments, large doses of substances must be used because evidence shows conclusively that as the size of the dose increases, so does the number of animals that get cancer. If a dose used in testing is too high, research animals may die of poisoning, but not cancer.

Since humans metabolize substances more slowly than these animals, some substances persist much longer in the human body. No level of small exposure to a carcinogen, such

---

[14]Douthitt, R. A. (1993) Biotechnology and the Consumer Interest. In T. Mauldin, *Proceedings of the American Council on Consumer Interests* (p. 17). Columbia, MO: University of Missouri.
[15]Ibid.

as radiation and asbestos, has ever been shown to be safe. In addition, since humans are exposed to a number of different carcinogens, exposure to one may add to the risk associated with the others. The overwhelming consensus is that science must rely on animal tests to make prudent public-policy decisions even though science does not yet have definitive answers to the health questions that environmentalists and consumerists are asking.

How Consumers Get Confused When Food Shopping

In today's complex marketplace, the food industry seems to have made it difficult for consumers to get what they pay for in grocery items. The shopper can easily get confused when food shopping, and as a result, many consumers buy the wrong items year after year because they do not know better. Efforts at self-regulation have not resolved these situations.

Absence of Prices on Food Products. On over 95 percent of all food products there is a **bar code** or **universal product code (UPC)**, which is a grid of lines, bars, and numbers representing a 10-digit number. Electronic scanning machines at checkout counters use these patterns to record purchases by means of a computer. The UPC is used in the company's perpetual stock-control program, and at the checkout counter to provide a correct charge for the product.[16]

Supermarket consumers are delighted that the electronic price scanners allow the typical grocery store to stock some of their 16,000 goods more efficiently, speed up checkout procedures, and reduce pricing errors, but consumers also want to keep prices marked on the products. Many consumers have difficulty remembering prices of goods they purchase week to week, and they also have difficulty trying to compare prices within the store. For example, once you have bought a can of corn for 79 cents, will you remember the price when you get to the freezer section to compare with the price of frozen corn? Or to the fresh produce section? The result of this concern has been passage of **item pricing laws** in many localities that require grocery retailers to mark the prices on individual items in a store.

Absence of Unit Prices. Unit pricing is the cost calculation for a small unit of measure, such as an ounce or a pound, used to compare the costs of a product in different-sized packages. It is provided to consumers by about one-quarter of the grocery stores as information on a shelf-tag along with the total price of the product. Some states and cities legally require that unit prices be posted in grocery stores. For example, a six-pack of 12-ounce Coke priced at $1.79 may have a unit price of 2.49 cents per ounce, while a 2-quart bottle of Coke priced at $1.19 may have a unit price of 1.86 cents per ounce.

With the availability of computers, there is no excuse for grocery stores not putting unit-price information on the shelves to help consumers make price comparisons so as to avoid overpaying for their purchases. Be alert to the fact that unit prices are not always lowest for the larger-sized products; frequently, the medium-sized grocery items have the lowest unit prices.

---

[16]A 1995 investigation by the Chicago Department of Consumer Services revealed that 55 percent of over 200 stores examined allegedly overcharged consumers due to scanning errors.

**CONSUMER UPDATE:
Privacy (?!) at the Checkout Counter**

Over 4000 grocery stores, including most major chains, offer a system called **Checkout Coupon**. It is a little box at the checkout counter that gives out coupons to encourage future purchases based upon the food items you have just purchased. When you buy hot dogs, for example, it might print out a coupon for mustard. When you buy snack chips, it might give you a coupon for bean dip. Some systems give automatic discounts without clipping coupons.

Billions of pieces of information are collected by the supermarket industry on consumer purchases. For example, the A. C. Nielsen Company's Advanced Information Technology Center uses such purchasing choices to infer behavior from what goes into a consumer's marketbasket. That knowledge allows food sellers to more accurately market their products and pricing.

It also raises some tough privacy questions. Now when you charge your groceries with a bank credit card or with an automated teller machine (ATM) card, you can wonder if the stores are combining your grocery purchasing information with personal information about you (perhaps from your credit file) and selling it.

Absence of Open Dating. Open dating is a system of ensuring quality and freshness by placing a date on perishable products that indicates either when the product should be sold or when it should be consumed. Alternative dates include the **pack date** (when the product was manufactured or packaged, but this information usually is of little value to consumers), the **pull date** (the last day the product should be sold by the store), the **expiration date** (the last date the product should be used by the consumer), and the **quality assurance date** (the date when the product will last be at its peak of condition, such as "for maximum enjoyment, use before March 15, 1998").

Studies show that sellers save money when open dating is used because losses are lower. Some states and cities legally require grocery stores to use open dating of perishable products, such as milk, cheese, and eggs. Only about one-quarter of all grocery stores provide open-dating information for consumers, so we buy lots of old merchandise thinking it to be fresh.

Illusionary Net Weights. Canned and frozen foods present special labeling problems for consumers. The **net weight** is the legal requirement that food products indicate the weight of the contents, exclusive of the container. The net weight typically represents a combination of both the food and the packaging liquids or syrups. This makes it impossible to compare, for example, a canned food product with its frozen-food counterpart. Mushrooms and olives are exceptions, since they must list their **drained weight** on the labels, which is the weight of the food after the liquid is drained. Drained weights represent the best weight comparison method for consumers, yet most canned and frozen foods are not labeled in this informative manner.

Illusionary Grade Labeling. The federal government has a series of grade labels that give the impression of ensuring some level of quality, but this is not the case. Labeling of beef, eggs, poultry, fruits, and the like is voluntary, and more than half the time the grades are not put on the final food products. Sometimes the grades are totally illusionary as well. For example, less than one-half of the nation's beef is graded according to the USDA's system of grading for eating-quality or palatability. Plus, the USDA grades emphasize maturity and *marbling* (the flecks of fat within lean muscle that apparently contribute to juiciness and tenderness of meat).

About 2 percent of meat is graded "U.S. Prime" (which you will never see in a supermarket because the best restaurants purchase all of it for its rich marbling and tenderness), about 45 percent is graded "U.S. Choice" (marbled and tender), about 22 percent is graded "U.S. Select" (which has less marbling than prime or choice and is more lean), and the remaining 31 percent is standard or ungraded.

Confusing Grade Labels. Grade labels are helpful to wholesalers, processors, and retailers because the system helps these buyers get the products they want. Consumers like the idea of product grading, but the current approach leaves much to be desired. Consider, for example, the USDA grades for fruits and vegetables, since they are probably the easiest to comprehend. The top grade for apples in all states but Washington is "U.S. Extra Fancy" and the second grade is "U.S. Fancy." In Washington state, it is "Washington Extra Fancy" and then "Washington Fancy." "U.S. Fancy" is the top grade for corn, grapefruit, and oranges, but it is "U.S. Extra No. 1" for lima beans and "U.S. No. 1" for turnips. It is more confusing for other produce.

Why can't government decide on a scale of "A, B, C, D, F" or "1, 2, 3, 4, 5," assuming that consumers would understand that "A" and "1" would be the highest? Also, why can't such systems be mandatory instead of voluntary for fruits and vegetables, beef, poultry, eggs, cheeses, canned fruits, and other food products?

CONSUMER UPDATE:
Consumer Responsibilities in the Food Marketplace

The food economic marketplace in America is complex. Thousands of product choices are available. Most of what consumers eat is heavily processed and then thoroughly packaged. As a consequence, consumers must trust industry and government to look out for their interests concerning the safety, cleanliness, and wholesomeness of the food supply.

Consumers, too, must accept significant responsibilities. Consumers should read product labels carefully, follow directions, learn more about how to obtain daily nutritional requirements, examine food carefully for cleanliness, assume proper precautions when storing and preparing food, heed warnings, inform sellers when food products are not satisfactory, seek out useful information about food, speak up when errors occur and when the quality of products or services is inferior, seek to redress wrongs and assert their consumer rights, encourage the government to improve food regulations, and become better informed about how to get their money's worth in the food marketplace.

Review and Summary of Key Terms and Concepts

1. Distinguish between **malnourishment** and **obesity**.

2. Summarize the intake of **calories** for most Americans.

3. Why do children eat so many **junk foods**?

4. Summarize the relationship between **disease** and **diet**.

5. Why do some **poor Americans pay more** for food than middle-income people?

6. Put into lay words a description of the **blood cholesterol problem**.

7. What should a person **eat less of for better nutrition**?

8. List two things that the **Nutrition Labeling and Education Act** is to accomplish.

9. What are **daily values (DVs)**?

10. Summarize the essence of the **USDA's Food Guide Pyramid**.

11. Briefly identify two **questionable food selling practices** that occur in the marketplace.

12. Distinguish between **calendar marketing agreements** and **allocation agreements**.

13. Define the following terms: **adulterated** and **misbranded**.

14. Distinguish between: **recall** and **seizure**.

15. Why has the FDA decided to approve **food biotechnology products**?

16. What is the essence of the FDA's new **seafood inspection program**?

17. Define **food additive**, and give an example of an **intentional additive** and an **incidental additive**.

18. Distinguish between **action levels** and **food filth tolerances**.

19. Why was the **generally recognized as safe (GRAS) list** ever created?

20. Summarize the argument of **negligible risk** versus **zero-risk**.

21. What would it take to have a completely **risk-free society**?

22. Choose two examples of **how consumers get confused when food shopping** that negatively affect consumers, and explain each.

Useful Resources for Consumers

Center for Science in the Public Interest
1875 Connecticut Avenue, NW, Suite 300
Washington, DC 20009-5728
202-332-9110

Community Nutrition Institute
910 17th Street, NW, Suite 413
Washington, DC 20006
202-776-0595

FDA's Seafood Hotline
800-332-4010

Public Voice for Food and Health Policy
1101 14th Street, NW, Suite 710
Washington, DC 20005
202-371-1840

USDA's Meat and Poultry Hotline
800-535-4555
Updated news about food safety

"What Do You Think" Questions

1. Look at Figure 14-2, and after reviewing the detail of the **Nutrition Labeling and Education Act**, write two paragraphs summarizing what the new law is expected to accomplish.

2. From your life experiences, which three **questionable food selling practices** have you seen? Describe the circumstances of those situations, and what you did about them at the time.

3. What do you think the government ought to do about the number of **anti-competitive practices** in the food industry? Why?

4. Describe your reactions to the text topic, **"Does Everything Cause Cancer?"**

Chapter 15

Health Care Issues

OBJECTIVES

After reading this chapter, you should be able to

1. Recognize the challenges consumers have when purchasing health care services.

2. List some guidelines on how to purchase health care services.

3. Identify what is wrong with the U.S. health care system.

4. Understand how health care reform has begun, is spreading, and why it must continue.

5. Explain how prescription and over-the-counter drugs are developed, approved, and marketed to American consumers.

6. Understand the dangers of smoking to individuals and society.

7. Recognize some of the social costs and benefits of consuming alcohol.

Unquestionably your health is your most important asset. Americans today are leading healthier lives than years ago, they live longer than ever, and yet many say they are feeling worse than ever. Americans are increasingly conscious of health care and are showing growing interest in the concepts of preventive care, wellness, and self-care. At the same time, our expectations for good professional health care keep rising. Consumers want and need reliable information on the price and quality of health care; they want to be able to evaluate and compare available products and services. More than ever before, consumers are actively involved in the health care consumption process, rather than remaining passive recipients of therapy. Most Americans want some form of national health reform, too.

This chapter begins with a review of the challenges of purchasing health care services, one of the most complicated and confusing areas of consumer consumption. Following are guidelines on how to purchase services. Next is a section examining what is wrong with today's U.S. health care system followed by a discussion of the calls to reform it. Another section discusses purchasing prescription and over-the-counter drugs. The chapter closes with an examination of the effects of tobacco and alcohol on individuals and society.

The Challenges of Purchasing Health Care Services

Planned buying has to do with rationally defining the problem, identifying values and goals, identifying alternatives, comparing costs and benefits, negotiating, selecting the best alternative, and accepting and evaluating the final action. This approach works well when one is buying products or services, but it is more difficult with services. Buying consumer health care services is especially demanding.

Consumer health deals with the decisions consumers make with regard to the purchase and use of available health products and services. Sometimes decisions must be made in a hurry because of emergency situations. Health information is often confusing and complex, and redress mechanisms are inefficient. This causes many transactions to be based on presumed confidence in sellers instead of proven competence. Another difficulty lies in the fact that many health problems are private and personal, resulting in a human tendency not to want to discuss such matters.

CONSUMER UPDATE:
Fewer Americans Concerned About Being Fit and Healthy

Over the past five years, Americans have changed their views on being healthy. Yankelovich's latest Annual Lifestyle Survey revealed that 53 percent of Americans were not concerned about watching their weight (up from 49 percent), only 30 percent strongly committed to maintaining fitness (down from 42 percent), and 30 percent reporting that they smoke (up from 25 percent).

Buying health services is confusing because: (1) there are so many providers of similar health services (even though there may be few actual choices), (2) price information is not standardized and sometimes is difficult to obtain, and (3) it is hard to determine reliability. Throughout the health care field there is an historical American tradition of keeping consumers uninformed about the process.

Untrained medical swindlers and unscrupulous individuals without adequate training, or **quacks,** also exist in the health field. Quacks typically warn of the dangers of conventional treatments, use testimonials, promote secret cures, and claim persecution by the established medical community. A consumer organization concerned about quacks is the National Council Against Health Fraud.

Health information is complex because scientific evidence is technical and not always clear to unsophisticated consumers. Also, few mechanisms exist that provide information for a fair comparison of health providers. When consumers experience problems with health care services, they have to use nontraditional forms of redress, such as complaining to a county medical board or hospital self-regulatory organization. This results in many complaints, especially small ones, never being resolved, while a number of big grievances are settled with expensive lawsuits. The challenges of buying all types of services include finding quality information, finding price information, making choices when few exist, and obtaining redress through unfamiliar sources.

DID YOU KNOW? Life Expectancies in Years*

Women

Japan	82.5
France	81.3
Switzerland	81.3
Netherlands	80.5
Sweden	80.4
United States	78.6

Men

Japan	76.2
France	74.3
Switzerland	74.2
Netherlands	74.1
Sweden	73.8
United States	71.6

*Source: World Health Organization

Guidelines on How to Purchase Services

Nearly half of all consumer expenditures are for services, as opposed to products. A **service** is work or an action performed at the request of a consumer. In every instance, what consumers are buying from service providers is performance. It is difficult for consumers to learn enough about each of these individual services (and dozens of others), and then recall meaningful evaluative comments when necessary. Some guidelines on how to purchase services are offered here.[1]

1. Learn about the service area of interest. It is foolish for consumers to remain ignorant about a service area when considering spending $20 or $2000, and perhaps enduring health risks in the process. Consumers need to systematically seek and use relevant facts and other information about a service area when it is going to be needed. A good place to start is to talk with friends and acquaintances and those who work in particular service areas. Magazines in the library are another good source. Reading about the service topic, including health problems, permits you to ask questions and help the provider get good feedback from you.

2. Check for registration, certification, and licensure. There are more than 1500 state boards and commissions that license or register professions and occupations. **Registration** is the formal recording of names suggesting that a person in a particular profession or occupation is qualified to perform certain tasks because he or she meets minimum established standards. Registration may be through a voluntary membership association or through state and local governments. Government registration generally requires only that a person inform the agency that they wish to practice the profession. Registered occupations are rarely restricted to any significant extent. Television and automobile repair shops are examples of registered occupations.

Certification is a formal confirmation that something is true, accurate, or genuine, especially as in having met a particular standard. Certification of occupations asserts positive assurances about the qualification of those people to perform certain tasks. It usually includes a document testifying to the facts or truth of something. People often receive certificates when they complete a course of study not leading to a diploma. Both private organizations and government regulatory agencies which offer certification either: (1) examine the credentials of individuals wanting to practice an occupation, or (2) give them an examination. Examples include: accountants, nurses, nutritionists, financial counselors, and physical therapists. However, anyone who wants to can practice these occupations without certification. Consumers can purchase services from certified practitioners or from those who generally charge lower prices and are not certified.

Licensure is an official recording of names by a state board, commission, or other government agency that provides legal permission or authorization to do a specific thing, such as practice a particular profession or occupation. The applicant either presents appropriate credentials or takes an examination. This is the most restrictive form of occupational regulation, and non-licensed people may not practice these occupations. Examples include: physicians, lawyers, cosmetologists, barbers, and dry cleaners.

These are all indicators of a person's qualifications to provide quality services, and they are not mutually exclusive. People in some occupations choose to be registered, certified, and licensed. Many also hold memberships in appropriate professional organizations. For example, when comparison shopping for a physician to perform knee surgery, consumers may prefer to select a surgeon who is board-certified in his or her specialty. Standards for registration, certification, and licensing vary widely, so consumers must seek answers related to what groups are doing the certifying and what standards are being met. Be aware that **grandfathering** also occurs in most occupational regulation.

---

[1]Adapted from Heinzerling, B. & Barsness, A. (1985). The Consumption of Services: A Proposed Framework. In Lawrence, F. C. (Ed.), *Proceedings of the Annual Conference for Family Economics and Home Management* (pp. 81-83). Baton Rouge, LA: Louisiana State University. Reprinted with permission.

This is a practice which permits current, and usually older, practitioners to be registered, certified, or licensed without being examined for competence.

3. Identify consumer problems unique to the service area. When learning about a service area, determine the consumer problems that are unique to purchasing those services. For example, when comparison shopping for a physician to perform cosmetic surgery, consumers should learn about the dangers of anesthesia, alternative surgical techniques being utilized, and the types of post-operative swelling problems that typically occur. Asking the physician about consumer problems is helpful, but it is not enough. Responsible consumers seek out and utilize a variety of sources to identify problems unique to a service area.

4. Inquire about complaint procedures. Consumers thinking about purchasing in a service area should find out the levels and channels appropriate for complaining should it become necessary. Service providers themselves should be happy to discuss complaint procedures in their profession or occupation, although some are overly sensitive to the topic. While learning about complaint procedures, consumers can also learn about problems unique to each service and what standards are met in the profession or occupation.

5. Develop a short list of criteria that are most important to you. Comparing performance in service areas is difficult. To help in the selection process, consumers are advised to list and rank two or three criteria they feel are most important. Then base a service selection decision primarily on only those factors.

What Is Wrong with the U.S. Health Care System

The U.S. health care system is in a state of great disrepair, however, the national government has been unable to seriously address any of its problems. President Bill Clinton's proposal for **universal health insurance** put the issue on the national agenda for discussion, but the supporters of the status quo—who continue to profit from today's system—killed all efforts at reform. Since state governments face a similar health care crisis, a number have provided leadership in legislating change.

Health Care Costs in the U.S. Are the Highest in the World

Health care consumes 1 of every 7 dollars of the nation's goods and services. Total health care spending in 1980 was $250 billion; this year it is expected to be over $1 trillion. Health care is a major expense of governments, businesses, and consumers. Today Americans spend nearly 15 percent of the nation's gross domestic product (GDP) on health care. This is projected to rise to 18 percent by the year 2000.[2] No other industrialized country spends more than ten percent; Canada, France, and Germany are under 9 percent, while Japan and Britain are under 7 percent.

Per capita spending on health care is approximately $3,000 in the U.S., $2,000 in Canada, $1,700 in Germany and France, $1,300 in Japan, and $1,100 in Great Britain, reports the Organization for Economic Cooperation and Development. Thus, health care

---

[2]In 1960, health care consumed 5 percent of the gross domestic product of the United States.

spending by an American family of four equals $12,000 each year. Twenty cents of every dollar of federal spending is for health care. Health care costs in the United States have been going up very rapidly in the last decade, at least twice the general inflation rate.

Health care for certain groups is much more expensive than for others. For example, a recent report in *Health Affairs* revealed that, "The healthiest 50 percent of Americans account for only 3 percent of annual health costs." Further, "the sickest 10 percent account for 72 percent of costs." Former U.S. Surgeon General Joycelyn Elders observes that 90 percent of medical care spending occurs during the last three months of life.

Such ruinous spending can bankrupt the country and its citizens. Such expenditures also severely strain the abilities of governments and consumers to make choices among competing budget alternatives. Rising expenditures on health care prevent increased government spending, for example, on education, housing, job training, and police protection. Rising health insurance premiums similarly depress workers' take-home pay.[3]

One-Quarter of Americans Are Without Health Insurance

Capitalism is the main reason why we have the most advanced care in the world. However, basic health care does not reach all the people in the capitalistic United States. Last year there were 157 million people with private health coverage. Meanwhile, over 42 million Americans were without health insurance—almost all are the poor, near-poor, and the working poor. This amounts to 17.4 percent of the non-elderly population. The uninsured are left to their own devices, or to chance or to charity. Another 19 million Americans were without health coverage during some part of last year because about 2 million Americans lose their health insurance every month[4] or become underinsured because they cannot afford to pay the premiums.

More than half of the uninsured live in homes where the head of the household has a full-time job. More than half are over age 24, and 22 percent are children. Seven in 10 have incomes above the poverty line; half are in families earning more than $20,000 annually. They lacked coverage because: (1) it was not offered by their employers,[5] (2) they could not afford to pay high health insurance premiums (individual policies cost about twice what group policies, offered through employers, charge), and (3) they were dropped by their insurers because of certain illnesses or because of old age.[6]

---

[3]The Labor Department reports that the average hourly wages for non-supervisory positions are 46 cents lower than what wages would be without the rising health care costs paid by employers. Thus, the average family lost about $900 in wages last year because health premiums rose more rapidly than the overall economy. Moreover, actual wages would be higher in the absence of rapidly rising health care costs.

[4]A nationwide survey in 1994 by A. Foster Higgins & Company shows that most companies cut employees off from health insurance coverage as soon as they retire; those that continue coverage shift most of the cost onto the retirees.

[5]Only 40 percent of firms with fewer than 25 employees offer their workers health insurance.

[6]A study by the National Institutes of Health reveals an eight-year gap between the life expectancy of the poorest and the richest white males in the U.S.; the gap among females was four years.

We Already Pay—Through Hidden and Real Taxes—the Health Care Costs of the Uninsured

Uninsured people actually do get a certain amount of medical care, but primarily through hospital emergency rooms.[7] Americans are already paying the high medical costs for those who do not have health insurance because such expenses are passed onto patients already insured. This is cost-shifting. Health insurers raise the premiums about an extra 25 percent to cover the cost of care to the uninsured—and those costs are among the highest provided, since most is given in emergency situations. (You didn't think those doctors and nurses at community hospitals worked for free, did you?) Thus, we pay what is in effect a hidden tax—especially on young people because they generally are quite healthy—to care for the uninsured.[8] This experience of the population violates a key principle of any insurance plan: The great majority of people in a plan must be healthy to cover the small number of those who are unhealthy. Plus, a full 20 percent of everyone's federal and state income taxes goes for various public health services, such as Medicare (covering most of the elderly) and Medicaid (covering 37 million people).

Calls to Reform the U.S. Health Care System

Every president of the United States since Franklin Roosevelt—both Democrats and Republicans—have proposed major health care reform for the nation. All have failed.

Why National Health Care Reform Failed

Numerous incentives exist for the special-interest groups to protect the status quo. The major special-interest groups involved in health care include: doctors, hospitals, insurance companies, drug companies, big business, small business, and labor. Those providing care are motivated to spend more, not less, on health care. This conflicts with an almost unlimited demand for services from consumers. Employers—who receive tax subsidies to provide workers with health insurance—have dealt with the rising cost problem by transferring increases in health premiums to employees, providing coverage using a managed care program (discussed below), and reducing benefits to retirees. A number of additional reasons for failure are listed in the feature titled "The Medical Care Market Has Characteristics That Make It Difficult to Reform." The ills of today's political system

---

[7]The National Center for Health Statistics study reveals that the top reasons patients give for an emergency room visit are in descending order: stomach pain and cramps, chest pain, fever, headaches, cuts on the upper body, shortness of breath, coughing, back problems, throat problems, and vomiting. The number one diagnosis by emergency room physicians is ear infection.

[8]Bureau of Labor Statistics data reveal that spending on health care by age group is: people under age 25: 2.0%; age 25-34: 3.9%; age 35-44: 4.5%; age 45-54: 4.4%; age 55-64: 6.6%; age 65-74: 11.0%; and age 75+: 15.7%.

were revealed when Congress could not even bring a health care bill to the floors of the House and Senate for debate.[9]

Congressional failure to seriously consider health care reform[10] only postpones the inevitable head-on collision with the younger generation who one day will wake up to discover that (1) 22, 25 or 30 percent of all wealth in America is going to status-quo profiteers, (2) 90 percent of the money will be spent on behalf of recipients over age 60, and (3) many millions of Americans without health insurance will continue to overtax the economics of the health care system. At that time, the economic costs will be even more difficult to turn around than now (if that is even imaginable!).

Calls to Reform Health Care Are Answered by Some States

The ways in which health-care costs can be reduced are: (1) requiring consumers to pay more, (2) reducing unnecessary surgery and procedures, as well as wasteful practices and fraud, (3) cutting payments to hospitals, doctors and other providers, and (4) delivering care more efficiently. Other factors that drive up health costs are personal indulgences in unhealthy behaviors—which are avoidable—such as smoking, being overweight, alcohol and drug abuse, driving without seat belts, and unsafe sex.[11] These are **lifestyle risk factors**.

Reform without effective cost containment assures the continued failure of the U.S. system of health care. Some medical procedures have to be considered optional, such as infertility services, traumatic brain injuries, acute cirrhosis of liver transplants, and some types of cosmetic surgeries. This is a form of **rationing**, a system that prioritizes the types of medical services covered.[12] With rationing, those who want optional services will have to pay out-of-pocket money for them.

Piecemeal solutions will result in few changes that will not go far enough to reverse the systemic problems and wrong-headed incentives in the health-care system. To develop a better health care system for all Americans requires a willingness to make sacrifices, on the part of all special-interest groups, that so far has been lacking. Moving towards genuine reform will be difficult for all. Economist Robert J. Samuelson observes that, "All our goals can't be met. No health plan can be perfect. All need to be judged against the alternatives, including doing nothing."[13]

---

[9]An insightful analysis of the failure to reform health care can be found in *The System: The American Way of Politics at the Breaking Point* (1996; Little, Brown), by Haynes Johnson and David S. Broder.

[10]The Kennedy-Kassebaum bill provides for **portability** of health insurance which means that one could take an existing polity from one employer to another with insurers being prohibited from basing premiums on medical history or pre-existing conditions. This will actually worsen the national health care crisis because those who will use portability mainly will be consumers who are not well or have potentially serious health problems who without portability would not have the financing to spend thousands of dollars. Thus, the aggregate national cost will rise. Such feel-good fake reform from politicians is shameful.

[11]The U.S. Public Health Service says that, "Approximately 50 percent of the deaths in people under 75 are due to personal behaviors which can be modified."

[12]Rationing already exists in today's health care system—if you do not have health insurance or money, you do not get health care. States that have adopted health-care reforms, particularly for Medicaid recipients, such as Oregon and Tennessee, have established rationing systems.

[13]Samuelson, R. J. (1994, February 2). The Dishonest (and Nasty) Health Care Debate. *The Washington Post*, p. A-19.

The Medical Care Market Has Characteristics That Make It Difficult to Reform*

The unique nature of the medical care market is recognized by health economists because a basic principle of economic theory—supply and demand—historically has not worked in health care. In most commodity markets, prices tend to fall as supply increases and some high-cost firms will be forced out of business. In contrast, an excess supply of medical professionals, hospital beds, and high-tech equipment tend not to affect the prices of medical care; the charges and fees remain high.

Economic theory also assumes an independence between demand and supply. In the medical care market, however, the demand can be created by providers. Studies have found that physicians can boost consumer demand for their services.

The distinctive characteristics of the medical care market—including an almost insatiable demand—are as follows:

1. The demand for medical services has considerable uncertainty. It is possible to predict the rate of illness for a population based on past experiences and scientific data, but, except for hereditary disease, illness is not predictable for an individual.

2. Consumers think they have a "right" to good health care, including the newest medical technologies.

3. Many health care providers focus on the welfare of individuals, rather than on keeping the cost of services in check. Most physicians and many non-profit providers have the same anti-profit perspective. Society expects physicians to treat illness of consumers at almost any cost.

4. Financing mechanisms, such as insurance, provide enormous ability to buy medical care. These include Medicare and Medicaid (federal programs for the elderly and poor, respectively), and private health insurance. Since insurance lowers the out-of-pocket cost for medical care to individual consumers, this may result in a moral hazard where consumers utilize more medical services than if they had to pay the entire price themselves.

5. Third-party control over payment is unique in medical care market. Until recent years, insurance companies simply paid charges from providers without questioning the cost or the quality.

6. An aging population consumes four times as much health care as the rest of the population.

7. Prices are kept high because entry to the medical profession is restricted. There are three entry barriers in the physician's market: graduation from an approved medical school, licensure, and continual training.

8. Physicians keep prices high by restricting price competition because they rarely cut prices.

9. Uncertainty in product quality is a serious problem in purchasing medical care products. Consumers in the medical care market tend to be poorly informed about the products. Many consumers are not able to evaluate the quality of services because of its scientific language or complexity. Thus, the information and knowledge gap between providers and consumers in the medical care market leads to poor decision making on the part of consumers.

10. Health care has positive external benefits. Externalities occur when actions of one individual in a market affects the welfare of others. In the case of communicable disease, for example, provision of a preventive or curative care to an individual yields a benefit beyond the prevention or cures of the illness itself. Moreover, when a sizable proportion of a population is immunized to a disease, the risk of infection for other people is reduced. The impact of a broken chain of infection on the health of the general population is manifold: the number of infected people will be fewer, public health care expenditures on the disease will be saved, and community well-being will be improved.

These unique characteristics distinguish the medical care markets from other commodity markets. Its complexity and uniqueness have contributed to the current national health care crisis. Many aspects of the health care market need change to better serve consumers and society.

*Gong-Soog Hong, Assistant Professor, Purdue University

A number of states have accepted the challenge of health care reform—primarily because of the run-a-way costs of the federally mandated Medicaid program for the poor—and approved radically new approaches. Examples include Florida, Maryland, Massachusetts, Minnesota, Oregon, Tennessee, and Washington.[14] Formulated and put together in only a few months, Tennessee's new "TeenCare" near-universal managed care program is getting good reviews from its users, former Medicaid patients and the uninsured.[15] Every managed care operation gets a fixed amount of money ($1416) per person-patient per year.

Those Who *Have* Health Care Coverage Utilize Managed Care and Managed Competition

The term **managed care** refers to health-care organizations, such as health maintenance organizations (HMOs) and Preferred Provider Organizations (PPOs). They seek to control costs largely by coordinating care through a primary-care generalist and by carefully assessing the necessity for health care. This is accomplished in several ways: closely monitoring how physicians treat specific illnesses; insisting upon appropriate, rather than expensive, medical care; limiting referrals to costly specialists; and requiring pre-authorization for hospital care.

Seventy percent of the people with health insurance are *already* being served by the managed care of a HMO or a PPO; four years ago it was 30 percent. Americans are witnessing a transformation of health care from a professional calling to a business. The mythical family physician has been largely replaced by employees of large health enterprises. The managed care transformation revolution—with its aims to cut costs, to ensure quality control, and to demand efficiency—will continue whether or not the role of government increases. The managed care system is rapidly replacing the traditional **fee-for-service** medical system where individuals saw any doctor and used any hospital, paying only a deductible and a co-payment with the insurer paying the rest. Managed care plans do allow patients to go outside the network of approved doctors if they pay more.

Health Maintenance Organizations Provide Managed Care

Health maintenance organizations (HMOs) are organizations that offer health and treatment services to their members using a philosophy of preventive medicine from a medical team for a specified prepayment fee. Unlike the fee-for-service approach of traditional private health care in America, HMO members pay a flat monthly fee, called a premium. Then almost all medical costs are paid for in advance regardless of the amount of use. Patients go to health care providers on an approved list. Referrals are controlled by a **primary care physician (PCP)**, who gives routine care and limits patients' access to specialists and often can only refer patients to certain specialists; he or she is a gatekeeper or care manager. Policyholders pay either nothing or very small co-payments for the services. When a policyholder chooses to go to a non-HMO health professional, any extra charges must be paid by the user.

---

[14]Hawaii has had universal coverage for all state citizens since 1974.

[15]Brown, D. (1996, June 9), Struggling to stem Medicaid deluge, open bigger umbrella, *The Washington Post*, A-1+.

CONSUMER UPDATE:
Questions to Ask Your HMO

To stand up for your rights, here are some questions you might want to ask your health maintenance organization:

1. Are financial incentives offered to physicians that might discourage them from referring patients to specialists?
2. What conditions and notification requirements are serious enough to warrant hospitalization?
3. Under what conditions will the plan not pay for a hospital bill?
4. Are there limits on how much a covered person can spend on prescription drugs annually?
5. How much are the co-payments for drug refills?
6. Does the plan cover expensive medical equipment, such as wheelchairs?
7. Does the plan cover oral surgery?
8. Does the plan cover cosmetic surgery?

The theory of HMOs is that consumers are likely to visit their physicians more frequently so that early detection and treatment of illnesses can occur. This allows people to remain healthier and avoid hospitalization, most often with the result of lower overall costs. Doctors are usually paid a salary instead of earning a fee for each patient visit. HMOs try to reduce inefficient practices, such as ordering more tests than necessary, sending patients to the hospital for tests that could have been conducted in the physician's office, and keeping patients in hospitals longer than necessary.

HMOs usually offer a full range of medical services. Regular examinations are encouraged to keep members healthy. Members of HMOs are assigned a primary care physician who becomes responsible for the patient's total care. Cost containment procedures of managed care plans means that you have to talk with your primary-care physician to obtain permission to see specialists or go to a hospital (except on an emergency basis). Your doctor or you occasionally must get approvals for medical care from outside reviewers, using 800-telephone numbers; denials occur too.

HMOs are not a new concept; the Kaiser-Permanente HMO in California was started in 1933. HMOs got a boost with the passage of the Health Maintenance Act of 1973. It requires that employers with 25 or more workers who offer a traditional health insurance plan as a fringe benefit must allow workers to join an HMO if there is a qualified plan located nearby. The monthly HMO premium is usually a little higher than that for traditional health insurance plans, but it covers almost all medical expenses.

Managed Competition Also Is Present Today

Managed competition is a system that permits customers (consumers, employers, and governments) to purchase health insurance from large, pre-approved, managed-care networks that compete for customers in given geographic regions. Capitalism provides the current form of managed competition in health care because large buyers of such services—mostly employers with large numbers of employees—increasingly are getting competitive bids for health care services from various providers.

One of the downsides of managed competition is the urge of the new breed of health care providers "to profit," therefore, many are engaged in **alarmist advertising** to generate dollars for optional, non-emergency services. These are media ads designed to purposefully create consumer anxiety so that people will want various medical services. Illustrations include: (1) as a small boy tugs at his father's pantleg, "Go ahead, ignore your chest pain. What have you got to lose?"; (2) as a woman gives herself a breast exam, "This woman just missed the cancer that will kill her."; and (3) "If you don't have a mammogram by age 40, you're at risk for cancer."[16] As if the system is not overburdened with excessive demand already!

Prescription Drugs

A key element of the health care industry is the purchase of medicines. The Food and Drug Administration (FDA) is responsible for ensuring the safety and effectiveness of both prescription and over-the-counter drugs. Its authorities include the Food, Drug and Cosmetic Act of 1938 (which supersedes the 1906 Food and Drug Act) and the Kefauver-Harris Drug Amendments of 1962. The FDA regulates over 300,000 drugs produced by over 3000 firms. As a regulatory agency, the FDA is limited in what it can do to safeguard the public good. The FDA cannot order a recall of products, so they must negotiate with sellers instead. The FDA can seize misbranded or adulterated products.

What Are Drugs?

A **drug** is defined by the FDA as a product intended to affect the structure or function of the human body or to treat, prevent, or ameliorate a disease. Drugs must: (1) be tested for safety and effectiveness before being marketed, (2) be labeled with its purpose, directions for use, warnings, active ingredients, and expiration date, (3) be made by a registered manufacturer who must be responsible to the FDA, and (4) meet established standards for purity, quality, potency, and dissolvability.

The ethical drug industry sells both prescription and over-the-counter drugs. A **prescription** is a written instruction usually from a physician for the preparation and administration of a drug. **Prescription drugs** are prepared and/or sold by **registered pharmacists**, who are persons trained in pharmacy and registered with a state government to sell such products. Prescription drugs are sold to consumers by pharmacists in retail drug stores and through mail-order facilities, the latter making up over 10 percent of the total U.S. prescription drug market, primarily because of low prices. **Over-the-counter drugs (OTC)** are less powerful medicines capable of being sold legally without a prescription in places such as supermarkets, discount stores, pharmacies, airports, convenience stores, and vending machines. The FDA requires that OTC drugs be generally recognized by experts as being safe and effective.

---

[16]The average American faces a one in four lifetime risk of getting cancer, reports the Environmental Working Group, a non-profit organization.

CONSUMER UPDATE:
Prescription Drugs Cost More in the United States

All industrialized countries in the world except the United States have some form of price regulations on prescription drugs. Prescription drug prices in the United States cost more than prices in Great Britain, according to a study reported last year by the U.S. General Accounting Office for the Senate Special Committee on Aging. In Great Britain, of 77 frequently prescribed drugs, 66 cost more in the U.S.; 47 cost more than twice as much.

In Canada, the provinces use their massive buying power and regulations to keep drug prices down. Canadians pay only 62 percent as much as U.S. consumers for the same drugs. Canada's review board tries to ensure that drug prices "are not excessive."

Profits from prescription drugs are used to finance research that benefits everyone. U.S. Drug companies spend more on marketing and advertising ($11.3 billion) than on research and development ($10.3 billion). Between 1985 and 1991, consumer prices in general rose 26 percent while prescription drug prices jumped 67 percent. Critics want a better accounting of costs to justify such prices.

Drug companies respond that development of prescription drugs is expensive, risky, and marketing often require one-on-one sales presentations. Because of patent laws, the companies have only 10 to 15 years to recoup research expenses. Thus, they market aggressively. The ethical drug industry has grown because of innovative basic research; companies say they need high markups to maintain research efforts.

Premarket Review of Prescription Drugs

The FDA requires probably the most rigorous **premarket review** and clearance of prescription drugs in the world. It is designed to ensure the safety and efficacy of drugs for human use. Prescription drug products may not be sold until approved by the FDA as safe and effective, which must be proven by substantial evidence conducted in well-controlled clinical investigations. The aim of the FDA's new drug application premarket clearance process, which averages six to seven years (but can go up to twelve years), is to prevent the marketing of unsafe drugs, rather than removing such products from the market after they have been found to be unsafe. Two in ten finally get to market.

There are two reasons for pretesting drugs: (1) to prevent injuries and deaths, and (2) to prevent people from using fraudulent drugs that will not help them. American drug policy is aimed at preventing people from using medications that will do them no good when they could be using approved drugs that might help.

When a new drug is discovered, the manufacturer obtains a **patent**, which is a grant by the government assuring the inventor of the sole right to make, use, and sell the product for a certain time period, usually 17 years. Several clinical tests follow. The manufacturer conducts animal tests, and later human tests, and submits the results to the FDA along with the results of all other studies associated with the drug, including tests run by other companies and in other countries. The FDA does no testing of its own.

When the FDA, with the help of its scientific advisory committees, is convinced of the safety of a new drug, the drug is approved. The FDA cautiously makes its decision by balancing the scientific and social benefits and risks of a new drug.

If a drug is later deemed questionable in effectiveness, FDA procedures call for the drug company to provide further information, during which time the manufacturer is still allowed to market the product. Then, if the drug is still deemed questionable, the FDA begins withdrawal procedures. Prescription drugs recently removed from the market, under FDA pressure, include Zomax and Nomifensine. If a drug is later found to be unsafe, the FDA can ban it by showing it to be an imminent hazard, a power previously used only once.

The FDA now has procedures—called **expedited process**—to permit faster evaluation of drugs to treat life-threatening illnesses, such as cancer and acquired immunity deficiency syndrome (AIDS). For example, final approval of the AIDS drug AZT was given in 32 months. Some are alarmed with the speeded-up process because they remember that it was the conservative FDA that kept the baby-deforming sedative thalidomide off the U.S. market in the 1960s.[17]

A drug approved by the FDA for one use is not necessarily safe or effective for other uses. Once a drug is on sale, a physician generally may prescribe it in any dosage and for any purpose whether or not that purpose has been scientifically evaluated. Some recent examples: (1) Retin-A, approved for severe acne, has not been approved for facial wrinkles; (2) collagen cannot be promoted to enlarge the lips; and (3) silicone cannot be used in injectable form. Many patients who have used drugs inappropriately have suffered. Most physicians prescribe drugs according to FDA guidelines.

Generic Drugs

A **generic drug** is a copycat version of an expensive brand name prescription drug that has come to the market because the brand name product's patent protection expired. Generic drugs are sometimes called **no-name drugs** or **substitution drugs** because they do not have a trademark or trade name. When a new drug is patented, it is given a generic name that usually is descriptive of its chemical composition. However, the manufacturer sells the drug under its brand name or trade name. The brand name of a drug is typically something shorter, easier to pronounce, uncomplicated for physicians to remember, and more marketable. For example, Lomotil is the trade name for a popular drug used to help control diarrhea; it is also sold by other manufacturers under the generic name diphenoxylate hydrochloride with atropine sulfate. The brand names of drugs are used to promote drugs to physicians, and sometimes to the general public.

Generic drugs can be sold after a manufacturer's patent expires, usually 20 years after a patent is first granted. Any company, including the original maker, that meets the standards of the FDA can manufacture generics. Such drugs must meet similar standards for strength, purity, effectiveness, and safety. All manufacturers must comply with the FDA's Good Manufacturing Practices (GMPS) and follow their Standard Operating Procedures. To gain approval for a generic drug, firms are required to submit test data to show that a sample batch is equivalent to the brand name drug being copied. Other than conducting a single human study with 20 to 24 people to ensure that the generic and the brand name drugs are absorbed into the bloodstream at about the same rate, the new maker of the drug does not have to carry out clinical studies to establish safety and efficacy for drugs.

---

[17]Thalidomide is illegally used in Brazil to treat leprosy as up to 500,000 Brazilians have what is also known as Hansen's Disease. Produced domestically, the drug is creating a new generation of deformed infants, with upwards of 30 thalidomide-caused deformed children so far. Thalidomide shows promise for treating cancer, rheumatoid arthritis, multiple sclerosis, and in some forms of blindness. Thalidomide is generally considered to be a safe drug, however, it should never be used by pregnant women.

Generic drugs received a boost with the 1984 passage of the Drug Price Competition and Patent Term Restoration Act. This law allows the FDA to approve generic versions of pioneer or brand name drug products already found to be safe and effective by the FDA. Generic drugs account for more than forty percent of all prescriptions. A federal law requires that pharmacists offer Medicaid patients counseling when they pick up a prescription. They are to explain drug interactions, side effects, and proper storing procedures. Most states require druggists to advise all consumers.

Some researchers argue that the equivalency of generic and brand name drugs is not precisely the same because the base or filler ingredients (ingredients other than the active ingredients in the drug itself) vary by product. The amount of drug that gets into the bloodstream can vary between brand name and generic drugs because: (1) it depends on where and how rapidly the pill disintegrates, which then permits the active ingredient to dissolve; (2) absorption into the bloodstream can happen no faster than the ingredient dissolves; and (3) some of the active ingredient may be excreted before it can get into the bloodstream. The FDA permits generic products to be therapeutically equivalent when they have a **bioavailability**, the rate and extent that a drug is absorbed, of no more than plus or minus 20 percent; the average difference is only 3.5 percent.

The FDA tests all generic and brand name drugs for purity and strength. The FDA believes that the over 2000 generic drugs are therapeutically equivalent to brand name drugs of the same strength and dosage form. Details are listed in the *United States Pharmacopeia (USP)*, which is a book published by a nonprofit organization of the same name that sets minimum quality standards that must be met by all drugs marketed in the United States. Drugs that do not meet the standards are subject to seizure by the FDA.

The former head of Bolar Pharmaceutical Company was recently sentenced to five years in prison and fined $1.25 million. This was the result of a four-year scandal in the generic-drug industry. A number of generic-drug pharmaceutical manufacturers (those who pride themselves as being pro-consumer alternatives to the brand name drug companies) bribed FDA officials, cheated on safety tests in order to win approval for their products, falsified production records, and sold drugs different from those accepted by federal regulators. After 11 companies were charged, more than 100 generic drugs were pulled off pharmacy shelves. Then the FDA began extensive safety tests of the 30 top-selling generic drugs. Still, most experts agree with pharmacologist Joe Graedon, author of the *People's Pharmacy*, that overall, generics still appear safe and effective, and represent an extraordinary price savings.[18]

Contrasted with brand name drugs, generic drugs generally cost 20 to 80 percent less. These discounts, which average 30 percent, occur because the generic manufacturers do not have the heavy marketing costs associated with the brand name. About half the most popularly prescribed drugs have generic equivalents available. Illustrative mail-order and retail price differences for packages of 100 pills are shown in Table 15-1.

Generic Substitution Laws

Recognizing the equivalency of brand name and generic drugs, most states have passed laws permitting generic substitutions. The most common approach is permissive as the law allows pharmacists to substitute a generic equivalent for a brand name

---

[18]Silberner, J. (1989, September 18). Why Generic Drugs Are O.K. *U.S. News & World Report*, pp. 21-22.

Source	Zantac 150 mg. For ulcers	Ibuprofen 600 mg. Pain reliever	Prozac 20 mg. Antidepressant
Metropolitan Retail Pharmacy	$187.57	$15.85	$242.69
American Association of Retired Persons (mail)	127.67	11.61	172.73
Action Mail Order	127.19	7.41	153.05
Medi-Mail	138.81	7.37	182.27
Pharmail	187.57	15.85	242.69

TABLE 15-1   Illustrative Mail Order and Retail Prices for 100 Pills

prescription unless the prescribing physician objects. More than one-third of the states have a mandatory substitution law that requires pharmacists to make substitutions unless the physician specifically disallows it, perhaps by writing "dispense as written" on the prescription or checking a box to that effect.

The major result of generic substitution laws has been that consumers are paying less for prescription drugs than they were a few years ago. Generic drugs now account for 40 percent of prescriptions written for drugs that are available from competing manufacturers and 25 percent of all prescriptions dispensed in the United States. In an apparent attempt to protect their profit margins, pharmacists in many states do not substitute the generic product unless the consumer makes a specific request. Alert consumers also need to be aware that, in an effort to maintain profit margins, many pharmacies have raised their prices for generic drugs. The odd result is that in those pharmacies, generic drugs cost almost as much as brand name drugs. It still pays to comparison shop for prescription drugs because prices vary widely. Generally, suburban discount drug stores have the lowest prices, while other sellers may charge 10, 30, or even 200 percent more for the same prescription, generic or brand name.

Some Pharmacists Prescribe Drugs

The state of Florida has a law that permits pharmacists to prescribe a limited number of drugs to their customers. The legislature recognized that a large proportion of the elderly population desires hemorrhoid medications and strong pain relievers without having to get a note from a physician. Consumer advocates are working toward getting other states to allow similar savings and convenience.

Over-the-Counter Drugs

Self-medication with over-the-counter drugs is an important part of our health care system. Without OTC nonprescription drugs, consumers would be standing in long lines in front of every doctor's office seeking relief from minor aches and pains. More than 300,000 non-prescription drugs are sold in the United States; over 400 use ingredients and dosages that were available only by prescription 15 years ago.

CONSUMER UPDATE:
Selecting the Proper Sunscreen

Ultra violet rays that damage the skin, UVA and UVB, also foster skin cancer and premature wrinkling.[1] Each year in the U.S., there are 7300 skin cancer deaths, 800,000 cases of basal cell carcinoma (usually disfiguring), and 100,000 cases of squamous cell carcinoma. To reduce burning and obtain protection, consumers should use a sunscreen, yet only 1 sunbathers in 3 bothers with a lotion.

Virtually all products are the same, so buy the least expensive one that has a **sun protection factor (SPF)** that meets your needs. The SPF is an index reporting the degree of protection that a sunscreen product offers from UVB (the rays that burn). If your skin normally takes 10 minutes to burn, it will take 150 minutes with SPF 15. The two main ingredients, equally effective, are PABA (or its derivatives) and benzophenones. The latter sometimes stains clothes. Despite claims that they are waterproof, consumers should reapply the lotions often. Start with a SPF number 15 product, that blocks about 93 percent of the sun's rays. Very dark skinned people can use a sunscreen with an SFP of six or eight. A recent Australian study demonstrated that using SPF 17 sunscreen actually prevents skin cancer.

---

[1]The active ingredient in Retin-A and Renova skin creams, tretinoin, has been shown to be effective as a remover of wrinkles and "age spots" in sun-damaged skin; however, it makes skin more likely to sunburn.

Problems and Dangers

The dangers of self-medication include overuse of drugs, reactions to drug combinations, and failure to get professional care when symptoms persist. Another problem is the lack of **efficacy** of many over-the-counter drugs. This is the power or capacity to produce a desired effect. People get the idea from advertising that over-the-counter drugs are going to cure their problems. The fact is that over-the-counter drugs (and many prescription drugs too) can only relieve symptoms.

Over 20 years ago, the FDA commissioned panels of expert advisors to review the effectiveness of OTC drugs, and they found evidence of safety or effectiveness to be lacking in 69 percent of the 1200+ products examined. Public Citizen has sued the FDA seeking enforcement of the drug-effectiveness requirements of the 1962 Kefauver-Harris Drug Amendments, which states that all drugs must be proven safe and effective before being marketed. In 1990, the FDA banned 223 ingredients in OTC products, as they were deemed ineffective since the manufacturers offered no proof that they were effective for the problems they were supposed to treat. The following year, the FDA banned another 111 diet pill ingredients. Another ban of 415 ineffective ingredients went into effect in 1993. That list included calamine lotion that many moms said was good for bug bites and poison ivy; it can be sold as a skin protectant but not as an external analgesic. Manufacturers of products with these ingredients may continue to make the products, but they are prohibited from shipping them across state lines.

CONSUMER UPDATE:
Consumer Cautions About Cosmetic and Beauty Products

Former Senator Thomas Eagleton summed up the situation in cosmetics quite well: "The number of grooming substances we rub, pour, sprinkle, spray, and otherwise apply to ourselves under the assumption they are safe is staggering. The majority of these, when used properly in moderation, are safe. Other products are only a waste of our time and money. But still others contain poisonous or dangerous substances. As the law stands now, we have no way of knowing. What we do know is that keeping Americans beautiful can have some ugly consequences."

The rule for consumers and cosmetics is still caveat emptor—"let the buyer beware." Consumers are advised to read product labels in the hope of identifying ingredients that may be personally harmful, although since most are chemicals, the average consumer probably will recognize none of them. Those who are allergic to specific chemicals probably can avoid them by reading the label. Be careful about sharing cosmetics because of the increased likelihood of bacterial infections. Before buying any cosmetics, carefully inspect the product for signs of **tampering**, which is illegal interfering with food, drug, and cosmetic products in a harmful manner. Watch for broken seals and damaged containers." The Federal Anti-Tampering Act, passed in 1983, provides for penalties for anyone who tampers with foods, drugs, cosmetics, or the labeling of such containers. Consumers should report any problems with cosmetics to the seller, manufacturer, and Food and Drug Administration.

Aspirin and Similar Pain Relievers

Analgesics are pain-relievers available without a prescription. All nonprescription analgesics relieve pain, but they cannot cure its underlying cause. Analgesics relieve headaches and provide temporarily relief from minor arthritic or rheumatic pain, pain of menstrual cramps, toothache, muscular aches and pains, backache, and the aches and pains of colds or flu. Not all analgesics work on the same health problems.

Aspirin is the most common over-the-counter analgesic drug sold in the United States. Each year consumers take 30 billion aspirin tablets with a total weight of 45 million pounds. **Aspirin** is defined in the *United States Pharmacopeia* as acetylsalicylic acid, its active ingredient. Aspirin, which is unpatented, comes in many different forms, such as plain, buffered, effervescent tablets or powders, or in other analgesics, antacids, antihistamines, and decongestants.

Aspirin is a powerful wonder drug used in tablet form since 1899 for fevers, headaches, and arthritis pain. Aspirin reduces pain, inflammation, and fever. No one knows the exact mechanism by which aspirin works, but it does work.

Findings concerning aspirin published in the *New England Journal of Medicine*, based on a nationwide study of more than 22,000 physicians, confirms earlier suggestions that for healthy men over the age of 50, small quantities of aspirin can reduce the risk of heart attacks by nearly half. Aspirin's ability to keep blood platelets from sticking together may be useful in reducing heart attacks. Low doses of aspirin thin the blood, therefore, it also may increase the chances of a stroke caused by bleeding in the brain. Since taking aspirin as a preventive is definitely not a do-it-yourself project, interested consumers should visit their personal physician for appropriate advice.

Side Effects of Aspirin

Aspirin leads all over-the-counter drugs as a cause of serious side effects. It is so strong that if it were a new drug, aspirin would have to be prescribed. Aspirin has some serious **side effects**, which are undesirable secondary effects of a drug or therapy. Generally, drugs that are more potent and effective have more associated side effects. In the case of aspirin, too much can cause ringing in the ears, vertigo, loss of hearing, gastrointestinal bleeding, and some allergic reactions. Typically, from 1 to 10 percent of aspirin users complain of mild upset stomach. Less than 1 percent of users are allergic to aspirin and may experience reactions, such as shortness of breath, skin rash, swelling, hives, asthma, or shock. Details on side effects of all drugs can be found in the *Physician's Desk Reference (PDR)*, a volume listing all approved drugs and their uses that is available in most libraries and offices of health professionals.

Aspirin slows down the rate of blood coagulation, and it can completely negate the effect of drugs used to control gout or enhance those used for diabetes. To hasten the absorption of aspirin, always take it with a full glass of water. Do not take aspirin (or a buffered aspirin product) if it has a strong vinegar-like odor; this means the medicine is breaking down and losing its potency.

CONSUMER UPDATE:
Over-the-Counter Drugs and Children's Deaths

No child under age five has died in the past eight years from poisoning by accidental ingestion of aspirin. In 1970, the Poison Prevention Packaging Act ordered child-resistant packaging on aspirin, vitamins, and a number of other over-the-counter and prescription drugs. FDA regulations require that of a sample group of children, 85 percent must not be able to open the container in 5 minutes. At the same time, at least 90 percent of the adults must be able to open it. Accidental poisonings have dropped approximately 50 percent.

Misleading OTC Drug Advertising

Misleading advertising occurs in the area of over-the-counter drugs. For example, advertisements for Frution, a Nestle Company product, claim that since the product contains the chemical beta carotene, it "may protect against a variety of cancers." But the label makes no mention of cancer. Also, Fleischmann's margarine advertising claims that the fact that it has no cholesterol means that, "it helps fight heart disease." The label makes no such claim.

Research shows that nearly half the population relies on advertising as their primary source of information about over-the-counter drugs. The Food and Drug Administration regulates prescription drug labeling, while the responsibility for regulating the advertising of over-the-counter drugs is assigned to the Federal Trade Commission. The FDA has strict rules about what can and cannot be said about health claims in labels. The FDA standard is that a company may make health claims only when the totality of scientific evidence supports the position. Further, a health claim may not be made for one nutrient when another ingredient in the same product is not healthy. The FDA does voluntarily pre-screen drug advertising before they are run.

The Federal Trade Commission regulates advertising, and it is much more lenient than the FDA in what it allows food and drug companies to say when promoting products. The FTC's standard is that companies must have a reasonable basis for believing there is a connection between a product and prevention of a certain disease. Therefore, new and controversial scientific findings are often used to make health claims in advertising. In general, the Federal Trade Commission has been ineffective in stopping over-the-counter advertising that exaggerates the need for an OTC drug, creates a problem in the minds of consumers that does not exist, or promises more results than people should realistically expect. OTC drug advertising is saturated with puffery claims and statements that are true, but leave false impressions.

Another example occurs in analgesics. Bayer was found by an FTC judge to be neither qualitatively nor therapeutically superior to any other aspirin products, despite its ads to the contrary. The Federal Trade Commission found that Bayer aspirin is "one of a number of high-quality 5-grain aspirin brands available to consumers.[19] Such misleading ads must work because an FTC study found that 40 percent of consumers believe Bayer's advertising that it is the most effective aspirin. Moreover, the conclusion of non-industry-sponsored scientific studies about aspirin, and other pain relievers, is that two 5-grain aspirin tablets are just as good as anything else in dealing with pain, fever, and inflammation. *Consumer Reports* says that, "all aspirin is equally effective, so buy the cheapest."[20] Note that timed-release aspirin is not suitable for relieving pain or fever because relief depends on rapid absorption.

The Main OTC Pain Relievers

Nearly 40 percent of the $1 billion consumers pay each year for headache remedies goes for advertising almost 200 different brand names of products. Most consumers have not learned much about the major types of pain-relief products, probably because of so much misleading advertising. Many pain-relief products claim that they are "gentler, stronger, or faster than aspirin," when in fact aspirin is often their major ingredient.

Aspirin

The first type of pain reliever is aspirin, which is acetylsalicylic acid. It is sold by nearly 400 companies, such as Bayer, Squibb, Norwich, and K-Mart. Aspirin is a major ingredient in such products as Bristol-Myers' Bufferin and Excedrin, American Home Products' Anacin and Arthritis Pain Formula, and Sterling Drug Company's Cope, Vanquish, and Midol. The "extra active ingredient" in Anacin is caffeine, and each tablet gives you 325 milligrams of aspirin and 32 milligrams of caffeine (the amount of a quarter cup of coffee). According to a Nielsen marketing survey, aspirin has about 42 percent of the market.

---

[19]Is Bayer Better? (1982, July). *Consumer Reports*, p. 347.
[20]Ibid.

Acetaminophen

A second popular OTC pain reliever is acetaminophen, which has about 36 percent of the market. It is sold under many brand names, including Tylenol, Datril, Anacin-3, and Bayer Acetaminophen. This analgesic is sometimes described as an aspirin substitute. Since acetaminophen is a non-aspirin product, it totally lacks an ability to reduce inflammation. Yet this is frequently the cause of pain in the first place, as in arthritis, tooth extraction, pulled back muscle, or a sprained ankle. Acetaminophen cannot reduce inflammation, but it has virtues. Acetaminophen can be used by the small number of people who are allergic to aspirin because it does not cause gastric bleeding or slow blood clotting. Also, it can be prepared in liquid form. Acetaminophen analgesics are less likely than aspirin-containing products to cause the nausea, stomach upset, or allergic reactions. Both acetaminophen and acetylsalicylic acid can cause liver damage or death if a substantial overdose is taken. Acetaminophen also has been linked with kidney problems.

Ibuprofen

A third type of OTC pain reliever, ibuprofen, has about 21 percent of the market and is sold under the brand names Advil, Motrin, Nuprin, and Medipren. This analgesic fights pain and fever but may not have anti-inflammatory properties at nonprescription doses. Research suggests that ibuprofen relieves headaches and the pain of menstrual cramps better than doses of regular-strength aspirin and acetaminophen. Also, ibuprofen is more effective for very high fevers because it lasts a couple of hours longer. Ibuprofen has been related to stomach ulcers. The FDA is examining findings indicating that ordinary doses of ibuprofen can cause kidney failure in people with mild kidney disease. People who are allergic to aspirin generally are allergic to ibuprofen.

Naproxen Sodium

The fourth type of over-the-counter pain reliever was recently approved by the Food and Drug Administration. Naproxen sodium previously had been available only as a prescription arthritis drug, using the trade names Naprosyn and Anaprox. Marketed by Syntex and Procter & Gamble, Aleve is a lower dosage version of Anaprox. A dose lasts for 8 to 12 hours. High doses can cause digestive problems and might cause kidney damage. Naproxen sodium can be used like other **nonsteroidal anti-inflammatory drugs (NSAIDs)** to alleviate minor pain and to reduce inflammation and fever. Other analgesic manufacturers are suing the makers of Aleve for allegedly making false advertising claims.

Ketoprofen

The fifth type of pain relievers is Ketoprofen, the newest on the market. It, too, is an NSAID product.

Independent research shows that, except for inflammation control, where aspirin products are superior, all other products work equally well as pain relievers. In fact, the FTC ordered the manufacturers of all the top-selling pain reliever manufacturers to stop their false advertising. The FTC concluded that some advertisements for these products were misleading because they imply one is better than another when relying upon invalid evidence. These FTC decisions have been appealed and likely will take a number of years to be settled. In the meantime, you can choose to spend perhaps 1 cent to cure a headache with an aspirin tablet or perhaps 25 cents to cure the same headache with another product. For unknown reasons, you may respond better to one drug instead of another.[21]

Vitamins and Food Supplements

Vitamins and food supplements are classified as foods, not drugs. If you eat a balanced diet, you probably do not need to spend money on supplemental vitamins. The FDA's **U.S. Recommended Dietary Allowances (RDAs)** generally represent the highest levels of the National Research Council's recommended dietary allowances for each of 13 nutrients. Few, if any, people need more than the U.S. RDA. Most people can get along just fine with less. Despite this advice, about 40 percent of Americans take supplements.

Problems occasionally arise with food supplements. L-tryptophan was banned after being linked to 27 deaths. GHB, gamma hydroxy butyrate, has caused 57 serious poisoning cases. The "natural high" promoted by Herbal Ecstacy, which contains the stimulant ephedrine, was linked to 15 deaths. Amino acid supplement pills, such as tyrosine and carnitine, when ingested in large quantities, cause unexpected and unwanted effects. The FDA is not allowed to limit the dosages in which vitamins and mineral supplements are sold. A *Money* magazine study concluded that, "More than 90 percent of the products sold by health stores...were of questionable value."[22] Further, "You waste money following most health store recommendations."

Difficult questions arise in this area because science does not have all the answers. Just how the body uses a vitamin pill is, for example, not completely understood. One thing is known, however—a vitamin is a vitamin. The body does not know if it comes from food or from a synthetic capsule. Also, the body cannot tell if a vitamin is a brand name or generic product or whether it was expensively advertised on television or inexpensively sold through the mail.

Congress passed the Dietary Supplement Health and Education Act in 1995 and it goes into effect in 1997. The FDA has the authority to require prior approval for health claims and wild health claims ("cures cancer") are prohibited. Producers of supplements must submit proof of "significant scientific agreement" among qualified experts to support a health claim touting the relationship between a substance and a disease or health-related condition before it can be on a label. Early FDA approvals were given to calcium as it "may help prevent osteoporosis" and folic acid which "may help prevent birth defects." The burden of proof is now on the FDA to show that a supplement presents "significant or unreasonable risk of illness or injury."

The supplement industry is still permitted to produce and distribute point-of-sale articles on the health value of supplements (without review by the FDA), but they are also supposed to provide articles with contrary views. Unfortunately, the law permits nutritional claims other than those previously established for foods, provided a disclaimer is included that, "This statement has not been evaluated by the FDA." Seventy-five days before selling a new supplement, the FDA must be notified.

---

[21]For menstrual cramps, ketoprofen, ibuprofen and naproxen sodium do have the edge.

[22]Rock, A. (1995, September). Vitamin Hype: What We're Wasting $1 or every $3 We Spend, *Money*, 84.

Smoking and Health

One point should be recognized about the issue of tobacco and health: Millions of Americans became addicted to tobacco products before the hazards of smoking became widely recognized and before consumer products sold to the public were adequately reviewed by government officials for safety. Millions of others have taken up smoking since the dangers were well known. One's genes may influence smoking habits, too. People continue to smoke because of ignorance or addiction, or both.

DID YOU KNOW? Official and Underlying Causes of Death*

Top 10 Official Causes of Death		Top 9 Underlying Causes of Death	
Heart Disease	720,000	Tobacco	400,000
Cancer	505,000	Diet/inactivity	300,000
Stroke	144,000	Alcohol	100,000
Unintentional injuries	92,000	Certain infections	90,000
Chronic lung disease	87,000	Toxic agents	60,000
Pneumonia & influenza	80,000	Firearms	35,000
Diabetes	48,000	Sexual behavior	30,000
Suicide	31,000	Motor vehicles	25,000
Liver disease & cirrhosis	26,000	Illegal drugs	20,000
AIDS	25,000		

Conclusion: In a recent year, nearly half of the 2.148 million deaths could have been prevented through behavioral changes, such as stopping smoking, eating healthier food, exercising more, avoiding alcohol, and practicing safe sex.

*Source: National Center for Health Statistics and *Journal of the American Medical Association* (November 10, 1993)

Today, 25.7 percent of Americans smoke, compared to 40 percent 20 years ago; that's 46 million smokers. Only 3 percent of physicians smoke. The average smoker consumes about 150 packs of cigarettes annually. More than 40 million Americans have quit smoking since the 1964 Surgeon General's report warning that cigarettes are lethal; nearly half of all those who have ever smoked. In Japan, 63 percent of men smoke; 70 percent do in China. Outside the United States, cigarette smoking has been growing steadily at a pace of two percent per year.[23]

Ninety-nine percent of U.S. smokers started before age 21, and the average age of first use of cigarettes is 14. Seventy percent of teenagers who smoke become regular smokers by age 18. The three most heavily advertised cigarette brands—depicted by the

---

[23]The rate of increase is 4.5 percent in China, and it is estimated by 900,000 Chinese will die of lung cancer between now and 2025.

Marlboro Man, Joe Camel, and the fun couples of Newport—have 86 percent of the teenage market. A recent study in the *Journal of the American Medical Association* established that, "cigarette advertising, despite industry assertions to the contrary, lures children to start smoking."[24]

Smoking and Death

Worldwide, "sixty million deaths have been caused by smoking since the 1950s," reports the World Health Organization (WHO) in *Mortality From Smoking in Developed Countries*. Three million deaths annually are attributable to smoking, says WHO, and this will rise to 10 million a year by 2020 because smoking in developing countries (especially women) continues to attract young people. The report observes that, "Smoking is like no other hazard. It will kill one in two smokers eventually."

In the United States, tobacco companies have to recruit at least 3000 new smokers every day to replace the 2000 who quit and 1100 who die daily. In the U.S., the Center for Disease Control reports that every year about 2,000,000 people die and at least 434,000 of those deaths are directly attributable to smoking.[25] This means that one out of every five deaths in the United States occurs because of smoking, a preventable cause of death. The state of Oregon records on death certificate whether or not tobacco was a contributing factor; one death in four has been related. The chemical NNK apparently is the most important tobacco-related carcinogen linked to lung cancer.

The American Council on Science and Health reports that cigarette smoking is responsible for about 30 percent of all cancer deaths, including about 90 percent of all lung cancers. Among women, lung cancer, rather than breast or uterine cancer, is the leading cause of cancer death. The American Medical Association reports that the likelihood of contracting lung cancer is 17 times higher for people who smoke than for nonsmokers—lung cancer is almost exclusively a smoker's disease. The number of deaths per 100,000 American people averages 130 nationally; Kentucky, a tobacco-producing state, has the highest, with a rate of 175.

The State Mutual Fund Life Assurance Company has followed the actual death experience of smokers and nonsmokers covered by life insurance for over 30 years. Like many insurance firms, the company developed new actuarial tables because "nonsmokers are better life insurance risks than cigarette smokers." Smokers experience 30 percent higher death rates than shown in traditional mortality tables, while nonsmokers experience only half the industry estimates for mortality. In other words, death rates for smokers are 2.5 times those for nonsmokers, with evidence showing up in younger age ranges in particular.

In another study of more than 8000 deaths, researchers writing in the *American Academy of Actuaries*, found that nonsmoking males lived 18 years longer than males who smoked, with life expectancies of 82 and 64 years, respectively.[26] A forty-year study of British physicians showed that smokers were three times more likely to die before the

---

[24]Brody, J. (1994, March 29). Cigarette Ads Linked to Rise in Smoking by Teenage Girls. *Roanoke Times & News-World*, p. Extra 1.

[25]Cancers (142,800 of lip, mouth, pharynx, esophagus, lung, etc.), cardiovascular diseases (200,100 of hypertension, heart disease, etc.), respiratory diseases (82,800 of pneumonia, influenza, bronchitis, emphysema, etc.), pediatric diseases (2,500 of infants under a year old by smoking parents).

[26]Specter, M. (1990, May 13). Male Smokers Seen Losing 18 Years. *The Washington Post*, p. A-4.

age of 70 than non-smokers.[27] The U.S. Center for Disease Control and Prevention reports that smokers have "an average loss of about five years in projected life expectancy."[28]

CONSUMER UPDATE:
Kids Love Old Joe Camel

Cigarettes—the product with no beneficial effects and when used as intended kills you—is well known among children. A 1992 article in the *Journal of the American Medical Association (JAMA)* reported that the cartoon dromedary that advertises cigarettes is just as recognizable to first grade students as is the Mickey Mouse silhouette; it also is familiar to 30 percent of 3 year-olds. The Camel brand is smoked by 33 percent of smokers under age 18, up from 1 percent before the ad campaign began.

The "Just say 'yes' to smoking!" camel cartoon is familiar to many preschoolers (3-year olds) too. Three subsequent studies have found that kids love Old Joe, confirming the notion, "It is now clear that children thoroughly absorb the message of tobacco advertisements long before they are capable of lighting a cigarette."[1] The issue of persuading children to smoke—R. J. Reynolds' "Joe Cool" multi-media advertising campaign—has gained the attention of policy makers; however, in 1994 the Federal Trade Commission (on a 3 to 2 vote) rejected a complaint about the advertising campaign because of a lack of hard evidence that the campaign lures children into smoking. A 1996 *Journal of Marketing* study revealed that minors are three times as likely as adults to be influenced by cigarette advertising.

A 1996 study of high school smoking revealed that teenage smoking rate is the highest it has been in over 30 years—35 percent. The rates for teenagers are 38 percent for whites, 34 percent for Hispanics, and 19 percent for black teens; only 5 percent of black high school seniors smoke compared to 23 percent of their white classmates. Teens who smoke are 16 times more likely to smoke as adults than those who did not smoke when they were teenagers. Research shows that no matter what one's race or gender, people with less education consistently have higher smoking rates than those with more education.

Fewer than 5 percent of high school smokers believe that they will be smoking five years in the future. Federal health surveys reveal that teenage boys who take up smoking and eventually quit do so at a median age of 33; it is age 37 for girls.

---
[1]Rovner, S. (February 9, 1993), Student Smoking Survey Favors Camel Mascot Ad, *Washington Post Health*, 5.

Related Negative Effects of Smoking

Smoking is the chief cause of lung cancer and has been specifically linked with other cancers, heart disease, stroke, and such respiratory diseases as pneumonia, chronic bronchitis, asthma, emphysema, and various lung disorders. Smoking during pregnancy increases the frequency of low-birthweight infants, premature births, lung disorders in newborns, mental retardation, and sudden infant death syndrome (SIDS). Smoking triples the likelihood of premature facial wrinkling. Smoking also has been linked with

---
[27]Study Finds Smoking Deadlier Than Believed (1993, February 18). *Roanoke Times & World-News*, p. A-8.

[28]Rich, S. (1993, August 27). Cigarette-related Deaths Decline. *The Washington Post*, p. A-4.

depression. It is linked with cataracts and leukemia. Smoking raises the skin cancer incidence rate by 50 percent.

The Tobacco Companies Lied for Fifty Years

The truth about the dangers of tobacco products finally started coming out in 1996. For decades, tobacco company executives lied to the public, the Congress, and probably their spouses. For years, the tobacco company executives told the public and the Congress under oath that: (1) Smoking is not addictive—anyone can quit smoking anytime they want, (2) smoking does not conclusively cause cancer or any other illness, and (3) tobacco companies do not advertise to entice new smokers."[29] They lied!

Since the 1950s, the tobacco companies have known that cigarettes were addictive and cause vascular and other diseases, but they kept the knowledge secret for financial reasons. The truth began to come out when some former tobacco company executives testified to their own past misdeeds, judges ordered the unsealing of tobacco company research papers and internal memorandums, boxes of incriminating company files kept in a garage were turned over to the government by a spurned girlfriend, and the smallest of the tobacco companies (Leggett) agreed to settle a liability lawsuit.

Former Secretary of Health and Human Services, Louis W. Sullivan, said that the tobacco companies have been "trading death for corporate profits" and their charitable support for various projects is "blood money." Sullivan says that he is disgusted with tobacco companies that align their products with the healthy image of athletes. Sullivan also said that cigarettes are "the only legal product that when used as intended causes death." The country of France has banned all cigarette advertising, and the European Union is considering the same action. The American Medical Association has called for "the removal of this scourger from our nation."

After winning 600 lawsuits by covering up the facts contained in the tobacco companies' own corporate files, the times are changing. Now numerous states are suing the tobacco companies to recover tobacco-related Medicaid costs, federal and state grand juries are investigating the industry, and numerous top-notch trial lawyers in several states have filed class-action lawsuits seeking damages for addiction and for diseases allegedly caused by smoking.

Secondhand Smoke Kills 40,000+ Every Year

The National Academy of Sciences reviewed the studies of environmental tobacco smoke (ETS) and held that nonsmokers were being endangered. Recent studies of nonsmokers show that they are being harmed by the smoke of others in buses, trains, subways, planes, offices, restaurants, and other public places. Secondhand smoke is very harmful.

Passive smoking, breathing secondhand smoke, causes 3800 lung cancer deaths among non-smoking Americans every year, reports both the Surgeon General and the

[29]Merzer, M. (1993, November 7). Smoking Ills Not Proven Swear Tobacco Czars. *Roanoke Times & World-News*, p. A-1.

CONSUMER UPDATE:
Smokeless Tobacco Also Kills

The federal government requires warning labels on smokeless tobacco (also called snuff, dip, plug, or chewing tobacco) products, although the Smokeless Tobacco Institute says that there is no proven link between oral cancer and snuff. They have lied just like the companies that sell cigarettes.

In reality, researchers have found that smokeless-tobacco users are four times as likely to develop mouth or throat cancer. A recent study released by the U.S. Surgeon General found that 75 percent of the 30,000 new cases of oral cancer were caused by snuff. The American Lung Association's research reveals that, "Within a year or two, most people who chew tobacco will develop some sort of mouth abrasions or cancers."[1]

Ten million people currently use smokeless tobacco—an eightfold increase in the last 15 years. One survey found that the average age for snuff initiation is 9 1/2. "Dipping," sucking on ground tobacco, has increased 15 times among 17- 19-year-old males since 1970. Experts predict an oral cancer epidemic by 2010. The best-selling brands have the highest nicotine levels. No one should doubt the additive power of nicotine.

The Federal Trade Commission has proposed that makers of smokeless tobacco add warning labels at auto races, monster truck rallies, and tractor pulls when vehicles are painted with the tobacco company's logo.

---

[1]Borgman, A. (1995, July 6), Trying to Snuff Out Teens' Tobacco Use, *The Washington Post*, B-3.

Environmental Protection Agency. Also, it greatly increases the likelihood of respiratory illnesses in children. Passive smoking causes 37,000 heart-disease deaths each year.

Exposure to secondhand smoke narrows the arteries of non-smokers, increasing the risk of heart disease. The chemical in second-hand smoke responsible for causing lung cancer has been shown to be NNAL. The Environmental Protection Agency concludes that environmental tobacco is "a 'Class A' human carcinogen—a group that includes a handful of substances such as asbestos, arsenic, and benzene."[30] Secondhand smoke is the third leading preventable cause of death; active smoking and alcohol use are first and second. Non-smokers who grew up with two smoking parents are twice as likely as other non-smokers to develop lung cancer. A recent report in the *Journal of the American Medical Association* revealed that women who have lived for years in the household of a smoker have a 30 percent greater chance of developing lung cancer than women living in a smoke-free environment. A 1996 Center for Disease Control and Prevention study showed that, "second-hand smoke invades the lungs of about 88 percent of America's non-smokers."

Smoke is hazardous to human health, and for this reason, a nationwide campaign has banned smoking in public areas, such as federal buildings, work places, restaurants, airplanes, trains, and rest rooms. More than 320 communities and a number of states have adopted laws restricting smoking. Now nearly all public places must have smoke-free areas. Maryland was the first state in the nation to ban smoking in restaurants, bars and the workplace. Smoking-permitted areas, as well as nonsmoking areas, may be designated, but if there is not room for both, smoking is often prohibited. The National Institute for

---

[30]Kenworthy, T. (1993), Secondhand Smoke Peril Affirmed. *The Washington Post*, A-1.

Occupational Safety and Health states that, "all available preventive measures should be used to minimize occupational exposures."[31] The American Heart Association agrees.

What About Smoking Is Harmful?

The long-sought "smoking gun" direct evidence that links cigarettes and heart disease was reported in the *Journal of the American Medical Association* in 1989. Smoking causes arteries to narrow. Heart disease patients who smoke are three times more likely to have chest pains and restricted blood flow to their hearts than nonsmokers. Such ischemic episodes damage the heart and can lead to heart attacks. Tobacco contains more than 800 elements, including 40 cancer-causing agents.

Tar is the element in cigarette smoking that causes cancer, according to the National Cancer institute. Tobacco products also contain nicotine, a poisonous stimulant. It is both a poison and a stimulant. Nicotine affects your heart rate and blood pressure, and it can restrict blood circulation and lower skin temperature. Tobacco company executives deny that they "spiked" their cigarettes with nicotine. They also denied that smoking is addictive, although evidence from a 1981 study from the Philip Morris Company's own research labs (stolen by someone with a conscience) suggests otherwise. Internal documents from Brown & Williamson's research labs show alarming concerns about the health hazards, although these too were not reported to the U.S. Surgeon General over thirty years ago when the research was conducted.

Surprise (NOT!), Nicotine Is As Addictive As Heroin

In the form of cigarettes, tobacco is the most addictive substance known. A report from Dr. C. Everett Koop, President Bush's Surgeon General, concluded that nicotine is as addictive as heroin! A recently uncovered confidential internal Philip Morris report likens nicotine to such drugs as cocaine and morphine in its addictive powers. Of those who try to quit, generally only 10 percent are successful; about 20 percent of "patch" users are successful six months later. People who smoke are often overly sure of their ability to stop; they misjudge the addictive power of smoking. **Nicotine dependence** means that you have a physical need or craving for the nicotine obtained from smoking. Smokers who quit usually have uncomfortable withdrawal symptoms, such as headaches, dizziness, stomach upset, nervousness, restlessness, and irritability. Nicotine is a prime suspect as a cause of heart attacks.

The Future of Smoking

Smoking is under attack in the United States as a serious health hazard. People are being encouraged to give up smoking; children are being encouraged to never begin. In the United States, smoking remains a choice. People still can choose to ignore the warnings and increase the risks of harming themselves. The existence of so-called

---

[31]Agency Urges Tighter Smoking Rules on Job. (1991, July 18). *Roanoke Times & World-News*, p. B-5.

CONSUMER UPDATE:
Ex-Smokers Lower Risks Immediately

Non-smokers lead healthier and longer lives. A 1994 study in the *Archives of Internal Medicine* shows that quitting smoking would extend an average male smoker's life 2.6 to 4.4 years, and the average female smoker's life 2.6 to 3.7 years.

The earlier one quits smoking the greater the benefits, but even older smokers who quit also gain. The Surgeon General reports that half of the excess risk of heart disease disappears within the first year of quitting smoking. Someone who stops smoking before age 50 is only one-half as likely to die as a non-smoker. A reduction in cancer risk is much more gradual. A study of nurses found that after 10 to 14 years of non-smoking, the statistical health risk was the same as if they never smoked.

---

smoker's rights, however, does not mean that the ill-effects of smoking—to smokers and nonsmokers alike—will be ignored by society.

In 1995, a Food and Drug Administration panel concluded that nicotine is an addictive drug. Then—for the first time in history and with the required approval of President Clinton—the FDA decided to regulate since "nicotine in cigarettes and smokeless tobacco products is a drug." The FDA is waiting for the U.S. Congress to provide guidance. The FDA will probably propose a system to gradually reduce the amount of nicotine in cigarettes, perhaps to about 1/6 of what it is today. The government is expected to issue sweeping regulations to curb underage smoking and restrict advertising and promotion of tobacco products in general.[32] Our constitution permits commercial speech to be restricted to advance a compelling state interest if the ban is narrowly tailored.

Critics have suggested that the cigarette warning labels required on each package be strengthened, perhaps to read: "Smoking may result in your death!" or "Smoking may result in horrible health during the last ten years of your life!"

One of the heirs of the R. J. Reynolds Tobacco Company fortune, Patrick Reynolds, also the founder of Citizens for a Smokefree America, laments that his father died in 1964 from emphysema caused by his smoking addiction. Several other family members have died from cigarette smoking, including his older brother, R. J. Reynolds Jr.

Taxes paid by cigarette smokers pay for only a fraction of the increased health costs caused by smoking. American smokers pay an average price of less than $2 per pack, of which 27 percent is taxes. The highest price is in Norway where the average pack costs $9, of which 77 percent is taxes. Canadian prices are over $4.00 a pack.

As cigarette taxes go up, smoking consumption goes down. A study by the National Cancer Institute found that cigarette consumption drops by about 4 percent with each 10 percent price increase.

Many health care professionals in the United States believe that cigarette taxes ought to go up, from the present 24 cents per pack to $2 or $3. States like California and Minnesota that have established public information programs to discourage smoking report that the rate of quitting or cutting back has tripled, along with reductions in the likelihood

---

[32]The tobacco company flooded Congress with a record $4 million in political campaign contributions in 1995 (overwhelmingly to Republicans); more is expected this year as Congress deliberates how to regulate the industry.

of teens beginning to smoke. California, which uses tax money from cigarette taxes to fund its non-smoking programs, aims to reduce smoking to 6.5 percent by the year 2000.

Many new smokers can be found in overseas markets as smoking is up 70 percent over the past 25 years. According to the World Health Association, smoking kills 3 million people a year. This is triple the number three decades ago. The World Health Organization says that 1/2 of all smokers will die from cancer.

CONSUMER UPDATE:
Why Do Some People Persist in Harming Their Health?

People process information differently about risks and make rationalizations. Many people reason that catastrophic events, such as airplane crashes, will happen to others, not to them. Such a deduction about catastrophic events is probably correct from a statistical point of view. Comparatively speaking, very few people die in airplane crashes, train wrecks, or fires. The odds are extremely low that the average American will die in a plane crash or flood, perhaps a million to one.

People are inclined to make similar rationalizations about such perils as radon, dioxin, pesticides, certain chemicals and colors added to foods, radiation, smoking, and alcohol. There is a human tendency to believe they are immune from such dangers. The thinking goes, "Oh, the odds are certainly against any of that stuff hurting me." Such thinking is false! This is an example of where human logic falls apart. People have a tendency to personalize the odds of something happening to them even when reality shows otherwise.

Such thoughts are simply **rationalizations**. This is the theory that the exercise of personal reasoning, rather than the acceptance of empirical evidence, provides the only valid basis for action or belief. Many people rationalize about health and safety risks. It occurs, in part, because: (1) people do not want to think about death and danger, (2) the odds of many calamities and dangers are unknown to consumers, (3) people often fail to add their behavior patterns to the factor of chance, and (4) most of us are incapable of making mathematically correct risk assessments.

As a result, many people smoke cigarettes, eat fatty foods, avoid regular exercise, choose not to wear seat belts, drink excessively, and sometimes drive too fast, all the time falsely assuming that the "odds are with them." Such people often believe they are making informed decisions, but they are not. Parents, schools, and governments need to do a better job helping consumers make valid and reliable risk assessments so they can make more informed decisions about what to eat, what behaviors to avoid, and where to live, work, and play.

Alcohol and Health

Among the general population, 40 percent report that they never drink and over 80 percent say they never drink and drive. Over 80 percent of the nation's collegians drink regularly. College students report alcohol consumption as the prime means of getting high. Half of all college freshmen get smashed during their first week on campus. A U.S. Department of Education survey of 58,000 college students revealed that about one-third of male and female students drink primarily to get drunk; nearly half of college students under age 21 reported binge drinking in the past two weeks. Drinkers should be aware that taking aspirin before drinking significantly increases the concentration of alcohol in the blood.

A recent report from Columbia University's Center on Addiction and Substance Abuse revealed that 20 percent of college students abandoned safe-sex practices after drinking. Sixty percent of college women with sexually transmitted diseases were drunk when infected.

Alcoholic beverages contain intoxicating compounds. Many people assume that alcohol makes them funny, brave, more sociable, sexier, or better in some other ways. While these statements are being debated by individuals personally and by professional researchers, it is well known that alcohol use leads to arrests, injuries, vandalism, and drunk-driving deaths. Traffic crashes are the number one cause of death for teenagers. Sweet drinks containing alcohol, such as Hooper's Hootch and a number of **alcopops** (lemonades, colas, and orange flavored drinks containing alcohol) are being blatantly marketed at young teenagers, much in the same way Camel cigarettes are advertised to underage people. Manufacturers deny such allegations.

Beer, wine, and liquor are consumer products which when ingested can negatively affect health. Evidence shows that each drink reduces the oxygen supply through the blood to the brain. The result is a deterioration of brain cells, of which each of us has about 12 billion, and these are irreplaceable. Alcohol contains a number of chemicals, some of which cause long-lasting birth defects from fetal alcohol syndrome. Two drinks a week during pregnancy have been shown to increase the chances of miscarriage. Alcohol is "the most common known cause of mental retardation;"[33] it only occurs when pregnant women drink alcohol. There also are a number of alcohol-related diseases and problems, such as automobile crashes, cirrhosis of the liver, pancreas difficulties, cancer, hypertension, depression, and suicide. Lower productivity occurs when workers have been drinking, and people with drinking problems also lose income because they miss too much work.

DID YOU KNOW? How the Young Die

Monthly Vital Statistics reports that in the United States the leading causes of death for people under age 44 are: accidents—39 percent, cancer—18 percent, heart disease—16 percent, homicide—14 percent, and suicide—13 percent.

Research suggests that drinking alcohol increases a woman's chances of developing breast cancer but helps protect against heart attacks and strokes. Approximately 3 million people have allergic reactions to the more than 50 additives allowed in beers and the more than 80 additives allowed in wines. About 15 million people are addicted to alcohol to the point where they are classified as alcoholics or as people with serious drinking problems; 100,000 of them die each year of the disease.

Research studies suggest that people, especially the elderly, who have one or two five-ounce drinks a day (one for women and two for men) enjoy greater protection against heart disease. Red wine, or what is in it (resveratrol), appears to have positive benefits. This may occur because drinkers have higher levels than non-drinkers of the good cholesterol, HDL. A recent study reported in the *New England Journal of Medicine* found

---

[33]Vobejda, B. (1994, April 20). Sobering Look at Alcohol and Pregnancy. *The Washington Post*, p. A-3.

that, "Those who consumed one to three drinks daily had half the heart attack risk of people who never drank."[34] TPA, tissue-type-plasminogen, a clot-dissolving enzyme physicians use to block a heart attack, seems to be increased among drinkers, too.

CONSUMER UPDATE:
Alcoholic Beverage Labeling

The consumer's right to information about alcoholic beverages is seriously limited. The labeling of beer, wine, and liquor does not tell the consumer much about anything, even though these products use numerous ingredients, some of which are harmful. Ten states require posters in liquor stores or sales areas warning of the dangers of alcohol to pregnant women. Proponents of improved labeling want to require labeling of ingredients in alcoholic beverages.

For years, the position of the government's Bureau of Alcohol, Tobacco and Firearms (ATF) has been that ingredient labeling regulations would result in increased costs to consumers, and burdens on industry which are not commensurate with the benefits which might flow from the additional label information. Congress has been unable to pass a law requiring that consumers be informed about the composition of the alcoholic products they consume.

Too much alcohol is not healthy. Alcohol is blamed for over 108,000 deaths annually, including over 17,000 alcohol-related traffic deaths. There are 10 million alcohol-related accidents[35] and 2 million arrests for public drunkenness reported each year. Nearly half of all accidental deaths, suicides, and homicides are alcohol-related; about one-third of all drowning victims were intoxicated at the time of death. Alcohol kills three times as many people in the U.S. as all other drugs combined. An estimated 40 percent of people in the United States will be in an alcohol-related automobile crash during their lifetimes.

CONSUMER UPDATE:
The Social Price Tag for Tobacco and Alcohol Abuse

The National Public Services Research Center, a non-profit research institute, regularly calculates the social cost of how Americans live their lives. Of all abused substances, tobacco takes a $94 billion toll on health-care costs. That amounts to $350 per person per year. The alcohol-related costs to society (including medical care, lost wages, and lost hours of work) total $128 billion. That is the equivalent, says the Center, of 50 cents per drink consumed annually.

---

[34]Associated Press. (1993, December 6). Moderate Drinking Cuts Heart Risk, Study Finds. *The Washington Post*, p. A-22.

[35]About one in nine drivers involved in fatal crashes do not have a valid driver's license.

Review and Summary of Key Terms and Concepts

1. Why is **buying health services** confusing?

2. Describe two **guidelines on how to purchase services**.

3. Distinguish among: **registration, certification**, and **licensure**.

4. Cite some facts suggesting that there are some things wrong with the U.S. **health system**.

5. Explain how Americans with insurance are really already paying the health care costs for those who are **uninsured**.

6. What factors lead to the failure of President Clinton's **health care reform proposals**?

7. List three of the unique aspects of the **medical care market** that makes it difficult to reform.

8. What is a **health maintenance organization**, and how does it function?

9. What is **managed care** and how does **managed competition** affect a managed care system?

10. Distinguish between **prescription** and **over-the-counter (OTC)** drugs.

11. Summarize the **pre-market drug-approval** and marketing process, starting with a **patent** and ending with the product turning **generic**.

12. What is a **generic drug**, and what does the term **bioavailability** have to do with generic drugs?

13. Summarize the differences in effectiveness among: **aspirin, acetaminophen**, and **ibuprofen**.

14. Offer a summary comment upon the allegations of **misleading advertising** of OTC drugs.

15. Who should take **vitamins**?

16. What does the government's **new labeling law** have to say about dietary supplements?

17. Describe the relationship between the top ten **official causes of death** and the top nine **underlying causes of death**.

18. Cite some facts and arguments against **tobacco smoking** and using **smokeless tobacco**.

19. Offer some comments about **children and teenagers smoking**.

20. Why do some people persist in **harming their health**?

21. Offer some observations on the costs and benefits of **alcohol consumption**.

Useful Resources for Consumers

American Association of Retired Persons
Consumer Affairs Section
601 E Street, NW
Washington, DC 20049
202-434-6030

American Council on Science and Health
1995 Broadway, 2nd Floor
New York, NY 10023-5860
212-362-7044

Action on Smoking and Health
2013 H Street, NW
Washington, DC 20006
202-659-4310

Families USA Foundation
1334 G Street, NW, Suite 300
Washington, DC 20005
202-628-3030

National Council Against Health Fraud
P.O. Box 1276
Loma Linda, CA 92354

Public Citizen Health Research Group
2000 P Street, NW, Suite 708
Washington, DC 20003
202-588-1000

"What Do You Think" Questions

1. Select one of the **guidelines on how to purchase services** that you believe is especially difficult for consumers to follow. Offer suggestions to government and the health care profession on how to improve the situation.

2. If you were the "United States dictator for the year" and supported **health care reform**, what steps would to take? List some possible actions.

3. What should a smart consumer do to select the best **pain reliever**?

4. What additional actions do you think government could take to discourage young people from not **smoking**?

5. What are your views on why some people persist in **harming their health**?

Chapter 16

Product Safety Issues

OBJECTIVES

After reading this chapter, you should be able to

1. Comprehend that many products cause injuries and deaths and a number of causal factors may be involved.

2. Understand how complex and difficult it is for government to make cost-benefit decisions on product safety issues.

3. Realize that so-called "tort reform" is against the consumer interest.

4. Explain the important role of the Consumer Product Safety Commission in protecting consumers in America.

5. Describe how the National Highway Traffic Safety Commission reduces highway deaths, injuries, and property losses caused by motor vehicle accidents.

6. Understand several criticisms of product safety efforts in America.

Some consumer products have built-in hazards, such as knives that cut, motor vehicles that crash, matches that burn, and skateboards that tip allowing riders to get hurt when falling. Other consumer products have hazards that are not so apparent, perhaps hidden. For example, it is almost impossible for consumers to know that their motor vehicle brakes or steering were defectively manufactured. Small children have difficulty recognizing the hazardous nature of playing with matches, drinking bottles of home-use pesticides, or riding on an all-terrain vehicle. The result of product dangers such as these is a considerable number of injuries and deaths.

This chapter begins by examining the topics of product safety and effectiveness and the causal factors in injuries. The concept of cost-benefit analysis also is examined since it is fundamental to government involvement in product safety regulation. The importance of product safety to the consumer interest is then examined in the context of the concept of strict liability. Next the chapter focuses on the role of two major federal agencies involved in product safety: the Consumer Product Safety Commission (CPSC) and the National Highway Traffic Safety Administration (NHTSA). The chapter concludes with a review of the criticisms of product safety efforts.

Product Safety and Effectiveness

Public awareness of the hazards of everyday products has increased in recent years. Part of the reason for this is frequent publicity about widely used hazardous products. Surveys show that more than two-thirds of the public believe there are dangers in such products as pesticides for home use, children's toys, power equipment, motor vehicles, and food additives.

Consumers, government, and industry strongly support the self-regulatory efforts of product manufacturers as they go to considerable efforts to design, develop, and sell safe products. They want increased sales and profits, not lawsuits and bad publicity. Still the competitive marketplace has not been an effective mechanism for providing the degree of safety that American society demands because millions of injuries and thousands of deaths occur each year. Whenever innocent consumers, especially children, are being killed or injured, it is the absolute responsibility of the government to intervene to protect the public health. While federally mandated safety standards cost manufacturers hundred of millions of dollars, they save lives and reduce injuries.

A constant tension exists between safety advocates and product manufacturers, with the government acting as referee. As a result, a number of federal laws and regulations have been passed to help protect consumers from unsafe products. Many government agencies are involved in product safety, such as the Consumer Product Safety Commission, Food and Drug Administration, Environmental Protection Agency, and National Highway Traffic Safety Administration.

Many Products Cause Injuries

Each year about 60 million, or one in four Americans, are injured. Research by Cristine Russell of *The Washington Post* reveals that this includes 143,000 deaths, 2.3 million hospitalizations, and 54 million less severe injuries. The associated causes of death include motor vehicle crashes, 41,700; firearms, 32,000 (39 percent are homicides); falls, 13,000; poisonings, 12,000; fires and burns, 6,000; drownings, 6,000; consumer products, 29,000. Thirty of the 60 million annual injuries are caused by consumer products commonly found around the home, such as bicycles, toys, lawn mowers, household chemicals, furniture, appliances, and power tools. Such injuries often require medical treatment and/or absence from work. The total cost is estimated at $42 billion a year.

The child's world of reality is filled with too many sharp edges (instead of rounded ones), objects that are breakable, and some toxic materials. It seems that nothing is "childproof." Accidents are the leading killer of children. More children die from preventable injuries each year than from all childhood diseases combined. Each year, nearly 8000 children under age 15 die from accidents associated with consumer products; another 50,000 are permanently disabled. Today's complex technology certainly poses threats to the physical security of Americans, both children and adults.

CONSUMER UPDATE:
Toy Safety Recommendations for Parents and Gift Givers

Last year there were over 30 toy-related deaths. More than half were from choking; another 160,000 were treated in hospital emergency rooms. Parents and gift givers should never assume that the toys they find on store shelves are safe, although the great majority are safe.

The $14 billion industry adds about 5000 new toys every year to the 150,000 choices already available. Heavy use and abuse of toys is normal.

Be skeptical of prepackaged toys unless a sample is available to examine. Parents and gift givers should avoid buying a toy with small parts that can be pulled off and ingested. Also refrain from buying anything with small parts (including balls), such as anything less than 1 1/4 inches in diameter or smaller than a child's fist. Avoid items with a long cord, chain, string or elastic band, as it could encircle a child's neck.

Products with sharp edges and points should be avoided too. While shopping, consumers should vigorously shake a toy before purchasing it, because if it comes apart, lacerations are likely to occur with use. Children cannot be supervised all the time, so screen toys for safety before purchasing them. Know that age labeling on toys is not designed for a child's mental age, but for his or her chronological age.

Causal Factors in Injuries

People interested in product safety are primarily concerned with two aspects of product safety: (1) reducing the incidence of injuries by preventing them from occurring in the first place, and (2) reducing the severity of injuries when they do occur.

A number of factors must be examined before government can attempt to regulate and improve product safety. Foremost is the need for adequate information. Reliable systems of epidemiologic information need to be in place to provide useful and meaningful data regarding deaths and injuries.

Casual factors also need to be clearly identified. People often "blame the product" for an injury, and sometimes poor product design *is* the cause of injuries that result through normal product use. Some defective products have production defects that occur during the manufacturing processes. A product designed with no safety flaws in normal use may result in injury if it is damaged or used beyond some safe product life. Other factors include: new scientific information about dangers from materials previously thought safe, accidental contamination, tampering, unforeseen misuse of products, or failure to meet safety standards.

Even though user behavior is often the proximate cause of accidents associated with consumer products, rather than the product, injuries often occur when a product that is safe to use is misused. Environmental factors also may be involved, such as weather or darkness. For example, when a child is riding his or her bicycle home at dusk, it is difficult to see loose stones and potholes in the road, which may "cause" an accident.

Incorrect age use is another causal factor. Children sometimes use an adult-styled product, such as an all-terrain vehicle (ATV), and get injured or die. Over the past twelve years, the CPSC reports that ATVs have been responsible for 872 deaths of children under age 16; 24,000 children are injured every year. Critics want an outright ban on the sale of ATVs for use by children under age 16.

Another causal factor may be the psychological or physical condition of the consumer. For example, a man who is physically and mentally tired from a long workday, and who is also in a hurry so he can go out for supper, may not be in the safest condition at 7 o'clock in the evening to mow his lawn.

Product manufacturers sometimes say that human behavioral and environmental conditions are beyond their responsibility in terms of product safety design because it is impossible to figure all the ways consumers can use or abuse products. They also argue that reliable product safety data suggest that less than half the injuries associated with consumer products result primarily because of the product itself. The reality is that consumer misuse is foreseeable or easy to anticipate.[1] Consumer advocates argue that it is futile to rely solely on trying to modify consumer behavior when increased government regulation of product safety features can quickly reduce injuries. It has been estimated that perhaps 20 percent of all product injuries could be prevented if the manufacturers sold better-designed products.

Cost-Benefit Analysis and Safety

Failure to use rational principles in decision making means that some consumers will suffer needless injuries and deaths. Thus, governments and businesses try to use rational principles in making safety decisions so society can save lives and reduce injuries for a given level of spending on safety. **Cost-benefit analysis** (or **benefit-cost analysis**) is an approach to policy recommendation that permits analysts to compare and advocate policies by quantifying *all* their total monetary costs and total monetary benefits, including various intangibles that are not easily measured. The economically rational policy recommendation, therefore, is to choose actions that maximize social welfare by yielding the highest net benefits given limited time and money. A **net benefit** is the total of all the benefits of a course of action less all the costs.

For example, if the costs of a proposal (such as adding design and material changes) add up to $1.00 and the benefits (such as reduced injuries and fewer deaths) are expected

---

[1]Some hazards seem almost impossible to deal with, such as when children choke and die as a result of ingesting pieces of uninflated balloons.

to amount to $1.10, the proposal passes the test. In effect, the opportunity costs of an investment are calculated on the basis of what net benefits might be gained. Since it is impossible to pin down precisely *all* the marginal benefits associated with proposed changes (such as how to measure risk or the value of nature), it is extremely unwise to make final policy decisions based solely on quantitative cost-benefit analysis.

Here is another illustration. Corporations often fix faulty designs in future products, but they usually do not want to correct old problems, preferring instead to fight lawsuits because the cost is frequently less than that of recalls. (This is an application of cost-benefit analysis.) A **recall** is a request by a manufacturer (done either voluntarily or mandated by government) of a product specified as defective for its return to the seller for necessary repair, exchange, adjustment, or refund.

How Much Risk Is Acceptable?

How society answers the question "How much risk is acceptable in consumer products?" reveals a lot about how the economic resources of the country are going to be spent. Years ago the National Commission on Product Safety made observations about the reasonableness of product hazards. They reported that **reasonable risks** occur "when consumers understand that risks exist, can appraise their probability and severity, know how to cope with them, and voluntarily accept them and get the benefits that could not be obtained in less risky ways." The commission report further observed that **unreasonable risks** occur "when consumers do not know that they exist; or when, though aware of them, consumers are unable to estimate their frequency and severity; or when consumers do not know how to cope with them, and hence are likely to incur harm unnecessarily; or when risk is unnecessary in that it could be reduced or eliminated at a cost in money or in the performance of the product that consumers would willingly incur if they knew the facts and were given the choice."

In essence, the question is whether or not consumers can be expected to make rational decisions regarding safety. Other factors to consider are how well known is the risk, if all user groups (such as children, the elderly, and other adults) understand the risks, and the likelihood of abnormal uses of the product. Compounding the difficulty of risk determination is the fact that consumers must make risk decisions many times every day, which lessens their appreciation of each individual risk. There is some doubt about whether or not consumers have the ability to understand their exposures to risk and the expected value of losses associated with product choices.

Another difficulty about unreasonable risks occurs when government attempts to decide how much risk is acceptable for each particular product. Government does this with the realization that any action taken will infringe upon the free choice of people to make personal decisions about their welfare. Advocates of minimal marketplace intervention suggest that consumers should be given choices between safer, more expensive products and cheaper, less safe products. Government intervention also places the burden of future risk evaluation on government, rather than on consumers.

Measuring Risk for Public-Policy Decisions

An important aspect of the public-policy decision making process is to assess the magnitude of the risk. One must first know the perils and hazards associated with a product. Then it is possible to define the degree and nature of the risk of injury that a proposed rule is designed to eliminate. Once the risk is defined, it may be possible to predict how effective a standard will be in reducing injuries and deaths and improving public health and safety.

Consider the hypothetical example in Table 16-1. Chain saws have a much higher level of risk than electric power drills and may be a more likely candidate for government regulation. One of the biggest difficulties in trying to objectively measure the magnitude of risk is establishing and assigning values for both injuries and deaths with injury-severity numbers and dollars.

Product	Probability of Injury	Injury Severity	Market Size	Level of Risk
Electric power drills	0.001	1	5 million	5,000
Chain saws	0.10	5	1 million	50,000

TABLE 16-1   Hypothetical Measurement of the Magnitude of Risk

Criticisms of Cost-Benefit Analysis

Many economists and consumer advocates dislike the mathematics of benefit-cost analysis for several reasons:

1. Benefit-cost analysis cannot possibly include all the variables. It should be a summation of all identifiable costs and benefits, but cost-benefit analysis is not a precise science.

2. A number of variables are almost impossible to measure. For example, how much is the beauty of the California redwood forest worth? Or, what is the value of having fish swim in a lake? Answers to these questions require much guesswork.

3. The benefits of reduced injuries and deaths are difficult to calculate. For example, what is the value of a lost finger, arm, or leg? What is the value of pain, as in the painful suffering and anguish of a severe burn victim? What is the value of a life? Or, the life of a child? (Economic studies of occupational deaths suggest that an appropriate statistical value of a life is between $4 and $5 million.)

4. Assignment of increased costs for safety is often arbitrary. The costs of products almost always increase as a result of decisions to improve safety because safer products are more expensive to make and/or because increased spending is needed for better product design and quality control. Estimating these additional costs, whether caused by performance standards or product-design standards, is not a precise science.

5. Assignment of the costs to consumers for decreased utility, satisfaction, availability, and usefulness is often arbitrary. For example, what is the worth of the inconvenience and additional time spent using a lawn mower with a government-approved safety device? This must be factored into the cost-benefit decision.

6. Reducing unreasonable risks involves difficult predictions as to the effectiveness of proposed alternatives. Calculations may involve engineering, scientific, and human factors, enforcement determinations, and predictions about the behavior of businesses and the public in response to a proposed rule.

7. Many researchers are biased and their interpretations of data are often heavily political. In such instances, the benefit-cost formulas and models tell researchers exactly what they want to hear because they purposely overestimate values to agree with their assumptions, which prejudices the findings. Thus, cost-benefit studies from industry support their views, while advocates for regulation have studies that support their positions. Government regulators who do, or do not, want to regulate, have been known to assign peculiar values in their studies, too. One critic observed that, "cost-benefit analysis is one of the techniques most prone to misunderstanding and misapplication in the hands of the uninitiated (not to mention the unscrupulous)."

8. Benefit-cost analysis often slows corrective regulatory action. This occurs when government officials order study after study on the benefits and costs of a particular action while injuries and deaths continue to mount.

9. By law, regulators often must consider some political and economic impacts of alternative product safety proposals. For example, the Consumer Product Safety Commission must consider "minimizing adverse effects on competition or disruption or dislocation of manufacturing and other commercial practices consistent with the public health and safety."

10. It is impossible to make a good regulatory decision based solely on findings from benefit-cost studies because of limitations on the quality of the inputs. Effective and appropriate regulatory decisions are based on good judgments of both quantitative and qualitative information. Cost-benefit analysis should be a part of good decision making.

Using Benefit-Cost Analysis

The result of a benefit-cost analysis is usually presented in one of two ways: (1) in the form of a ratio of costs-to-benefits or benefits-to-costs, or (2) as a remainder of net benefits after subtracting the total costs from the total benefits.

Benefit-cost analysis should be a tool in the decision making process, not a commandment. The resulting cost-effectiveness analysis forces government regulators, however superficially, to consider alternative means of meeting safety goals. Benefit-cost analysis is only one of many inputs government uses in making product safety regulation decisions. It is a vital tool that can help regulators decide which problems to attack with their limited resources, assist in choosing priorities, provide guidance in rulemaking, and assist in developing effective and efficient compliance and enforcement activities. Most federal regulatory agencies are required by a 1981 Executive Order of the President (Number 12291) to apply cost-benefit formulas during formal rulemaking.

Factors to Consider in Making Product Safety Decisions

Government uses several factors when considering whether to make a public-policy decision to regulate product safety:

1. There must be a known hazard.
2. There has to be some probability that the hazard causes injuries or deaths.

3. The magnitude of the loss must be such that the problem warrants attention.
4. There must be one or more preferably inexpensive alternatives to reduce the incidence and severity of losses.
5. The benefits must seem to outweigh the costs of implementing a safety regulation.
6. An industry group must fail to establish voluntary regulatory product safety standards or take other self-regulatory steps to address the hazard.
7. There must be a political willingness among government officials to take action to regulate.

CONSUMER UPDATE:
Responsibilities of Consumers in Product Safety

Consumers have the responsibility to:
- Examine merchandise for safety features before buying.
- Question sellers about the safety attributes of products before purchase.
- Complete and return postage-paid registration cards on purchases so you can be notified in case of a recall.
- Carefully read product labels and literature, and heed warning labels.
- Read and follow care and use instructions carefully.
- Use products as intended and with reasonable caution and care.
- Assume personal responsibility for normal precautions when using a product.
- Inform retailers, manufacturers, trade organizations, and government agencies when a product does not perform safely.
- Identify possible defects and report them to the proper government authorities.
- Respond to recalls.
- Support efforts to improve safety for all consumers.

Products Needing Safety Regulations

Product safety areas ripe for government action (i.e., warning labels, safety standards, bans, recalls) include: swimming pool covers that trap and drown (26 dead so far); accordion-style baby gates (8 deaths so far); child-resistant mouthwash bottles (3 deaths so far); small balls and toys (186 choking deaths in 11 years); empty 5-gallon buckets (1 child dies every nine days in a few inches of water); hand-held hair dryers that electrocute about 20 people each year, usually when the dryers are dropped into the bathtub with the switch in the incorrectly presumed-safe "off position"; baby walkers that pose serious risks of injury (29,000 emergency room visits annually);[2] and bicycle helmets (300 children die annually with another 50,000 suffering bike-related head injuries); playgrounds (200,000 injuries from falls annually); and ordinary rubber balloons (131 deaths in the last 20 years).

Other consumer products that cause concern include recliner chairs that entrap necks and heads of children; portable liquid-fuel space heaters that are dangerous; riding lawn mowers that are unstable; vehicle child seats that are not firmly anchored; "Slip 'N Slide"

---

[2]One out of three infants who use these walkers is injured.

toys; and amusement parks that have unsafe rides. Short of banning dangerous products, government may demand improvements in design and/or require warning labels. Government may or may not take action to regulate in these areas.[3]

CONSUMER UPDATE: Warning Labels Are Often Ignored

People are bombarded with warning labels on household products, signs in restaurants and bars cautioning that common items may cause cancer or birth defects, and recall notices from auto and consumer product manufacturers. These are often misinterpreted and/or ignored because many consumers are bombarded by notices, the warnings are written in difficult-to-comprehend legalese and people feel overwhelmed. Businesses seem to put too many warnings, disclosures and instructions on products. Metal ladders, for example, have over 30 such pieces of information.

Product Liability Lawsuits—A Powerful Weapon of Consumers

One of the consumer's most important rights is to remedy a wrong. A **tort** is a wrongful act resulting in injury to a person or property, for which the injured party may seek compensation. Our current product liability "system compensates for injuries, deters conduct that results in unsafe products, and leads to the disclosure of outrageous corporate practices."[4] As consumers in America, people are supposed to have their problems listened to, and, if necessary, to have their day in court. A Rand Corporation research study found that just 1 in 50 persons hurt by products outside of work make a claim for compensation. Vital to the right of redress or remedy is being able to file a lawsuit to recover damages for injuries from defective products. According to a study in the *Journal of Consumer Affairs*, sixty percent of Americans believe that companies should make sure products are safe, regardless of the cost.

Product liability lawsuits are generally filed on a **contingency basis** where the attorney's fee is zero unless the consumer-plaintiff wins. Consumers win about 50 percent of the cases that go to trial, although 95 percent of such lawsuits are settled out of court. The contingency fee in a product liability lawsuit is surely the poor consumers's key to equity and redress at the courtroom door. Otherwise, consumers would have no voice to represent them in cases where companies sell them toxic, hazardous, mislabeled products that injure and kill people. Product liability lawsuits have through the discovery process often turned up unscrupulous, often criminal, and sometimes murderous corporate behavior. Consider the tobacco companies, for example.

The vast majority of product liability cases, including class-action lawsuits, would never be filed without a sufficiently motivated legal staff. Money is the motivation in contingency lawsuits because attorneys typically collect one-third of the amount of any

---

[3]The CPSC mandated that child-resistant cigarette lighters go on the market in 1994. Historically, 150 people have been killed and 1,000 injured every year from fires started by children playing with lighters. The new lighters cost about 10 cents more.

[4]Nye, P. (1992, November/December). The Faces of Product Liability. *Public Citizen*, p. 21.

settlement. The alternative is to pay $100 to $200 a hour for legal and investigative fees for the months and years it takes to get a case to court. Without the contingency fee system, the economics of bringing most product liability cases would be prohibitive.

Punitive Damages Penalize the Worst Manufacturers

Consumer-plaintiffs in product liability lawsuits typically win **compensatory damages** which are assessed to cover a plaintiff's medical bills, lost wages, and pain and suffering. Plaintiffs also usually win attorney's fees. Only in some cases are punitive damages awarded by a judge or jury. **Punitive damages** are those which inflict or aim to inflict punishment against people and companies who have consciously and flagrantly done wrong. The awarding of punitive damages is fundamental to protecting the consumer interest in obtaining equity for other consumers.

Over the past 25 years, only 355 product liability cases involved the awarding of punitive damages, reports Suffolk University's Michael Rustad. That is an average of only 14 cases per year, nationwide. However, because they usually involve popular consumer goods, they attract disproportionate attention from consumers, regulators, and reform-minded critics. Tort court filings account for only 9 percent of the 14 million civil cases filed annually, and just 4 of that 9 percent are product liability lawsuits. The Rand Corporation found in a survey that large courts find punitive awards in only 2.6 percent of product-liability cases.

Data from the National Association of Insurance Commissioners show that less than one half of product liability lawsuit litigants receives any compensation. The average winning claim over the past decade was $13,200; the winning plaintiff averaged $8600 and the plaintiff's attorney averaged $4600. The "prize winning awards" that receive all the media attention averaged less than $500,000 over the past decade, according to Jury Verdict Research. According to the Consumer Federation of America, "the entire cost in 1994 of all product liability settlements and verdicts, insured, and uninsured, totaled $4.1 billion."

When the Ford Motor Company was ordered to pay $3.5 million in punitive damages in the Grimshaw case, the jury tried to recover the money that Ford should have spent on properly designing the Pinto fuel tanks that killed and maimed so many consumers. The silicone breast implant class action settlement in 1995 penalized the manufacturer for continuing to sell defective products; 400,000 women filed claims. The Exxon Company was punished economically for the Valdez oil spill.

Examples of recent liability lawsuits where the defendant companies lost to plaintiff-consumers include breast implants that leaked silicone gel; General Motors 1983-87 full-size pickup trucks with gas tanks mounted outside the frame (which have claimed over 300 lives in crashes that became gasoline infernos); Dalkon Shield, a plastic contraceptive device that left many women sterile; Suzuki Samurai vehicle rollovers in sharp turns; Medtronic heart pacemakers that failed; and the General Electric Coffeematic Brew Starter that turned itself on, but not off, and started fatal fires. These cases often involve hundreds of thousands, and sometimes millions, of wronged consumers.

Other examples include defective cars that were not crashworthy enough; football helmets that did not have enough resistance to shock to prevent head and neck injuries; children's sleepwear that did not have sufficient flame retardancy; recliner chairs that were not designed well enough to prevent children from strangling as they became trapped between the seat and the leg rest; side effects of a prescription drug that caused a birth deformity; and upholstered furniture that failed to stop a fire started by a smoldering cigarette.

CONSUMER UPDATE: Breast Implant Lawsuit

The class-action lawsuit (400,000 plaintiffs) against manufacturers of silicone breast implants that have caused such problems as autoimmune diseases and hardened breasts reached a settlement in 1995. This permits distribution of some of the $3 *billion* settlement to compensate the more than 48,000 women who received the devices over the past 25 years and filed claims as part of a class-action lawsuit. The fund also will provide medical monitoring and surgical expenses.

The FDA declared a moratorium on silicone breast implants in 1992, except for reconstructive surgery as part of a clinical study. Last year the FDA announced that it was considering similar restrictions on saline-filled breast implants.

Punitive damage awards puts firms on notice to improve their behaviors. In addition, punitive damages often lead to product recalls, redesigns, and warnings about product dangers. Thus, some form of equity is achieved for all consumers. In 1991, the Supreme Court upheld the concept of punitive damages.

Today's Product Liability Laws

Product liability is generally a matter of state law and variations exist throughout the country. Some lawsuits are brought as a breach of warranty under contract law. Most product liability cases are brought to court under the concepts of negligence or strict tort liability. The legal doctrine of **strict liability** provides that plaintiffs only have to show that a defective product was the cause of their injury.[5]

Strict liability was cited in the 1963 *Greenman v. Yuba Power Products* case which held that, "a manufacturer is strictly liable in tort when an article it places in the market, knowing that it is to be used without inspection for defects, proves to have a defect that causes injury to a human being." Further, "The purpose of such liability is to insure that the cost of injuries resulting from defective products are borne by the manufacturers that put such products rather than the injured persons who are powerless to protect themselves." Thus, the strict liability theory allows plaintiffs to collect damages without having the burden of proving actual negligence. The emergence of the concept of strict liability has made it easier for consumers to prove and collect damages from a manufacturer.

Because of strict liability, manufacturers today have little choice except to make safer products. Absolute safety is impossible, so manufacturers will continue to test their products and purchase sufficient liability insurance. The price of every consumer product includes an amount to cover liability insurance premiums, just as there are amounts to provide for salaries of executives and profits for shareholders. Society has become more

---

[5]Prior to the 1960s, plaintiffs had to convince juries that the product manufacturer had acted in a negligent manner, an extremely difficult standard.

conscious of the need to demand safe products and to penalize those manufacturers who refuse or are unable to sell safe goods.

CONSUMER UPDATE:
Court Secrecy Using "Protective Orders" Hides Safety Concerns

Does a corporation's right to keep its business affairs confidential outweigh the consumer's right to information about potentially harmful products? Should companies be forced to give up their privacy rights when they are dragged into court? Should corporations be forced to give up information on trade secrets? On proprietary information? On incriminating research and memorandums?

In defending itself against scores of lawsuits filed by victims of fiery car crashes and other product safety problems, General Motors Corporation has succeeded in suppressing controversial documents in state courts across the country by obtaining **protective orders** from judges. As part of the settlement of these court cases, GM has obtained agreements that prohibit opposing lawyers from disclosing details, thus creating, in effect a **secret settlement**.

On the request of numerous defendant companies, judges have issued sealing orders that remove entire lawsuit files from the public record. Sometimes courts have allowed the records to be destroyed. This keeps health, environmental, and safety concerns out of the public spotlight and forces other litigants to try to uncover the same information again and again, at appreciable expense.   This tactic designed to keep sensitive information out of the public record also has been used by many companies involved in product safety lawsuits. Such protective orders have sealed information, at least temporarily, for the manufacturers of accutane, cigarettes, dangerous playground equipment, grain elevators, defective heart valves, Agent Orange, unsafe all-terrain vehicles, breast implants, and butane lighters.

Such secrecy undermines the right to know of all Americans. It keeps vital information hidden from the public. Arthur H, Bryant, director of the Trial Lawyers for Public Justice, says that, "by making sure that nobody knows about injuries that are caused, manufacturers can influence the state of scientific knowledge by controlling access to the data on which scientific opinions are based."[1]

Seven states have passed laws that encourage judges to permit disclosure of internal company documents that detail health and safety problems to lawyers with similar lawsuits. In effect, lawyers can share confidential documents obtained from companies under protective orders with other attorneys. Thus, attorneys with similar cases will not have to litigate the same issues. If an objection is raised, a hearing is held and a judge may impose restrictions if necessary. Although the law does not permit attorneys to share the information with the public, it increases the chances that safety information will reach government safety regulators and be aired at trial. Congress is considering similar legislation.

Judges in Florida, New York, New Jersey, and Texas have refused to keep such court records secret. They have ordered the release of sealed records, ruling that, "labeling corporate negligence a 'trade secret' hides vital facts from the public" and that authorities "may have access to anything under seal that may be helpful and beneficial for the protection of public health."[2] The New Jersey Supreme Court concluded that, "there is a profound public interest when matters of health, safety, and consumer fraud are involved," and, therefore, "there must be careful scrutiny prior to sealing records and documents filed with a court in a high public-interest case."[3]

---

[1]Weiser, B. & Walsh, E. (1988, October 25), Drug firm's strategy: Avoid trial, ask secrecy. *The Washington Post*, p. A-12.
[2]Weiser, B. (1994, July 29), Lawsuits spur a debate over secrets vs. safety. *The Washington Post*, p. A-1.
[3]Court Rejects Secrecy for Accutane; Cites "Profound Public Interest" (1995, September-October), *Public Citizen*, 2.

Critics of Product Liability Lawsuits

Critics of tort liability argue that the system creates too many uncertainties about manufacturers' liabilities and the size of damage awards. The notorious cases of McDonald's coffee (where a woman was awarded $6 million after spilling hot coffee on herself) and BMW (where the purchaser of a new car was awarded $4 million after discovering that part of the vehicle had been surreptitiously repainted by the seller) are the exception rather than the rule. (In most of these cases, including the two just cited, judges often reduce the award [although the media never seem to get that corrected message to the people]).[6] Critics want the system changed so businesses could reduce their insurance and litigation costs.

Opponents have been pushing for weak federal legislation that would preempt strict state laws. They also advocate eliminating or constraining strict liability lawsuits. As a result, 30 states have passed laws that put caps on punitive damages. Leading the battle is the Product Liability Coordinating Committee, a coalition of 700,000 firms. It is dominated by Union Carbide, Ford Motor Company, and a number of motor vehicle, drug, chemical, and insurance companies.

Opponents of product liability lawsuits, which include most Republicans and the business community, seek to place caps on punitive damages in *all* civil cases, eliminate strict liability, and impose a negligence standard for injuries caused by design defects or failure to warn. They want plaintiffs to be restricted to collecting no more than $250,000. That would allow manufacturers to simply budget certain amounts for future fines as a cost of doing business. They also propose a **loser pays** provision that would require the losing party to pay the winner's legal fees. Such a provision would effectively end this important type of consumer protection litigation as most consumers would not be willing to accept such financial risk.

Supporters of the Consumer's Right to Sue

Consumer organizations, labor groups, and trial lawyers support the current legal concept of strict liability to obtain just compensation. Consumer advocates see product liability lawsuits as the single most important threat to keep manufacturers in line. If strict liability were abolished, the poorest manufacturers would have no incentive to avoid making defective products. Such manufacturers would become free riders if they were not required to pay compensation. Also, it is not unrealistic to figure that as business steps away from paying legitimate claims to wronged consumers, business will ask government to bear the cost of such claims. "After all," would be the argument, "if the FDA approved the drug, shouldn't the government have to pay the damages?"

Ralph Nader, who opposes tort reform, says that, "Injured plaintiffs must be able to hold their perpetrators accountable." Efforts to limit the threat of a consumer product liability lawsuit are against the consumer interest. In 1996, President Clinton wisely vetoed Congress' bill to weaken product liability laws.

---

[6]In 1996, the U.S. Supreme Court threw out the BMW award was "grossly excessive."

The Consumer Product Safety Commission

At the time the Consumer Product Safety Commission (CPSC) was created, unsafe products were abundant and widely distributed. Voluntary safety standards to protect consumers were not working very well. Consumer groups were actively involved throughout the 1960s in publicizing product safety shortcomings until Congress finally got into the act to preempt weak and non-existent state laws. Until creation of the CPSC, government had taken a piecemeal approach to product safety, attacking problems in response to individual tragedies and public outcries. The CPSC was formally established in 1973 to protect consumers against unreasonable risks of injuries associated with consumer products. It is currently chaired by Ann Brown. The more serious risks include amputation, electrocution, burns, asphyxiation, and cancer.

Creation of the CPSC was a major step forward because it established for the first time an agency dedicated to ensuring that consumers are protected from unreasonable product risks. The responsibilities for a number of existing fragmented product safety efforts were centralized and a reasonably comprehensive approach to product safety evolved. The main goal of the commission is to provide for a safer public market of consumer goods.

The CPSC is a five-member independent regulatory agency. Its members are appointed by the President for 7-year terms and approved by the U.S. Senate. One commissioner serves as chair. The CPSC has a staff of 487 and an annual budget of $42 million; that amounts to 44 cents per year per household.[7]

The CPSC is empowered to: (1) set safety standards for consumer products; (2) ban products; (3) issue administrative recall orders to compel repair, replacement, or refunds for products found to present substantial hazards; and (4) seek court orders to require the recall of imminently hazardous products.

The commission regulates only products that are sold in the United States. Examples include: bicycles, chain saws, toys, coffee makers, television antennas, baby cribs, and stereos. The CPSC regulates through standard-setting, product bans, refunds, and recalls. Few products are not under its control. Other federal agencies have developed special expertise with certain products and have legal jurisdiction over them, such as motor vehicles, bullets, fireworks, food, drugs, cosmetics, medical devices, alcohol, tobacco, aircraft, boats, and pesticides.[8]

CPSC Legal Mandates and Responsibilities

The CPSC has two key legal authorities: the Consumer Products Safety Act (1972) and the Federal Hazardous Substances Act (1960). It also enforces the Flammable Fabrics Act (1953 and amendments in 1967 and 1976), the Child Protection Act (1966), the

---

[7]The CPSC budget is just over 1 percent of the $3.1 billion of the Environmental Protection Agency and less than 5 percent of the Food and Drug Administration's $920 million.

[8]Despite the fact that firearms kill twice as many people as all household products combined, there is no federal agency responsible to ensure that defectively designed guns are not sold. This is because firearms were exempted from CPSC responsibility in 1972. Thus, firearms are legally exempt from federal safety regulation. CBS says that 1500 people are accidently killed or injured each year, in addition to the murders and suicides.

Poison Prevention Packaging Act (1970), the Refrigerator Safety Act (1956), and the Child Safety Protection Act (1994). The broad responsibilities of the CPSC are:

- To gather and disseminate information related to product injuries;
- To protect the public against unreasonable risks of injury associated with consumer products used in and around the home, in schools, and in recreation areas;
- To promote the use of uniform safety standards;
- To help consumers evaluate the comparative safety of products;
- To require manufacturers of CPSC-regulated products to conduct a testing program to ensure that their products are safe and meet appropriate safety standards; and
- To promote research and investigation into the causes and the prevention of product-related deaths, injuries, and illnesses.

The CPSC works with industry to develop voluntary safety standards. The Consumer Product Safety Act requires the agency to defer to voluntary standards instead of promulgating mandatory standards where there is a voluntary standard that adequately addresses a product safety problem and there is substantial compliance with that standard.

The CPSC also issues and enforces mandatory safety standards, bans unsafe products, encourages and/or orders recalls and repairs of unsafe products, conducts research on potential product hazards, and conducts information and education programs. The CPSC has a toll-free hotline (800-638-2772) to receive reports about potentially hazardous consumer products and provide safety information to the public about product recalls. The commission also answers questions about product safety problems.

CPSC Authorities and Powers

The Consumer Product Safety Commission has several important legal powers:

1. It has the authority to set mandatory product safety standards under Section 7 of the Consumer Products Safety Act. Standards may set forth requirements as to product performance, composition, content, construction, finish, packaging, and design. Products may also be required to carry warnings or instructions. Standards that have the force of law must be reasonably necessary to prevent or reduce an unreasonable risk of injury associated with such products. CPSC standards may preempt state or local product safety standards when it is in the public interest to do so.

2. It can seek court action to declare a product an imminent or substantial hazard. The CPSC can do this when it determines that there is no feasible standard that will protect the public from unreasonable risk of injury. An **imminent hazard** is a product that presents an impending and unreasonable risk of death, serious illness, or severe personal injury. An imminent hazard presents the highest risk to the public. For example, several years ago one particular brand of a mechanic's trouble light was declared an imminent hazard because its poor design allowed people to easily become electrocuted. The lights were withdrawn from the market and recalled from consumers who had purchased them.

A **substantial hazard** is a product that fails to comply with applicable consumer product safety rules and which creates a substantial risk of injury to the public. Substantial hazards also include product defects which, because of the pattern of the defect, the number of defective products distributed in commerce, the severity of the risk, or otherwise, creates a substantial risk of injury to the public. Items found to be substantial hazards under Section 15 of the CPSA are usually one particular branch of a manufacturer's product line, such as a defective electric lamp. Here the CPSC can initiate action to ban the product from the marketplace. Upon approval by a U.S. District Court, hazardous products are then **banned**, which means that the product can no longer be sold. **Banning** is an official decree of prohibition by a federal court issued when no feasible safety standard would adequately protect the public.

Most products that are banned are removed from the market under Section 8 of the CPSA because they present an unreasonable risk of injury to the public by failing to meet known standards and regulations. Examples of banned products include: flammable imported rayon scarves, unstable refuse bins that fell on people, flammable contact adhesives used on floor tiles, paints containing leads, patching compounds containing asbestos, and lawn darts (a game similar to horse-shoes). The values of these products in the market were far outweighed by the number of serious accidents and unnecessary deaths.

3. It can order a recall of hazardous products. After a hearing, the CPSC can compel manufacturers to recall a product, refund the purchase price of a hazardous product, repair or modify it to proper safety standards, or replace it with a comparable item that meets appropriate safety standards. The CPSC can suggest a voluntary recall to a manufacturer or order a mandatory one, but most recalls are voluntary. Recalls and repairs are ordered for products that fail to comply with mandatory standards or that present substantial hazards or imminent hazards to consumers. This approach is called **managing by exception**, since most consumer products are safe. When a product is recalled, the manufacturer is required to make an effort to notify buyers that a safety defect has been discovered, often by mail or with radio and television announcements and advertisements.

Examples of products that have been recalled are: hair dryers that expelled asbestos, paint strippers that were too powerful, baby cribs that could cause strangulation of infants, toys with parts that could be swallowed by small children because they failed an established regulation, smoke detectors that failed to operate in the presence of smoke, and weak portable child safety seats. The CPSC makes about 250 product recalls each year.

4. If necessary, the CPSC can file a legal request in federal court to have goods seized that do not comply with a regulation.

5. Manufacturers are required to notify the CPSC within 24 hours about hazardous products. Section 15 of the CPSA requires that manufacturers notify the CPSC if they become aware that any product either fails to comply with appropriate product safety rules and standards or contains a defect that could create a substantial hazard to consumers. Failure to report can subject a company to fines of up to $1.25 million.[9]

6. The CPSC can impose both civil and criminal penalties. Under the CPSA, civil fines for CPSA violations are $2,000 for each offence up to $500,000 for multiple infractions. People who knowingly and willfully violate the laws are subject to 1 year in prison.[10]

---

[9]American corporations paid over $2.5 million in civil penalties to the U.S. Treasury since 1985 to settle CPSC allegations that they failed to notify the federal government about defective consumer products they were manufacturing or importing.

[10]Individual consumers also can sue in a U.S. District Court for enforcement of CPSC rules and orders.

CPSC Injury Data-Collection System

To help determine the nature and scope of injuries from consumer products, the CPSC has a national data-collection system known as the National Electronic Injury Surveillance System (NEISS, pronounced "nice"). NEISS serves as the backbone of the commission's injury reporting system. It collects data from 62 statistically representative hospital emergency rooms located across the country, which permits the CPSC to calculate national injury estimates by associated product. Research shows that approximately 38 percent of all injuries are treated in hospital emergency rooms, 41 percent are treated in doctors' offices, 18 percent are treated at home, and 3 percent become inpatient cases.

Participating hospitals classify injuries according to about 1000 product codes. The information from hospitals is processed by the CPSC and extrapolated into national statistics. NEISS projections can then help identify those products most often related to injuries. For example, recent data show that the products or activities that caused injuries most frequently as reported by hospital emergency rooms included in descending order: stairs; bicycles; baseball; football; basketball; nails, carpet tacks, and screws; chairs, sofas, and sofa beds; skating; non-glass tables; and glass doors, windows, and panels.

The CPSC collects data from death certificates and from interviews with nurses, physicians, and injury victims. Consumer products that are frequently involved in injuries or which cause severe injuries are usually considered priority items for regulation.

CPSC Rulemaking Procedures

In recent years, the CPSC has written rules to establish performance, design, composition, packaging, and construction standards for a number of products. Examples of products with mandatory safety standards include: bicycles, matchbooks, walk-behind lawn power mowers, residential garage door openers, baby cribs, baby rattles, child-resistant packaging, swimming pool slides, power lawn mowers, chain saws, matches, home-use pesticides, and cellulose insulation. Other rules were written on the flammability of such products as children's sleepwear, general wearing apparel, furniture, mattresses, carpet, and rugs. The CPSC issues standards in an effort to reduce injuries and save lives. For example, think about how much easier it is to see a bicycle at night because of the mandatory safety reflectors.

The Administrative Procedures Act Governs
Federal Regulatory Agency Rulemaking

Regulations are often adopted by single-purpose, mission-oriented agencies such as the Consumer Product Safety Commission and the National Highway Traffic Safety Administration. The basic procedures governing rulemaking were adopted in 1946 under the federal Administrative Procedures Act (APA).

Rulemaking by various agencies can be done informally or formally by administrative agencies, depending on their enabling legislation. Informal rulemaking involves publication in the Federal Register of a "Notice of Proposed Rulemaking." This provides reasons for the action, as well as a time and place for proceedings to be held by the agency, followed by a comment period, during which interested parties can submit their views, culminating with publication of the final rule in the *Federal Register*.

A less quick and inefficient approach is **formal rulemaking**. This provides for the adoption of rules to be made based on the evidence on the record after several opportunities have been provided through agency hearings. Formal administrative rulemaking generally requires a number of time periods for "an announced intention for possible rulemaking," a "notice and comment" time period, evidentiary rulemaking hearings, and additional months for "notices of comment" until a regulation is formalized. Interested members of the public, such as businesses, unions, and consumers, are permitted to participate in the proceedings.

DID YOU KNOW? Childproof Cap Wins Award

In 1994, the Consumer Product Safety Commission gave its first "Chairman's Commendation for Significant Contributions to Product Safety" to the Proctor & Gamble Company for its new childproof cap that, "uses adult reasoning skills rather than brute force" to open containers. The **adult-friendly cap** is used on mouthwash and some pain medications.

CPSC Rulemaking Authority

The CPSC can promulgate regulations under authorities granted from the Consumer Product Safety Act (CPSA). It also can issue regulations under authorities granted from the Federal Hazardous Substances Act and the Flammable Fabrics Act, although these can only be used for toys or other articles intended for use by children that present electrical, mechanical, or thermal hazards. In rulemaking, the CPSC must follow the standard government rulemaking procedures under the guidelines of the federal Administrative Procedures Act. It takes a minimum of about 1 1/2 years for the CPSC to issue informal regulations and even longer using formal rulemaking procedures.

Any interested person, including a consumer or consumer organization, may petition the CPSC to commence a proceeding for the issuance, amendment, or revocation of a consumer product safety rule as described in the APA. The CPSA itself calls for the use of performance standards whenever possible, rather than specification of design standards. Thus, consumers, industry, and government may play a vital role in the development of a trade regulation.

The CPSC can participate in a voluntary standards proceeding as a nonvoting member. **Voluntary standards** are those adopted by industry organizations. Since 1981, the CPSC has been required by law to get industry to develop reasonable voluntary safety standards whenever possible. Accordingly, many well-qualified industry groups have been intimately involved in the rulemaking process. Examples include the Underwriters' Laboratories (UL), the American Society for Testing and Materials (ASTM), and the American National Standards Institute (ANSI). Although voluntary standards can be implemented more quickly than mandatory standards, critics allege that the standard-setting bodies often fail to consider the consumer interest thoroughly enough and that voluntary standards may represent the least common denominator.

Rulemaking to develop a standard is a very technical, complex, and expensive process that requires the cooperative efforts of manufacturers and sellers. In general, hearings must be held to allow citizens to make inputs to the process. Often state and federal governments rely on voluntary standards because they lack the expertise and resources to develop their own. When writing standards, particularly mandatory standards, it is not uncommon to have an official record in a rulemaking procedure amount to thousands of pages, including research data, testimony, and comments.

Factors That Must be Considered in CPSC Rulemaking

Before any product safety standard can be promulgated, the law requires that several factors be considered: (1) the incidence and severity of injuries or illnesses associated with a product, (2) the nature of the risk of injuries that will be reduced or eliminated, (3) the expected support from the public given their attitude toward the proposed rule, (4) the effect of the proposed rule on the public's need for the product, and (5) the effect of the proposed rule on competition and manufacturing. The CPSC also must use cost-benefit analysis in the decision making process. Any rule developed by the CPSC may be overruled or reversed if Congress passes a law to that end; this is loosely called a **congressional veto.**

The National Highway Traffic Safety Administration

The National Highway Traffic Safety Administration (NHTSA) is an administrative unit in the Department of Transportation (headed by Frederico Peña) created in 1966. NHTSA's single administrator is appointed by the President.

NHTSA Legal Mandates and Authorities

The NHTSA enforces the National Traffic and Motor Vehicle Safety Act (1966), Highway Safety Act (1966), Motor Vehicle Information and Cost Savings Act (1972), and Intermodal Surface Transportation Act (1991). The NHTSA was established to reduce highway deaths, injuries, and property losses caused by motor vehicle accidents. The NHTSA establishes and enforces minimum safety and performance standards for motor vehicles and related equipment called the **Federal Motor Vehicle Safety Standards (FMVSS).** NHTSA's budget is $307 million and it has 667 employees. Since the NHTSA was established, it is estimated that 250,000 lives have been saved and millions of injuries reduced.

Last year 41,700 Americans died in motor vehicle accidents (one of the lowest in history); two-thirds of the deaths were passengers. The estimated 6.8 million crashes resulted in 3.3 million injuries.[11] About 10,000 suffer permanently disabling injuries in

---

[11]The consequences of faster travel can be counted in lives lost. In the 40 states where speed limits were raised to 65 mph on rural interstate highways (before the 1996 federal speed limit law was abolished), deaths on those interstates were 28 percent higher than when the speed limit was 55 mph. The higher speed limit is projected to result in an additional 4750 deaths annually; this equates to increasing a societal cost of $19 billion. Speed is blamed for one-third of all highway fatalities.

motor vehicle accidents each year. Motor vehicle crashes are the leading killer of Americans under the age of 35 and the leading cause of head injuries, epilepsy, quadriplegia, paraplegia, and facial injuries. People are now surviving vehicle accidents that a few years ago would have been fatal. A result is rising medical costs for crash survivors with serious injuries.

DID YOU KNOW?
The Death Rates in Vehicles

The death rates per 10,000 registered vehicles by the size of autos are: very small, 2.9; small, 2.1; small midsize, 2.1; medium midsize, 1.4; large, 1.1; very large, 0.7. Both size and weight are factors. The incidence of severe injuries and death increases as the length of the wheelbase decreases. The laws of physics dictate that, everything else being equal, the larger the car the safer the occupants. Rollover deaths are five times greater in small cars than in large cars.

When yesteryear's heavier cars averaged 14 miles per gallon, the death rate per 10,000 was 3.5; the death rate on last year's 28 mpg lighter-weight models was 2.1. Both the Insurance Institute for Highway Safety and the Center for Auto Safety say that automobiles can be downsized without trading off safety.

Even though twice as many miles are driven annually compared to 25 years ago, the fatality rate in cars has dropped from 5.7 deaths per 100 million vehicles to a recent 1.7 rate, a 68-year low. That is a difference of between 50,000 and perhaps 130,000 deaths that would have occurred without government motor vehicle safety laws. Why has this occurred? Ralph Nader's answer is: "Regulations."

Recent fatality rates per 100,000 deaths by age group were: ages 15-24 (38), ages 25-39 (14), ages 40-69 (10), ages 70-79 (15), and ages 80+ (25); the average is 15. Teenagers comprise 10 percent of the U.S. population, but 14 percent of all motor vehicle deaths; more than twice as many male teenagers are killed as females. Sixty-six percent of Americans use seat belts. Men account for 76 percent of fatalities, women 24 percent.

Of all motor vehicle deaths, the proportion of fatally injured drivers with high blood alcohol concentrations (0.10 percent or more) remains about 40 percent. Among fatally injured male drivers, 44 percent had blood alcohol levels above 0.10 percent; compared to 22 percent of women.

The NHTSA has jurisdiction over all types of motor vehicles, such as automobiles, trucks, buses, recreational vehicles (RVs), motorcycles, and mopeds. It handles complaints about the safety of motor vehicles and failures of associated vehicle equipment and accessories. The NHTSA conducts investigations looking for safety-related defects and equipment failures that cause safety problems. NHTSA has rulemaking authority. It also enforces laws and regulations requiring recalls and associated remedies for motor vehicles and vehicle equipment, and it is empowered to force manufacturers to recall and repair unsafe vehicles.

NHTSA Programs

The NHTSA is legally required to perform several mandated programs:

- Investigate safety defects in motor vehicles.
- Establish and enforce federal motor vehicle safety standards.
- Promote the use of safety belts, child safety belts, and air bags.
- Help states and communities reduce the threat of drunk drivers.
- Investigate odometer fraud.
- Establish and enforce vehicle anti-theft regulations.
- Set and enforce fuel economy standards.
- Conduct research on driver behavior and traffic safety.
- Provide the public with information on motor vehicle safety topics.

CONSUMER UPDATE:
Rollover Risk Ratings Coming on Vehicles

The National Highway Traffic Safety Administration has proposed that window stickers on new cars and trucks also include a rollover rating. This would be a score indicating how likely the vehicle is to turn over in an accident. Rollover accidents kill about 9,000 people a year—28 percent of the total. Judith Lee Stone, president of the Advocates for Highway and Auto Safety says that, "Information won't do much to prevent rollover deaths and injuries. The solution is more-stable vehicles and more-forgiving interiors." NHTSA has issued a regulation—to be phased in by 2003—that will require overpadding of pillars, side rails, roofs, and the frames around windshields, doors, and windows.

NHTSA Recalls

The NHTSA has the authority to order recalls whenever substantial numbers of a safety-related defect are observed that present an unreasonable risk of accident or injury. Examples of recalls include ignition switches that could cause fires, unsafe seat belts, rear hatch latch popping open, defective steering mechanisms, failure of pins to hold seats in place, motor vehicle tire treads separating, gasoline tanks that explode in rear-end collisions, transmissions jumping from the park gear into reverse in unattended vehicles, and sudden acceleration of cars while in gear.[12] The success rate for NHTSA recalls in a recent five-year period was 68 percent of all vehicles, 51 percent of equipment problems, and 28 percent for difficulties with tires.

When the NHTSA suspects a safety-related defect, a **preliminary low-level safety investigation** is conducted. This informal inquiry asks manufacturers to provide information about an alleged problem. The NHTSA then conducts an engineering analysis of the safety consequences. Most often, such investigations are dropped for lack of persuasive evidence. Should an analysis be negative, the manufacturer may be sent a **recall request letter** which asks the company to conduct a voluntary recall in an effort

---

[12]The Center for Auto Safety (CAS) estimates that the five million 1973-87 GM full-side pickups with side saddle gas tanks mounted outside the frame were involved in over 300 fire crashes. The Secretary of Transportation signed an unprecedented agreement with GM that closed the investigation into the gas tanks in exchange for a commitment by GM to spend $51 million on safety education programs. Years ago, the infamous Ford Pinto fire crashes claimed only 27 lives. GM has a "consumer be burned" attitude in refusing to recall those pickup trucks, says CAS.

to get a defective product off the market quickly. About half such requests result in voluntary recalls, since manufacturers often contest the NHTSA's findings. Most recalls supervised by the agency are initiated voluntarily by the manufacturers, not in response to government defect investigations. Court-ordered recalls are rare.

If the manufacturer declines to recall and the evidence points to a safety-related defect, the NHTSA opens a **formal defect investigation**. This serious investigation may take two months or two years. After the investigation is complete, NHTSA makes its initial defect determination. It then holds a public meeting at which the public and the manufacturers present their views. The agency later makes a final decision on the matter. When a problem is judged to be serious, the NHTSA orders a recall of the product, and requires that the manufacturer remedy the difficulty.

The NHTSA can make recalls: (1) when specific safety defects are discovered, (2) when a manufacturer fails to comply with a FMVSS safety standard, and (3) when safety problems are observed that are common to a number of similar vehicles.

After a product is manufactured, the NHTSA has eight years to take action to recall vehicles and vehicle equipment and three years for tires before the agency's legal authority expires. Owners of recalled vehicles must be notified by first-class mail of any safety defects. Defective vehicles that are recalled under government order must be repaired by an authorized dealer for free. Manufacturer's policies vary when there is a voluntary recall even though the manufacturers pay the dealers to make the repairs.

CONSUMER UPDATE:
The United States Does Not *Require* Daytime Running Lights

Canada requires all new vehicles to have **daytime running lights** as a safety feature. These automatically keep the vehicle's highbeam headlights on at a reduced brightness. This is a safety feature designed to make cars more visible to pedestrians and other drivers during daytime hours. NHTSA recently began *permitting* daytime running lights on new vehicles, but not requiring them.

It is possible that a vehicle may be one of the 20 million that has some unrepaired safety defect. The NHTSA can provide these data to consumers, as well as information on safety defect investigations and new car crash test results. You can get a report on an motor vehicle and find out if it is part of a recall by calling the NHTSA's toll-free hotline (800-424-9393) and giving them the make, model, year, and **vehicle identification number (VIN)**. The VIN number is the numeral indicating a specific vehicle made by a manufacturer. It is visible on the dashboard when you look through the front windshield on the driver's side. Only the manufacturers' computers can tell if the defects in any particular recalled vehicle have been repaired.

The NHTSA also can assist callers who are having difficulty obtaining repair work for an existing safety recall. Manufacturers are obligated to repair recalled vehicles no matter how old the cars or who owns them. The NHTSA also accepts complaints about safety problems in motor vehicles, tires, and vehicle equipment; copies of complaints are forwarded to the manufacturers. (The Environmental Protection Agency has the authority to order recalls when motor vehicles fail emission control system standards.)

NHTSA Vehicle Crashing and Testing

The NHTSA has a New Car Assessment Program (NCAP) for **crashworthiness** to determine a vehicle's overall ability to protect seat-belted front-seat drivers and passengers. To simulate a head-on crash, the NHTSA tows vehicles at 35 miles per hour into a stationary barrier and measures the impact on dummies' heads, chests, and thighbones; more than 80 percent of all crashes occur at speeds less than 40 miles per hour. Large cars are better at absorbing energy and maintaining structural integrity than small vehicles because they have more body to take the crush of the impact. The NHTSA annually publishes the results of safety tests it conducts by make and model, and these data also can be obtained from the non-profit Center for Auto Safety. The data are now converted into a single rating of one to five stars, although safety advocates point out that "three stars under the current system equals a failing grade under the old system." The new system disguises less safe vehicles. The old method published an index that measured the human body's ability to withstand these crashes, called the **hic score** (for head-injury criteria).

CONSUMER UPDATE:
Light Trucks Are Dangerous

Light trucks—a term that includes sport-utility vehicle, pickups, minivans, and some vans—account for 40 percent of the vehicles on the road today. These vehicles tend to roll over, flip, or spin out of control more easily than automobiles. During a recent five-year period, the Geo Tracker, for example, had the highest driver death rate of any vehicle, 3.2 deaths per 10,000 registered vehicles.

For years these vehicles have been exempt from many federal automobile safety standards. Some sport and utility vehicles are nearly 20 times more likely than cars to experience a fatal rollover. Light trucks *began* to meet *some* of the auto safety standards in 1993. They probably will remain exempt from proposed requirements for rear-seat shoulder harnesses, new child booster-seat standards, and revised standards for pedestrian safety that could alter the front-end designs of light trucks.

NHTSA Safety Standards

A number of Federal Motor Vehicle Safety Standards (FMVSS) are in effect on motor vehicles today. Examples include: rear center-mounted brake signals, shatterproof windshields, collapsible steering columns, energy-absorbing bumpers, headrest restraints on the front seats, padded dashboards, non-protruding interior appliances, collapsible arm rests, seat-belt warning systems, over-the shoulder and lap seat belts, and front-seat air bags.[13]

A **passive restraint system** is an automatic safety device that requires no special effort from the protected vehicle passenger to operate in the event of an accident. Air bags and automatic seat belts both are illustrations of passive restraint systems. Air bags inflate in a crash (within 30 milliseconds—less time than it takes to blink) to cushion the heads of

---

[13]Side-impact and knee-impact air bags that are coming on the market are not mandated by the government.

drivers and in some cases front-seat passengers. Automatic seat belts wrap around occupants as the car doors are closed. With either of them a person can enter a motor vehicle without having to perform any tasks whatsoever and, in the event of an accident, be restrained from hitting the steering wheel, steering column, dashboard instrument panel, side doors, or windshield. Your chances of being killed in a car accident are almost 25 times greater if you are thrown from the vehicle. Insurance companies understand the value of passive restraint systems and the effect on reducing deaths and injuries, and most offer substantial discounts to drivers of cars with air bags.

One safety standard of the NHTSA is to require air bags or automatic seat belts in motor vehicles.[14] This requirement is being phased in over several years. All passenger vehicles are expected to have both driver-side air bags and manual lap-and-shoulder belts by the 1998 model year; light trucks by 1999. The downside of air bags is that while the devices save lives, they kill some small children who are not seated properly (raised up like an adult) and a number of survivors have serious lower-body injuries. The bag offers good protection against fatal head and upper-body injuries. However, leg and foot injuries are causing long hospital stays and big medical bills for those who once would have died in such crashes. Safety advocates are calling for improvements in body design to better protect the lower portion of the passenger cabin.

Some people are confused about the value of air bag systems, yet the Coalition for Consumer Health and Safety, a group of more than two dozen health and consumer organizations reports that, "25 percent of all injuries—primarily brain trauma—could be prevented with air bag use. Some even fear air bags, mistakenly believing that they could inflate or explode when driving over a bump in the road."[15] Consumers need to understand that safety belts provide only limited protection in frontal collisions. Maximum protection is obtained by using both safety belts and air bags. Department of Transportation studies show that 9000 lives would be saved each year and another 110,000 injuries would be prevented if all vehicles were equipped with air bags.

CONSUMER UPDATE:
Brain Protection in Motorcycle Helmets

Laws requiring motorcycle riders to wear protective helmets existed in almost all states 25 years ago. Over the years, many states have weakened or repealed the laws. The Insurance Institute for Highway Safety and the Highway Loss Date Institute report that, "repeals were associated with about 40 percent more cyclist deaths, compared with the years the laws were in effect."[1] When a helmet law went into effect recently in California, helmet use, according to the Insurance Institute for Highway Safety, doubled to 100 percent. The first full year the law was in effect, there were 327 motorcycle deaths compared to 523 the year earlier. The National Public Service Research Institute calculates that the injury cost to the public due to nonuse of helmets is $375 million a year, or about 40 cents per motorcycle mile.

---

[1]25 Years of Work (1994), Insurance Institute for Highway Safety and the Highway Loss Date Institute, Arlington, VA, 12.

---

[14]The National Public Service Research Institute calculates that the cost for people injured in accidents who failed to buckle their seat belts is $12 billion. "Every adult who uses his safety belt religiously currently is paying $110 a year to cover the nonusers."

[15]Ploachek, L., Nelson, J. & Muira, S. (undated), Motor Vehicle Safety. *Consumer Health and Safety Agenda* (Washington, D.C.: The Coalition for Consumer Health and Safety), p. 6.

Criticisms of Government Product Safety Efforts

Critics of regulatory efforts make the usual arguments that: (1) regulations limit the freedom of people to make individual choices by themselves because government issues mandates about some product designs and bans particular products from the marketplace, (2) standards and recalls increase the cost of all products, and (3) regulatory efforts lead to a government that is bigger, more expensive, and more restrictive. Criticisms of the Consumer Product Safety Commission and the National Highway Traffic Safety Commission go beyond these concerns.

Few People Respond to Recalls

Recalls have always been a major problem area for the CPSC and the NHTSA as they attempt to improve product safety. A good recall often results in no more than 30 to 35 percent of the defectively dangerous products being returned, often 10 percent or lower. Recalls are unsuccessful because they are expensive, it is difficult to track down consumers (fewer than 10 percent of purchasers fill out warranty-registration cards), and often the perceived danger of a defective product is low.

Serious Time Delays Exist

Time delays are immense at both the CPSC and the NHTSA. Negotiations over what constitutes a proper repair of a dangerous product can go on for months while companies benefit from the delay, because they have fewer products to repair. Getting effective regulations into effect can take an enormous amount of time. For example, it took 18 years for the NHTSA to approve motor vehicle tire grading standards. The passive restraint systems to protect drivers and front-seat passengers were supposed to be in all automobiles in 1987, but the NHTSA has allowed delays for twelve years. Similar problems occur at the CPSC.

Too Much Reliance on Voluntary Efforts

Critics are concerned that both the CPSC and the NHTSA rely too much on the voluntary efforts of manufacturers and sellers. In recent years, this has been the primary regulatory approach taken by government. Writing product standards is a complex task requiring the inputs of many specialists in an effort to reach consensus. General agreement on a voluntary safety standard is reached through the process of compromise, and it simply may not lead to a good standard. Critics suggest that voluntary standards are usually weaker than mandatory standards imposed by the government and they are often inadequate.

There have been few mandatory standards written by CPSC and NHTSA in recent years. Consumer groups say that the agencies focus so much on voluntary safety standards that there is no realistic threat that mandatory rules will be adopted if businesses cannot agree on their own guidelines. Lacking a willingness to exercise regulatory authority, it seems like the agencies no longer have a threat, a "big stick," to motivate manufacturers and sellers to exhibit a serious interest in product safety.

Critics argue that businesses are more careful when the CPSC and the NHTSA are more vigilant. After all, they say, the reason government established these agencies in the first place and gave them the authority to issue mandatory regulations was because voluntary efforts by industry failed.

Too Much Politics

Critics also complain that these two federal agencies are politicized so much that they have lost much of their potential effectiveness. Internal battles and political infighting hamper the work of regulators. Too much time is wasted arguing with other administration officials and congressional committees.

Independence is a related issue. The CPSC is an independent regulatory agency, but it recently lost some of that independence because a new law requires the CPSC to submit all safety rules to particular Senate and House committees for approval before official adoption. Both the CPSC and the NHTSA lack enough independence to candidly speak their views in public because they first have to submit their budget requests for approval to the White House Office of Management and Budget.

Inclination Not to Prosecute

Another difficulty of the CPSC and the NHTSA is an inclination not to prosecute. In some instances, the commissioners on the CPSC have voted to punish violators and their staff attorneys have recommended certain courses of action only to have the Justice Department refuse to prosecute. Critics observe that the Justice Department frequently does not prosecute violations of product and motor vehicle safety laws and regulations, contrary to the desires of the heads of the CPSC and the NHTSA. Since the NHTSA is an executive agency, the Justice Department must represent its cases in court. The CPSC retains latitude to prosecute its own cases because it is an independent regulatory agency. In general, if the Justice Department does not proceed on a case recommended to them by the CPSC within 45 days, attorneys for the CPSC can then pursue the case themselves.

Not Enough Resources to Do the Job Properly

Budget cutbacks in recent years have greatly reduced the effectiveness of the CPSC and the NHTSA to regulate product safety. For example, staffing of the CPSC was cut 50 percent during the Reagan and Bush Administrations, from 978 to less than 500. Similar budget reductions were made at the NHTSA. Under President Bill Clinton, CPSC and the NHTSA have received small budget increases.

Review and Summary of Key Terms and Concepts

1. List four **government agencies** that are involved in product safety.

2. Offer a few statistics on **product injuries** affecting adults and children.

3. Give two examples of **causal factors** in injuries.

4. What is **cost-benefit analysis**, and how does that relate to **reasonable risks** and **unreasonable risks**?

5. Identify three **criticisms of cost-benefit analysis**.

6. Explain why attorneys collect **contingency fees** from consumers who win product liability lawsuits.

7. Distinguish between: **compensatory damages** and **punitive damages**.

8. Explain the legal doctrine of **strict liability**.

9. What are **secret settlements**, and why do they occur?

10. Identify two **key roles** of the Consumer Product Safety Commission.

11. Distinguish between: **imminent hazard** and **substantial hazard**. Give two examples of each.

12. Distinguish between: **informal rulemaking** and **formal rulemaking**.

13. What is a **voluntary standard**, and why does the Consumer Product Safety Commission seek these instead of mandatory standards?

14. Cite some **statistics** that indicate that the efforts of the National Highway Traffic Safety Administration are needed.

15. Briefly outline the **NHTSA recall process**.

16. What is a **hic score**, and why is more valuable than the NHTSA's star rating system?

17. Define **passive restraint system**, and name some pluses and minuses of **air bags**.

18. Give three reasons why people **criticize product safety** as a slow process.

Useful Resources for Consumers

Center for Auto Safety
2001 S Street, NW, Suite 410
Washington, DC 20009
202-328-7700

Insurance Institute for Highway Safety
1005 North Glebe Road
Arlington, VA 22201
703-247-1500

Mothers Against Drunk Driving
511 E. John Carpenter Freeway, Suite 700
Irving, TX 75062
214-744-6233

"What Do You Think" Questions

1. There are a number of **criticisms of cost-benefit analysis**. What one criticism listed do you believe is most likely to result in additional harm to consumers? Why?

2. The concept of **punitive damages** ranks as a key factor in why many businesses are trying to restrict **product liability lawsuits**. Describe your views on punitive damages as a method to improve product safety in the marketplace. Assume for the moment that punitive damages were prohibited, then explain what other factors would provide the motivation for a reduction in product safety problems.

3. Looking over the list of **products that need safety regulations** and the list of **needed vehicle safety regulations**, select two from each list that you agree might be serious problems. Recommend whether to ban each product or redesign each in some ways. If appropriate, give some suggestions for redesign and appropriate labeling.

4. Which **criticism of product safety** is one that could be improved upon with some serious attention? Explain what might be done to improve the situation and lessen that criticism.

Chapter 17

Banking, Credit, and Housing Issues

OBJECTIVES

After reading this chapter, you should be able to

1. Examine a number of consumer problems and issues in the area of banking with a view toward improving the rights of consumers.

2. Review several consumer problems and issues in credit.

3. Recognize a number of consumer problems and issues in housing.

Banking, credit, and housing are areas of consumer spending vital to the consumer interest. Getting banking services for a fair price is a genuine challenge for consumers; it is extremely difficult for economically disadvantaged consumers. The complex world of credit often confuses consumers about issues such as credit terms, interest rates, ripoff charges, hidden fees, and some unfair and misleading practices. Consumers who use credit regularly fall victim to excessive charges resulting from the use of credit. Additionally, all consumers experience a need for suitable housing, yet the small supply and low quality of available housing presents consumers with additional dilemmas. A number of consumer problems and issues, such as illegal redlining of neighborhoods, ripoffs of escrow funds, and kickbacks compound the consumer's housing problems.

This chapter focuses upon problems and issues of consumers in banking, credit, and housing transactions. It begins by examining problems and issues in banking: truth in savings (almost), the impact of deregulation, problems of access to banking services by the poor, and fallout from the savings and loan/banking scandal. Next, it overviews problems and issues in credit, including credit-card solicitations, high interest rates, privacy violations, discrimination, and mistakes in credit files. The chapter concludes with an examination of consumer problems and issues in the area of housing: high costs, supply and demand, redlining, and a number of dilemmas related to disclosure. The reader is encouraged to analyze each of the consumer problems using the model that follows.

Banking Problems and Issues

There are a number of consumer problems and issues in the world of banking. Several are examined below.

Truth in Savings, Almost

The Truth in Savings Act (TIS), effective in 1993, requires depository institutions to disclose the annual percentage rate on interest-bearing accounts, along with any fees that may be assessed, so that depositors can easily compare various savings options. The **annual percentage yield (APY)** is the total amount of interest that would be received on a $100 deposit, based on the annual rate of simple interest and the frequency of compounding for a 365-day period, expressed as a percentage. The APY must be used in advertising and other disclosures to savers.

Banks used to pay consumers $4.90 or $4.40 a year on accounts that they claimed were "earning 5% percent." Columnist Jane Bryant Quinn says savers now "get an honest accounting of the interest rate they earn; bankers can no longer fudge."[1] Her column argues against Republican efforts to repeal the Truth in Savings Act.

When financial institutions calculate interest on deposits, it is primarily based on four variables: how much money is on deposit, the method of determining the balance, the interest rate applied, and the frequency of compounding, such as annually, semiannually, quarterly, weekly, or daily. The more frequent the compounding, the greater the effective return for the saver.

---

[1]Quinn, J. B (1996, April 21), It's Time to Fight for Your Interest, *The Washington Post*, H-3.

Depository institutions are now required to calculate interest on the full balance in an account once any minimum balance requirements have been reached. In addition, banks must show the **annual percentage yield earned (APYE)** on periodic statements. While the APY tells what one can expect to earn, the APYE tells what one really did earn. As a result, differences in accounts, such as the frequency of compounding and minimum balance requirements, which can make a lot of difference in the final cost of an interest-bearing account, will be properly reflected in the APYE. Wise money managers should select the savings option that pays the highest APY and avoid institutions that assess lots of costs and penalties. Comparison shopping could easily earn you an extra $15 to $30 a year on a $1500 savings account balance.

However, TIS is a bit of hoax for consumers because: (1) banks can "average" the daily balances (instead of using the exact balance every day), and (2) verification of accounts remains impossible. Correctly programmed computers generate the calculations for the financial institutions—so the correct amount of interest can be paid—but depository institutions are not required to show these details to consumers. Consumer advocate Richard L. D. Morse, father of Truth in Savings, calls this "unverifiable truth."

How would you know if your bank made a mistake in your checking or savings account? Presumably, you could "put the pencil" to the figures in your account and recompute the interest rate paid, as well as all fees paid. You are encouraged to try it! Go see your bank and ask to see the mathematics that verify your interest calculation. Most likely you will discover that your bank statement does not tell you what you need to know. Your banker likely will not be able to explain it either. Don't accept a final calculation, see the math.

A MODEL TO ANALYZE CONSUMER PROBLEMS AND ISSUES

1. Specify the issue or problem that negatively affects consumers.

2. Which consumer right(s) does this problem or issue affect? List.

3. Explain how this problem or issue negatively affects each consumer right.

4. For each listed right, suggest alternative(s) to improve the status quo.

5. Which of the suggested alternatives might be most acceptable to the interests of consumers, governments, and businesses? Why?

Deregulation of Banking

The deregulation issue is one of choice: Banks want more freedom to compete in the industry (to underwrite and sell stocks and bonds, as well as sell insurance[2] and real

---

[2]Nationally chartered banks generally cannot sell insurance; however, a 1916 law upheld by the U.S. Supreme Court in 1996 says that banks located in towns with populations of 5000 or less are permitted to sell insurance.

estate), and outsiders (Gulf and Western, American Express, J. C. Penney, Sears, General Electric, Ford, and Merrill Lynch) want the latitude to enter the banking business. A range of institutions have already moved into the traditional banking business. These outsiders are called **nonbank banks**. These financial institutions make commercial loans or accept consumer deposits, but not both, because in this manner they can escape being defined as banks. Thus, non-banks are not subject to a number of banking laws and controls.

In recent years, Congress, regulatory agencies, and the courts have been supportive of continued deregulation of the financial services industry. President Clinton recently signed into law legislation that makes it easier for banks to operate branches across the nation. It goes into effect in 1997, except in states that pass legislation to forbid out-of-state branches from operating in their states. This decade will bring new groups of players in the industry, an evolving redefinition of banking, the availability of new products and services, rapid technological developments, and full-scale national banking.

CONSUMER UPDATE:
Restructuring the Nation's Banking Industry

General reform of the structural aspects of the banking industry has been necessary for more than a decade. The industry remains in the regulated utility model born in the 1930s, while the world of banking has been changing dramatically. Many agree that yesterday's Depression-era approach to setting "firewalls" between banking, insurance, securities, and real estate, in the name of safety and soundness, no longer serves the nation well. The difficulty is getting political agreement on how to change it. To do so will require profound changes in the way America views its financial systems and their roles in the economy. Efforts center around making banking a more competitive industry with government continuing to serve as the ultimate guarantor of deposits.

Letting well-capitalized banks compete head-to-head with non-banks, in particular the insurance companies and securities firms, would quickly result in lower prices for consumers buying stocks, bonds, mutual funds, and insurance. Unleashing the nation's banking giants without safeguards also would lead to hundreds of smaller, ill-equipped institutions going out of business. Consumers might face greater risk to their savings, as well as face misleading sales techniques by banks selling securities and insurance. Such concentration of ownership, says respected financial management consultant Henry Kaufman, would rapidly "produce a corporatist type of state, in which power is concentrated in fewer decision makers, free markets are suppressed, and economic dynamism is stifled."

The impacts of deregulation on consumer banking are numerous. Today's banking industry has consumers thinking and acting differently:

- Consumers must search harder and longer for banking services.
- Consumers must deal with explicit pricing services previously offered without charge.
- The increased price competition for deposits and credit accounts requires that consumers compare savings rates across products.
- Consumers must be more alert to the safety of their deposits.
- Consumers are having difficulty finding smaller banks because many have gone out of business and many have lost their local flavor because of mergers.
- Consumers must deal with fewer branch banking offices.

- Consumers wonder about what "banking" is (Is it just checking and savings? Is it money market accounts? Is it mutual funds? Insurance? Real estate brokerage?) and where to bank.
- Consumers are wondering about the validity and purposes of cross-subsidizations by savers who subsidize borrowers.
- Consumers are irritated at having to pay $2 to $3 to ask simple questions, like "Has my social security check cleared?" or "How much do I have in savings?"
- Consumers are concerned about the plight of the poor, who have been shut out of the traditional banking system and must rely on high-cost alternative banking services.

CONSUMER UPDATE:
Automatic Overdraft Loans—Ripoff Charges!

It does help your credit rating to avoid writing bad checks. But using an automatic overdraft loan can be expensive. Suppose, for example, that a $10 charge was assessed on a check that overdrew an account by $50. That is 20 percent interest ($10 / $50) for only a few days of credit! Annualized, the imputed interest rate is a couple thousand percent. Alternatively, if you write a check for insufficient funds you could wind up paying $20 or $30 in charges.

Rising Fees

Numerous factors contribute to the current pricing schemes used in the banking industry: rising operating costs, deregulation of interest rates, managing in a competitive environment, and loss of cross-subsidies among accounts. The result is that financial institutions are charging explicit prices for some services and charging for other services that previously were free. Fees now represent 30 percent of bank revenue, and they will eventually account for 50 percent of bank revenue.

Surveys show that 2 in 5 Americans prefer to withdraw their money from an **ATM (automated teller machine)**. There are three possible types of ATM fees: (1) A charge by one's own bank to use its machines, typically 50 cents to $1; (2) A fee if you access your bank from an ATM owned by another bank, usually $1; and (3) a special surcharge for non-customers, up to $2.50. Thus, when using a bank other than your normal one, you pay twice for the same transaction! The fee may be as much as $8 or $10 on a cruise ship or in a casino. A study by the Consumer Federation of America shows that fees for ATM devices jumped 37 percent over the previous year. Further, CFA says that 78 cents out of every dollar consumers spend at an ATM is pure profit for banks. CFA reports that the average bank profit per ATM customer is $37.

Smart Money magazine reports that the average annual cost for maintaining a regular checking account is $202.[3] The typical bank charge for a bounced check—and all banks assess such fees—is $20, but the cost the bank incurs is a paltry $2.68. The U.S. Public Interest Research Group reports that the minimum balance requirement averages over

---

[3]The Fee World (1996, March), *Smart Money*, 80.

$1200. With such a high threshold, it is easy to see why so many households are forced to pay fees to an industry that already enjoys record profits. Data from the U.S. General Accounting Office shows that virtually all consumers earning under $30,000 annually experience a net cost for their checking services, even when they have interest-bearing accounts. On savings accounts, a CFA study reveals annual fees averaging $28; therefore, those with savings balances of less than $1000 are likely to lose money by keeping it in a financial institution.

DID YOU KNOW? Bounced Checks are Profitable

Banks collected over $4.35 billion in profits in a recent year from penalty fees on bounced checks, reports the Consumer Federation of America. Costs were only $685 million, thus, the banks realized a profit of $3.67 billion. The markup over cost ranges from about 300 percent to almost 1,000 percent. The administrative cost to process a bad check is typically less than $3; therefore, consumers should complain about excessive fees and request their banks to waive or greatly reduce such fees when assessed.

A *Consumer Reports* survey "shows that banking fees can easily vary by $40 a month between the lowest- and the highest-cost accounts."[4] There are so many costs associated with banking today that some are calling for a "truth-in-banking fees" law to provide needed uniform disclosures for consumers regarding terms, prices, and features of financial products.

Discrimination Against Small Depositors and Nondepositors

Federal Reserve Board data reveal that over time a declining proportion of the population, currently 79 percent, has banking accounts. Census data show that 76 percent of families without checking accounts earn less than $20,000 per year. The growing number of consumers without access to the traditional banking system—one fifth of all consumers—cannot pay bills with inexpensive checks and are not able to build up a savings fund at a federally insured institution.

The banking industry has some discriminatory practices for opening accounts. Many institutions require a driver's license, employer photo IDs, or credit card—something many young people do not possess—to open an account. Only three-quarters of all households have credit cards. A Consumer Federation of America survey revealed that three quarters of all banking institutions are unwilling to cash checks for nondepositors.

To make payments and cash checks, low-income consumers are forced to patronize commercial check-cashing outlets, convenience stores, and liquor stores. A study by the American Association of Retired Persons found that 9 out of 10 banks refused to cash government checks for people without an account.

To cut costs, banks are closing lots of offices, especially branch banks. Over the past decade, the number of banks has shrunk from 14,500 to about 10,000, and nearly half of all branch banks have closed. This discriminates against consumers living in low- and moderate-income neighborhoods because these are the locations of least profitability. In

---

[4]How Good is Your Bank? (1996, March), *Consumer Reports*, 10-15.

CONSUMER UPDATE:
Consumer Frustrations With Electronic Banking

Consumers have several concerns about electronic funds transfers and the use of ATM machines.

- Although use of ATM machines at banks and stores was initially offered as a free service, a growing number of financial institutions are charging 50 cents or $1 for each transaction.
- An annoying problem exists when ATM machines lack reliability and are nonfunctional.
- Mechanical failure of ATM machines sometimes results in consumers' losing money, being shortchanged, or having an account double debited, and there is little recourse in such disputes except to rely on the goodwill of the financial institution or retailer to reimburse the consumer.
- Some machines do not provide a printed record of each transaction.
- Electronic funds transfer point-of-sale transaction refusals can be embarrassing for the consumer.
- A problem of potential unauthorized access to personal financial information also exists.
- Low-income consumers are unlikely to embrace EFT eagerly because they currently do not use credit cards very often.
- Some occasionally have difficulties using ATMs, such as ethnic minorities (because the machines are in English) and elderly and disabled people (because the machines are sited badly or are difficult to manipulate).
- Compared with suburban areas, ATM machines are not nearly as widely available in inner-city neighborhoods and rural communities.
- The consumer's ability to make pre-transaction comparisons in his or her own best interest is diminished by the complexity and pseudo-differentiation of EFT financial services.

New York City, 65 percent of bank branches closed over a 7-year time period, while branches in suburbs increased 8 percent. This has left 16 city neighborhoods with no bank branches and 8 neighborhoods with only one. The branch banks that remain are raising the minimum amount required to open checking and savings accounts.

Basic Banking Is a Reality in Some States, But Not All

The Federal Financial Institutions Examination Council has determined that the three most fundamental needs in banking are: (1) a safe and accessible place to keep money, (2) a way to obtain cash, and (3) a way to make payments to third parties.

Yet, millions of adults do not have bank accounts. Various studies reveal reasons why: (1) did not have enough money to open an account and meet the substantial minimum balance requirements, (2) lacked personal identification (such as a driver's license with a photograph), (3) had a previous account closed for improper use or fraud, (4) believed they didn't write enough checks to make it worthwhile, (5) lacked mathematical and reading skills, (6) distances were too long between the institution's offices and work or home, (7) believed banks had high service charges, and (8) mistrusted financial institutions in general.

CONSUMER UPDATE:
The Poor Pay More to Cash Checks

Millions of low-income people have to pay high fees to cash their social security and welfare checks each month because they do not have bank accounts. People without checking accounts are forced to cash government checks at places other than banks, various check-cashing facilities, where they pay fees from $2 to as high as $25 to cash a $500 check. Some firms charge an unconscionable 10 percent of the face value of the check. The **fringe-banking system** (also called **poor people's banks**) is comprised of over 5000 check-cashing outlets and some other high-fee places to cash checks, such as liquor and grocery stores. Most states do not regulate check-cashing facilities.

One can calculate that the household that cashes a $400 check every two weeks and writes four money orders monthly can expect to pay between $152 and $408 annually for these two services—and the charges may be even higher. "The impact of check cashing on the limited public benefits and meager paychecks of these families is severe...charging 2 percent to cash a welfare check is equivalent to a 2 percent cut in benefits."[1]

---

[1]Leech, I. (1994, April 28), Testimony Before the Subcommittee on Consumer Credit and Insurance, Committee on Banking, Finance and Urban Affairs, Commonwealth of Virginia, 5.

The concept of **basic banking** (also called **lifeline banking**) is that banking institutions would be required to offer universal access to certain minimal financial services that every consumer must have, regardless of income, in order to function in society. The Virginia Citizens Consumer Council defines a basic account as one that: (1) costs $3 or less per month, (2) permits up to ten free checks to be written monthly, (3) has low minimum balance requirements, (4) permits unlimited and free ATM usage, and (5) has a flexible policy on identification requirements.

Consumer Federation of America's Stephen Brobeck says that, "Consumerists believe that institutions enjoying the special privileges and protections provided by the federal bank regulatory system have an obligation to make essential banking services available to all communities." A spokesperson for the American Bankers Association, Virginia Stafford, argues that banks are not public utilities, and should not be treated like one. Consumer advocates observe that any industry that takes a $500 billion bailout, like the banks and savings and loan associations have done, should be regulated like a public utility.

Banks claim that basic banking would increase their costs substantially, that they would have to add tellers on certain days, that they would have to have extra cash available, and that they would run an increased risk of fraud. Critics accuse the banking industry of not wanting low-income consumers in their lobbies mingling with their usual customers. If basic banking services cannot be made available to low-income consumers, millions of consumers are forced to bank under their mattresses and use high-cost alternatives.

A few states (IL, MA, NJ, NY, and MN) require banks operating within their borders to offer basic banking. The New Jersey "Consumer Checking Accounts Law" provides an illustration. For a $3 a month fee, the law requires banks to offer checking accounts with an opening balance of $50 or less, permit eight free checks to be written per month, and the right to make an unlimited number of withdrawals at teller windows.

Related is the concept of **electronic benefits transfer (EBT)**. It is designed to include recipients of state-administered assistance programs into a complete network of electronic banking. Many recipients of government assistance now participate in both direct deposit systems and electronic funds transfer withdrawal systems. Consumers use magnetic-stripe photo identification cards with electronic point-of-sale systems in supermarkets and other businesses, as well as perform banking transactions with bank tellers and ATM machines.[5]

Largely for cost reasons, low-income consumers are kept out of most other parts of the financial services industry, too. The **alternative financial sector (AFS)** "provides low-income consumers with a range of services in much the same way that the traditional financial services sector provides services to more affluent individuals."[6] Elements in the AFS include check cashing outlets, money orders, post-dated checks, pawn shops, refund anticipation loans, rent-to-own stores, and rental-purchase agreements. These financial services are offered to consumers, primarily those with low incomes, at much higher prices than charged in the traditional financial sector. Since the poor have little economic weight in both the economic marketplace and the political system, few improvements in consumer protection in the financial services area are expected.

Paying for the Savings and Loan/Banking Scandal

During the Great Depression of the 1930s, 182 savings and loans failed; between 1982 and 1995, 1207 institutions failed. Deregulation of the savings and loan (S&Ls) and banking industries in the 1970s and 1980s created opportunities for bad judgments, fraud, mismanagement, and bureaucratic ineptitude, creating the greatest financial fiasco in the history of this country.

Columnist George Will notes that, "Never in history have we had the government spend $500 *billion* of the taxpayers' money and not get anything for it." This is, he continues, "another instance of no-fault entrepreneurship, wherein profits are private and losses are socialized."[7]

The $500 billion ($300 billion in bailouts plus $200 billion in interest) amounts to about $5000 for every adult taxpayer. Sadly, most of the money is gone forever and cannot be recovered. Much of the money has been spent, lost in devalued real estate, or stashed in foreign bank accounts. Only a modest amount can be recovered through criminal and civil restitution.

How It Happened: Recklessness, Bad Regulation, Fraud, and Coverups

These failures, says conservative business publication *U.S. News & World Report*, "can be laid directly at the feet of two Republican administrations: One that created it, another that did not act decisively to fix it."[8] "Congress and the White House waited until after the election of 1988 before confronting the terrible truth."[9] *U.S. News* continued,

---

[5]The Federal Reserve Board voted to extend the safeguards provided debit card holders through Regulation E to consumers receiving electronic benefits transfers. Low-income consumers who lose an EBT debit card may gain the benefit of having a $50 liability limitation for unauthorized use beginning in 1997.

[6]Swagler, R., Burton, J., and J. K. Lewis (1995, Fall), The Alternative Financial Sector: An Overview, *Advancing the Consumer Interest*, 7,2, 7.

[7]Will, G. (July 31, 1990). Nothing Inevitable About S&L Mess. *Roanoke Times & News-World*, p. A-9.

[8]Zuckerman, M. B. (1990, August 6). This is a "Thrift" Industry? *U.S. News & World Report*, p. 64.

[9]Glassman, J. K. (1994, June 1). The U.S. Banking System is all Better-or Maybe Not. *The Washington Post*, p. C-1.

"The Reagan-Bush administration promised to get the government off the back of the people. What it did instead was to get the government off the back of the crooks."

As interest rates climbed to historic highs in the 1980s (short-term interest rates were over 15 percent) and real estate prices collapsed, the value of assets owned by thrifts declined (**thrifts** are savings and loan associations). With no revenue coming in from real estate investments and having to pay out interest each day on depositor's funds, the S&Ls needed to find money elsewhere. They promised savers extraordinarily high rates to attract new money, and instead of investing these funds, the new deposits were used to pay the interest on earlier deposits. Continuing losses were paid for by attracting even more funds through even higher rates.

The government guaranteed every $100,000 deposit, regardless of the financial soundness of the institution. The existence of deposit insurance created what economist Paul Krugman called an "epidemic of **moral hazard**," where institutions, especially those in financial trouble, take on riskier investments only because they are insured. (It is as if a consumer had a diamond ring insured for $5,000 and then became complacent about keeping it safe, only rarely putting it in a safe deposit box.) Virtually all the losses were insured by the government, so the bank managers didn't actually lose any money. In retrospect, this honestly sounds like a federally-sponsored Ponzi investment scheme (described in Chapter 4), doesn't it? To compete, financially healthy S&Ls and banks had to pay high rates too. All depositors gained from earning higher interest rates on savings because the falling S&Ls were offering sky-high interest rates.

Weak government oversight allowed land to be resold at higher prices to justify even bigger loans and make subsequent losses larger. Phony appraisals were made to permit developers to make more profits by borrowing rather than by building. Risky futures and options trading helped bring down more than one S&L. In one spectacular failure, Seapoint S&L, in Carlsbad, California, lost half its depositors' money in one day. The infamous Lincoln S&L had stakes in some risky junk bonds.

The Justice Department says there have been 5506 convictions of those who "looted" financial institutions. More than 3700 high-profile senior executives and owners of failed thrifts have been sent to prison for fraudulent activities. One expert says that only about 3 percent of the total cost was the result of criminal behavior, and that there was an incredible amount of incompetency. Prosecutions of an additional 2500 are in process. The conviction rate has been 95 percent.

American consumers should be incensed, angry, and outraged that the costs for this fiasco will be paid by them, through higher taxes and higher banking costs passed along to customers. Consumers are paying this money back through higher banking fees, reduced interest rates earned on deposits, and higher prices on loans.

Another Multi-Billion Dollar Bailout Is Imminent

Taxpayers are continuing to take the risk of another bailout. Because of the continuing existence of $100,000 insurance coverage and the fact that banks pay much lower premiums than S&Ls for that coverage (92 percent of banks pay the statutory minimum requirement of $2000 a year for deposit insurance in the Bank Insurance Fund [BIF]), it is expected that most S&Ls will convert to banks. This puts increasing pressure on the S&Ls undercapitalized Savings Association Insurance Fund (SAIF). Another bailout will have to occur before both banks and S&Ls have a single insurance fund. One bank president observed, "There is going to be no future for the S&L industry."

How to Clean Up America's Banking System

The Bush bailout legislation in 1991 paid some big bills of the S&L and banking scandal but did not alter the federal deposit insurance system, which is a root cause of the industry's problems. It may help to recall that the original concept of the insurance system was to protect only individual savings, not institutional investors.

Two vital changes are needed to reform the banking system, and both eliminate the custom of placing the full risk on government (really the taxpayers since consumers pay 85 percent of all revenues of the federal government):

First, restore the power of private market forces to punish unnecessary risk taking by offering only co-insurance on banking deposits. If deposit insurance were limited to only a part of the deposit, perhaps to 80 percent on amounts above $100,000, affected depositors would be impelled to find ways of ensuring that the institutions holding their money had adequate equity, liquidity, and diversification. In this way the problem would be genuinely resolved because big depositors (businesses, other financial institutions, those with funds deposited in retirement plans, and wealthy consumers) would be motivated to assure the safety of the uninsured portion of their deposits. Shaky financial institutions would be forced to purchase additional private insurance for the remaining 20 percent of risk or be unable to attract large deposits.

Second, establish a risk-based insurance system for bank deposits. Well-run, safe institutions would pay low insurance premiums to the FDIC, while riskier banks and S&Ls would have to pay higher premiums. Congress has taken no action to lower the insured amount below the present $100,000 or establish risk-based premiums.

Credit Problems and Issues

This section examines consumer problems and issues in credit.

Unnecessary Credit-Card Solicitations

"Congratulations! You have been preapproved for credit!" How does this happen? All large credit reporting organizations, such as TRW, Equifax, and Trans Union, are capable of creating a computer-generated review of credit files to locate names of people who pass certain tests of credit worthiness. Each company has files on over 150 million Americans. Oftentimes, these lists are sold to marketers that wish to offer people credit accounts. To purchase such a list, the user must have a legitimate business interest. This service is particularly useful when a branch of a store opens in a new area and management wishes to open new local accounts. This also is the concept behind **prescreening**, where an application for new credit is mailed to consumers who have a good credit record. Credit very likely will be granted after the consumer mails in the completed application. Sometimes a person's credit history is of such high quality that companies send a **preapproved** (also called **preauthorized**) line of credit that can be used almost immediately.[10]

---

[10]Federal legislation is pending to create a system to allow consumers to opt out of prescreening and direct marketing.

Such marketing techniques seem to flatter consumers into falsely thinking that they are "worth" more credit. The thinking goes, "I know that I can't afford more credit, but if the bank figures that I can, it must be all right." Many consumers accept a second or third Visa card when they really do not want or need it.

To sweeten the deal for consumers, credit-card companies also offer a number of enhancements and pile on new features, such as rebates on purchases, extended warranties on purchases, travel discounts, rental car insurance, airline frequent-flier points, travel accident insurance, price-guarantee refunds for products purchased at a lower price within 60 days, and merchandise replacements when purchased goods are lost, stolen, or damaged within 90 days. These deals have loads of restrictions, and since it is difficult to meet the conditions many consumers do not collect.

Marketers have little concern for the number of credit cards consumers already possess. Roper CollegeTrack reports that 55 percent of undergraduates already have major credit cards. One observer noted that, "There are only two things you need to get a credit card: a college ID and a pulse."

Solicitations often go to consumers who are already carrying too much debt. Crediholics who cannot resist grab those preapproved lines of credit like candy and soon get into deeper financial difficulties. It is not unusual that a person earning $30,000 a year can run up $40,000 in credit card bills, get cash advances from one card to pay another, never make late payments, and pay over $20,000 in finance charges. Creditors love such people.

DID YOU KNOW?
Free Credit Counseling Advice

For those who are overindebted or having severe budgeting problems, excellent counseling advice can be obtained at the 1000+ offices of the Consumer Credit Counseling Service (CCCS), a non-profit organization affiliated with the National Foundation on Consumer Credit, 8611 Second Avenue, Ste. 100, Silver Spring, MD 20910. Telephone: 800-388-2227.

Paying Interest Rates That Are Too High

Credit card rates can only be brought down by competition, and this will not happen until consumers choose not to use credit at certain prices.[11] People must comparison shop for the best deals and interest rates. Consumer behavior, however, often suggests that many people really don't care about paying high interest rates. Many people seem indifferent, especially about interest rates on credit cards or special fees. Rational consumers do some comparison shopping for credit rates and terms. Many consumer advocates support national **interest-rate caps**, usury limits on credit card rates, although such state laws have not worked in the past. (See "An Economic Focus on Usury Laws" later in this chapter.)

Tiered lending is the credit industry's idea of price discrimination in that they charge different customers different interest rates. A person with an excellent credit history might

---

[11]Variable-rate credit card issuers are not legally required to tell customers that the rate has changed, so they can raise rates anytime.

have a credit card rate of 8 percent, while someone with a less-than-perfect credit history might have an interest rate of 24 percent. Critics believe that these punitive interest rates are another way of discriminating against women and minorities.

To get a reduced interest rate on your credit cards, you simply need to telephone your card issuers and ask. Most requests are approved.

Making Credit Payments Increases Total Costs

Never forget that lenders are interested in consumers who pay their bills on time, but they relish those who maintain balances. Since banks make money on the **spread** between what lending costs them and the interest rate they charge, the industry's motivation is to keep interest rates high. Banks that pay 3 percent interest on savings accounts and charge 18 percent interest on their Visa or MasterCard accounts are enjoying quite a profitable spread.

More than one-half of American credit cardholders do not pay their card balances in full each month. Because of financing costs, these people also pay more for everything bought on credit rather than using cash. Finance charges often amount to about 18 percent of the cost of items purchased on credit, since this is a typical rate on credit-card purchases.

Some call buying on credit and making a series of repayments (instead of paying cash) a **negsale**, short for "negative sale," because after adding up all the charges and fees, credit-card expenditures become the opposite of buying things on sale. The result is as if the lender says, "Please repay us slowly so we can mark up your purchases an additional 18 percent!" Surveys show that at least forty percent of credit cardholders do not know how much interest they were charged in the past year for revolving purchases on their bankcards.

DID YOU KNOW?
How to Refinance Your Education Loans

You may look into options to restructure a student-loan payment schedule by contacting the government's Federal Student Aid Information at 800-433-3243.

Paying Only the "Low Minimum Monthly Payment"

Guess what happens if you have a credit balance of $2,000 at 18.5 percent interest (perhaps a Visa or MasterCard balance) and choose to pay only the "required low minimum monthly payment"? It will take 11 years to pay off the $2,000 debt, plus interest charges of $1,934 (assuming a minimum payment of 1/36 of outstanding balance or $20, whichever is greater). Some consumers accept such enticing offers thinking that they are good deals; they are simply ignorant of the facts. Lenders boost their profits by lowering their minimum monthly required payments, now often as low at 2 percent of the outstanding balance. Repayment takes a decade or more.

Some direct-mail lenders want to loan you money that, "takes the sting out of paying back your loan." One legitimate offer was from First Deposit National Bank of Tilton, New Hampshire. They would loan a consumer $3,000 and allow repayment according to the bank's low minimum monthly payment schedule, only two percent of the outstanding balance. At their interest rate of 21.7 percent, it would take 63 years and $22,748 to repay the loan. "Because payments are so low," says the bank, "many customers use this money to pay off credit-card balances, bills, and other loans that demand high payments."

AN ECONOMIC FOCUS ON...Usury Laws and the Supply and Demand for Consumer Credit*

Adam Smith wrote in 1776, "The man who borrows in order to spend will soon be ruined..."[1] (Smith, 1776, 105).Smith was generally against government interference in the marketplace, but made an exception for the regulation of credit. A **usury law** is a ceiling on the price of credit, usually expressed as a maximum interest rate that can be charged on a particular type of loan or credit card. Usury laws typically are applied to particular types of loans. There has been controversy about usury laws because the effect includes benefiting some consumers who are able to obtain credit at a more reasonable rate, while hurting others, who may be denied credit that they want.

The Supply and Demand for Credit

The price of credit is the interest rate, and can be expressed as:

Interest Rate = Cost of Lender's Funds + Cost of Operation + Risk Premium + Lender's Profit

The cost of the lender's funds will vary with general economic conditions, including the effect of government monetary policies and the anticipation of future inflation. The cost of the lender's operation will depend on many factors, including how difficult it is for the lender to evaluate loan applicants. The **risk premium** is an amount charged to compensate a lender for the likelihood of some failure to repay. It includes the expected loss from borrowers who are late in repaying the loan, or who never repay. The lender's profit will, if the market is competitive, be just sufficient to provide the same rate of return as the next best investment, such as safe government bonds.

Because lenders have other ways to invest their money, there is a supply curve for credit of any particular type, and the higher the interest rate, the more money will be lent (Figure 17-1). There is a demand curve for credit, based on the value different types of consumers place on borrowing money. At the equilibrium point (a) supply equals demand. In the hypothetical example shown in Figure 17-1, the supply and demand for credit for consumers with poor credit records is illustrated. The equilibrium interest rate is 25%. At this level, the amount of money lent might be 50 million dollars. If the government does not allow interest rates for this type of loan to be higher than 10%, the demand for credit might be 80 million dollars (b), but the supply of credit might be 20 million dollars (c). There will be a shortage of credit amounting to 60 million dollars.   (continued)

---

[1]Smith, A. (1964; 1776). *The Wealth of Nations* in George W. Wilson (ed.) *Classics of Economic Theory*, 105, Indiana University Press.

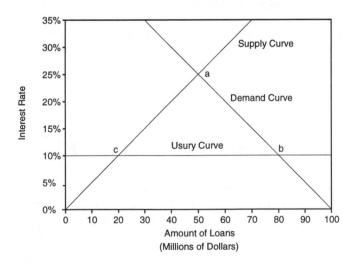

FIGURE 17-1   Supply and Demand for Credit

(continued)
Usury Laws

Usury laws are an interference with the free operation of a market. Based on standard economic theory, usury laws may lead to inefficient allocation of society's scarce resources. Some consumers may see a short-term gain, as the amount they have to pay in finance charges will be reduced. Other consumers will be denied credit, and some consumers will be subject to inconvenience because they cannot obtain a credit card.

Protecting Middle-Income Consumers

Usury laws affect middle-income consumers when they apply for home mortgages and credit cards because rates are usury laws set rates at below-market levels. If inflation is increasing, a low limit on home mortgage interest rates will result in a decrease in loans to home buyers and to home builders. A low limit on credit card rates will make it more difficult for consumers to obtain credit cards.

The most common justification for applying usury laws in a way to directly benefit middle-income consumers is that competition may be limited. When a pure monopoly exists, there is justification for the government to regulate rates. In consumer credit, competition does exist, even if it is not perfect.[2] Increasingly, non-financial corporations are entering the credit card business, so that conditions are right for competition. However, there is evidence that few consumers shop around for credit.[3] When lenders and credit card issuers vigorously compete advertising of interest rates may reduce the amount of time consumers have to spend shopping for credit.

During the early 1990s, there was some pressure on the U.S. Congress to set limits on credit card interest rates because the rates had not dropped as much as other interest rates had declined. Such legislation calls for an interest-rate cap on credit-card accounts, which would provide that interest rates on credit cards could not go higher than a certain amount. For example, interest charges on credit cards may be prohibited by law from exceeding 15 percent or from being higher than 5 percentage points above the average yield on recently sold U.S. Treasury bills. Six states (Connecticut, Iowa, Kansas, Rhode Island, Virginia, and Washington) have passed some form of credit-card interest rate cap legislation. Most laws peg the interest-rate cap to an economic index, such as the rate on 1-year U.S. Treasury bills, the prime rate, or the federal discount rate.

Defenders of the credit card industry claimed that 15 million individuals would lose cards if national ceilings were imposed.[4] An example of a breakdown of the actual costs of a typical retail credit card seemed to show that even a 21.5% annual interest rate might be reasonable.[5] One justification given for the slowness of decreases in credit card rates in the 1980s was that the cost of funds comprised only 30% of the total cost of credit cards, compared to 90 percent of the cost of mortgage loans.[6]

The Costs of Usury Laws for Middle-Income Consumers

Many studies have found that usury laws reduce the supply of credit in states, cause job losses and reduce housing production.[7] Usury laws tend to hurt young consumers the most, as they tend to need credit to acquire furniture and other durable goods, but have not yet established a good credit record.

Protecting Low-Income Consumers

Usury laws may be designed to help "...the uneducated, the impetuous, and the poor."[8] Research has shown that consumers with low levels of education are much less likely to shop for credit than are more educated consumers. Therefore, competition may be less likely to operate effectively for less educated, lower income consumers than it might for more educated, higher income consumers.

Even if lenders compete vigorously and honestly communicate the relative cost of credit to consumers, some consumers may decide to take on credit at very high interest rates. Consider an annual percentage rate (APR) of over 30% per year. It is very unlikely that a safe, productive investment would give this high a return. Most people seeking to borrow at a rate that high are either poorly informed or want to finance spending today.

A consumer may want to enjoy relatively high consumption today, even if he or she knows that in the future, the burden of repayment may reduce the level of living to a very low level.[9] Perhaps usury laws are a reasonable way to protect the consumer from his or her own folly.

Other consumers may feel sure that their incomes will be much higher next year than this year. If a consumer is certain that family income will be much higher next year, borrowing at a very high interest rate may be rational.[10] There may be situations where a consumer would willingly pay very high APRs to finance consumption now. An example is when a family member will return to work next year, but the family has pressing needs now. Further research is needed to determine the proportion of families who mistakenly take on credit at high interest rates, versus those who might be acting rationally. It is likely at most consumers who borrow at an APR higher than 30% are acting out of ignorance or irrational optimism.

Conclusions on the Supply and Demand of Credit

Usury laws may protect consumers from making mistakes in obtaining credit, but they also may hurt consumers, especially if the limits are set too low. An APR of 30% for unsecured credit (if inflation is about 5% per year) might be a reasonable compromise, protecting some consumers and only reducing the supply of credit to those with poor credit records. Vigorous consumer information and education efforts and enforcement of disclosure laws, such as Truth-in-Lending, would still be needed, as some consumer borrowing at or below the usury limit might be based on ignorance.

---

[2]Nathan, H.C. (Winter, 1980). Economic Analysis of Usury Laws, *Journal of Bank Research*, 10(4), 209.

[3]Chang, Y.R. & Hanna, S. (1992). Consumer Credit Search Behavior, *Journal of Consumer Studies and Home Economics*, 16, 207-227.

[4]Becker, M. (February, 1988). Credit Card Ceilings: Illusory Gains and real Costs, 76, 42-47.

[5]Ibid. 45.

[6]Chaudoin, G.S. (February, 1987). Are Credit Card Interest Rates Too High?, *Illinois Business Review*, 44, 3-6.

[7]Nathan, Economic Analysis.

[8]Avio, K.L. (1972). An Economic Rationale for Statutory Interest Rate Ceilings, Quarterly Review of Economics and Business, 13(1), (Spring), 63.

[9]Ibid, 61-72.

[10]Chang, Y.R., Fan, X.J. & Hanna, S. (1992). Relative Risk Aversion and Optimal Credit Use with Uncertain Income, *Proceedings of the American Council on Consumer Interests*, 14-22.

*Sherman Hanna, Professor, The Ohio State University

Grace Periods Are Confusing Because the Methods of Assessing Interest Are Perplexing

The annual study for American Express conducted by Princeton Survey Research Associates shows that three-quarters of cardholders do not know how their grace period works. A **grace period** is the number of days a consumer has before a credit card company starts charging interest on new purchases, often 20 to 25 days. In essence, the credit customer receives a free ride by not having to pay finance charges. However, credit companies have different policies that are confusing to many consumers.

Finance charges on credit card accounts are typically calculated by first computing the **average daily balance**. This is the sum of the outstanding balances owned each day during the billing period divided by the number of days in the period. Then the periodic rate is applied to that balance. The **periodic rate** is the annual percentage rate (APR) divided by the number of billing periods per year, usually 12. For example an annual percentage rate of 18 percent divided by 12 months would equal a periodic rate of 1.5 percent.

To illustrate, during a 31-day month a credit card account showed the following: a balance of $120 for 10 days and $70 for 21 days (reflecting a $50 payment). The average daily balance is $86.13 [(10 X $120 = $1200) + (21 X $70 = $1470) =$2670; $2670\31 = $86.13]. Thus on an account with an APR of 18 percent, a periodic rate of 1.5 percent is multiplied times the average daily balance of $86.13, resulting in a finance charge of $1.29 ($86.13 X 0.015).

There are two key elements in determining finance charges on credit cards. First is the number of days in the grace period (usually zero or 20 to 25 days). Second is whether the balance includes or excludes new purchases. Variations using these two popular ways of assessing finance charges on credit cards are described immediately below.

First, no grace period with interest calculated on the "average daily balance that *includes* **new purchases."** Here the consumer has no grace period because interest is assessed every day on the balance owed. When a balance is carried forward from a previous month, interest is calculated on the average daily balances left over from the previous month and on *every* purchase or cash advance from the exact date of each transaction. This method of assessing credit costs is growing in popularity with lenders, and it results in credit cardholders paying lots of interest. The key phrase to look for in the small print of any credit card agreement is "It *includes* new purchases."

Second, full grace period with interest calculated on the "average daily balance that *excludes* **new purchases."** This is the most common type of grace period and, depending upon use, it can result in the cardholder (A) never paying interest because the consumer pays the bill in full each month, or (B) paying interest on the previous month's unpaid balance (but not on new purchases) because the consumer sometimes or always chooses to pay less than the full balance owed.

Here the cardholder pays interest only on any balance carried forward from the previous month. The consumer gets the benefit of a full grace period because new purchases are *excluded* when figuring the amount of interest owed for the current month. Credit cards offering this method are for people who pay their credit card balances in full each month because they never pay interest and they get an interest-free loan for purchases made. It is also useful for people who do not always pay their bill in full because they too get an interest-free loan for purchases made each month. Credit card companies typically assess finance charges *on new purchases* immediately whenever a balance is carried forward from the previous month. As a result, only those consumers who have an account that uses the average daily balance method that excludes new purchases and who pay off their current balance completely enjoy the benefits of a full grace period. The key phrase to look for in the small print of any credit card agreement is "It *excludes* new purchases."[12]

A promotion that misleads consumers occurs when the lender offers you a "special grace period" allowing you to skip one month's credit-card payment. This usually happens at income tax time or just after the Christmas holidays. If you accept, the lender will not only charge interest on that month's purchases, but will deprive you of the grace period for the following month. An unpaid balance on one month's bill automatically results in interest charged against the next month's purchases, even if the second month's bill is paid within the grace period. Thus, you will be charged interest on all purchases during the two months, and likely from the day you made them. Now you know why lenders occasionally send you a notice saying, "Because of your excellent credit rating, you are eligible to skip your payment this month." Also, this "slow payment" may be reported to credit bureaus.[13]

The "Two-Cycle Method of Assessing Interest" Legally Doubles the Effective Interest Rate

Yet another method of assessing finance charges on credit cards is the **two-cycle average daily balance method**. It eliminates the grace period on new purchases and *retroactively* eliminates the grace period received for the previous month each time the account carries a balance. The result is often a doubling of the interest charges, a ripoff. This misleading and horribly unfair method permits advertising of one interest rate, perhaps 15 percent, and effectively charging another, more like 30 percent.

Here is an example that illustrates how cardholders get legally overcharged. A cardholder makes two purchases of $200 each, one on November 2nd and one on December 2nd. The lender sends out bills on the first of the month and charges an APR of 18 percent, or a periodic rate of 1.5 percent. The cardholder makes no payment on the December bill but pays the January bill in full. Under the favorable method of calculating interest (the average daily balance that excludes new purchases noted above) the cardholder pays $3 in finance charges (.015 X $200 [on the balance from November]); under the least favorable method (the two cycle approach) the cardholder pays $9.00 (.015 X $400 [on the average daily balance from December] + .015 X $200 [on the average daily balance from November]).

The typical cardholder in the U.S. carries a balance averaging $2700 on nine cards and pays about $529 ($2700 X .196 [not 18 percent because of the required

---

[12]To keep consumers confused and take in more money in interest charges, some credit card companies say that they "exclude new balances" where in reality they *only* do so when the previous month's balance was paid in full by the consumer. The result on such accounts is that when the customer has not paid a bill in full interest is assessed on all new purchases as they are made, plus, of course, interest is charged on the balance carried forward. Sound perplexing? It is.

[13]The "Optima True Grace Card™" credit card marketed by American Express (no annual fee as long as the card is used three times annually) offers a grace period that begins after the monthly billing period ends, thus sparing cardholders some interest charges if they do not pay their whole bill each month. Some other credit cards offer a similar deal.

compounding]) in annual finance charges. Some consumers pay two or three times that amount—$1058 to $1587 (and these figures are not made up!)—depending upon the method used to determine the outstanding balance. This occurs even though both cards may have a stated APR of 18 percent and the pattern of purchases and payments by the cardholders is the same. Moreover, the result of using the two-cycle average daily balance including new purchases method of calculating the interest charges is an effective rate of interest of 30 or 40 percent or more! The key phrases to look for in the small print of any credit card agreement are "It *excludes* new purchases" and "*two cycle*" method. Both Discover and First USA use this method.

The "Rule of 78s" Is a Prepayment Penalty

The **rule of 78s**, sometimes called the **sum-of-the-digits method**, is a commonly used method of calculating rebates of finance charges and the prepayment penalty charged the borrower who pays off an installment loan early. It assumes that you pay more in interest in the beginning of a loan when you have the use of more money and that you pay less and less interest as the debt is reduced.

CONSUMER UPDATE:
Some Check-Cashing Companies Offer Illegal
(and Exorbitantly Priced) "Credit"*

Some check-cashing companies offer credit—at ripoff rates!—and such transactions are not illegal in all states. The typical deal offered by check-cashing businesses is to loan money to people who are short of cash by accepting a post-dated check from them. A **post-dated check** is a check written against a consumer's account and dated sometime in the future. The expectation is that the consumer will have sufficient funds in the account at that future point so the check will be honored by the bank. The check-cashing company (the "lender" here) charges exorbitant fees to advance funds against post-dated checks.

A typical transaction: On June 16th the customer presents a post-dated check for $260 and the company gives the consumer $200 in cash agreeing to hold the check until July 1st, two weeks later. On July 1st the consumer either pays the company $260 in cash or lets the check go through the banking system. The effective rate is 730 percent for two weeks, 1095 percent for ten days, and 2190 percent for five days.

One Attorney General observed that, "These companies are offering what are short-term loans with effective annual percentage rates of more than 2000 percent in some cases." They are targeting people who are experiencing temporary financial difficulties.

Check-cashing companies are not legal lenders in most states. Consumers should avoid obtaining loans from such businesses, especially at exorbitant interest rates. The fees charged are a form of interest which should make the businesses subject to government regulation that would protect consumers.

*This was written by Greg O'Donoghue, Manager, Personal Financial Management Program, Seymour Johnson Air Force Base, North Carolina

---

To illustrate, suppose on a $500 loan for 12 months, $80 in finance charges were scheduled to be paid. If the loan is paid off after only 6 months, the borrower will not have the interest reduced $40. To calculate the reduction, first add together all the numbers between 1 and 12 (1 + 2 + 3 + 4 + 5 + 6 + 7 + 8 + 9 + 10 + 11 + 12 = 78). If the loan is paid off after 1 month, the amount of interest paid is assumed to be 12/78 of the total, with a reduction of 66/78 due the borrower. For a loan paid in full after 2 months, the amount of interest paid is assumed to be 23/78 of the total (12/78 for month 1 plus 11/78 for month 2). So, much of the early payments goes for interest. In this example, after 6 months, the lender assumes that $58.46 (57/78 has been paid in interest, and the interest is reduced $21.54 (21/78). Thus, the borrower does not get 50 percent of the interest as a reduction for paying the loan off in half the time, but only 27 percent ($21.54/$80).

The rule of 78s method was designed before the days of computers, and it is nothing more than a prepayment penalty charged borrowers who pay off installment loans early. A loan with this credit clause effectively winds up doubling the effective annual percentage rate for consumers who pay off loans early. In extreme cases, a consumer may even pay more in interest than the principal amount of the loan.

The rule of 78s penalty situation arises whenever a consumer pays off a loan, most commonly through refinancing. A common example is trading in a car with an existing auto loan for a new one. Poor consumers often default on loans, pay the 78s penalties, and refinance.

The Truth in Lending law does not require that lenders disclose this clause in advance. Consumers must ask for the information or scan a credit contract to see if it is there. Consumer advocates want to make the rule of 78s illegal. A non-refundable service charge would be much fairer to creditors and borrowers.

Credit- and Debit-Card Registration Services

In case of lost credit and debit cards, the cardholder should notify debit and credit card companies to avoid legal liability for fraud and misuse. Some firms sell a **card registration service** that registers all the credit- and debit-card numbers of a consumer and arranges for cancellation and replacement of any lost or stolen credit cards. For $25 to $60 a year, you only need to make one telephone call to report all card losses. While this may be a useful service to those consumers who do not keep a record of their credit cards, this is not an efficient purchase decision.

The Fair Credit Reporting Act (see Chapter 10) limits cardholder's liability to $50 in the event of a fraudulent use, and most creditors waive all costs in the event of fraudulent usage. In addition, every card issuer has a telephone number (most are toll-free) that you can call yourself to report a lost or stolen card and to get a replacement card. Further, almost all renter's and homeowner's insurance policies provide automatic coverage of up to $500 for lost or stolen credit and debit cards.

Credit Insurance (Life/Disability/Unemployment)

Most consumers are asked when they complete and sign a credit agreement whether or not they want to purchase credit life, disability, and unemployment insurance. Should the borrower die, become disabled or unemployed (according to the definition in the policy), the insurance pays off the unpaid balance of the consumer debt.

Finance companies and auto dealers sell this overpriced product to more than half their installment loan customers. The main reason is that sales commissions can exceed 70 percent of the premium. Some consumers do not even realize that they have purchased credit life, disability, or unemployment insurance. Others are mistakenly led to think that they cannot borrow without purchasing the insurance. Even if a lender requires coverage to secure a loan, the law says that the consumer need not purchase insurance from lender-recommended sources.

Credit life insurance is the nation's worst ripoff reports the Consumer Federation of America. An estimated $500 million is wasted annually on overcharges. State insurance commissioners have the power to regulate payout ratios, but most are lax. A **payout ratio** is the proportion of premium dollars paid out as benefits to insurance purchasers. A 65 percent payout ratio is the standard recommended by the National Association of Insurance Commissioners. Companies in some states pay out as little as 15 cents of every dollar in premium collected. What a ripoff!

The consumer's cost per $1000 of term life insurance purchased through a local insurance agent—those reputable people with an office on main street—likely would be 1/6 to 1/10 the amount of the so-called "small monthly premium" charged for most of these policies. The credit disability and unemployment coverage are equally costly. It is not uncommon for consumers to unnecessarily pay $2000 for life, disability, and unemployment insurance premiums over the life of an installment loan.

Advice: Do not listen to the commission salesperson selling any of these insurance policies. Inexpensive term life insurance is available through credit unions and the military. Action recommendation: Before signing on the dotted line, use a pen to draw lines through anything that is not wanted; initial the changes. A few minutes of inattention can add up to many dollars of wasted money. If you need a policy, contact local insurance sources, examine the coverage, read the policy, and compare prices.

CONSUMER UPDATE:
Some Retailers Still Record Race on Checks!

The ugly face of racism continues in the 1990s. Well-known retail companies like Safeway Stores, Merry-Go-Round Enterprises, and Sears, Roebuck Company were recently caught recording the race of customers on personal checks. Confused, angered and rightfully indignant patrons complained about the race-coding symbols "W," "A," "B" and "H" (for white, Asian, black or Hispanic) written by store employees on their checks, sometimes after the customers had left the premises. Years ago, retailers identified a customer's race on checks, ostensibly to help identify those who wrote bad checks. If needed for an arrest warrant, racial information may be obtained from the Department of Motor Vehicles, using driver's license numbers; similarly motivated, some stores take photographs of all checkwriters.

Merry-Go-Round, a 700-store apparel retailer, began apologizing for the practice, saying, "We feel we have done nothing wrong. But we've decided to quickly clear the air and be responsive to customer's concerns." Showing a more realistic understanding of the insensitive discriminatory practice, one shopper observed that, "racial coding puts everyone into a wronged position."

Mistakes in Credit Files

After receiving a completed credit application, the lender conducts a **credit investigation,** an inquiry undertaken to verify information supplied by a borrower on a credit application. One's **credit history** is a continuing record of a borrower's debt commitments and how well these have been honored. Lenders often obtain information about a person's credit history from a credit bureau. A **credit bureau** is a reporting agency which assembles credit repayment history and other information on consumers to supply to others concerning a consumer's creditworthiness, credit standing, and/or capacity to repay a debt. One's **creditworthiness** is the ability to repay debts. Credit bureaus provide lenders with financial information on millions of Americans, compiling information primarily from court records, various merchants, and creditors.

One's **credit rating** largely determines whether credit is granted. This is an evaluation of a person's previous credit experience. Generally, the lender decides on your credit rating. To help assess potential borrowers, most lenders use a **credit scoring system**. This is a statistical measure used to rate credit applicants on the basis of various factors relevant to creditworthiness. Scoring systems help reduce subjectivity in decision making, avoid discrimination, and improve the likelihood of making correct decisions. Since types of credit and credit applicants vary, each lender uses different scoring techniques. Lenders typically use computers to analyze credit files and determine credit scores.

Members of credit bureaus (lenders and others who provide data to a credit bureau) pay both an annual charge and a specific fee for each credit report requested. This fee can vary from $2.50 for a verbal credit report and $1.50 for access to a file via a computer terminal to $8 for a printed copy of the file on hand; it costs $25 or more for an updated comprehensive report. Nonmember lenders must pay higher fees for these reports.

DID YOU KNOW?
How to Contact the Major Credit Bureaus and Get a
Free Copy of Your File

Most of the more than 2000 local credit bureaus belong to national groups that have access to credit histories of over 80 million people, such as Equifax (P.O. Box 4081, Atlanta, GA 30302; 800-685-1111), Trans Union (P.O. Box 7000, North Olmsted, OH 44070; 800-851-2674), and TRW Complimentary Report, P.O. Box 8030, Layton, UT 84041-8030; 800-682-7654). Laws in Maryland and Vermont allow consumers to get their credit histories for free. TRW gives all consumers a *free* report once a year, just for the asking. Nice pro-consumer corporate policy, TRW!

A credit bureau in New York analyzed 1500 reports and found errors in over 40 percent of the credit files. Sometimes the mistakes are minor, such as an incorrect address. Other times the mistakes are major, as when the credit files of two people with similar names are mixed together. A study by *Consumer Reports* revealed that one out of five credit reports contained major inaccuracies that could adversely affect a credit application. The Maryland Consumer Credit Commission recently examined all 1,018 written complaints from consumers about irregularities in their files at the three largest credit bureaus, and they found that 56 percent had not been corrected. Credit bureau mistakes, such as having someone else's data mixed in a credit report, have been the number one consumer complaint to the Federal Trade Commission in recent years. To correct an error, one must contact each credit bureau (including local) that has your file.

Each year about nine million people ask to see their credit files; over three million ask to have their files corrected because of invalid or stale information.[14] Credit bureaus are protected against lawsuits for financial damages by consumers who have been wronged (i.e., lost job opportunities, being refused home rentals, rejections for mortgages and automobile loans) when they have made "honest" mistakes. Gross negligence is about the only grounds for legal action.

CONSUMER UPDATE:
Don't Waste Money on TRW's "Credentials Service"

The nation's largest credit reporting company, TRW Credit Data, is profiting nicely by selling consumers its "Credentials Service" for an annual fee of $39. TRW will send you regular reports about your own credit file, particularly when your credit file has been prescreened by a lender to check your credit. Equifax and TransUnion have similar programs. Over 95 percent of prescreening is done by creditors wanting to send you another credit card.

These companies are selling people something they do not need because the information already belongs to consumers. If you ever want to know what is in your file, the Fair Credit Reporting Act requires that your local credit bureau provide you with the same information for a small fee, usually $5 to $15. (See Chapter 5 for more information.)

Privacy

Privacy, the condition of being secluded or isolated from the sight, presence, or intrusion of others, is under threat. Many people inadvertently supply firms with personal information. This occurs when you send in a warranty-registration card, buy an automobile, or order a magazine. When such data are combined with one's social security number, it can be overlaid to develop detailed pictures of almost anyone. It might include employment history, preference for breakfast cereal, list of magazines read, school records, and more. Such information helps companies develop improved products, offer better packaging, and conduct more precise advertising. Gaining a little extra information per consumer costs the seller a little more but it is supposed to increase the accuracy of marketing. For example, it is more efficient for a company selling storm windows to telephone only people who own their homes.

Credit reporting agencies and other specialized businesses collect an amazing amount and range of data about people. Combined with a person's social security number and the details in one's credit file, a firm could tell a lot about a consumer's life. For a price, this kind of information is readily available. Names and addresses of consumers who meet certain criteria might sell for 30 cents a name for orders of 1000 names or less to six cents per name for larger orders.

Target marketing is a carefully orchestrated effort to single out particular segments of consumers for purposes of marketing. Supporters argue that computers are used to generate mailing lists, not to look up personal information about individuals. That, however, may not be entirely true.

---

[14]In 1995, the Federal Trade Commission is expected to issue regulations requiring credit reporting agencies to provide raw credit scores to consumers upon their request, plus give a clear explanation of the individual's risk score ranked against thousands of others.

CONSUMER UPDATE:
Your Right to Privacy Is Being Invaded*

An individual's right to privacy is rooted in the Fourth Amendment to the U.S. Constitution. With increasingly powerful technology, consumers are experiencing two types of privacy invasion: (1) control over one's personal information, and (2) freedom from intrusion.

Laws created for privacy were written in an era that did not have worldwide access to data, high-speed transmission, and instant feedback. It is questionable whether government regulation or even self-regulation can effectively police today's sophisticated information superhighway. Even if regulation were possible, the penalties for misuse of personal information probably would not be severe enough to discourage profiteers from illegally seeking substantial financial gains.

Although you cannot always determine who has access to your personal information, you can establish safeguards to impede unwanted access: (1) Before giving out information, know how it is to be used; (2) Ask how the user will protect the information; (3) Provide only the information that is absolutely required; and (4) Before using new technology, you must possess an understanding of how using it may invade your privacy. Moreover, you must consider whether providing personal information about yourself is worth the risk of any misuse.

The Privacy Act of 1974 requires that government, when requesting a social security number, must tell the consumer what authority it has for making the request, whether the number is required or optional, how the number will be used, and what the consequences would be if the number is not provided. Businesses, however, have no required guidelines regarding social security numbers. So, again, you should consider being cautious about releasing your social security number.

In addition to trying to control who has access to your personal information, you can reduce the number of unwanted telephone calls and mail solicitations by contacting the sources listed in chapter 5. You also may ask your credit reporting company to block sending credit information for promotional purposes.

*Joan Kinney, Lecturer, University of Wisconsin-Madison

The three dominant companies in the data business are R. L. Polk, Donnelley Marketing, and Metromail. The three large credit reporting agencies, which constantly update their files, are TRW Inc., Equifax, and Trans Union Corporation. All three sell their data to marketers. Telephone companies are getting into the business too with the **"caller ID"** technology that identifies callers by telephone number. Later, these are easily matched with names and addresses. The advent of caller ID raises the issue of whose right is more compelling: the caller or the person being called.

Privacy advocates have unsuccessfully sought for laws to require companies to obtain a person's permission before collecting or selling the information. Presently, some companies voluntarily inform consumers that their names may be sold.

Congress is expected to pass the Consumer Credit Reporting Reform Act to update federal privacy laws and extend more rights to credit consumers. Issues under discussion include: (1) disclose information in credit reports only with the permission of the consumer, (2) consumers to receive a free copy of his or her credit report every year, (3) require credit reporting agencies to correct errors within 30 days, (4) require creditors to notify consumers when and what information from their monthly statements is routinely forwarded to credit bureaus, (5) require creditors to tell consumers (right on their credit statements) about any negative information that is being reported, (6) require credit bureaus to notify consumers after adverse information is placed on their records, and (7) provide a toll-free number for consumers to call to correct mistakes.

Housing Problems and Issues

A number of consumer problems and issues exist in the area of housing. These range from the high cost of housing, to the supply and demand for housing, to the need for defect-disclosure laws.

Discrimination in Housing and Credit

Discrimination is acting on the basis of bias or intentional prejudice. It is illegal to discriminate in credit financing, as well as many areas of housing and employment. Various laws prohibit discrimination on the basis of race, color, religion, national origin, sex, marital status, age, disability, elderliness, or parenthood. As a country, Americans seek a society in which each person is evaluated on his or her worth, not a community based upon factors that cannot be changed. Still, discrimination goes on."Discrimination is very subtle and can often be defined by the lack of assistance someone receives," says Shanna Smith, director of the National Fair Housing Alliance.[15]

DID YOU KNOW?
How to Report Credit Discrimination

If you suspect that you have been discriminated against because of your race, gender or age, telephone any of the following: Housing Discrimination Hotline of the Department of Housing and Urban Development (800-669-9777); Justice Department (202-514-4713); National Fair Housing Alliance (202-898-1661).

A survey by five federal regulatory agencies, prepared by the Federal Financial Institutions Examination Council, reports that "banks, savings institutions, and credit unions last year turned down 33.4 percent of mortgage applications received by blacks, 31.6 from American Indians, 24.6 percent from Hispanics, 16.4 percent from whites, and 12.0 percent from Asians." Mortgage denial rates for minority applicants, according to the Mortgage Bankers Association, were in a recent year at least twice as great as denial rates for white borrowers. This finding occurred regardless of income. A recent Federal Reserve Board study found that black mortgage applicants were rejected for loans at double the rates of whites, regardless of income. A report of the American Bankers Association studying mortgage lending data showed similar disturbing patterns.

The overwhelming amount of evidence makes it appear that society now believes that discrimination in mortgage lending really exists. Another study revealed that, "one of out every eleven recent home loan borrowers felt they were discriminated against even as their mortgages were approved."[16] A recent nationwide study that utilized interracial pairs of testers

---

[15]Fickenscher, L. (1993, April). Don't Let Bias Slam the Door to a Home Loan. *Money*, p. 42.
[16]Mariano, A. (1994, March 10). One in 11 Mortgage Seekers Sense Bias. *The Washington Post*, p. B-11.

found that African Americans and Hispanics were discriminated against about half the time. A study of 25 metropolitan areas by the Department of Housing and Urban Development study found that Hispanics encountered bias half the time they tried to rent and more than half the time they attempted to buy a home; blacks faced even higher rates of discrimination.

Examples of discrimination against the minorities included: being told they were in the wrong office, being urged to consider another lender, being falsely told that much more information was needed before they could receive an indication of how likely they were to qualify, having housing ratios falsely computed, and being incorrectly discouraged from applying for a loan. Also, minorities were less likely to be told of little tips and hints about how to qualify.

Discrimination also occurs in buying homeowners insurance, which is required when one finances a home. Testers in Chicago, says the National Fair Housing Alliance, found that Latinos "ran into problems more than 95 percent of their attempts to obtain insurance." Discrimination occurs in rental housing, too.

CONSUMER UPDATE
How to Identify Discrimination: Examples

To help combat discrimination, the Clinton Administration in 1994 directed that all federal agencies meet and develop a uniform "Policy Statement on Discrimination in Lending" for detecting and preventing the many forms subtle discrimination can take. The newly approved policy statement applies to all lenders, including mortgage brokers, issuers of credit cards, and any other person who extends credit of any type. The agencies define **discrimination in lending** as lending on the basis of race or other prohibited factors and that such discrimination is destructive, morally repugnant, and against the law.

The agencies also offered a series of examples of discrimination, some of which are summarized below:

- A lender rejected a loan application made by a female applicant with flaws in her credit report but accepted applications by male applicants with similar flaws.
- Two minority applicants were told that it would take several hours and require the payment of an application fee to determine whether or not they qualified for a home loan, while non-minority applicants were given no such requirements.
- When a non-minority couple applied for a loan, upon questioning the lender recommended that the adverse information in their credit report be challenged because it was incorrect and the loan was later approved. A minority couple with similar adverse information were simply denied credit without having an opportunity to discuss the report.
- Two minority borrowers inquired about a mortgage loan and were given applications for fixed-rate loans only and were not offered assistance in completing the applications; later their application was turned down. Two similarly qualified non-minority applicants made an identical inquiry, were given information about adjustable-rate and fixed rate loans and were given assistance in filling out the application which the lender later approved.
- A lender's longtime policy has been not to extend loans for single family residences for less than $60,000. However, this policy is shown to disproportionately exclude potential minority applicants.

For those against whom discrimination is practiced, the hope of renting or buying housing without bias remains slight. Efforts are underway in the industry and in government to increase credit availability to minority and low- to moderate-income communities while assuring that discrimination no longer is a factor in home financing.

Housing lenders are turning to **credit scoring** to reduce bias considering applications.[17] Instead of evaluating loan applicants face-to-face, this method offers a computerized "artificial intelligence" method to predict a loan's likelihood of defaulting based upon the lender's historical delinquency data. This method of evaluating housing loan applications is designed to eliminate bias and speed up the process. When a computerized system is used, loan approval time generally is cut in half from the traditional 28 days.

Redlining

Credit availability is a crucial concern, particularly for low- and moderate income consumers. **Redlining** is the illegal practice of a financial institution outlining an area by drawing red lines around disfavored neighborhoods where money would reluctantly be lent or refused, regardless of the creditworthiness of individual loan applicants. Illegal redlining also occurs in insurance sales. It is a form of discrimination. Laws prohibit discrimination in housing or housing financing. A growing number of communities additionally prohibit discrimination based on sexual orientation. A study of 24 million mortgage records by *U.S. News & World Report* reveals that both blatant and subtle forms of redlining continue.[18]

Redlining is prohibited by federal and state laws. An insurance representative summed up a common view on the situation by saying that, "There really isn't evidence of intentional discrimination by insurers against urban residents. What you have are neutral underwriting rules that have a disproportionate impact upon minority, urban residents."

CONSUMER UPDATE:
Community Reinvestment Act Ratings

Because of the 1977 Community Reinvestment Act (CRA), banks, savings banks, and savings and loan associations are required to serve the credit needs of the entire communities where they have offices—rich or poor, white or black—especially low- and moderate-income neighborhoods. The CRA regulations, described in Chapter 5, require a dialogue between the financial institutions and all segments of the communities they serve.

The CRA requires that financial institutions play a vital role in revitalizing neighborhoods. Because of CRA, over $60 billion has been invested into inner cities. The accountability of the banks, savings banks, and savings and loan associations is made clear to the public through posting of regular performance evaluations, **CRA ratings**, that are used to grade each institution's efforts to serve its community. This rating is based upon proper documentation reviewed by federal inspectors. Interested consumers need only visit a local financial institution to determine its CRA rating and review the institution's CRA Public File for a description of recent efforts.

De facto redlining of mortgage loans occurs when financial institutions close their branch offices in poor and middle-income neighborhoods. If one cannot get access to a mortgage loan, there is no alternative.

---

[17]Harney, K. R. (1994, January 15). Automated Credit Scoring Screens Loan Applicants. *The Washington Post*, p. E-1.

[18]The New Redlining, *U.S. News & World Report*, April 17, 1995, 52.

The High Cost of Housing in America

The cost of the average new home sold in the United States is over $121,000. Prices for single-family dwellings in Orange County, California, are above $250,000, and prices are not far behind in Los Angeles, San Francisco, Honolulu, New York, District of Columbia, Hartford, Connecticut, and Providence, Rhode Island. Census data reveal that 85 percent of households headed by persons under age 25 are renters compared with only 19 percent of those headed by persons aged 55 to 64. Recent data from the Joint Economic Committee of Congress reveal that home ownership declined in the 1980s for the first time in 50 years, and now only 63.9 percent of Americans own their homes.

Lower mortgage rates in the 1990s has helped enormously with housing affordability. With household income averaging about $36,000, after making a 20 percent downpayment that household could afford a $120,000 home. If interest rates should jump up two percent, that same income could qualify for only a $100,000 home.

CONSUMER UPDATE:
Need Help Buying a Home: Government Program Assists
Recent College Graduates

A number of housing loan programs exist for low-income consumers. Key among them is the Federal National Mortgage Association (Fannie Mae). Its newest program allows borrowers to make a down payment of as little as $1000, or three percent of the sales price. Participant's income is not to exceed 60 to 80 percent of the area's median income. The Washington, D.C. area has the highest median income in the program, over $59,000.

All states have funds reserved to subsidize interest rates for low-income home buyers. For example, if housing loans are 8 percent and require a $440 monthly repayment amount for a $60,000 loan, a government subsidy could reduce the interest rate perhaps to 6 percent. Then the monthly payment for principal and interest would be only $359, much more affordable than $440. The maximum income ceiling for participation may be about $29,000 for a single and $35,000 for a couple.

A great number of housing loan programs are community based and can only be learned about by contacting local housing officials. If interested, see the telephone book blue pages to find out about income requirements and other details.

The maximum loan amount on the low-downpayment housing loans insured by the Federal Housing Administration (FHA) recently rose to $151,725 in high-cost areas of the U.S. The new rule sets the price cap at 95 percent of the local median price or 75 percent of the loan limit set by the secondary mortgage companies, Federal National Mortgage Association and Federal Home Loan Mortgage Corporation. Since the FHA handles more than 700,000 loans a year, this opens up more higher-priced housing to people who have the income but not the often required 20-percent down payment money to buy a home. The Veterans Administration (VA) recently broadened the eligibility for no-downpayment VA-insured loans to include members of the military reserves and the national guard who have spent six years on inactive duty. The Federal National Mortgage Association (Fannie Mae) recently announced that it will make $1 trillion available to low-income families for the next six years.

Congressman Henry B. Gonzales of Texas recently proposed that government step in with very specific financial help for all potential first-time home buyers. Gonzales has introduced legislation to establish a $3 billion National Housing Trust offering low-interest mortgages to first-time home buyers. A number of groups also support the proposed concept of **housing vouchers**, which are federal government financial supplements designed to bridge the gap between income and housing costs.

Another housing plan targeted at first-time lower- and moderate-income home buyers who otherwise would be priced out of the market has been proposed by the Chicago-based National People's Action group. This organization is trying to get Congress to support a program called Home Ownership Made Easier (HOME), which would encourage consumers to save money to eventually pay for mortgage costs. The plan would reward the lenders by providing federal matching funds for every dollar saved by a home buyer.

Reports by the Center on Budget and Policy Priorities indicate that the growing lack of affordable housing has reached a crisis stage for low-income Americans, particularly African Americans and Hispanics. Unless and until special funds become available, it will continue to be difficult for many people to buy housing in America. A recent survey of 44 cities by the same organization found that three-quarters of the nation's poor are paying more than what the government says is affordable in rent. Of the households earning less than $10,000 a year, 75 percent were paying more than 30 percent of their incomes for rent. Fewer than one-third of urban poor are receiving rent subsidies. The affordable housing problem is serious.

AN ECONOMIC FOCUS ON...The Supply and Demand for Housing

Each housing market is local, and composed of many participants, including builders, landlords, lenders, government regulators, and consumers.[1] Each housing market is local, and each local market is composed of sub-markets: (1) owner-occupied housing of different types and price levels, and (2) rental housing at different rent levels. For simplicity, the following discussion uses the assumption that all housing is rental and identical.

The Supply of Housing

The supply of housing in a private market is determined by the interest of builders in making a profit, and the availability of land, labor, and materials needed to build a housing unit, whatever the actual structure type—single family, townhouse, apartment building, etc. There is rarely any absolute limit on the inputs of land, labor and materials for building housing. Even when the supply of land is limited, builders can build up, with multilevel housing. The higher the market price of housing, the more units will be built. If there are not enough workers for building homes, wages will increase and workers will come into the industry. New homebuilding firms will start, with some builders working nights and weekends after their regular jobs.

Credit. The availability of credit is one of the most important limitations on the supply of housing. If the government, especially the Federal Reserve Board in the United States, is trying to control inflation, there may be a decrease in the availability of housing. The supply of housing will be sharply decreased during these times when credit is expensive and difficult to obtain. At other times, the government will try to stimulate the economy and plenty of credit will be available.

The Demand for Housing

The demand for housing is determined by the number of households and the amount of money they want to spend for housing. Obviously, rich consumers can spend more for housing than poor consumers. Families with many children will want different types of housing and different locations than will single persons and childless couples. The demand curve for housing of a particular type and general location is the sum of the quantity each household would want at each price or rent. The demand curve will shift up if incomes increase or if people move into an area. The demand curve will shift down if incomes decrease or if people move out of an area.

Effect of Increase in Demand for Housing. Consider the example of a housing market shown in Figure 17-2. If supply and demand are in balance in the market, the average rent is $250 and there are 50,000 rental units, at the intersection of supply and demand (point a). Assume that the demand in the market increases, for instance, because of a sudden increase in population (shown by the change in the demand curve from D to D'). The short run supply curve is almost vertical, as shown by S_0. Within the first month after the sudden increase in demand, no new housing units can be built. The supply curve will not be completely vertical, because there may be some vacant units, and some units may be converted from other uses (e.g., commercial space or parts of owner-occupied housing may be rented out). Most of the effect of the increase in demand will be seen in the increase in the rent, shown in the example as an increase from $250 to $355. The number of rental units will increase from 50,000 to 52,000 units.   (continued)

---

[1]Lindamood, S. & Hanna, S. (1979). *Housing, Society and Consumers: An Introduction* (West Publishing), 132.

(Continued)

Short-run Market Response. The change in equilibrium to point b has very little increase in the number of units available and a large increase in rent. A large increase in rent will outrage consumers, but it will also attract builders and landlords because of the opportunity for above average profits. Before new units can come on the market, some consumers will have to "double-up", living with relatives or others, and others will have long commutes to work.

Medium-run Market Response. If there are not excessive limitations on building and renovations, many new rental units will become available. If building can proceed very quickly, within one year the supply curve may have shifted to what is shown by S_1. The new equilibrium point will be point c, which will have a lower rent ($320) and a larger quantity (63,000 units).

Long-run Market Response. After two years, the supply curve will shift to S_2 and the new equilibrium point will be at point d. The rent level will drop to $320 and the quantity will increase to 80,000 units. After five years, it is possible that rents (after general inflation is subtracted) will drop back to the original level ($250). It is even possible that builders will be over-optimistic and overbuild, in which case rents will be driven down below the original level.

Rent Control. Some cities respond to a sudden increase in the demand for housing by passing rent control laws to protect tenants from increases in rents. This effort will inevitably hurt some consumers, as a shortage will continue as long as the rent control is in effect. The ultimate result can be seen in New York City, where the government must spend billions of dollars to build housing for low and moderate households, because the private market will not supply it.

Regulations. Regulations such as building codes and zoning restrictions have stated purposes of protecting consumers and of improving the environment of residents. In many cases, however, such regulations also have resulted in higher rents and home prices. Some regulations, such as minimum sizes for building lots, may benefit existing homeowners at the expenses of young families and others who would like housing in the area. Even when regulations are at moderate levels, they will tend to shift up the supply curves shown in Figure 17-2, leading to some reduction in the amount of affordable housing for low and moderate income families. If society has a concern for the housing of these families, some type of housing programs or income supplements may be needed.

Conclusion: There Is No Free Lunch

The fundamental truth to consider about housing is that there is no free lunch. Provision of adequate housing for people costs money. The private market can deal efficiently with shifts in demand and supply, and adjust to regulations, but some families will have to pay high fractions of their incomes to obtain housing considered adequate by society. Efforts to improve housing of low and moderate income families will cost money, and ultimately middle and upper income consumers will pay, either through higher prices and rents or by higher taxes.

*Sherman Hanna, Professor, The Ohio State University

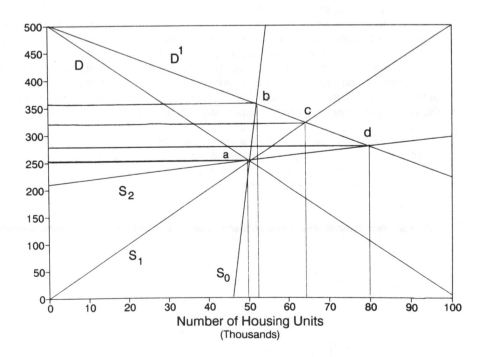

FIGURE 17-2 The Effect of an Increase in Demand (D to D¹) on the Price and Amount of Rental Housing

Appraisers Are Regulated, but Not for Most Consumers

Almost all real estate appraisers must be licensed or certified. A federal law requires that states enact their own licensing or certification laws. In 21 states, appraisers must be licensed; in the other 29, licensed appraisers are only required for deals involving the federal government. Ninety percent of all real estate sales involved the federal government in one way or another. The federal government, however, largely exempts the need for an appraisal on loans under $250,000; that amounts to 80 percent of all loans. Therefore, most residential properties that consumers purchase will no longer be evaluated by an appraiser. Instead, an alternative appraisal called an *evaluation* may be performed, and this person may not be a licensed appraiser. It remains "caveat emptor" for middle- and low-income home buyers![19] Regulators are considering raising the standard to $250,000, thus excluding 80 percent of all housing transactions from proper appraisals.

CONSUMER UPDATE:
Predatory Home Mortgage Abuses Against Poor Homeowners

Property values soared during the 1980s, giving even poor homeowners a measure of wealth in home values. For example, many homes in South Central Los Angeles have values of $100,000 or more. The 1990s has home repair hustlers working all across the nation stealing homes from thousands of poor people who own them.

The ripoff occurs when borrowers, often poor, minority, or under-educated, are persuaded to take out high rate, high fee, home-secured loans, in order to finance home improvements, pay property taxes, consolidate debts, or pay for personal emergencies. Such scandalous transactions benefit the home-repair companies, the real estate agents, and legitimate banks. These people specialize in high-interest mortgages to poor and elderly people who need credit but whose income or credit histories might not allow them to obtain a bank loan.

In a matter of months or a year or so, for one reason or another (often the payment is two or three times what the consumer was led to believe), the consumer misses a payment or two. That's it. After 20 or 25 years of ownership, foreclosure results. The lender takes over the home, puts the people on the street, and sells the home for a good price and keeps the profits.

High-interest second mortgage scams against homeowners include sales of overpriced satellite dishes, vinyl siding, water purifiers, air conditioners, solar heating systems, exterior stucco coating, carpeting, and drapes. The High Cost Mortgage Act of 1995 offers consumers protections when they refinance their home or take out a home equity loan.

---

[19]On a related matter, the Federal Reserve Board has proposed that appraisers, including mortgage lenders, be required to give a copy of any appraisal to the consumer who paid for it within 15 days after receipt of a written request.

Mandatory Defect-Disclosure Laws

Even though real estate agents typically represent sellers, over the years many agents have been successfully sued by buyers who believed the agent "should have known about defects and informed them." Real estate agents support home warranty programs and use of disclosure forms for the same reason: protection of real estate agents from lawsuits blaming them about undisclosed defects in homes.

Six states require sellers to complete a **defect-disclosure form** that sets forth what a seller really knows about the condition of a home when selling it. The form requires the seller to complete a detailed, two-page form. Often included on the list are such items as the condition of appliances; presence of termites, carpenter ants, asbestos, lead-based paint; noise in the neighborhood; whether or not the well has gone dry; and if the property had ever been involved in a dispute over property-lines. Disclosure forms are not warranties of a home's condition; they are simply supposed to list defects that could affect a potential buyer's perception of the value of the property. Sellers are urged to be precise in describing flaws. One often used response to a form question is, "Don't know." The liability for undisclosed defects rests with the seller.

The idea is strongly supported by the National Association of Realtors (NAR). Disclosure benefits both the sellers and the buyers. Over 30 states have voluntary disclosure forms. Some Realtors[R] (an agent or broker who is a member of the NAR) and agents require the forms for any home they list for sale.

The Residential Lead-Based Paint Hazard Reduction Act of 1992, effective in 1996, aims to educate residents about the dangers of lead paint in older homes, particularly the 64 million dwellings built before 1978, when lead paint was outlawed. The rules require sellers, landlords, sales agents, and rental agents to provide disclosure forms and pamphlets written by HUD and EPA that tell people how to protect themselves from lead paint.

Laws to Require Agents to Disclose to Buyers Whom They Represent

A study by the Federal Trade Commission revealed that three-quarters of all home buyers mistakenly believe that the agent driving them around to see homes and presenting their purchase offers represents their interests. While state laws require agents to treat buyers and sellers honestly and fairly, long-standing legal precedent provides that the agents almost always work for the seller, not the buyer. The whole idea is to sell the home for the seller because the seller pays the sales commission. If a potential buyer divulges any confidential information to the agent, such as the price they would be willing to pay if they couldn't get it for less, the agent is legally obligated to pass the information on to the seller. The result: buyers paying too much for housing, contributing to price inflation everywhere.

Because of the confusion in the minds of so many consumers, a number of areas have regulations requiring that home buyers be notified in writing—at the first substantive meeting between the agent and the consumer—that the real estate agent who shows them homes is representing only the sellers. States have been slow to mandate such disclosures.

CONSUMER UPDATE:
Some Agents Solely Represent the Buyer

Less than five percent of all real estate agents solely represent the home buyer. A study by U.S. Sprint found that consumers who hired **buyer's brokers**, those who represent only the buyer in a real estate transaction, paid an average of 91 percent of a home's list price; those using traditional agents paid 96 percent. Buyer's brokers are paid by the hour or a flat fee, often two to three percent of the buyer's target purchase price. Listing agents sometimes discriminate against buyer brokers by not showing homes or splitting commissions with them. To determine if a buyer's agent is in your geographic area, check the local Board of Realtors or telephone the Buyer's Broker Registry (800-729-5147).

Bargaining Is Necessary to Reduce Sales Commissions

Tradition provides that real estate agents earn a standard six (or even seven) percent commission when selling a home. Sellers pay a **listing agent** (the person who reaches an agreement with a seller to place the home for sale) the commission. This amount is shared with other agents, especially **selling agents** (persons working with potential buyers). Since both agents are paid by the seller they represent the seller. The great majority of homes are sold using a **multiple-listing service (MLS)**, a shared database that lists and describes homes for sale available to most agents. Assuming that the seller pays a 6 percent commission upon the sale of a home, the real estate agent who originally listed the property receives 3 percent, probably splitting 50/50 with the owner of the agency; the selling agent receives the remaining 3 percent, and shares 40 percent to the owner of the agency.

The commission is paid regardless of the quality of service received, and there is a wide range. The commission pays for the earnings of the agent, advertising the property, and office backup support of the full-service real estate firm. Occasionally, a real estate agent will agree to accept a reduced commission, but consumers have to ask. No laws require agents to disclose that they will work for less than the so-called standard commission rate. Also, no laws exist to require real estate agents to disclose their selling experience, such as number of homes sold in the past year.

A growing number of realty firms work for flat fees far below the usual six percent commission. **Discount real estate firms** generally charge a flat fee ranging from $3400 to $3950 and require that the homeowner show the home to prospective buyers. The discounters, such as the fast-growing 600-office Help-You-Sell firm, usually provide "for sale" signs, do the advertising, provide advice throughout the process, and handle most or all of the paperwork. It is estimated that perhaps one-third of today's residential sales are made for less than the standard six percent. Nationally, 20 percent of homeowners sell their own homes without the use of a realty agent.

Kickback Fees to Help Arrange Other Services

When a consumer purchases a home all of the financial aspects of the deal come together. On the day of **closing** or **settlement**, the business aspects are managed by lawyers, realty companies, real estate agents, and title companies. Then the consumer signs all the documents.

DID YOU KNOW?
Women and African Americans Pay Higher Prices

A three-year study in Chicago revealed that African Americans and women pay the highest prices for new cars. Higher prices were routinely quoted to the undercover researchers, and differences ranged from $142 to $875.

Federal investigators are currently examining the amount of fees charged to women and minority applicants compared with the fees charged their white counterparts. Rather than focusing on lending, which remains important, they are focusing on fees. On a related matter, a series of class action lawsuits are pending that challenge the fees lenders routinely charge borrowers who pay off their loans early.

Recent rules of the Department of Housing and Urban Development (HUD) adopted under the Real Estate Settlement Procedures Act (RESPA) interpret what Congress meant in the 1983 law. RESPA attempts to protect consumers from abusive real estate closing practices, especially where kickback fees are given to various service providers. A **kickback fee** is a percentage payment to a person able to influence or control a source of income, often by confidential arrangement or coercion. The types of related services that a consumer might purchase when buying a home include a loan application, home inspection service, mortgage loan, title insurance, life insurance, and property and casualty insurance. Many large companies are interested in providing most or all of these services and offering "one-stop shopping" for consumers.

One example occurs in **computer mortgage-shopping services**, which occurs when a real estate agent collects a fee from a consumer for providing detailed information on financing rates and then refers that client to a particular lender. To illustrate, a real estate agency has access via computer to a large number of mortgage loan rates through a mortgage broker. If a mortgage loan is arranged, the consumer-borrower pays a fee to cover the cost of the computer link. The real estate agent also may receive a commission for referring the client to the mortgage broker. (It is illegal, under the Real Estate Settlement Practices Act, to require home purchasers to use a subsidiary's financing.)

The HUD regulation permits these charges, places no limits on the amount, and does not require that mortgage shopping be open to all lenders. (The lowest-priced lenders may choose not to participate.) In larger communities, the same detailed financing information can be found by making a few telephone calls; oftentimes the facts are available in newspapers.

Under the rules, as independent contractors, real estate agents will be prohibited from receiving a bonus for referring business. However, an employer can pay an employee for referring business to an affiliate. Therefore, all companies that participate in packaging services with other firms to offer them at a discount to consumers will no longer be prohibited from paying each other fees arising from the arrangements. In 1993, Sears affiliate Coldwell Banker Residential Real Estate settled out of court with Housing and Urban Development (HUD) for steering 700 home buyers in New Jersey to Sears-owned subsidiaries without telling consumers about the financial links between the firms. Kenneth Harvey, noted real estate columnist, observes that many illegal under-the-table kickbacks continue.

Consumer advocates are worried about anti-competitive practices where firms will be motivated to steer borrowers to lenders and other providers in the system that give them the biggest kickbacks, rather than offer the best prices for consumers. For consumers, the question is, "Am I being taken advantage of by getting ripped off with high prices at the time of settlement?"

Regulations do require written disclosure of any special fees, kickbacks, rebates, or other forms of payment for related services. Consumers also must be told they have the legal right to shop elsewhere for alternatives. Home buyers are well-known for trusting the advice of their realty agent on financing and settlement. Without comparison shopping, consumers are more likely to pay too much.

HUD officials estimate that a system of affiliated networks will save about 10 percent on settlement costs. The president of Countrywide Funding Corporation, Angelo Mozilo, argues that the economies of scale argument is fallacious and calls the bundling of services a "fraudulent concept."[20] As independent service providers are squeezed out of business because of a lack of referrals within the system, consumers in the future will have fewer choices in a marketplace with no constraints on pricing.

Locked-in Mortgage Loans

Disclosure also is important to consumers who apply for a mortgage loan, wait a number of weeks for all the approvals, and then discover that the mortgage lender is raising the interest rate at the last minute before closing the deal. To illustrate the impact of apparently small increases, a $130,000 thirty-year mortgage loan at 9 percent requires a $1046 monthly repayment for principal and interest; a loan at 9 1/2 percent costs $1093 a month, not to mention the extra $42,080 in interest costs. Some states have disclosure laws to protect consumers in these situations. They require lenders to disclose whether they offer **locked-in mortgage commitments** that will not change within the time period between quotation and closing. Other laws permit consumers to sue for damages should the mortgage lender fail to refund lock-in fees when the mortgage does not close on time or fail to give legally required disclosures.

Settlement Date May Lack Meaning

When a home buyer and a seller agree on a price for a home, they both sign a contract agreeing to a variety of terms. Consumers should pay attention to the details of such contracts. Fortunately, many states require builders to disclose a clearly estimated **settlement date**, or **closing date**, (which is the day when a home is legally and financially transferred to a new buyer). Also, some states require disclosure of a **contract termination date**, the day the builder expects to complete all work on a home. Provisions for a settlement date written by builders sometimes prohibit home buyers from inspecting homes before settlement or prohibit an inspector to accompany the consumer buyer.

Problems also arise between new home contractors and buyers when the settlement date is on one page and a provision for a much later contract termination date is on another page. A provision might allow the builder to take an additional 12 months to complete the work. Consumers who do not realize the differences in the dates might have

---

[20]Lehman, H. J. (1992, December 12). New Rules on Settlement Procedures Could Alter Buying, Borrowing Process. *The Washington Post*, p. E-1.

to arrange to live elsewhere should the home not be ready or live in a partially completed residence (if permitted by a building inspector).

Escrow Ripoffs Exist

Escrow payments are monthly prepayments made by a homeowner to a lender to accumulate and later be used to make annual payments for real estate property taxes and homeowner's insurance. More than three-quarters of all outstanding loans have escrow requirements. The idea is to protect the lender and prevent foreclosure if, for example, a homeowner fails to pay those bills in a timely manner. If a homeowner expects to owe $400 for homeowner's insurance and $800 for real estate taxes at the end of a year, he or she may give the lender $100 a month to build up a sufficient amount. These funds go into an escrow account. Consumers should earn interest income on such amounts held in escrow or have the amounts temporarily applied to the outstanding balance to reduce interest paid. In the example above, this could save perhaps $50 a year. The Clinton Administration has announced that it favors mandatory, nationwide interest payments on escrow accounts.

A recent study by seven attorneys general reported by Robert Abrams, attorney general of New York, revealed that two out of three homeowners nationwide are being taken advantage of by the mortgage lenders of America. Since savings and loan associations are not legally required to pay interest on escrow accounts, most are not paying consumers the interest income that the financial institutions actually earn on such deposited funds. Thus, the industry gets a free loan. Abrams says mortgage lenders in many states are charging homeowners billions of dollars in excess escrow payments and holding the funds in accounts that bear little or no interest income.[21] Fleet Mortgage, one of the nation's largest mortgage companies, reached a settlement with attorneys general from 26 states that required it to return $150 million in escrow payments to customers. Fleet overcharged its customers nearly 90 percent of the time.[22]

Escrow ripoffs would occur quite rarely if the lenders would give the consumers the same information they have. Consumer advocates want to require that financial institutions send mortgage loan customers a detailed monthly statement. It should show the prior loan balance, amount of the last payment, how the interest was calculated on that payment, and the new balance. Why shouldn't consumers have the same information lenders do?

Canceling Private Mortgage Insurance

Because many consumers are unable to make a 20 or 30 percent down payment on a home, they must purchase private mortgage insurance. The cost typically amounts to an extra one-half of one percent of the mortgage, paid monthly. **Private mortgage insurance (PMI)** requires the borrower to purchase a policy that insures the first 20 percent of a loan in case of default. If the borrower fails to pay, the insurer reimburses the lender for losses should the foreclosed home not resell for the full amount of the loan. Over ten percent of all loans have private mortgage insurance.

---

[21]Mortgage Ripoffs Claimed. (1990, April 25). *Roanoke Times & World-News*, p. A-1.
[22]Singletary, M. (1993, February 9). *The Washington Post*, p. D-3.

Consumers should not have to pay these insurance premiums forever, but some policies and regulations prohibit this from happening. To illustrate, assume a home that cost $100,000 five years ago has increased in value to $130,000 because of inflation and other factors. Since the lender's 20 percent risk no longer exists because the value of the home has risen, some private mortgage insurance companies are willing to cancel a PMI policy. Getting an appraisal of the higher value is usually required. Cancellation could save the homeowner in this illustration from paying perhaps $600 or more in unnecessary premiums a year. However, some insurers will not cancel the private mortgage insurance policies until the mortgage loan is "paid down" 20 percent. Even the Federal Home Loan Mortgage Corporation has taken a restrictive stand. Consumer advocates are asking for legislation requiring PMI companies to cancel unnecessary policies when a homeowner shows that the value of an insured home has increased substantially so as not to warrant coverage.

Review and Summary of Key Terms and Concepts

1. What has the **Truth in Savings Act** accomplished for consumers?

2. What is lacking in the **Truth in Savings** regulations?

3. Give three examples of some **negative impacts** of deregulation of the banking industry.

4. List some **consumer frustrations** with electronic banking.

5. Summarize how **discrimination against small depositors and nondepositors** occurs.

6. Summarize why the **poor pay more** for banking services.

7. What is **basic banking**?

8. List some key factors that lead to the **savings and loan scandal/banking** scandal.

9. What is a **moral hazard**, and how did the concept apply in the banking industry?

10. What is a key to **eliminating any future banking scandal**?

11. Distinguish between **prescreened** and **preapproved**.

12. Explain how paying on credit **increases total costs**.

13. What is **spread**, and what does that concept illustrate in consumer credit?

14. Explain how the **rule of 78s** penalizes consumers.

15. What is the central idea behind how **credit, disability and unemployment insurance** are ripoffs.

16. Why are **credit- and debit-card registration services** ripoffs?

17. How does one go about correcting **mistakes** in a credit file?

18. In a sentence, explain why the **two-cycle average daily balance method** is a ripoff.

19. What is the **rule of 78s**, and why is it unfair to consumers?

20. Explain the idea of **payout ratio** and how that is such a clear indicator of insurance companies that sell overpriced policies.

21. Explain why **credit-card registration services** are a poor deal for consumers.

22. Give some examples of **privacy violations** in credit.

23. Summarize how **usury laws** affect the supply and demand for credit for middle-income consumers and low-income consumers.

24. Give two examples of the high **cost of housing** in America.

25 What factors influence creating a greater **supply of housing**?

26. List three factors that determine the **demand for housing**.

27. Summarize the reality of **discrimination in housing** as revealed in recent housing research.

28. What is **redlining** in housing?

29. What is a **CRA rating**?

30. What is a **defect disclosure form**, and why is it used?

31. Distinguish among: **buyer's broker, listing agent**, and **selling agent**.

32. What are **kickback fees**? Give two examples.

33. Distinguish among: **locked-in mortgage commitment, settlement date**, and **contract termination date**.

34. Briefly explain the problem of ripoffs in **escrow payments**.

35. What is **private mortgage insurance (PMI)**, and why is it used?

Useful Resources for Consumers

Bankcard Holders of America
560 Herndon Parkway, Suite 120
Herndon, VA 22070
703-481-1110

Department of Housing and Urban Development
451 Seventh Street, SW, Room 9272
Washington, DC 20410
202-708-2700
800-347-3735 (fraud hotline)
http://www.hud.gov/places.html

National Foundation for Consumer Credit
8611 2nd Avenue, Suite 100
Silver Spring, MD 20910
301-589-5600
800-388-2227

"What Do You Think" Questions

1. The concept of personal **privacy** seems to be growing in importance to consumers. What are your thoughts on privacy concerns? In particular, how do they balance the rights of consumers against the rights of sellers?

2. The **rising prices of banking** affect all consumers, including the poor. What do you think should be done to lower the cost of banking for the economically disadvantaged? Consider actions that both government and sellers might take.

3. What do you think should be done to increase the supply of **affordable housing** in America? Make a short list of your suggestions along with the cost effects of each idea.

4. List three factors that might make a genuine improvement in reducing **discrimination** in housing.

Chapter 18

Insurance and Investment Issues

OBJECTIVES

After reading this chapter, you should be able to

1. Recognize that there are a number of consumer problems and issues in insurance.

2. Describe a number of consumer problems and issues in investments.

Insurance and investments are important parts of consumer living. Insurance is a necessity, yet most consumers are mystified about how insurance rates are set and often feel that rates are excessive. Like insurance, the world of investments also uses complicated terminology. About one-third of all adults own stocks, and many more Americans invest through employer pension plans. Consumers must learn enough about insurance and investments in order to avoid being defrauded by swindlers, avoid being ripped off by advisors who are only interested in earning commissions, and be confident that one's insurance and investments will be there when needed.

This chapter provides an overview of the major consumer problems and issues in the areas of insurance and investments. It begins with insurance problems and issues that negatively affect consumers, such as anti-competitive practices, high prices, and rental car insurance ripoffs. It concludes with an examination of consumer problems and issues in investments, including insider trading, fairness in arbitration, and recognition of the biases of most financial planners.

Consumer Problems and Issues in Insurance

This section begins by identifying consumer rights in insurance. It follows with a number of consumer problems and issues in insurance, including auto insurance industry reforms, defacto price-fixing, no-fault auto insurance, life insurance suggestions, and what happens when an insurance company goes broke.

The Insurance Consumer's Bill of Rights

Federal and state laws provide consumers with a number of rights. Insurance companies may not: (1) refuse, cancel, or not renew your policy for discriminatory reasons (such as race, gender, age, disability, handicap, and marital status); (2) refuse coverage because another company turned you down; (3) offer you higher rates than originally quoted when you applied; (4) charge you a different rate than someone in a similar class unless they have sound reasons; (5) refuse, cancel, or not renew your homeowner's policy solely because of location or age of the property; (6) refuse automobile insurance because you once purchased insurance through the assigned-risk program; and (7) cancel your automobile policy after 60 days or more after being in effect except for your failure to pay premiums or if you provided inaccurate driver's license information on the insurance application.

Consumers have additional rights in that you may: (8) cancel (or lapse) a policy at any time, but you must pay for the time the policy was in force; (9) at your own expense, hire your own appraiser or public adjuster to contest the value of items damaged or lost; (10) request a report on the types and uses of information collected about you by an insurance company; (11) find out the reasons why an insurance company canceled your coverage or raised your premiums, although medical reasons are disclosed to your physician rather than to you; and (12) correct misinformation in the insurance company's files.

Also, consumers have some moral rights: (13) a "good driver right" to affordable insurance; and (14) a right to a ratings and a classification system based on relevant not arbitrary characteristics.[1]

Automobile insurance rates should be based on the factors of miles driven, previous accidents, driving violations, and type of vehicle, not on gender, race, marital status, and residence, because use of the latter factors is unfair. Commitment to traditional forms of rating and classification is a block in the path of competition, as well as enlightened regulation. For example, the automobile insurance industry has known for years that the concept of a "safe driver" is a myth because even at-fault accidents are mostly random events—having the bad luck or conditions under which a mistake is made.

Since insurance rates go up when cars are not crashworthy (automobile repairs cost 40 percent of the total premium dollar), insurance companies should pressure the automobile manufacturers to build better cars, with stronger bumpers for example. To secure and assert these rights, contact your insurance agent, insurance company, state insurance regulatory agency, and various consumer organizations.

A MODEL TO ANALYZE CONSUMER PROBLEMS AND ISSUES

1. Specify the issue or problem that negatively affects consumers.

2. Which consumer right(s) does this problem or issue affect? List.

3. Explain how this problem or issue negatively affects each consumer right.

4. For each listed right, suggest alternative(s) to improve the status quo.

5. Which of the suggested alternatives might be most acceptable to the interests of consumers, governments, and businesses? Why?

The Automobile Insurance Rebellion and Resulting Reforms

The topic of automobile insurance rates, said one state Attorney General, "is as important to average consumers as electricity and running water." Where driving is a necessity, the availability of automobile insurance is as much a necessity as shelter and utilities. If it is not available at reasonably fair prices, consumers will be overcharged and they will be upset. Some consumers, often 50 percent or more in large metropolitan areas, even make the choice to drive without insurance. This puts them at risk legally and financially, and it also ultimately adds to the rates paid by other consumers.

Consumers across America are rebelling at high automobile insurance premiums. Today, the average cost to households with automobile insurance is about $640; ranging from about $1,000 in New Jersey, Hawaii, and Connecticut to less than $350 in South Dakota, North Dakota, and Wyoming. According to a national opinion poll, 72 percent of the public believe these rates are too high.

---

[1]You can be legitimately turned down for auto insurance because of a poor credit history.

The Florida State Supreme Court struck down an **anti-rebate law** that prohibited insurance agents (the retailers) from offering discounts to consumers. Thus, agents in Florida became the first in the nation to be able to offer a rebate of some of their commissions to customers. Efficient agents in Florida can go after a larger market share. In all other states except California, agents are prohibited by law from refunding any portion of a commission to a consumer. Commissions are established by the insurers, who set them high enough to provide a profit to the least efficient agent, which, logically, drives up prices. Some agents offer to work for an hourly fee and rebate 50 to 75 percent of the commission. An example is Direct Insurance Services in San Diego (800-622-3699).

CONSUMER UPDATE:
Automobile Insurance Premiums Vary Widely

Premiums from the California Insurance Department *1994 Automobile Insurance Survey* reveal widely varying prices for all types of consumers purchasing minimum amounts of coverage. For comparison, Table 18-1 shows illustrative prices to insure a 19 year-old male and a 30 year-old married couple in different communities. Rural prices are lowest although they range among five companies from $285 to $647 for a 30-year old; urban prices for a 19 year-old male ranged from $2,320 to $9,270.

Patrick Butler, Director of the Insurance Project for the National Organization for Women, says, "These prices explain two things: (1) why there are lots of uninsured cars on the highways, and (2) insurance reform in California has not been a success for urban drivers."

	Customer A			Customer B		
Company	Rural (No. Calif.)	Suburban (Sacramento)	Urban (Los Angeles)	Rural (No. Calif.)	Suburban (Sacramento)	Urban (Los Angeles)
AAA	$1717	$1717	$3201	$647	$647	$1166
MercG	768	962	2320	320	398	978
Safeco	639	931	2396	285	409	1048
GEICO	2090	2525	9270	502	614	2224
Hartf	1634	2248	5634	556	766	1928

Customer A is a single male driver, who has had one chargeable accident and drives a new Pontiac Firebird 15 miles to work; Customer B is a married couple, both age 30, driving a 2-year old Chevrolet Caprice less than 20 miles to work.

TABLE 18-1 Illustrative Auto Insurance Premiums

Insurance Industry Accounting Logic

Consumers everywhere are fed up with "insurance company accounting logic" that says they are losing money and have to raise premiums every year. For example, the industry claims that in a recent year they paid out $110 for every $100 brought in through premiums. While this may be technically true, it does not begin to tell half the story. Insurance companies also earn income by investing those premiums. Further, their accounting procedures allow them to project losses, but the losses arguably do not turn out to be as big as projected. *Consumer Reports* says that, "the average household spent $8910 on auto insurance over the past 10 years but filed just one claim, typically for about $600."[2] This is a very profitable industry with loads of unnecessary overhead costs. The industry is regulated by each of the 50 states through state insurance departments.

According to the A. M. Best Company, a leading insurance company evaluator, automobile insurers received $70 billion in premiums and $7 billion in investment income in a recent year. With $77 billion to spend, 23 percent was allocated to payments for injuries (medical expenses, economic payments, noneconomic damages), 35 percent to payments for damages to or replacement of cars, and 42 percent for expenses of underwriting, selling, claims settling, profits, dividends, and taxes.

Anti-Group Laws

Premiums could be cut if the companies lowered their sales and administrative costs. **Anti-group laws** are state prohibitions against selling automobile insurance (unlike health or life insurance) in any manner except by one policy at a time. This causes inefficiency and unnecessary costs. Author Andrew Tobias says, "Why sell insurance one policy at a time when we require everyone, by law, to have it?"[3] If states allowed firms to sell group automobile insurance and let agents offer a discount by giving up part of their commissions, which average 12 to 17 percent of the premium, premiums could drop even lower.

Massachusetts does permit group sales, and they are generally offered through employers, although people who belong to credit unions may participate. Discounts range from 5 to 10 percent.

It is likely that group sales will not increase unless and until automobile insurance is a fringe benefit of employment, much like today's health and life insurance, where employers can take a tax deduction to offset some of the costs.

Insurance Industry is Exempt from Anti-trust Laws

Entry barriers also limit competition. State laws prohibit banks from entry into the automobile insurance market, although they would likely be strong competitors. The lobbying power of the insurance industry is focused at the state level, since that is where McCarran-Ferguson requires that it be regulated, and that is precisely where critics say insurance regulation is inadequate. The insurance lobby is powerful at the federal level too, as evidenced by the law they got passed that expressly prohibits the FTC from even conducting research on the insurance industry.

A special commission of the American Bar Association has called for repeal of the insurance industry's exemption from federal antitrust laws, calling it "inconsistent with the concept of free-market competition."[4] The Federal Trade Commission has joined the

---

[2]Auto Insurance. (1992, August). *Consumer Reports*, p. 489.
[3]Tobias, A. (1989, February 17). Fill 'er Up With No-fault, Please. *Time*, p. 52.
[4]Hines, M. (1988, December 28). U.S. Urged to Regulate Insurers. *New York Times*, p. D-1.

Justice Department, state officials, small business representatives, and consumer organizations in supporting repeal of the McCarran-Ferguson Act. It is looking likely that repeal may occur soon. The Chairman of the House Judiciary Committee, Jack Brooks, author of a bill to repeal McCarran-Ferguson, says that the current antitrust exemption creates "an invitation to price-fixing arrangements that stifle product choice and comparison shopping among consumers.[5]

Price Fixing Among Insurers is State Approved

State-approved price fixing occurs because few insurance companies (automobile, fire, homeowner's, or liability insurers) do not base their rates on their own loss experience and expectations. Instead, they pool their loss information and rely on industry-wide advisory guidelines constructed by rate-making bureaus. The Insurance Services Office (ISO) creates average loss figures based on information obtained from hundreds of insurers' past claims, projected claims, overhead costs, and estimated profit data. Insurers then set their rates above or below the industry guidelines. Consumers who are customers of companies with low expenses can end up paying as much as people who insure with inefficient firms. As a result, in so-called competitive markets, prices for equivalent products often range no more than 25 percent. If state regulators would outlaw the use of profit and expense data from these averages, it should lead to more diversity in insurance rates and lower them from 5 to 15 percent according to the National Association of Insurance Commissioners. To save people money, critics also want insurers to help accident victims shop for lower repair prices by providing price information on area body shops and garages.

A new California law prohibits insurance companies from fixing prices, limits automobile insurance rates based on place of residence (**redlining**), and requires that companies get regulatory approval before raising rates. Several insurers stopped writing new policies and have threatened to leave the state; similar threats were made in Florida and other insurers moved in to take the business. Consumers want competitive pressures to exist in the insurance industry so that insurance rates can be kept at reasonably low levels. Competition will yield some surprises too. For example, if place of residence is outlawed as a rating factor, rates in rural areas may rise to subsidize urban drivers.

Price Fixing Between the Automobile Repair and Insurance Industries

There is **de facto price fixing** between the automobile repair and insurance industries in America, meaning it occurs in reality. Price fixing is illegal in all states, and this includes managing marketplace events that cause price fixing to exist. Investigation can easily show that a conspiracy exists, yet, so far the nation's attorneys general apparently are not interested in stopping it.

Here is how the system works: In most states when the consumer has an automobile accident, the consumer simply notifies his or her insurance company. The consumer's insurance agent has a company adjuster look at the vehicle to assess the damages. Then

---

[5]Ibid, F-6.

the adjuster prepares a written estimate of the damages that the insurance company thinks it should pay for, and that estimate is given to the consumer. The consumer is expected to then go to an automobile repair shop and have the repairs made. If the repair shop finds things that need fixing that were not on the adjuster's estimate, perhaps because the damage was hidden, the shop calls the insurance adjuster, who authorizes an additional necessary amount. Thus, the consumer goes away happy that the insurance company paid for all the repairs, not realizing that he or she paid too much for the repairs.

This is a nice system for the insurance companies and the major automobile repair shops, which are usually those associated with new car dealerships. The insurance companies win because their own adjusters make fairly competitive estimates. Most important under this system is that the insurance companies do not have to contend with their insured policyholders "shopping for the highest estimate," which occurred under the old system.

CONSUMER UPDATE: What is the Difference Between Uninsured Motorist and Underinsured Motorist Coverages?

Most vehicle insurance policies contain **uninsured motorist (UM) coverage**. This covers losses sustained in accidents where the at-fault driver is not insured. A victim with UM coverage is allowed to sue his or her own company for losses if there is no one else to sue. All states require companies to offer UM coverage.

In many states, more than 1/4 of the accidents involve uninsured drivers. In some urban areas (like the San Ysidro zip code in Los Angeles) the uninsured level is above 95 percent.[1]

Underinsured motorist (UIM) insurance coverage (not *un*insured) pays up to the limits of the vehicle policy when the at-fault driver has insufficient coverage to cover the cost of a victim's expenses. For example, a driver with minimum liability coverage hits your car causing damage in excess of his policy limits. Your underinsured motorist coverage will pay you the excess amount above his policy limits, up to the limit of your coverage.

Many states require that insurance companies offer the coverage, but few mandate that policyholders purchase it. A few states routinely include underinsured motorist coverage whenever uninsured motorist coverage is purchased. For most Americans, underinsured motorist coverage is just an option.

[1] State Updates (1995, May), *Crossroads* (University of Wisconsin-Milwaukee), 2.

Under the previous way of settling claims, the insurance company wrote a check to the consumer for the lower of two estimates. As a result, many consumers went around from shop to shop trying to find two high estimates. Then, after receiving the insurance check, the consumer had the repairs done at some place less expensive and kept the difference. For example: when a consumer turned in repair estimates of perhaps $900 and $880 the insurance company would issue the consumer a check for $880. Then the consumer would have the vehicle repaired at some less expensive place, perhaps for $700, and pocket the difference of $180 ($880 - $700).

The participating repair shop dealers also win with the current system. They have far fewer people coming in asking for estimates, so this saves them lots of time. Most important, under today's system, is that the repair shops will not give a written estimate for repairs of a vehicle that has already had an estimate prepared by an insurance adjuster. The repair shop manager demands that the consumer turn over the adjuster's estimate and the work is done for that amount. Thus, there is absolutely no incentive for the repair shop to do the work for a lesser amount because they are always paid at least the amount of the insurance company's estimate. If additional repairs are needed, the shop only has to telephone the friendly adjuster for approval.

It is a cozy arrangement, but it is not in the consumer interest. This is de facto price fixing because the marketplace systems put into place by the insurance companies and the major repair shops have resulted in implicit agreements on pricing. In addition, the companies are restraining trade because the systems put in place by the two industries cause consumers to mostly patronize major repair shops associated with new car dealerships rather than the smaller, independent automobile repair shops. Which state attorney general will challenge the system?

CONSUMER UPDATE:
Unisex Automobile Insurance Law Penalizes Women

About a decade ago, Montana became the first state to prohibit insurance companies from using gender or marital status to set premium rates for all types of insurance. A recent study of Montana's unisex insurance law shows that insurance costs have risen for female drivers. Average rates for women drivers under age 25 have increased $91 to $274 a year.

The National Organization for Women (NOW) notes that, "at every age in their driving lifetime, men as a group drive twice as many miles as women, are twice as exposed to risk of accident, and consequently are twice as frequently involved in accidents as women." NOW concludes that since "women average half men's mileage but are deceptively charged unisex prices, they are paying on average twice as much as men per mile for identical coverage on their cars." Further, NOW Insurance Project Director Patrick Butler observes that, "this is the reality behind the insurers' claim that women get a 'break' in auto insurance." The National Safety Council says that 70 percent of all driving miles are driven by men.

No-Fault Automobile Insurance

In most states, consumers live with the "sue-me, sue-you insurance system." When people have accidents they file lawsuits to determine who was at fault and whose insurance company will pay. This is called the **fault system**. This system overcompensates the slightly injured, undercompensates the gravely hurt, clogs the courts with lawsuits that take years to reach verdicts, and returns to victims only half of the premiums paid in. The rest goes to lawyers and to people who administer the system. The Insurance Information Institute reports that 11 cents of the traditional premium dollar goes for lawyer fees and another 12 cents goes for pain, suffering, and noneconomic damages.

The Basic Idea of No-Fault Insurance

A **no-fault automobile insurance system** allows the consumer to collect medical expenses and wage losses directly from his or her insurance company for losses resulting from an automobile accident without regard to who was at fault and without making a claim against the other driver (unless that driver was drunk). In addition, under no-fault, the victim must show that any injuries are severe before being allowed to sue another driver. A driver's no-fault coverage also pays for injuries to his or her passengers and to pedestrians struck by the car. In effect, no-fault guarantees that consumers get compensation for injuries and lost wages. Except in Michigan, no-fault insurance states do not deal with collision, theft, and other coverages.

In exchange for guaranteed compensation for injuries and lost wages, injured drivers give up the right to sue for damages unless their injuries exceed a **dollar threshold** (actually a test of the severity of the injury), such as $3000, specified in the no-fault law. Since this will keep millions of lengthy, expensive minor injury cases out of the courts, proponents of no-fault insurance argue that delays in the payment of claims and claims-handling expenses would be greatly reduced, thereby lessening the pressure to increase premiums.

Benefits of No-Fault Insurance (Compared with Fault-Based Systems)

Compared to the traditional fault-based system of auto insurance, there are a number of benefits of no-fault insurance:[6]

- No-fault compensates more people (roughly twice as many).
- No-fault provides greater benefits (79 percent more).
- Payments are made more quickly (almost all no-fault payments, as opposed to only half of tort awards, are made during the first year following injury).
- Drivers get more coverage for their no-fault premium dollar (since vast administrative costs are reduced).
- Thousands of accident-related small claims have been kept out of court (automobile accident suits have been reduced by as much as two-thirds in some states), representing millions in saved taxpayer dollars.

No-Fault Today

Only 14 states now have some variation of the no-fault concept, though none of these are strictly no-fault because they do not forbid lawsuits. The results have been mixed because most states just tacked no-fault coverage onto the existing liability system. Studies have shown that in states with strong no-fault automobile insurance laws, payment delays have been reduced, claims-handling expenses have come down as a proportion of the premiums collected, and premiums, although continuing to rise, have done so at a lower rate than in states without a no-fault system.

In general, the benefits envisioned after the enactment of no-fault plans have not been fully realized because only a few states (such as Michigan, Florida, and New York) have seriously attempted to implement the no-fault concept by severely restricting lawsuits.

The most successful no-fault law, the one in Michigan, requires insurance policies to provide unlimited medical and rehabilitation benefits, three years' worth of wage-loss benefits (where an injured person receives 80 percent of gross income up to a maximum, currently $2670 a month), survivors' benefits, and a $20 daily benefit for replacement services. Lawsuits for damages to vehicles are severely restricted. Lawsuits for personal injury can only be brought if a victim dies or suffers permanent and serious disfigurement

---

[6]O'Connell, J. (1986, April 20), Minor adjustment could tune up no-fault insurance, *The Daily Progress*. Reprinted by permission of *The Daily Progress*.

or serious impairment of bodily function. Policyholders can buy collision coverage to pay for damage to their own cars and enough property damage liability coverage to protect them when out of state.

The most liberal of the no-fault systems provides unlimited medical coverage and substantial compensation for loss of income but does not pay victims for pain and suffering. Opponents attack this as an unfair limit on compensation. However, instead of 32 percent of consumers' insurance premiums going for court costs and legal fees, as was the case before passage of the Michigan no-fault law, the amount is now four percent.

Pay-at-the-Pump No-Fault Insurance

Andrew Tobias, author of *Auto Insurance Alert!* and *The Invisible Bankers: Everything the Insurance Industry Never Wanted You to Know*, has proposed **pay-at-the-pump no-fault (PPN)** coverage. The primary source of funds would be from a less-than-30-cents-a-gallon surcharge. Another charge would be paid when consumers annually registered their cars. Presto! Everyone has generous insurance coverage. Bad drivers would have to pay higher annual registration fees for their cars. PPN would eliminate most sales and underwriting costs, the uninsured motorist problem, and the need for consumers to shop for insurance. Insurers would competitively bid to provide coverage for perhaps 5000 customers at a time, much as they now do for health insurance. If necessary, after being involved in an accident you would get your car fixed right away, receive lost income benefits, and have all medical expenses paid because a genuine no-fault system would be established.

PPN "would be good for almost all drivers (except those who now drive uninsured and pay nothing) who would have better coverage for less money."[7] Tobias says that pay-at-the-pump will cut insurance costs 20 to 40 percent for most drivers. Good drivers would not be discriminated against because of age, gender, or residence. Everyone would pay the same until some were identified as bad drivers. Fraudulent bodily injury claims would cease to exist. PPN also would be good for those insurance companies that are efficient because they'd win even more business than they have now.[8] Prices would be even lower if the state took over the processing of claims, which would eliminate the need for insurance agents and trial lawyers. Supporters of this idea are trying to get a proposal made into law in California by getting it passed in a referendum vote.

Which Remedy for the Auto Insurance Mess Do You Want?

Remedies to the problem of rising automobile insurance premiums might include: (1) requiring no-fault coverage for all drivers and eliminating the traditional fault system, (2) installing a pay-at-the-pump premium collection system, (3) allowing elective no-fault insurance where drivers could choose true no-fault coverage or the traditional liability automobile insurance, (4) using odometers as the exposure unit, (5) repealing laws that prohibit insurance salespersons from offering a discount on their commissions, and/or (6) creating a more competitive automobile insurance market that would vigorously compete on price, as well as new products. The current vehicle insurance system is broken: it charges millions of consumers unfair premiums and does not insure all. What reforms will society choose?

---

[7]Here's an Idea to Slash the Costs of Insurance. (1993, February). *Money*, p. 23.
[8]Tobias, pp. 52-53.

A CONSUMER UPDATE:
A Proposal to End Discrimination in Auto Insurance — Use the Odometer-Mile As the Exposure Unit

Charges for automobile insurance currently are calculated at a lump sum dollars-per-year price varied only by (1) coverage amount, and (2) cost classifications, such as owner's residence territory, car use, and driver characteristics, with token discounts for unverifiable "low future mileage" estimates. Homeowners insurance is priced much the same way using the house-year as the exposure unit.

Unlike a home, however, a car's exposure to the chance of an accident is virtually zero when it is not being driven. Drivers intuitively know that a car's exposure to risk increases with every mile it travels.

Some cars are driven much more than the average for their classification and some much less. Driving twice the mileage doubles gasoline expense but has little or no effect on insurance expense because charges are calculated in **time-period** rather than **distance units**. By taking two or three years to drive the same mileage others drive in a year, such car owners pay two or three annual premiums for the same amount of insurance protection others get for one annual premium.

To end this kind of price discrimination, it might seem sensible to switch from the "car-year" to the "gasoline gallon" as the unit for measuring the amount of each car's exposure.

Unfortunately, because cars could no longer be cost-classified, the gasoline gallon approach to auto insurance would still result in discrimination, i.e., consumers whose cars averaged 15 miles per gallon would pay twice as much as those whose cars can get 30 miles per gallon and people with older cars would subsidize those with more expensive vehicles.

This dilemma can be resolved by adopting the **"mile exposure unit,"** measured by odometer, as the basis for insurance reform. This unit makes it possible to combine measurement of a car's individual exposure with its price classification. Both are essential for determining appropriate auto insurance charges. For example, the price of full driving coverage for a particular kind of car might be 5 cents a mile for owners living in a rural-class territory and 9 cents a mile for urban owners. At the rural price, 10,000 miles of insurance protection would cost $500 (10,000 X 5 cents), and 5,000 miles at the urban price would cost $450 (5,000 X 9 cents).

Reform has already been proposed in several states. It would require a one-sentence **"exposure unit"** amendment to state insurance law. The effect would be to convert driving coverage prices from "dollars per year" to "cents per mile" for each cost classification. As now, car owners would pay in advance to keep insurance protection in force. Premium at per-mile prices would be pre-paid in mileage amounts and at times chosen by owners to suit their own needs. The car's insurance identification card would display both **odometer-mile** and **date limits** of prepaid protection, as automobile service contracts and mechanical breakdown insurance policies now do.

Policy renewal would be conditional on taking the car to one of hundreds of garages previously approved by the company for an annual odometer check. Theft of insurance protection would be controlled because tampering with the odometer—which is already a federal crime—or with the company-applied seals (detectable during claim investigation) would automatically void the policy's protection.

Annual mileage correlates strongly with income and newer cars are driven twice as far annually as cars ten years and older are. As a result, retaining the car-year price unit forces many women, older people, and poorer people to pay two to ten times more per mile for insurance than owners of cars with the same classification driven above-average mileage. Note also that in each age group, men drive about twice the annual miles women drive, which explains why men average about twice as many accident involvements as women do.

At present, however, despite the large difference between men's and women's average annual miles of exposure, insurers in the 44 states that still permit sex-pricing of auto insurance nevertheless choose to favor men by charging **"unisex"** prices to adult men and women. Paying the same per-year prices to insure half as many miles of driving exposure means that women on average are paying twice as much per mile as men pay.

Changing to the mile exposure unit would eliminate price discrimination against all owners of cars driven less than the average mileage of their class and would simultaneously produce genuine unisex auto insurance. All owners of cars in the same cost class—women and men—would pay the same class price for each mile driven. Odometers would become the measure of exposure and the guarantee of equal treatment.

*Patrick Butler, Director, Insurance Project, National Organization for Women

Good Buys in Term Life Insurance[9]

Many consumers purchase the wrong type of life insurance and pay too much for the coverage they receive. It is easy to pay too much for life insurance because consumers who do not comparison shop almost always do. The National Insurance Consumer Organization (NICO) suggests that the best way to judge a *term* life insurance policy is by the cost each year for each $1000 of coverage. A **term life insurance** policy is often called pure protection because it pays benefits only if the insured party dies within the time period of the contract. (Cash-value life insurance is examined later in this chapter.) NICO says that the rates shown in the box below present good values. Multiply the rate by each $1000 of coverage desired and then add $60 to cover estimated administrative fees.

CONSUMER UPDATE:
Avoid Overpriced Life Insurance

It is easy to pay too much for life insurance because consumers who do not comparison shop almost always do. The National Insurance Consumer Organization (NICO) suggests that the best way to judge a *term* life insurance policy is by the cost each year for each $1000 of coverage. NICO says that the rates shown in the following table represent good values. Multiply the rate by each $1000 of coverage desired and then add $60 to cover estimated administrative fees.

Age	Nonsmokers		Smokers	
	Male	Female	Male	Female
18 to 30	$0.76	$0.68	$1.05	$1.01
35	0.80	0.74	1.36	1.26
40	1.03	0.95	2.06	1.65
45	1.45	1.20	2.95	2.30
50	2.60	1.76	4.16	3.30

Source: National Insurance Consumer Organization

NICO advises the majority of consumers to purchase *annual renewable term (ART)* insurance coverage. A Consumer Federation of America report suggests that American consumers spend $5 to $10 billion unnecessarily each year on life insurance. This amounts to $50 to $100 per household, which should compel consumers to evaluate more carefully their life insurance purchases.

---

[9]The odds of premature death in an accident are about 1 in 20,000; in an automobile crash, 1:100; in a tornado, 1:30,000; in a flood, 1:40,000; in a small plane, 1:2,000,000; and in a large commercial airplane, 1:7,000,000. The odds of catching the AIDS virus from a blood transfusion is 1:500,000.

Beware of Life Insurance Being Sold as a Retirement Plan

A recent scandal in the insurance industry occurred when for five years one of the largest and seemingly most reputable life insurance companies repeatedly lied to customers. The giant Metropolitan Life Insurance Company, with over 16 million policies in force, sold millions of dollars of so-called "guaranteed retirement savings plans" all over the country to consumers who unknowingly purchased cash-value life insurance policies. Typical was the comment from one New York couple, "The agent never once mentioned the word 'insurance.'" Instead of making monthly payments to an investment plan, the money went for insurance premiums. MetLife has paid $20 million in civil fines to government agencies and has offered $75 million in refunds to approximately 65,000 clients. MetLife has not revoked the commissions earned by the sales agents for selling the policies. Since MetLife is a mutual company, the fines will be paid by policyholders.

A reputable actuary commented that, "persuading individuals to use insurance in lieu of other, more appropriate retirement investments could actually prevent them from accumulating the assets necessary to retire."[10] Reputable financial planners recommend tax-sheltered retirement plans to build up assets instead of life insurance.

Arguing that the problem was not just MetLife, Joseph M. Belth, professor emeritus at Indiana University, says that, "this is an industry in which various forms of deceptive practices flourish, and the regulators have not done anything about it."[11] New York's Superintendent of Insurance, Salvatore R. Curiale, says, "There's no doubt in my mind that the scope of this is broader than just MetLife and some other companies mentioned."[12] Many critics want to shift the responsibility of insurance regulation from states to the federal government where it is expected that supervision would be greatly improved.

Title Insurance for Homes: A Ripoff

Title insurance is a policy that protects the lender's interest in a loan if the title to real estate is later found to be faulty, i.e., have "defects" that might involve a legal claim that are not in the public record about which the buyer is unaware. Consumers who buy homes or refinance mortgages often are required to purchase title insurance. Many homeowners also purchase a separate title insurance policy to protect themselves from possible loss. State rating bureaus, made up with the participation of the title insurance companies themselves, generally set (fix!) the prices of title insurance. Since 75 to 92 percent of the average $500 one-time premium typically goes as a kickback commission to the local title company or attorney who arranged the business, very few dollars, often $40 or $50, actually go to the insurance company. Actual industry losses over decades have amounted to 4 or 5 percent of premium income; that's 4 to 5 percent of $40 or $50, or $2.50 or less per policy. Such a small payout-ratio suggests a profiteering industry overripe for proper regulation.[13]

---

[10]Quinn, J. B. (1994, February 13). Beware of Life Insurance Firms Selling Policies as Annuities. *The Washington Post*, p. H-3.

[11]Crenshaw, A. B. (1994, March 13). *The Washington Post*, p. H-1.

[12]Policies of Deception. (1994, January 17). *Business Week*, p. 24.

[13]For an excellent article on the subject, see Lindamood, S. (1993, Spring). Title Insurance and the Consumer Interest. *Advancing the Consumer Interest*, 5, pp. 18-23.

CONSUMER UPDATE:
Excellent Tips About Buying Life Insurance

Here are some tips from consumer-minded insurance experts for those considering a life insurance purchase:

1. If you have no dependents, you probably do not need life insurance at all. Life insurance is essentially protection against loss of income for dependents.
2. There is no mathematical advantage to buying life insurance at an early age. Premiums increase at the same rate for everybody regardless of the age at which you start the policy.
3. If you need protection for your dependents, term insurance can do the job at the lowest cost.
4. Be wary of offers of free insurance or cash-value policies for only a few dollars the first month or year. Agents who make such claims are probably hiding vital details. A small initial premium may be only a down payment on a sizable loan for the rest of the first year's cost.
5. There are disadvantages to financing the first year's premium. Signing a promissory note binds you to a long-term debt and substantially raises the price of insurance. If you cannot afford to pay the full first year's premium, you probably should not sign up.
6. If you fail to pay any premium on time during the years when a promissory note is in force, the entire note becomes due immediately.
7. Before you buy life insurance, get the advice and approval of people you trust—such as a consumer economics professor—and at least one insurance expert other than the agent selling the policy.
8. Read everything carefully. If an agent does not allow you time to read, don't sign anything. Do not be afraid to ask questions or take a few days to think it over.
9. Bring a friend with you when you meet with an agent. Take notes on the sales presentation. An agent will be less likely to misrepresent the policy if he or she realizes you are paying close attention.
10. Don't be pressured into buying anything you do not want. If you think an agent is misleading or dishonest, report him or her to state insurance officials.
11. If you buy a policy and then run into a problem that cannot be solved by the insurance company, call your state insurance department. Many companies will make adjustments in hardship cases referred to them by state insurance officials.
12. If you need life insurance, it may be purchased through agents who represent one company exclusively who will earn a commission averaging 50 to 125 percent (the 25 percent comes out of the second year's premium). Alternatively, life insurance is also sold directly through the mail with little or no agent commission. The National Insurance Consumer Organization recommends the following no-load or non-commission direct-mail life insurance companies: USAA Life (800-531-8000), Bankers National Life (800-631-0099, 201-267-2540 in New Jersey), and Amica Life (800-992-6422). Wholesale Insurance Network (800-808-5810) will send you free quotes from two or more no-loan companies.
13. You might consider calling a **rate-screening company** to purchase life insurance. It specializes in finding consumers the best buy in life insurance, typically term coverage, by scanning their database of insurers. You only need to telephone a toll-free number and supply the company relevant information (age, gender, residence, smoking history, and desired coverage). Within a week you will receive a computer printout listing four or five competitive insurers and the prices. Rate-screening companies do not charge a fee, but they do receive a commission from the life insurance company if you buy a policy. Rate-screening companies include Insurance Quote (800-972-1104), Life Quote (800-521-7873), Quotesmith (800-556-9393), Select Quote (800-343-1985), and Term Quote (800-444-TERM).

What Happens When Insurance Companies Go Broke?

The number of bankrupt property-casualty and liability insurance companies going broke is on the increase. Property insurers have failed at a rate of 35 per year over the past five years. Historically, the small high-risk companies went broke; now big companies do too. Most of the insurance company bankruptcies each year are caused by mismanagement, fraud, excessive price cutting to meet the competition, and unwise diversification into other lines of business. Another contributing factor is the high cost of claims for environmental damage, such as asbestos removal, pollution, and chemical spills. Recent insurance company failures include Executive Life Insurance Company, Mutual Security Life, Bankers Life Insurance Company of Richmond, Mutual Benefit Life in New Jersey, and Blue Cross and Blue Shield of West Virginia.

The National Association of Insurance Commissioners annually identifies a number of the nation's 3500 insurance companies that have financial conditions that may impair short-term or long-term financial survival. In a recent year, 600 life/health insurance companies were cited for immediate regulatory attention because of concerns about financial solvency. Another 140 life/health companies also were on NAIC's list. An industry-sponsored study observed in 1990 that, "the quality of regulation in the life insurance industry is disturbingly similar to that existing in the thrift industry during the early 1980s. The absence of effective solvency regulation is frequently cited as a major factor contributing to the S&L crisis."[14]

State guaranty laws provide for the indemnification of losses suffered by policyholders through assessments against other insurers doing business in that state. All states have a state-supervised guaranty program that attempts to cover losses when an insurance company goes broke and cannot pay claims. Either each company licensed to do business in a state is required to contribute to a supervised fund (often 2 percent of premiums) or each company is assessed after an insolvency occurs. Thus, "healthy companies are taxed to support those that fail."[15] The state fund then pays the claims on the failed carrier, although a delay of one to two years is not uncommon. Also, each fund has a cap on how much it will pay for each claim. These programs are not publicly funded; however, since most states give companies a credit on their income tax for the premiums, they are subsidized with taxpayer money.

State guaranty funds usually have severe limitations on what claims they will pay. Often excluded are Blue Cross/Blue Shield plans, companies that self-insure, and some group-health plans.[16] Many states limit the amount claimants may collect, regardless of the loss. A number of states do not insure guaranteed investment contracts contained in many retirement plans. (This is discussed below.) If you live in the wrong state, you could lose. It is wise to check *Best's Key Ratings Guide* for information on the financial solvency of insurance companies to avoid firms that have shaky finances. Other prominent firms also rate the financial solvency of insurance companies, including Standard & Poors, Moody's Investors Service, Duff & Phelps, and Weiss Research. Weiss Research has the toughest standards. These ratings can be found in books in larger libraries.

The Coming Insurance Industry Scandal

The savings and loan scandal and banking bailouts are the nation's worst financial disasters. Some worry that the insurance industry is next. Insurance company insolvencies have tripled in the last decade. Some failures were rooted in fraud. Since the insurance

---

[14]Belth, J. (1987, October 22). Press release. Bloomington, IN: University of Indiana, p. 1.

[15]Poff, M. (1994, May 9). Man Invests in Annuity, Learns a Costly Lesson. *Roanoke Times & World-News*, p. Extra-4.

[16]Lord, M. (1993, May 24). Checking Your Coverage. *U.S. News & World Report*, p. 55.

industry has been regulated by the states for the past 50 years, the federal government has provided no oversight in spite of the multi-state nature of the business. *U.S. News & World Report* says that the FBI has "some 100 investigations underway of possible insurance fraud worth hundreds of millions of dollars, and the number is expected to grow."[17] The taxpayer picks up part of the losses since many of the insurance companies go bankrupt owing income taxes. When the General Accounting Office compared insurance company insolvencies to savings and loan bankruptcies, they found ten of the eleven root causes "were the same for both insurance companies and the thrift institutions."[18]

Consumer Problems and Issues in Investments

You are solely in charge of investing to build your own retirement fund, so you must beware of the many pitfalls. This section begins by identifying consumer rights in investments. It follows with a number of consumer problems and issues in insurance, including biased financial planners, insider trading, fairness in arbitration, problems with guaranteed investment contracts putting investment pensions at risk, and leveraged buyouts (LBOs).

The Investing Consumer's Bill of Rights

A number of self-regulating investment organizations have developed an investor's bill of rights that suggest consumer investors are entitled to: (1) honesty in advertising, (2) full and accurate information about investments, (3) prior disclosure of risks, (4) advance explanation of obligations and costs, (5) time to consider actions, (6) responsible advice that is suitable for particular needs, (7) ethical management of an investor's funds, (8) complete and truthful accounting, (9) easy access to funds and full information on any restrictions, and (10) recourse, if necessary, for dishonesty or unfairness.

The U.S. Securities and Exchange Commission (SEC), chaired by Arthur Levitt Jr., is an independent, nonpartisan, quasi-judicial federal regulatory agency that oversees most securities transactions and financial intermediaries. Its mission is to protect investors and ensure market integrity by having the highest disclosure standards in the world. The SEC has explicit powers to bring remedial and preventive action to the field of corrupt stock exchange and corporate practices. The SEC consistently wins praise for its fairness and highly practical approach to regulation. Complaints about investing may be directed to the SEC, 450 5th Street, NW, Washington, DC 20549 (202-942-7040).

---

[17]Prediction: Big Fraud Crimes Will Explode. (1992/1993, December 28/January 4). *U.S. News & World Report,* p. 68.

[18]Risky Business. (1991, January/February). *Public Citizen,* p. 21.

DID YOU KNOW?
Divorced Women Sometimes Have Rights to
a Former Husband's Pension

Only about one-quarter of divorced older women (age 62+) receive a pension from a former spouse. Survivorship rights are not automatic. Useful details can be found in *Your Pension Rights at Divorce, What Women Should Know* (Pension Rights Center, 918 16th Street, NW, Washington, DC 20006). The American Association of Retired Persons publishes "A Women's Guide to Pension Rights" and "A Guide to Understanding Your Pension Plan: A Pension Handbook," which can be obtained from AARP, 601 E Street, NW, Washington, DC 20049.

Banks Sell Investments That Are *Not* Federally Insured

Banks, savings and loan associations, brokerage firms, insurance companies, and credit-card companies all sell various types of investments; some are selling insurance.[19] Problems exist when uninformed consumers are too trusting of the sellers and their products. Most investing consumers are neophytes in an investing world of well-trained salespeople. Investing consumers are not likely to realize that they could lose some of their original investment if the mutual fund or bond does poorly. They also are largely unaware of investment fees being charged.

What Bank Products Are Insured?

A lot of confusion among the investing public occurs because they do not realize that only two types of investments are insured by the federal government against the loss of principal: (1) U.S. savings bonds, notes, and bills, and (2) certificates of deposit. A **certificate of deposit (CD)** is an interest-earning savings instrument offered by an institution that accepts deposits of money for a fixed amount of time, commonly ranging from seven days to eight years, with no fees charged. Investors who put money into certificates of deposit often do so because they are insured by the federal government's Federal Deposit Insurance Corporation (FDIC).[20]

Three Types of Bank Products Are Not Insured

In many states, the banking laws permit affiliates to operate inside the bank lobby. As a result, institutions with "FDIC" on all the doors, windows, and tables are selling certain investments that have zero insurance. Consumers who unknowingly put money into uninsured investments run the risk of losing all their money. Savers and investors should know that not all financial institutions have federal deposit insurance, and many

---

[19]Banks located in towns with populations of 5000 or less are permitted to sell insurance. Through 800-numbers and other techniques, most banks are expected to soon be selling insurance.

[20]Many banks pass along to their investments departments the names of depositors with maturing CDs, and critics think this is a violation of the trust between banks and their customers.

so-called investments sold inside these institutions are not insured at all. Deposits at federally insured institutions are insured by the U.S. government; however, investments are not, even if purchased at a financial institution. Banks sell three investments that are not insured: annuities, cash-value life insurance, and mutual funds.

CONSUMER UPDATE:
Disclosures Are Needed in Financial Planning

A Truth in Financial Planning bill has been proposed in Congress by U.S. Representative Rick Boucher. It would require disclosure of the planner's background plus details about services offered and commissions earned. The bill also requires the planner to tell prospective investors about any previous disciplinary incidences and conflicts in behavior. Planners will be required to: (1) disclose in advance estimates of any commissions or fees investors will pay on every transaction, including other third-party income; (2) maintain written records of your finances, goals, and recommendations; and, (3) once a year report the total of his or her charges for all services to each client. Without this kind of information, consumers are unable to effectively judge a financial advisor's motivations and objectivity. Unfortunately, the bill excludes stockbrokers and insurance agents, people who often call themselves financial consultants.

---

1. Annuities Are *Not* Insured

Annuities are contracts, underwritten by insurance companies, that provide for a series of payments to be received at stated intervals for a fixed or variable time period in return for the payment of a premium or premiums. These investments, which have substantial early-withdrawal penalties are issued by insurance companies and sold by brokerage firms, banks, and financial planners. American Express is selling annuities, which are described in their mail advertising as a "Preferred Assets Tax Deferred Savings Plan." The American Express ad uses the word "savings plan" six times, "account" nine times, and "annuity" once.[21] Annuities are underwritten by insurance companies, and in a recent 16-month time period, "five major life insurers and 36 smaller ones have collapsed...."[22] Annuities are never insured by the government.

2. Cash-Value Life Insurance Policies Are *Not* Insured

Cash-value life insurance pays benefits upon the death of the insured (like all life policies, including term-life examined earlier in the chapter) and it has a savings element (called a **cash value**) that slowly builds up within the policy as long as the insured lives. If desired, the cash value may be borrowed by the policyholder, but, of course, any amount not repaid would be withheld from any death benefit. For this "living benefit," the premiums for cash value policies are much higher than for term policies. Cash-value life insurance polices are sometimes called **permanent life insurance** because the time period of coverage under such policies is the entire life of the insured; term policies are for a

---

[21]Schultz, E. E. (1991, February 27). *The Wall Street Journal*, p. C-1.
[22]Editor's notes. (1992, April). The Empty Promise of Annuities. *Money*, p. 7.

specific amount of time, such as 1 year or 20 years. Different types of cash-value life insurance include: *whole-life*, *ordinary life*, *adjustable life*, *universal life*, *variable life* and *variable-universal life*. Such life insurance policies are never insured by the government.

3. Mutual Funds Are *Not* Insured

Besides offering check and savings accounts, many banks also are selling mutual funds. A **mutual fund** is an open-end investment company that combines the funds of investors who have purchased shares of ownership in the investment company and invests that money into a diversified portfolio of securities issued by other corporations or governments. While many mutual funds perform well as investments, particularly when held within a retirement plan, those sold by banks have below-average performance records. Mutual funds, including those sold by banks, are not insured by the government.

Consumers Buying Bank Investments Are Misinformed

A 1996 study of bank customers by the Federal Deposit Insurance Corporation found that more than one out of four banks do not properly warn consumers that their investment in a mutual fund was not federally insured. A similar study by the Securities and Exchange Commission revealed similar confusion among the investing public. A study by the American Association of Retired Persons revealed that perhaps one-third of bank customers investing in mutual funds are unaware of any commissions or costs involved. A study by *Consumer Reports* found that two-thirds offered inappropriate investment advice.[23] Many investors who purchased mutual funds from banks have already lost a substantial part of their principal. Regulators put out two guidelines in 1994 on how banks can better inform customers, but apparently the suggestions are being ignored by many banks.

Critics argue that either banks must explain more or government regulation must be implemented to protect investing consumers, such as requiring that sales of uninsured investments be done in a separate portion of a bank, savings and loan association, or credit union. The bank's salesperson puffery statements that a mutual fund investment is "completely safe" and that the fund would "lock in 10 percent" with "hardly any risk" must come to an end! The federal government has a program of "testers" or "mystery shoppers" that go to banking institutions to find out whether or not fund salespersons are misleading investors.

Most Financial Advisors Are Biased

In the past, financial advice was only provided for the rich. However, with inflation, tax-law changes, deregulation of much of the financial industry, an increase in dual-income families, and an industry willing to lower prices for financial planning advice, many consumers now find themselves in need of professional advice. Middle-income consumers today often have questions about taxes, cash management, budgeting, planning for children's education, insurance, retirement planning, and estate planning. Evaluating

---

[23]Should You Buy Mutual Funds From Your Bank? (1994, March). *Consumer Reports*, p. 148.

your assets systematically and repositioning them to your best advantage, with or without a financial planner, is crucial to long-term personal financial success.

You can buy financial planning advice from attorneys, accountants, insurance salespersons, stockbrokers, and people just calling themselves financial planners. There are perhaps 500,000 people in America who call themselves financial planners. A **financial planner** is any person who calls himself or herself by that title. Many are sales personnel who sell financial products, such as insurance and investments. The term financial planner roughly describes a variety of professionals who suggest coordinated solutions that seem to fit situations of various consumers. They plan and/or promise to manage a client's financial affairs and investments. They work with clients to help them establish and achieve financial needs and objectives. Financial planners typically provide information for tax savings, insurance coverage, investment plans, and referrals for more complicated financial topics. The SEC says that an **investment advisor**, a more narrow term than financial planner, is anyone who is paid for giving advice on the purchase or sale of securities to more than 15 people a year. You can find out about the disciplinary history of any brokerage firm and sales representative by calling the National Association of Securities Dealers (800-289-9999).

Method of Compensation Indicates Potential Bias

Part of the confusion on the consumer's part is knowing how the advice is being compensated. Most financial planners are biased because they sell something. The financial advice obtained from a banker, stockbroker, or insurance salesperson is always slanted toward the transactions and/or products sold by the firm he or she represents. It is in the economic interest of a financial planner working for a brokerage firm to sell you stocks, bonds, or some other service from which a commission is earned. In a similar way, the insurance salesperson earns a commission and the banker gets a year-end bonus for successfully promoting their products.

Consumers should not be deceived by people calling themselves an "investment advisor," "Investment analysis," or "financial consultant" in an effort to appear as an objective adviser. Such terms should not hide the truth about the source of someone's income. The Securities and Exchange Commission recently released a report concluding that the industry's virtual universal reliance on commissions and other sales incentives "inevitably leads to conflicts of interest" that can hurt investors.[24]

There are three types of financial planners, and they are categorized by the manner in which they charge their clients.

1. A **fee-only financial planner** offers his or her advice for a fixed fee, which is either an annual fee based on the amount of assets managed, income earned, and/or investment advice, or an hourly fee. Fee-only planners do not sell any products themselves and they refer clients to other providers to actually purchase investments or insurance products. Therefore, fee-only planners can offer unbiased advice.

For $400 a fee-only planner might interview you, collect details on your interests and goals, develop a rather uncomplicated comprehensive financial plan, and discuss it with you. A more complex situation would cost more, but the amount of the fee would be decided and agreed upon in advance. Hourly fees might range from $50 per hour to $200 or more. The

---

[24]Simon, R. (1995, June), Be Sure Your Broker Works for You, Not Against You, *Money*, 26.

major fee-only professional association is the National Association of Personal Financial Advisers (1130 Lake Cook Road, Suite 150, Buffalo Grove, IL 60089; 800-366-2732).

2. A **commission-only financial planner** is a person who offers advice on financial topics and receives remuneration only in the form of commissions for products and services sold, such as stocks, insurance, and real estate partnerships. For example, a commission-only planner might earn a 1 1/2 percent commission on stocks sold and 8 1/2 percent on a mutual fund. These persons are biased toward selling consumers "something."

3. A **fee-and-commission financial planner** is paid by charging a fee for financial advice in addition to receiving commissions on the direct or indirect sale of products. These persons also are biased toward selling consumers "something."The Securities and Exchange Commission says that 85 percent of all financial planners sell products to clients.

Stockbrokers sometimes push particular investments because they receive hidden sales incentives in the form of secret bonuses and extra commissions. A broker who can win a trip to a resort, jewelry, or a television set is a person you want to avoid at all costs because he or she is motivated to "sell" you something you may not need. Here your broker works against you, instead of for you. Bonuses and prizes are a scandalous and abusive selling practice of the "legitimate" investment industry.[25]

DID YOU KNOW?
Beware of Insurance and Securities Companies Selling

Over the past decade, Prudential Securities sold $10 *billion* worth of misrepresented high-risk partnership investments as safer income-producing investments to unsuspecting investors. Prudential Securities was forced to pay $41 million in fines and another $330 million in compensation to hundreds of thousands of investors who were steered into risky investments. The Securities and Exchange Commission said that Prudential defrauded its customers. Prudential had previously paid $260 million in the scandal. Not a single Prudential employee has ever been charged with a criminal action. None!

The Securities and Exchange Commission recently issued rules to require that all investment advisors study their clients' finances before recommending any investments. Advisors are to make sure that any suggested investments are suitable for the needs of each investing consumer.

Other big-name companies that have paid multi-million dollar fines for a variety of improper advertisements and sales practices include New York Life, Paine Webber, Prudential Insurance Company of America, John Hancock Mutual Life Insurance Company, and Metropolitan Life. Be wary when you are being "sold" something expensive!

Insider Trading

An **inside trader** is a person who buys or sells securities while possessing material non-public information or data capable of moving a company's stock prices. Insider

---

[25]Seventy to 80 percent of individual investors in commodities (a commission-based product) lose money, yet neither the Commodity Futures Trading Commission nor the Securities and Exchange Commission stock trading regulations require brokers to stop clients from making bad investments. What a comment on the ethics of the industry.

trading is against the law, and violators are subject to both civil and criminal penalties. Inside traders have unfair advantages over the typical consumer-investor that generally results in substantially greater, but illegal, profits.

The government has recently expanded the definition of insider trading to include the **misappropriation doctrine**, which bars trading on the basis of stolen information. Insider trading regulations prohibit trading by a tender offertory, any officer, their confidants, or those whom they tip. Still legal is the long-controversial practice of **dual trading,** which allows stockbrokers to trade for themselves at the same time they are handling orders for their customers. Insider trading and dealing with privileged information are at odds with the goal of insuring investor confidence in the stock market.

Fairness in Arbitration

Investor complaints against brokers are often serious, amounting to losing part or all of ones's life savings, and the number of grievances is increasing. Nearly 10,000 securities arbitration cases are expected to go to arbitration this year. For details about going to arbitration, call the National Association of Securities Dealers (212-858-4400). In general, claims must be filed within three years of investing in a security or one year of discovering a problem, whichever is less.

Virtually all contracts that investing consumers sign with stockbrokers contain mandatory arbitration clauses that require customers to agree that they will not sue the firm, even in cases of fraud, but instead will submit to arbitration. The agreements attempt to eliminate an aggrieved customer's rights to jury trials and curtail the chances for punitive damages and appeals; however, the U.S. Supreme Court ruled in 1995 that contracts may not bar punitive damages. Such **forced arbitration clauses** for jury trials are common practice, but only for investors using a margin (credit) account at a stockbroker. Investing consumers do not have to sign the agreement if they have a cash account. The U.S. Supreme Court recently upheld the validity of these contracts to require investors with complaints to appeal only to arbitration systems controlled by the brokerage industry.

Critics argue that the arbitration panels are dominated by individuals with direct or indirect ties to the securities industry. In addition, there are no formal rules of evidence, no consistent standards of judgment, and little outside oversight of the disposition of cases. A recent U.S. General Accounting Office study found no indication of pro-industry bias in decisions, although it also concluded that the arbitration forums lacked internal controls to assure the competence and independence of arbitrators. Since punitive damages are rarely awarded, the most an aggrieved investor can hope for is to recover money lost. The Consumer Federation of America reports that, "one study revealed that only 13 percent of those filing claims were awarded as much as 60 percent of claimed losses."[26] Consumer groups are lobbying Congress to pass legislation outlawing mandatory arbitration contracts and to require that arbitration cases be handled by the more neutral American Arbitration Association (888-237-6275).

---

[26]Vise, D. A. (1993, February 3). Pension Agency's Records Are in Disarray, GAO Says. *The Washington Post*, p. F-1.

CONSUMER UPDATE:
Shareholder Activists Speak for Consumers

Securities and Exchange Commission rules that went into effect in 1993 improve the balance of power between corporate managers and the investors. The corporate managers are going to have to listen better to the shareholders, the ultimate owners of those companies, especially those who own large blocks of shares. Pension funds, labor groups, churches, universities, and other institutional investors own more than half of all publicly traded U.S. stock. Previously, investors were precluded from exercising much influence over corporate operations.

Rules will encourage communications among institutional shareholders and propose reforms. More authority is being given to **outside directors**, members of a corporate board of directors whose full-time employment has not been with the corporation itself. Most boards in the U.S. are stacked with executives from inside the company. Getting more attention will be issues like astronomical executive pay packages, especially among companies that are losing money, and instead basing executive compensation on performance. Shareholders want corporate directors to be more accountable for their actions when they stand for re-election. This new activism will mark a dramatic change from how U.S. corporations operated in the past. More participatory democracy is on its way.

State Guarantee Funds Often *Exclude* So-Called "Guaranteed Investment Contracts"

One form of investment sold is a **guaranteed investment contract (GIC)**. This is a contract backed by an insurance company's assets that is supposed to pay the investor a fixed rate of return for a certain number of years. In this manner, GICs are similar in design to certificate of deposit. GICs are usually sold to institutions that then resell them to investing consumers. GICs often are an option in retirement plans offered by employers.

Guaranteed investment contracts are backed solely by an insurance company's assets, and they are not insured by the federal government. In point of fact, GICs are not "guaranteed" because when an insurer goes bankrupt, the investor (including retirement plans that have purchased GICs) loses all or part of the principal. Recent insurance company bankruptcies have left "as many as a million customers dependent on a state-by-state patchwork of guarantee funds that don't hold any money."[27] More than half of the state guaranty funds exclude coverage for guaranteed investment contracts. GICs are not what they are often implied to be.

Some Retirement Investment Pensions Are at Risk

The Employee Retirement Income Security Act (ERISA) requires companies to prudently invest pension funds in diversified instruments, mostly stocks and bonds. However, company pensions for employees may or may not be there at retirement time.

---

[27]Ibid.

The fundamental safety of a company pension rests first on the financial stability of the firm. If the company goes bankrupt, the federally chartered Pension Benefit Guaranty Corporation (PBGC) *may* step in to provide assistance. PBGC *only* insures **defined-benefit pension plans**, those that base the level of benefits on the income and years of employment of the worker. PBGC covers about 40 million workers in 85,000 plans. It guarantees a maximum benefit of $2250 a month, indexed annually.

The pension that most workers have, defined-contribution plan, is not covered by any insurance. A **defined-contribution plan** is an account into which employers and employees may contribute pre-tax money that is permitted to grow beyond the reach of income taxes until the money is withdrawn. Workers often invest this pension money into mutual funds, stocks, and guaranteed investment contracts. These pension plans are excluded from the PBGC insurance program.

CONSUMER UPDATE:
Socially Conscious Investing

Many socially responsible consumers choose investments consistent with their values. There are a number of **socially conscious mutual funds** available that invest only in companies that meet their shareholders' ethical or moral standards. Businesses that treat customers, employees, shareholders, and the earth with respect have fewer legal problems. Dreyfus Third Century, New Alternatives, and Calvert Social Investment are mutual funds that do not invest in companies that have a poor environmental record, a history of poor labor relations, or manufacture weapons. Comparatively, these funds perform as well as most mutual fund companies.

The Federal Deposit Insurance Corporation limits deposit insurance to $100,000 per person on money in all retirement accounts on deposit at a single insured financial institution. Those who have pension funds should spread the investments around at different federally insured institutions so that one stays under the $100,000 limitation. Several limitations apply on the $100,000 in FDIC insurance; therefore, any consumer with $100,000 or more should carefully discuss the limitations with an officer of a depository institution.

Many defined-benefit pension programs are underfunded by the companies that run them; some firms deliberately underfund their pensions. Well-known firms that have underfunded pension plan include General Motors, Chrysler, CSX, Reynolds Metals, Uniroyal Goodrich Tire, TWA, Pan Am, Continental Air, Bethlehem Steel, and Kellogg. A recent General Accounting Office (GAO) study reports the gap between employers' promises and the funds set aside to pay pensions is $53 billion. Almost three-quarters of the underfunding is in plans sponsored by just 50 companies. The GAO refused to certify the PBGC's annual financial statements "due to insufficient and sloppy records."[28]

When the firms go bankrupt, they unload their pensioners and current workers rights to pensions onto the PBGC. Critics charge that the PBGC itself is based on unsound actuarial principles, claiming it does not have sufficient funds to pay for future liabilities. They want the PBGC to raise the premiums it charges companies for pension insurance, especially those firms in risky industries. PBGC makes payments to 125,000 retirees from over 1500 bankrupt businesses. The PBGC audits about one percent of the pension plans annually. In 1995, the PBGC was technically insolvent; it was in the red $2.7 billion. Finances got a bit better in

---

[28]Ibid.

1996, but there still is not enough money in the fund to pay any significant amount of claims to retirees. The taxpayers may soon be asked to bail out the $2 trillion in private pensions, perhaps at a level equivalent to the savings and loan debacle.

Workers' Pensions Can Get "Stolen" in Leveraged Buyouts

Workers and pensioners lose when their pension plan is used to help finance someone else's effort to buy their company. An **employee stock ownership plan (ESOP)** is a method through which employees can own shares of the company they work for which they typically use later for retirement purposes. Oftentimes the ESOP shares are part of the money invested in the employee's defined-contribution retirement plan.

Managers of the money in many defined-contribution pension funds, including ESOPs, made some excellent investments during the run up of the stock market in the 1980s and 1990s. This resulted in a large number of funds that had more money than needed to pay the claims of present and future retirees; the terminology is "surplus assets."

Although the Employee Retirement Income Security Act largely prohibits American companies from borrowing from their pension plans or investing in their own businesses, pensions can still be effectively stolen by corporate raiders. This can be accomplished via a **leveraged buyout**. This is a takeover of a company, usually by its officers and other private investors, in which the company's assets are used as collateral to finance the takeover. Financing is accomplished is obtained by selling **junk bonds**, which are high-risk, high-interest-rate bonds

Leveraged buyouts permit people to: (1) buy out companies with fat pension plans; (2) change the pension plans from defined-contribution to defined-benefit; (3) enforce mandatory retirement on many workers; (4) reinsure the pension plan with reckless investments in guaranteed investment contracts purchased from insurance companies that bought lots of unstable junk bonds (to technically meet legal obligations to workers and pensioners); and (5) break the company into pieces and sell its parts for high profits.

When junk bonds default, guaranteed insurance contracts fail, and insurance companies go bankrupt, the pensioners are often left having their checks slashed by 30 percent or more. The interests of pension fund trustees often diverge from those of the workers and pensioners. The corporate raiders are not legally responsible to make the pensions whole. Supporters of LBO's note that they do more good than harm because the effect is to put a true value on corporation for the stockholders.

Timesharing Vacation Real Estate Is *Not* An Investment

Timesharing is promoted as investment property; however, most of the time it turns out to be a ripoff for the investor because profits for consumers in this industry rarely exist. **Timesharing** is the use of a vacation home for a limited, preplanned time. About 14 million consumers own timeshares. For $5000 to $20,000 buyers can purchase one week's use of luxury vacation housing furnished right down to the salt and pepper shakers. Vacationers also pay an annual maintenance fee for each week of ownership, perhaps $400 or $500 a year. Many people buy, falsely thinking that they are making a real estate purchase that will appreciate in value when what they are really making is a decision on where to spend future vacations.

A serious problem arises in **non-deeded timesharing**. This is a right-to-use purchase agreement entered into between the seller and the consumer that permits a limited, preplanned timesharing period of use that is actually only a vacation lease, license, or club membership, which only last a certain number of years. It does not grant legal real estate ownership interests to the purchaser, but instead provides a long-term lease of a hotel, suite, condominium, or other accommodation. When the lease runs out, often in 20 to 25 years, the non-deeded timesharing consumer has no legal claim to anything. The bad news begins earlier if the real owner of the property (the developer) goes bankrupt, because the purchasers (the lessees) have a zero ownership claim to the property. The consumers have no more legal rights than other unsecured creditors, and in all likelihood, they lose previous payments and their leases on their vacation properties. Timeshare purchasers should only buy **deeded timesharing** units because the buyer actually owns part of the property.

It is almost impossible to sell a timeshare, even if your lifestyle changes and you no longer want to own it. Resort Property Owners Association says that 58 percent of survey respondents had tried to sell their timeshares, but "only 3.3 of them have succeeded, and the average resale took 4.4 years."[29] Resale of timeshare properties generally sell for about 50 to 70 percent of what the owner paid, according to the head of a trade association trying to clean up the industry's image. A reputable and large broker of timeshares, Vacation Concepts, reports that it sells only 10 to 15 percent of its listings. A large Florida seller of timeshares, Independent Timeshare Sales, reports that its commissions are 20 to 25 percent. At any point in time, about 60 percent of all timeshare owners are trying to sell.

Some consumers buy timeshares because they believe that they can easily and inexpensively trade use of their properties for use of other properties in more exotic places. The largest timeshare exchange business is Resort Condominiums. It charges a $200 initiation fee, a $59-a-year membership fee, and another $84 for each week of an exchange. Consumers sometimes wind up paying substantial fees to advertise and trade use of their properties.[30]

So-called **real estate liquidators** are scam artists that take advantage of people with hard-to-sell properties, such as undeveloped land and timeshares. The promise is to connect the owner with prospective buyers. Some operators tell owners that their nationwide computer network contains the names of several buyers who are interested in their properties. Other promoters promise to sell the timeshare during the following twelve months for a price equal to or greater than the amount originally paid. They sometimes promise to give the property owner a $1000 savings bond certificate if they fail to sell the property (and from reading this book, you know the savings bond is worthless). After collecting a $250 to $1000 **advance fee**, the promoters simply do not refund the money, even though property owners were "guaranteed a 100% refund" if a sale did not occur.

Florida has a law that puts time-share resale agents under the direct authority of a state regulatory agency. Licensed agents have to spell out in writing all services, conditions, and fees and are prohibited from offering guarantees to sell time-shares by a specific time or at a set price. Many states now have cooling-off period laws, often 3 to 5 days, during which consumers can change their minds about investing in timeshares. Such legal protections for investing consumers, however, are not available in all states.

---

[29]Lehman, H. J. (1995, September 30), Time on Their Hands—But No Buyers, *The Washington Post*, E-1+.

[30]The entry of Disney, Hilton, and Marriott into the timesharing business may help improve the industry's image, but reselling will remain extremely difficult.

Review and Summary of Key Terms and Concepts

1. List three important examples in the **insurance consumer's bill of rights**.

2. Give an example of how prices vary on **auto insurance premiums**.

3. Distinguish between an **anti-rebate law** and an **anti-group law**.

4. What is occurring in the insurance industry since it is exempt from **anti-trust laws**.

5. Outline how **de facto price fixing** occurs between the auto insurance companies and some auto repair shops.

6. Distinguish between the **fault system** and the **no-fault auto insurance system**.

7. Explain why most state **no-fault systems** have not been successful.

8. Summarize how the **pay-at-the-pump no-fault insurance** plan would work.

9. Summarize how the **personal protection policy (PPP)** auto insurance plan would work.

10. Distinguish between **uninsured motorist (UM)** coverage and **underinsured motorist (UIM)** coverage.

11. How much should a properly priced **life insurance policy** for a 21-year-old cost if he/she purchased $50,000 worth?

12. Explain what happens **when insurance companies go broke**.

13. What is the role of the **Securities and Exchange Commission**?

14. Give some examples of some investments that are not **federally insured**.

15. Why do some financial advisors have a **bias**?

16. Distinguish between: **financial planner** and **investment advisor**.

17. Distinguish among: **commission-only financial planner**, **fee-only financial planner**, and **fee-and-commission financial planner**.

18. What is **inside trading**, and how does it differ from **dual trading**?

19. Explain the concept: **forced arbitration clause**.

20. What is a **guaranteed investment contract**?

21. Distinguish between a **defined-benefit pension plan** and a **defined-contribution pension plan**.

22. What is a **socially conscious mutual fund**?

23. Outline how a **leveraged buyout** works, and who does these things.

24. What is an **employee stock ownership plan (ESOP)**, and how do these plans sometimes get into danger?

Useful Resources for Consumers

National Association of Insurance Commissioners
120 West 12th Street, Suite 1100
Kansas City, MO 64105-1295
816-842-3600

National Council of Individual Investors
1990 L Street, NW, Suite 610
Washington, DC 20036
202-467-6244
http://www.ncii.org.ncii

National Insurance Consumer Organization
1424 16th Street, NW, Suite 604
Washington, DC 20036
202-387-6121

"What Do You Think" Questions

1. **Unisex automobile insurance laws** discriminate against females drivers while subsidizing male drivers. Design a multi-part program to attack the pricing problems in auto insurance and describe how your plan all fits together.

2. Do some **comparison shopping** for automobile insurance by telephoning four different insurance agencies. After making a table of your findings, make some observations about why there were price differences.

3. Use the table on **avoiding overpriced life insurance** to calculate how much $25,000 of term life insurance should cost if fairly priced. To obtain some price comparisons, telephone some local insurance agents and some of the 800-numbers for life insurance companies. After making a table of your findings, make some observations about why there were price differences.

4. What do you think about the **pay-at-the-pump no-fault (PPN)** auto insurance idea? Offer some pluses and minuses about it.

5. There seem to be some serious cracks in the safety of some of our nation's **private retirement programs**. What suggestions can you offer to improve the likelihood that workers today will receive the benefits to which they may be entitled?

Careers in Consumer Affairs

Career Opportunities in Consumer Affairs

Career opportunities exist for professionally trained college graduates interested in the field of consumer affairs. This appendix describes consumer affairs as an academic area of study, typical curriculum requirements, expected competencies of graduates, job responsibilities, career development responsibilities, and career options.

Most people work and that's it. Lots of people also give some of their time to helping others. Consumer affairs allows one to be paid in a career helping consumers.

Consumer affairs is an area of study at a college or university that prepares students to reasonably advocate the consumer interest and help consumers improve their well-being. The primary responsibilities of consumer affairs professionals are to champion the consumer's viewpoint to their employing organization and to convey information about the organization's products and services to the consumer.

Although the consumer affairs area of study deals with concerns of business, it is people-oriented, with emphasis on the consumer perspective. It focuses on the human viewpoint in problem-solving. Consumer affairs majors are expected to have a keen interest in people and the quality of life.

Furthermore, consumer affairs professionals are concerned with more than simply calculating the benefits and costs of alternatives. They also consider fairness, decency, kindness, compassion, and honor. Each student majoring in consumer affairs must identify his or her life mission and career aspirations, the answers to which are rooted in that person's values, goals, interests, and priorities. Majors are expected to develop clearer ideas about the way the world works and what needs to be done to make it better.

Job Responsibilities

The focus of work of consumer affairs professionals is on problems and issues that affect consumers. CAPs should be interested in prevention of customer complaints. The end result is to improve consumer welfare by positively affecting public policy, corporate behavior, and societal changes and/or working directly with individuals and families.

Consumer affairs professionals often interact with consumers, social service agencies, government agencies, educators, and persons with limited incomes. Many large organizations have consumer affairs professionals who also inform, update, and educate the firm's employees.

Major activities of consumer affairs professionals include responding to consumer inquiries and complaints; championing the interests of consumers within the organizational decision-making structures; developing promotional and informational programs; preparing leaflets and booklets on how to use products; monitoring and evaluating consumer trends; monitoring legislative issues; writing news releases, informational brochures, and newsletters; speaking to consumer, educational, professional, and government groups, as well as opinion leaders; helping others understand an employer's perspective (that of business, government, or a nonprofit agency); and being a change agent.

Career Development Opportunities

People who graduate from consumer affairs programs are qualified for employment in positions as consumer affairs professionals (CAPs). Careers follow six primary paths: (1) complaint-handling, (2) complaint prevention, (3) customer service, (4) public relations (including information and education and lobbying), (5) community outreach, (6) and sales. Jobs for consumer affairs professionals exist in most large businesses and government agencies.

Entry-level Job Titles in Consumer Affairs

Typical entry-level job titles include customer service representative, consumer information and education specialist, consumer investigator, complaint mediator, product information specialist, quality assurance representative, consumer researcher, consumer writer, product testing specialist, human resources specialist, consumer service specialist, hospital patient representative, ombudsman, community reinvestment act officer, retail sales and management, restaurant management, securities sales, real estate sales, publicist, community relations representative, consumer communication specialist, insurance agent, insurance claims adjuster, insurance cost-containment specialist, cooperative extension agent, telemarketing sales, travel agent, loan officer, credit or financial counselor, financial planning assistant, income tax preparation specialist, entrepreneur, consumer education coordinator, public relations representative, lobbyist, legislative assistant, political staff assistant, and public information officer.

Entry-level Employers of Consumer Affairs Graduates

Typical employers for entry-level consumer affairs majors include public utility companies, Better Business Bureaus, Chambers of Commerce, non-profit community organizations (United Way, Community Chest, etc.), banks, savings and loan associations, credit unions, consumer credit counseling services, hospitals, marketing research firms, advertising firms, automobile dealerships, mortgage lenders, creditors, collection agencies, credit reporting organizations, supermarkets, personnel management firms, life insurance companies, property and casualty companies, financial planning firms, income tax preparation services, securities firms, mutual fund companies, advertising agencies, cooperative extension services, telemarketing firms, travel agencies, real estate firms, various retail businesses, government agencies (federal, state and local), and professional and trade associations.

Lifelong Career-Development Opportunities

Lifelong career-development opportunities as a consumer affairs professional exist. Advanced positions, which require several years of successful consumer affairs experience, include directing and training a consumer affairs staff, representing an organization at meetings, monitoring legislative and regulatory issues, addressing legislative hearings, coordinating research on consumer complaints, and reasonably advocating the consumer interest to top management within an organization. Top job titles in the consumer affairs profession include manager of consumer affairs, vice president for consumer affairs, vice president for global consumer affairs, and director-consumer affairs worldwide.

Career Options

Consumer affairs graduates are employed in business firms, government agencies, and nonprofit agencies. Consumer affairs positions are more likely to be found in large organizations rather than in smaller firms. Potential employers are located throughout the country, although the greatest number of employment opportunities are in urban areas.

Jobs in Business

Many employment positions are available in businesses concerned with manufacturing, processing, and marketing. Graduates often find employment in such industries as savings, investments, food, housing, retailing, entertainment, insurance, oil, agriculture, radio, television, journalism, travel, transportation, textiles, household appliances, labor, medical care, and credit. Graduates may work for business trade associations, such as the American Gas Association, National Turkey Federation, American Association of Retired Persons, Better Business Bureau, or American Bankers Association. Some graduates work for regulated utilities, such as the telephone, water, gas, and electric industries.

Jobs in State and Local Government

Graduates may work for state and local government agencies, such as a county office of consumer affairs, state office of consumer affairs, housing authority, department on aging, weights and measures office, tourism, licensing, registration, bureau of automotive regulation, social services, energy agency, cooperative extension service, attorney general's office, insurance commission, financial institutions bureau, utilities commission, or for a legislator.

Jobs with the Federal Government

Employment opportunities are also available with the federal government working for members of Congress, as well as for various agencies, such as the Office of Management and Budget, Consumer Product Safety Commission, Food and Drug Administration, U.S. Department of Agriculture, Environmental Protection Agency, and U.S. Office of Consumer Affairs.

Jobs in Federal Offices in Local Communities

Employment positions for consumer affairs majors are also available in federal offices located in local communities, such as the Farmers Home Administration, the Housing and Urban Development Office, Army Community Services, Navy Family Services, Social Security, and an area energy office.

Jobs in Nonprofit Agencies

Other graduates may work for nonprofit agencies, such as Public Citizen, Center for Auto Safety, Public Voice for Food and Policy, Common Cause, community services agency, solar energy center, legal services, or a public interest research group.

Curriculum Requirements

Consumer affairs majors study the role of consumers in the economy and analyze the information needed for individuals and families to become more knowledgeable and assertive consumers. They seek answers to questions such as, "How can I get my money's worth?" "How can I contribute to improving communication and respect between consumers and producers?" and "How can I personally help improve the world in which I live?" The subject matter is taught from the consumer point of view, not from the perspective of marketing interests in consumption. For example, students learn which styles of nutritional information on food labels are most helpful to consumers rather than which format sells the most products.

The concepts and skills of the consumer affairs profession come from a wide range of academic disciplines and applied areas, including political science, law, finance, insurance, management, marketing, accounting, economics, family economics, psychology, sociology, credit, statistics, research methods, computer technology, health, foods, clothing, household equipment, media, and communications. This broad range of knowledge is used by the professional to help consumers get the best products and services for their money, to promote the availability of choices for consumers, to assess consumer complaints and suggest fair solutions, and to help consumers better manage their money. The curriculum provides students with a liberal education rather than a technical education.

Courses in the department offering the major in consumer affairs generally have a family perspective with which students can examine problems and issues to improve the level of living of individuals and families. Issues and problems are studied from the perspectives of consumers, businesses, and governments. Students learn a variety of terms, concepts, processes, and applications relevant to employment in careers as consumer affairs professionals.

Specialized course offerings in the consumer affairs major often include such titles as Consumer Problems, Consumer Protection, Family Finance, Budget and Debt Counseling, Debtor/Creditor Relationships, Resource Management, Family Economics, and Professional Seminar in Consumer Affairs.

Consumer affairs majors are provided a variety of in- and out-of-class learning experiences. Opportunities for self-development exist with student professional associations on campus, as well as relevant state and national organizations, such as the Consumer Education and Information Association of Virginia (CEIAV), Consumer Educators of Michigan (CEM), Illinois Consumer Education Association (ICEA), American Council on Consumer Interests (ACCI), Society of Consumer Affairs Professionals in Business (SOCAP), and National Association of Consumer Agency Administrators (NACAA).

Students are expected to develop independence and initiative. Because the curriculum is designed with the ultimate goal of developing skills and confidence, students progressing through the consumer affairs curriculum have increasing responsibility to individualize aspects of their educational program. Majors in consumer affairs often are required to complete an individual study experience, such as research, a field study, or an internship.

Competencies of Graduates

Students develop competencies that enable them upon graduation to: (1) make rational buying decisions, (2) efficiently resolve consumer problems, (3) advise people to manage resources more effectively, (4) be familiar with major problems and issues confronting consumer affairs professionals, (5) understand how to operate a consumer complaint-handling system, and (6) advocate the consumer interest to superiors in an organization.

Graduates of consumer affairs programs generally seek employment as a consumer affairs professional (CAP). Employers look for the ability to communicate effectively orally and in writing. They want employees who possess strong analytical decision-making skills, being able to take into consideration a number of complicated, subjective factors. CAPs should have a thorough knowledge of consumer-related problems and issues, utilize economics in analyzing alternatives, know survey research techniques, appreciate the American free-enterprise system, understand consumer behavior and public relations, appreciate the legislative and regulatory processes, and understand ways of affecting changes in legislation and public policy. They should also be able to plan, research, and develop consumer education and information materials, and implement such programs.

Graduates should be motivated, resourceful, and self-determined. Employers prefer those who are willing to work and demonstrate curiosity, dependability, open-mindedness, competence, confidence, leadership, and a positive professional attitude. CAPs need to see both the short- and long-term view of a situation. In addition, graduates should possess the desire to increase knowledge and skills and stay up-to-date in the field of consumer affairs.

Sample Letters for Employment

Two samples letters follow. One is to seek an internship and the other is to seek a job.

SAMPLE LETTER SEEKING INTERNSHIP

Return Address
Today's Date

Name/Address of Addressee

Dear Mr./Ms. XXXXX:

I am writing to inquire about an internship with your office this coming summer. I am currently a junior attending _____ college majoring in Consumer Affairs. This major provides a broad background in business and human relations. In addition, the major emphasizes the importance of supporting the consumer interest.

The courses in my major have helped prepare me to deal with the problems and challenges experienced by consumers. My courses in Consumer Affairs, particularly the class in Consumer Protection, has given focus to my desire to help promote the interests of consumers. My communications classes have taught me a variety of writing styles and interpersonal skills to use when dealing with the public. In addition, I have strengths in the academic areas of consumer economics, credit, personal finance, family relations, economics, marketing and political science. For one of my upper-division classes, Professionalism in Consumer Affairs, we researched the importance of effectively handling consumer complaints. My studies have helped me develop a sense of professionalism and sharpened my ability to make rational decisions where the consumer interest is concerned.

Last summer, I worked as an office assistant for _____, a credit reference company. One of my duties was to perform credit checks on personal credit card accounts. This required that I deal with individuals by telephone to verify purchases, handle any complaints, and determine account status. The previous summer I worked in retail sales for a furniture company, where I learned to deal with the public on a one-to-one basis listening to and analyzing their wants and needs while conveying the company's total quality management perspective to each sales contact. During the academic school year, I have worked 15 hours a week as an analyst in the Registrar's Office, mostly dealing with the confidential details of graduation analysis. These experiences, combined with the knowledge I have learned in my classes, have prepared me for an internship with _____.

I will contact you within two weeks to ensure that you have received this letter and the enclosed resume. I hope an interview can be arranged so that I might personally convey to you some idea of my abilities and interest in an internship at _____. I will require a salary to offset my living expenses over the summer.

I will contact you within two weeks to ensure that you have received this letter and the enclosed resume. Should you have any questions, please feel free to communicate with me. I look forward to hearing from you soon.

Sincerely,

Your Name

Enclosure

SAMPLE LETTER SEEKING JOB

Return Address
Today's Date

Name/Address of Addressee

Dear Mr./Ms. XXXXX:

I am writing to pursue the opportunity of becoming a customer service representative with _____. My major at _____ college was Consumer Affairs.

My senior year at _____ college has been very rewarding for me. I have sharpened my writing and public speaking skills in several ways. My greatest opportunity in this area came in February when I co-presented a paper with my academic advisor and professor, Dr. _____, who has helped me in my professional development. The paper, "_____," was based on a class research project. It was presented at the _____ meeting and published in the conference proceedings. This year also afforded me the opportunity to serve as Vice President of the Consumer Interest Organization, a student group. In addition, I had the privilege of doing weekly volunteer work helping to build homes for Habitat for Humanity.

For the past four years I have worked for different companies that ultimately are concerned with the same objective-customer satisfaction. Through my employment experiences as an office assistant, salesperson, analyst, and research assistant, I have been able to develop and enhance a number of job-related abilities. These include word processing, spreadsheet, financial software, organizational skills, technical writing, and platform speaking. My internship last summer with the Better Business Bureau enhanced my interpersonal and telephone skills while I learned more about reasonably advocating the consumer interest; my fluency in Spanish also improved. Moreover, my experience and education make me confident that I can be a successful employee at _____.

I expect to be in the _____ geographic area soon, and I would enjoy an opportunity to visit your office to discuss the possibilities of a position at _____. I look forward to hearing from you.

Sincerely,

Your Name

Enclosure

Index

Note: Terms are **defined** on page numbers highlighted in **bold**.

"as is" (154)
800-number **(108)**
900-number **(108)**
900-Number regulations (134)
976-numbers **(108)**

A

Absolute advantage **(237)**
Academia
  and student consumer rights (62)
Acceptable quality **(9)**
Acceptance
  revocation of and used cars (144)
Access to credit
  a consumer right (63)
Acesulfame
  sweetener (444)
Acetylsalicylic acid (470)
  aspirin (472)
Acquired immunity deficiency
      syndrome (AIDS)
  speeded-up drug approval process
    (466)
Action for Children's Television (ACT)
  (382)
Action levels **(440)**
Addictive substance
  tocacco (480)
Additional dealer markup (ADM) **(414)**
Additives
  Color Additive Amendments (444)
  incidental (440)
  intentional (440)
Adjudicatory power **(300)**
Adjusted market value (AMV) **(414)**
Administrative agencies **(296)**
Administrative law judge (ALJ) **(300)**
Administrative Procedures Act (APA)
  (503)
Adulterated **(438)**
Adverse selection **(352)**
Advertisement
  informational (377)

puffery (378)
Advertisements
  comparative (378)
  deceptive (379)
  regulation of (375)
  types of (377)
Advertising
  alarmist (463)
  and Channel One (383)
  and comparative claims (377)
  and deception (104)
  and false impressions (377)
  and prescription drugs (465)
  and testimonial (376)
  as part of selling expenses (375)
  at its worst (374)
  bait and switch (380)
  cigarettes to children (477)
  corrective (342)
  costs for headache remedies **(374)**
    (472)
  expenditures per person (374)
  food to kids (427)
  FTC environmental guidelines
    (371)
  health claims (427), (471)
  misleading (104), (378)
  misleading, Bayer aspirin (472)
  of over-the-counter drugs (471)
  prescription drugs (379)
  purpose of (374)
  relied upon for information about
    OTC drugs (471)
  standards (266)
  types of truth in (376)
Advertising code
  of CBBB (375)
Advertising dollars
  and the consumer interest (380)
Advertising guidelines
  of the FTC (376)
  advertising of drug FTC (471)
Advertising practices
  considered deceptive (380)
Advertising substantiation **(267)**
Advertising, false

in automobiles (414)
Affordability
  illustrated (400)
Age discrimination
  Human Rights Act (75)
Agricultural marketing orders **(436)**
AIDS
  speeded up approval procedures
    (466)
Air bags (509)
Airline (140)
  lost baggages rules (141)
Airline bumping regulations (140)
Alarmist advertising **(463)**
Alcohol
  and aspirin (483)
  and auto accidents (506)
  and health (482)
  social costs (484)
Alcoholic beverage labeling (484)
Aleve (473)
Allocation agreements **(436)**
Alternate operator services (AOS)
  and high telephone bills **(97)** (135)
Alternative financial sector (523)
Alternatives identified
  illustration (402)
Ameristroika
  type of capitalism (185)
Analgesics **(470)**
Anger
  at the political system (322)
Annual lease rate (140)
Annual percentage yield (APY) **(516)**
Annual percentage yield earned (517)
Annuities **(570)**
Anti-competitive practices
  Allocation agreements (436)
  calendar marketing agreements
    (436)
  in the food industry (435)
Anti-group laws **(557)**
Anti-rebate law **(556)**
Anti-trust
  and food industry (435)
Antitrust

barriers in health care (461)
Antitrust laws
  aims of (275) **(278)**
  exemptions from (277)
  goals of (278)
  lack of success (279)
Antitrust tools (285)
Antitrust violations
  examples of (281)
Appraisers
  housing (544)
Arbitration **(72), (343)**
  forced arbitration clauses (574)
  in investments (574)
Arguments
  types of (336)
As is **(59), (146)**
Aspartame
  sweetener (443)
Aspirin
  acetylsalicylic acid (472)
  and children's deaths (471)
  and drinking alcohol **(470)** (483)
  heart attacks (470)
Aspirin and similar pain relievers (470)
Asymmetric information **(360)**
ATM machines
  consumer problems with (521)
Attentive public **(321)**
Attitudes
  of consumers (202)
Auto
  see vehicle (145)
Automated teller machine
  fees (519)
Automated teller machines
  consumer problems with (521)
Automatic debit (88)
Automatic debiting (134)
Automatic overdraft loans
  ripoff charges (519)
Autombile
  national dealer advertising (414)
Automobile
  additional dealer markup (414)
  adjusted market value (414)
  balloon loan (410)
  buying service (417)
  cash rebate (411)
  daytime running lights (508)
  dealer sticker price (414)
  executive driven (413)
  factory-direct rebate (415)
  holdback (413)
  invoice price (414)
  leasing (409)
  manufacturer's suggested retail
    price (414)
  Markup (414)
  No haggle dealerships (415)
  one-price shopping (415)
  Profit margin (414)
  Rebate (411)
  Rebates (415)

repair-cost histories (403)
  rollover rating (507)
  safety ratings (403)
  secret warranties (406)
  seller financing (410)
  sticker price (414)
Automobile accidents
  numbers (505)
Automobile advertising
  false (413)
Automobile broker **(416)**
Automobile bumpers
  weak (405)
Automobile insurance
  factors affecting rates (556)
  premiums vary widely (556)
  unisex law (560)
Automobile Leasing Act (139)
Automobile manufacturers
  and arbitration (72)
Automobile prices
  and discrimination (547)
Automobile purchases
  breaking the contract (78)
Automobile repairs (119)
Automobile size
  and death rates (506)
Automobiles
  and planned buying (399)
  bargaining (414)
  cost of driving (407)
Automotive Consumer Action Program
    (AUTOCAP) (73)
Average propensities
  relationship with marginal
    propensities (222)
Average propensity to consume (APC)
    (222)
Average propensity to save (APS)
    (222)
Average revenue (AR) **(273)**
Award
  for quality (264)

B

Bait and switch advertising **(105),
    (380)**
Balance of trade **(241)**
Balloon automobile loan **(410)**
Balloon loans **(168)**
Bandwagon effect **(365)**
Bank examiner (102)
Bank Watch (295)
Bankcard Holders of America
  and lobbying (295)
Banking
  alternative financial sector (523)
  basic banking (521)
  cost of checking (520)
  Deregulation (517)
  Discrimination against small

depositors and
    nondepositors (520)
  fundamental consumer needs (521)
  problems of consumers (521)
  reasons why people do not have
    accounts (521)
  restructuring the industry (518)
  Savings and loan scandal (523)
Banking problems and issues (516)
Bankruptcy **(263)**
Banks
  and mutual funds (571)
  CRA ratings (540)
  selling uninsured products (569)
Banned **(502)**
Banned products
  examples of (502)
Bargaining (393)
  and automobiles (413)
  no haggle auto dealerships (415)
Barriers to free trade **(243)**
Base price
  automobile **(414)**
Basic banking **(522)**
Baumol's disease **(268)**
BBB Autoline (73)
BBB National Consumer Arbitration
    (73)
Beliefs **(323)**
Benefit rights **(11)**
Benefit-cost analysis **(311)**
  use of (493)
Benefits and costs
  and planned buying (392)
  food additives (444)
  illustration (403)
Best buy **(63), (392), (404)**
Better Business Bureau
  as a self-regulatory group (266)
  information services (398)
  source of buying information (398)
Bias
  in financial planning (571)
Biases in the U.S. (19)
Bill of rights
  in investing (568)
Bioavailability **(467)**
Biotechnogy
  food (439)
  risk assessments (446)
Birth control (186)
Blacklisting **(42)**
Blockbusting **(158)**
Blood cholesterol problem (429)
Blue Book (401)
Boiler rooms **(108)**
Borrowing **(4)**
Boycott **(24)**
  global (258)
  organizing a (80)
Boycotts, group **(282)**
Branch banking law (518)
Brand name
  of drug (466)

Brand names **(396)**
Brands
    generic **(396)**
    store (396)
Brazzein (444)
Break-even point **(222)**
    household income and
        consumption (222)
Breast implants (497)
Budget constraint **(361)**
Budget constraint information **(363)**
Budget deficits (240)
Budget line **(225)**, **(361)**
Bumping
    off airlines (140)
Bureau of Economic Research (200)
Business
    and the consumer interest (18)
Business costs
    of labor (202)
Business cycle **(200)**
Business Cycle Dating Committee
    (200)
Business day **(137)**
Business interest **(9)**
Businesses **(262)**
    helps consumers (23)
Buy-domestic policies **(245)**
Buyer beware
    slogan in developing countries
        (254)
Buyer's broker **(546)**
Buyer's remorse **(351)**
Buying behaviors (388)
Buying clubs (114)
Buying power (189)
Buying service **(417)**

C

Cable television industry
    and price regulation (273)
Calendar marketing agreements **(436)**
Caller ID
    and privacy (537)
Calorie **(425)**
Calorie intake (425)
Camground contracts
    cooling-off laws (139)
Campground memberships (102)
Cancellation rights
    and door-to-door sales (138)
Cancer
    and sunscreens (469)
    does everything cause it? (445)
    skin (469)
    Smokeless tobacco (479)
Capital
    cost to business **(187)**, (202)
Capital flight **(236)**
Capitalism
    American (184)
    defects of **(182)**, (184), **(196)**
    new trend (185)

rewards efficient firms (184)
    worst aspects of (253)
Carcinogens **(443)**
Card registration service **(95)**, **(161)**,
    (533)
Careers in consumer affairs (585)
Carpet and Rug Institute (73)
Cartel **(246)**, **(278)**
Cartels
    and predatory pricing (246)
Cash on delivery (137)
    and mail-order rules (137)
Cash-value life insurance **(570)**
Caveat emptor
    cosmetics **(30)**, (470)
Caveat venditor **(36)**
Cease and desist order **(277)**
Cellar-Kefauver Act (284)
Cemetery Consumer Service Council
    (73)
Censureship
    using advertising dollars (380)
Center for Auto Safety
    and consumers who have trouble
        with cars (407)
Center for the Study of Commercialism
    (374), (375)
    and product placements (375)
Center for the Study of Responsive
    Law
    and lobbying (295)
Certificate of deposit **(569)**
Certification **(456)**
Certification programs (395)
Ceteris paribus **(190)**, **(212)**
Chain letters (127)
Chain store act (284)
Chamber of Commerce
    primary tasks of (265)
Change
    and marginal propensities (222)
    incremental (38)
Channel One **(383)**
Charge back (162)
Charities
    quasi-charities (112)
    signs of problems (112)
    source to verify claims (113)
Check-Cashing companies
    illegally offering credit (111),
        (532)
Checking
    race-coding (534)
Child-resistant packaging
    aspirin (471)
Children
    and cigarette advertising (477)
    and cigarettes (477)
    and Old Joe Camel (477)
    and smoking (479)
    and television (381)
    deaths and injuries from products
        (489)
    deaths by aspirin (471)
Children's Advertising Review Unit
    (CARU) (267), (382)

Children's Television Act (CTA) (382)
China
    consumer movement in (256)
Chlorofluorocarbons (CFCs) **(372)**
Choice
    and product safety (491)
    and state lotteries (306)
    and the poor (354)
    as a consumer right (13)
    right to (61)
Cholesterol **(428)**
    recommendations on intake (429)
    uses of (429)
Cigarettes
    and children (477)
Circular flow **(190)**
Citizen roles **(17)**
Citizen utility boards (CUBs) **(43)**,
    (342)
Citizen-consumers **(16)**
Citizens
    planatary (254)
Citizenship (25)
Civics **(328)**
Civil courts and small claims courts
    (74)
Civil fines
    for product safety violations (502)
Civil law **(274)**
Civility (322)
Class action lawsuits **(77)**
Clayton Act (281)
Clinton
    Hillary Rodham, on citizenship
        (328)
    President Bill, and communitarian
        views (331)
    President Bill, on national service
        (328)
    Presidential supports for skills
        (241)
Closing **(546)**
    date **(548)**
Coalition **(43)**
Coalition for Environmentally
    Responsible Economies
    (CERES) (368)
COD (cash on delivery) rule (137)
    of the Postal Service (137)
Codes
    for proper corporate behavior (255)
Coin-operated customer-owned
    telephones
    and high telephone bills (135)
Coin-operated telephones (98)
Collection agencies (166)
Collection practices
    and the law (166)
Collective society (331)
College
    has opportunity costs (221)
Collegial group **(298)**
Collision-damage waiver (CDW) **(94)**
Color Additive Amendments (444)
Comfort ranking
    illustrated (412)

Commerce clause (**297**)
Commercial-free television
    programming (382)
Commercialism (350), (374)
Commercials
    number aimed at children (381)
    per year on television (374)
Commericialism
    Center for the Study of (375)
Commission-only financial planners
    (**573**)
Commissions
    of auto insurance agents (558)
    regulatory (273)
Common Cause
    and lobbying (295)
Common law (**56**)
Communications industry
    and price regulation (273)
Communism (**181**)
Communitarian
    a political ideology (**331**)
Community property (166)
Community Reinvestment Act (157)
Comparative advantage (**238**)
    illustrated (239)
Comparative advertisements (**378**)
Comparison
    rebate of low interest rate? (411)
Comparison shopping (**392**)
    how much (356)
    illustrated (404)
Compensatory damages (**77**), (**275**),
    (**496**)
Competencies of consumer affairs
    graduates (589)
Competition
    and its two virtues (290)
    as a government goal (275)
    benefits to consumers (**183**), (275)
    effects of little (275)
    imperfect (279)
    prohibited in contact lens sales
        (303)
    unfair companies (284)
Complain
    percent who do (67)
Complaining
    fighting and winning (78)
    five channels of (69)
    why people don't (67)
Complaining effectively
    procedures to (69)
Complaining process
    should follow a sequence (69)
Complaint letters
    how to write (83)
    sample (84)
Complaint procedure
    illustrated (70)
    in services (457)
Complaints
    common of consumers (304)
    in investing (574)

insurance (565)
    reasons for (67)
    reasons sellers handle (68)
Complaints to BBB
    source of information (399)
Compliment whenever possible (65)
Compromise
    to resolve an issue (336)
Concentration of ownership
    dangers of (518)
Concentration ratio (**279**)
Confidence
    economic (202)
Conglomerate merger (**282**)
Congress Watch
    and lobbying (295)
Congressional veto (**505**)
Consent agreement (**277**)
Consent decree
    and the FTC (308)
Consequential expenses (**77**)
Conservatism (**328**)
Conservative's
    attack on consumer protection (45)
Conservatives
    percentage of the population (330)
Conspicuous consumption (**389**)
    effect (**365**)
Consume
    average propensity to (222)
    marginal propensity to (222)
Consumer (**3**)
    pro-environmental (366)
    risk assessments (482)
Consumer action agencies (**73**)
Consumer action panels (CAPs) (**72**)
    list of (73)
Consumer activists (**34**)
Consumer advisory panels (**45**)
Consumer advocates
    and utility companies (**25**), (**34**),
        (272)
    differences between an
        environmentalist and (367)
    reformists (333)
Consumer affairs (**585**)
    department (**45**)
    departments state level (291)
    entry-level job titles (586)
    professionals (CAPs) (**37**)
Consumer Attitudes (202)
Consumer Bill of Rights (**34**)
    in investing (568)
    of President Kennedy (61)
Consumer citizens (16)
Consumer consumption (**242**)
Consumer counsels (**272**)
Consumer credit
    a right of consumers (63)
Consumer decision (**350**)
Consumer economics (**25**)
Consumer education
    as a consumer right (13)
    consumers flunk test (344)

need for (343)
    right to (62)
Consumer efficiency (**8**) (**198**)
Consumer expectations (49)
Consumer Federation of America
    (CFA)
    and lobbying (295)
Consumer fraud acts (**302**)
Consumer health (**454**)
Consumer Information
    source of buying information (398)
Consumer interest
    and business (18)
    and government (20)
    and state lotteries (306)
    as a special-interest group (14)
    conflicts with public interest (21)
        (**9**)
    functions of (16)
    in conflict with itself (21)
    in international trade (239)
    institutionalization (47)
    is biased (14)
    morality aspect (11)
    who determines? (12)
Consumer interest issues (**20**)
Consumer issues
    evolution of (341)
    how Congress voted (331)
    moving it forward (337)
    public support for (49)
    resolving (334)
Consumer knowledge
    consumers flunk test (344)
Consumer Movement
    1890s through 1920s (31)
    and organized labor (**34**), (239)
    future (52)
    goals of (34)
    in China (256)
    international rights (252)
    participants in (34)
    today (44)
    today's primary concerns (44)
    under challenge today (45)
    upon being successful (39)
Consumer organizations
    around the world (258)
    basis of support (48)
    in the consumer movement (48)
    what they do (49)
Consumer payoffs (**354**)
Consumer price index (CPI) (**199**)
Consumer problems
    and the poor (354)
    beliefs about resolution (**6**), (324)
    in service area (457)
Consumer Product Safety Commission
    (CPSC) (500)
Consumer protection
    attack by conservatives (45) (**296**)
Consumer protection agency
    in China (256)
Consumer protection proposals

support for (332)
Consumer Reports (33), (43)
    and buying an automobile (403)
    and planned buying (392)
    testing magazine (394)
Consumer Reports Buying Guide Issue
    (403)
Consumer Reports Used Car Price
    Service (417)
Consumer rights (13)
    and state lotteries (306)
    in insurance (556)
    international (252)
    of students (62)
Consumer sovereignty **(5)**, **(326)**
Consumer statement
    to credit report (161)
Consumer watchdogs **(304)**
Consumer's Resource Handbook
    address to obtain (71)
Consumerism
    1960s (33)
    as a social movement (33)
    business response **(33)**, (35)
    early years (30)
    excessive (331)
    future (50)
    not in disagreement with business
        interest (51)
    response of government (37)
    says Esther Peterson (258)
    today (39)
    why it emerged (34)
Consumers
    aggressive-assertive (23)
    and lobbyists **(17)**, (295)
    in China (256)
    in developing countries (253)
    low income and rent-to-own (115)
    poor (354)
    should organize (22)
    who are vulnerable (12)
Consumers International (43), (252)
Consumers Research Magazine
    and product testing (395)
Consumers Research, Inc. (32)
Consumers Union
    on free trade (239)
Consumers Union, Inc. (CU) (33) (43)
Consumers' Research Magazine (32)
Consumers' Union of the United States
    and lobbying (295)
Consumption **(3)**, **(188)**
    explained by Smith (183)
    simultaneous (188)
    successive (188)
Consumption expenditure
    determinant of (222)
Consumption function **(222)**
Contact lens laws (303)
Contempt of court
    and consent decrees (277)
Contests (110)
Contests, prizes, and free gifts (109)
Contingency basis **(495)**
Contracts

getting out of (78)
    how to break (76)
    revoking acceptance (76)
Cooling-Off laws
    health spas, timeshares, etc. (139)
Cooling-off period **(138)**
    state laws (139)
Cooperation
    to resolve consumer issues (339)
Corporate behavior
    product liability (495)
Corrective advertising **(310)**, **(342)**
Corvair (36)
Cosmetics
    and Senator Thomas Eagleton
        (470)
    tampering (470)
    waste of money (470)
Cost
    and product safety (511)
Cost containment procedures
    in health care (460)
Cost of driving (407)
Cost-Benefit analysis
    criticisms of **(311)**, **(490)**, (492)
Cost-shifting **(12)**, (459)
Costs and benefits
    and planned buying (392)
    food additives (444)
    illustration (403)
Council of Better Business Bureau
    and Children's Advertising Review
        Unit (382)
Coupon books (116)
CPSC
    Authorities and powers (501)
    hotline (501)
    Injury data-collection system (503)
    Legal mandates (500)
    National Electronic Injury
        Surveillance System (503)
    responsibilities (501)
    rulemaking authority (504)
    voluntary standards (504)
CRA ratings **(540)**
Credence goods **(366)**
Credit
    a right of consumers (63)
    affects availability of housing
        (542)
    and rent-to-own (115)
    card registration service (533)
    Check-Cashing companies (111),
        (532)
    credit bureau addresses (162),
        (535)
    demand curve (528)
    for low-income home buyers (542)
    high interest rates (526)
    interest-rate cap (529)
    interest-rate caps (526)
    Investigation (534)
    low interest or cash rebate? (411)
    negsale (527)
    paying only the minimum balance
        (527)

preapproved (526)
prescreening (525)
privacy concerns (538)
refund anticipation loan (93)
risk premium (528)
Rule of 78s (532)
shopping for (529)
spread (527)
supply curve (528)
two-cycle daily balance method
    (531)
Unnecessary credit-card
    solicitations (525)
usury laws (528)
Credit bureaus **(161)**
    addresses and telephone numbers
        (162), **(535)**
Credit card
    registration services (95), (533)
Credit card disclosures
    state laws (167)
Credit cards
    limited liability (158)
    variable-rate (526)
Credit counseling advice (526)
Credit discrimination
    how to report (539)
Credit history **(535)**
Credit insurance
    payout ratio (534)
Credit investigation **(534)**
Credit problems and issues (525)
Credit rating **(535)**
Credit Report
    investigative (162)
Credit reporting agencies (161)
Credit scoring **(540)**
Credit scoring system **(535)**
Credit-card liability **(158)**
Credit-card telephones (98)
Credit/debit card liability
    covered by homeowner's/renter's
        insurance (161)
Creditworthiness **(535)**
Criminal law **(275)**
Criteria
    for decision making (412)
Cross-subsidization **(12)**, (22)
Currency devaluation **(245)**
Curriculum in consumer affairs (588)
Customs and ceremonies (357)

D

Daily Values (DVs) **(433)**
Daytime running lights **(508)**
De facto price fixing **(558)**
De minimis
    policy (444)
Dealer sticker price **(414)**
Death
    leading cause for teens (483)
    leading causes (483)
    odds (564)

Death rate
in vehicles (506)
Deaths
traffic and alcohol (484)
Debit cards
new protections (523)
Debt
growing external (235)
Debt crisis
reasons for (235)
Debt relief (**236**)
Debt service (**235**)
Deceit (**103**)
Deception
current FTC definition (**103**), (**379**)
historical definition of FTC (103)
Deceptive act (**379**)
Decision making
accepting and evaluating (418)
and environmental issues (367)
and time (355)
chart (412)
getting difficult (350)
illustrated (411)
is irrational (352)
Model of consumer choice (358)
selecting the best alternative,
illustrated (417)
Decision Making Matrix
for pro-environmental consumers
(370)
Decision making model
of planned buying (391)
Decisions, incorrect
conditions for (393)
Defect-disclosure form (**545**)
Defendant (**75**)
Deficits
of U.S. (240)
Defined-benefit pension plans (**576**)
Defined-contribution plan (**576**)
Deflation (**199**)
Delaney Clause
food (443)
Deliveries and installations laws (142)
Demand
affects prices (210) (**211**)
of housing (542)
Demand curve (**212**)
for credit (528)
housing (543)
showing different elasticities (214)
Demand drafts (134)
Demand for health services (461)
Democracy (**196**)
true (196)
Democrat
number of (330)
Democratic
beliefs (331)
Democratic National Committee (294)
Dependability ranking
illustrated (412)
Dependent agencies (**298**)

Depreciation
and auto leasing (409)
Depression (**200**)
Deregulation
and the consumer interest (305)
banking (**305**), (517)
effects of (307)
failure in airlines? (309)
impacts on consumer banking
(518)
of the airline industry (279)
techniques of (307)
which raised search costs (252)
Design ranking
illustrated (412)
Design standards (**313**)
Devaluation of currency (245)
Developed countries (**233**)
Developing countries
and capital flight (**233**), (236),
(249)
good trading partners (237)
Diet
and cancer (426)
and disease (426)
and weight (425)
disease (428)
improvement in (430)
Diminishing Marginal Utility (**224**)
Direct deposit
regulations (159)
Direct Marketing Association (73)
Direct Selling Association (73)
and computer mailing lists (92)
Disability insurance ripoffs (534)
Disclosure
by real estate agents (545)
in financial planning (570), (572)
Discount rate (**194**), (**353**)
Discount real estate firms (**546**)
Discount window (**194**)
Discrimination
against small depositors and
nondepositors (520)
against young persons (68)
and airline rates (309)
and automobile prices (547)
and the Equal Credit Opportunity
Act (166)
and the poor (**157**), (354), (**538**)
examples of (539)
how to report (539)
Human Rights Act (75)
in auto insurance rates (560)
in credit (63)
in housing (157)
some examples (539)
testers (539)
Discrimination in housing
exclusions (158)
Discrimination in lending (**539**)
Disease
and diet (426)
Disposable income

and consumption and savings (222)
Disputes with automatic billing (160)
Dissatisfaction
causes of (67)
in marketplace transactions (351)
Dissolution (**285**)
Divestiture (**285**)
Divorce
pension rights (569)
Divorcement (**285**)
Dollar votes (17)
Door-to-Door sales cooling-off-period
state laws (139)
Door-to-door sales regulations
of Federal Trade Commission
(138)
Douthitt, Robin A.
on consumer risk assessments
(446)
Downsizing (**203**)
Drugs (**464**)
application process (465)
pretesting reasons for (465)
unsafe (466)
Dumping
and the United Nations (**246**),
(255)
Dunning letters (165)
Duty free (243)

E

Earning (**3**)
Economic belief systems (324)
Economic community (**248**)
Economic concerns
of consumers (11)
Economic Confidence
indicators of (202)
Economic cycle (**200**)
stages in (200)
Economic development (**234**)
Economic efficiency (**197**)
Economic frauds
protection from, as an government
goal (291)
Economic freedoms (**197**)
Economic goals
of society (195)
Economic growth (**199**)
measurement of future directions
(202)
sluggish (200)
Economic ideology (**323**)
Economic objective
of a consumer (198)
Economic problems
world (232)
Economic productivity (**202**)
Economic questions (180)
Economic resources
types of (185)

Economic security **(203)**
Economic system **(180)**
Economic systems
   mixed (184)
Economic vote **(187)**
Economic well-being **(187)**, **(198)**,
   (275)
Economics **(180)**
Economies of scale **(237)**
   in housing (548)
Economy **(180)**, **(200)**
Education loans
   how to refinance (527)
Effective demand **(211)**
Efficacy **(469)**
Elastic **(213)**
Elasticity **(213)**
   determinants (214)
   of demand coefficient **(213)**
Electric power industry (273)
Electronic benefits transfer (EBT)
   (522)
   new regulations (523)
   propsed regulation (523)
Electronic funds transfer
   Act (159)
   correcting errors (160)
   liability for (160)
   regulations (159)
Electronic Industries Association (73)
Embargo (243)
Employee Retirement Income Security
   Act (ERISA) (575)
Employee stock ownership plan
   (ESOP) **(185)**, **(577)**
Employment, full (198)
Endorsement **(376)**
Entitlements (331)
Entrepreneur **(262)**
Environmental concerns
   which affect the worldwide
      consumer movement (252)
Environmental health
   as a consumer right (13)
   right to (62)
Environmental problems
   examples of (367)
Environmental Protection Agency
   on secondhand smoking (479)
Environmental tobacco smoke (ETS)
   (478)
Environmentalist
   differences between a consumer
      advocate and (367)
Equal Credit Opportunity Act (166)
Equilibrium price **(218)**
Equity **(10)**, (204)
   interests (11)
   tax (204)
Escrow payments **(549)**
Ethics **(263)**
European Union (250)
Evaluation
   and planned buying (393)
Excess profits **(183)**
Exclusive dealing agreements **(282)**

Executive agencies **(298)**
Executive branch **(274)**
Expansion (200)
Expansion stage
   results of (200)
Expenditure
   determinant of (222)
Experience goods **(366)**
Express warranties **(56)**
   created when... **(58)**, **(153)**,
      (406)
Extended service contracts
   cancelling (78)
Extended warranties **(149)**, (407)
External benefits **(270)**
External costs **(269)**
Externalities **(269)**

F

Factors of production
   in housing (542)
Factory service bulletins **(406)**
Factory-direct rebate **(415)**
Fair Credit and Charge Card Disclosure
   Act (167)
Fair Credit Billing Act (60), (162)
Fair Credit Reporting Act
   and credit reporting agencies (161)
   Medical information (159)
Fair Debt Collection Practices Act
   (166)
Fair Housing Act (157)
Fair price (8)
Farm Prices (219)
Fat
   easy ways to reduce (431)
Fault system **(560)**
Fed (192)
Federal Communications Commission
   (FCC)
   and advertising to children (382)
Federal Deposit Insurance Corporation
   limiting insurance on pension plans
      (576)
Federal funds rate **(194)**
Federal Information Center
   source of buying information (398)
Federal Motor Vehicle Safety
   Standards (FMVSS) (505)
Federal Open Market Committee
   (FOMC) **(194)**
Federal Reserve System
   functions of (193)
Federal Trade Commission
   and drug advertising (471)
   authorities (283)
   responsibilities of (308)
Federalism (303)
Fee-and-commission financial planner
   (573)
Fee-only financial planner **(572)**
Fertility rate (233)
Financial consumer associations (FCA)

   (342)
Financial planner **(572)**
   fee-and-commission (573)
   fee-only (572)
Financial planners
   and bias (572)
   commission-only (573)
   types of (572)
Financing
   low interest or cash rebate? (411)
   seller (410)
Financing of an auto
   illustrated (401)
Financing options
   for automobiles (410)
Financing ranking
   illustrated (412)
First Amendment
   and political advertising (376)
First world countries **(232)**
Fiscal policy **(192)**
Flat tax (204)
Food
   additives (440)
   advertising (427)
   advertising to kids (427)
   agencies and laws (437)
   and health hazards (427)
   and the poor (428)
   Anti-Competitive practices (435)
   biotechnology (439)
   calorie intake (425)
   Color Additive Amendments (444)
   confusing grade labels (449)
   contaminants (440)
   Delaney Clause (443)
   filth (440)
   generally recognized as safe
      (GRAS) (441)
   grade labeling (448)
   item pricing laws (447)
   junk (427)
   label (432)
   laws and agencies (437)
   Low-Fat meals (428)
   Miller Pesticides Chemicals
      Amendment (442)
   mislabeling (438)
   nutritional labeling requirements
      (431)
   open dating (448)
   packaging costs (435)
   questionable selling practices (433)
   Reference Daily Intakes (433)
   sweeteners (444)
   unit pricing (447)
Food additive **(439)**
Food additives
   benefits and costs (444)
Food Additives Amendment (439)
Food and Drug Administration
   overview (438)
   seafood inspection program (442)
Food filth tolerances **(440)**
Food Guide Pyramid
   Food (433)

Food irradiation (**439**)
Food label
    sample (432)
Food preservatives (**444**)
Food safety
    concerns (438)
Food Safety and Inspection Service
    (FSIS) (437)
Food shopping
    confusions (447)
Foreign-exchange controls (**245**)
Formal rulemaking (**504**)
Fractional reserve system (**193**)
Fraud (**103**), (**291**)
    economic (276)
    elements to prove (103)
Frauds
    cause two bad things (291)
    guidelines to avoid (89)
    how they work (86)
    of large corporations (105)
    why they exist (87)
Frauds and misrepresentations
    home repair hustlers (544)
Free enterprise (**197**)
Free market bias (**19**)
Free riding (**16**)
Free trade
    and the interests of consumers
        (243)
    benefits of (**243**)
Free-rider (**369**)
Freedom of choice
    product safety (511)
Freedoms (**188**)
Freezer meat (102)
Frequent-buyer progarm (356)
FTC
    standard for health claims (472)
Fuel economy ranking
    illustrated (412)
Full employment (**198**)
Full warranty (58), (**147**), (**154**)
Funeral rule
    and the FTC (310)
Funeral Service Consumer Action
    Program (FSCAP) (73)
Furniture Industry Consumer Action
    Panel (FICAP) (73)

G

Games
    food (435)
Gas industry (273)
GATT (251)
    and the consumer movement (239)
Geistfeld Model of Consumer Choice
    (358)
Gender
    price discrimination (547)
General Agreement on Trade and

Tariffs
    how it came into being (251)
General Motors
    in Mexico (244)
Generally recognized as safe
    definition (441)
Generation X
    social activism (50)
Generic brands (**396**)
Generic drug (**466**)
Generic drugs
    and patents (466)
Generic substitution laws (467)
Genetically engineered food products
    (439)
Ghetto
    shopping (354)
Globalization
    of the economy (252)
Goals
    economic goals of U.S. (195)
    of the U.S. (195)
    social and economic (195)
Goals and values
    illustrated (400)
Good Manufacturing Practice
    Regulations
    FDA (438) (466)
Government
    economic goals of (200)
    fundamental purposes of (267)
    how it influences the economy
        (191)
    involvement in solutions (337)
    protecting consumers (20)
    visible hand (183)
    why it gets involved in consumer
        issues (337)
    why they exist (267)
Government agencies
    source of buying information (398)
Government organizations
    when active (41)
Government regulation
    of the economy (200)
Governments
    help consumers (23)
Grace period (**530**)
Grade labeling
    confusing (449)
    illusionary (448)
Grading
    of foods (437)
Grandfathering (**456**)
Green labeling (**371**)
Greenhouse effect (**373**)
Gross domestic product (GDP) (**201**)
Group boycotts (**282**)
Growth
    measured by economists (201)
Guarantee (**56**), (**152**)
Guaranteed investment contract (GIC)
    (**575**)
Guarantees (**405**)

Guidelines
    how to purchase services (455)

H

Habit buying (388)
Habitability of rental property (156)
Haggling (393), (**415**)
Hart-Scott-Rodino Act (285)
Hazard Analysis and Control Points
    for meat and pountry (437)
Hazard Analysis Critical Control Point
    (HACCP)
    seafood (442)
Health
    and nutritional labeling (431)
    environmental, right to (62)
Health and safety standards (**245**)
Health care
    aspirin and similar pain relievers
        (470)
    calls to reform (460)
    cost containment procedures (460)
    costs (458)
    demand for (459)
    generic drugs (466)
    managed care (462)
    National health reform (457)
    Over-the-Counter drugs (468)
    prescription drug pricing (465)
    prescription drugs (464)
    rationing (460)
    special-interest groups (459)
    unique market (461)
    vitamins and food supplements
        (474)
Health claims
    dietary supplements (474)
    FDA standard (471)
    in nutrition (431)
Health club (102)
Health insurance
    number without (458)
    why people do not have (458)
Health maintenance organizations
    (HMOs) (**462**)
Health spas
    cooling-off laws (139)
Health-care costs
    ways to reduce (460)
Heard
    and state lotteries (306)
Heart attacks
    and aspirin (470)
Heath care issues (453)
Heclo, H. (321)
Hic score (**509**)
High Cost Mortgage Act (544)
High school students
    smoking (477)
High-balling (**119**)
HMOs (462)

Holdback **(413)**
Home Equity Loan Consumer
     Protection Act (168), (169)
Home Mortgage Disclosure Act (157)
Home Owners Warranty Program
     (HOW) (73)
Home shopping **(389)**
Home-equity loan (168)
Homeowner's insurance (161)
     and lost credit cards (159)
Horizontal division of markets **(282)**
Horizontal merger **(282)**
Hospital
     Patient's bill of rights (463)
Hotline
     CPSC (501)
     NHTSA (508)
Household Goods Dispute Settlement
     Program (73)
Household production (3)
Housing
     affordability (541)
     agents work for (545)
     appraisers (544)
     buyer's brokers (546)
     Community Reinvestment Act
          ratings (540)
     contract termination date (548)
     credit affect availability (543)
     Defect-Disclosure laws (545)
     demand (542)
     demand determinants (542)
     disclosure by agents (545)
     discount real estate firms (546)
     discrimination (538)
     high costs (541)
     kickback fees (547)
     listing agent **(546)**
     loan programs (541)
     mortgage abuses (544)
     private mortgage insurance (550)
     problems and issues (538)
     Real Estate Settlement Procedures
          Act (RESPA) (547)
     redlining **(540)**
     Regulations (543)
     rent control affects demand (543)
     selling agent (546)
     supply (542)
Housing discrimination laws
     state (158)
Housing vouchers **(542)**
Human capital **(187)**
Human resources **(187)**
Human rights **(14)**
Human Rights Act
     and age discrimination (75)
Hyperinflation **(236)**

I
_____

Ibuprofen
     and aspirin (473)
Ideology

communitarian **(323)**, (331)
Imminent hazard **(501)**
Imperfect competition (279)
Implied warranties
     and used car regulations (147)
     cannot be disclaimed **(56)**, (149),
          (406)
     disclaiming (154)
Implied warranty **(57)**
Import duty (243)
Import quota (243)
Impulse buying **(388)**
Incidental additives **(440)**
Incidental expenses **(77)**
Income **(222)**
     household data (198)
     per capita (202)
     predicting consumption (222)
     real (199)
Income effect **(220)**
Independent agencies **(298)**
Indifference curve **(225)**, **(358)**
Indifference curve analysis **(225)**
Individualism
     excessive (331)
Industrial policy **(247)**
Industrialized countries **(238)**
Inelastic **(213)**
Inequity **(11)**
     wage inequality (203)
Inflation **(192)**
Infomercials (378)
Informal dispute procedure
     and warranties (58) **(155)**
Informal rule-making **(299)** **(504)**
Information
     and alcoholic beverages (484)
     and censorship by advertisers (380)
     as a consumer right (13)
     as a government goal (291)
     asymmetric (360)
     inadequate (363)
     right to (61)
Information age (252)
Information highway
     and used cars (416)
Information highway scams (114),
          (123), (125), (128)
Information processing (353)
Information, buying
     sources of (393)
Information, objective **(394)**
Informed
     and state lotteries (306)
Ingredient labeling
     AFT (484)
Injunction **(77)**, **(302)**, **(439)**
Injuries
     and motor vehicles (506)
Injury data-collection system
     CPSC (503)
Inside trader **(573)**
Institutionalization
     as part of change (38)
Insurance
     accounting methods (556)

anti-group laws (557)
anti-rebate law (556)
auto claims (558)
auto premiums vary widely (556)
bankrupt companies (566)
barriers to entry (557)
cash-value (570)
fault system (560)
financial stability figures (567)
guaranteed investment contract
     (GIC) (575)
how premium dollar is spent (557)
investment income of industry
     (557)
limited on retirement accounts
     (576)
no-fault (561)
pay-at-the-pump no-fault coverage
     (562)
payout ratio (100), (534)
premiums average on autos (556)
problems (556)
rate-making bureaus (558)
rebellion in auto insurance (555)
redlining (558)
remedy for auto problems (563)
rental car ripoffs (94)
rider (95)
scandal is coming (567)
sellers lie (574)
state approved price fixing (558)
state guaranty laws (567)
underinsured motorist coverage
     (559)
unisex law (563)
Insurance issues (555)
Insurance policies
     breaking the contract (78)
Insurance rates
     for autos (556)
Intentional additives **(440)**
Interactional space **(188)**
Interest rate
     punitive (167)
Interest-rate cap **(526)**, (529)
Interests
     conflicting (19)
     value for money (11)
Interlocking directorships **(281)**
International Association for Financial
     Planning (73)
International Codes
     for proper corporate behavior (255)
International Organization of
     Consumers Unions (IOCU)
     and lobbying (295)
     goals of (252)
International Organization of
     Consumers Unions
Interstate commerce **(297)**
Interstate land sales (157)
Intrastate commerce **(297)**
Investigative power **(299)**
Investigative report (162)
Investing
     arbitration (574)

certificate of deposit (569)
consumer bill of rights (**5**), (568)
defined-benefit pension plans (576)
Employee Retirement Income
    Security Act (575)
Employee Retirement Income
    Security Act (ERISA) (575)
employee stock ownership plan
    (ESOP) (577)
financial planner (572)
financial planner disclosures (570)
forced arbitration clauses (574)
guaranteed investment contract
    (GIC) (575)
Insider trading (573)
investment advisor (572)
Pension Benefit Guaranty
    Corporation (PBGC) (576)
Pensions at risk (575)
problems (568)
shareholder activism (575)
shareholder activists (575)
underfunded pension plans (576)
Investment (**242**)
    required in monopoly businesses
        (273)
    social (242)
Investment advisor (**572**)
Investment fraud
    in Russia (126)
Investment swindles
    tips to avoid (122)
Investments
    and sales incentives (573)
    hidden fees (572)
    potential bias (572)
    sellers lie (574)
Invoice price (**414**)
Iron triangle
    of public policy (322)
Issue (**323**)
Issue networks (**321**)
Issues of the day (337)
Item pricing laws
    food (447)

J

Job-search company (**97**)
Joe Camel
    cigarettes (477)
Joe Cool
    cigarette advertising campaign
        (477)
Joint ventures (**282**)
Judgments (**76**)
Judicial branch (**274**)
Junk calls
    and the Direct Selling Association
        (92), (**107**)
Junk fax (132)
Junk food (**427**)

Junk mail
    and the Direct Selling Association
        (92)
Justice (204)

K

Keynes, John Maynard, on propensity
    to consume (222)
Kickback fee (**547**)

L

Labeling
    of alcoholic beverages (484)
Labor
    and the consumer movement (239)
    cost to business (202)
    supply and demand (244)
    supply in developing countries
        (244)
Labor economics (244)
Labor union membership (204)
Laissez faire (**182**), (**263**)
    capitalism (197)
Latent public (**321**)
Law of demand (**211**)
Law of Diminishing Marginal Utility
    (**224**)
Law of supply (**215**)
Laws
    that limit the sale of contact lenses
        (303)
Laws and regulations
    on sales transactions (132)
Lead or Leave
    organization (50)
Leading economic indicators (LEI)
    (**201**)
Lease
    closed-end (410)
    open-end (409)
Leasing
    and residual value (**409**)
    rules (139)
    who should consider (410)
Legal-aid attorneys (**79**)
Legislative branch (**274**)
Legislative process (338)
Lemon **by state laws** (**143**)
Lemon car branding laws (145)
Lemon clause (**154**)
Lemon law (**143**)
Lemon laws (76)
    and used cars (144)
Less developed countries (LDCs) (**233**)
Letter of complaint
    how to write it (83)
    sample complaint (84)
    suggestions (83)

Level of living (**188**)
    differs from standard of living
        (188)
Leveraged buyout (**577**)
Leveraged buyouts
    employee stock ownership plans
        (ESOP) (577)
Liability
    on credit cards (158)
Liability for lost EFT cards (159)
Liberalism (**329**)
Liberals
    percentages of populations (330)
Libertarianism (**328**)
Licensure (**456**)
Life cycle hypothesis (**229**)
Life expectancies
    in different countries (455)
    smokers and nonsmokers (476)
Life insurance
    and smoking (476)
    good buys (564)
    tips for students (566)
Lifeline banking (**522**)
Lifestyle (**357**)
Limitational space (**188**)
Limited warranty (58), (**148**), (**155**)
Line of business reporting (283)
List price (**118**)
Listing agent (**546**)
Literacy
    in the United States (202)
Little FTC act (**302**)
Lobbying
    consumer organizations (295)
    forms of (339)
    the legislature (338)
Lobbyists (**293**)
    job of (338)
Locational space (**188**)
Lock-out agreements
    food (436)
Loser pays (499)
Loss of use (LOU) waiver (94)
Loss-damage waiver fee (**94**)
Lottery (108)
    consumer safeguards (306)
    state monopoly (306)
Low income consumers
    and rent-to-own (115)
Low price (8)
Low-balling (**119**)
Low-income
    housing loan programs (541)
Low-income consumers
    usury laws (529)

M

M1 (**193**)
Magnuson-Moss Warrant Act (152)
Magnuson-Moss Warranty Act

and products costing $15 (58)
Mail fraud **(107)**
Mail Order Action Line
    mediation group (73)
Mail order prescription drug prices
    table (468)
Mail-Order insurance (100)
Mail-order merchandise regulations
    of Federal Trade Commission
    (136)
Mailing lists
    and the Direct Selling Association
    (92)
    removing your name from (133)
Maintenance agreement **(407)**
Major Appliance Consumer Action
    Panel (MACAP) (73)
Malcolm Baldrige National Quality
    Award **(264)**
Malnourished **(424)**
Malnutrition **(426)**
Managed care **(462)**
Managed competition **(463)**
Managed trade **(248)**
Managerial belief system **(326)**
Manufacturer's suggested retail price
    (MSRP) **(414)**
Manufacturers brands **(396)**
Manufacturing
    jobs (241)
Margin **(414)**
Marginal cost **(221)**
Marginal propensities
    relationship with average
    propensities (222)
Marginal propensity to consume
    (MPC) **(191)**
Marginal propensity to import (MPI)
    (191)
Marginal propensity to save (MPS)
    (191), **(222)**
Marginal rate of substitution **(225)**
Marginal utility **(224)**
Marginal utility theory
    and indifference curve analysis
    (225)
Market **(210)**
    unique in health care (461)
Market economy **(210)**
Market Equilibrium (216)
Market failures **(7)**, **(368)**
Market price **(210)**
    system **(2)**
Market trade-off **(361)**
Market-oriented economy **(210)**
Marketing orders'
    food (436)
Marketplace
    failure in product safety (488)
    imperfections (184)
Markets and lousy choices (352)
Markup
    for auto dealers (414)
Mass media
    source of buying information (398)
Material information **(103)**

Materialism (350)
    and children's advertising (382),
    (391)
McCarran-Ferguson Act
    groups against it (558)
Mediation **(72)**, **(343)**
Medical Information Bureau (159)
Member banks **(193)**
Merger **(282)**
Mexico
    site for manufacturing firms (244)
Military Spending
    excessive (234)
Milk
    hormone-supplemented (439)
Miller Pesticide Chemicals Amendment
    (442)
Misbranded **(438)**
Misrepresentation **(103)**
Model to analyze issues (517)
Moderate
    ideology of communitarians (331)
Monetary policy **(192)**
Money
    and its symbols (390)
Money supply **(193)**
    velocity of (194)
Money's worth
    illustrated (401)
Monopolies
    and large-scale production (273)
    why they arise (279)
Monopolistic competition **(279)**
Monopolization (defined by the
    Supreme Court) **(279)**
Monopoly (278)
    power (279)
    state lottery (306)
Moral rights **(60)**
    in insurance (557)
Mortgage
    abuses (544)
Motorcycle helmets
    and brain damage (510)
Multi-level network marketing **(125)**
Multiple-listing service (MLS) **(546)**
Multiplier **(191)**
    multiplier effect **(191)**
Mutual fund **(571)**
    socially conscious (576)
Mutual funds
    government insurance (571)

N

Nader, Ralph (36)
    on free trade (239)
Nader's Raiders **(35)**, **(36)**
NAFTA (249)
    and the consumer movement (239)
National Advertising Division (NAD)
    (266)
    of Council of Better Business
    Bureaus (73)

National Advertising Review Board
    (NARB) (266)
National Association of Attorneys
    General (NAAG) (304)
National Bureau of Economic Research
    (200)
National Coalition for Consumer
    Education (NCCE)
    and lobbying (295)
National Consumers League (NCL)
    (31)
    and lobbying (295)
National Council Against Health Fraud
    (455)
National dealer advertising (NDA)
    (414)
National debt (240)
National Electronic Injury Surveillance
    System (NEISS)
    CPSC (503)
National Foundation on Consumer
    Credit (526)
National Fraud Information Center
    (108)
National Highway Traffic Safety
    Administration (NHTSA) (505)
National Institute for Consumer
    Education (NICE)
    and lobbying (295)
National Insurance Consumer
    Organization
    good prices for term life insurance
    (564)
    recommended direct-mail life
    insurance companies (564)
National Traffic and Motor Vehicle
    Safety Act (36)
Natural monopolies **(271)**
Needs and wants
    worksheet (402)
Neg-Reg (295)
Negative amortization **(168)**
Negative externalities **(7)**
Negative externality **(369)**
Negative option **(136)**
Negative option plans **(93)**
Negligible risk **(442)**
Negotiating
    and planned buying (393), **(414)**
Negotiation
    goal of (413)
    process of (414)
Neoclassical belief system **(324)**
Net weights
    illusionary on foods (448)
NHTSA
    crash-worthiness (509)
    formal defect investigation (508)
    hic score (509)
    hotline (508)
    Legal mandates and authorities
    (505)
    passive restraint system (509)
    recalls (507)
    safety investigation (508)
    slow (511)

Vehicle crashing and testing (509)
vehicle identification number (508)
Nicotine dependence **(480)**
Nitrites
and food preservatives (444)
Nitrosamines **(444)**
No-fault automobile insurance system **(560)**
history (560)
pay-at-the-pump (562)
No-frills brands **(396)**
Non-deeded timesharing **(578)**
Non-economic issues (11)
Non-price determinants of demand (212)
Normative economics **(180)**
North
the industrialized countries (254)
North America Free Trade Agreement (249)
Nutrients **(424)**
Nutrition
and good health (427)
Nutritional labeling
restaurant menus (441)

O

Obesity
and children's television (381), **(424)**
results of (426)
Obligations (331)
Occupational licensing boards **(265)**
Odometer fraud **(120)**, **(143)**
Office of Consumer Affairs (OCA) (42)
state level (304)
statewide network (304)
U.S. (41), (291)
Olean (439)
Olestra (439)
Oligopolistic industries (279)
Oligopoly **(279)**
On the record rule-making **(300)**
ON...Free riders
and pollution (368)
ON...Information search
in the buying process (360)
ON...Large-Scale production
and price regulation (273)
On-line shopping (416)
One-price shopping
auto dealerships (415)
OPEC (246)
Open dating **(448)**
Open-door economic policies **(256)**
Open-end auto lease (409)
Open-market operations **(194)**
Opportunity cost **(220)**, (491)
of college (221)
of time (356)

Opportunity line **(225)**
Opportunity rights **(11)**
Optimal consumer purchase decision **(358)**
Optimal purchase (361)
Optimizin **(221)**, **(354)**
Ordinal utility theory **(225)**
Organization of Petroleum Exporting Countries (OPEC)
cartel (246)
Over-the-Counter drugs (OTC) **(464)** (468)
Oversight function **(297)**

P

Packaging costs
food (435)
Parens patriae **(285)**
Pareto efficiency **(237)**
Parity price **(219)**
Passive restraint system **(509)**
Passive smoking **(478)**
Patent **(465)**
and generic drugs (466)
Patent laws
in prescription drug industry (465)
Patient's bill of rights
in hospitals (463)
Payout ratio **(100)**, **(534)**
Pension Benefit Guaranty Corporation (PBGC) (576)
Pensions
Employee Retirement Income Security Act (575)
Federal Deposit Insurance Corporation (576)
spousal rights (569)
underfunded (576)
Pensions at risk (575)
Per se actions **(281)**
Perfect information
in decision making (354)
Perfectly elastic demand **(214)**
Perfectly inelastic **(214)**
Performance
comparing in services (457)
Performance ranking
illustrated (412)
Performance standards
and CPSC **(313)**, (504)
Permanent income hypothesis (229)
Personal trade-off **(361)**
Pesticide **(442)**
legal residue level (442)
Pesticides
cumulative effects (445)
negligible risk (442)
tolerance levels (442)
Pet Lemon Laws (141)
Picketing (79)
Pigeon drop (102)

Plaintiff **(76)**
Plane of living **(188)**
Planned buying
decision making model **(391)**
for automobiles (399)
health care (454)
Point of zero savings **(222)**
Point-of-purchase information **(399)**
Poisonings
by aspirin (471)
Political action committees (PACs) **(294)**
and soft money (294)
Political advertising techniques
examples of unscrupulous (376)
Political belief systems (328)
Political ideology **(328)**
Political party
affiliations of populations (330)
Political perspective
communitarian (331)
Political votes (17)
Politically correct buying (357)
Politics
and product safety (512)
Pollution (233)
and its customers (370)
and market failure (368)
ways of controlling (370)
Pollution-permit rights (370)
Ponzi schemes **(123)**
Poor
and usury laws (529)
consumer problems of (354)
mortgage abuses (544)
pay more for banking (522)
pay more for food (428)
Poor Economic Conditions
contribution to consumer movements (44)
Poor people's banks (522)
Popcorn in theaters (430)
Population
of the world (186)
that strains resources (233)
Population projections (186)
Positive economics **(180)**
Positive externalities **(369)**
Possessions **(188)**
Postal Service
COD (cash on delivery) rule (137)
unordered merchandise regulations (135)
Postcards saying "You Definitely Have Won!" (111)
Poverty (204), **(234)**
Power clusters **(320)**
patterns of behavior (323)
Powers
quasi-judicial, of the FTC (309)
Preapproved **(526)**
Predatory marketing practices (184)
Predatory pricing **(278)**
Preemption

CPSC standards (501)
doctrine (297)
Premarket clearance
of prescription drugs (465)
Prescreening (525)
Prescription drug pricing (465)
Prescription drugs (464)
and advertising (379), (464)
Price
additional auto dealer markup
(414)
as a determinant of demand (212)
as a reference point (211)
base, in autos (189), (414)
determining what you want to pay
(416)
in auto advertising (414)
market (210)
Price caps (271)
Price ceilings (219)
Price controls
on monopolies (273)
Price discrimination (355)
Price elasticity of demand (213)
Price fixing (276)
de facto, in auto insurance and
repairs (105), (220), (558)
horizontal (286)
retail price maintenance (286)
state approved (558)
types of (286)
vertical (286)
Price gouging (93)
Price manipulation
food (434)
Price mechanism (189)
Price ranking
illustrated (412)
Price regulation
and large-scale production (273)
can reduce prices (273)
Price stability (199)
Price supports (219)
price-fixing
meatpacking industry (437)
Price-quality conceptual model (8)
Prices
absent on food products (447)
Pricing
of prescription drugs (465)
Priorities
illustration of choosing (411)
Privacy
at the checkout counter (448)
being invaded (536), (538)
legislative proposals (537)
Private brands (396)
Private enterprise (197)
Private mortgage insurance (550)
Private organizations
active (42)
Privatization (236)
Privatizing (307)
Pro se court (75)
Pro-environmental consumer
how to be (366)

Problems
defining illustrated (399)
economic (233)
percentage of consumers
experiencing (67)
the real ones in society (332)
Producer sovereignty (5)
Producers (262)
Product discrimination (355)
Product injuries
most frequent (503)
Product liability (495)
compensatory damages (496)
consumer point of view (499)
court secrecy (498)
examples of lawsuits (496)
future (499)
liability laws (497)
punitive damages (496)
Product safety
and children (489)
and cost-benefit analyis (490)
and design (489)
and politics (512)
award for cap (504)
banned products (502)
civil fines (502)
Consumer Product Safety
Commission (CPSC) (500)
consumer responsibilities (494)
cost (511)
criticisms of (511)
effectiveness (488)
examples of product liability
lawsuits (496)
factors to consider in decision
making (493)
imminent hazard (501)
Injuries (488)
limited resources (513)
measuring risk (491)
motorcycle helmets (510)
National Highway Traffic Safety
Administration (NHTSA) (505)
notification requirements (502)
primary concerns (489)
product liability (495)
products needing safety regulations
(494)
prosecution (512)
reasonable risks (491)
recall (491)
risk acceptability (491)
rulemaking factors that must be
considered (505)
rulemaking procedures (503)
secrecy of court records (498)
toy safety suggestions (489)
uninflated balloons (490)
unsafe products (494)
voluntary efforts (511)
voluntary standards (504)
Production (185)
Productivity
and literacy (202)
Productivity increases (202)

Products
defective, and lawsuits (495)
that are unsafe (489)
with built-in hazards (488)
Professional licensing boards (265)
Profit (262)
in an accounting sense (182)
in an economic sense (182)
normal (183)
Profit margin (414)
Profit motive
negative results of (184)
Profits
excess (183)
in prescription drugs (465)
Progressive tax (192)
Progressives (329)
Propensity to consume (222)
Property report (157)
Property rights (182)
Protectionism (245)
Protective order (498)
Psychological recession (200)
Public (16)
Public bad (369)
Public Citizen
and lobbying (295)
and subgroups (43)
Public good (16), (369)
Public interest (16), (17)
concerns (20)
disputes (19)
Public Interest Research Group
and lobbying (295)
Public issues (20)
differ from consumer issues (337)
Public members (304)
Public participation
in regulatory proceedings (341)
Public policy (195), (268)
how shaped (322)
Public safety
as a government goal (290)
Public utility (271)
commission (271)
Public Voice for Food and Health
Policy
and lobbying (295)
Public well-being
as a government goal (290)
Puffing (105)
Punitive damages (77), (275), (496)
not limited by Supreme Court (77)
Pure monopoly (278)
Push money (402)
Pyramid schemes (124)
differences from multi-level
marketing (126)

Q

Quacks
in health care (455)
Quality

acceptable (9)
and brand names (396)
broadening definition of (367),
   (392)
indicators of (360)
Quality award
   Malcolm Baldrige (264)
Quality indicators
   in schools (62)
Quasi-charities **(112)**
Quasi-judicial power **(300)**
Quasi-legislative power **(299)**
Quasi-Legislative powers
   of the FTC (310)
Quota (243)
   set by OPEC (246)

R

Race
   and auto insurance rates (558)
   price discrimination (547)
Racism
   and retailers (534)
   in political advertising (376)
Radiation ionization **(439)**
Railroading industry (273)
Rain checks **(380)**
Ranking
   illustrated (412)
Rate-of-return regulation **(271)**
Rational consumer
   reflects on decisions (418)
Rational self-interest **(350)**
Rationing (219), **(460)**
Real Estate Settlement Procedures Act
   (RESPA) (547)
Real gross domestic product **(201)**
Real income **(199)**
Real per capita gross domestic product
   (201)
Reasonable consumers
   and deception (104)
Reasonable risks **(491)**
Rebates **(405)**
   factory-direct (415)
   or take a low rate of interest (411)
   reasons why offered (415)
Recall request letter **(507)**
Recalled products
   Examples of (502)
Recalls (438) **(491)**
   NHTSA (507)
   response to (511)
Recession **(194)**, (200)
   defined by National Bureau of
      Economic Research **(200)**
   economists' definition (200)
   phase in economic cycle (200)
   psychological (200)
Reciprocal dealing agreements **(282)**
Recision (76)

Recovery
   phase **(200)**
   room scam (133)
Recycling **(372)**
Redlining **(158)**, **(540)**
Redress
   as a consumer right (13)
   as a government goal (291)
   right to (62)
Reference Daily Intakes (RDIs) **(433)**
Reformation **(76)**
Reformist belief system **(327)**
Refund anticipation loan (93)
Regional trade agreement **(248)**
Registered pharmacists **(464)**
Registration **(456)**
Regressive tax **(192)**
Regulation
   affecting housing (543)
   and auto death rates **(262)**, (506)
   and cost-benefit analysis (493)
   children's television (382)
   costs of (312)
   incentive-based (272)
   Neg-Reg (295)
Regulatory Agencies
   powers of (298)
Regulatory commissions
   and prices (273)
Remedies
   for warranty problems (76)
   right to (62)
   to resolve consumer problems (68)
Rent control laws
   and demand for housing (543)
Rent-to-own **(115)**
   laws (142)
Rental car insurance **(94)**
Rental car lawsuit (76)
Renter's insurance (161)
   and lost credit cards (159)
Renter's security deposits (156)
Repair laws
   vehicles (145)
Repair-cost histories
   of automobiles (403)
Repairs
   reasonable number of (155)
Republic **(196)**
Republican
   beliefs (331)
   number of (330)
Republican National Committee (294)
Reputation ranking
   illustrated (412)
Research
   and a risk-free society (446)
   on animals (446)
Reserve requirement **(193)**
Residual value **(409)**
   in leasing (140)
Resource
   allocation (187)
   availability (186)

Resources **(180)**, **(187)**, (232)
   nonhuman (187)
Responsibilities
   and communitarians (331)
   in product safety (494)
   of consumers in food marketplace
      (449)
Responsibilities of consumers (62)
Restaurant menus
   nutritional labeling (441)
Restitution **(77)**
Results-based trade **(248)**
Retail price maintenance (286)
Return
   normal, in monopoly businesses
      (273)
Return on investment (ROI) **(189)**
Return policy **(68)**
Revocation of acceptance **(144)**
Right to be heard
   responsibilities of (64)
Right to choose
   responsibilies of (63)
Right to consumer education
   responsibilities of (66)
Right to environmental health
   responsibilities of (65), (66)
Right to information
   responsibilities of (64)
   secret settlements (498)
Right to redress
   responsibilities of (65)
Right to remedy
   responsibilities of (65)
Right to safety
   responsibilities of (64)
Right to service
   responsibilities (66)
Right to voice
   responsibilities of (64)
Rights
   human (14)
   in insurance (554)
   of students (62)
   Patient's bill of rights (463)
   says IOCU (253)
   that people just know about (50)
Rights for all Americans (61)
Rights of consumers (56)
Ripoffs
   against poor homeowners **(92)**,
      (291), (544)
   and service contracts (408)
   automatic overdraft loans (519)
   escrow payments (549)
   guidelines to avoid (89)
   health, diet and fitness (96)
   how they work (86)
   in insurance (534)
   poor people banking (522)
   Rule of 78s (532)
   title insurance (565)
   why they exist (87)
Ripoffs and frauds

things in common (88)
Risk acceptability (491)
Risk assessments
by consumers (482)
Risk premium **(528)**
Robinson-Patman Act (284)
Rollover rating **(507)**
Rule **(299)** 703
of Federal Trade Commission
(155)
Rule of 78s (532)
Rule of reason **(281)**
Rulemaking
factors that must be considered
(505)
formal (504)
informal (504)
Rulemaking procedures
of CPSC and NHTSA (503)
Rules of thumb **(352)**
Rural
shopping (354)
Rural communities
and airline discrimination (309)

S

Saccharin
carcinogen (443)
Safety
and health standards (245)
and state lotteries (306)
as a consumer right (13)
right to (61)
Safety ratings
on automobiles (403)
Safety seals **(395)**
Safety standards
examples for autos (509)
examples of mandatory standards
(503)
FVMSS (509)
mandatory (501)
voluntary (501)
Sales transactions
laws and regulations (132)
Salmonella (438), (440)
Satisfaction (3)
and indifference curves (226)
maximizing (361)
Saturated fats **(428)**
Save
average propensity to (222)
marginal propensity to (222)
Savings **(4)**
and loan scandal (523)
in the U.S. and Japan (242)
point of zero (222)
Scandals
contribution to consumer
movements (39)
Scarcity **(196)**, (232)
Scholarship aid (117)
Seafood inspection program

of FDA (442)
Seals and certification programs (395)
Search
and cost-benefit analysis (360)
illustrated (405)
Search and seizure orders **(299)**
Search costs
and deregulation (252)
Search goods **(366)**
Searching
is complicated (351)
Second world countries **(233)**
Secret settlement (498)
Secret vehicle warranties (145)
Secret warranty **(406)**
Section 5
of the Federal Trade Commission
Act (283)
Securities and Exchange Commission
(SEC) (568)
Security deposit
of renters (156)
Seizure
defined by FDA **(438)**
Selecting the best alternative
illustrated (417)
Self-regulation **(264)**
examples of (265)
Self-Regulatory organizations
how to complain to (71)
Seller financing **(410)**
Seller financing ranking
illustrated (412)
Selling agent **(546)**
Selling practices
in food industry (433)
Service
as a consumer right (13)
right to (62)
Service contract **(149)**
cost **(407)**, (408)
profitability (408)
questions to ask (409)
Service department reputation ranking
illustrated (412)
Services
guidelines for purchasing (455)
Settlement **(546)**
Settlement date **(548)**
Sexual orientation
and housing laws (540)
Shopping
confusions in food area (447)
criteria illustrated (402)
for credit (529)
one-price auto dealers (415)
Silicone breast implant (496)
Silicone breast implants (497)
Simplesse (439)
Simultaneous consumption **(188)**
Small claims court **(75)**
procedures (75)
Smokeless tobacco (479)
Smoker
living with one (479)
quitters gain health benefits (481)

Smoking
and health (475)
and heart disease (480)
bans (479)
benefits of quitting (481)
by teenagers (477)
carcinogen (479)
consumption (475)
future of (480)
harmful aspects of (480)
negative effects of (477)
passive (478)
secondhand smoke (478)
Smoking gun
of smoking (480)
Social activism
of twenty-something generation
(50)
Social goals
of society (195)
Social responsibilities of business (263)
Socialism **(181)**, **(328)**
Soft-sell
of free trial memberships (93)
South
the developing countries (254)
Sovereignty (5)
Space
and level of living (188)
interactional (188)
limitational (188)
locational (188)
Spanish language sales
and used cars (152)
Special-interest group **(14)**, **(293)**
health care (459)
Specification standards
and CPSC (504)
definition (313)
Speed limits (505)
Spending
and the poor (354)
policies (191)
Spiff **(402)**
Stages
in the economic cycle (200)
Stagflation **(200)**
Standard
of living (188)
Standards
uniform, as a government goal
(291)
Standards-setting organizations **(266)**
Standing (301)
Standing to sue **(301)**
State attorneys general
and consumer problems (303)
State guaranty laws **(567)**
State utility consumer advocates **(272)**
State-sponsored lotteries **(306)**
Status quo
and alternative solutions (336)
Sticker price **(414)**
Stop payment order (90)
Store brands **(396)**
Strict liability **(497)**

Student activism (328)
Student attorney (79)
Students
    in post-secondary education (62)
Style (358)
Subpoena **(75)**, **(299)**
Subsidies **(245)**
Substantial hazard **(501)**
Substitutability **(211)**
Substitution drugs **(466)**
Substitution effect **(220)**
Successive consumption **(188)**
Sulfite **(441)**
Summons **(75)**
Sun protection factor (SPF) **(469)**
Sunscreen
    selection of (469)
Sunset laws **(307)**
Super 301
    trade policy (247)
Supplemental health insurance
    sold through the mail (100)
Supply **(215)**
    nonprice determinants (216)
    of housing (542)
    of labor (244)
Supply Affects Prices (215)
Supply and demand
    and usury laws (528)
    doesn't work in health care (461)
    for credit (528)
Supply curve
    for credit (528)
Supremacy clause **(297)**
Sweepstakes **(108)**
    food (435)
    odds of winning (109)
Sweeteners
    food (444)
Swindler **(121)**

T

Tampering **(470)**
Target marketing **(537)**
Tariff (243)
Tax equity (204)
Taxes **(5)**
    progressive and regressive (192)
Taxing policies (191)
Taxpaying **(5)**
Technological changes (252)
Tele-Consumer Hotline (98)
Telefrauds **(107)**
Telemarketing **(107)**
Telemarketing solicitations laws (132)
Telephone charges
    fight back (135)
Telephone companies
    and caller ID (537)
Telephone company
    may help with bills (135)

Telephone dumb cards **(99)**
Telephone industry
    and price regulation (273)
Television
    and false promises (51)
    watching patterns (374)
Television advertising supporters (381)
Television and children (381)
Television programming
    commerical-free (382)
Term life insurance **(564)**
    good prices (564)
    sold through the mail (100)
Term papers (102)
Testimonial **(376)**
Testimonial advertisements **(378)**
Testing magazines (394)
Thalidomide (466)
The Conference Board (202)
Third world countries **(233)**
Third-party complaint-handling sources
    (71)
Third-party payers in health care (461)
Thrifts **(524)**
Time
    is limited (355)
Timesharing **(577)**
    cooling-off laws (139)
    how long to resell (578)
Title insurance **(565)**
Tobacco
    as an addiction (480)
    social costs (484)
Tobacco company
    and Joe Cool (477)
Tobacco, smokeless (479)
Tolerance levels **(442)**
Totalitarian **(181)**
Toy safety suggestions (489)
Toy-mercials (382)
Trade
    is a necessity (237)
    managed (248)
Trade agreement
    regional (248)
Trade associations **(267)**
    government-sponsored (437)
Trade deficit (242)
Trade embargo (245)
Trade name
    of drugs (466)
Trade regulation rule **(299)**
Trade war **(245)**
Tradeoff **(10)**, **(221)**
    inefficient (10)
Trading stamps
    food (435)
Trading up **(105)**
Traditional economic system **(181)**
Transfer payments **(191)**
Transnational company (TNC) **(255)**
Transportation
    difficulties of the poor (354)
Transportation, local street industry

    (273)
Trust **(278)**
Trusts **(32)**
Truth in Financial Planning Act (570)
Truth in Savings Act (TIS) (516)
Twenty-somethings (50)
Two-cycle average daily balance
    method **(531)**
Tying agreements **(281)**, **(282)**

U

U.S. Department of Agriculture
    overview of (437)
U.S. Office of Consumer Affairs
    (USOCA) (298)
U.S. Public Interest Research Group
    and lobbying (295)
Unconscionability (79), **(303)**
Unconscionable (93)
    contract clauses (292)
    practices prohibited (302)
    sales practices (184)
Underemployed
    in Mexico (244)
Underinsured motorist (UIM) **(559)**
Unemployed
    in Mexico (244)
Unemployment insurance ripoffs (534)
Unfair and deceptive sales practices
    statutes (302)
Unfairness
    and advertising (310)
    and the FTC (310)
    current FTC definition **(283)**
Unfunded mandates (311)
Uniform Commercial Code (UCC)
    (302)
Uniform consumer sales practices act
    (302)
Uniform Deceptive Trade Practices Act
    (302)
Uniform Trade Practices and Consumer
    Protection Law **(302)**
Uninsured motorist coverage (559)
Union membership (204)
Unit elasticity **(215)**
Unit pricing **(447)**
United Nations Guidelines on
    Consumer Protection
    purposes of (256)
United Nations Population Fund (186)
Universal product code (UPC) (447)
Unordered merchandise regulations
    of the Postal Service (135)
Unreasonable risk
    examples of banned products (502)
Unreasonable risks **(491)**
Unregulated firm (273)
Unsafe at Any Speed (36)
Unsafe products
    examples (494)

examples of successful lawsuits (496)
Unsatisfactory goods (164)
Unsaturated fats **(428)**
USDA
    Food Guide Pyramid (433)
Used car lemon laws (144)
Used car rule
    of Federal Trade Commission (146)
Used cars
    on information highway (416)
Usury
    cost to middle-income consumers (529)
Usury laws **(528-529)**
    and supply and demand (528)
    justication for (529)
    Low-Income consumers (529)
Utilities
    as regulated industries (271)
Utility **(221)**, **(350)**
    subjective expected (356)
Utilizing **(4)**
Utils **(224)**

V

Vacation certificates (116)
Valdez Principles (368)
Value
    customer (350)
Value for money
    expended (8)
    interests (11)
Value judgments
    illustrated (412)
Value-for-Money/Equity Model (11)
Values
    American export (249)
Values and goals
    and planned buying (392)
    illustrated (400)
Vegetarians (430)
Vehicle crashing and testing (509)
Vehicle identification number (VIN) **(508)**
Vehicle laws (143)
Vehicle repair laws (145)
Verifiable authorization (133)
Vertical merger **(282)**
Vertical restraint on distribution **(282)**
Vitamins and food supplements (474)
Voice
    as a consumer right (13)
    right to (61)
Voluntary standards
    CPSC **(504)**
Voters
    and consumers (22)
Voting records
    of politicians (331)

W-Y

Wage inequality (203)
Wages
    in developing countries (241)
    in U.S. and Mexico (244)
Wants and needs
    worksheet (402)
Warning labels
    ignored (495)
Warranties
    and service contracts (408)
    and spoken promises (148)
    attempts to disclaim (59), **(405)**
    disclaiming implied (154)
    unexpired (148)
    views of consumers (406)
    views of sellers (405)
Warranty
    consumer remedies **(56)**, (76), **(152)**
    extended (407)
    viewed by consumers (153)
    viewed by the seller (153)
Warranty information
    used vehicles (146)
Warranty of fitness for a particular purpose **(57)**, **(147)**
Warranty of merchantability **(57)**, **(147)**
Warranty problems (153)
Warranty ranking
    illustrated (412)
Warranty-Registration cards (58), (511)
Water industry (273)
Weight and diet (425)
Weight loss (96)
Weight-Loss center laws (142)
Weights and measures departments (291)
Weights and measures offices **(304)**
Welfare
    middle-class (204)
Well-being
    economic (187)
Wheeler-Lea (283)
    amendment to the Federal Trade Commission Act (283)
Whistleblower Protection Act (40)
Whistleblowers **(40)**
Whistleblowing
    Prudential Insurance Company of America (40)
Whitelisted **(42)**
Willingness to trade **(359)**
Window shopping **(402)**
Work at home (102)
Work-at-Home scams (127)
Working conditions **(188)**
World Health Assembly (255)
World Trade Organization (251)
Writ of execution **(76)**
Written express warranties **(58)**
WTO (251)

Z

Zero population growth **(234)**
Zero-risk standard **(443)**
Zero-sum game **(237)**
Zero-tolerance level standard **(442)**
Zone office **(71)**